The

TRO

The
Prophet Armed

TROTSKY: 1879–1921

ISAAC DEUTSCHER

OXFORD UNIVERSITY PRESS

Oxford University Press, Walton Street, Oxford OX2 6DP

Oxford New York Toronto
Delhi Bombay Calcutta Madras Karachi
Petaling Jaya Singapore Hong Kong Tokyo
Nairobi Dar es Salaam Cape Town
Melbourne Auckland

and associated companies in
Berlin Ibadan

Oxford is a trade mark of Oxford University Press

First published 1954 by Oxford University Press
First issued as an Oxford University Press paperback 1970
Reprinted 1979, 1987 (twice), 1989

ISBN 0–19–281064–2

Printed in Hong Kong

PREFACE

WHEN I first contemplated the writing of a biographical trilogy on the leaders of the Russian revolution I intended to include a study of Trotsky in Exile, not a full-scale biography of Trotsky. Trotsky's later years and the tragic close of his life stirred my imagination more deeply than did the earlier and more worldly part of his story. On second thoughts, however, I began to doubt whether Trotsky in Exile could be made at all comprehensible if the earlier part of the story was not told. Then, pondering historical materials and biographical sources, some of them new to me, I came to realize more clearly than before how deeply the drama of Trotsky's last years was rooted in the earlier and even the earliest stages of his career. I therefore decided to devote to Trotsky two separate yet interconnected volumes: *The Prophet Armed* and *The Prophet Unarmed*, the first giving what might be described as Trotsky's 'rise', the second his 'fall'. I have refrained from using these conventional terms because I do not think that a man's rise to power is necessarily the climax of his life or that his loss of office should be equated with his fall.

The titles to these volumes have been suggested to me by the passage from Machiavelli printed on page xii. The present study illustrates the truth of what is there said; but it also offers a somewhat ironical commentary on it. Machiavelli's observation that 'all armed prophets have conquered and the unarmed ones have been destroyed' is certainly realistic. What may be doubted is whether the distinction between the armed prophet and the unarmed one and the difference between conquest and destruction is always as clear as it seemed to the author of *The Prince*. In the following pages we first watch Trotsky conquering without arms in the greatest revolution of our age. We then see him armed, victorious, and bent under the weight of his armour—the chapter portraying him at the very pinnacle of power bears the title 'Defeat in Victory'. And when next the Prophet Unarmed is contemplated, the question will arise whether a strong element of victory was not concealed in his very defeat.

My account of Trotsky's role in the Russian revolution

will come as a surprise to some. For nearly thirty years the powerful propaganda machines of Stalinism worked furiously to expunge Trotsky's name from the annals of the revolution, or to leave it there only as the synonym for arch-traitor. To the present Soviet generation, and not only to it, Trotsky's life-story is already like an ancient Egyptian sepulchre which is known to have contained the body of a great man and the record, engraved in gold, of his deeds; but tomb-robbers and ghouls have plundered and left it so empty and desolate that no trace is found of the record it once contained. The work of the tomb-robbers has, in this present instance, been so persistent that it has strongly affected the views even of independent Western historians and scholars.

Despite all this, the record of Trotsky's life is still intact, preserved in his own voluminous but now mostly forgotten writings and in his Archives; in numerous memoirs of friendly and of hostile contemporaries; in files of Russian periodicals published before, during, and after the revolution; in minutes of the Central Committee; and in verbatim reports of the Congresses of the party and of the Soviets. Nearly all these documentary sources are available in public libraries in the West, although a few of them can be found only in private libraries. I have drawn on all these sources. Together with my wife, who shared equally with me in research and has in many other respects contributed greatly to this work, I made a special study of the rich collection of Russian pre-revolutionary periodicals in the Hoover Library at Stanford, California, where I found sources scarcely used before by historians of Russian revolutionary movements. Together with my wife I also studied the Trotsky Archives at the Houghton Library, Harvard University, by far the most important collection of original documents on Soviet history existing outside the U.S.S.R. (A brief description of the Archives is given in the bibliography at the end of this volume.)

I have therefore no ground for complaining here, as I complained in the Preface to my *Stalin*, about paucity of biographical material. This is due largely to the contrast between my chief characters. Trotsky was as communicative about his life and activities as Stalin was secretive. He allowed complete strangers to delve freely into almost every aspect of his life; he himself wrote an autobiography; and, what is more important, a strong,

unconscious autobiographical streak runs through his scores of
published volumes, through his innumerable articles and essays
not reprinted in book form, and through some of his unpublished writings. Wherever he went he left footprints so firm that
nobody could later efface or blur them, not even he himself,
when on rare occasions he was tempted to do so.

A biographer is not usually expected to apologize for narrat-
ing the life of a political leader who has himself written an autobiography. I feel that this case may be an exception to the rule,
for after a close and critical examination I still find Trotsky's
My Life as scrupulously truthful as any work of this kind can be.
Nevertheless, it remains an apologia produced in the middle of
the losing battle its author fought against Stalin. In its pages the
living Trotsky wrestled with his tomb-robbers. To wholesale
Stalinist denigration he responded with a peculiar act of self-
defence which savoured of self-glorification. He did not and
could not satisfactorily explain the change in the climate of the
revolution which made his defeat both possible and inevitable;
and his account of the intrigues by which a narrow-minded,
'usurpatory', and malignant bureaucracy ousted him from
power is obviously inadequate. The question which is of absorbing interest to the biographer is: to what extent did Trotsky
himself contribute to his own defeat? To what extent was he
himself compelled by critical circumstances and by his own
character to pave the way for Stalin? The answer to these
questions reveals the truly classical tragedy of Trotsky's life,
or rather a reproduction of classical tragedy in secular terms
of modern politics; and Trotsky would have been more than
human if he had been able to reveal it. The biographer, on the
other hand, sees Trotsky at the climax of his achievement as
being as guilty and as innocent and as ripe for expiation as
a protagonist in Greek drama. This approach, presupposing
sympathy and understanding, is, I trust, as free from denunciation as from apologetics.

In *My Life* Trotsky sought to vindicate himself in terms
imposed upon him by Stalin and by the whole ideological situation of Bolshevism in the 1920s, that is, in terms of the Lenin
cult. Stalin had denounced him as Lenin's inveterate enemy,
and Trotsky was consequently anxious to prove his complete
devotion to, and his agreement with, Lenin. His devotion to

Lenin after 1917 was undoubtedly genuine; and the points of agreement between them were numerous and important. Nevertheless, Trotsky blurred the sharp outlines and the importance of his controversies with Lenin between 1903 and 1917, and also of later differences. But another and much stranger consequence of the fact that Trotsky made his apologia in terms of the Lenin cult was that in some crucial points he belittled his own role in comparison with Lenin's, a feat extremely rare in autobiographical literature. This applies especially to the account of the part he played in the October uprising and in the creation of the Red Army, where he detracted from his own merits in order not to appear as Lenin's detractor. Free from loyalties to any cult, I have attempted to restore the historical balance.

Finally, I have paid special attention to Trotsky the man of letters, the pamphleteer, the military writer, and the journalist. Most of Trotsky's literary work is now wrapt in oblivion and inaccessible to a wider public. Yet this is the writer of whom Bernard Shaw, who could judge Trotsky's literary qualities only from poor translations, said that he 'surpassed Junius and Burke'. 'Like Lessing', Shaw wrote of Trotsky, 'when he cuts off his opponent's head, he holds it up to show that there are no brains in it; but he spares his victim's private character. . . . He leaves [his victim] without a rag of political credit; but he leaves him with his honour intact.'[1] I can only regret that considerations of space and composition have not allowed me to show this side of Trotsky's personality in greater detail; but I hope to return to it in *The Prophet Unarmed*.

I. D.

---

[1] *The Nation*, London, 7 Jan. 1922.

CONTENTS

PREFACE V

ACKNOWLEDGEMENTS X

I. HOME AND SCHOOL 1

II. IN SEARCH OF AN IDEAL 22

III. AT THE DOOR OF HISTORY 57

IV. AN INTELLECTUAL PARTNERSHIP 98

V. TROTSKY IN 1905 117

VI. 'PERMANENT REVOLUTION' 145

VII. THE DOLDRUMS: 1907–1914 175

VIII. WAR AND THE INTERNATIONAL 211

IX. TROTSKY IN THE OCTOBER REVOLUTION 249

X. THE PEOPLE'S COMMISSAR 325

XI. THE DRAMA OF BREST LITOVSK 346

XII. ARMING THE REPUBLIC 405

XIII. REVOLUTION AND CONQUEST 448

NOTE ON TROTSKY'S MILITARY WRITINGS 477

XIV. DEFEAT IN VICTORY 486

BIBLIOGRAPHY 523

INDEX 529

MAP
(following page x)
Territories Occupied by Anti-Bolshevik
Armies in 1919 and 1920

ACKNOWLEDGEMENTS

I AM greatly indebted for criticism and friendly encouragement to Professor E. H. Carr and Mrs. Barbara Ward-Jackson, who read parts of my manuscript; and to Mr. Donald Tyerman, who read the whole. Mr. Bernard Singer helped me with his intimate knowledge of Russian life. To Mr. D. M. Davin and members of the Editorial Staff of the Oxford University Press I am grateful for many suggestions for improvements in style. Mr. Hugo Dewar and Mr. Jon Kimche kindly assisted me with materials and books, some of which are now bibliographical rarities. My thanks are given to Professor Wm. A. Jackson and his assistants at the Houghton Library, Harvard University, who helped my wife and me to find our way through the dossiers of the Trotsky Archives. I am similarly obliged to the Staffs of the Hoover Library, the London Library, the British Museum, and the National Central Library.

The generosity of the Oxford University Press and the Humanities Department of the Rockefeller Foundation enabled my wife and me to spend many months in the United States and to carry out that part of our research programme which depended entirely on our access to the above-mentioned American libraries.

My debt to other authors is acknowledged in footnotes. The quotation from Machiavelli's *The Prince* on page xii is taken by permission of J. M. Dent & Sons Ltd., from the translation by W. K. Marriott in the Everyman's Library.

I. D.

Murmansk

FINLAND

Archangel

YUDENICH
(1919)

Petrograd

Riga

Vologda

Vilna

MOSCOW

Perm

Ekaterinburg

Omsk

Minsk

P
O
L
E
S

(1920)

Gomel

Orel

Kazan

Samara

K O L C H A K

(1919)

Kiev

D
E
N
I
K
I
N

(1919)

Kharkov

Tsaritsyn

Odessa

Rostov
on Don

Astrakhan

Sebastopol

Batum

Tiflis

Baku

Krasnovodsk

T U R K E Y

Ashkhabad

TERRITORIES OCCUPIED
BY ANTI-BOLSHEVIK ARMIES
IN 1919 AND 1920

Fronts of anti-Bolshevik
armies in 1919-20
Territories under
White governments
Foreign intervention
troops
Mainly no man's land
Soviet Russia's
frontiers of 1921
Railways

Miles
0   100 200 300 400 500

R. W. FORD

'. . . there is nothing more difficult to take in hand, more perilous to conduct, or more uncertain in its success, than to take the lead in the introduction of a new order of things. Because the innovator has for enemies all those who have done well under the old conditions, and lukewarm defenders in those who may do well under the new. . . .

'It is necessary, therefore, if we desire to discuss this matter thoroughly, to inquire whether these innovators can rely on themselves or have to depend on others: that is to say, whether, to consummate their enterprise, have they to use prayers or can they use force? In the first instance they always succeed badly, and never compass anything; but when they can rely on themselves and use force, then they are rarely endangered. Hence it is that all armed prophets have conquered, and the unarmed ones have been destroyed. Besides the reasons mentioned, the nature of the people is variable, and whilst it is easy to persuade them, it is difficult to fix them in that persuasion. And thus it is necessary to take such measures that, when they believe no longer, it may be possible to make them believe by force.

'If Moses, Cyrus, Theseus, and Romulus had been unarmed they could not have enforced their constitutions for long—as happened in our time to Fra Girolamo Savonarola, who was ruined with his new order of things immediately the multitude believed in him no longer, and he had no means of keeping steadfast those who believed or of making the unbelievers to believe.'

MACHIAVELLI, *The Prince*, CHAPTER VI

CHAPTER I

Home and School

THE reign of Tsar Alexander II (1855–81) was drawing to its gloomy end. The ruler whose accession and early reforms had stirred the most sanguine hopes in Russian society, and even among émigré revolutionaries, the ruler who had, in fact, freed the Russian peasant from serfdom and had earned the title of the Emancipator was spending his last years in a cave of despair—hunted like an animal by the revolutionaries, and hiding in his imperial palaces from their bombs and pistols.

The Tsar was paying the penalty for the frustration of the hopes he had stirred: he had deceived the expectations of almost every class in society. In the eyes of many landlords he was still subversion itself, crowned and dressed in imperial robes. They had never forgiven him the reform of 1861, which had deprived them of their feudal mastery over the peasants. From the peasants he had lifted the burden of serfdom only to let them be crushed by poverty and debts: the ex-serfs had, on their emancipation, to yield to the gentry much of the land they had tilled, and for the land they retained they had over the years to pay a heavy ransom. They still looked up to the Tsar as to their well-wisher and friend and believed that it was against his intentions that the gentry cheated them of the benefits of the emancipation. But already there had been aroused in the peasantry the hunger for land, that great hunger which for more than half a century was to shake Russia and to throw her into a fever, body and mind.

The gentry and the peasantry were still the main classes of Russian society. Only very slowly was the urban middle class growing. Unlike the European bourgeoisie, it had no social ancestry, no tradition, no mind of its own, no self-confidence, and no influence. A tiny portion of the peasantry was detaching itself from the countryside and beginning to form an industrial working class. But, although the last decade in the reign of Alexander brought the first significant industrial strikes, the urban working class was still looked upon as a mere displaced branch of the peasantry.

From none of these classes could there come an immediate threat to the throne. Each class hoped that its claims would be met and its wrongs redressed by the monarch himself. In any case, no class was in a position to air its grievances and make its demands widely known. None could rally its members and muster its strength in any representative institution or political party. These did not exist. State and Church were the only bodies that possessed a national organization; but the function of both, a function which had determined their shape and constitution, had been to suppress not to express social discontent.

Only one group, the intelligentsia, rose to challenge the dynasty. Educated people in all walks of life, especially those who had not been absorbed in officialdom, had no less reason than had the peasantry to be disappointed with the Tsar—the Emancipator. He had first aroused and then frustrated their craving for freedom as he had aroused and deceived the muzhiks' hunger for land. Alexander had not, like his predecessor Nicholas I, chastised the intelligentsia with scorpions; but he was still punishing them with whips. His reforms in education and in the Press had been half-hearted and mean: the spiritual life of the nation remained under the tutelage of the police, the censorship, and the Holy Synod. By offering the educated a semblance of freedom he made the denial of real freedom even more painful and humiliating. The intelligentsia sought to avenge their betrayed hopes; the Tsar strove to tame their restive spirit; and, so, semi-liberal reforms gave way to repression and repression bred rebellion.

Numerically the intelligentsia were very weak. The active revolutionaries among them were a mere handful. If their fight against the ruler of ninety million subjects were to be described as a duel between David and Goliath, that would still exaggerate their strength. Throughout the 1870s, this classical decade of the intelligentsia's rebellion, a few thousand people at the most were involved in the peaceful, 'educational and propagandist' phase of the *Narodnik* (Populist) movement; and in its final, terroristic phase less than two score men and women were directly engaged. These two score made the Tsar a fugitive in his own realm, and kept the whole might of his empire in check. Only against the background of a discontented but mute

nation could so tiny a group grow to so gigantic a stature. Unlike the basic classes of society, the intelligentsia were articulate;
they had the training indispensable for an analysis of the evils
that plagued the nation; and they formulated the programmes
that were supposed to remedy those evils. They would hardly
have set out to challenge the ruling power if they had thought
that they were speaking for themselves alone. They were at first
inspired by the great illusion that they were the mouth-piece
of the nation, especially of the peasantry. In their thoughts their
own craving for freedom merged with the peasants' hunger for
land, and they called their revolutionary organization *Zemlya
i Volya*—Land and Freedom. They eagerly absorbed the ideas
of European socialism and strove to adjust them to the Russian
situation. Not the industrial worker but the peasant was to be
the pillar of the new society of their dreams. Not the publicly
owned industrial factory but the collectively owned rural commune—the age-old *mir* which had survived in Russia—was to
be the basic cell of that society.

The 'men of the 1870s' were foredoomed as precursors of a
revolution. No social class was in fact prepared to support them.
In the course of the decade they gradually discovered their own
isolation, shed one set of illusions only to adopt another, and
tried to solve dilemmas, some peculiar to their country and
generation and some inherent in every revolutionary movement.
At first they attempted to move the peasantry to action, either
by enlightening the muzhiks about the evils of autocracy, as did
the followers of Lavrov, or by inciting them against the Tsar, as
Bakunin had urged them to do. Twice in this decade men and
women of the intelligentsia abandoned homes and professions
and tried to settle as peasants among the peasants in order to
gain access to their mind. 'A whole legion of socialists', wrote a
general of the gendarmerie, whose job it was to watch this
exodus, 'has taken to this with an energy and a spirit of self-
sacrifice, the like of which cannot be found in the history of any
secret society in Europe.' The self-sacrifice was fruitless, for the
peasantry and the intelligentsia were at cross purposes. The
muzhik still believed in the Tsar, the Emancipator, and received
with suspicious indifference or outright hostility the words of
Narodnik 'enlightenment' or 'incitement'. Gendarmerie and
police rounded up the idealists who had 'gone to the people';

the courts sentenced them to long terms of imprisonment, hard labour, or deportation.

The idea of a revolution through the people was gradually replaced by that of a conspiracy to be planned and carried out by a small and determined minority from the intelligentsia. The forms of the movement changed accordingly. The exodus of the intelligentsia to the countryside had been spontaneous; it had not been guided from any centre. The new conspiracy required a strictly clandestine, closely knit, strongly led, and rigidly disciplined organization. Its leaders—Zhelyabov, Kibalchich, Sofia Perovskaya, Vera Figner, and others—were not at first inclined to terroristic action; but the logic of their position and the events drove them that way. In January 1878 a young woman, Vera Zasulich—one day she was to influence the chief character of this book—shot General Trepov, head of the gendarmerie in Petersburg, in protest against his maltreatment and humiliation of a political prisoner. At her trial horrible abuses of which the police had been guilty were revealed. The jury were so shocked by the revelations and so moved by the sincere idealism of the defendant that they acquitted her. When the police attempted to seize her outside the court, a sympathetic crowd rescued her and enabled her to escape. The Tsar ordered that henceforth military tribunals, not juries, should try political offenders.

Zasulich's unpremeditated deed and the response it evoked pointed the way for the conspirators. In 1879, the year in which this narrative begins, the party of *Land and Freedom* split. One group of members, bent on pursuing terroristic attempts until the overthrow of autocracy, formed themselves into a new body, the *Narodnaya Volya*, the *Freedom of the People*.[1] Their new programme placed far greater emphasis on civil liberties than on land reform. Another and less influential group, setting no store by the terroristic conspiracy, broke away to advocate *Black Partition* (*Chornyi Peredel*)—an egalitarian distribution of the land. (From this group, headed by Plekhanov, who presently emigrated to Switzerland, was to come the first Marxist and Social Democratic message to the revolutionaries in Russia.)

The year 1879 brought a rapid succession of spectacular

---

[1] *Narodnaya Volya* is often translated as the *Will of the People*. *Volya* means in fact both 'will' and 'freedom' and can be translated either way.

terroristic attempts. In February Prince Kropotkin, the Governor of Kharkov, was shot. In March an attempt was made on the life of General Drenteln, head of the political police. In the course of the year the Tsar himself narrowly escaped two attempts: in March a revolutionary fired five shots at him; and in the summer, while the Tsar was returning from his Crimean residence, several mines exploded under his train. Mass arrests, hangings, and deportations followed. But on 1 March 1881 the conspirators succeeded in assassinating the Tsar.

To the world Tsardom presented a glittering façade of grandeur and power. Yet in April 1879 Karl Marx in a letter written from London to a Russian friend pointed to the disintegration of Russian society concealed behind that façade; and he compared the condition of Russia at the close of Alexander's reign with that of France under Louis XV.[1] And, indeed, it was in the last decade of Alexander's reign that most of the men were born who were to lead the Russian revolution.

. . . .

Far away from the scenes of this grim struggle, in the peaceful and sunlit steppe of the southern Ukraine, in the province of Kherson, near the little town of Bobrinetz, David Leontievich Bronstein was—in the year 1879—settling down on a farm which he had just bought from a Colonel Yanovsky, after whom the farm was called Yanovka. The Colonel had received the land, about a thousand acres, from the Tsar as a reward for services. He had not been successful as a farmer and was glad to sell 250 acres and to lease another 400 to Bronstein. The deal was completed early in the year. In the summer the new owner and his family moved from a nearby village to the thatched cottage which they had acquired together with the farm.

The Bronsteins were Jews. It was rare for a Jew to take up farming. Yet about two score of Jewish farming colonies—an overspill from the crowded ghettoes of the 'pale'—were scattered over the Kherson steppe. Jews were not allowed to live in Russia outside the pale, outside, that is, the towns that lay mostly in the western provinces annexed from Poland. But they were allowed to settle freely in the southern steppe near the Black Sea. Russia had come into possession of that sparsely

[1] *Perepiska K. Marxa i F. Engelsa s Russkimi Politicheskimi Deyatelami*, p. 84.

populated but fertile land towards the end of the eighteenth century, and the Tsars were anxious to promote colonization. Here, as so often in the history of colonization, the foreign immigrant and the outcast were the pioneers. Serbs, Bulgarians, Greeks, Jews were encouraged to conquer the wilderness. Up to a point, the Jewish settlers improved their lot. They struck roots in the country; they enjoyed certain privileges; and they were relieved of the menace of expulsion and violence which always hung over the Jewish pale. It had never been quite clear just how far that pale extended. Alexander I had allowed it to spread a little. Nicholas I had no sooner ascended the throne than he ordered the Jews to be driven back. Towards the middle of the century he expelled them again from Nikolayev, Sebastopol, Poltava, and the towns around Kiev. Most of those expelled resettled within the shrunken and congested pale, but a few went out to the steppe.[1]

It was probably during one of these expulsions, in the early 1850s, that Leon Bronstein, the father of the new owner of Yanovka, had left with his family a small Jewish town near Poltava, on the east side of the Dnieper, and settled in the Kherson province. His sons and daughters when they grew up stayed on the land; but only one, David, became prosperous enough to detach himself from the Jewish colony and set up as an independent farmer at Yanovka.

As a rule, the colonists came from the lowest orders of the Jewish population. Jews had been town dwellers for centuries; and farming was so foreign to their way of life that very few of those able to eke out a living in town would take to it. The merchant, the craftsman, the money-lender, the middle-man, the pious student of the Talmud, all preferred living within the pale, in an established if miserable Jewish community. They despised rural life so much that in their idiom *Am Haaretz*, 'the man of the land', also meant the boor and the vulgar who did not even have a smattering of the Scriptures. Those who went out into the steppe had had nothing to lose; they were not afraid of hard and unfamiliar work; and they had few or no ties with the Synagogue.

The new owner of Yanovka would certainly have been described by his co-religionists as an *Am Haaretz*: he was

[1] S. M. Dubnov, *History of the Jews in Russia and Poland*, vol. ii, pp. 30–34 and *passim*.

illiterate, indifferent to religion, and even a little contemptuous of the Synagogue. Although a ploughman in the second generation only, he had in himself so much of the peasant and of the child of nature as to appear almost completely un-Jewish. At his home not Yiddish, that amalgam of old German, Hebrew, and Slavonic, was spoken but a mixture of Russian and Ukrainian. Unlike most muzhiks, however, the Bronsteins had no memories of serfdom; here in the open steppe serfdom had never been firmly established. David Bronstein was a free and ambitious, tough, and hard-working farmer, of the frontiersman type. He was determined to develop his farm into a flourishing estate, and he drove himself and his labourers hard. His opportunities still lay ahead: when he moved to Yanovka he was only about thirty.

His wife Anna came from different stock. She had been brought up either in Odessa or in some other southern town, not in the country. She was educated enough to subscribe to a lending library and occasionally to read a Russian novel—few Russian Jewish women of the time could do that. In her parental home she had imbibed something of the orthodox Jewish tradition; she was more careful than her husband to observe the rites, and she would not travel or sew on the Sabbath. Her middle-class origin showed itself in an instinctive conventionality, tinged with a little religious hypocrisy. In case of need, she would sew on the Sabbath, but take good care that no stranger should see her doing so. How she had come to marry the farmer Bronstein is not clear; her son says that she fell in love with him when he was young and handsome. Her family was distressed and looked down upon the bumpkin. This was, nevertheless, not an unhappy marriage. At first the young Mrs. Bronstein fretted at rustic life, but then she did her best to shed her urban habits and to become a peasant woman. Before they came to Yanovka, she had borne four children. A few months after the family had settled at Yanovka, on 26 October 1879, a fifth was born, a boy. The child was named after his grandfather, Lev or Leon, the man who had left the Jewish town near Poltava to settle in the steppe.[1]

By a freak of fate, the day on which the boy was born, 26 October (or 7 November according to the new calendar) was

[1] L. Trotsky, *Moya Zhizn*, vol. i, chapter ii.

the precise date on which thirty-eight years later, as Leon
Trotsky, he was to lead the Bolshevik insurrection in Petrograd.[1]

. . . .

The boy spent his first nine years at Yanovka. His childhood,
as he himself put it, was neither like a 'sunny meadow' nor like
a 'dark pit of hunger, violence, and misery'. The Bronsteins led
the stern life of industrious and thrifty upstarts. 'Every muscle
was strained, every thought set on work and savings.' 'Life at
Yanovka was entirely governed by the rhythm of the toil on the
farm. Nothing else mattered, nothing except the price of grain
in the world market';[2] and this was just then falling rapidly.
However, the Bronsteins's preoccupation with money was no
heavier than that of most farmers; they were not stingy where
their children were concerned, and were doing their best to
give them a good start in life. When Lyova[3] was born, the elder
children were at school in town; the baby had a nursemaid, a
luxury very few peasants could afford. Later there would be a
teacher of music at Yanovka, and the boys would be sent to the
universities. Both the parents were too absorbed in their work
to give their youngest child much tenderness, but for this he
had instead the affectionate care of his two sisters and of his
nanny. Lyova grew into a healthy and lively boy, delighting his
parents and sisters and the servants and labourers on the farm
with his brightness and good temper.

By the standards of his environment, he had a comfortable
childhood. The Bronsteins's cottage was built of clay and had
five rooms; some of these were small and dim, with uncovered
clay floors and ceilings which leaked in heavy rain; but peasant
families usually lived in mud huts and hovels of one or two
rooms. During Lyova's childhood the family grew in wealth and
importance. The crops and the herds of cattle were on the
increase; new farm buildings sprang up around the cottage.
Next to the cottage stood a big shed containing a workshop, the
farm kitchen, and the servants' quarters. Behind it was a cluster
of small and large barns, stables, cowsheds, pigsties, and other
outbuildings. Farther off, on a hill beyond a pond, stood a big
mill, apparently the only one in this part of the steppe. In the

[1] In the same year, more than two months later, Joseph Djugashvili Stalin was
born in the little Georgian town of Gori.
[2] Trotsky, op. cit., loc. cit.   [3] Lyova is the diminutive of Lev or Leon.

summer, muzhiks from nearby and remote villages would come to have their corn ground. For weeks they waited in queues, slept in the fields when the weather was dry or in the mill when it rained, and paid the mill owner a tithe in kind for the grinding and threshing. David Bronstein traded with local merchants at first; but later, as his wealth grew, he sold his goods through his own wholesaler at Nikolayev, the grain harbour rapidly developing on the Black Sea. After a few years at Yanovka, he could easily have afforded much more land than he owned, were it not for the new *ukase* of 1881 which forbade Jews to buy land even in the steppe. He could now only rent it from neighbours; and this he did on a large scale. The neighbours belonged to the 'downstart' Polish and Russian gentry, who lightheartedly wasted their fortunes and were deep in debt, even though they still lived in splendid country residences.

Here the boy watched for the first time a social class in decay. 'The quintessence of aristocratic ruin was the Ghertopanov family. A large village and the entire county were once called by their name. The whole district had belonged to them. Now the old Ghertopanov owned only a thousand acres, and these were mortgaged over and over again. My father leased this land, and paid the rents into the bank. Ghertopanov lived by writing petitions, complaints, and letters for the peasants. When he came to see us, he usually hid tobacco and lumps of sugar up his sleeve. His wife did the same. Dribbling, she would tell us stories about her youth, and about the serfs, pianos, silks, and perfumes she had possessed. Their two sons grew up almost illiterate. The younger, Victor, worked as an apprentice in our workshop.'[1] It is easy to imagine the sense of their own competence and dignity that the Bronsteins felt when they compared themselves with such neighbours. Much of their own self-confidence and optimistic industriousness they passed on to their children.

Parents and sisters tried to keep the little Lyova in or near the cottage, but the bustle and commotion on the farm were too much for him, except during the quiet monotonous winter months, when family life centred on the dining-room. The magic of the workshop next door lured the boy: there Ivan Vassilyevich Grebien, the chief mechanic, initiated him into the

[1] L. Trotsky, *Moya Zhizn*, vol. i, pp. 46–47.

uses of tools and materials. Ivan Vassilyevich was also the
family's confidant; he lunched and supped at the cottage, at
his master's table, a thing almost unimaginable in an ordinary
Jewish home. The mechanic's tricks and jokes and his jovial
temper captivated Lyova: in *My Life* he recollects the
mechanic as the main influence of his early childhood. But at
the workshop the boy now and then also came up against an
outburst of puzzling ill temper on the part of other labourers.
Time and again he would overhear harsh words about his
parents, words which shocked him, set him thinking, and sank
into his mind.

From the workshop he would wander to the barns and cowsheds, play and hide in shady lofts, grow familiar with men and
animals, and with the wide spaces of the prairie. From his
sister he learned the alphabet, and got his first inkling of the
importance of figures as he watched the peasants and his father
wrangling in the mill over grain and money. He stared at
scenes of poverty, cruelty, and helpless rebellion; and he watched
the strikes of half-starved labourers in the middle of the harvest.
'The labourers left the fields and gathered in the courtyard.
They lay in the shade of the barns with their faces turned
downward, brandishing their bare, cracked, straw-pricked feet
in the air, and waited to see what would happen. Then my
father would give them some whey, or water melons, or half
a sack of dried fish, and they would go back to work and even
sing.'[1] Another scene he was to remember was that of a group of
labourers coming from the fields, in the twilight, with uncertain
steps and with their hands stretched out in front of them—they
had all been struck by night-blindness from undernourishment.
A health inspector came down to Yanovka, but found nothing
wrong there: the Bronsteins treated their labourers no worse
than did the other employers; the food, soup and *kasha*, was
not inferior to that served on any other farm. The impression
all this made on the child need not be exaggerated. Many have
seen such and worse scenes in their childhood without later becoming revolutionaries. Other and more complex influences
were needed to kindle in Lyova indignation against social
injustice and to turn his mind against the established order.
But when those influences appeared, they recalled vividly the

[1] L. Trotsky, *Moya Zhizn*, vol. i, p. 42.

pictures and scenes stored in his memory, and played all the more strongly on his sensitivity and conscience. The child took his environment for granted. Only when he was disturbed by an extreme instance of his father's harshness would he burst into tears and hide his face in the pillows on the sofa in the dining-room.

He was seven when his parents sent him to school at Grom-okla, a Jewish-German colony only a couple of miles away from Yanovka. There he stayed with relatives. The school he atten-ded may be described as a *kheder*, a Jewish private religious school, with Yiddish as its language. Here the boy was to be taught to read the Bible and to translate it from Hebrew into Yiddish; the curriculum also included, as sidelines, reading in Russian and a little arithmetic. Knowing no Yiddish, he could neither understand his teacher nor get along with his school-mates. The school was almost certainly a dirty and fetid hole, where the boy accustomed to roam the fields must have nearly choked. The ways of the adults also bewildered him. Once he saw the Jews of Gromokla driving a woman of loose morals through the main street of the village, pitilessly humiliating her and shouting vehement abuse. Another time the colonists meted out stern punishment to a horse-thief. He also noticed a strange contrast: on one side of the village stood the wretched hovels of Jewish colonists; on the other shone the neat and tidy cottages of German settlers. He was naturally attracted to the gentile quarters.

His stay at Gromokla was brief, for after a few months the Bronsteins, seeing the boy was unhappy, decided to take him back home. And so he said goodbye to the Scriptures and to the boys who would go on translating, in a strange sing-song, versets from the incomprehensible Hebrew into the incomprehensible Yiddish.[1] But, during his few months at Gromokla, he had learned to read and write Russian; and on his return to Yanovka he indefatigably copied passages from the few books at hand and later wrote compositions, recited verses, and made rhymes of his own. He began to help his father with accounts and book-keeping. Often he would be shown off to visiting neigh-bours and asked to recite his verses and produce his drawings.

[1] Later, during his stay in Odessa, he once again took lessons in Hebrew, but the result was not much better.

At first he ran away in embarrassment, but soon he grew accustomed to receiving admiration and looked for it.

A year or so after he had left the Jewish school there came to Yanovka a visitor who was to have a decisive influence on him as boy and as adolescent. The visitor was Moissei Filipovich Spentzer, Mrs. Bronstein's nephew, one of the remote, town-dwelling, middle-class branch of the family. 'A bit of a jour-nalist and a bit of a statistician', he lived in Odessa, had been touched by the liberal ferment of ideas, and had been debarred from the University for a minor political offence. During his stay at Yanovka, which lasted a whole summer—he had come there for his health—he gave much of his time to the bright but untutored darling of the family. Then he volunteered to take him to Odessa and to look after his education. The Bronsteins agreed; and so, in the autumn of 1888, equipped with a brand new school uniform, loaded with parcels containing all the delicacies that the Yanovka farm-kitchen could produce, and amid tears of sadness and joy, Lyova left.

The Black Sea harbour of Odessa was Russia's Marseilles, only much younger than Marseilles, sunny and gay, multi-national, open to many winds and influences. Southern ebullience, love of the spectacular, and warm emotionalism predominated in the temperament of the people of Odessa. During the seven or so years of his stay there it was not so much the city and its temper, however, as the home of the Spentzers that was to mould Lyova's mind and character. He could hardly have come into a family which contrasted more with his own. At first the Spentzers were not too well off; Spentzer himself was handicapped by his expulsion from the University, and, for the time being, his wife, headmistress of a secular school for Jewish girls, was the family's mainstay. Later Spentzer rose to be an eminent liberal publisher. Max Eastman, the American writer who knew the couple about forty years later, described them as 'kindly, quiet, poised, intelligent'.[1] They began by teaching the boy to speak proper Russian instead of his homely mixture of Ukrainian and Russian; and they polished his man-ners as well as his accent. He was impressionable and eager to transform himself from a rustic urchin into a presentable pupil. New interests and pleasures were opening before him. In the

[1] Max Eastman, *Leon Trotsky: The Portrait of a Youth*, p. 14.

evenings the Spentzers would read aloud the classical Russian poets—Pushkin and Lermontov and their favourite Nekrasov, the citizen-poet, whose verses were a protest against the miseries of Tsardom. Lyova would listen entranced and would demur at being compelled to descend from the golden clouds of poetry to his bed. From Spentzer he first heard the story of Faust and Gretchen; he was moved to tears by *Oliver Twist*; and stealthily he read Tolstoy's drastic and sombre play, *The Power of Darkness*, which the censorship had just banned and which was the topic of much hushed conversation among the grown-ups.

The Spentzers had chosen a school for him, but he was too young. This difficulty was overcome, however, when the registrar at home made out a birth certificate declaring him to be a year older than he was. A greater obstacle was that the year before, in 1887, the government had issued the ill-famed *ukase* on *numerus clausus*, under which admittance of Jews to secondary schools was so restricted that they might not exceed 10 and in some places 5 or 3 per cent. of all pupils. Jewish entrants had to sit for competitive examinations. At the examination Lyova, who had not attended any primary school, failed. For a year he was sent to the preparatory class at the same school, whence Jewish pupils were admitted to the first form with priority over outside Jewish applicants.

At St. Paul's *Realschule*—this was the name of the school—no Greek or Latin was taught, but pupils got a better grounding than in the ordinary *gymnasium*, in science, mathematics, and modern languages, German and French. To the progressive intelligentsia this curriculum seemed best calculated to give their children a rationalistic and practical education. St. Paul's had been founded by the German Lutheran parish of Odessa, but it had not escaped Russification. When Lyova joined it the teaching was in Russian, but pupils and teachers were of German, Russian, Polish, and Swiss origin—Greek Orthodox, Lutheran, Roman Catholic, and Jewish. This variety of nationalities and denominations resulted in a degree of liberalism uncommon in Russian schools. No single nationality predominated, and no denomination, not even the Greek Orthodox, was favoured. At the worst, a Russian teacher would surreptitiously pester a Polish pupil, or a Roman Catholic priest would annoy with subdued malice a Jewish boy. But there was no open discrimination or persecution to give a sense of inferiority to non-Russian pupils. To be sure, the discrimination was inherent in the fact that Russian had been made the official language; but only German parents and children would have been likely to resent this. And, in spite of the *numerus clausus*, the Jewish pupil, once he had been admitted, was treated with fairness. In a sense, St. Paul's gave Lyova his first taste of cosmopolitanism.

He at once became the top pupil in his class. 'No one had to take charge of his training, no one had to worry about his lessons. He always did more than was expected of him.'[1] His teachers were quick to acknowledge his gifts and diligence, and soon he also became popular with the boys of the higher forms. Yet he shunned sports and physical exercise, and during his seven years on the Black Sea he never went fishing, rowing, or swimming. His aloofness from the school playground was perhaps due to an accident during an early escapade, when he fell from a ladder, hurt himself badly, and 'wriggled on the ground like a worm', and perhaps also to his feeling that the proper place for outdoor exercise was Yanovka: 'the city was for studying and working.' His excellence in the class-room was enough to establish his self-confidence.

In the course of the seven years of the *Realschule* he was involved in a few school rows, none of which ended too badly. Once he produced a school magazine, nearly all written by himself; but, as such magazines had been forbidden by the Ministry of Education, the teacher to whom he presented a copy warned him to desist. Lyova paid heed to the warning. In the second form, a group of boys, including Lyova, booed and hissed a disliked teacher. The headmaster detained some of the offenders, but he let off the first pupil as being quite above suspicion. Some of the detained boys then 'betrayed' Lyova. 'The best pupil is a moral outcast', said the insulted teacher, pointing at the boy of whom he had been proud; and the 'outcast' was expelled. The shock was softened by the understanding and sympathy which the Spentzers showed their ward and by the indulgence of his own father, who was more amused than indignant.

Next year Lyova was readmitted, after examination; he became again the favourite and the pride of the school and took

[1] M. Eastman, *Leon Trotsky: The Portrait of a Youth*, p. 17.

care to avoid further trouble, though in one of the upper forms, together with other pupils, he refused to write compositions for a sluggish teacher who never read or returned the exercise-books; but this time he suffered no punishment. In the auto-biography, he himself describes, in a somewhat self-indulgent tone, the sequel to his expulsion: 'Such was my first political test, as it were. The class was henceforth divided into distinct groups: the talebearers and the envious on one side, the frank and courageous boys on the other, and the neutral and vacillating mass in the middle. These three groups never quite disappeared even in later years. I was to meet them again and again in my life....'[1] In this reminiscence the second form at the Odessa school is indeed made to look like the prototype of the Communist party in the 1920s with its divisions for and against Trotsky.

The boy's appearance and character were now becoming formed. He was handsome, with a swarthy complexion and sharp but well-proportioned features, short-sighted eyes lively behind their spectacles, and an abundant crop of jet black, well-brushed hair. He took unusual care with his appearance: neat and tidy, well and even stylishly dressed, he looked 'highly bourgeois'.[2] He was buoyant, sprightly, but also dutiful and well mannered. Like many a gifted youth, he was also strongly self-centred and eager to excel. To quote his own words, he 'felt that he could achieve more than the others. The boys who became his friends acknowledged his superiority. This could not fail to have some effect on his character.'[3] Max Eastman, his not uncritical admirer, speaks about his strong and early de-veloped instinct of rivalry, and compares it to a well-known instinct in race-horses. 'It makes them, even when they are ambling along at a resting pace, keep at least one white eye backwards along the track to see if there is anything in the field that considers itself an equal. It involves an alert awareness of self, and is upon the whole a very disagreeable trait—especially as it appears to those horses who were not bred for speed.'[4] Although Lyova had many followers among his school mates, none became his intimate friend.

At school he came under no significant influence. His teachers,

[1] L. Trotsky, *Moya Zhizn*, vol. i, p. 94.
[2] M. Eastman, *Leon Trotsky: The Portrait of a Youth*, pp. 15, 31.
[3] L. Trotsky, op. cit., vol. i, p. iii.   [4] M. Eastman, op. cit., p. 19.

whose personalities he sketches so vividly in the autobiography, were a mixed lot: some reasonably good, others cranky, or notorious for taking bribes; even the best were too mediocre to stimulate him. His character and imagination were formed at the Spentzers' home. There he was loved as well as admired, and he responded with warmth and gratitude. From his first weeks there, when he watched rapturously the Spentzers' baby and observed its first smiles, until the last days of his stay nothing clouded the affectionate relationship. The only discordant story his mentors would tell after many years was how once, at the beginning of his stay, Lyova sold a few of their most precious books to buy himself sweets. As he grew, he appreciated more and more his good fortune in having found such excellent guides and he shared increasingly in their intellectual interests. Editors of local liberal newspapers and men of letters were frequent visitors. He was mesmerized by their talk and by their mere presence. To him 'authors, journalists and artists always stood for a world more attractive than any other, open only to the elect';[1] and this world he beheld with a thrill known only to the born man of letters when he first comes into contact with the men and the affairs of his predestined profession.

Odessa was not one of the leading or most lively literary centres; the giants of Russian literature were not among the friends of the Spentzers. All the same, the boy of fifteen or sixteen stood reverently at the threshold of the temple, even if he saw none of the high priests at the altar. The local liberal press, much molested by the censorship, had its courageous and skilful writers such as V. M. Doroshevich, the master of that semi-literary and semi-journalistic essay at which Bronstein himself was one day to excel. Doroshevich's *feuilletons* were Lyova's and his elders' favourite reading. After Spentzer had started his publishing business, the house was always full of books, manuscripts, and printers' proofs which Lyova scrutinized with devouring curiosity. It excited him to see books in the making, and he inhaled with delight the fresh smell of the printed word, for which he was to retain a fond weakness even in the years when he was conducting vast revolutionary and military operations. Here he fell ardently in love with words; and here he first heard an authentic author, a local authority on Shakespeare who had

[1] L. Trotsky, *Moya Zhizn*, vol. i, p. 86.

read one of his compositions, express rapturous admiration for the way the boy handled and marshalled words.

He was spellbound by the theatre as well. '. . . I developed a fondness for Italian opera which was the pride of Odessa. . . . I even did some tutoring to earn money for theatre tickets. For several months I was mutely in love with the coloratura soprano, bearing the mysterious name of Giuseppina Uget, who seemed to me to have descended straight from heaven to the stage boards of Odessa.'[1] The intoxication with the theatre, with its limelight, costumes, and masks, and with its passions and conflicts, accords well with the adolescence of a man who was to act his role with an intense sense of the dramatic, and of whose life it might indeed be said that its very shape had the power and pattern of classical tragedy.

From Odessa, Lyova returned to Yanovka for summer holidays and for Christmas, or sometimes to repair his health. At every return he saw visible signs of growing prosperity. The home he had left was that of an ordinary well-to-do farmer; the one he came back to looked more and more like a landlord's estate. The Bronsteins were building a large country house for themselves and their children; yet they still lived and worked as of old. The father still spent his days bargaining with muzhiks over sacks of flour in the mill, inspecting his cowsheds, watching his labourers at the harvest, and occasionally himself grasping the scythe. The nearest post-office and railway station were still twenty or so miles away. Nobody read a newspaper here—at the most his mother would slowly and laboriously read an old novel, moving her toil-worn finger across the pages.

These homecomings filled Lyova with mixed feelings. He had remained enough of a villager to feel constricted in the city and to enjoy the wide and open steppe. Here he uncoiled himself, played, walked, and rode. But at each return he also felt more and more a stranger at Yanovka. His parents' pursuits seemed unbearably narrow, their manners coarse, and their way of life purposeless. He began to perceive how much ruthlessness towards labourers and muzhiks went into the making of a farmer's prosperity, even if that ruthlessness was, as it seems to have been at Yanovka, softened by patriarchal benevolence. While on holidays, Lyova helped with book-keeping and calculating wages; and some-

[1] L. Trotsky, op. cit., vol. i, p. 85.

times father and son quarrelled, especially when the calculations seemed to the old Bronstein unduly favourable to the wage-earners. The quarrels did not escape the attention of the labourers, and this incensed the farmer. The boy was not inclined to behave with discretion, and his spirit of contradiction was enhanced by a feeling of superiority, not unusual in the educated son of an illiterate peasant. Rural life in general struck him now as repulsively brutal. Once he tried, unavailingly, to protest against the rudeness of a policeman who came to deport two labourers because their passports had not been quite in order. He had a glimpse of the savage cruelty with which the poor themselves treated one another. He felt a vague sympathy for the underdog and an even vaguer remorse for his own privileged position. Equally strong, or perhaps even more so, was his offended self-esteem. It hurt him to see himself as the son of a rustic moneygrubber and illiterate upstart, the son, one might say now, of a *kulak*.

His stay in Odessa ended in 1896. A *Realschule* normally had seven forms, but St. Paul's only six, so he had to attend a similar school at Nikolayev to matriculate. He was now nearly seventeen, but no political idea had so far appealed to him. The year before, Friedrich Engels had died; the event did not register in the mind of the future revolutionary—even the name of Karl Marx had not yet come to his ears. He was, in his own words, 'poorly equipped politically for a boy of seventeen of that time'. He was attracted by literature; and he was preparing for a university course in pure mathematics. These two approaches to life, the imaginative and the abstract, lured him—later he would strive to unite them in his writings. But for the time being politics exercised no pull. He pondered the prospects of an academic career, to the disappointment of his father, who would have preferred a more practical occupation for him. Least of all did he imagine himself as a revolutionary.

In this the spirit of the time undoubtedly showed itself. At other times young people often plunged into clandestine revolutionary groups straight from school. This happened when such groups were astir with new ideas, animated by great hopes, and naturally expansive. During the 1880s and the early 1890s the revolutionary movement was at its nadir. In assassinating Alexander II the *Freedom of the People* had itself committed suicide. Its leaders had expected that their deed would become the signal for a nation-wide upheaval, but they failed to evoke any response and the nation maintained silence. Those directly and indirectly connected with the conspiracy died on the gallows, and no immediate successors came forward to continue it. It was revealed once again that, despite its discontent, the peasantry was in no revolutionary mood: to the peasants the assassination of Alexander II was the gentry's revenge on the peasants' benefactor.

The new Tsar, Alexander III, abolished most of his predecessor's semi-liberal reforms. His chief inspirer was Pobedonostsev, his tutor and the Procurator of the Holy Synod, in whose sombre and shrewd mind were focused all the dread and fear of revolution felt by the ruling class. Pobedonostsev egged on the Tsar to restore the unimpaired 'domination of the father over his family, of the landlord over his countryside and of the monarch over all the Russias'. It became an offence to praise the previous Tsar for the abolition of serfdom. The gentry's jurisdiction over the peasantry was restored. The universities were closed to the children of the lower classes; the radical literary periodicals were banned; the nation, including the intelligentsia, was to be forced back into mute submission.

Revolutionary terrorism proved itself impotent, and thus another *Narodnik* illusion was dispelled. An attempt to assassinate Alexander III—Alexander Ulyanov, Lenin's elder brother participated in it—failed. The survivors of the *Freedom of the People* languished in prisons and in places of exile, cherished their memories and were lost in confusion. Characteristic of the time was the repentance of one of the *Narodnik* leaders, Tikhomirov, who came out, in western Europe, with a confession under the title 'Why have I ceased to be a revolutionary?' Some former rebels found an outlet for their energies and talents in industry and commerce, which were now expanding at a quicker tempo than before. Many found their prophet in Leo Tolstoy, who rejected with disgust the evils of autocracy but preached that they should not be resisted with force. Tolstoy's doctrine seemed to give a moral sanction to the intelligentsia's disillusioned quiescence.

In *My Life* Trotsky ascribes his political indifference to this general mood. The explanation is only in part correct. The

truth is that well before 1896, the year in which he left Odessa,
a revival had begun in the revolutionary underground. The
Marxists expounded a new programme and method of action;
and groups of students and workers who considered themselves
social democrats were rapidly springing up. From a contemporary Russian report to the Socialist International we know
that by the middle of the decade such groups had been active in
Odessa.[1] The young Bronstein was not aware of their existence.
Evidently no socialist circle existed among the pupils of St.
Paul's, otherwise it would have tried to attract the school's most
popular and gifted pupil. Nor did the stirrings of the new movement find any echo in the prosperous and well-sheltered home
of the Spentzers. The Spentzers belonged to those on whom the
Narodnik débâcle had left a deep impression. They shunned the
really dangerous topics or spoke about them in muffled voices.
Their radicalism shaded off into a broad-minded but timid
liberalism which was, no doubt, implicitly opposed to Tsardom.
This was too little to impress their ward. Only clear-cut, bold,
and expressly stated ideas can enthuse young minds and hearts.
When in 1895 Nicholas II ascended the throne and bluntly told
the very moderate 'liberal' *Zemstvos* to give up 'nonsensical
dreams', Lyova's heart was with the 'dreamers'; but, like the
Spentzers, he took it for granted that it was quixotic to strive for
any change in the established system of government.

In this ill-defined, quiescently liberal mood one sentiment
was felt very keenly: a wistful yearning for Europe and its civilization, for the West at large and its freedoms. That 'West' was
like a vision of the promised land—it provided compensation
and comfort for the sorry and shabby reality of Russia. Especially on the Jewish intelligentsia, that part of the world which
knew no pogroms, no pale, and no *numerus clausus*, exercised
immense fascination. To a large section of the gentile intelligentsia, also, the West was the antithesis of all they detested at
home: the Holy Synod, the censorship, the *knout*, and *katorga*.[2]
Many of the educated Russians first approached the West with
that exalted reverence with which the young Herzen had

[1] *Doklad Russkikh Sots. Demokratov Vtoromu Internatsionalu* (Geneva 1896) states
that in Odessa these groups had been more active than elsewhere in the south of
Russia. See also P. A. Garvi, *Vospominanya Sotsialdemokrata*, pp. 20-1.
[2] *Katorga*: hard labour, penal servitude.

viewed it before bourgeois liberalism, seen at close quarters, disillusioned him. In later years Lyova, too, would, as a Socialist, grow aware of the limitations of liberal Europe and turn against it: but something of his youthful enthusiasm for the 'West' was to survive and colour his thoughts to the end.

This, then, was the frame of mind in which he left Odessa, 'the most police-ridden city in police-ridden Russia'. His only vivid political memory of the city was that of a street scene dominated by Odessa's Governor, Admiral Zelenoy, a man who exercised 'absolute power with an uncurbed temper'. 'I saw him but once and then only his back. But that was enough for me. The Governor was standing in his carriage, fully erect, and was cursing in his hoarse voice across the street, shaking his fist. Policemen, with their hands at attention, and janitors, caps in hand, marched past him in review, and behind curtained windows frightened faces peeped out. I adjusted my school bag and hurried home.'[1]

The spark of rebellion had not yet been kindled in the young man who watched the satrap—he merely shrank in horror from the ruling power and went his way, as if in a mood of Tolstoyan non-resistance.

[1] L. Trotsky, *Moya Zhizn*, vol. i, p. 79.

CHAPTER II

In Search of an Ideal

IT was a casual influence that first set the young Bronstein on his revolutionary road. In the summer of 1896 he arrived at Nikolayev to complete his secondary education. He was lodging with a family whose sons had already been touched by Socialist ideas. They drew him into argument and tried to impress their views on him. For several months they seemed to make no headway. He superciliously dismissed their 'Socialist Utopia'. Assailed with arguments, he would adopt the posture of a somewhat conservative young man, not devoid of sympathy with the people but distrusting 'mob ideology' and 'mob rule'. His passion was for pure mathematics and he had no time or taste for politics. His hostess, apprehensive because of her sons' dangerous views, was delighted by this good sense and tried to induce them to imitate him. All this did not last long. The talks about prevailing social injustice and about the need to change the country's whole way of life had already started a ferment in his thoughts. The Socialists' arguments brought out and focused the scenes of poverty and exploitation that had since childhood been stored in his mind; they made him feel how stifling was the air he had breathed; and they captivated him by their novelty and bold high-mindedness. Yet he continued to resist. The stronger the pull of the new ideas the more desperately he clung to his assumed conservatism and indifference to politics. His spirit of contradiction and his eagerness to excel in argument did not easily allow him to yield. But his defences and vanity had to give way. In the middle of the school year he suddenly acknowledged his 'defeat', and at once began to argue for socialism with an ardour and acuteness which took aback those who had converted him.[1]

Again and again we shall see this psychological mechanism at work in him: He is confronted with a new idea to which up to a point he is conditioned to respond; yet he resists at first with stubborn haughtiness; his resistance grows with the attraction; and he subdues incipient doubt and hesitation. Then his inner

[1] Trotsky, op. cit., vol. i, p. 120.

defences crumble, his self-confidence begins to vanish; but he is still too proud or not convinced enough to give any sign of yielding. There is no outward indication yet of the struggle that goes on in his mind. Then, suddenly, the new conviction hardens in him, and, as if in a single moment, overcomes his spirit of contradiction and his vanity. He startles his erstwhile opponents not merely by his complete and disinterested surrender, but by the enthusiasm with which he embraces their cause, and sometimes by the unexpected and far-reaching conclusions which he draws from their arguments.

The cause to which he had just adhered was dim in his mind. He had embraced a mood rather than an idea. He would 'side with the underdog'. But who was the underdog? How did he become one? And what was to be done? Nobody could offer him guidance. No significant Socialist group or organization existed in Nikolayev. Immediately, his socialism showed itself in a freshly awakened interest in social and political matters and in a corresponding weakening of his passion for mathematics. He began to seek those with similar views and interests; but in doing so he at once stepped out of the sheltered environment in which he had spent his childhood and adolescence.

Through his co-lodgers he met a certain Franz Shvigovsky, a poor gardener renting an orchard on the outskirts of the town, who, in his hut in the orchard, held a small discussion-club for radically minded students and working men. Shvigovsky, a Czech by origin, was a curious character. He read in many languages, was well versed in the classics of Russian and German literature, subscribed to foreign newspapers and periodicals, and was always ready to oblige his friends with a banned political book or pamphlet. Old *Narodniks*, living in the town under police surveillance, would sometimes join the group at the orchard. There were no prominent men among these *Narodniks*, and they formed no organization; but they imparted something of their own romantic revolutionary outlook to Shvigovsky's circle. Nearly all its members considered themselves to be *Narodniks*. The meetings, as one of the participants says, had a 'harmless character'. People came to the orchard because they felt at ease there and could speak freely. In the town Shvigovsky's garden soon had 'a most odious reputation ... as a centre of all sorts of the most terrible conspiracies'. The police sent in spies, disguised as labourers working in the garden; but these could only report that Shvigovsky kept serving his visitors apples and endless cups of tea and having harmless and cranky discussions with them.[1]

These, we know, were years of revolutionary revival. In March 1895 the Minister of the Interior, Durnovo, wrote to Pobedonostsev that he was alarmed by the new trends, especially among students who had zealously and with no expectation of reward taken to lecturing on all sorts of social themes. In the Minister's eyes this idealistic disinterestedness augured nothing good. All the repressive legislation of previous years had failed to make the schools and universities immune from subversive influences. For years now the ministry had been appointing professors over the heads of the faculties, dismissing suspects, and promoting obedient nonentities. Scholars of world fame such as D. Mendeleyev, the chemist, I. Mechnikov, the biologist, and M. Kovalevsky, the sociologist, had been found disloyal and dismissed or forced to resign their chairs. The eminent historian Klyuchevsky had had to recant his liberal opinions. The works of John Stuart Mill, Herbert Spencer, and Karl Marx had been forbidden. Students' libraries and clubs had been closed; and informers had been planted in the lecture halls. Entry fees had been raised fivefold to bar academic education to children of poor parents. Yet in spite of everything resurgent rebellion stalked the universities. At the end of 1895 and at the beginning of 1896 students were asked to take an oath of loyalty to the new Tsar, Nicholas II. In Petersburg, Moscow, and Kiev most students refused. The Tsar's coronation (during which thousands of onlookers were trampled upon, maimed, and killed in a stampede for which the police were blamed) was followed, in May 1896, by a strike of 30,000 Petersburg workers, the first strike on this scale.[2]

In these events the influence was already felt of the Union of Struggle for the Emancipation of the Working Class recently founded by Lenin, Martov, and Potresov. The revived movement was wholly influenced by the Marxists—the *Narodniks* scarcely took part in it. The new socialism relied primarily on the industrial worker. It repudiated terrorism. It recognized

[1] G. A. Ziv, *Trotsky, Kharakteristika po Lichnym Vospominanyam*, p. 8.
[2] Sibiryak, *Studencheskoye Dvizhenie v Rosii.*

the need for further capitalist industrialization in Russia, through which the working class would grow in numbers and strength. Its immediate purpose, however, was to fight for civil liberties and to move the workers to economic and political action and organization.

These developments had so far made only a ripple on the Nikolayev backwater. At the time when Bronstein joined Shvigovsky's circle (in the late autumn or early winter of 1896) its members must still have been agitated by the events that had taken place earlier in the year. They collected information and discussed it. But they did not go beyond that. They were not in a position to gauge the import of the new movement, and they had only a hazy notion of the Marxist critique of the *Narodnik* doctrines. They went on calling themselves *Narodniks*. Only one member of the circle, a young woman, Alexandra Sokolovskaya, herself the daughter of a *Narodnik*, claimed to be a Marxist and tried to persuade the circle that proletarian socialism offered them the real philosophy and science of revolution. She made little impression at first. But soon the hut in the orchard resounded with heated arguments. When Bronstein entered he found himself at once in the middle of a fierce controversy. At once he was pressed to make a choice. At once he labelled himself a *Narodnik*. And almost at once he assailed the solitary Marxist. G. A. Ziv (a friend of his youth and later his enemy, who has written vivid reminiscences of these days) tells us that when he, Ziv, first came to the orchard in the winter of 1896 Bronstein, not yet eighteen, 'was, because of his eminent gifts and talents, already attracting the attention of all Franz's visitors'; he was already the 'most audacious and determined controversialist' of the group and spoke with 'pitiless sarcasm' about the theories of Karl Marx, as expounded by the young woman.

He had only very little knowledge of either of the two contending doctrines. He had just borrowed from Shvigovsky a few outdated clandestine pamphlets, the first he ever read, and some files of radical periodicals; and he had scanned these nervously, impatient to grasp at a glance the substance of the arguments they contained. The authors who excited his enthusiasm were John Stuart Mill, Bentham, and Chernyshevsky, though their books had no direct bearing on the new controversy.

For a time Bronstein proudly described himself as a Benthamist and had no inkling how ill his infatuation fitted any revolution- ary, whether *Narodnik* or Marxist. Of Marx himself and of the lesser lights of the Marxist school he had not even a smattering of knowledge. A more cautious or reflective young man would have sat back, listened to the arguments, perhaps gone to the sources and weighed the pros and cons before he committed himself. (It was in this manner that Lenin first approached the teachings of Marx.) But Bronstein was precocious and had a volatile and absorptive mind. He had, 'like richly intellectual people who can think rapidly, a wonderful gift of bluff. He could catch so quickly the drift of an opponent's thought, with all its . . . implications, that it was very difficult to overwhelm him with mere knowledge.'[1] From school he had brought the self-confidence of the brilliant pupil and the habit of outshining his fellows. The last thing he would do when buttonholed by his new associates and urged to take sides was to plead ignorance. He did take sides; and, incapable of lukewarm reserve, he dashed headlong into the fray.

He made his choice instinctively. The *Narodnik* outlook ap- pealed to him precisely through that which distinguished it from the Marxist. The Marxists insisted that all social phenomena are directly or indirectly determined by society's economic condition. The *Narodniks* did not altogether reject this view— they had twenty years earlier been the pioneers of historical materialism in Russia. But they did not dwell on it with the same implacable emphasis; and many of them accepted the so- called subjectivist philosophy, which stressed the supremacy of the 'critical mind' and of the will of the individual. This philo- sophy accorded well with the traditions and the legends of a party which had refused to defer its assault on Tsardom until the economic conditions had 'ripened' or until the mass of the people had been aroused, and which had sent out its lonely fighters and martyrs, its strong-minded and strong-willed con- spirators, to hunt down, bomb in hand, the Tsar, his ministers, and his governors. To the young Bronstein Marxism seemed narrow and dry as dust—an offence to the dignity of man, whom it portrayed as the prisoner of economic and social circumstances,

[1] Max Eastman, *Leon Trotsky, The Portrait of a Youth*, p. 68; A. G. Ziv, op. cit., pp. 9–12; L. Trotsky, op. cit., vol. i, chapters vi–vii.

the plaything of anonymous productive forces. This, he himself was to say later, was a simplification and a parody of Marxism; and, at any rate, no other modern political creed was to inspire as many people as Marxism would with the will and determination to fight, to suffer, and to die for their cause.[1] But the parody was not altogether unreal. Many of those who professed Marxism were indeed adopting the dry and quietist parody as their creed. The first version of Marxism which the young Bronstein encountered was probably of that sort. Against this the attraction of the romantic *Narodnik* tradition was overwhelming. It held up inspiring examples to imitate, the memory of heroes and martyrs to cherish, and a plain, unsophisticated promise for the future. It offered glories in the past and it seemed to offer glories in the future. It only seemed so. In its decay, the *Narodnik* movement was incapable of repeating its past exploits, incapable, at any rate, of repeating them with the old, pure, and heroic illusions. But even while the sun of that great romantic movement was setting, it cast a purple afterglow on to the Russian skies. The eyes of the young Bronstein were filled with that glow.

Having thrown himself into the controversy he was Sokolovskaya's most bitter antagonist. Into their relationship there crept an ambivalent emotion almost inevitable between two young and close political opponents of different sex, meeting regularly in a tiny group, attracted and repelled by each other and incapable of escaping from each other. Sokolovskaya, several years older than Bronstein—six according to some, ten according to others—had, of course, a wider and more serious political experience than had the pupil of the top form of the *Realschule*. Modest, firm in her convictions, and altogether free from vanity, she would stubbornly explain her views and keep her temper even when her adolescent opponent was making her the butt of his jibes. The situation took on a farcical twist. Everybody in the orchard was a little infatuated with the girl; and some of the boys wrote love poems. The great 'isms' and problems, the budding love and the rhymes all became mixed up—and the more perverse grew the discussions. 'You still think

---

[1] In his late years, Trotsky often compared Marxism with Calvinism: the determinism of the one and the doctrine of predestination of the other, far from weakening or 'denying' the human will, strengthened it. The conviction that his action is in harmony with a higher necessity inspires the Marxist as well as the Calvinist to the highest exertion and sacrifice.

you are a Marxist?' Bronstein teased her, 'How on earth can a young girl so full of life stand that dry, narrow, impractical stuff!'—'How on earth', Sokolovskaya would answer, 'can a person who thinks he is logical be contented with a headful of vague idealistic emotions?' Or Bronstein would mock at her girlish sentimentality which scarcely harmonized with her adherence to Marxism, that 'doctrine for shopkeepers and traders'.[1]

Yet her arguments were beginning to find their way to his mind. His inner confidence was shrinking. All the more 're-lentless' was he in debate, and all the more boorish were his jibes. On the last day of December 1896 the group met for a discussion and celebration of the New Year. Bronstein came and, to the surprise of his friends, declared that he had been won over to Marxism. Sokolovskaya was elated. Toasts were drunk to the rapid emancipation of the working classes, to the downfall of Tsarist tyranny, and so on. When Bronstein's turn came, he stood up, lifted his glass, and turning towards Sokolovskaya, without apparent reason or provocation, burst out: 'A curse upon all Marxists, and upon those who want to bring dryness and hardness into all the relations of life!' The young woman left the orchard swearing that she would never shake hands with the brute. Soon afterwards she left the town.[2]

The new year had come, and the group had not yet gone beyond talk. Bronstein wrote a polemical article against Marxism, 'more epigrams, quotations, and venom than content' and sent it off to a periodical with *Narodnik* leanings. The article never appeared. Jointly with Sokolovskaya's brother, he was writing a drama on the Marxist-*Narodnik* controversy, but got stuck after the first or second act. The play was intended to show the *Narodnik* in a favourable light and to contrast him with the Marxist. As the plot was unfolding the authors noticed with astonishment that it was the Marxist who was shaping into the attractive character: he was almost certainly endowed with some of Sokolovskaya's features. The group also staged a 're-volt' in the local public library, the board of which had intended to raise readers' fees. The 'orchard' rallied the 'public', brought

---

[1] G. A. Ziv, op. cit., p. 15; M. Eastman, op. cit., p. 46.

[2] These incidents are related by both Eastman and Ziv. In *My Life* Trotsky omits them; but as in his preface to Eastman's book he confirms its factual accuracy, he thereby also testifies to the truthfulness of these stories, for which Ziv is the original source.

in new subscribers and overthrew the board at an annual meeting—no small event in the dormant town.[1]

Bronstein now neglected his school work; but he had learned enough to graduate in the summer of 1897 with first-class honours. However, his father sensed that something had gone wrong. On a vacation at Yanovka Lyova had talked about freedom and the overthrow of the Tsar. 'Listen, boy. That will never happen, not even in 300 years!' the farmer replied, wondering where his son had picked up such ideas. Soon he was on the track of Lyova's new associates and briskly ordered him to keep away from Shvigovsky's orchard. Lyova now asserted his 'critical mind' and 'free will'. He was free, he said, to choose his own friends; but as he would not submit to paternal authority he would not go on living on his father's money. He gave up his allowance, took up private tutoring, and moved from his comfortable lodgings to Shvigovsky's hut, where six students, some tubercular, had already been living. The change was exhilarating; freedom at last! Gone was the neat and dutiful bourgeois son, the object of admiration and envy to other boys' parents. His place was taken by a real *Narodnik*, who, like the pioneers of old, 'went to the people' to become one of them, lived in a little commune where everybody dressed like a farm labourer, put his few *kopeyeks* into the pool, drank the same thin soup, and ate the same *kasha* from a common tin bowl.

Old Bronstein sometimes came from Yanovka to see whether Lyova, weary of privation and discomfort, might not mend his ways. There was no sign of this. One of Shvigovsky's lodgers, later a well-known communist editor, was to remember the 'big, whiskered farmer . . . coming into the hut at dawn and standing over him aggressive and implacable. "Hello!" he shouts with a loud voice like a bugle: "You, too, ran away from your father?" '[2] Angry scenes alternated with half-hearted reconciliation. The father, seeing the ruin of his fond hopes for Lyova, was inconsiderate and impatient. The son, humiliated in front of his comrades, among whom he aspired to be the leading light, reacted with vehemence and disrespect. On both sides came into play the same temperaments, the same sense of righteousness, the same stubbornness, the same pride, and the same bugle-like voices. When Lyova entered the University of

[1] L. Trotsky, loc. cit.   [2] M. Eastman, op. cit., p. 55.

Odessa to study mathematics, it seemed that things might yet
be patched up: even pure mathematics was in his father's eyes
preferable to playing in obscure company at the overthrow of the
Tsar. At the university Lyova began to show an exceptional
gift for his subject.[1] But the university could not compete in
attraction with Shvigovsky's orchard; nor could calculus get
the better of revolution. His stay in Odessa was brief, but long
enough for him to make contact with revolutionaries there and
to get from them clandestine papers and pamphlets, with which
he returned in triumph to Nikolayev.

Then came the turbulent spring of 1897. In March a student-
girl imprisoned for her political convictions in the Peter–Paul
fortress in St. Petersburg committed suicide by burning herself in her cell. The event provoked a storm of protests and
demonstrations in the universities. In reprisal the authorities
deported large numbers of undergraduates. New protests and
demonstrations followed. Even 'police-ridden' Odessa was astir.
Students coming from Kiev brought fresh excitement and indignation to Shvigovsky's orchard. This, Bronstein and his
friends felt, was the time to pass from words to deeds.

'Bronstein . . . suddenly called me aside and proposed in
great secrecy that I join a working-men's association, organized by himself', writes Ziv, then a student of medicine just
arrived from Kiev. 'The *Narodnik* idea, Bronstein said, had been
discarded; the organization was planned to be social democratic, although Bronstein avoided using this term . . . and proposed to call it the *Southern Russian Workers' Union*.' 'When I
joined the organization', Ziv goes on, 'everything had already
been arranged. Bronstein had already established his contacts
with the workers and also with revolutionary circles in Odessa,
Ekaterinoslav, and other towns. . . .'[2]

About 10,000 workers were employed in the docks and factories of Nikolayev, mostly skilled and well-paid craftsmen with
enough leisure to read books and newspapers. So far, however,
they had had no organization, not even a trade union. The

[1] Eastman quotes a prominent Russian technician, one of Trotsky's university
colleagues, who, even after the revolution, regretted the loss to science of so exceptionally gifted a mathematician. Ibid., p. 59.

[2] A. G. Ziv, op. cit., p. 18. About this time social democratic groups were reviving
or being formed in most towns in the south. See M. N. Lyadov, *Kak Nachynala Skła-
dyvatsia R.K.P.* (*Istorya Ross. Sots.-Dem. Rab. Partii*), pp. 310 ff.

working-class quarters were teeming with religious sects opposed to the Orthodox Church. These sectarians Bronstein approached. He quickly saw which of them were concerned with religious dogma mainly and which were more preoccupied with the political implications of their opposition to Greek Orthodoxy. Among the latter he recruited the first members of the South Russian Workers' Union. He grouped them in small circles which met regularly to discuss current events and read clandestine papers. Before the year was out the Union counted about 200 members. From a contemporary Russian report, published after their arrest, we have a detailed view of the organization. Its members were locksmiths, joiners, electricians, seamstresses, and students, most of them in their early or middle twenties but some well over forty.[1] Among the founding members was also Sokolovskaya. Unmindful of the New Year's Eve scene, she returned to the orchard as soon as she had learned about the new beginning.

The name of the organization was evidently borrowed from another which had existed a quarter of century before and had had its centre in Odessa. The old South Russian Workers' Union, founded by a student, E. O. Zaslavsky, had been *Narodnik* in character and followed Lavrov's educational-propagandist line. It had been, as far as can be ascertained, roughly of the same size as its successor. In 1875 it was routed out by the police. Its leaders were tried by the Senate and most of them were convicted to forced labour. Zaslavsky and some of his associates died in prison. One of the founders, N. P. Shchedrin, was twice condemned to death and twice had his sentence commuted to life-long forced labour. For many years the prisoner was chained to his wheel-barrow, until his mind became deranged; then he was transferred to the Schlusselburg fortress, where for another fifteen years he was subjected to the sort of torture of which Dostoyevsky's *Notes from the House of the Dead* perhaps gives an idea. The legend of this martyrdom lived on in southern Russia; and it was probably as a tribute to it that Bronstein called his organization the South Russian Workers' Union. He himself assumed his first pseudonym—Lvov.

---

[1] *Rabocheye Delo, Organ Soyuza Russkikh Sotsial-Demokratov*, Geneva, 1 April 1899, pp. 150–2, gave a long and detailed list of the arrested members of the Union, with data about age, occupation, &c.

This transformation of the boy, who only the year before seemed a rich man's worldly son, into the founder of a clandestine organization, volunteering to take the revolutionary's thorny path, was startlingly rapid. He had evidently been overflowing with an inborn exuberant energy and with an ardour and imagination for which conventional pursuits provided little or no outlet. He needed a cause to serve, a cause exacting sacrifice; and when he found it, his youthful and passionate temperament came into the open. Both his friends and his enemies agree that he was the moving spirit, the mouthpiece, the organizer, and also the most energetic and devoted worker of the Union. 'Our group was the first social democratic organization at Nikolayev', says Ziv in reminiscences coloured by retrospective hostility. 'We were so excited by our success that we were in a state . . . of chronic enthusiasm. For the major part of these successes we were undoubtedly indebted to Bronstein, whose energy was inexhaustible and whose many-sided inventiveness and untiring drive knew no bounds.' The organization, Ziv goes on, many years afterwards looked back with pride to its hey-day when it was led by the eighteen-year-old boy, who by his faith, eloquence, and personal example cast a spell upon its members and induced them to forget all their private attachments and preoccupations and wholly devote to the cause themselves, their thoughts, energies, and time. After Bronstein's departure the nerve of the organization snapped. The Union could not recapture the ardour of its beginnings.[1]

The Union was, of course, a tiny group compared with any normal party or organization. In relation to the power against which it set itself it was like a microbe assailing a huge and decaying body; it was in fact one of a score or so of the microbes of revolution that were just going into action.

The groups set up in the docks and factories circulated leaflets and a sheet called *Nashe Delo* (*Our Cause*). The leaflets commented on matters of local interest, conditions in factories and shipyards, and abuses by employers and officials. The exposures made an impression; those exposed were compelled to reply; and the Union fought back with new leaflets. 'What satisfaction I had when I received the information from factories and workshops that the workers avidly read the mysterious leaflets

[1] A. G. Ziv., op. cit., p. 21 and *passim*.

printed in purple ink. . . . They imagined the author as a strange and powerful person who had . . . penetrated into all the factories, knew what was happening in the workshops, and within twenty-four hours reacted to events with fresh leaflets.'[1] *Nashe Delo*, the 'organ' of the Union, also met with encouraging response. The group was too poor to print the clandestine sheet. Bronstein is said to have proposed to produce it secretly in Spentzer's printing shop in Odessa—in his fervour he was un-mindful of the harm he might have done to his relative—but his own comrades persuaded him not to. Then a somewhat cranky well-wisher came along with a 'scheme' for revolution: what was needed to overthrow the Tsar, he said, was 100,000 roubles, for which a thousand little clandestine printing shops could be set up all over Russia to flood the working-class quar-ters with anti-Tsarist proclamations. As a beginning the well-wisher presented the group with a mimeograph; and Bronstein set to work. He himself wrote the sheet and the leaflets; he him-self calligraphed them in purple ink (so that the workers should not need to strain their eyes); he himself illustrated the text with cartoons; he himself produced, in the wretched dwelling of a blind comrade, the stencils and the several hundred copies of each issue; and he himself looked after the distribution.[2] It used to take him about two hours to print a page. 'Sometimes I did not even unbend my back for a week, interrupting my work only for meetings and group discussions.'

Politically, the Union was a parochial fraternity of rebels, innocent of any sophistication. Some members still described themselves as *Narodniks*, others called themselves Marxists; but this division did not interfere with their work. They could act together because they acted on a narrow basis. They called the workers to fight for higher wages and for shorter hours and in this no difference showed itself between the *Narodnik* and the Marxist. They avoided addressing the workers on the political issues over which they were arguing at the orchard. This sort of activity, at this time characteristic of most of the clandestine groups, was later labelled 'Economist', because of its one-sided concentration on matters of 'bread-and-butter'. But it was its

---

[1] L. Trotsky, op. cit., vol. i, pp. 133–4.
[2] 'All the important technical, not to speak of the literary part of the work was done by Bronstein.' A. G. Ziv, op. cit., p. 21 and *passim*.

one-sidedness that secured its rapid success. If two groups, each advocating another 'ism', had come out and tried in competition with each other to win the workers, the result would have been confusion and failure. Only within a broader and more firmly established movement could the differences be seriously fought out. All the same, the Union of Nikolayev became known to the leaders of more advanced groups in other centres, who were preparing to call a Congress and to found the Social Democratic Workers' Party. They wondered whether to invite the Nikolayev group to send its delegate: would his age not detract from the solemnity of the occasion? Before the doubt was resolved the Nikolayev group was in prison.[1]

The success of this first venture demonstrated to the young revolutionary the 'power of the written word'. The town was astir with rumour; the Union, admired or feared, was a factor to be reckoned with; and friend and foe imagined it to be much stronger than it was. All this was the effect of his, Bronstein's, written word. The belief in the power of the word was to remain with him to the end. In every situation he would turn to it as to his first and his last resort; and throughout his life he would wield that power sometimes with world-shaking effect, and sometimes with lamentable failure. In this small fraternity of rebels he also first tried out his oratory; but the first attempt ended in humiliation and tears. It was one thing to speak sharply and bitingly in argument and quite another to make a set speech. 'He quoted Gumplowitz and . . . John Stuart Mill . . . and he got himself so terribly wound up in a sliding network of unintelligible big words and receding hopes of ideas that his audience sat bathed in sympathetic perspiration, wondering if there was any way under the sun they could help him to stop. When he finally did stop and the subject was opened for general debate, nobody said a word. Nobody knew what the subject was.' The speaker 'walked across the room and threw himself face down in the pillow on the divan. He was soaking with sweat, and his shoulders heaved with shame and everybody loved him.'[2]

In this small group none of Bronstein's qualities, good or bad,

[1] L. Trotsky, *Pokolenie Oktyabrya*, p. 20; M. N. Lyadov, *Kak Nachala Skladyvatsia RKP*, p. 324; Akimov, *Materialy dla Kharakteristiki Razvitya RSDRP*, pp. 39, 75.
[2] M. Eastman, op. cit., p. 70; Ziv relates that Bronstein carefully studied the techniques and tricks of polemics in Schopenhauer's *The Art of Debating*.

escaped his comrades. Their recorded observations agree with one another in almost everything except the emphasis. Soko-lovskaya, who was to become his wife and whom he was to abandon, recollected after nearly thirty years that he could be very tender and sympathetic but also very assertive and arro-gant; in one thing only he never changed, in his devotion to the revolution. 'In all my experience I have never met any person so completely consecrated', she said. His detractor speaks with more emphasis about his self-centredness and domineering temper: 'Bronstein's Ego', writes Ziv, 'dominated his whole behaviour', but, he adds, 'the revolution dominated his Ego.' 'He loved the workers and loved his comrades . . . because in them he loved his own self.' Having cheerfully given up the comforts of a settled life and the prospects of a good career he could not see how others could behave differently. When Ziv, anxious to finish his university course, began to neglect the group, Bronstein gave him a telling though tactful admonition. He presented Ziv with a picture on which he wrote a dedication: 'Faith without deeds is dead.'[1]

The hero who inspired him more than anybody else was Ferdinand Lassalle, the founder of the first mass movement of German socialism. In those days Lassalle's influence on Euro-pean socialism was very strong—later the disclosure of his am-biguous political dealings with Bismarck dimmed the lustre. That the young Bronstein should have been so strongly impres-sed by Lassalle was due to an indubitable affinity. Lassalle, too, had been the son of a wealthy Jewish family and had abandoned his class to strive for the emancipation of the workers. He had been one of the greatest orators and one of the most colourful and romantic characters of his age. His meteoric career had come to a tragic end: he found his death in a romantic duel. As the founder of the first modern Labour party—the first not only in Germany—he had made history. The greatness, the brilliance, and the drama of such a life could not but stir the young Bronstein's imagination. He spoke about his hero with rapturous admiration; he swore to follow in his footsteps; and, if we are to believe Ziv, he boasted that he would become the Russian Lassalle. The young man was not addicted to modesty, false or real. He hid neither his faults nor his pretensions.

[1] M. Eastman, op. cit., p. 87; A. G. Ziv, op. cit., pp. 12, 19-21.

He used to think and dream and indulge his ambition—aloud.

.　　.　　.　　.　　.　　.　　.　　.　　.

The first spell of his clandestine activity lasted from the spring of 1897 till the end of the year. The police at first refused to believe that all the agitation in the factories and docks emanated from the few adolescents and cranks in Shvigovsky's garden; and they searched for a more impressive source. This gave the Union time to spread its influence, until the police recovered from incredulity and began to watch the comings and goings of Bronstein and his friends. Towards the end of the year the leaders of the Union, expecting repression, agreed to disperse and to resume work after an interval. They decided, however, to reappear in town if in their absence the police arrested workers belonging to the Union: the police must not be in a position to tell the rank and file that the leaders had deserted them.

In the first weeks of 1898 Bronstein left Nikolayev to seek refuge on an estate in the country, where Shvigovsky had just taken a new job. No sooner had he arrived there than both he and Shvigovsky were seized by the police. Most members of the Union were arrested in Nikolayev and in the neighbourhood. From the country Bronstein was transferred to the prison at Nikolayev and then to a prison at Kherson, where he was kept for several months. The police had no doubt that he was the animator of the group. Through a bitterly cold winter they kept him in strict isolation in a tiny, unheated, unaired, and vermin-ridden cell. A straw mattress was brought for the night and removed at dawn so that in daytime he had neither couch nor seat. He was not allowed to walk and take exercise in the prison yard, nor to receive a newspaper, a book, soap, or a change of linen. Starved, dirty, covered with lice, he paced his cell, knocked at the walls to see whether there was a living soul in the neighbouring cells—there was none; he resumed his walk, counted his steps and tried to shake off the vermin. The monotony of these months was not even interrupted by an official interrogation; the prisoner was not even told what were the charges brought against him. This treatment, intended to break his spirit, was still milder than that meted out to a few other members of the Union, who under torture were committing suicide, becoming insane, or breaking down and agreeing to serve as informers. 'There were times . . . when I was sick with loneliness', he confessed. But he found moral satisfaction in his sacrifice and he composed revolutionary limericks which later were sung as folk-songs. Towards the end of his stay in this prison the police relented, and his mother succeeded in bribing his guards and sending in food parcels and such 'luxuries' as soap, linen, and fruit.

For depositions and examination he was at last transferred to a prison in Odessa, in which he was to remain a year and a half, until the end of 1899. There, too, he was kept in solitary confinement, but he could secretly communicate with his friends.[1] The prison was overcrowded and alive with constant movement, plotting, and practical jokes. He was in high spirits and poked fun at the colonel of the gendarmerie who conducted the investigation. To prepare himself for his interrogator he had to ascertain how much the gendarmes had discovered about the Union and he communicated about this with his associates in other cells. 'His task . . . was not easy . . . he had to tell me the the whole story of his arrest and the circumstances attending it and to summarize his own deposition. . . . All this had to be expressed so that I should get the fullest possible idea of what had happened and so that the communication should contain no clue against himself in case of interception. He performed this in a masterly fashion. He wrote an essay full of scintillating wit and satirical irony, a brilliant pamphlet.'[2] He began to transform his own experience into literature.

The interrogation dragged on without producing incriminating evidence. In the meantime Bronstein avidly read whatever he could lay hands on, at first only books and periodicals available in the prison library but, later, books sent from outside as well. The prison library contained only religious literature and church periodicals. For linguistic exercise he read the Bible simultaneously in German, French, English, and Italian. Then he got hold of files of Greek Orthodox periodicals, which were full of polemics against agnostics, atheists, and especially freemasons. 'The polemics of the learned Orthodox writers', he

[1] It was in this prison that the members of the Union learned about the founding 'Congress' of the Social Democratic Party, which had just taken place in Minsk; and in excitement they passed on this news from window to window. L. Trotsky, *Pokolenie Oktyabrya*, p. 20.

[2] A. G. Ziv, op. cit., p. 28.

wrote later, 'against Voltaire, Kant, and Darwin, led me into
a world of theological thoughts which I had never touched before and I had never even distantly imagined in what fantastic,
pedantic, droll forms these thoughts poured out.' 'The research on the devils, daemons, their princes, Satan himself and
the Kingdom of Darkness constantly amazed me. . . . The
copious descriptions . . . of Paradise with details about its . . .
internal lay-out ended on a melancholy note: "Exact directions
about the location of Paradise are not available"; and at dinner
and tea and during my walks I kept repeating this sentence: as
to the geographical location of Paradise precise directions are
lacking.'[1] Theological bickering with a bigoted jailor was his
favourite diversion. Rationalistic rejection of religion was, generally speaking, characteristic of the educated Russian of this time,
whether he was Radical or Socialist or only moderately Liberal,
whether he came from a Greek Orthodox or a Jewish family.
In Bronstein's upbringing the Jewish creed had played no part
at all, and only in the prison did he acquaint himself with Greek
orthodoxy. Both the Jewish and the Greek orthodoxies were so
obscurantist and stubborn in their refusal to take notice of any
new idea—they were in this respect far behind the Protestant
and even the Catholic Churches—that they violently repelled
the educated or even half-educated man. He could not compromise with a religion which itself refused to compromise with
any modern trend in the human mind.

As he delved with amusement into this theological literature
he also tried to extract from its polemical summaries and distortions the main lines of the unfamiliar philosophies and sociological systems which the Church condemned. He searched for
clues which would enable him to reconstruct his own versions
of these evil theories and then to evaluate them, according to
his lights, in a Marxist manner. From outside he received a few
books which helped him more directly. He read Darwin's
works, and these confirmed him in his instinctive atheism.
Twenty-five years later he recalled how Darwin's description
of the way in which the pattern on the peacock's feathers
formed itself naturally, banished for ever the idea of the Supreme Being from his mind; and how shocked he was to learn

[1] See Trotsky's letter to Eastman in Eastman, op. cit., p. 113, and L. Trotsky,
Moya Zhizn, vol. i, p. 141.

that Darwin himself had not been an atheist.[1] Then the philosophical essays of Antonio Labriola, the Italian Marxist, brought him a little nearer to his goal: Labriola's thought and style, undogmatic, lucid, and graceful, left a lasting impression. He now only half understood the subject matter of Labriola's book, but he obtained more solid clues to Marxist theory.

From such precarious points of view, and using a loose tissue of fact drawn from Greek Orthodox sources, he then attempted to write a materialist history of freemasonry and in this concrete historical analysis to put to a test his homespun version of Marxism. This was his first copious literary work and one for which he preserved a lifelong attachment: he remained unconsoled after its loss in one of his early wanderings. We need not share the author's tenderness for his first-fruits; but we may assume that in these writings he first tried his hand at Marxist history writing. Among his many essays, which he used to put into a hiding place in the prison latrine for his friends to read, was one on the role of the individual in history, the subject of ever-absorbing debate for the Marxist and the *Narodnik*. 'I made no new discoveries; all the conclusions . . . at which I arrived had been made long ago by others. . . . But I reached them gropingly and, up to a point, independently. This influenced the whole course of my development. In the writings of Marx, Engels, Plekhanov, and Mehring, I later found confirmation for what in prison seemed to me only a guess. . . . I had not at the outset accepted historical materialism in a dogmatic form.'[2]

These efforts occupied his mind and kept his spirit buoyant as his second year in prison was drawing to a close. Mentally, the adolescent was passing into manhood; and the transition was hastened by the fact that nothing was left to the captive in his cell but thought and reflection.

. . . .

[1] In an address to the students of the Sverdlov University in Moscow, in 1923, he said: 'To the end of my life I shall wonder whether Darwin was sincere in this, or whether he merely paid his tribute to conventional beliefs.' *Pokolenie Oktyabrya*, pp. 55–56.

[2] L. Trotsky, *Moya Zhizn*, vol. i, p. 147. Ziv claims that in the Odessa prison Bronstein also wrote a treatise on wages, in which he argued that piece-wages were preferable to time-wages, because they were more conducive to high productivity. It seems almost impossible that he should have dealt with so specific an economic subject at this time. Ziv was again imprisoned with Bronstein in St. Petersburg in 1906–7; and he probably ascribes to his friend in Odessa an essay written several years later.

Towards the end of 1899 the prisoners received their administrative verdict, that is, a verdict without trial. Bronstein and
three of his associates were to be deported to Siberia for four
years; others were exiled for shorter terms; some were released.
Soon the trek of the deportees began. They were first taken to
Moscow, and there they waited six months in a 'transfer
prison'. Not only had they been given no fair hearing or trial,
the two and a half years of their detention were not to be de-
ducted from their terms.

In the prison in Moscow Bronstein met older and more experienced revolutionaries from all parts of Russia who were also
awaiting final deportation. New faces, new impulses, new ideas.
Here he first heard about Lenin and read his solid book, just
published, *The Development of Capitalism in Russia*. Here he first
became aware of the more advanced stages the clandestine
movement had reached in the north of the country. Even
battles of ideas fought in western Europe found an immediate
echo within the walls of this prison. Among the many books
passed on from cell to cell was Edouard Bernstein's famous
work *The Premisses of Socialism*, the first explicit attempt made
by an eminent German Social Democrat to dissociate the labour
movement from the revolutionary conceptions of Marxism and
to impart to it an evolutionary, reformist character. Bernstein's
work provoked what seemed at the time a Homeric struggle
between two wings in European socialism, the 'orthodox Marxist' and the 'revisionist'. It caused no flurry among the inmates
of the transfer prison: not one of them was in a mood to abandon
the road of revolution for a peaceful pedestrian march towards
socialism.

In these new surroundings Bronstein lost none of his self-
confidence. He went on reading and arguing, and produced a
continuous stream of essays and pamphlets. He planned to set
up a printing shop inside the prison under the very noses of the
police. This seemed too risky to his comrades and he had to
content himself with circulating his output in manuscript. Already to his fellows his imagination at times seemed too bold
and his willingness to challenge authority too rash. At Kherson
he had, in the teeth of opposition, persuaded his comrades to
start a hunger strike in protest against a proposal from the
police that juvenile prisoners be released on condition that their

parents would give them a good thrashing and keep them from meddling in politics—this was 'an insult to the honour of the juvenile revolutionary'. Here again, in Moscow, he defended with *bravura* the prisoner's dignity. A prisoner had failed to take off his cap to the governor of the prison and had been punished with solitary confinement. Bronstein at once staged a demonstration of solidarity:

At a brief meeting it was decided that we should all come out with our hats on and ask the guard to give the alarm signal for the governor. When the governor comes we shall, of course, not take off our hats. Circumstances will dictate what to do next. The guard . . . refused to give the alarm signal. We crowded around him, and Bronstein, standing in front of us, took out his watch and said with supreme confidence: 'I give you two minutes to make up your mind.' . . . Then . . . pushing aside the disconcerted jailor, he pressed the button with a magnificent flourish. We put on our hats and went out to the yard. The governor, surrounded by a huge band of armed guards, came running into the yard. 'Why don't you take your hat off?', he burst out, jumping at Bronstein, who stood in front of us with the most defiant mien. 'And you, why don't you take off yours?', Bronstein replied proudly.[1]

A few giant guards carried away the struggling rebel to solitary confinement.

Harsh and defiant towards authority, or, as he himself would have said, towards the class enemy, he was warm-hearted and even sentimental with his comrades and their relatives. The convicts were allowed to receive their relatives twice a week. At these visits Bronstein 'showed a moving tenderness not only to his own girl and future wife . . . but to all the other women who came to see their husbands or brothers; he charmed them all with his chivalry'.[2] The women usually took home the men's linen; but Bronstein refused to benefit from such comforts, washed and repaired his own linen, and mocked at revolutionaries so ensnared in bourgeois habits and prejudices as to burden their womenfolk with such work. Returning from the visitors' room to the cell, he 'used to spend all the excess of his tenderness on us, caressing and kissing and embracing us'. So much was he remembered for the warmth of his friendship that years later his friends, who had in the meantime become his

[1] A. G. Ziv, op. cit., p. 39.   [2] Ibid., p. 36.

opponents, were puzzled by his ruthlessness in the revolution and in the civil war.

During this spell in the Moscow prison, in the spring or summer of 1900, he married Alexandra Sokolovskaya. A Jewish chaplain conducted the wedding in the cell; and the bridegroom borrowed a wedding ring from one of his jailors. The story of this marriage is a little obscure. Quite often political deportees arranged fictitious marriages, because a married couple were entitled to be deported to the same place and could thus escape complete isolation. The fictitious connexions often developed into real ones. It is not clear how Bronstein and Sokolovskaya at first viewed their marriage. In *My Life* he devoted to this only one curiously detached and cool phrase, suggesting that it was meant to be a sham. 'Common work', he says, 'had bound us closely together, and so, to avoid separation, we married. . . .'[1] The eye-witness account denies the prosaic character of the connexion. It describes how the ambivalent feeling between the former antagonists had given place to love, how in the prison and *en route* from Moscow to Siberia Bronstein was full of affection, and how, during the journey under military escort which lasted nearly a fortnight, he was so absorbed in that affection that he completely neglected his friends and discussions. This eye-witness account seems, on internal evidence, truthful. The marriage, incidentally, was not easily concluded. Bronstein first thought of it in the Kherson prison, but not having yet come of age he had to get parental permission. His father objected: he would not allow his son to marry a girl so much older, a girl who—the old Bronstein had no doubt about this—had led his son on to the evil path. 'Lyova raged and thundered' writes Ziv, 'and fought with all the energy and stubbornness of which he was capable. But the old man was no less stubborn, and having the advantage of being on the other side of the prison bar, he won.' In Moscow Lyova renewed his efforts and this time he succeeded. He would perhaps not have 'raged and thundered' so much for the sake of a fictitious wedding.

The journey from Moscow to the place of exile, interrupted by short stops in various transfer prisons, lasted from the summer till the late autumn. The whole party of deportees travelled by

[1] Trotsky, op. cit., vol. i, p. 148.

rail to Irkutsk, where they were separated and dispatched in different directions. The Bronsteins were sent down the Lena river on a large barge, which was crowded with Skoptsy,[1] dressed in white clothes, chanting prayers, and dancing wildly. The Bronsteins were ordered to disembark in the village of Ust-Kut, which during the gold rush on the Lena had served as a base for east Siberian settlers. The gold-diggers had by now moved farther east and north, and Ust-Kut was a god-forsaken place with about a hundred peasant huts, dirty and plagued by vermin and mosquitoes. The inhabitants, sick with unfulfilled dreams of wealth, were madly addicted to *vodka*. Here the Bronsteins stayed for a time, during which he studied *Das Kapital*, 'brushing the cockroaches off the pages' of Karl Marx. Later they obtained permission to move to another place, 150 miles farther east, where he worked as book-keeper for an illiterate millionaire peasant–merchant. His employer conducted business over a vast area and was the uncrowned ruler of its Tunguz inhabitants. Bronstein watched this huge capitalist enterprise growing on virgin Siberian soil—he would cite it in the future as an illustration of that combination of backwardness and capitalist development which was characteristic of Russia. Sociological observation and attentive book-keeping did not go well together, and an error in the accounts cost Bronstein his job. In the middle of a severe winter, with temperatures about ninety degrees below freezing-point, the Bronsteins went on sledges back to Ust-Kut. With them was their baby daughter, ten months old, wrapped in thick furs. At the stops the parents had to unwrap the baby to make sure that in protecting her from freezing to death they had not suffocated her.

From Ust-Kut they moved to Verkholensk, half-way on the road to Irkutsk, in the mountains towering over the Baikal Lake. There they occupied a little house and settled down in relative comfort. Verkholensk was one of the oldest eastern Siberian settlements—thirty-five years earlier Polish insurgents had been

---

[1] The Skoptsy were a persecuted sect of fanatics who castrated themselves to live in saintliness ('Holy eunuchs'). They lived in communes and were mostly gardeners, dressed in white, and spent night hours in prayer. The sect based itself on Isaiah: 'For thus saith the Lord unto the eunuchs that keep my sabbaths, and choose the things that please me, and take hold of my covenant; even unto them will I give in mine house and within my walls a place and a name better than of sons and of daughters.' (lvi. 4, 5.) According to legend, some of the Tsars (e.g. Alexander I) belonged to the sect.

deported there to build roads—and it now had a large colony
of deportees and good postal connexions with Irkutsk, the most
important town in this part of Siberia. Here Bronstein had a
fair opportunity to continue his studies and develop his ideas,
to establish useful contacts and to make himself known in more
ways than one. Soon he was up to his ears in the disputes which
were going on in the exiles' colonies and he wielded a growing
influence. He lectured, argued, and wrote, pleading for socialism against anarchism, for mass struggle against terrorism, and
for Marxism against the subjectivist philosophy. In the preceding years he had accepted the main lines of the Marxist philosophy: now, in Siberia, he finally and firmly identified himself
with the social-democratic trend. A Social Democratic Siberian
Union was just then growing up, recruiting members among
deportees and among workers employed in the building of the
Trans-Siberian Railway. The Union approached Bronstein and
asked him to write leaflets. He readily agreed, and soon the
organization came to regard him as their leader and mouthpiece. Two years later he was to represent this Siberian Union
in Brussels and London at the momentous Congress during
which the party split into Mensheviks and Bolsheviks.

The spring of 1901 brought one of those sudden commotions
which marked the flux and reflux of public opinion in the Tsarist Empire. There were again stormy demonstrations in the
universities and strikes in the factories. Thousands of students
were arrested; many were conscripted into the army—this was
a new punishment decreed in 1899—and many were deported.
The Holy Synod excommunicated Leo Tolstoy. In February
1901 an undergraduate named Karpovich shot the Minister
of Education, Bogolepov. The Writers' Association protested
against brutal police control over academic life. The Socialist
International denounced the Tsar in a solemn manifesto.
The clandestine groups got fresh blood, and new deportees
brought a fresh breeze into the Siberian colonies. From the new-
comers' tales Bronstein tried to gauge the strength of the anti-
Tsarist opposition. He reached the conclusion that the political
ferment, intense though it was, was about to fizzle out largely
because the clandestine groups did not know what use to make
of it or how to direct it against autocracy. The mushrooming
underground organizations led a disjointed existence, each being

engrossed in local affairs and ambitions. National co-ordination and leadership were needed. Bronstein was not the first to advance this idea. Abroad older Marxists, Plekhanov, Lenin, Martov, and others were expounding it in the newly-founded *Iskra* (*The Spark*). But *Iskra*, the first issue of which had appeared in Germany a few months before, had not yet reached the exiles at Verkholensk. Bronstein set down his views in an essay which was widely circulated and hotly debated in the Siberian colonies. The biographical interest of this now little-known essay lies in the fact that in it he expounded broadly a view of the organization and the discipline of the party identical with that which was later to become the hall-mark of Bolshevism, and which he himself then met with acute and venomous criticism.[1]

The revolutionary movement, so he argued in 1901, would be a Frankenstein monster, unless it came under the rule of a strong Central Committee which would have the power to disband and expel any undisciplined organization or individual. 'The Central Committee will cut off its relations with [the undisciplined organization] and it will thereby cut off that organization from the entire world of revolution. The Central Committee will stop the flow of literature and of wherewithal to that organization. It will send into the field . . . its own detachment, and, having endowed it with the necessary resources, the Central Committee will proclaim that this detachment is the local committee.' Here, one might say, was in a nutshell the whole procedure of purge, expulsion and excommunication, by which he himself was eventually to be 'cut off from the entire world of revolution'. Yet, it was true that at this time the revolutionary movement in Russia could not advance a single step without national integration and discipline and that a national leadership was sometimes bound to impose this discipline sternly on reluctant groups.[2] When Bronstein first formulated this view, he brought down upon himself the very charges with which he

[1] See his *Vtoroi Syezd RSDRP* (*Otchet Sibirskoi Delegatsii*), p. 32. He quoted his Siberian essay in 1903 in an appendix to his report to the Siberian Union on the second congress of the party, in which he tried to explain why he sided with the Mensheviks against the Bolsheviks, despite the views he had advocated in Siberia. The Siberian Union at first was, like the South Russian Union, 'economist' in character; and only in 1902 did it recognize the supremacy of revolutionary politics over economics and join, under Bronstein's influence, the *Iskra* organization. Later it was affiliated with the Mensheviks.

[2] L. Martov, *Istorya Ross. Sotsial-Demokratii*, pp. 62–72.

would one day confront Lenin. Some of the deportees argued that
Bronstein's view was a relapse from the Marxist into the *Narodnik* attitude; that Social Democrats set their hopes on the mass
of the workers and not on a handful of leaders; and that they
had, consequently, no need to invest a Central Committee with
those dictatorial powers which had been indispensable in a
narrow conspiracy. We shall not now go farther into the controversy which at its more advanced stage will become one of
the major motifs of this narrative. But it is important to notice
that its first appearance goes back as far as 1901.

These activities are, however, less well known to us than
Bronstein's literary achievements of the Siberian years. Very
soon after his arrival he began to write for the *Eastern Review*
(*Vostochnoye Obozrenie*), a progressive newspaper appearing at
Irkutsk. He signed his contributions Antid Oto. The pen-
name (from the Italian *antidoto*) well suited the spirit of opposition which permeated his writings. As Antid Oto he became
very popular in the Siberian colonies and through exiles returning to Russia his fame presently reached revolutionary
circles in Petersburg, Kiev, and even the émigrés in western
Europe.[1] His contributions, which are reprinted in volumes iv
and xx of his *Works*, were on the borderline of literature and
journalism—by the standards of the short-winded, asthmatic
journalism of the mid-twentieth century they would certainly
be classed as literature. He wrote social reportage and literary
criticism. The former consisted of essays mainly on the life of the
Siberian peasantry, composed in a mixed style at once leisurely
and descriptive and sharply satirical. In these writings he was
strongly influenced by Gleb Uspensky, the talented and tragic
Narodnik whose realistic yet profoundly melancholy descriptions
of the life of peasants, artisans, and petty officials tore open the
wounds and revealed the miseries of the Tsarist empire, and set
a very high standard for the 'literature of exposure'.

'Nearly a quarter of a century has passed since the old writer
surveyed the scene, and it is time to see how much has changed
in the Russian countryside and small town since his days': with
this direct invocation Antid Oto stepped into Uspensky's shoes.

---

[1] The author knew personally old ex-deportees, who, in the 1920s and 1930s
would in conversation still refer to Trotsky as Antid Oto and ask, for instance, 'What
does Antid Oto say about the situation?'

He dealt with the same characters, the peasants and the petty officials, the injured and the dejected; and he treated them with the same sympathy and pity—only his indignation was sharper and more bitter. As his writings had to be laid before the censor, he did not directly attack the Government. But this restraint made his subdued anger and mockery even more effective. His language was easy and fluent, and despite its mannerisms—it was often verbose, sometimes pompous and over-elaborate— it was colourful and expressive; and full, penetrating observation, vivid portraiture, and unexpected contrasts and images made up for his mannerisms. 'Our village is economically devastated by the *kulaks*, physically by syphilis and all sorts of epidemics, and spiritually it lives in a dense concentrated darkness . . .', he wrote in an essay on the insanitary state of the Siberian countryside and on the lot of the village doctor. 'In thoughtful silence our village is dying from disease.' The mentally ill were kept for observation in the prisons, which, because of the lack of hospitals, formed 'the psychiatric department of the local sanitary authority'. In one case two homeless invalids, an old insurgent and an old gendarme—the same gendarme who had once escorted the insurgent to the place of deportation— lived in the same prison cell, for lack of any other asylum. The doctors were cut off from the world, helpless and dejected. Perhaps regional conferences of the medical personnel would shake them from their apathy.[1] Another time he demanded local government for Siberia. In European Russia, he wrote, the *Zemstvos* (rural assemblies) had at least some say in local matters. But east of the Urals the administration sensed rebellion in every *Zemstvo*, and even if a nucleus of local government existed here and there, the peasants were in it as 'silent symbols' only. The gentry sent one representative for every 3,000 roubles of income, while the peasants sent one for every 43,000.

He illustrated the anachronistic nature of the administration in a character-sketch of a clerk in a Siberian *volost* (an administrative district comprising several villages). The clerk was burdened with an incredible variety of jobs: he acted on the spot for the Ministry of the Interior; he was responsible to the Ministry of War for the call-ups; he collected taxes for the Ministry of Finance; he prepared statistics for the Ministry of

[1] L. Trotsky, *Sochinenya*, vol. iv, pp. 17–42.

Agriculture; he was the local agent for the Department of Justice, and for the Ministry of Education and Religious Denominations. Only the Navy and the Foreign Office left him in peace; but even this was not sure. Financial agent, statistician, agronomer, road engineer, architect, notary, legal officer, all in one person, the clerk did not even receive his salary regularly. The result? 'The half-fictitious statistical figures he supplies to higher authority are processed there, made the basis of many an official . . . survey or investigation, which then becomes the object of passionate polemics for the responsible leaders of opinion.'[1] A series of Bronstein's articles was devoted to the 'martyrdom of the womenfolk': the muzhik beat his wife mercilessly, and so did the wealthy Siberian merchant.

Half a century later these essays still retain their documentary value, and one can imagine the effect they produced at the time. The censor pored over them with increasing suspicion and more and more often cut out paragraphs or entire sections. The writer was constantly compelled to resort to new tricks of evasion and to convey his purpose by hint and allusion. When his 'unprotected fingers' were no longer able to grasp the nettle of fact, he would, with an apology, make his style shade off into semi-fiction.

Opposition writers often found in literary criticism some refuge from the assaults of censorship. This was so with Bronstein, yet to him literary criticism was much more than a convenient pretext for expounding political views. He was a literary critic as by vocation. Even his first attempts to approach literature from the Marxist angle were untainted by that narrow political utilitarianism which so-called Marxist criticism often makes its chief virtue. His approach was analytical rather than didactic, and it was enriched by a vivid appreciation and enjoyment of aesthetic values. He was a voracious reader. In the course of his two years in Siberia he wrote on Nietzsche, Zola, Hauptmann, Ibsen, D'Annunzio, Ruskin, Maupassant, Gogol, Herzen, Belinsky, Dobrolyubov, Uspensky, Gorky and others. The range of his historical and literary reminiscence and allusion was extremely wide, even if some of it must be dismissed as a youthful showing-off of erudition. His prime interest was, as with the Marxist it must be, in the social impulse behind the literary

[1] L. Trotsky, *Sochinenya*, vol. iv, pp. 3–7 and *passim*.

work, in the moral and political climate to which the poet or the novelist gives his individual expression, and in the effect which the literary work, in its turn, has on that climate.

But there was nothing in this of the vulgar Marxism which pretends to discover an economic or political class-interest hidden in every poem or play or novel. He was also exceptionally free (quite exceptionally for a man of 20–22 years) from the sectarian attitude which may induce a revolutionary to denounce any spiritual value which he cannot fit to his own conception and for which he has therefore no use. In the young Marxist this attitude is usually a symptom of inner uncertainty: he has not genuinely assimilated his new-found philosophy; the principles he professes are up to a point external to his thinking; and he is an historical materialist from duty rather than from natural conviction. The more fiercely he denounces anything that seems to contradict his ill-digested philosophy, the easier is his conscience, the more gratified is his sense of duty. In the young Bronstein it was therefore a sign of how intimately he had made the Marxist way of thinking his own, and a measure of his confidence in it, that he was singularly free from that dutiful sectarianism. He usually paid generous tribute to the talent or genius of a writer whose ideas were remote from or directly opposed to the doctrines of socialism. He did so not merely from fairness but from the conviction that the 'spiritual estate of man is so enormous and so inexhaustible in its diversity' that only he who 'stands on the shoulders of great predecessors' can utter a truly new and weighty word. The twenty-one-year-old writer insisted that revolutionary socialism was the consummation, not the repudiation, of great cultural traditions—it repudiated merely the conservative and conventional conception of tradition. He was not afraid of finding that Socialist and non-Socialist views might overlap or coincide and of admitting that there was a hard core, or a grain, of truth in any conception which as a whole he rejected.[1]

His first literary essay, a critical obituary on Nietzsche,

[1] He concluded an essay on Gogol, 'the founder of the Russian novel' as follows: 'If Gogol tried to weaken the social significance of his own writings . . . let us not hold this against him. If in his publicist writings he tried to appeal to the petty minds—let us forgive him this! And for his great inestimable artistic merits, for the loftily humane influence of his creative work—eternal, inextinguishable glory to him!' *Sochinenya*, vol. xx, p. 20.

appeared in the *Eastern Review*, in several instalments, in December 1900, a month or two after his arrival in Siberia. He could have chosen no subject more embarrassing than the work of Nietzsche whose hatred of socialism was notorious and whose cult of the Superman was repugnant to the Socialist. Bronstein began his obituary with an apology for its critical tenor: 'We ought to behave dispassionately towards the personalities of our . . . adversaries, and we ought to . . . pay due tribute to their sincerity and other individual merits. But an adversary—sincere or not, alive or dead—remains an adversary, especially if he is a writer who survives in his works. . . .' He showed how the idea of the Superman grew out of normal bourgeois morality and in what way it was opposed to that morality. Nietzsche, he held, generalized and drew to its last logical, or rather illogical, conclusion the contempt of the masses which was deeply rooted in normal bourgeois thinking. To prove this point, the critic showed how many of Nietzsche's views were either implied or expressly stated in the writings of Herbert Spencer, that representative philosopher and sociologist of the Victorian middle class. The idea of the Superman was opposed to bourgeois morality only as the excess is opposed to the norm. The immoral Superman stood in the same relation to the virtuous middle class in which the medieval *Raubritter* (with his maxim: Rauben ist keine Schande, das tuhn die Besten im Lande) had stood to the feudal lord. Nietzsche's ideal was the rapacious bourgeois freed from inhibition and stripped of pretences. Despite this, the Socialist could not but admire the brilliant originality with which Nietzsche had shown how brittle were the normal workaday ethics of the middle class.[1]

To this issue Bronstein returned in an essay on Ibsen, in whom he saw the immortal artist at loggerheads with the false moralist.[2] 'The historian of European social thought will never forget the slaps, those truly glorious slaps, which Ibsen has inflicted on the well washed, neatly brushed, and shiningly complacent physiognomy of the bourgeois philistine.' In *An Enemy of the People*, for instance, Ibsen had shown how subtly, without committing a single act of violence, a bourgeois democracy could isolate and destroy a heretic ('as effectively as if they had deported him to Siberia'). But the Socialist cannot approve the

[1] L. Trotsky, *Sochinenya*, vol. xx, pp. 147–62. [2] Ibid., pp. 181–95.

superman-like attitude of Ibsen's hero, his distrust of the people, and his contempt of government by majority. The people, the majority—the Socialist agrees—is not the fount of all-embracing wisdom: 'If the "crowd" were called upon to pronounce on the merits of a scientific theory or of a philosophical system . . . Ibsen would have been a thousand times right. . . . The view of a Darwin on problems of biology is a hundred times more important than the collective opinion expressed at a meeting by a hundred thousand people.' (The author did not imagine that fifty years later it would be customary in his country for mass meetings to denounce 'disloyal' biologists or linguists.) 'But when we go out into the field of practical social policy, where so many deeply antagonistic interests are at play, the problem is quite different. . . . There the subordination of the minority to the majority, if it corresponds to the genuine balance of social forces and is not temporarily brought about by artificial means, is of infinitely superior merit.' Nevertheless, Ibsen's distrust of 'the people' expressed an artistic opposition to bourgeois society, an opposition towards which Marxists ought to behave with understanding and sympathy, although they themselves revolted against that society from different premisses and in a different way.

As a Marxist, Bronstein was not impressed by the pretensions of art for art's sake. 'Like a paper kite [that art] can soar to heights from which all earthly matters are drowned in grey indifference. But even after it has reached the clouds, this poor "free" art still remains tied to a strong rope, the earthly end of which is tightly gripped by the philistine.'[1] 'Literature without the power of great synthesis', he wrote on another occasion, 'is the symptom of social weariness and is characteristic of sharply transitional epochs.'[2] He therefore viewed critically the then fashionable symbolist trend; but he did so not because he favoured narrow realism. On the contrary: 'Artistic creation, no matter how realistic, has always been and remains symbolist. . . . The purpose of art . . . is not to copy reality in empirical detail but to throw light on the complex content of life by singling out its general typical features. . . . Every artistic type is broadly a symbol, not to speak of such highly symbolical images as

[1] See the essay on Hauptmann, ibid., pp. 170–81.
[2] Essay on Balmont, ibid., pp. 167–70.

Mephisto, Faust, Hamlet, Othello, artistically embodying definite "moments" of the human soul. . . .' The symbolist school, however, he held, was trying to elevate the means into an end in itself and, so, was degrading the symbol from an intensified expression of human experience into a means of escaping from that experience.

His interest in European letters was as intense as was his reaction against the national self-centredness of official, and in part also of *Narodnik*, Russia. He ridiculed the boast of the Slavophiles that they had no need to learn from the West and that the Russians themselves made all the great discoveries and inventions—'the Russian land can rear its own Platos and quick-witted Newtons'.[1] This 'westernizing', then common to all Marxists and liberals, did not imply any repudiation of the Russian spiritual heritage of the nineteenth century—Russia's great literary tradition did not go back any farther. Most of Russia's thinkers and writers had been rebels, and the revolutionary intellectual was steeped in their works. It was the influence of the literature of rebellion that helped Bronstein to cut himself adrift from his own childhood and adolescence in which there had been so little experience likely to make of him a revolutionary. He had been, we know, profoundly impressed by Gleb Uspensky. In 1902, when Uspensky died insane, Bronstein quoted with self-revealing approval Uspensky's remark that there had been almost no link between his adult life as a rebel and his childhood and adolescence, and that he had had 'to forget his own past' before he could form his new identity. This was, of course, even truer of the writer of the obituary. 'With terrible suicidal perspicacity', he wrote, 'Uspensky grasped life such as it was and he burned himself out in the craving for life such as it should be. He searched for truth and found the lie; he searched for beauty and found ugliness; he searched for reason and found unreason.'[2]

In the other leaders of the literary revolt, Belinsky, Dobrolyubov, and to a lesser extent in Herzen, Bronstein admired their identification with the oppressed, their indifference to worldly

[1] L. Trotsky, *Sochinenya*, vol. xx, pp. 116–18, the satirical article on 'The Russian Darwin' published in November 1901.

[2] Bronstein wrote two obituary essays on Uspensky, one for the *Eastern Review* and another for *Nauchnoye Obozrenie* (Scientific Survey), *Sochinenya*, vol. xx, pp. 33–40 and 41–67.

success, their imperviousness to banality, and the self-immolat-
ing integrity with which they searched for truth. Uspensky, the
Narodnik, had risen above *Narodnik* prejudices and illusions:
'A lonely figure, the martyr of his own fearless thought, he looks
with painfully penetrating eyes above the heads of his contemporaries and comrades . . . into the face of the future.' Belinsky,
'the godfather of modern Russian literature' held that 'nothing
that appears and succeeds at once and is met with . . . unconditional praise can be important or great—significant and great
is only that which divides opinion . . . which matures and grows
through genuine struggle, which asserts itself . . . against living
resistance'. In Dobrolyubov the critic valued the extreme sensitivity to any false note and the impatience with platitudes, even
when they were innocuous. Nothing was more embarrassing
to Dobrolyubov than to have to listen to a man who argued
heatedly about the inhumanity of cannibalism or the usefulness
of education. Dobrolyubov's satire, Bronstein concluded, would
remain acutely topical 'as long as the great heroism for petty
affairs raised its head so high . . . and as long as it was
considered a social merit to preach the rudiments of a cheap
liberalism'.[1]

This summary of Bronstein's literary criticism may, through
inevitable compression, give a somewhat exaggerated idea of the
maturity of his writings. His style, over-elaborate, over-rhetori-
cal, and over-witty, was still adolescent; but his judgement was,
on the whole, mature. To the biographer the value of these
essays is enhanced by the many flashes of the author's implied
self-analysis and self-portrayal. However, the young Bronstein
epitomized more directly his own outlook in an invocation to the
twentieth century (written early in 1901, under the title 'On
Optimism and Pessimism, on the Twentieth Century, and on
Many Other Things').[2] There he analysed various types of optimism and pessimism and stated his preference for the view
which was pessimistic about the present but optimistic about the
future. It is, Bronstein argues, the man who holds this view who
opens new vistas to the human mind and makes history. More
than once this peculiar optimist has had to brave a Holy In-
quisition. 'More than once has the collective Torquemada devoted exclusive attention to him.' Yet he, the optimist, rises

[1] Ibid., pp. 12, 29-31.   [2] Ibid., pp. 74-79.

C

from the ashes and 'as passionate, as full of faith and as militant as ever, confidently knocks at the gate of history'. On his way he meets the philistine, whose strength lies in numbers and un-diluted vulgarity and who is 'armed to the teeth by an experi-ence which does not range beyond the counter, the office desk, and the double bedroom'. To the mockery of the philistine and to his pseudo-realistic conservatism ('There is nothing new under the moon'), the optimist who looks to the future replies:

Dum spiro spero! . . . If I were one of the celestial bodies, I would look with complete detachment upon this miserable ball of dust and dirt. . . . I would shine upon the good and the evil alike. . . . But I am a *man*. 'World history which to you, dispassionate gobbler of science, to you, book-keeper of eternity, seems only a negligible moment in the balance of time, is to me everything! As long as I breathe, I shall fight for the future, that radiant future in which man, strong and beautiful, will become master of the drifting stream of his history and will direct it towards the boundless horizon of beauty, joy and happiness! . . .

The nineteenth century has in many ways satisfied and has in even more ways deceived the hopes of the optimist. . . . It has compelled him to transfer most of his hopes to the twentieth century. Whenever the optimist was confronted by an atrocious fact, he exclaimed: What, and this can happen on the threshold of the twentieth century! When he drew wonderful pictures of the har-monious future, he placed them in the twentieth century.

And now that century has come! What has it brought with it at the outset?

In France—the poisonous foam of racial hatred; in Austria—nationalist strife . . .; in South Africa—the agony of a tiny people, which is being murdered by a colossus; on the 'free' island itself—triumphant hymns to the victorious greed of jingoist jobbers; dramatic 'complications' in the east; rebellions of starving popular masses in Italy, Bulgaria, Rumania. . . . Hatred and murder, famine and blood. . . .

It seems as if the new century, this gigantic newcomer, were bent at the very moment of its appearance to drive the optimist into absolute pessimism and civic nirvana.

—Death to Utopia! Death to faith! Death to love! Death to hope! thunders the twentieth century in salvoes of fire and in the rumbling of guns.

—Surrender, you pathetic dreamer. Here I am, your long awaited twentieth century, your 'future'.

—No, replies the unhumbled optimist: You—you are only the *present*.

.   .   .   .

After four and a half years of prison and exile Bronstein longed for a scene of action broader than the Siberian colonies. In the summer of 1902, the underground mail brought him a copy of Lenin's *What is to be done?* and a file of *Iskra*. He read these with mixed feelings. Here he found ideas on the shape and character of the party, ideas which had been maturing in him, set out with supreme confidence by the brilliant émigré writers. The fact that he had in his backwater reached the same conclusions independently could not but give him a thrill and confirm him in his self-reliance. But he was intensely restless: he could no longer bear the sight of the muddy, cobble-stoned, narrow streets of Verkholensk. Even the arguments within the colonies of deportees and his literary successes with the *Eastern Review* filled him with boredom. If only he could get away to Moscow or Petersburg . . . and then perhaps to Geneva, Munich, or London, the centres where the intellectual weapons of the revolution were being forged. . . .

He shared his impatience and his secret ambition with his wife. Alexandra had no doubt that her husband was destined to greatness, and that at twenty-three it was time for him to do something for immortality. She urged him to try to escape from Siberia and in doing so she shouldered the burden of a heavy sacrifice. She had just given birth to their second daughter and was now undertaking to struggle for her own and her children's lives, unaided, with no certainty of a reunion. In her own conviction she was, as his wife and as a revolutionary, merely doing her duty; and she took her duty for granted without the slightest suggestion of melodrama.[1]

On a summer night in 1902, Bronstein, hidden under loads of hay in a peasant cart rumbling along bumpy Siberian fields, was on his way to Irkutsk. In his bed, in the loft of his house at Verkholensk, there lay the dummy of a man. Next evening the police inspector who came, as usual, to check whether the Bronsteins were in, climbed a ladder to the loft, glanced at the bed and, satisfied that everything was in order, went away. In

[1] L. Trotsky, *Moya Zhizn*, vol. i, p. 157; Ziv, op. cit., p. 42; M. Eastman, op. cit., pp. 142–3.

the meantime the fugitive, supplied by his friends at Irkutsk
with new, respectable-looking clothes, boarded the Trans-Siberian railway.

Before he left Irkutsk his comrades provided him with a false
passport. He had to inscribe hastily the name he was to assume,
and he scribbled that of one of his former jailors in the Odessa
prison. In this hazardous escape did the identification with his
jailor perhaps gratify in the fugitive a subconscious craving for
safety? It may be so. Certainly the name of the obscure jailor
was to loom large in the annals of revolution: it was—Trotsky.[1]

The journey west was unexpectedly quiet. The passenger
killed time reading Homer's hexameters in a Russian translation.
He alighted at Samara on the Volga, where *Iskra's* organization
had its Russian headquarters. He was heartily welcomed by
Kzhizhanovsky-Clair, the prominent technician, Lenin's friend
and future chief of the Soviet *Gosplan* (State Planning Commission). Bronstein's literary reputation had preceded him, and
Kzhizhanovsky-Clair nicknamed him *The Pen* (*Piero*) and sent
a glowing report on his talents and activities to *Iskra's* headquarters in London. Straightway Bronstein was sent to Kharkov, Poltava, and Kiev to inspect groups of Socialists. He found
that most of the groups persisted in their local patriotisms and
refused to co-operate with one another or to submit to any central authority. With a report to this effect he returned to Samara.
There an urgent message from Lenin was awaiting him: The
Pen was to report as soon as possible at *Iskra's* foreign headquarters.

[1] Ziv, op. cit., pp. 25–26; M. Eastman, op. cit., p. 143. In his autobiography
Trotsky does not mention the bizarre origin of his pseudonym. As if a little ashamed
of it, he merely says that he had not imagined that Trotsky would become his name
for the rest of his life.

CHAPTER III

At the Door of History

EARLY one morning, almost at dawn, in October 1902, the fugitive from Siberia knocked violently at a door in London, at 10 Holford Square, near King's Cross. There, in one room and a kitchen, lived Vladimir Ilyich Lenin and his wife, Nadezhda Konstantinovna Krupskaya—Mr. and Mrs. Richter to their lower-middle-class neighbours. The early hour was hardly suitable for a visit, but the caller was too full of the importance of his mission and too impatient and self-confident to think of the minor courtesies. He had travelled in feverish excitement from Irkutsk to London, stealing across frontiers and surmounting all obstacles on the way. In Vienna he had roused the famous Victor Adler, the founder of the Austrian Socialist Party, from a Sunday rest and got from him the help and the money he needed for the rest of his journey. In Zurich he had knocked, in the middle of the night, at the door of Paul Axelrod, the veteran of Russian Marxism, in order to introduce himself and make arrangements for the last lap. Now, at his final destination, alone in the grey mist of an early London morning, with only a cabman waiting behind him for the fare— the passenger had no money—he expressed his inner agitation by his loud knocking. He was indeed 'knocking at the door of history'.

Krupskaya, guessing a countryman in the early and noisy visitor, and a little worried lest her English neighbours might be annoyed by this instance—not the only one—of the extravagant behaviour of the foreigners in the house, hurried out to meet the newcomer. From the door she exclaimed: 'The Pen has arrived!' Lenin, she later recollected, 'had only just awakened and was still in bed. Leaving them together I went to see to the cabman and prepare coffee. When I returned I found Vladimir Ilyich still seated on the bed in animated conversation with Trotsky on some rather abstract theme. But the cordial recommendations of the "young eagle" and this first conversation made Vladimir Ilyich pay particular attention to the

newcomer.'[1] The visitor was to remember the 'kindly expression
on Lenin's face . . . tinged with a justifiable amazement'.

Breathlessly the visitor made his report on the political
trends and moods among the Siberian exiles; on the impressions
he had formed from his recent trip to Kiev, Kharkov, and
Poltava; on the reluctance of local groups there to consider
themselves as parts of an integrated national movement; on the
work at Samara headquarters; on the degree of reliability of
the clandestine channels of communication; on defects in the
arrangements for illegal frontier crossings; and on much more.
Lenin, who had recently been exasperated by the unbusinesslike and muddled communications that had been reaching him
from the underground in Russia, was delighted to obtain from
the young man an unusual amount of precise and definite
information, to listen to his 'lucid and incisive' remarks and to
find in him a convinced adherent of the idea of a centralized
party.[2]

Anxious to examine him more closely, Lenin took him for
long walks and talks, in the course of which he showed him
London's historical and architectural landmarks. But Trotsky—
so he began to be called—was so full of the clandestine struggle
in Russia that his mind was closed to anything that had no
direct bearing on it. He noticed the peculiar mannerism Lenin
used in trying to acquaint him with some of the landmarks:
'This is *their* Westminster' or 'This is *their* British Museum', he
would say, conveying by the inflection of his voice and by
implication both his admiration for the genius embodied in the
grand buildings and his antagonism to the ruling classes, to
whose spirit and power those buildings were a monument.
Trotsky was eager to return from these digressions to topics
nearer to his heart: In what way did the *Iskra* men propose to
weld the disconnected groups into a centralized party? How
were they faring in the campaign against the Economists, who
were trying to keep the movement within the bounds of non-
political trade unionism? How would they counter the attempts
just begun by others to revive a *Narodnik*-like terrorist party?
What were they going to do to combat Peter Struve's 'legal

[1] N. K. Krupskaya, *Memories of Lenin*, p. 60.
[2] Lenin, *Sochinenya*, vol. xxxiv, pp. 89–92; Krupskaya, loc. cit.; L. Trotsky, *Moya
Zhizn*, vol. i, chapter xi.

Marxists', who were drifting away from revolutionary Marxism? Lenin listened with discreet satisfaction to the story of how in jail Trotsky and others had studied his *Development of Capitalism in Russia*, how impressed they had been by the enormous mass of statistical material he had marshalled to show that capitalist industry had been transforming Russian society so radically that it had killed all hope of agrarian socialism and set the scene for the proletarian movement. And above all there was the question: Why was Trotsky so urgently asked to report to London and what was he to do here?

In truth, no special assignment had been awaiting him. Lenin was usually anxious to meet everyone who had gained distinction in underground work. Only a few weeks before he had written: 'In order that the centre should always be able not only to advise, persuade, and argue . . . but actually to conduct the orchestra, it is necessary that it should be known precisely who is playing which fiddle, and where, and how he does it; where any person has been trained to wield an instrument and which instrument; who strikes a false note, and where and why . . ., who ought to be shifted, and how and whither, in order to eliminate the discordant tone. . . .'[1] His idea of the centralized party included a close interest in the living people who were fighting the party's battles on the spot, an interest characteristic of the true leader of men. Trotsky, he knew, had 'played first fiddle' in Siberia, and so he wished to meet him, to find out 'where and how he had learned to wield his instrument'. At this time Lenin was complaining, in letters to friends, about the inadequacies of *Iskra's* editorial staff, and he must have pondered whether The Pen would not be best employed on *Iskra*. On the day of Trotsky's arrival Lenin found him accommodation in a neighbouring house, where the other editors of *Iskra*, Martov and Zasulich, were living. No sooner had the newcomer moved in than he wrote his first contribution to the paper—it appeared in the issue published immediately after his arrival and dated 1 November 1902.[2]

The editorial board of *Iskra* consisted of six: Plekhanov, Vera Zasulich, and Axelrod, the three émigré pioneers of social democracy; and the much younger Lenin, Martov, and Potresov,

[1] Lenin, *Sochinenya*, vol. vi, pp. 205-24.   [2] *Iskra*, no. 27.

who had only recently left Russia. Most of the editors were living in London, in the borough of St. Pancras; Plekhanov and Axelrod lived in Switzerland, but Plekhanov made frequent trips to London. From this group, especially from Lenin's home, ran all the threads to the underground movement in Russia, whose agents appeared at Holford Square with messages and went back with instructions. Thus, the young Trotsky found himself transferred from Verkholensk straight into the directing centre of Russian socialism and placed under the constant influence of outstanding and contrasting personalities.

Zasulich and Martov shared with him their home, their meals, and their thoughts. It was Vera Zasulich who had, the year before Trotsky's birth, fired at General Trepov, and had unwittingly inspired the *Freedom of the People* to follow her example. After the jury acquitted her she escaped abroad, kept in touch with Karl Marx, and, although she did not accept his teaching without mental reservations, became one of the founders of the Russian Marxist school. Disregarding Marx's doubts, she was among the first to proclaim that the proletarian socialism he had advocated for western Europe would suit Russia as well.[1] She was not only a heroic character. Well read in history and philosophy, she was essentially a heretic, with a shrewdly feminine mind working by intuitive impulses and flashes rather than by reasoning. In all the portraits of her drawn by contemporaries, we also find the comic touches of the old-style Russian Bohemian. 'She wrote very slowly, suffering truly all the torments of literary creation'; and as she wrote or argued she paced thoughtfully up and down her room, with her slippers flapping, rolling cigarettes, chain-smoking, throwing butts on the window sills and tables, scattering ash over her blouse, arms, and manuscripts or into her cup of tea, and sometimes over her interlocutor. To the young Trotsky she was the heroine of a glorious epic—he had come to stay under one roof with the living legend of revolution.

Martov was only a few years older than Trotsky. He, too, was a Jew. The descendant of an old family of great Hebrew scholars—his real name was Zederbaum—he had been one of the initiators of the Bund, the Jewish Socialist party; but then he abandoned the idea of a separate Jewish Labour party, and,

[1] *Perepiska K. Marxa i F. F. Engelsa s Russkimi Politicheskimi Deyatelami*, pp. 240-2.

together with Lenin, founded the *Association for the Struggle for the Emancipation of Workers*, in Petersburg. He followed Lenin into exile, where they joined hands with the veteran émigrés to found *Iskra*. A subtle analyst, a writer with a satirical bent, a fluent and prolific commentator on the topics of the day, he was *Iskra's* journalistic mainstay, while Lenin was its political inspirer and organizer. Both Martov and Zasulich belonged to the romantic breed of rebels, guided less by theoretical principle than by moral indignation at social injustice. Full of charm, generosity, and modesty, both were by temperament artists rather than politicians.

Lenin was made of different stuff. Not that he was entirely free from romanticism—no one who was so could be a revolutionary while the revolution was still nothing but idea and dream. But Lenin had suppressed the romantic streak in himself and was contemptuous of the usual unworldliness of the Russian rebel. The brother of the *Narodnik* martyr, he knew the price in blood and frustration which revolutionaries had paid for that unworldliness. His task, as he saw it, was to infuse in them a spirit of realism, to blend their fervour with sobriety, and to train them in precise, efficient methods of work. For this he reserved his own energy and time. Self-disciplined, absorbed in study and work, he was rarely seen at the gatherings of the exiles and rarely took part in their interminable, often fruitless arguments. He appreciated and enjoyed discussion as preparation for action, not for its own sake. In a sense, his mind moved along a single track, but that track was as broad as society itself and it led to the transformation of society.

It was almost inevitable that Trotsky should be drawn closer to Zasulich and Martov, whose roof he shared and who exercized their influence on him constantly, than to Lenin whose influence was intermittent only. Still in his formative years, he needed close social intercourse and argument on which he could whet his mind. This need Zasulich and Martov, but not Lenin, generously satisfied. They also struck a deeper chord in him, the chord which the *Narodniks* had struck when he had first joined Shvigovsky's circle. Lenin's conduct, for all the curiosity and respect it aroused, could not but seem to him dry and prosaic. Years were to pass before he discovered greatness in that prosaic character.

Soon after he had arrived in London, he also met Plekhanov, who, like Zasulich, had been an almost legendary figure to him. Plekhanov, too, had been one of the founding fathers of Russian Marxism and had stood close to Engels. He was the philosopher and ideologue of the new school, its great, erudite stylist and orator, enjoying European fame. But Plekhanov was also full of his own fame and brilliance—remote and haughty. At their first meeting he showed an instinctive dislike of the new contributor to *Iskra*, and the dislike grew into intense antipathy. The two men possessed many similar gifts and characteristics. Both were imaginative writers and sharp-witted controversialists; both had a theatrical manner of speaking and behaving; both were full of themselves, their ideas, and their doings. But while the junior's star was only beginning to rise, the senior's had just begun to decline. Trotsky was overflowing with immature yet captivating enthusiasm; Plekhanov was becoming sceptical and over-ripe. Lunacharsky relates an anecdote, current among the émigrés, which, though obviously untrue, does in part indicate Plekhanov's attitude. When he arrived in London, Zasulich expansively praised in his presence Trotsky's talents. 'The lad', she exclaimed, 'is undoubtedly a genius.' Plekhanov sulked, turned aside and said: 'I shall never forgive him this.'[1]

The *Iskra* team still spoke with one voice. But it had its dissensions, of which Trotsky presently became aware, and in which he was unwittingly becoming involved. The editorial board was equally divided between the three veterans and the three younger editors. Controversial matters were decided by vote and, as each group voted solidly against the other, a deadlock arose. Issues of editorial policy had often to be left in abeyance. Lenin, anxious to break the deadlock, thought of adding a new, a seventh, member to the board. As early as March 1903, four months after Trotsky's arrival, Lenin, in a memorandum sent to all editors, emphatically recommended his appointment. Beforehand he disposed of objections concerning Trotsky's age and qualifications: he underlined Trotsky's 'rare abilities', 'conviction and energy', and added that his

---

[1] A. Lunacharsky, *Revolutsionnye Siluety*, pp. 19–22. Some memoirists (Zelikson-Bobrovskaya) say that when Trotsky's first unsigned articles appeared in *Iskra*, readers attributed them to Plekhanov.

contributions were 'not only very useful but absolutely necessary'.[1] Zasulich and Martov agreed. 'His [Trotsky's] literary
works', Martov wrote to Axelrod, 'reveal indubitable talent . . .
and already he wields great influence here thanks to his uncommon oratorical gifts. He speaks magnificently. Of this both
I and Vladimir Ilyich [Lenin] have had sufficient proof. He
possesses knowledge and works hard to increase it. I endorse
Lenin's proposal without reservation.'[2] Axelrod, too, accepted
the candidature. On this at least there was no division between
the veterans and the others. The whole team, with one exception, eagerly welcomed Trotsky. The exception was Plekhanov.
He objected vehemently on the ground that Trotsky's contributions, with their florid rhetoric, lowered the standard of the
paper. That Trotsky's style was flowery and full of flourishes
was true. Lenin had gently tried to prune it; and, in recom-
mending Trotsky's appointment, he wrote that if the latter
became a regular member of the editorial team it would be
easier to impress on him the need for stylistic simplicity: he
would then see that this was the view of the whole team, not
merely Lenin's preference for austerity. But, to the indignation
of all his colleagues, Plekhanov was unmoved. After much
bickering, Zasulich brought the unsuspecting Trotsky to an
editorial conference, hoping that Plekhanov would give in.
Plekhanov snubbed the 'intruder' and persisted in his veto.

In *My Life* Trotsky says that Plekhanov suspected that he,
Trotsky, would join Lenin in his opposition to the veterans.
This could hardly have been Plekhanov's main motive. All the
other veterans treated Trotsky with almost paternal pride and
tenderness; and he in his turn showed them an affectionate
reverence, becoming the Benjamin of the group. Such was his
attitude not only towards Zasulich but also, and especially,
towards Axelrod, whose home in Zurich presently became
Trotsky's favourite retreat during his trips to the Continent.
It is difficult to imagine characters more contrasting than those
of Plekhanov and Axelrod, who had for nearly twenty-five
years worked together in close friendship. Axelrod was a south
Ukrainian Jew, like Trotsky. He had started as a *Narodnik* in the
original South Russian Workers' Union, from which Trotsky had

---

[1] Krupskaya, op. cit., p. 65; Trotsky, *Moya Zhizn*, vol. i, chapter xii.
[2] *Pisma Axelroda i Martova*, pp. 79–80.

borrowed the name of his first organization. Then he had emigrated and pioneered for Marxism. With none of Plekhanov's gifts, poor as a writer and poorer still as a speaker, he was the inarticulate originator of many of the ideas which his friend brilliantly expounded. While Plekhanov's socialism was intellectual, Axelrod's sprang from absolute confidence in the working class. He believed fanatically that the workers would find their way to socialism and emancipation, and he instinctively distrusted the intelligentsia's aspiration to lead them—this was later the main motive of his unflagging opposition to Bolshevism. While Plekhanov, a polished European and an aristocrat in appearance, led a rather bourgeois life, Axelrod earned his living as a worker, producing in his home a special kind of buttermilk and delivering it to his customers. Over his milk-cans he argued with fugitives from Russia to whom his home was a haven of rest, and whom he fed and often clad. With his broad dishevelled beard, he looked more like a saintly Russian rabbi than a revolutionary politician. Yet the revolutionary leaders, including until quite recently Lenin, had all regarded him as their teacher and inspirer. To this man the young Trotsky became strongly attached, and the attachment was to have a bearing on his political fortunes.[1]

Ties of mutual friendship also bound him to another pioneer, Leon Deutsch, once also a southern Russian *Narodnik*, who had recently, after thirteen years of *katorga*, escaped from Siberia and made a journey around the world. Although at the height of his fame—his courageous escape had earned him world-wide admiration—Deutsch was regarding the new time, its problems, and its men, with weary and somewhat uncomprehending eyes. A little uneasy about Trotsky's exuberant radicalism and optimism, he nevertheless attached himself tenderly to the brilliant 'Benjamin', as if to the embodiment of his own youthful hopes, watched his first steps abroad with admiration, and sought to help him and to advance him in every way.

The dissension inside the *Iskra* team had as yet no political significance. Only a short time before, Lenin and Martov,

[1] L. Trotsky, loc. cit. and *Lenine*, pp. 9–60; A. Lunacharsky, op. cit., pp. 35–40; F. Dan, *Proiskhozhdenie Bolshevisma*, pp. 191–4, 288–9; N. Alexeyev in *Proletarskaya Revolutsia*, no. 3, 1924; L. N. Meshcheryakov in *Pechati Revolutsia*, vol. ii, 1924; V. Medem, *Von Mein Leben*, vol. ii, chapter i; John Mill, *Pioneers and Builders*, vol. i, pp. 205–7.

as we have seen, had sat at the veterans' feet with the same feelings which animated Trotsky now. But their apprenticeship had come to an end; and, as often happens, the pupils were more acutely aware of this than the masters. The whole work now centred on *Iskra*, and as editors and contributors the veterans, with the exception of Plekhanov, were more or less ineffectual. They wrote rarely and not very well; and they took little or no part in organizing the clandestine movement in Russia. Lenin and Martov shared day-to-day editorial duties; and Lenin, assisted by Krupskaya, bore the brunt of the drudgery that had to be done in order to keep and develop the contacts with Russia.[1] Inevitably, the veterans felt that they were being by-passed.

The jealousies were focused in the antagonism between Plekhanov and Lenin, each of the two being the most assertive man in his group. This antagonism had appeared at the moment of *Iskra*'s foundation, and it had grown since. Lenin was acquiring confidence in his own ideas and methods of work, and he did not conceal it. Plekhanov treated him with patronizing irony or with schoolmasterly offensiveness. Some months before Trotsky's arrival, in May 1902, Lenin had written to Plekhanov: 'You have a fine idea of tact. . . . You do not hesitate to use the most contemptuous expressions. . . . If your purpose is to make mutual work impossible, then the way you have chosen will very rapidly help you to succeed. As for our personal relations . . . you have finally spoilt them, or more exactly, you have achieved their complete cessation.'[2] This rift had since been patched up by Zasulich and Martov. But clashes recurred and the latest was connected with Trotsky's work for *Iskra*. 'Once [Lenin] returned from an editorial meeting', writes Krupskaya, 'in a terrific rage. "A damned fine state of affairs", he said, "nobody has enough courage to reply to Plekhanov. Look at Vera Ivanovna [Zasulich]! Plekhanov trounces Trotsky, and Vera just says 'Just like our George. All he does is to shout.'" "I cannot go on like this", Lenin burst out.'[3]

---

[1] In a hostile memoir, written in 1927, Potresov admitted: 'And yet . . . all of us who were closest to the work . . . valued Lenin not only for his knowledge, brains, and capacity for work but also for his exceptional devotion to the cause, his unceasing readiness to give himself completely, to take upon himself the most unpleasant functions and without fail to discharge them with the utmost conscientiousness.' A. N. Potresov, *Posmertnyi Sbornik Proizvedenii*, p. 299.

[2] *The Letters of Lenin*, pp. 155–6.   [3] Krupskaya, op. cit., p. 65.

Almost imperceptibly this dissension was being superseded by another arising from it. Lenin, Martov, and Potresov (the latter's role, important at first, was now insignificant) still acted and voted together against the veterans. But as the rivalry developed, Lenin began to alienate his contemporaries also, especially Martov. Convinced that he was right, he would not turn back, and went on in total disregard of the veterans' susceptibilities. Martov, less definite in his views and less determined to enforce them, tried to make peace. His ideas were usually the same as Lenin's; but as soon as he tried to put them into effect and met with resistance, he began to vacillate, and, swayed by second thoughts, to retreat. This was so not only in the quarrel with the veterans. In other matters as well, he usually first agreed with Lenin to 'strive uncompromisingly' for a certain objective. Then he would balk at Lenin's uncompromising manner, and would finally abandon the objective. He was by temperament 'soft' and was repelled by Lenin's 'hardness'. At meetings 'Lenin would glance at Martov, for whom he had a high esteem, with a critical and slightly suspicious eye, and Martov, feeling this glance, would look down and his shoulders would twitch nervously. . . . Lenin would look beyond Martov as he talked, while Martov's eyes grew glassy behind his drooping and never quite clean pince-nez.'[1]

These, then, were the influences under which Trotsky came. The fact that Lenin defended him and tried to promote him, against Plekhanov's opposition, might have brought him close to Lenin and turned him against the veterans. But this did not happen. For one thing, the veterans, as we know, did not on this point support Plekhanov—they, too, did their best to sponsor and encourage Trotsky. For another, he was nearly ten years younger than Lenin and ten times as sensitive to the veterans' romantic appeal. So far he had had no time to become disillusioned with them and to notice that, for all their virtues, they were ineffectual in day-to-day work. Lenin's opposition to them seemed to him boorish, and his motives personal and mean.

However, he considered the discord as the trivial side of a glorious and momentous venture. The internal squabbles did not prevent *Iskra* from being the great rallying centre of the nascent party—its name alone was a stirring summons to

[1] Trotsky, *Moya Zhizn*, vol. i, p. 176.

revolutionaries. Nobody believed in *Iskra*'s mission more ardently than Trotsky; and his writings pulsated with this belief. The distinctive mark of his early contributions to *Iskra* lies not so much in originality of ideas as in the force of the emotional current that runs through them, in the passionate character of his revolutionary invocations, and in the almost dramatic vehemence of the invective which he poured out on Russia's rulers and on socialism's enemies. He was now writing without the inhibitions of censorship, and he gave free vent to his temperament, a fact which did not necessarily improve the quality of his writing—his articles for *Iskra* were often inferior to his Siberian essays.

His first contribution to *Iskra* was devoted to the bi-centenary of the ill-famed Schlüsselburg fortress, which Peter the Great had built near his capital—'his window on Europe and his most important prison'. The writer evoked the shades of the martyrs who had been murdered or driven to madness within its walls, among them Alexander Ulyanov, Lenin's brother. And he ended with a ringing apostrophe to the Tsar and his servants: 'You may still indulge in your patriotic bacchanals—to-day you are still the masters of Schlüsselburg.' In the same issue he flayed the quasi-liberal gentry, who in the *Zemstvos* hardly dared to breathe a word against authority: 'What other Egyptian plagues, what other Russian scorpions are needed to straighten the meekly bent backs of the liberal *Zemstvo* men?'[1] In connexion with Slavophile demonstrations against Turkey, sponsored by the Tsar, he wrote about the 'Sharks of Slavophilism': 'Again, O Russian citizen, an attempt is made to open the safety valve of official Slavophilism and to provide an outlet for the excess of your civic emotions. Again, as twenty-five years ago [during the Russo-Turkish war of 1878], the journalistic purveyors of patriotism drag out of their archives . . . ideas of Pan-Slav fraternity and put them into circulation with pomp and chiming of bells.' Yet the Tsarist government treats its own people no better than the Sultan treats his non-Moslem subjects. 'Are our own prisons', the writer asked, 'better than the Turkish . . . have the soldiers of our punitive expeditions not raped the wives and daughters of the Poltava peasants? Have they not looted their property?' Why then were so-called Liberals

[1] *Iskra*, no. 27, 1 November 1902.

lending support to the Tsar's 'civilizing mission' in Turkey, why 'do not they call for a crusade against the barbarians . . . of Tsardom?' The semi-liberal opposition, 'that lawful opposition to a lawless government' was already, and would remain for many years, the favourite butt of his irony.[1] In the *Zemstvos*, whose function it should be to judge the actions of the administration, the 'defendant in fact assumes the role of the presiding judge and arrogates the right to adjourn the court at any moment'. Tsardom was offering the *Zemstvos* 'the *knout* wrapped in the parchment of Magna Charta', and the *Zemstvos* were contented. What do they understand by freedom—'freedom from political freedom?' 'One may confidently say that if Russian freedom were to be born from the *Zemstvos*, it would never come to life. Fortunately Russian freedom has more reliable parents: the revolutionary proletariat and the inner, self-destructive logic of Russian absolutism.' 'Many political trends will succeed one another, many "parties" will emerge and fade, each pretending to improve upon the Social Democratic programme and tactics, but the future historian will say: these trends and these parties were only insignificant, secondary incidents in the great struggle of the awakened working class . . . already advancing with clumsy but faithful steps on the road of political and social emancipation.'[2]

In a similar vein he wrote about the Tsar's attempts to force the Russian language on the Finns and to destroy their autonomy; the expulsion of Maxim Gorky from the Imperial Academy; the futility of the newly formed Social Revolutionary party, reverting to *Narodnik* terrorism; or the attempt by the police to set up puppet clandestine organizations to compete with the real underground. His attacks on the terrorism of the Social Revolutionaries, especially one made after the execution of a young student Balmashev, who had killed Sypiagin, the Minister of the Interior, provoked indignant protests from Liberals and Socialists. The Liberal intelligentsia had much more sympathy with the terrorists than had the Marxists. But

---

[1] *Iskra*, no. 28, 15 November and no. 29, 1 December 1902. It is noteworthy that as early as March 1901 Trotsky wrote in the *Eastern Review*: 'Pure liberalism with all its Manchester symbols of faith has faded in our country before it has blossomed: it did not find any social ground for itself. It was possible to import Manchester ideas . . . but it was impossible to import the social environment which produced those ideas.' *Sochinenya*, vol. xx, pp. 85–86.   [2] *Iskra*, no. 29, 1 December 1902.

even Socialists held that Trotsky's polemics were too vehement and that he ought to have written with more respect or warmth about the executed Social Revolutionary.[1]

Only nine months were to elapse between his arrival in London and the opening of the second congress of the Russian Social Democratic party. In this short time his reputation was established firmly enough to allow him, at the age of twenty-three, to play a leading role at the congress, in the momentous split between Bolsheviks and Mensheviks. This was perhaps due more to his lecturing and speech-making than to his writing. No sooner had he arrived in London than Lenin and Martov pitted him in debate against venerable old *Narodnik* and anarchist émigrés in Whitechapel. The novice was pleasantly surprised at the ease with which he swept the floor with his grey-bearded opponents. After that he toured the Russian colonies in western Europe. Contemporaries have described the first sudden and irresistible impact of his oratory, the élan, the passion, the wit, and the thunderous metallic voice, with which he roused audiences and bore down upon opponents. This appears all the more remarkable as only a few years before he could only stammer in blushing perplexity before a tiny, homely audience and as he had spent most of the time since in the solitude of prison and exile. His oratory was quite untutored: he had hardly yet heard a single speaker worthy of imitation. This is one of those instances of latent unsuspected talent, bursting forth in exuberant vitality to delight and amaze all who witness it. His speech, even more than his writing, was distinguished by a rare intensity of thought, imagination, emotion, and expression. The rhetoric which often spoilt his writing made his speaking all the more dramatic. He appeared, as it were, with the drama in himself, with the sense of entering a conflict in which the forces and actors engaged were more than life-size, the battles Homeric, and the climaxes worthy of demi-gods.[2]

---

[1] In the summer of 1902, Miliukov, the future leader of the Constitutional Democrats, paid a visit to *Iskra*'s editors in London, praised *Iskra* but objected to its campaign against terrorism. 'Why', he said, 'let there be another two or three such attempts on the Tsar's ministers and we are going to get a constitution.' The moderate constitutionalist often regarded the terrorist as a useful agent for exerting pressure on the Tsar. N. Alexeyev in *Proletarskaya Revolutsia*, no. 3, 1924.

[2] In August 1902, just before his flight from Siberia, he had written in the *Eastern Review*: 'The laws of social life and the principles of party . . . are also a force

Elevated above the crowd and feeling a multitude of eyes centred on him, himself storming a multitude of hearts and minds below—he was in his element. A contemporary describes the lean, tallish man, with large fierce eyes and large, sensual, irregular mouth, perched on the platform like a 'bird of prey'.[1]

.   .   .   .

In the admired speaker and writer there lived on, as he himself put it, a 'barbarian struggling for self-preservation'. Having found himself among the élite of the movement, he had to lift himself intellectually by his bootstraps. He diligently studied Marxism, which in this its golden age gave the adept a solid mental equipment. Just before he escaped from Siberia he had explored the intricacies of 'capitalistic circulation', with its periodic crises, as they are analysed with seeming dryness and yet with the utmost dramatic effect in the second volume of *Das Kapital*. Abroad he resumed this study. But the fascination of Marxism kept his mind closed to any extraneous idea or phenomenon. On his arrival in London it had seemed to him strange that Lenin should try to interest him in English historical monuments. When he first visited Paris he similarly defended himself against the assault of novel impressions. He summed up his first view of Paris grotesquely: 'Very much like Odessa, but Odessa is better.' The art treasures of the Louvre bored him. What excited him most in France was the controversy between the orthodox Marxists, led by Jules Guesde, and the reformists who followed Jaurès. He plunged into a crowd of Parisian workers demonstrating against Millerand, the first Socialist to become a minister in a bourgeois government and then engaged in suppressing strikes. Marching in the crowd he shouted 'all sorts of unpleasant things against Millerand'.

In Paris he met his second wife. She was Natalya Sedova, a girl student who had taken him to the Louvre and tried to open his eyes to paintings and sculpture. A few years younger than his first wife, she, too, was a revolutionary. She had been expelled from a boarding school for young ladies of noble birth at Kharkov, where she had persuaded her classmates not to attend

not second in its grandeur to the antique Fatum. Social principles in their pitiless compulsion, not less than Aeschylus' Fate, can grind into dust the individual soul if it enters into a conflict with them.' *Sochinenya*, vol. xx, p. 241.

[1] V. Medem, op. cit., vol. ii, pp. 7–9; P. A. Garvi, *Vospominanya Sotsialdemokrata*, p. 385.

prayers and to read, instead of the Bible, Russian radical literature.[1] She was at this time studying the history of art at the Sorbonne. She was to remain his companion for the rest of his life and to share with him to the full triumph and defeat. Sokolovskaya, however, remained his legal wife and bore his name. To all three the legal niceties of their connexion did not matter at all—like other revolutionaries they disregarded on principle the canons of middle-class respectability. At heart, perhaps, Trotsky never quite freed himself from a qualm over the manner of his separation from Sokolovskaya; and this, more than alleged reluctance to expatiate on his private life, may explain why in his autobiography he devoted no more than a single sentence to the whole affair. As an émigré he himself could not do much for his wife and two children. His parents, who in 1903 went to Paris for a reconciliation, took care of the children, helping to bring them up. As far as we know, the question of a reunion between Trotsky and his first wife never arose. When he and Sedova returned to Russia there was no suggestion of discord. Ties of respect and of a high-minded friendship were to bind the three of them to the end; and eventually his political fortunes affected with equal tragedy both the women and the children of both.

. . . .

While he was working and lecturing in France, Switzerland, and Belgium, there came from clandestine headquarters in Russia insistent demands that he should be sent back. The Russian underground and the émigré centre competed intensely for personnel. Trotsky knew nothing of these demands. When old Leon Deutsch learned about them, he used all his influence to prevent Trotsky's return. With the burden of his own thirteen years of hard labour in Siberia still on his mind, he pleaded with the editors of *Iskra* to leave the 'Benjamin' abroad, so that he might widen his education, see the world, and develop his talents. Deutsch found an ally in Lenin, who was reluctant to lose his contributor. Lenin wrote back to Russia that Trotsky was showing no desire to return. This was a subterfuge by which Lenin hoped to put off Russian headquarters, and Krupskaya leaves no doubt that it was Lenin who decided against sending Trotsky back. Thus, Trotsky's fate was settled for the

[1] Eastman, op. cit., p. 153.

time being: he would stay abroad for the forthcoming congress of the party.[1]

.   .   .   .

In July 1903 the congress was at last convened in Brussels. This was actually to be the foundation assembly—the so-called first congress of 1898 had been a meeting at Minsk of eight people only, who were soon arrested, and had left nothing behind except a stirring *Manifesto*, written by Peter Struve. Only now, in 1903, had the network of clandestine organizations become close enough, and the contacts of *Iskra* with it solid enough, for everybody to feel that the time had come to form a regular party with a well-defined constitution and an elected leadership. It was taken for granted that that leadership would remain with the *Iskra* team, which alone had supplied the organizations with a political idea and alone had co-ordinated their activities. For the whole team the congress was a solemn occasion. To the veterans it was the materialization of a dream long cherished in prisons, and in places of deportation and exile.

It was also taken for granted that the *Iskra* men would appear at the congress as a single body, bound by solidarity in ideas, in achievement, and in the aspiration to leadership. Before the congress there was some discord over the drafting of a programme, but this was easily settled. Opposition was expected from two groups: from the Economists, who would fight a rearguard skirmish against the triumphant advance of revolutionary politics; and from the Jewish Bund, claiming for itself a special status within the party. These two groups were in a minority, and all *Iskra* men were united against them. Just before the opening of the congress the editors of *Iskra* began to wrangle over the manner in which the leading bodies of the party should be set up; but this seemed a minor detail of organization.

At the beginning of July forty-four delegates with voting rights, and fourteen with consultative voice, met at the Socialist *Maison du Peuple* in Brussels. Trotsky arrived from Geneva to represent, together with another delegate, the *Siberian Social Democratic Workers' Union*.[2] Seated in a drab warehouse in the

[1] N. Krupskaya, *Memories of Lenin*, p. 60; Lenin, *Sochinenya*, vol. xxxiv, p. 114.
[2] In *My Life* he describes humorously how he and Dr. Ulyanov, Lenin's younger

back of the *Maison du Peuple*, the delegates listened in exaltation to Plekhanov's opening speech. By their presence, they felt, they were creating a landmark in the history of that submerged Russia which had for more than three-quarters of a century struggled against the Tsars and was now heading for the final battles. Neither the humble setting of the congress, nor its obscurity from the world, could, in the eyes of the participants, deprive the moment of its historic consequence.

The first controversy on the floor concerned the Bund. The Jewish organization demanded autonomy within the party, with the right to elect its own central committee and to frame its own policy in matters affecting the Jewish population. It asked further that the party should recognize the Bund as its sole agency among the Jewish workers. It urged the party that it should advocate not merely equal rights for Jews, as it had done, but that it should acknowledge the right of the Jews to 'cultural autonomy', their right, that is, to manage their own cultural affairs and to maintain their own schools in the Jewish (Yiddish) language. On behalf of the *Iskra* men, Martov, who had been one of the Bund's founders, indignantly repudiated these demands. Trotsky repeated the repudiation even more vehemently. The debate was taking place only a few months after the great pogrom of the Jews at Kishynev. Jewish suscepti- bilities and suspicions were aroused; and they were indirectly reflected in the Bund's attitude.[1] The non-Jewish spokesmen of *Iskra* kept in the background in order to spare those suscepti- bilities; and so the rebuff to the Bund came from the Jews. Martov tabled the motion against the Bund; and only Jewish delegates put their signatures to it. Trotsky himself spoke on behalf of the *Iskra*ites of Jewish origin, and, making the most

brother, at a small station near Geneva, hurriedly boarded an express train for Brussels after the train had begun to move, and how the station-master stopped the train to take the strange passengers off the buffers. Trotsky travelled on a false Bulgarian passport as Mr. Samokovlieff. These precautions were intended to keep the Russian secret police in the dark. But the *Okhrana* had its agents among the delegates, and the Belgian police closely watched the congress and its participants. Trotsky describes, in the style of a good film scenario, his race with a police agent through the empty streets of Brussels in the middle of the night. Finally, the con- gress was transferred to London.

[1] An illuminating account of the mood among Jewish socialists after the pogrom is found in the correspondence of Y. M. Sverdlov, the future Soviet President, in *Pechat i Revolutsia*, vol. ii, 1924. See also Medem, op. cit., vol. ii, pp. 29–32.

of this circumstance, he lashed the delegates of the Bund into a fury. They protested vehemently against his speech, suggested that he was out to affront the Jews, and appealed to the chairman to protect them. When the chairman found Trotsky's remarks unexceptionable, the Bundists tabled a motion censuring the chairman.

This was one of the stormiest scenes at the congress, and one of the very rare occasions on which Trotsky referred to himself as a Jew and spoke on a specifically Jewish issue That he was doing so only to refute Jewish demands must have seemed almost caddish to the highly-strung delegates of the Bund. He pleaded, however, that more than a Jewish issue was at stake. Claiming for itself autonomy within the party, with the right to elect its own Central Committee, the Bund was, in fact, setting a precedent for others: if the party had granted such privileges to the Bund it could not later refuse them to other groups. It would then have to abandon the idea of an integrated organization and to transform itself into a loose federation of parties and groups. In short, the Bund was trying by devious means to induce the *Iskra* men to abandon their guiding principle and the practical work they had done to put it into effect. The other demand that the Bund be recognized as the party's sole agency among Jewish workers amounted to a claim that only Jews were entitled to carry the Socialist message to Jewish workers and to organize them. This, Trotsky pointed out, was an expression of distrust in the non-Jewish members of the party, a challenge to their internationalist conviction and sentiment. 'The Bund', Trotsky exclaimed amid a storm of protests, 'is free not to trust the party, but it cannot expect the party to vote no confidence in its own self.'[1] The party as a whole could not renounce its right to address the Jewish toiling masses without yielding to Jewish separatism. The Bund's demand for 'cultural autonomy' sprang from the same separatism, confronting with its claims first the party and then the state and the nation. Socialism was interested in sweeping away barriers between races, religions, and nationalities—it could not turn its hand to putting up such barriers. He granted the Jews the right to have schools in their own language, if they so desired. But these, he added, should not be outside the national educational system,

[1] *Vtoroi Syezd RSDRP*, pp. 52–55.

and Jewish cultural life at large should not be centred on and closed in itself. He tabled a motion to this effect, supplementing Martov's general resolution. Both resolutions were carried by an overwhelming majority.[1]

Like Martov, Axelrod, Deutsch, and other Socialists of Jewish origin, Trotsky took the so-called assimilationist view, holding that there was no future for the Jews as a separate community. The ties that had kept the Jews together were either those of religion, which, according to the prevalent Socialist conviction, were bound to dissolve; or those of a semi-fictitious nationalism culminating in Zionism. The Bund was strongly opposed to Zionism, for it conceived the future of the Jews to lie in the countries of the so-called diaspora. But, Trotsky argued, in its opposition to Zionism the Bund absorbed from the latter its nationalist essence.[2] He saw the solution of the Jewish problem not in the formation of a Jewish state, still less in the formation of Jewish states within the non-Jewish ones, but in a consistently internationalist reshaping of society. The premiss for this was mutual unreserved confidence between Jews and non-Jews, whether in the party or in the state. To this attitude he was to adhere till the end of his life—only the impact of Nazism was to induce him to soften a little his hostility towards Zionism.[3] He would not grant the tragic truth contained in the Jews' distrust of their gentile environment. Neither he nor any other Socialist could imagine even in a nightmare that the working classes of Europe, having through generations listened to the preachings of international solidarity, would, forty years later, be unable or unwilling to prevent or stop the murder of six

[1] Ibid., p. 198.
[2] Some time after the congress Trotsky published in *Iskra* a bitter attack on Zionism. The occasion was a conflict between the original Zionists who were led by Theodore Herzl and those Zionists who, led by Max Nordau, were prepared to abandon Palestine for Uganda as a Jewish homeland. Herzl tried to buy the land of Palestine from the Sultan, while Nordau conducted a campaign for the acquisition of Uganda. A fanatical follower of Herzl made an attempt on Nordau's life. Trotsky wrote in this connexion about Herzl as a 'shameless adventurer' and about 'the hysterical sobbings of the romanticists of Zion'; and he saw in the conflict the bankruptcy of Zionism. (*Iskra*, no. 56, 1 January 1904.)
[3] In an interview with the American-Jewish *Forward* (28 January 1937) Trotsky stated that after the experience of Nazism, it was difficult to believe in the 'assimilation' of the Jews, for which he had hoped. Zionism by itself, he went on, would not solve the problem; but even under Socialism, it might be necessary for the Jews to settle on a separate territory.

million Jewish men, women, and children in Hitler's gas chambers. To this problem the formulas of the Bund could, of course, provide no answer. Trotsky came out as a Jew against Jewish separatism, because his vision of the future was as remote from mid-century European 'civilization' as heaven from earth.

The next dispute at the congress was between the *Iskra* men and the Economists. The Economists protested against the supremacy which revolutionary politics had gained in the mind of the party over trade unionism and the struggle for reforms. They also objected to the centralized organization in which they, the Economists, were reduced to impotence. Their spokesmen, Martynov and Akimov, upbraided *Iskra* for its dictatorial, 'Jacobin-like' attitude.[1] It should be noted that this is the first time the charge appears in the records. The *Iskra* men answered the critics in unison. Trotsky spoke against the Economists with an aggressive zeal which earned him the epithet of 'Lenin's cudgel'.[2] The struggle for small economic gains and reforms, he said, made sense only in so far as it helped to muster the forces of the working classes for revolution. 'The Social Democratic Party, as it struggles for reforms, carries out a fundamental reform of itself—a reform in the minds of the proletariat, which is being prepared for a revolutionary dictatorship.' The ruling classes, in any case, agree to reforms only when they are confronted by a threat of revolution, and so the supremacy of revolutionary politics was needed even in the struggle for reforms.[3] He defended the centralistic mode of organization, saying that the party needed strict statutes, enabling the leadership to keep out noncongenial influences. Ridiculing the charges of Jacobinism, he said that the statutes should express '*the leadership's organized distrust*' of the members, a distrust manifesting itself in vigilant control from above over the party.[4]

This idea was soon to become Lenin's exclusive property, the hallmark of Bolshevism. Trotsky, we remember, had advocated it as early as in 1901; and this idea was still *Iskra*'s common property. It summed up, to quote the most authoritative Menshevik historian, the reaction of all forward-looking Socialists against the 'shapelessness and federative looseness' of the move-

[1.] *Vtoroi Syezd RSDRP.*, p. 137.   [2] N. K. Krupskaya, op. cit., p. 70.
[3] *Vtoroi Syezd RSDRP.*, pp. 136–7.   [4] Ibid., p. 168.

ment.[1] But this was the last time that all *Iskra* men, including the future Mensheviks, were in complete accord in defending this idea, although perhaps none of them spoke for it as vigorously as Trotsky did. None of them would have been more surprised than he if he had been told that a few sessions later he would angrily renounce his own words. It was, generally speaking, not Lenin but the future leaders of Menshevism, especially Plekhanov, who at this congress, during the debate on the programme, spoke with the greatest determination for proletarian dictatorship. Plekhanov urged the delegates to adopt formulas that left no doubt that in a revolutionary situation they would not shrink from the destruction of parliamentary institutions or from restricting civil liberties. *Salus revolutionis suprema lex esto*— Plekhanov used these words as his text when he argued that if, after the overthrow of Tsardom, a constituent assembly hostile to the revolutionary government were to be elected, that government should, after the manner of Cromwell, disperse the assembly. It was on this principle that Lenin and Trotsky acted in 1918, unmoved by the vituperation of an old and sick Plekhanov. The latter now also pleaded that the revolutionary government should not abolish capital punishment—it might need it in order to destroy the Tsar. These views evoked one single protest from an obscure delegate and gave rise to a feeble doubt in a few others, but they were generally received with acclamation.

Behind the scenes, however, the solidarity of the *Iskra* men was beginning to vanish. The discord did not at first appear over any problem of policy, not even over the famous paragraph 1 of the statutes, on which they were eventually to divide, but over a matter in which no principle of policy or organization was involved. Lenin proposed to reduce the number of *Iskra*'s

---

[1] L. Martov, *Istorya Rossiiskoi Sotsial-Demokratii*, pp. 62–72. Martov describes how much the concept of a centralized organization was then 'in the air'. The idea was first formulated in detail not by Lenin but by an underground worker in Petersburg, who wrote a letter to Lenin about this, and who after the split joined the Mensheviks. In the year before the congress a scheme of organization similar to Lenin's was proposed to *Iskra* by Savinkov, who later left the Social Democrats to form the Social Revolutionary Party. Even after the split Martov wrote: 'In the problem of organization we are first of all adherents of centralism, which as revolutionary social democrats we must be.' Ibid., p. 11. See also Lenin, *Sochinenya*, vol. vi, pp. 205–24, Martov's preface to Cherevanin, *Organizatsionnyi Vopros*, and V. L. Akimov, *Materialy dla Kharakteristiki Razvitya RSDRP*, p. 104.

editors from six to three. The three editors were to be: Plekhanov, Martov, and himself. Axelrod, Zasulich, and Potresov
were to be left out. Historians of the opposed schools are eager
retrospectively to read into this proposal profound, far-reaching
intentions, baleful or benign, according to the viewpoint. In its
actual setting, Lenin's intention was simple. He was seeking to
make the editorial work of *Iskra* more efficient than it had lately
been. As the board of six had tended to divide equally, he had,
in order to break the deadlock, proposed Trotsky's appointment;
but, since Plekhanov's objections had ruled this out, he now
tried to achieve his purpose by reducing, instead of increasing,
the number of editors. The three whom he was proposing had
been *Iskra*'s real pillars. Zasulich, Axelrod, and Potresov had contributed very little—none of them was a fluent writer—and had
done even less in the work of administration and organization.[1]
On grounds of efficiency alone, Lenin's proposal was justified.
But considerations of efficiency clashed, as they often do, with
acquired rights and sentiment. Lenin had his qualms before he
decided on this step; Plekhanov had little or no scruple. To
Trotsky this attempt to eliminate from *Iskra* Axelrod and
Zasulich, two of its founders, seemed 'sacrilegious'; he was
shocked by Lenin's callousness.

This narrow issue at once became entangled with other and
wider questions. *Iskra*'s editorial board was to remain, as it had
been, the party's virtual leadership. A central committee, to be
elected at the congress, was to operate in Russia. But, working
underground and exposed to arrest, it could not secure continuity in leadership—only an émigré centre, such as the
editorial board, could do that. Lenin further proposed the election of a Council which was to act as arbiter between the
central committee and the editorial board. That Council was
to consist of five members: two from *Iskra*, two from the central
committee, and a chairman who was to be elected by congress.
It was a foregone conclusion that Plekhanov would be the
chairman; and so *Iskra*'s editorial board was sure to wield the
decisive influence in the Council. It was because of this scheme

---

[1] Explaining in a letter to his follower his own motives, Lenin stated that to the
45 issues of the 'old' *Iskra* Martov had contributed 39 articles, Lenin 32, Plekhanov
24; Zasulich had written only 6 articles, Axelrod 4, and Potresov 8. Lenin, *Sochinenya*,
vol. xxxiv, p. 164.

that Lenin brought upon himself the charge that he was seeking
to dominate the party. Yet, as events showed, the scheme by
itself could not give Lenin more influence than he had had
under the old dispensation. If it tended to accord a privileged
position to any single person then that person was Plekhanov,
Lenin's future enemy. All that was to be achieved was the
elimination of the least effective members of the old team, in
the first instance of Axelrod and Zasulich. Lenin was willing to
pay these veterans the homage they had well deserved; but he
was not prepared to do so in a manner that would have inter-
fered with the effective conduct of business, the brunt of which
he himself had anyhow borne. The two veterans, not unnatur-
ally, were shocked. Martov was anxious to soothe them. Trotsky, not well informed about the inner workings of the team,
could not understand Lenin's motives. He sensed a sinister
conspiracy.

While behind the scenes the initiated whispered about the
'family scandal', the statutes of the party came up for debate
in full session. The *Iskra* team had discussed them before the
congress and had noticed a difference between Lenin and
Martov. Lenin's draft ran as follows: 'A member of . . . the
Party is any person who accepts its programme, supports the
Party with material means, and *personally participates* in one of
its organizations.' Martov's draft was identical with Lenin's,
except that where Lenin demanded that a member should
'personally participate' in one of the party's organizations,
Martov required him more vaguely to 'co-operate personally
and regularly under the guidance of one of the organizations'.
The difference seemed elusively subtle. Lenin's formula pointed
towards a closely-knit party, consisting only of the actual
participants in the clandestine bodies. Martov's clause envisaged
a looser association, including those who merely assisted the
underground organization without belonging to it. When the
two formulas were first compared, the difference did not seem
important; and Martov was prepared to withdraw his draft.[1]
There seemed to be no reason why the party should split over
two words of a paragraph in its rules and regulations.

In the meantime the personal clashes connected with Lenin's
editorial scheme generated behind the scenes ill feeling and

[1] Pavlovich, *Pismo k Tovarishcham o Vtorom Syezde*, p. 5.

bitterness which caused the protagonists to approach one another with petulance and growing suspicion.[1] Martov, Trotsky, and others angrily assailed Lenin for his rudeness and lust for power, while Lenin could not see why this abuse should be heaped on him when all he had done was to suggest a workable and self-explanatory plan for *Iskra*'s overhaul. Each side began to scent intrigue and machination in every move made by the other. Each side was on the look-out for the traps that the other was laying for it. Each began to rehash old and half-forgotten differences; and although these had seemed puny only yesterday, they now appeared meaningful and portentous. In this mood the antagonists faced one another when the congress moved on to examine the statutes. There could be no question now of patching up the different formulas and submitting only one draft. On the contrary, the author of each draft was bent on bringing out the most deeply hidden implications of his clause, on making them as explicit as possible, on impressing the bewildered delegates with the gulf, the unbridgeable gulf, between the alternatives; and on emphasizing and over-emphasizing the practical consequences that the adoption of the one clause or the other would entail. Martov and Lenin, the two friends and comrades, confronted each other as enemies. Each spoke as if in a trance; each wondered at his own strange behaviour; each was surprised and bewildered by it; yet neither was capable of pausing and retracing his steps.[2]

The mood of the chief protagonists communicated itself to the delegates. The congress was split. Instead of founding one party it gave birth to two. At this moment, Plekhanov, the future irreconcilable enemy of the Bolshevik revolution, was Lenin's closest ally; while Trotsky was one of Lenin's most vocal opponents. He charged Lenin with the attempt to build up a closed organization of conspirators, not a party of the working

[1] The *Iskra* men held their closed sessions outside the congress. At one of these, when the division first became apparent, Trotsky presided because the opponents could not agree on any other chairman. Trotsky, *Moya Zhizn*, vol. i, chapter xii.

[2] In a letter to Potresov, Lenin wrote shortly after the Congress: 'And now I am asking myself: for what reason should we part to become life-long enemies? I am reviewing all the events and impressions of the congress, I am aware that often I acted and behaved in terrible irritation, "madly", and I am willing to admit this my guilt to anybody—if one can call guilt something that was naturally caused by the atmosphere, the reactions, the retorts, the struggle, etc.' Lenin, *Sochinenya*, vol. xxxiv, p. 137.

class. Socialism was based on confidence in the workers' class-instinct and in their capacity to understand their historical mission—why then should the party not open its gates wide to them, as Martov advised? Lenin, surprised to see his 'cudgel' turning against him, made repeated attempts to detach Trotsky from Martov. In full session he mildly and persuasively appealed to Trotsky, saying that from lack of experience Trotsky was confusing the issues and misinterpreting the differences. In the working class, too, he went on, there was confusion, wavering, and opportunism; and if the party were to open its gates as widely as Martov urged it to do, then it would absorb into its ranks all those elements of weakness. They should organize only the 'vanguard of the proletariat', its most class-conscious and courageous elements. The party must lead the working class; it could not, therefore, be as broad as the class itself.

This argument failed to persuade Trotsky. Lenin then met him outside the conference hall and for hours tried to answer charges and to explain his behaviour. Later he sent his followers and his own brother to 'bring over Trotsky'.[1] All was in vain. Trotsky was stiffening in hostility.

The congress adopted by a majority Martov's draft of the statutes. But this majority included the delegates of the Bund and the Economists, who, having been defeated by the votes of all *Iskra* men, were about to leave the congress and secede from the party. After their secession Lenin presented his scheme for the overhaul of *Iskra*'s staff. Trotsky countered the scheme with a motion emphatically confirming in office the old editorial board.[2] This time Lenin won with a majority of only two votes. With the same majority the congress elected Lenin's candidates to the Central Committee. The opposition abstained from voting. Thus it came about that Lenin's followers were labelled *Bolsheviki* (the men of the majority), while his opponents were described as *Mensheviki* (the men of the minority). The leaders of the minority, shocked and almost horror-stricken by the audacity with which Lenin had deprived Axelrod and Zasulich of their status in the party, announced that they would boycott the newly elected Central Committee and *Iskra*. Martov at once resigned from the editorial board. Lenin denounced this as intolerably anarchic behaviour. He was determined to enforce

[1] L. Trotsky, loc. cit.   [2] *Vtoroi Syezd RSDRP*, p. 364.

the authority of the newly-elected bodies: he insisted that, however narrow the margin by which they had been chosen, they constituted the legitimate leadership: in any democratic body, the majority, be it ever so slight, is the repository of constitutional power. The congress broke up in uproar and chaos.

In spite of its outwardly fortuitous character, this division initiated a long and irreversible process of differentiation, in the course of which the party of the revolution was to become separated from the party of the moderates. In western Europe the most moderate elements in the Labour movements were already frankly describing themselves as reformists, opposed to revolution. It was natural that such a division should appear in Russia as well. But under Tsarist autocracy even the most moderate of Socialists could not openly constitute themselves into a party of reform: the parliamentary democratic setting for this was lacking. They went on to profess, more or less sincerely, revolutionary socialism and Marxist orthodoxy. This, even more than the bewildering circumstances of the split, concealed its true nature. The division assumed an involved, irrational, and befogged aspect. What Trotsky saw in 1903 was two groups professing the same principles of policy and organization. He perceived nothing that would cause them to drift apart, except Lenin's ruthlessness in dealing with comrades, with such exalted comrades as Axelrod and Zasulich. This superfluous split, he reasoned, could not but become a source of weakness to the party and the working class.

On the face of things this was quite true. So far the protagonists were divided only by a difference in temper, although every one of them would soon try to rationalize this difference into a deeper controversy over ideas and conceptions. But the difference in temper was not without significance. In his 'disrespect' for the veterans, Lenin had shown that he would subordinate every sentiment, no matter how praiseworthy, and every other consideration to higher requirements of policy and organization. If the founding fathers of the party had to be sacrificed to efficiency, he would sacrifice them. An underground movement, assailing the ramparts of Tsardom and savagely persecuted, could not afford to give honorary sinecures even to those who had started the movement. This was, of course, a fanatical and in a sense an inhuman attitude. The man who so acted would not hesitate to sacrifice other persons and other considerations to what he regarded as the vital interest of the revolution. But a revolutionary party cannot do without a large dose of fanaticism of this sort. It must take seriously the maxim, proclaimed by Plekhanov, that the preservation of the revolution is its supreme law. Lenin's opponents, on the other hand, gave to their private sentiments the same weight which they had promised to attach to that law alone. They would, in the future, give the same weight to all sorts of other sentiments and considerations, clashing with their avowed revolutionary aspiration. They would prove themselves conciliators, not revolutionaries.

It is no wonder, however, that the symptomatic significance of this difference, so obvious in retrospect, was hidden from many, if not from most, of the actors. Trotsky did not perceive the revolutionary frame of mind behind Lenin's personal ruthlessness. Other motives probably confirmed him in his attitude. By Lenin's side he saw the haughty, aggressive Plekhanov, who had snubbed him on every occasion for no apparent reason. On the other side were all the warm-hearted and unassuming men and women to whom he had owed so much. His choice was clear; it was a choice he would one day grievously regret.

Almost immediately after the congress, 'not yet cooled off from the heat of the clash', he wrote the *Report of the Siberian Delegation*, 'a human document for the future historian', as he described it. In it he expressed with much affectation his disillusionment, his new hostility towards Lenin, and the contradictions in his own attitude.

The congress thought that it was doing constructive work; it was only destructive. . . . Who could suppose that this assembly, convened by *Iskra*, would mercilessly trample over *Iskra*'s editorial board . . .? Which political crystal gazer could forecast that Martov and Lenin would step forth . . . as the hostile leaders of hostile factions? All this has come like thunder from the blue[1] . . . this man [Lenin], with the energy and talent peculiar to him, assumed the role of the party's disorganizer. . . . Behind Lenin . . . stood the new compact majority of the 'hard' *Iskra* men, opposed to the 'soft' *Iskra* men. We, the delegates of the Siberian Union, joined the 'soft' ones, and

[1] N. Trotsky, *Vtoroi Syezd RSDRP* (*Otchet Sibirskoi Delegatsii*), pp. 8–11.

. . . we do not think that we have thereby blotted our revolutionary record. . . . The confirmation of the old editorial board of *Iskra* had been taken for granted. . . . The next day, comrades, we were burying *Iskra*. . . . *Iskra* is no longer, comrades. About *Iskra* we can speak only in the past tense, comrades.

Echoing Martov, he wrote that Lenin, impelled by a yearning for power, was imposing upon the party a 'state of siege' and his 'iron fist'.[1] 'We suffered defeat because fate has decreed victory not for centralism but for [Lenin's] self-centredness.' Like a new Robespierre, Lenin was trying to 'transform the modest Council of the party into an omnipotent Committee of Public Safety'; and, like Robespierre, he was preparing the ground for the 'Thermidorians of socialist opportunism'.[2] For the first time, Trotsky now made this significant analogy, to which, throughout his life, in different contexts and changed circumstances, he would come back over and over again. What he now intended to convey was this: Robespierre's terror brought about the Thermidorian reaction, which was a setback not merely to the Jacobins but to the French Revolution at large. Similarly, Lenin was carrying the principle of centralism to excess, and in doing so he would not only bring discredit upon himself, but provoke a reaction against the principle of centralism, a reaction which would favour the opportunists and the federalists in the movement. In a postscript Trotsky added mockingly that he had not intended to compare Lenin with Robespierre: the Bolshevik leader was a mere parody of Robespierre, whom he resembled as 'a vulgar farce resembles historic tragedy'.[3] Once he had made up his mind against Lenin he did not mince his words. He attacked with all his intensity of feeling and with all the sweep of his invective.

The leaders of the minority, the Mensheviks, carried out their threat to boycott the Central Committee and *Iskra*. Trotsky, among others, ceased to contribute. In September 1903 the Mensheviks assembled in Geneva to decide on the forms of further action: how far should they carry the boycott? Should they incur the risk of expulsion, and, if expelled, form a rival party? Or should they conduct themselves so as to remain within the party and try to unseat Lenin at the next congress?

[1] N. Trotsky, *Vtoroi Syezd RSDRP* (*Otchet Sibirskoi Delegatsii*), pp. 20–21.
[2] Ibid., p. 30.   [3] Ibid., p. 33.

Views were divided. For all the violence of his public attacks on Lenin, Trotsky advocated moderation. The purpose of the boycott, in his view, was to exert pressure on Lenin and Plekhanov, to bring back the veterans to their positions of influence and to re-establish unity. The conference adopted a resolution written jointly by Martov and Trotsky. That part of the declaration of which Trotsky was the author stated: 'We consider it our moral and political duty to conduct . . . the struggle by all means, without placing ourselves outside the party and without bringing discredit upon the party and the idea of its central institutions . . . . [We shall strive] to bring about a change in the composition of the leading bodies, which will secure to the party the possibility of working freely towards its own enlightenment.'[1] But, although the Mensheviks stopped short of final schism, they formed a shadow central committee which was to conduct the campaign against the Leninist committee and against *Iskra*, and which, in case of a final break, would undoubtedly have emerged as the leadership of the new party. That committee, or 'bureau', consisted of Axelrod, Martov, Trotsky, Dan, and Potresov. Except for Trotsky, these men were to lead Menshevism to the end.

The Mensheviks had, in fact, no need to take upon themselves the odium of breaking up the party. The boycott which they waged with a loud hue and cry quickly yielded results. Plekhanov, who had at first so firmly sided with Lenin, became anxious to appease the opposition and to remove its grievance. He tried to persuade Lenin that they should restore the old editorial board. Lenin would not budge: he could not, he said, under the pressure of informal émigré groups, reverse a formal decision taken by a national congress.[2] From the point of view of the procedure by which any party is normally guided, Lenin's argument was irrefutable. But Plekhanov was in a position to disregard it. He was the chairman of the party's Council, and he was still the more authoritative man on *Iskra*'s editorial board, which, after Martov's resignation, consisted of himself and Lenin only. Plekhanov decided to invite Axelrod, Zasulich, Martov, and Potresov to rejoin the editorial staff. Lenin resigned. The Mensheviks thus took over *Iskra*, still in a position of the greatest

[1] *Pisma Axelroda i Martova*, p. 94.
[2] Lenin, *Sochinenya*, vol. xxxiv, pp. 162–6.

influence. Soon Lenin's own followers wondered whether Lenin had not gone too far and whether it was not wiser to seek peace with their adversaries. Lenin was defeated and isolated, yet even more than before convinced of the rightness of his attitude and determined to defend it.

With the Mensheviks Trotsky returned to *Iskra*, much to Plekhanov's annoyance. But having made it possible for the veterans to return in triumph, Plekhanov could not straightway slam the door on their most devoted defender and protégé. At first he merely urged Martov, now the actual editor, to keep Trotsky in a more subordinate place than he had held in the old *Iskra* or the one which Martov would have liked to assign to him. Trotsky was apparently confined to commenting on more or less indifferent topics, especially after readers in Russia had objected to the offensive tone of his polemics against Lenin.[1] Plekhanov, although he himself was now severely attacking Lenin, would not countenance this tone in Trotsky. At length, he demanded that *Iskra* should cease to publish Trotsky's contributions; and he threatened to resign from the paper if his demand was rejected. It was 'morally repugnant' to him, he stated, to be editor of a paper for which Trotsky was writing.

The occasion of this 'ultimatum' was an article by Trotsky on the war between Russia and Japan, which had just broken out. The article, published in *Iskra* in the middle of March 1904, was confused in content and style—Plekhanov's objections to it were not quite groundless—but it also contained a few significant ideas. Much of it was devoted to an exposure of Russian liberalism, 'half hearted, vague, lacking in decision and inclined to treachery'. This attitude of the middle classes was bound to harm the cause of democracy, but it would have one redeeming consequence: liberalism would not be able to place itself at the head of the revolution; and it would by its behaviour speed up 'the self-determination of the proletariat'. In the main, however, the argument was a criticism of the party's attitude, a criticism which did not quite tally with Trotsky's anti-liberal invective. He attacked 'the majority of the party committees' for the crudities of their propaganda, which claimed that the war against Japan was being waged in the interest, and with the

[1] See, for instance, the protest from the party committee of Tver, *Iskra*, no. 60.

support, of the Russian bourgeoisie. This, Trotsky argued, was not true; the Tsar conducted the war in the exclusive interest of autocracy—the bourgeois liberals were in 'an anti-patriotic mood'. He protested against the 'pseudo-Marxist cliché' rampant in the party: 'The vital criterion of class interest is being transformed into a dead and deadening cliché . . . into a Procrustean bed for problems which are no longer analysed but chopped around . . . for the proletariat's consumption.' The criticism was directed mainly, though not exclusively, against the Bolsheviks.[1]

Plekhanov's 'ultimatum' placed the Menshevik *Iskra* team in a quandary. They had all approved the incriminated article. They were reluctant to dispense with Trotsky's services: he was one of their chief spokesmen and a member of their shadow central committee. They had, on the other hand, recaptured *Iskra* thanks to Plekanov; and to him, as to the chairman of the Council, they owed their newly-won predominance, as Plekhanov was constantly reminding them. At first they rejected his pretensions and chafed at his 'undignified behaviour', 'blackmail', and 'personal spite'. Trotsky, nevertheless, offered to resign and expressed the desire to return to clandestine work in Russia. Martov and the other Mensheviks prevailed upon him to ignore the insult and to go on working for *Iskra*. But Plekhanov, having staked his prestige in this vendetta, could not put up with this; he carried out his threat of resignation. At length, the Mensheviks, afraid of losing their most important ally, who had just enabled them to defeat and humiliate Lenin, came to terms with Plekhanov: Trotsky's name disappeared from *Iskra*.[2]

Thus began Trotsky's estrangement from the Mensheviks. Although he himself, to spare his friends an embarrassment, had offered to resign, their bargain with Plekhanov could not but irk him. Sulkily he left Geneva and for a few months disappeared from Menshevik circles. The personal resentment was mixed up with incipient political differences. The Mensheviks, as they tried to rationalize their motives in the feud with the

---

[1] *Iskra*, no. 62, 15 March 1904. See also Trotsky's half-apologetic comment in the Supplement to *Iskra* of June 1904.

[2] The incident is related on the basis of *Perepiska Plekhanova i Axelroda*, vol. ii, pp. 198–201; *Pisma Axelroda i Martova*, pp. 101–5, and of *Iskra*.

Bolsheviks, began to react away from the views to which they
had been committed before the split. The reaction spread from
matters of organization to issues of policy. Zasulich was dreaming aloud about an alliance between socialism and middle-class
liberalism. Theodore Dan, now gaining eminence, bluntly
advocated that alliance. Even now, when Dan and Trotsky
were the leaders of the same faction, they instinctively repelled
each other. Dan was by temperament as solid and pedestrian
as Trotsky was flamboyant and impetuous. The one could
thrive best in a climate of political compromise, as his role under
Kerensky's régime in 1917 would show; the other was made
for revolution. While the Mensheviks were beginning to grope
for more moderate formulas, Dan's influence among them was
naturally rising and Trotsky's declining. Martov himself fore-
bodingly watched his followers in their quest for moderation;
but he was overpowered by the process he had initiated. The
reaction against the spirit of the 'old' *Iskra* did not leave Trotsky
unaffected. It could not be otherwise, for Lenin, whom he was
opposing, embodied that spirit. Trotsky now found that the old
Iskra had not been free from the *Narodnik*-like, conspiratorial
attitude; that it had been unjust towards the Economists; and
that it had falsely preached the supremacy of organization over
the 'spontaneous' Labour movement. These were the stock conclusions which most Mensheviks reached as they reviewed their
own recent past; and thus far Trotsky went along with them.[1]
But at one point he balked and balked for good, the point at
which they made the first attempt to bridge the gulf between
socialism and liberalism. He stuck to the anti-liberal attitude
which had, on the whole, prevailed in the old *Iskra*. In long
arguments with the Mensheviks he began to realize how much,
in this crucial issue, divided him from them, and how little from
Lenin.

Yet, before parting with the Mensheviks he once again
assailed Lenin with a hailstorm of his most hurtful invective,
which made any reconciliation with him wellnigh impossible.
In April 1904 Trotsky left *Iskra*. In August there appeared in
Geneva his pamphlet *Our Political Tasks*, which he dedicated to
'My dear teacher Paul B. Axelrod'. The historical and bio-

----

[1] In this respect there was no difference between Trotsky (in *Nashi Politicheskye
Zadachi*) and the most right-wing Menshevik Cherevanin (in *Organizatsionnyi Vopros*).

graphical interest of the pamphlet lies in the fact that this was
the most strident bill of impeachment that any Socialist had
ever drawn up against Lenin. Its interest also lies in the train of
thought which it initiated and in the amazing flashes of historical
intuition scattered over more than a hundred closely-printed
pages of vituperation.

'Just at a time', so Trotsky began, referring to the Russo-
Japanese war, 'when history has placed before us the enormous
task of cutting the knot of world reaction, Russian social democrats do not seem to care for anything except a petty
internal struggle.' What a 'heartrending tragedy' this was, and
what a 'nightmarish atmosphere' it created! '. . . almost everybody was aware of the criminal character of the split, but
nobody could free himself from the iron grip of history'. The
deep cause of the division lay in the difficulty the party had had
in reconciling its democratic and its socialist tasks. Russia had
not yet gone through a bourgeois democratic revolution; and
the party's immediate interest was to overthrow Tsarist absolutism. Yet its real but more remote objective was socialism.
The party was constantly torn between the two pursuits.
Whenever a controversy arose in its ranks, each side charged
the other with abandoning the class interest of the proletariat in
favour of bourgeois democracy. 'Every group representing a
new trend excommunicates its predecessors. To those who come
with new ideas the previous period seems to have been but a
crude deviation from the correct road, an historical misunderstanding. . . .'[1]

Thus, he went on, had Lenin and the old *Iskra* as a whole
treated the Economists, who, for all their limitations, had
awakened the Russian working class. The Mensheviks were the
first group 'trying to establish itself on the shoulders, not on the
broken bones, of its predecessors'; and this alone was a sign of
maturity. The Economists 'had appealed to the proletariat, but
they did so not in the spirit of social democracy' but in that of
non-political trade unionism. *Iskra*, on the other hand, had
addressed its social democratic message to the intelligentsia, not
to the workers. Lenin had bullied the revolutionary intelligentsia
into a Marxist orthodoxy, into an unconditional surrender to
Marx's authority, hoping that in this way he would train the

[1] N. Trotsky, *Nashi Politicheskye Zadachi*, p. 4.

men of the intelligentsia into reliable leaders of an immature
and timid labour movement. But Lenin was merely trying to
force the pace of history: for to be in possession of a proletarian
doctrine, such as Marxism, 'was no substitute for a politically
developed proletariat'.[1] Lenin distrusted the masses and adopted
a haughty attitude towards their untutored activities, arguing
that the workers by themselves could not rise from trade unionism to revolutionary socialism, and that socialist ideology was
brought into the Labour movement 'from outside', by the
revolutionary intelligentsia. This, Trotsky wrote, was the theory
of an 'orthodox theocracy'; and Lenin's scheme of organization
was fit for a party which would '*substitute* itself for the working
classes', act as proxy in their name and on their behalf, regardless of what the workers felt and thought.

To this 'substitutism' (*zamestitelstvo*), as Trotsky called it, to
this conception of a party acting as a *locum tenens* for the proletariat, he opposed Axelrod's plan for a 'broadly based party',
modelled on European social democratic parties.[2] 'Lenin's
methods lead to this: the party organization [the caucus] at
first substitutes itself for the party as a whole; then the Central
Committee substitutes itself for the organization; and finally a
single "dictator" substitutes himself for the Central Committee. . . .'[3] 'The party must seek the guarantee of its stability
in its own base, in an active and self-reliant proletariat, and not
in its top caucus, which the revolution . . . may suddenly sweep
away with its wing. . . .' After an ironical travesty of Lenin's
'hideous, dissolute, and demagogical' style,[4] and after some
ridicule directed at Lenin's attempt to impose discipline on the
party, Trotsky asked: 'Is it so difficult to see that any serious
group . . . when it is confronted by the dilemma whether it
should, from a sense of discipline, silently efface itself, or,
regardless of discipline, struggle for survival—will undoubtedly
choose the latter course . . . and say: perish that "discipline",
which suppresses the vital interests of the movement.' History will
not say that discipline should have prevailed even if the world
had to perish; it will eventually vindicate those who had 'the
fuller and the deeper understanding of the tasks of revolution'.[5]

The most curious part of the pamphlet is its last chapter on

---

[1] N. Trotsky, *Nashi Politicheskye Zadachi*, p. 23.   [2] Ibid., p. 50.
[3] Ibid., p. 54.   [4] Ibid., p. 75.   [5] Ibid., p. 72.

'Jacobinism and Social Democracy'.[1] At the congress, Trotsky refuted the charge of Jacobinism when the Economists levelled it against *Iskra* as a whole. Now he turned the charge against Lenin. Lenin faced it almost with pride: 'A revolutionary Social Democrat', he rejoined, 'is precisely a Jacobin, but one who is inseparably connected with the organization of the proletariat and aware of its class interests.' Trotsky elaborated the charge in the light, as the pamphlet shows, of his recent detailed study of the French Revolution; and he pointed towards the future drama of the Russian Revolution. The characters of the Jacobin and of the Social Democrat, he stated, are mutually exclusive. The French Revolution, because of the limitations of its epoch, could establish only a bourgeois society with bourgeois property as its basis. Jacobinism (that 'maximum of radicalism of which bourgeois society has been capable') strove to perpetuate a fleeting, quasi-egalitarian climax of the revolution, which was incompatible with the fundamental trend of the time. This was a foredoomed Utopia: history would have had to stop in its course in order to save Jacobinism. The conflict between Jacobinism and its age explains the Jacobin mentality and method of action. Robespierre and his friends had their metaphysical idea of Truth, their *Verité*; but they could not trust that their *Verité* would win the hearts and the minds of the people. With morbid suspicion they looked round and saw enemies creeping from every crevice. They had to draw a sharp dividing line between themselves and the rest of the world, and they drew it with the edge of the guillotine. 'Every attempt to blur [this division] between Jacobinism and the rest of the world threatened to release inner centrifugal forces. . . .' His political instinct suggested to Robespierre that only through a permanent state of siege could he prolong the ephemeral climax of the revolution. 'They spared no human hecatomb to build the pedestal for their Truth. . . . The counterpart to their absolute faith in a metaphysical idea was their absolute distrust of living people.'

From the Jacobin, Trotsky went on, the Social Democrat differed in his optimism, for he was in harmony with the trend of his age. At the threshold of the twentieth century, with the growth of modern industry and of the working classes, socialism

[1] Ibid., pp. 97-107.

was no longer Utopia. The Social Democrat and the Jacobin stand for 'two opposed worlds, doctrines, tactics, mentalities. . . . They were Utopians; we aspire to express the objective trend. They were idealists . . . we are materialists . . . they were rationalists, we are dialectitians. . . . They chopped off heads, we enlighten them with class consciousness.'

Trotsky did not deny that there were similarities between the Jacobin and the Social Democrat. Both were irreconcilable: the Jacobin fought against *moderantisme*; the Socialist is opposed to reformist opportunism. But the Social Democrat had no use for the guillotine. 'A Jacobin tribunal would have tried under the charge of moderation the whole international Labour movement, and Marx's lion head would have been the first to roll under the guillotine.'[1] 'Robespierre used to say: "I know only two parties, the good and the evil citizens"; and this aphorism is engraved on the heart of Maximilian Lenin', whose 'malicious and morally repulsive suspiciousness is a flat caricature of the tragic Jacobin intolerance. . . .' (In the same passage he described Lenin as 'an adroit statistician and slovenly attorney'.)

A clear-cut choice—this was Trotsky's conclusion—must be made between Jacobinism and Marxism. In trying to combine them, Lenin was virtually abandoning socialism and setting himself up as the leader of a revolutionary wing of bourgeois democracy. This was the gravamen of Trotsky's accusation that Lenin was changing from a Socialist into a radical bourgeois politician, because only a bourgeois politician could distrust the working classes as intensely as Lenin did.[2] Lenin's followers went even farther and frankly envisaged their 'dictatorship over the proletariat' and when one read how some Bolsheviks (here Trotsky quoted their leaflets published in the Urals) were advocating the need for an absolutely uniform party, 'one felt a shiver running down one's spine'.

He wound up his argument with the following plea against uniformity:

The tasks of the new régime will be so complex that they cannot be

---

[1] N. Trotsky, *Nashi Politicheskye Zadachi*, p. 95.

[2] Trotsky here quoted Axelrod, who had compared Lenin's evolution to Struve's. In this pamphlet Trotsky also gave eulogistic sketches of the Menshevik leaders, especially of Axelrod and Martov, describing the former as 'a great Marxist and penetrating political mind' and the latter as the 'Dobrolyubov of his generation'.

solved otherwise than by way of a competition between various methods of economic and political construction, by way of long 'disputes', by way of a systematic struggle not only between the socialist and the capitalist worlds, but also between many trends inside socialism, trends which will inevitably emerge as soon as the proletarian dictatorship poses tens and hundreds of new . . . problems. No strong, 'domineering' organization . . . will be able to suppress these trends and controversies. . . . A proletariat capable of exercising its dictatorship over society will not tolerate any dictatorship over itself. . . . The working class . . . will undoubtedly have in its ranks quite a few political invalids . . . and much ballast of obsolescent ideas, which it will have to jettison. In the epoch of its dictatorship, as now, it will have to cleanse its mind of false theories and bourgeois experience and to purge its ranks from political phrasemongers and backward-looking revolutionaries. . . . But this intricate task cannot be solved by placing above the proletariat a few well-picked people . . . or one person invested with the power to liquidate and degrade.[1]

Among the writings that came from Trotsky's prolific pen in the course of four decades, this is perhaps the most amazing document, not least because it contains so odd an assortment of great ideas and petty polemical tricks, of subtle historical insights and fustian flourishes. Hardly any Menshevik writer attacked Lenin with so much personal venom. 'Hideous', 'dissolute', 'demagogical', 'slovenly attorney', 'malicious and morally repulsive', these were the epithets which Trotsky threw at the man who had so recently held out to him the hand of fellowship, who had brought him to western Europe, who had promoted him and defended him from Plekhanov's aspersions. Marxists, to be sure, especially the Russian ones, were wont to state their views with ruthless frankness. But, as a rule, they refrained from personal mud-slinging. Trotsky's offence against this rule cannot be explained merely by youthful ebullience—he now exhibited a characteristic of which he would never quite free himself: he could not separate ideas from men.

Nor did he support his accusations by any fact that would give them weight in the historian's eye. Lenin had so far not expelled a single member from the party. All he had done was to insist on the validity of the mandate which the congress had given him, and to warn the opposition that, if they persisted in

[1] Ibid., p. 105.

obstructing the formal decisions of the congress and boycotting
the elected leadership, he would have to take action against
them. In so doing, he behaved as any leader of any party would
have behaved in the circumstances.[1] Since, through a series of
accidents and personal shifts the Mensheviks had first recaptured *Iskra* and then virtually ousted Lenin from leadership, his
formal predominance lasted a very short time, in the course of
which he did nothing to implement his warnings to the opposition. Once the opposition was on top, its leaders confronted
Lenin with exactly the same warning, although, as they had not
been elected at a congress, they had less right to do so.[2]

Trotsky knew all this and he said as much in his pamphlet.
His accusations were therefore based merely on inferences and
on one point of theory. Lenin had argued that, historically, the
revolutionary intelligentsia played a special role in the Labour
movement, infusing it with the Marxist outlook, which the
workers would not have attained by themselves. Trotsky saw in
this view a denial of the revolutionary capacities of the working
class and an aspiration of the intelligentsia, whose mouthpiece
Lenin was, to keep the Labour movement under their tutelage.
Implied in this he saw a design for a Jacobin-like, or, as we
would now say, a totalitarian dictatorship. Yet many socialist
writers had stressed the special role of the intelligentsia in the
Labour movement; and Lenin had in fact drawn his view from
Kautsky, the recognized authority on Marxist theory.[3] Both
factions, Mensheviks as well as Bolsheviks, were led by intellectuals: at the recent congress only three workers had appeared

[1] When Rosa Luxemburg attacked Lenin in the *Neue Zeit* and then in *Iskra*
(no. 69, 10 July 1904), she criticized him for transplanting European, German, and
British (Fabian) models of organization to Russia. In the German Social Democratic Party centralism was upheld by the moderate leaders against the revolutionary wing. Karl Kautsky (*Iskra*, no. 66, 15 May 1904) criticized Lenin on the
same ground, saying that what was meat for Europe was poison for Russia. The
Russian Social-Revolutionaries, future enemies of Bolshevism, warmly approved
Lenin's attitude (see 'Evolutsia Russkoi Sots. Mysli' in *Vestnik Russkoi Revolutsii*,
no. 3). It can be seen from this how unhistorical is the view, held by both Bolsheviks
and many of their critics, that the brand of centralism which Lenin represented in
1903 was the exclusive feature of Bolshevism, its exclusive virtue or its original sin.

[2] Parvus, who stood nearer to the Mensheviks than to the Bolsheviks (see next
chapter), criticized the Mensheviks for adopting the dictatorial methods of organization which they attributed to Lenin. Parvus, *Rossya i Revolutsia*, pp. 182 ff.

[3] Lenin, *Sochinenya*, vol. v (*Chto Delat?*), pp. 354–5; K. Kautsky in *Neue Zeit*, no.
3, 1901.

among the several scores of delegates. There was no reason therefore why the odium of voicing the aspirations of the intellectuals should fall only on Lenin. In Lenin's conception of the revolutionary régime, as he had developed it so far, there was not a single point on which Trotsky could base his indictment. Now and for many years to come Lenin held that a revolutionary government in Russia would be formed by a coalition of parties, and that the Socialists could not even aspire to hold a majority of seats in it.[1] The idea of a monolithic state had not even occurred to him. Trotsky himself would presently come much nearer to this idea than Lenin: against Lenin he would soon begin to advocate the proletarian dictatorship as the direct objective of revolution in Russia, which need not necessarily have meant a monolithic state, but which inevitably implied an approximation to it. Briefly, neither in fact nor in theory could Trotsky find any important premiss for his anticipatory portrait of Lenin as the Russian Robespierre, drawing by the guillotine a line of division between his party and the world. It required a volatile and irresponsible imagination in the pamphleteer to show his adversary in so distorting a mirror.

And yet this was the faithful mirror of the future, although the Russian Robespierre shown in it was to be not so much Lenin as his successor, at this time still an unknown Caucasian Social Democrat. So faithful indeed was this mirror of the future that in it one finds, in confused assortment, all the elements of the drama of the Russian Revolution. There is, first of all, the dilemma between the bourgeois democratic and the socialist objectives of the revolution, a dilemma which was often to recur. There is further the conflict of the two souls, the Marxist and the Jacobin, in Bolshevism, a conflict never to be resolved either in Lenin, or in Bolshevism at large, or even in Trotsky himself. Much as Trotsky now pressed for a clear-cut choice between Marxism and Jacobinism, circumstances would not permit Lenin or Trotsky to make that choice. Moreover, the mirror showed in advance the stages through which, in its 'substitutism', the party of the revolution would move: 'The caucus substitutes itself for the party; then the Central Committee for the caucus; and finally a dictator substitutes himself for the Central Committee.' These are in fact headings for several yet remote chapters in the annals of the revolution. Here again, Trotsky could have no inkling that one day he himself would go much farther than Lenin in preaching and glorifying that 'substitutism', before he would shrink in horror from its consummation. And then there is the grim picture of that consummation: the image of the morbidly suspicious dictator, 'invested with the power to degrade and liquidate', who sees enemies creeping from every crevice around him, and who, sparing no human hecatomb, struggles to perpetuate a climax of the revolution and hermetically separates the revolution from the rest of the world. And, as in the prelude to classical tragedy, the omens appear which seem to point to Trotsky's own fate: He makes the plea for the free competition of ideas and trends, a plea he will repeat, almost in the same words, before the tribunals of Bolshevism twenty years later. He now confidently believes that 'a working class capable of exercising its dictatorship over society will tolerate no dictator over itself'; and he is unaware that he begs the gravest question of all: what will happen if, after the revolution, the working class is not capable of exercising its dictatorship over society? He trusts that history will eventually vindicate those who have 'the fuller and the deeper understanding' of the needs of their epoch, an assurance which he will go on expressing all his life, up to the moment when the rusty axe of an assassin cleaves his brain. And, finally, as if in premonition of that moment, he feels 'a cold shiver running down his spine' at the mere thought of what might become of Lenin's party.

We cannot reconstruct in any detail the mental process by which he arrived at this view of the future. The circumstance that he had lacked any solid factual premiss for his conclusions indicates that the process was one of imaginative perception, not of reasoning. We can only trace some of the external stimuli to which his imagination responded. In a general manner, the comparison between Bolsheviks and Jacobins had already been made by some of the Mensheviks. Plekhanov, even while he was Lenin's ally, had said about the latter: 'Of such stuff the Robespierres are made.' The *obiter dictum* was repeated by others, first in whispers and then publicly. But hardly anybody, not even its author, meant it literally—it was received as one of Plekhanov's polemical *bon mots*. Trotsky took the saying literally, or at any rate seriously enough to plunge into the history of Jacobinism and to explore it avidly with an eye to the parallel. His imagination, inflamed by the Jacobin tragedy and over-flowing with the freshly absorbed images, projected these upon the groups and individuals with whom he was in daily contact and—upon Russia's indefinite future. In the light of a strictly rational analysis, this projection may have been gratuitous and erratic. A cooler and better disciplined mind would not have lent itself to such visionary anticipations. But Trotsky was possessed of a sixth sense, as it were, an intuitive sense of history, which singled him out among the political thinkers of his generation, sometimes exposed him almost to derision, but more often found triumphant, if much delayed, vindication.

Behind his polemical pursuits and imaginative projections there was the pent-up emotion of the romantic revolutionary, who, much as he himself may have argued about the need for a closely-knit and disciplined party, broke into individualistic protest against the reality of that party as soon as he was confronted by it. His inclinations, his tastes, his temperament revolted against the prosaic and business-like determination with which Lenin was setting out to bring the party down from the clouds of abstraction to the firm ground of organization. Trotsky's present protest was little different from that which, as a boy of seventeen, he had, with so much ill temper, thrown at Sokolovskaya, the first Marxist he had met: 'A curse upon all of you who want to bring dryness and hardness into all the relations of life!' The cry into which he had burst at Shvigovsky's orchard on the last night of 1896, reverberated in his anti-Leninist philippic of 1904.

CHAPTER IV

An Intellectual Partnership

WHEN *Our Political Tasks* appeared in Geneva, in August 1904, the situation in the party was very different from what it had been the year before, immediately after the split. The Menshevik *Iskra* ceaselessly harassed Lenin, who for a time was not even in a position to counter the attacks: it was almost six months before he could publish his own paper, the *Vperyod (Forward)*. Plekhanov was pouring ridicule upon his erstwhile ally and was confident that he was destroying Lenin's reputation for good and all. The authorities of European, especially of German, socialism who had long known and respected Plekhanov and the other veterans, joined in condemnation of Lenin, who in their eyes was an obscure young intruder. Even the Bolshevik Central Committee disregarded Lenin's attitude and came to terms with the Mensheviks. However, on the day when Trotsky's pamphlet appeared, Lenin gathered in Switzerland those Bolsheviks who were prepared to follow him and laid before them a plan for the convocation of a new congress, with or without Menshevik participation.

Trotsky's broadside seemed surpassed by events—the enemy appeared to have scattered before he had pressed home the attack. By way of afterthought he therefore wrote in the preface to *Our Political Tasks* that the crisis in the party was over, and that those who stood for unity could look to the future with confidence, because the extremists among both Bolsheviks and Mensheviks had been discredited and isolated. A more experienced politician, or one inclined to give more thought to the wounding effect of his words, might in the circumstances have either refrained from publishing the pamphlet or at least pruned its polemical extravagances. Trotsky was too much enamoured of his own words to do that. However, he tried in the preface to make allowance for the new situation: he called upon the Mensheviks to wind up their own separate organization, that party within the party, of which he himself had been one of the secret leaders. The Mensheviks, he wrote emphatically, should accept 'organizational death', that is, a merger of

the hitherto opposed groups.[1] His call fell on deaf ears. The
schism was beginning to acquire its own momentum. Its
'fanatics' were active in both groups. Among the Bolsheviks,
Lenin's group considered the changes that had taken place
since the congress as Menshevik usurpations, to which a new
congress would put an end. The Mensheviks, having recaptured
positions of influence, would not risk losing them at a new
congress, let alone sharing them, through a merger, with their
adversaries. Having with so much thunder pilloried Lenin as
the 'disorganizer', Trotsky was shocked to find 'disorganizers'
among his Menshevik friends. He began, mildly enough, to
plead with them the need of reconciliation. He had joined the
Mensheviks in order to make good the injury Lenin had inflicted
on the founding fathers of the movement and through them on
the movement itself. The injury had been made good with a
vengeance. The Bolshevik Central Committee itself was anxious
to make it good. All that was now needed to close the painful
chapter was that the *ad hoc* arrangements which had been
necessary in order to defeat Lenin be scrapped and that the
men of good will in both sections of the party join hands. He
did not realize that the *ad hoc* arrangements had come to
stay.

In controversies like this the conciliator is unwelcome. He
threatens to upset well-laid plans and to mix all the cards.
His own friends look askance at him, considering him little
better than a traitor. Thus did some Mensheviks now look upon
Trotsky: his attitude was not stable; it was indistinguishable
from that of the moderate Bolsheviks; and nobody could say
where he would stand tomorrow. Indeed, Trotsky might easily
have become one of the Bolshevik 'conciliators' had not his
hurtful attacks on Lenin and Lenin's followers estranged him
from all Bolsheviks. In their eyes he was one of the most vicious
Mensheviks. And so he was breaking with his political friends
without much chance of agreement with his adversaries.

In this situation he came under the influence of a man who
was in a sense an outsider to the party and whose role in its
affairs was that of a brilliant interloper. He was A. L. Helfand,
a Russian Jew who had made his home in Germany and had
won distinction as an economist, publicist, and author of

[1] N. Trotsky, *Nashi Politicheskye Zadachi*, p. viii.

scholarly Marxist books.[1] Under the pen-name Parvus he contributed to Kautsky's *Neue Zeit*, the most important and sophisticated Socialist periodical in Europe, and to many other Socialist newspapers. He also published his own review *Aus der Weltpolitik*, in which, as early as 1895, he forecast war between Russia and Japan and foresaw that out of that war would develop the Russian revolution—the prophesy was much quoted in 1904–5, when it came true. In the German party Parvus stood on the extreme left, sharply opposed to the reformist trend and disdainful of the pretences of Marxist orthodoxy with which some of the leaders still covered their reconciliation with the established order. Shrewd and militant, he searched for ways and means to bring about the regeneration of the revolutionary spirit in German socialism.

The reformist leaders viewed him with fear and that special irony which is reserved for immigrants seeking to mend the ways of their adopted country.[2] Parvus compensated himself with more biting criticism and adopted, in his turn, a patronizing attitude towards his original countrymen: to the Russians in exile he eagerly pointed out their eastern 'backwardness and parochialism' and he tried to teach them western political manners. Despite these droll postures, the Russians regarded him as a sort of guide to world politics and economics. He contributed to *Iskra*, first under the pen-name Molotov and then as Parvus. His essays usually appeared on *Iskra's* front page—the editors gladly relegated their own writings to make room for him. They respected his massive knowledge, gifts, and judgement. But they were also apprehensive of a streak of unreliability in him. There was something Gargantuan or Falstaffian about him and his (to quote Trotsky) 'fat, fleshy, bulldog-like head'. For many years, however, nothing seemed to justify the apprehension: there was no distinct instance of misdemeanour on Parvus's part, nothing, at any rate, that

[1] His books were translated into Russian. One of them, *The World Economy and the Agricultural Crisis*, was reviewed with great admiration by Lenin in 1899. 'Parvus deals primarily with the development of the world market', Lenin wrote, 'and describes . . . the recent phases of this development connected with the decline of England's industrial predominance.' 'We strongly recommend . . . Parvus's book.' Lenin, *Sochinenya*, vol. iv, pp. 51–52.

[2] The irony gave way to enormous respect as soon as the immigrant had begun to conform. Towards the end of his life Parvus was the brain behind Ebert, the President of the Weimar Republic.

would allow anybody to impugn his Socialist integrity and conviction. He was a somewhat erratic contributor, writing his essays in long serials and rarely delivering them on time; all the same his contributions were most welcome. He had somewhat brittle financial schemes: he had tried to set up a Socialist publishing house and had failed; and he laid plans for a great Socialist daily, to be issued simultaneously in several European languages, which was to shake European socialism from its reformist coma. But to found such a paper he needed enormous funds, and these he could not obtain, probably because he was not yet prepared to plunge into dubious financial ventures. Enough that, for one reason or another, the respect in which he was held was mingled with a little irony and distrust. His later fortunes were to show that hidden in him was a snob and a political impostor. Nevertheless, his was one of the boldest and most penetrating political minds of his generation; and the political thinker still overshadowed the impostor.

In the controversy among the Russians, Parvus at first showed sympathy for the Mensheviks but later kept himself decently aloof from both groups, as befitted a man who cast himself for the role of peacemaker. He had once tried to reconcile the *Iskra* men with the Economists; now he attempted to bring about a truce between the former *Iskra* men. His relations with both groups were, at any rate, unspoilt. When somewhat later he launched into criticism of both, the antagonists, though unpersuaded, took his intervention with grace and accorded him the treatment due to a well-wishing and reputable outsider.[1]

When Trotsky, barred from *Iskra* and at loggerheads with everybody, left Geneva, he went to Munich, where Parvus was living; he stayed in Parvus's home, and there Sedova, his second wife, later joined him. In Parvus he found a man viewing with detachment internal Russian alignments, capable of taking in the whole international scene of socialism, a master at Marxist analysis, unsurpassed at visualizing for himself and others the broad vistas of class struggle. Last but not least, Trotsky

---

[1] Parvus, *Rossya i Revolutsia*, pp. 182 ff.; *Iskra*, nos. 111 (24 September 1905) and 112 (8 October 1905). See also Martov, *Istorya Ross. Sots. Dem.*, pp. 112 ff. Lenin's reply to Parvus was in a tone of the highest respect (*Sochinenya*, vol. viii, p. 261).

admired in Parvus his 'virile, muscular style', which he was to remember hankeringly long after their break. In brief, Parvus still towered above Trotsky in erudition, experience, and literary taste. It is not easy, however, to define the extent of his influence on Trotsky. To this day Trotsky's detractors attribute the exclusive authorship of the theory of 'permanent revolution', the hallmark of Trotskyism, to Parvus, and suggest either that Trotsky copied or plagiarized it or that a theory coming from so contaminated a source must be worthless. Trotsky himself never denied his debt to Parvus, although the warmth with which he acknowledged it varied with times and circumstances. What they both wrote in the hey-day of their association reveals how many of the ideas and views first formulated by Parvus left a deep mark on Trotsky, and how many of them he was to repeat through his life in a form not very different from that in which his older friend had first put them.

But Trotsky was possessed of certain qualities which enabled him to be from the outset more than Parvus's mere disciple. He had the fresh experience of Russia and of the underground struggle, which Parvus had not. He had an incandescent political imagination, while Parvus's analyses and prognostications sprang from a bold but cold mind. He had the revolutionary fervour which gave wings to his ideas, while Parvus was the cynical type of revolutionary. Trotsky, then, had his own individual contribution to make to their common fund of ideas. As in most associations of this sort, the respective shares of the partners cannot be unscrambled, not even by the partners themselves. The thinking is done in common; and even if sometimes it is possible to say who has first formulated in print this or that part of a theory, the invisible, two-way traffic of suggestions and stimuli that has passed between the partners can never be traced. All that can be said of Parvus and Trotsky is that at first the older of the two was well ahead, leading with ideas and formulas. At the next stage both seemed to advance *pari passu*. In the end the junior leapt forward with a contribution which was distinctly his own, and which made and rounded off a new political doctrine; and with this doctrine he came to the fore on the vast and confused stage of the revolution. It should be added that the whole process developed and was concluded rapidly. It began in the summer of 1904. It was consummated in 1906, when, awaiting trial in a Petersburg prison, Trotsky expounded in writing the theory of the permanent revolution in its finished form. The time of his apprenticeship with Parvus was briefer still: it hardly lasted longer than till the beginning of 1905, the opening of the first revolution. This was a time of condensed and rapid thinking; and the young Trotsky, who had already projected the image of Jacobinism on to the Russian revolution, was a quick learner.

. . . .

After the outbreak of the Russo-Japanese war, Parvus published a series of essays in *Iskra* on 'War and Revolution'.[1] Even before that his contributions, which he used to sign as Molotov, had strongly impressed Trotsky. But it was mainly the views which he put forward in 'War and Revolution' that made the lasting impression.

Parvus's central idea was that the nation-state, as it had developed with capitalism, had outlived its day. This view had belonged to the common stock of Marx's theory—it had been stated by Marx in the *Communist Manifesto*. But to most Socialist writers at the turn of the century this was one of the master's sayings, fit to be repeated on festive occasions, but bearing little relation to the realities of a late Victorian, nation-conscious, and empire-proud Europe. Only a very remote future, it was thought, might bring the eclipse of the nation-state. Parvus, on the contrary, saw the eclipse coming, pointed to its symptoms, forecast its cataclysmic intensification, and urged the Socialists to adjust their attitudes and policies accordingly. He placed an unusual emphasis on the interdependence of nations and states, and this emphasis gave to his reasonings a broad, worldwide sweep, rare in other Socialists. He saw the Russo-Japanese conflict of 1904 as the start of a long sequence of wars, in which the nation-states, impelled by capitalist competition, would fight for their survival. The fate of continents had become intertwined. The opening up of the American west had sharpened the competition for world markets between the agricultural producers. European, especially German, farming and industrial interests joined hands in order to do away with free trade and to impose a protectionist system on western Europe. 'The customs walls have become an economic barrier to the historical process

[1] The series began in *Iskra*, no. 59, 10 February 1904.

of the cultural unification of nations; they have increased the
political conflicts between states . . . and enhanced the power of
states and governments . . .—the stronger the power of governments, the easier do the states clash in arms.' These ideas were
to become for Trotsky axioms from which he would argue all
his life.

Russia's expansion in Asia and conflict with Japan, Parvus
held, were partly brought about by domestic pressures: Tsardom was seeking in external conquest an escape from internal
weakness. But more important were the external pressures to
which Russia was subjected. In the worldwide struggle between
capitalist nation-states only the great modern powers acted with
independence; and even an empire as vast as the Tsar's, was,
because of its industrial backwardness, merely 'a pensioner of
the French Bourse'. 'The war has started over Manchuria and
Korea; but it has already grown into a conflict over leadership
in east Asia. At the next stage Russia's entire position in the
world will be at stake; and the war will end in a shift in the
political balance of the world.'

Parvus concluded his analysis as follows: 'The worldwide
process of capitalist development leads to a *political upheaval* in
Russia. This in its turn must have its impact on the political
development of all capitalist countries. The Russian revolution
will shake the bourgeois world. . . . And the Russian proletariat
may well play the role of the vanguard of social revolution.'[1]

Thus already in 1904 Parvus viewed the approaching revolution not as a purely Russian affair but as a reflection in Russia
of worldwide social tensions; and he saw in the coming Russian
upheaval a prelude to world revolution. Here were the main

---

[1] *Iskra*, no. 82, 1 January 1905. In the same series Parvus wrote: 'One must
reach the paradoxical conclusion that the most decisive subjective factor of historical
development is not political wisdom but political stupidity. Men have never yet
been able fully to benefit from the social conditions they themselves have created.
They always think that they are far ahead, whereas they are far behind the objective
historical process. . . . History has often led by the noses those who have thought
that they could keep her in check.' 'The capitalist order in Europe has long since
been an obstacle to Europe's economic, political, and cultural development. It
survives only because the popular masses have not yet become sufficiently aware
of their tragic condition. The political energy of the proletariat is not concentrated
enough, the socialist parties lack decision and courage. One can imagine such a
turn of events that the Social Democratic Party will bear the political guilt for the
survival of the capitalist order.' To contemporaries this seemed a far-fetched
prophesy.

elements for the theory of permanent revolution. Yet, Parvus had so far spoken only about a 'political upheaval' in Russia, not about a 'social' or Socialist revolution. He apparently still shared the view, then accepted by all Marxists, that the Russian revolution by itself would, because of the country's semi-feudal and backward outlook, be merely bourgeois in character. Trotsky would be the first to say that the revolution would of its own momentum pass from the bourgeois to the Socialist stage, and establish a proletarian dictatorship in Russia, even before the advent of revolution in the West.

Not only were Parvus's international ideas and revolutionary perspectives becoming part and parcel of Trotsky's thinking, but, also, some of Trotsky's views on Russian history, especially his conception of the Russian state, can be traced back to Parvus.[1] Parvus developed the view that the Russian state, a cross between Asian despotism and European absolutism, had formed itself not as the organ of any class in Russian society, but as a military bureaucratic machine designed primarily to resist pressure from the more highly civilized West.[2] It was for this purpose that Tsardom had introduced elements of European civilization into Russia, especially into the army. 'Thus came into existence the Russian state organism: an Asian absolutism buttressed by a European type of army.' It was enough, he remarked, to cast a glance at the line of Russian frontier fortresses to see that the Tsars had intended to separate Russia from the West by a sort of Chinese wall. Some of these theories, as they were developed and refined by Trotsky, became the objects of heated historical and political disputes twenty years later.

Parvus's influence on Trotsky is felt also in the style and manner of exposition, especially in the characteristic sweep of historical prognostication. This is not to say that Trotsky played the literary ape to Parvus. He absorbed the influence naturally and organically because of his intellectual and literary affinity with Parvus, an affinity which was not lessened by contrasts in character and temperament.

During his first stay in Munich, towards the end of September

[1] In part, however, the original source of the views on Russian history held by both Trotsky and Parvus is the liberal historian P. Miliukov.
[2] *Iskra*, no. 61, 5 March 1904.

1904, Trotsky announced his break with the Mensheviks in an 'Open Letter to Comrades', which he sent for publication to *Iskra*. The letter was never published. We have only a Menshevik summary of it, which says that 'in a stilted and supercilious tone' Trotsky brought a number of charges against 'some comrades' and raised various demands. The gravamen of those charges was that the Menshevik group tended to place its sectional interests above those of the party. In addition, he wrote, the Mensheviks were reacting wrongly to Lenin's attitude in one important point: while Lenin was bent on giving the intelligentsia a privileged and dominant position in the party, the Mensheviks were inciting the workers against the Socialist intelligentsia. In a private letter to Martov and Zasulich, Trotsky explained that his criticisms were directed mainly against Theodore Dan, the politician of moderation; and that his intention was to promote the creation of a 'stable party centre' and an understanding with the Bolshevik Central Committee. He also complained that writers 'whom *Iskra* could not assimilate'—a hint at his having been squeezed out by Plekhanov—had no chance of reaching the Socialist public. Finally, he announced in a formal manner his secession from the Menshevik group.[1]

The Mensheviks responded with the anger of embarrassment. 'A very stormy correspondence' passed between Trotsky and Martov, which, so Martov wrote, 'if I had given him free rein would have ended in a complete breaking off of my relations with him.' Martov and other Mensheviks were anxious to prevent the breach, for if they became public the criticisms levelled against them by their most outspoken anti-Bolshevik controversialist, were likely to harm the group. A closed conference was arranged at Geneva, at which Trotsky's Open Letter was discussed in his presence. It was formally agreed that the further existence of the Menshevik émigré organization might become 'the source of new conflicts in the party', and that the organization should be disbanded, pending further instructions from Menshevik groups in Russia.[2]

This decision was clearly meant to appease Trotsky and to keep him quiet. It had no further repercussions: the Menshevik 'party within the party', just like the Bolshevik, was to function

[1] *Pisma Axelroda i Martova*, pp. 110–11.   [2] Ibid.

as before, although Trotsky may have consoled himself with the illusion that the Mensheviks had accepted his advice. At any rate, the formal decision to disband the Menshevik organization freed him from the group discipline by which he had been bound. Martov soon reported to Axelrod that Trotsky had at last 'calmed down', 'softened', and that he had resumed writing for *Iskra*—Trotsky's first contribution since the clash with Plekhanov did indeed soon appear in the paper.[1] As usual, personal resentments, pretensions, and political motives were so mixed up that it is well-nigh impossible to disentangle them. We cannot say whether Trotsky 'calmed down' because the Mensheviks seemed to yield to him on a matter of principle, or because they gave him some satisfaction for Plekhanov's rebuff, or for both these reasons. He was not now one of *Iskra's* policy-makers and editorial writers; he contributed a political note-book, which appeared on one of the back pages. But *Iskra* was still the Mensheviks' militant paper, and so to outsiders Trotsky remained a Menshevik.

. . . .

His differences with the Mensheviks were not really settled and news from Russia presently widened them. The Russo-Japanese war had taken a turn disastrous for Russia; and cracks were showing in the edifice of Tsardom. In July, the Minister Plehve, the inspirer of the Tsar's Far Eastern policy, was assassinated by Sazonov, a social revolutionary.[2] Plehve had banned and dispersed the *Zemstvos*, which were the strongholds of the Liberal and semi-Liberal gentry. His successor, Svatopolk-Mirsky, tried to appease the opposition and allowed the *Zemstvos* to hold a national convention in November 1904. The convention was followed by a long sequence of political banquets held in many towns. At these the Liberal leaders of the gentry and of the middle classes voiced their demands; but side by side with them there also appeared, for the first time, workers and members of the Socialist underground. Although all of them still spoke in unison against the government, the banquets afforded a glimpse of a deep division in the

[1] *Iskra*, no. 75, 5 October 1904. (Trotsky's only contribution in the interval had appeared in a discussion sheet published in June as a supplement to *Iskra*.)
[2] Azev, the *agent-provocateur* whom Plehve himself had employed to disrupt the clandestine terrorist organization, helped in preparing the assassination.

opposition. The workers suspected that the purpose of the Liberal spokesmen was not to overthrow the Tsar but to strike a bargain with him.

The émigrés in western Europe watched with hopeful suspense the banqueting campaign, which went on till the end of the year. Events pressed the Socialists to clarify their attitude towards liberalism. The division between socialism and liberalism existed in the émigré circles as well. Since the middle of 1902, Peter Struve had been publishing his *Osvobozhdenie* (Liberation) first in Stuttgart and then in Paris. At the outset the paper advocated 'legal Marxism', a diluted version of the doctrine; it placed particular emphasis on that part of the Marxist argument which was directed against *Narodnik* terrorism and agrarian socialism and it insisted that capitalist industrialization would bring social progress to Russia. In this phase the old *Iskra* and *Osvobozhdenie* were not yet openly opposed to each other. But soon it became clear that Struve's group used the Marxist argument to dispose of one brand of socialism, the agrarian, not to advocate proletarian socialism. *Osvobozhdenie* evolved from 'legal Marxism' towards liberalism; and the evolution became very marked just when the cleavage between the Socialists was deepening. The Mensheviks inclined towards the Liberals; the Bolsheviks were turning against them. Over this issue, in the autumn of 1904, Trotsky again fell out with the Mensheviks.[1]

In November and December he wrote a brochure on the problems raised by the banqueting campaign, and he submitted it to the Menshevik publishers. The latter were reluctant to bring it out, delayed publication, and, according to Trotsky, intended to suppress it. This was hardly their set intention, for they did bring it out in the end. But the brochure contained so sweeping and devastating a diatribe against the Liberals that it could not but arouse misgivings in men who had begun to see their chance in joint Socialist-Liberal action against the Tsar. The crux of Trotsky's argument was that the Liberals, more afraid of the revolution than of the Tsar, were incapable of such action.[2]

---

[1] L. Martov, *Istorya Ross. Sots. Dem.*, p. 102; Trotsky, *Moya Zhizn*, vol. i, chapter xiii.

[2] The brochure *Do 9 Yanvara* (*The Period up to 9 January*) is reprinted in *Sochinenya*, vol. ii, book 1.

In the first instance he flayed the pathetic and insincere patriotism which the Liberals had displayed in the Russo-Japanese war. Struve, he wrote, 'sacrificed the last remnants of his spirit of opposition and of his political dignity not to "patriotic feeling" but to patriotic hypocrisy'.[1] Because of its military defeats, Tsardom was in an impasse. 'All the more sharply and energetically . . . should the opposition have revealed the gulf that yawns between Tsardom and the nation. All the more firmly should it have tried to push Tsardom, the nation's real enemy, into the gulf. Instead, the liberal *Zemstvo* . . . harnesses itself to the rickety war-chariot, removes the corpses and sweeps away the trail of blood.' At heart the Liberals prayed for the Tsar's defeat which might induce him to meet the opposition half-way. 'But what does the liberal Press do? That miserable, mumbling, slick, mendacious, wriggling, corrupted and corrupting liberal Press? . . . Not believing its own words and concealing a slavish yearning for the Tsar's destruction [it speaks about] '*our* Monarch and *our* war.' The Liberal opposition was seeking to 'deserve the gratitude and the trust of absolutism, to become indispensable to it, and finally to bribe it with the people's money,—tactics as old as Russian liberalism, which has become neither more sensible nor more dignified with the years'.[2] The new Minister, Prince Svatopolk-Mirsky had initiated an era of spurious concessions by expressing ('stupidly and insolently') his government's confidence in the people, 'as if the question was whether the Ministry trusted the people and not whether the people trusted the Ministry'. But this was enough, Trotsky went on, for the *Zemstvos* to omit from their statements the demand for universal suffrage and constitutional government. They were afraid of the foreign word 'constitution'; and 'behind the fear of the word was concealed the fear of the deed. . . '. 'He who wants to be understood by the masses and to have them on his side, should above all express his demands clearly and precisely, call things by their proper names, call constitution—constitution, republic—republic, universal suffrage—universal suffrage.'[3] By their timidity the Liberals were unwittingly restoring in rulers and ruled alike confidence in the future of absolutism. They pretended to be the party of

---

[1] L. Trotsky, *Sochinenya*, vol. ii, book 1, p. 6.
[2] Op. cit., p. 9.   [3] Op. cit., p. 15.

democracy; but they were betraying their own principle. 'We have no democratic traditions; these have to be created. Only the revolution can do that. The party of democracy cannot but be the party of the revolution.'[1] Neither the Liberal intelligentsia nor the middle classes but the Socialist factory workers would deal the decisive blow to Tsardom.

The whole brochure is permeated with a triumphant sense of the imminence of the revolution. 'Barristers are demonstrating in the streets, political exiles are protesting in newspapers against their banishment, . . . a naval officer opens a public campaign against the naval department. . . . The incredible becomes real, the impossible becomes probable.'[2] So close a premonition of approaching events can hardly be found in the writings of any other émigré. The others were so immersed in their internecine struggles and so engrossed in manœuvring against one another, with the intention, no doubt, of securing for the party the best possible vantage-point in a revolution, that they almost missed the advent of the revolution. Because he stood almost alone, Trotsky turned his undivided attention to developments in Russia. He was, as Lunacharsky put it, less of an émigré than were other Socialists, who had, in varying degrees, lost contact with their country.[3] His sceptical friends shrugged their shoulders at his triumphant heralding of the upheaval not less than at the vehemence of his anti-Liberalism.

He saw the revolution developing from a general strike. This was a novel concept: the labour conflicts in Russia had so far been on a local scale; and even the industrial countries in the West, with their old trade unions, had not yet any real experience of a general strike. In *My Life* he says that he had mooted this idea since 1903, although he finally adopted it only in 1904.[4] He now sketched a 'plan of action' which he summed up as follows:

Tear the workers away from the machines and workshops; lead them through the factory gate out into the street; direct them to neighbouring factories; proclaim a stoppage there; and carry new masses into the street. Thus, moving from factory to factory, from workshop to workshop, growing under way and sweeping away police

[1] L. Trotsky, *Sochinenya*, vol. ii, book 1, p. 30.   [2] Op. cit., p. 3.
[3] A. Lunacharsky, *Revolutsionnye Siluety*, pp. 20–25.
[4] L. Trotsky, *Moya Zhizn*, vol. i, chapter xiii; *Sochinenya*, vol. ii, book 1, p. 521.

obstacles, haranguing and attracting passers-by, absorbing groups
that come from the opposite direction, filling the streets, taking
possession of the first suitable buildings for public meetings, en-
trenching yourselves in those buildings, using them for uninterrupted
revolutionary meetings with a permanently shifting and changing
audience, you shall bring order into the movement of the masses,
raise their confidence, explain to them the purpose and the sense of
events; and thus you shall eventually transform the city into a
revolutionary camp—this, by and large, is the plan of action.[1]

This was indeed the picture of the revolution which was to
materialize both in October 1905 and in February 1917. The
'plan of action' was not modelled on any precedent: in the
French Revolution the industrial-proletarian element had been
absent. The picture sprang from a fervent revolutionary imagination, in which romanticism was curiously blended with realism.
Some parts of this brochure read like passages·from Trotsky's
own histories of 1905 and 1917, only that the events are described
here in the future tense; and even the watchwords are those that
would resound in 1905 and 1917: 'End the war', and 'Convoke
a constituent assembly!'[2]

Finally, he surveyed the social forces that were coming into
action. 'The town will be the main arena of revolutionary
events.'[3] But the urban proletariat alone will not decide the issue.
The peasantry represented 'a major reservoir of potential
revolutionary energy'.[4] It is 'necessary to carry the agitation
into the countryside, without a day's delay and without missing
a single opportunity'.[5] Far from calling the urban proletariat,
as his later critics say, to brave Tsardom single-handedly and
court defeat, he strongly underlined the dangers of isolation
that threatened the working class.[6] He analysed the role of the
army, composed of peasants, and urged Socialists to watch
soberly what was going on in the barracks. When ordered to
fire at crowds, soldiers preferred to shoot into the air; the morale
of the army was under a strain:

Our ships are slow. Our guns do not fire far enough. Our soldiers
are illiterate. Our N.C.O.s have neither map nor compass. Our
soldiers go barefoot, naked and hungry. Our Red Cross steals.
Our supply services steal. Rumours about this reach the army and

[1] L. Trotsky, *Sochinenya*, vol. ii, book 1, p. 51.
[2] Ibid. and *passim*.   [3] Op. cit., p. 50.
[4] Op. cit., p. 20 and *passim*.   [5] Op. cit., p. 52.   [6] Op. cit., p. 46.

are avidly absorbed. Every such rumour corrodes like a sharp acid the rust of official indoctrination. Years of our peaceful propaganda could not achieve what one day of war does.

On the decisive day the officers should not be able to rely on the soldiers. . . . The same soldier who yesterday fired his shots in the air, will tomorrow hand over his weapon to the worker. He will do so as soon as he has gained the confidence that the people is not out merely to riot, that the people knows what it wants and can fight for what it wants. . . . We must develop the most intense agitation among the troops so that at the moment of the [general] strike every soldier sent to suppress the 'rebels' should know that in front of him is the people demanding the convocation of the constituent assembly.[1]

The Menshevik publisher was still withholding Trotsky's brochure from the press when news arrived of the first act of revolution in Russia. On 9/23 January 1905 the workers of Petersburg marched in an enormous but peaceful procession to the Tsar's Winter Palace. They were led by Father Gapon, a prison chaplain and a protégé of Zubatov, the chief of the gendarmerie, who had set up his own Labour organization to combat clandestine socialism. The demonstrators, carrying the Tsar's portraits, holy icons, and church banners, hoped to submit to the Tsar a petition, in which they humbly and plaintively begged him to redress their grievances. The Tsar refused to receive the petitioners and ordered the troops guarding the Winter Palace to fire into the crowd. Thus he ignited the revolutionary explosion.

The news found Trotsky in Geneva, whither he had just arrived from a lecturing tour. His forecasts, which he had in vain been trying to publish, began to come true. Full of hopeful excitement, he returned to Parvus in Munich, the galley proofs of the brochure in his pocket. Parvus read the proofs and was so impressed that he decided to put the weight of his authority behind Trotsky's views. He wrote a preface to the brochure and urged the Mensheviks to publish it. In his preface he stated a conclusion which Trotsky still hesitated to draw. 'The revolutionary Provisional Government of Russia', Parvus wrote, 'will be the government of a workers' democracy. . . . As the Social Democratic party is at the head of the revolutionary movement . . . this government will be social democratic . . . a coherent

[1] L. Trotsky, *Sochinenya*, vol. ii, book 1, p. 50.

government with a social democratic majority.' When the brochure at last appeared, it aroused much controversy, and it spurred on both Bolsheviks and Mensheviks to formulate their own anticipations. Disputation centred on Parvus's conclusion: both Mensheviks and Bolsheviks rejected it. The former advanced the view that as the revolution was bourgeois in character, directed against absolutism and residual feudalism, not aiming at socialism, the bourgeoisie, not the proletariat, was the legitimate heir to power. The Socialists, according to them, could not participate in any bourgeois government, even in one that emerged from a revolution. Their task was to guard, in opposition, the interests of the working class. Lenin agreed that the revolution was bourgeois in so far as it could not aim at socialism; but he did not believe in the revolutionary mission of the bourgeoisie. The Socialists, he held, were bound in duty to enter a revolutionary government. Yet he, too, contested Parvus's forecast about the Social-Democratic character of that government. 'This *cannot be*', Lenin wrote, 'if we have in mind not fleeting episodes but a halfway lasting revolutionary dictatorship, capable of leaving some mark on history. This cannot be, because only such a revolutionary dictatorship can have any stability . . . as is based on a great majority of the people. The Russian proletariat constitutes now a minority of Russia's population.' The revolutionary government would have to be formed by a coalition, in which 'petty bourgeois and semi-proletarian elements' would participate 'or even predominate. . . . It would be extremely harmful', Lenin added, 'to entertain any illusions whatsoever about this.'[1]

This was the first time that any group or individual laid, on behalf of Russian socialism, open claim to power, or to the major share in it. It was a curious freak that this claim should have been first made by Parvus, an outsider to the Russian revolution, and that it should have been repudiated almost in horror by Lenin. In Lenin's person the revolution seemed 'to shrink back appalled before the vague immensity of its own aims'. Yet even Parvus spoke about a 'workers' government', not a proletarian dictatorship. Nor did Trotsky yet question the common assumption that the revolution would be merely bourgeois, and that with the destruction of feudal and absolutist

[1] Lenin, *Sochinenya*, vol. viii, pp. 262–3.

institutions its role would be exhausted. At the same time it seemed to him as to Parvus irrefutable that if the urban proletariat was the chief driving-force of the revolution, then its representatives must, if the revolution succeeded, wield the major influence in the provisional government. No social class would be willing to bear the brunt of a revolution and then give up the fruits of its victory. The critics were incapable of effectively refuting this argument. But both Bolsheviks and Mensheviks asked two pertinent questions: How could this prospect be reconciled with the bourgeois character of the revolution? And how could one envisage a government by a proletarian minority, without abandoning the principle of representative democratic government, which none of the disputants was willing to abandon? To these questions neither Trotsky nor Parvus had any answer yet.

In January 1905, at Parvus's home, Trotsky began to write another series of essays, which appeared later under the title *After the Petersburg Insurrection*. The series consisted of rather disparate segments: of new, sarcastic polemics against the Liberals, of intensely enthusiastic passages greeting the revolution, and of highly sober reflections on the techniques of revolution. In his strictures on the Liberals he dwelt on the point that only two days before the demonstration in Petersburg, Struve had stated that 'no revolutionary people exists in Russia'. 'These words', Trotsky commented, 'should be engraved on Mr. Struve's forehead, if, even without this, his head did not already look like a gravestone, under which are buried so many plans, slogans, and ideas—socialist, liberal, "patriotic", revolutionary, monarchist, democratic, and others.'[1] Trotsky's conclusion was: *'Our struggle for the revolution, our preparation for it, will go hand in hand with our ruthless struggle against liberalism for influence on the masses, for the leading role of the proletariat . . .'*

The tenor of the passages in which he greeted the revolution may be gauged from these words:

Yes, she has come. We have awaited her. We have never doubted her. For many years she was only a deduction from our 'doctrine', at which the nonentities of every political shade mocked. . . . With her first sweep, she has already uplifted society. . . . Before 9 January our demand for a republic seemed fantastic, doctrinaire, and dis-

[1] L. Trotsky, *Sochinenya*, vol. ii, book 1, pp. 57 ff.

gusting to all liberal pundits. One day of revolution was enough, one magnificent contact between the Tsar and the people was enough for the idea of constitutional monarchy to become fantastic, doctrinaire, and disgusting. The priest Gapon rose with his idea of the monarch against the real monarch. But, as behind him there stood not monarchist liberals but revolutionary proletarians, this limited 'insurrection' immediately manifested its rebellious content in barricade fighting and in the outcry: Down with the Tsar. The real monarch has destroyed the idea of the monarch. . . . The revolution has come and she has put an end to our political childhood.[1]

At this stage problems of revolutionary technique acquired 'colossal importance'. 'The proletarians of Petersburg have shown great heroism. But the unarmed heroism of the crowd could not face the armed idiocy of the barracks.' Henceforth scattered efforts would lead to nothing—the movement must culminate in an all-Russian insurrection. The revolution must arm itself. Some people held that insurgents had no chance against a government armed with modern weapons; an English writer, for instance, believed that if Louis XVI had had a few batteries of machine-guns the French Revolution would not have occurred. 'What pretentious nonsense it is', Trotsky observed, 'to measure the historical chances of revolution by the calibre of weapons and guns. As if weapons and guns had command of men, as if men did not wield the weapons and guns.'[2] He granted that workers by themselves, even if armed, could not conquer in a rising—they must bring the army over to their side. But to be able to achieve this, they must first arm themselves and impress by their own determination the Tsar's vacillating soldiers. He developed this idea in passages which were in part instructions on how the workers should arm themselves and in part descriptive images illustrating the process by which the Tsar's troops would go over to the insurgent people. These anticipatory scenes again read like pages from his own histories of the revolution, written after the event. He concluded with an appeal to his own comrades framed in Dantonesque style: All that you needed, he said, in order to rise to the opportunity, was 'a few very simple qualities: freedom from organizational routine and from the miserable

[1] Loc. cit.   [2] Op. cit., p. 60.

traditions of a clandestine movement; a broad view; courageous initiative; the ability to evaluate situations; and once again, courageous initiative'.

.   .   .   .

Between the lines of these writings one can still feel the fever that consumed the author. He was burning with impatience to return to Russia and to plunge into the vortex. Not for him the stale air of the émigré colonies, where he was at cross-purposes with almost everybody. Not for him an exile from which the revolution could be only dimly watched as a storm on the high seas is watched from a remote shore. The return to Russia was bound up with grave risks. A fugitive from Siberia, if caught by the police, was automatically treated as an outlaw and deported for hard labour, even if his original sentence had not provided for this. All the same, he made up his mind to return. Sedova went ahead of him to prepare secret lodgings. In February 1905 he himself was on his way back. He stopped in Vienna and called on Victor Adler, the Austrian leader, in whose home he shaved off his moustache and beard to make it difficult for the Russian police to recognize him.

It was at Adler's home that he had first called for help while he was on his way from Siberia to England. Only two and a half years had passed since, but how crowded and full of portent those years were.

CHAPTER V

Trotsky in 1905

In February Trotsky arrived in Kiev, and there, having assumed the identity of a retired ensign, Arbuzov, he hid for several weeks. Kiev was then the hub of the clandestine organization; but the police were less alert there than in Petersburg and Moscow. There Trotsky met Leonid Krasin, with whom he was to be closely associated for the rest of the year. An eminent technician and prosperous industrial manager, Krasin was also a member of the Central Committee second only to Lenin in the Bolshevik hierarchy, and the actual manager on the spot of the clandestine organization. He was, however, a 'conciliator', anxious to overcome the breach in the party and therefore at loggerheads with Lenin. This made it easier for Trotsky to co-operate with him. And to Krasin, Trotsky, the only prominent Socialist policy-maker and writer then in Russia, soon became indispensable. In the spring, Krasin took him to Petersburg.

The other Socialist leaders stayed in western Europe until late in the year. In normal times, when events moved slowly, the clandestine organization could well afford to consult the émigrés and to wait for their instructions. But now the range of its activities was expanding feverishly; more and more often the party had to act under the compulsion of events and on the spur of the moment; consequently, routine contacts with the émigrés became too cumbersome and slow.

Having returned to Russia so early, Trotsky found himself at once at the very centre of clandestine affairs. This was to make him loom much larger in the revolution of 1905 than did any of the older leaders. But he was to loom larger for yet another, more fundamental, reason: The two trends in the party had not yet crystallized sufficiently to become two separate and hostile forces. Yet the controversy had advanced enough to absorb the minds and energies of the leaders. The turmoil in Russia came too late for the party to be able to act with the immediate initiative and massive vigour of a single body. But it also came too early—before the two parties, Bolshevik and Menshevik, had disengaged from each other and gained a new

freedom of movement. More than anybody else Trotsky represented that mood of indecision and that horror of division
which was still common to both sections of the party. In a sense,
he embodied the 'immaturity' of the movement, while the
'fanatics of the schism' were more representative of its future.
He expressed the party's strongest sentiment against the even
stronger logic of its development. But he also embodied the
highest degree of 'maturity' the movement had so far attained
in its broader aspirations: in formulating the objectives of the
revolution, Trotsky went farther than either Martov or Lenin;
and he was therefore better equipped for an active role in the
upheaval. An unfailing political instinct led him at the right
moments to the sensitive spots and the foci of the revolution,
and guided his steps.

During the first months after his return, he could do little
more than write and inspire Krasin, and through him the
organization. The turmoil of January and February was over;
and in the spring the Labour movement was in the doldrums.
The strikes had fizzled out; police repression and executions
had intimidated the workers. The political initiative passed to
the Liberal middle class. A long series of congresses and conventions, held by industrialists, merchants, bankers, doctors,
lawyers, and others, raised the cry for constitutional government and reform. Only later in the year, after the defeat of
Tsushima, the revolt of the crew on the *Potemkin*, and the end
of the war with Japan, was the initiative to slip back from the
middle class to the workers.

In the meantime Trotsky could not appear in the open. Even
in the clandestine circles of Petersburg he moved warily as
'Peter Petrovich'. The ground was shaky—the *Okhrana* had its
agents provocateurs in the organization. But from his hiding-
places he watched the political scene and produced an unending
stream of essays, sociological studies, letters to *Iskra*, leaflets,
pamphlets, polemical broadsides, and writings on the strategy
and tactics of revolution. He became confirmed in the views
he had expounded together with Parvus; and he went farther.
Immediately after his return, he wrote in *Iskra* that apart from
the Social Democratic Party 'there is nobody on the battlefield of
the revolution' capable of organizing a nation-wide insurrection:

Other groups in the urban population will play their part in the

revolution only in so far as they follow the proletariat. . . . Neither
the peasantry, nor the middle class, nor the intelligentsia can play
an independent revolutionary role in any way equivalent to the
role of the proletariat. . . . Consequently, the composition of the
Provisional Government will in the main depend on the proletariat.
If the insurrection ends in a decisive victory, those who have led the
working class in the rising will gain power.[1]

Abroad, Parvus, too, advocated armed insurrection; and
Lenin, of course, did likewise. The Mensheviks bided their
time, saying that an armed rising, like a revolution at large,
could not be organized—it would come of its own accord with
the growth of popular revolt. Behind this expectant Menshevik
attitude was a hardening conviction that the leadership in the
Russian revolution belonged not to socialism but to liberalism.
In the issue of *Iskra* in which Trotsky wrote that 'apart from
social democracy there is nobody on the battlefield of the
revolution', capable of leadership, Martov insisted that it was
the historical mission of the middle classes to bring about a
radical democratization of Russian society. 'We have the right
to expect', these were Martov's words, 'that sober political
calculation will prompt our bourgeois democracy to act in the
same way in which, in the past century, bourgeois democracy
acted in western Europe, under the inspiration of revolutionary
romanticism.'[2]

Trotsky countered Martov's view with a critique of the Liberal
attitude as it was expressed by such bodies as the Association of
Industrialists of Moscow, the Iron and Steel Industries of Petersburg, the provincial banks, the employers of the Urals, the
sugar-mill owners of the Ukraine, the national congresses of
surgeons, actors, criminologists, &c. He did not deny that the
middle classes were constrained by autocratic rule, and that
their interest in economic progress and free trade induced them
to demand political freedom. He even said that 'the liberal
régime becomes a class necessity for capital', and that 'the urban
merchant has shown that in opposition he is not inferior to
the "enlightened landlord" '.[3] But he added that in their demands the middle classes merely echoed the workers; and they
were inhibited by the fear of revolution. 'For the proletariat

[1] *Iskra*, no. 93, 17 March 1905.   [2] Ibid.
[3] L. Trotsky, *Sochinenya*, vol. ii, book 1, pp. 71, 79.

democracy is in *all* circumstances a political necessity; for the
capitalist bourgeoisie it is in *some* circumstances a political
inevitability.'[1] Their gestures of opposition were creating for
the middle classes a political prestige which was not without
peril to the revolution. The intelligentsia had until recently
looked down upon the industrialist and the merchant; now
they were hailing them as the heroes of a popular cause; and to
the Liberal spokesmen 'their own speeches sound so convincing
that they await the enemy's [the Tsar's] immediate surrender.
. . . But Jericho still stands, and, moreover, it is scheming evil.'[2]

'Jericho' was indeed scheming—on the initiative of Bulygin,
the Tsar's minister—for the convocation of a pseudo-parliament, the so-called Bulygin Duma. On 6 August the Tsar
announced the plan in a Manifesto. The Duma was to be his
consultative council, not a legislature; in the election each
Estate was to cast its vote separately; the vote was to be based on
property; and the Tsar reserved the right to prorogue or disband
the Duma. The working classes were virtually disfranchised.
Yet the Manifesto threw the opposition into some confusion.
Miliukov, the great historian, who was now assuming the leadership of liberalism, greeted the Manifesto and described it as the
crossing by the nation of the rubicon of constitutional government.[3] The Liberal leader's readiness to content himself with
the sop from the Tsar prompted Trotsky, who stood for boycotting the Duma, to write an 'Open Letter to Professor P. N.
Miliukov'.[4] Of all his philippics against liberalism, this was the
most biting and subtle; and it was widely circulated in semi-
secrecy. 'An historical Rubicon', Trotsky wrote, 'is truly crossed
only at the moment when the material means of government
pass from the hands of absolutism into those of the people. Such
things, Professor, are never achieved with the signing of a
parchment; they take place on the street and are achieved
through struggle.' He recalled how in the French Revolution
the great turns came not with declarations of constitutional principle but with real shifts of power. He further recalled events in
Germany in 1848—how middle-class liberalism had contented

[1] L. Trotsky, *Sochinenya*, vol. ii, book 1, p. 91.   [2] Ibid., pp. 98–99.
[3] The confusion cut across party lines: disagreeing with Miliukov, many Liberals
were preparing to boycott the Duma, the Mensheviks were for a time against the
boycott. The Bolsheviks were for it. See L. Martov, *Istorya Ross. Sots. Dem.*, p. 126.
[4] L. Trotsky, *Sochinenya*, vol. ii, book 1, pp. 196–205.

itself with the Prussian king's promise of freedom; how it had helped the autocrat to subdue the revolution; and how, in the end, on the ebb of the revolution, the autocrat had defeated and humiliated liberalism:

But history teaches the professors of history nothing. The mistakes and crimes of liberalism are international. You are repeating what your predecessors did in the same situation half a century ago. . . . You are afraid of breaking with the Duma, because to you this constitutional mirage seems real in the dry and barren desert through which Russian liberalism has been wading not for its first decade. . . . You, Professor, you will not tell the people this. But we shall. And if you try to debate with us not at liberal banquets but in front of the masses, we shall show that in our crude, harsh, revolutionary idiom we can be irrefutably convincing and eloquent. . . . If the revolution does not ebb away, the bureaucracy will cling to you as to its bulwark; and if you really try to become its bulwark, the victorious revolution will throw you overboard . . . [if, on the other hand, the revolution is defeated, then Tsardom will have no use for liberalism]. You propose not to be disturbed by the voices from the right and the voices from the left. . . . The revolution has not yet said its last word. With powerful and broad thrusts it lowers the edge of its knife over the head of absolutism. Let the wiseacres of liberalism beware of putting their hands under the glittering steel blade. Let them beware.

The style was the whole man in this 'Open Letter', at once scholarly, rhetorical, and implacable. In his attitude towards liberalism he was akin to Lenin. But Lenin had little or no inclination to engage in a direct ideological dialogue with liberalism, while Trotsky felt the need for a constant confrontation between revolutionary socialism and liberalism. He conducted this dialogue now, and he would do so to the end of his life, not because he had broken less decisively than Lenin with bourgeois liberalism, but in part because he was more aware of its attraction. Lenin instructed and led his followers, and in a sense preached to the converted, while Trotsky addressed the Liberal spokesmen directly and dissected and countered their arguments before large and undecided audiences. The dialogue with the adversary also best suited his polemical temperament and his dialectical style. Not for nothing was the Open Letter his favourite form of expression.

He addressed thus directly the most diverse audiences, speaking to each social group in its own idiom, with an extraordinary ease and *élan*. In his diatribes against liberalism he turned towards the intelligentsia and the advanced workers. In his 'Open Letter to Miliukov' he spoke to an academic public. Soon after his return to Russia he wrote peasant proclamations, which Krasin published, putting under them the signature of the Central Committee. In these proclamations Trotsky had before his eyes a primitive, illiterate mass of farm labourers, such as he could remember from his father's farm, a crowd in which a few individuals might be able to read his words aloud to the rest. He framed his appeal in the simplest terms and in the rhythm of a Slavonic folk-rhapsody, with characteristic refrains and evocations. The words and the rhythm were as if designed for recital by a semi-agitator, semi-bard in a village. Yet, he spoke to the muzhiks with the same logic and sweep with which he addressed his academic adversary. In the whole revolutionary literature written for or by peasants, there are very few, if any, documents which could compare, in folk style and directness of appeal, with a proclamation in which Trotsky related to the peasants the January massacre in Petersburg. He described how the workers had marched 'peacefully and calmly' to the Tsar's palace with the Tsar's pictures, icons, and church banners:

'What did the Tsar do? How did he answer the toilers of St. Petersburg?

'Hearken, hearken peasants. . . .

'This is the way the Tsar talked with his people. . . .

'All the troops of Petersburg were raised to their feet. . . . Thus the Russian Tsar girded himself for the talk with his subjects. . . .

'200,000 workers moved to the palace.

'They were dressed in their Sunday best, the grey and old ones and the young; the women went along with their husbands. Fathers and mothers led their little children by their hands. Thus the people went to their Tsar.

'Hearken, hearken peasants!

'Let every word engrave itself on your hearts. . . .

'All the streets and squares, where the peaceful workers were to march, were occupied by troops.

' "Let us through to the Tsar!", the workers begged.

'The old ones fell on their knees.

'The women begged and the children begged.

' "Let us through to the Tsar!"——
'And then it happened!
'The guns went off with a thunder. . . . The snow reddened with workers' blood. . . .
'Tell all and sundry in what way the Tsar has dealt with the toilers of St. Petersburg! . . .
'Remember, Russian peasants, how every Russian Tsar has repeated with pride: "In my country, I am the first courtier and the first landlord." . . .
'Russian Tsars have made the peasants into an Estate of serfs; they have made of them, like of dogs, presents to their faithful servants. . . .
'Peasants, at your meetings tell the soldiers, the people's sons who live on the people's money, that they dare not shoot at the people.'

Thus, in plain words, without weakening for a moment his grasp on the muzhik's imagination, he explained the ends his party was pursuing and the means it would employ; and he translated the alien term 'revolution' into the peasants' idiom: 'Peasants, let this fire burst all over Russia at one and the same time, and no force will put it out. Such a nation-wide fire is called revolution.'[1]

In a different manner again he addressed urban workers—for instance when they failed to respond to the party's call and demonstrate on May Day: 'You have taken fright before the Tsar's soldiers. . . . But you are not afraid of delivering your brothers to the Tsar's army so that they may perish on the great, unwept-for Manchurian cemetery. . . . You did not come out yesterday, but you will come out tomorrow or the day after.'[2]
A small masterpiece of revolutionary journalism was a very short article: 'Good morning, Petersburg Dvornik.'[3] He wrote it later in the year, after the Tsar had, in the so-called October Manifesto, promised a constitution and civil liberties. The dvornik (concierge) had usually served the political police as informer and stooge; but now he became infected with revolution. 'The Petersburg dvornik awakens from the police nightmare',

[1] Iskra, no. 90, 3 March 1905. Sochinenya, vol. ii, book 1, pp. 217–24. The manuscript of this proclamation was found, after 1917, in the archives of the gendarmerie of Kiev—it had been seized during a raid on Krasin's printing shop.
[2] L. Trotsky, Sochinenya, vol. ii, book 1, pp. 241–5. This proclamation, signed by the Central Committee was also found in the archives of the Kiev gendarmerie after 1917.
[3] Russkaya Gazeta, 15 November 1905; Sochinenya, vol. ii, book 1, pp. 300–1.

Trotsky wrote. '2500 *dvorniks* met to discuss their needs. The *dvorniks* do not wish to serve any longer as tools of police violence.' They put forward their demands and refused to sign a thanksgiving address to the Tsar, because in the Tsar's Manifesto 'freedom had been given but not yet proven'. 'Many sins and crimes', Trotsky wrote, 'weigh on the conscience of the Petersburg *dvorniks*. More than once have they, on police orders, manhandled honest workers and students. . . . The police have bullied them, and the people have come to hate them. But the hour of universal awakening has come. The Petersburg *dvornik* is opening his eyes. Good morning to you, Petersburg *dvornik*.'

Thus he spoke to every class of society, from the highest to the humblest, in its own language, but always in his own voice. The Russian Revolution never had, and never would have, another mouth-piece with such a variety of accent and tone.

.   .   .   .

During his stay in Kiev he shifted from one secret lodging to another, precariously concealing his identity under the mask of 'Ensign Arbuzov'. The 'ensign' looked respectable, even elegant; but he was strikingly busy, received odd visitors, was closeted with them for hours, or pored over piles of newspapers, books, and manuscripts. Some of his hosts took fright and he had to move out. Others sheltered him with courage and good humour. In *My Life* he describes how, posing as a patient, he found asylum in an ophthalmic hospital. The doctor in charge of the ward and some of his assistants were in the secret. An unsuspecting nurse conscientiously and tenderly struggled with the odd patient, urging him to take eye-drops and foot-baths and to stop reading and writing.

After he had moved to Petersburg, Krasin found him accommodation in the home of Colonel Littkens, the chief medical officer of the Imperial Military Academy, where Krasin, too, had his secret meeting-place with members of the underground. The colonel's sons were engaged in clandestine work, and he himself was a 'sympathizer'. In his home Trotsky and Sedova lived as the landowning family Vikentiev, escaping for a time the *Okhrana's* attention. Sedova, however, was arrested at a May Day demonstration; and the *agent provocateur* planted in the clandestine organization was on Trotsky's track. Trotsky hurriedly left for Finland, which was then part of the Tsarist empire but enjoyed much greater freedom than Russia. Amid the lakes and pine woods of the Finnish countryside, in a hotel called *Rauha* (Peace) he meditated, studied, wrote, and kept in touch with Krasin, until in the middle of October the news of a general strike in Petersburg broke into the quiet deserted hotel 'like a raging storm through an open window'. On 14 October, or at the latest on the 15th, he was back in the Russian capital.

The strike had begun with a printers' demand for shorter hours and higher wages; it then spread rapidly to other industries and from Petersburg to the provinces, assuming a markedly political character and taking by surprise the leaders of the Socialist underground. The workers clamoured for constitutional freedom as well as for better wages and shorter hours. As the strike developed there sprang into being an institution bred in the bone of the Russian Revolution: the first Council, or Soviet, of Workers' Deputies. The Soviet was not a Bolshevik invention. On the contrary, the Bolsheviks, led in Petersburg by Bogdanov and Knuniants-Radin, viewed it with suspicion as a rival to the party. Only in the first week of November (the third week, in the new-style calendar) when the Soviet was already at the peak of its strength and influence, did Lenin try from Stockholm to induce his followers to approach the Soviet in a more co-operative spirit.[1] The nucleus of the Soviet was set up by the strikers from fifty printing shops, who elected delegates and instructed them to form a council. These were soon joined by delegates of other trades. Paradoxically, the idea itself had, indirectly and unwittingly, been suggested by the Tsar who, after the events of January, had appointed a commission under a Senator Shydlovsky to investigate the causes of the trouble. The commission had ordered the workers to elect their representatives from the factories in order to voice grievances. The strikers in October followed this precedent. When the Soviet first met, on 13 October, only delegates of one district (the Neva district) attended. A stimulus was needed to induce other

---

[1] Lenin wrote a letter to this effect to the Bolshevik *Novaya Zhizn* (*New Life*), appearing in Petersburg, but the paper failed to publish the letter—it first saw the light in *Pravda* thirty-five years later—on 5 November 1940.

districts to join in. That stimulus was provided by the Mensheviks, who would one day bitterly oppose the institution to which they now acted as godfathers.

The Soviet instantaneously gained an extraordinary authority. This was the first elective body which represented the hitherto disfranchised working classes. Under a government which held in supreme contempt the very principle of popular representation, the first institution embodying that principle at once tended morally to overshadow the existing administration. The Soviet at once became a revolutionary factor of the first magnitude.

For the first time Trotsky appeared at the Soviet, assembled at the Technological Institute, on 15 October, the day of his return from Finland, or the day after. Deputies from several districts were present—about 200,000 people, nearly 50 per cent. of all workers in the capital, had taken part in the election. Later, after further elections, the number of deputies grew and varied from 400 to 560. The Soviet had just decided to publish its own paper, *Izvestya* (*Tidings*); and it negotiated with the municipal council for accommodation and facilities for work. In the halls and corridors of the Technological Institute there was an air of feverish agitation: strikers were coming and going, deliberating and waiting for instructions—a foretaste of the Soviet of 1917.

The Socialist parties and groups, however, were not yet agreed in their attitude towards the Soviet. The Mensheviks and Social Revolutionaries had decided to send their representatives immediately. The Bolsheviks were reluctant to follow suit and demanded that the Soviet should accept the party's guidance beforehand—only then were they prepared to join. Trotsky, invited by Krasin to a meeting of the Bolshevik Central Committee, urged its members to join the Soviet without any preliminary condition. No party or group, he pleaded, could aspire to exclusive leadership. The Soviet should be a broad representative body embracing all shades of working-class opinion, for only then would it be able to provide a united leadership in the general strike and in the revolutionary situation that might develop from it.

This wrangle was still on when on 17 October the Tsar, frightened by the general strike, issued a Manifesto promising a

constitution, civil liberties, and universal suffrage. The Manifesto was composed by Count Witte, a semi-Liberal Prime
Minister. The Bulygin Duma had been buried before it was
born; and the Tsar appeared to be renouncing the absolutism
that was as old as the dynasty itself. Petersburg was first stunned
and then intoxicated with joy. Festive crowds filled the streets
and read the Manifesto in amazement. In the government,
however, the opponents of the reform continued to wield effective power. General Trepov, Minister of the Interior, gave the
police the order: 'Spare no bullets!'; and this order was posted
on the walls side by side with the Tsar's Manifesto, as if it had
been intended to provide. a malicious comment on the 'new
era'. Just before the Tsar issued his proclamation, the police had
made numerous arrests.

On the morning of the 17th Trotsky moved with a huge and
excited crowd towards the Technological Institute, where the
Soviet had sat the previous two days. Gendarmes on horseback
rode into the crowd. Trepov's proclamation seemed to warn
everybody that it was too early for exultation. All the same, the
crowd, consisting of workers and middle-class people, gave
itself up to common rejoicing. The workers, however, were the
heroes of the day. It was their strike that had wrested from the
Tsar the promise of a constitution and freedom. The houses
were at first decorated with the white–red–blue flag of the
dynasty, but young workers tore off the white and the blue
strips of cloth, littered the pavements with them, and hoisted
the narrow and ragged red flags. The procession reached the
Technological Institute, but there it was halted by a barrier of
police and gendarmerie.

The crowd moved on towards the University, where meetings
were held. The swelling, good-humoured procession carried
with it the young man who had so long waited for this moment,
who had forecast it, and who was now full of misgivings and of
an impatient desire to warn the multitude against too early
rejoicing. The procession poured into the courtyard of the
University. From a balcony speakers were already haranguing
the crowds. Tense with his misgivings and with the emotion
absorbed from the procession, Trotsky pushed his way through
the vast and dense multitude up to the balcony: there was his
place! The organizers of the meeting knew him as the man who,

under the name Yanovsky (the man of Yanovka), had appeared
at the Soviet to represent the Mensheviks; some knew him as
the Trotsky of *Iskra*.[1] He eyed the mass of humanity, the like of
which he had never seen before; and in a voice which seemed
remote and strange to himself he exclaimed: 'Citizens! Now
that we have put our foot on the neck of the ruling clique, they
promise us freedom.'

He stopped, as if wondering whether the cold shower he was
about to pour on the crowd's enthusiasm would not freeze
them; and he searched for the words which would show the people
that he was rejoicing with them but which would also warn them
against their own credulity.

'It is this tireless hangman on the throne', he went on, 'whom
we have compelled to promise us freedom. What a great triumph
this is! But——do not hasten to celebrate victory: it is not yet
complete. Does the promissory note weigh as much as pure
gold? Is a promise of freedom the same as freedom? . . . Look
round, citizens, has anything changed since yesterday? Are the
gates of our prisons open? . . . Have our brothers returned to
their homes from the Siberian wilderness? . . .'

'Amnesty! Amnesty!', the crowd responded. But this was not
yet what he was driving at. He went on to suggest the next
watchword:

'. . . if the government were honestly resolved to make peace
with the people, they would first of all have granted an amnesty.
But, citizens, is this all? Today hundreds of political fighters
may be released, tomorrow thousands will be jailed. . . . Is not
the order 'Spare no bullets' posted side by side with the freedom
manifesto. . . . Is not the hangman Trepov the undisputed master
of Petersburg?'

'Down with Trepov!' came the cry from the crowd.

'Down with Trepov!' Trotsky resumed; 'but is Trepov alone?
. . . He dominates us by means of the army. His power and
mainstay is in the Guards, stained by the blood of 9 January.
Them he orders to spare no bullets for your bodies and your
heads. We cannot, we will not and we shall not live under the
gun barrels.'

The crowd replied with the demand for the removal of
troops from Petersburg. Then the speaker, as if exasperated by

[1] *Pervaya Russkaya Revolutsia v Peterburge 1905*, vol. i, p. 63; vol. ii, p. 68.

the unreality of this people's victory and excited by the unfailing response of the crowd and his own unsuspected mastery over it, concluded:

'. . . citizens! Our strength is in ourselves. With sword in hand we must defend freedom. The Tsar's Manifesto, however, . . . see! it is only a scrap of paper.'

With a theatrical gesture he flourished the Manifesto in front of the crowd and angrily crumpled it in his fist:

'Today it has been given us and tomorrow it will be taken away and torn into pieces as I am now tearing it into pieces, this paper-liberty, before your very eyes.'[1]

Thus the capital of Russia first heard the orator of the revolution.

In this speech Trotsky pointed to all the fatal weaknesses which were to frustrate the revolution. The Tsar's self-confidence, but not his massive machine of power, had been shaken. There was a ferment in the armed forces, especially in the navy. But the Cossacks, the Guards, and the endless ranks of the muzhik infantry were gripped by the age-old habit of blind obedience. Behind the army lay rural Russia, its whole immensity steeped in apathy and despair. The revolution was still a purely urban affair. And even in the towns its triumph was mixed with fear. The middle classes and their Liberal spokesmen, wistfully believing in the Tsar's promise of freedom and uneasy at the thought that they owed that promise to the workers' general strike, were anxious to stop the revolution. They were haunted by the spectre of plebeian 'anarchy', and by the fear that, if the revolution went on, the Tsar would listen to those of his advisers who counselled suppression not concession. 'If you do not call off the struggle', so the Liberals argued with the Socialists, 'our newly-won freedom will prove illusory.' 'But it *is* illusory', the Socialists retorted. To the working class the October Manifesto gave a sense not so much of victory as of strength and an impatience to use that strength for further assaults. Each class intended different aims for the movement. The middle classes hoped to gain most from a constitutional monarchy. The workers were republicans. The former desired nothing but political freedom. The latter raised

[1] L. Trotsky, *Die Russische Revolution 1905*, pp. 93-96.

social demands as well, directed against the middle classes more
than against Tsardom.

The fervour of the working class, hot and impulsive, out-
stripped even that of the Socialist leaders. The leaders counted
the ranks, laid plans, and marked time-tables. They expected
the struggle to reach its climax by 9 January 1906, the anniversary of the march to the Winter Palace.[1] But all phases and
dates were unexpectedly advanced by the impetuous temper
of the masses, easily inflamed by provocation and stampeded
into action. Yet the helplessness of the masses was as great as
their self-confidence; and the outcome could only be disastrous.
The working class was unarmed; and it could not get arms, in
sufficient quantity, until the army itself was in rebellion. Even
in conditions ideal for a revolution, it takes time before the
prevalent rebellious mood seeps through to the barracks. The
mood in the Russian army depended on the state of mind of the
peasantry. Only in 1906 did rural Russia become seriously
restive. By that time the revolution in the towns had been reduced
to cinders; and it had been put down by the uniformed sons of
the peasants, who, if the urban movement had been less hasty,
might have joined it. The revolution squandered its reserves
piecemeal. The working class lacked experience in insurrection.
The Socialist parties were too weak to curb the workers' impatience. And the basic fact behind all this was that the old
order was not yet quite at the end of its strength; it was still
capable of dividing the forces that might have converged on it.

The Soviet of Petersburg, the hub of this foredoomed revolution, was from the first placed in the very middle of all the cross
currents; and it was constantly torn between courage and
caution, between the volcanic heat of its surroundings and its
political judgement. The Soviet elected its Executive on 17
October. On that Executive sat, among others, three representatives of the Bolsheviks, three of the Mensheviks, and three
of the Social Revolutionaries. The chief Bolshevik spokesmen
were Knuniants-Radin and Sverchkov. (Sverchkov later wrote

[1] In his letter from Stockholm, which was published by *Pravda* only in 1940, and
which we have already quoted, Lenin wrote: 'On the anniversary of the great day
of 9 January, let there not remain in Russia even a trace of the institutions of
Tsardom.' Lenin, *Sochinenya*, vol. x, p. 11. Others hardly reckoned on such rapid
and radical results. On another occasion Lenin wrote that it would be best to delay
insurrection till spring 1906. (Ibid., vol. xxxiv, p. 311.)

a history of the Soviet.) Trotsky was the chief Menshevik representative, even though abroad he had resigned from the group. He had in the meantime come to sway the Menshevik organization in the capital and to turn it against the émigré leaders.[1] He was assisted by Zlydniev, a worker who had come to Petersburg from Nikolayev and who had earlier in the year represented his fellows on Senator Shydlovsky's commission. On Trotsky's initiative, the Bolshevik and Menshevik committees in Petersburg formed a Federal Council, which was to prepare the reunion of the two groups, and in the meantime to co-ordinate their activities in the Soviet.[2] The Social Revolutionaries were led by Avksentiev, who in 1917, as Minister of the Interior under Kerensky, was to order Trotsky's imprisonment. In 1905, however, all three parties co-operated harmoniously. None attempted to impose its will upon the other; and all agreed to elect as President of the Soviet Khrustalev-Nosar, a lawyer, who stood outside the parties and had gained the workers' confidence as their attorney in labour conflicts.[3] To the outside world, Khrustalev-Nosar represented the Soviet and momentarily he won great fame. The policies of the Soviet were, however, framed by the parties, mainly by the Social Democrats; and Khrustalev's role in the revolution was episodic. Politically, Trotsky, as the records and memoirs of participants testify, was the Soviet's moving spirit. On major occasions he spoke for both Bolsheviks and Mensheviks and for the whole Soviet. He wrote most of the Soviet's manifestoes and resolutions, and edited its *Izvestya*. Behind the scenes a silent rivalry developed between the formal President of the Soviet and its presiding spirit.[4]

On 19 October, two days after the Tsar had issued his

---

[1] L. Martov, *Istorya Russ. Sots. Dem.*, pp. 141–2.

[2] The agreement appeared under Trotsky's signature in *Izvestya*, no. 2. See also Martov, loc. cit.

[3] Khrustalev-Nosar later, however, joined the Social Democrats (Mensheviks).

[4] Khrustalev-Nosar's legend was cruelly dispelled when as an émigré he was arrested by the French police and charged with financial offences. In 1917 he turned up at the Soviet in Petersburg demanding admission, as a former President, but was disdainfully refused. During the civil war in 1918–19 he emerged as the head of a tiny republic, the so-called Khrustalev republic in one of the southern Russian provinces and was shortly thereafter killed. For Khrustalev's controversies with Trotsky see L. Trotsky, *Sochinenya*, vol. viii, pp. 190–7 and vol. ii, book 1, pp. 110–11, 508–9; N. Sukhanov, *Zapiski o Revolutsii*, vol. i, pp. 126, 129.

Manifesto, Trotsky urged the Soviet to call off the general strike. Its continuance offered no prospect of further success and might lead to more bloodshed. The Soviet unanimously accepted this view, and on 21 October the strike came to an end. The Soviet then announced that a solemn funeral of workers who had been killed during the strike would take place on 23 October. On the 22nd it was learned that General Trepov was preparing the gendarmerie to suppress the demonstration, and that the *Okhrana* was scheming a pogrom of Jews. The same night Trotsky stood before the Soviet, pleading for the cancellation of the funeral. 'The Soviet declares [ran a motion he submitted]: the proletariat of Petersburg will give the Tsarist government the last battle not on a day chosen by Trepov, but when this suits the armed and organized proletariat.'[1] The Soviet swallowed its pride and cancelled the funeral of its martyrs. There was anguish in this humiliation: would the proletariat be able to give battle on the day chosen by itself only if it had armed and organized itself? And how was it to be armed? On the same day the Soviet resolved to organize fighting squads, whose immediate task was to prevent the pogrom. Later, at the trial of the Soviet, conclusive evidence was to be produced that the pogrom had indeed been planned and that only the Soviet's action had averted it. But the fighting squads, even the one that guarded the Soviet, were at best armed with revolvers; and most had only sticks and pieces of iron. This call to arms was, nevertheless, to be one of the main counts in the indictment of the Soviet.[2]

The Soviet maintained a vigorous political initiative, however. The October Manifesto had promised freedom of the press; but the pseudo-liberal Prime Minister Witte ordered the censorship to function as before. In reply, the compositors and the printers, encouraged by the Soviet, declared that they would neither set nor print newspapers and books submitted to the censors; and, by forcing the hands of the government, the publishers, and the writers, they gave Russia her first taste of a free press. Then a clamour rose for the eight-hour day; and under the auspices of the Soviet the workers themselves began to introduce it in the workshops. Towards the end of October

---

[1] L. Trotsky, *Sochinenya*, vol. ii, book 1, p. 284.
[2] See Chapter VI, and Sverchkov, *Na Zarie Revolutsii*, p. 200.

the government proclaimed a state of siege in Poland; and the sentiment of revolutionary Petersburg was outraged. On 1 November the Soviet arranged a solemn reception for the 'delegates of oppressed Poland'. The assembly was disconcerted to find that the men who came to speak for Poland were Count Zamojski, Count Krasiński, Prince Lubomirski, a few Roman Catholic priests and merchants, and only one peasant and one worker. Trotsky, nevertheless, warmly welcomed the delegation, and solemnly proclaimed Poland's right to determine her own fate. The Soviet called for a new general strike in sympathy with Poland. The government at the same time announced that sailors of Kronstadt who had taken part in the October strike would be court martialled, and clamour for the release of the sailors merged with the cry for Poland's freedom.[1]

A mood so generous and heroic was not without its aggressive humour. The Prime Minister Witte issued an appeal to the strikers: '*Brother workers*, listen to the advice of a man who is well disposed towards you and wishes you well.' The appeal was brought to the Soviet in the middle of a stormy session and Trotsky proposed this immediate reply:[2]

'The proletarians are no relatives of Count Witte. . . . Count Witte calls us to have pity on our wives and children. The Soviet . . . calls upon . . . the workers to count how the number of widows and orphans has grown in the working class since the day when Witte took office. Count Witte speaks about the Tsar's gracious consideration for working people. The Soviet recalls . . . the Bloody Sunday of 9 January. Count Witte begs us to give him 'time' and promises to do 'everything possible'. . . . The Soviet knows that Witte has already found time to deliver Poland to military hangmen, and the Soviet has no doubt that he will do "everything possible" to strangle the revolutionary proletariat. Count Witte . . . wishes us well. The Soviet declares that it has no need for the good wishes of the Tsar's time-servers. It demands popular representation on the basis of universal, equal, direct, and secret suffrage.'[3]

The Liberals in their drawing-rooms, the students and professors in their lecture-halls, and the workers in their tea-shops

---

[1] Trotsky's speech of welcome to the Poles appeared in *Izvestya*, no. 5 (3 November).

[2] Sverchkov relates that the Soviet had commissioned him, Sverchkov, to draft the reply, but as nothing occurred to him, he asked Trotsky, who had just arrived, to write it. Trotsky produced the reply on the spot and read it out amid general applause. Sverchkov, *Na Zarie Revolutsii*, p. 28.   [3] Trotsky, op. cit., p. 287.

roared with laughter; and Witte himself was said to have suffered
a fit when he read the Soviet's riposte.[1]

On 5 November Trotsky, speaking at the Soviet for the whole
Executive, proposed to call an end to the second general strike.
The government had just announced that the sailors of Kronstadt would be tried by ordinary military courts, not courts
martial. The Soviet could withdraw not with victory indeed,
but with honour. Yet withdraw it had to, especially as strikers in
the provinces were growing weary. 'Events work for us and we
have no need to force their pace', Trotsky said. 'We must drag
out the period of preparation for decisive action as much as we
can, perhaps for a month or two, until we can come out as an
army as cohesive and organized as possible.' A general strike
could not be waged indefinitely. Its sequel ought to be insurrection, but for this the Soviet was not ready. One day, when the
railwaymen and the post and telegraph workers had joined in,
they would 'with the steel of rails and with telegraph wire bind
together all revolutionary bulwarks of the country into a single
whole. This would enable us to arouse when necessary the whole
of Russia within twenty four hours.'

Even while he tried to dam up the raging element of revolt,
he stood before the Soviet like defiance itself, passionate and
sombre. He related a conversation he had with an eminent
Liberal who had urged moderation:

I recalled to him an incident from the French revolution, when
the Convention voted that 'the French people will not parley with
the enemy on their own territory'. One of the members of the Convention interrupted: 'Have you signed a pact with victory?' They
answered him: 'No, we have signed a pact with death.' Comrades,
when the liberal bourgeoisie, as if boasting of its treachery, tells us:
'You are alone. Do you think you can go on fighting without us?
Have you signed a pact with victory?', we throw our answer in their
face: 'No, we have signed a pact with death.'[2]

[1] That Trotsky did not treat Count Witte unfairly Miliukov testifies. About this
time Miliukov visited Witte and expressed the view that the Tsar ought to promul-
gate a constitution at once, without waiting for the Duma. Witte answered that the
Tsar wanted no constitution, and that the October Manifesto had been issued in a
'fever'. Witte himself did not want a constitution either—he was interested only
in sham constitutionalism. Miliukov, *Istorya Vtoroi Russkoi Revolutsii*, vol. i, book 1,
pp. 18–19.

[2] The speech appeared in *Izvestya* no. 7, 7 November 1905; *Sochinenya*, vol. ii,
book 1, pp. 290–3.

A few days later he had again to impress upon the Soviet its own weakness and urge it to stop enforcing the eight-hour day: the employers had answered with the lockout of more than 100,000 workers. The Soviet was divided, a minority demanding a general strike; but Trotsky, supported by the metal workers, prevailed. These displays of weakness were becoming all too frequent, but the popular impulse to action made them inevitable. What was surprising was that the Soviet's weakness was not revealed with more disastrous results, especially as the Soviet's chief inspirer was a young man who had never led, or participated in, a mass movement of any size. When all the handicaps under which this revolution laboured are considered, the tactics of the Soviet, designed to harass the enemy without engaging him in general battle, appear almost faultless; and its results, the undiminished authority maintained by the Soviet and the concessions it contrived to wrest, must be judged impressive. It was not until twenty years later, during the struggle between Stalin and Trotsky, that Trotsky's 'moderation' in 1905 was held out against him. During the intervening years no such reproach was heard; and the Bolsheviks treated the Soviet's record as a proud chapter in the annals of the revolution.[1] Nor was any alternative line of conduct ever proposed by the Bolsheviks to the Soviet, or even as much as hinted at. In the political literature devoted to the subject, the failure of the revolution of 1905 was invariably attributed to the broad, 'objective' alignments in the country, never to the errors of any leader, least of all of Trotsky.[2]

The Soviet had with such breath-taking rapidity become the main focus of the revolution that the groups and factions did not even have time to ponder its significance or to adjust themselves to the new institution. By the middle of November all their leaders had at last returned from western Europe; and

[1] The Bolsheviks, however, cultivated with warmer sentiments the memory of the Moscow rising of December 1905, which had been led by members of their group.

[2] Lenin, *Sochinenya*, vol. xxiii, pp. 228–46; *Pervaya Russkaya Revolutsia v Peterburge 1905*, vols. i and ii. No differences over the Soviet's tactics came to light at the next congress of the party. See *Pyatyi Syezd RSDRP*; and Sverchkov, op. cit. Only about 1926 did the party historians (Lyadov and Pokrovsky) begin gradually to 'revise' this attitude until Stalin's *History of the C.P.S.U.*; *Short Course* (pp. 79–80) stated plainly that, under the influence of Trotsky and other Mensheviks, the Soviet was 'against preparations for an uprising'.

they watched in suspense and bewilderment this forum, which looked very much like the Russian Convention. But they had too much of the air of émigrés about them to gain a foothold in it—the Soviet had, in any case, constituted itself three or four weeks before their arrival. It was now Trotsky who, on behalf of the proletariat of Petersburg, paid a tribute in the Soviet to the martyrdom and heroism of the émigré elders.[1] When at the beginning of the year he had taken leave of the émigrés they still treated him with the mixture of admiration and condescension shown to the child prodigy. Now they viewed him with new respect, watched his dominating attitude on the platform and read in the rough and grave faces of the working men's assembly the authority and devotion he commanded. Lunacharsky recalls that when Lenin, after his return on 8 or 10 November, was told that 'the strong man in the Soviet is Trotsky', his face darkened somewhat but he said: 'Well, Trotsky has earned that with his fine and tireless work.' His face darkened, for the wounding epithets which Trotsky had flung at him must have flashed through Lenin's mind. The epithets rankled: only a short time before, Lenin had chided Parvus of all men for his partnership with Trotsky, that 'hollow bell', that 'phrase-monger' and 'Balalaykin'.[2] Yet he now acknowledged fairly Trotsky's merit and achievement.

For one further reason Trotsky seemed vindicated against his former adversaries. Both Lenin and Martov now admitted that their passionate controversies had been storms in so many émigré tea cups. The disputes over the prerogatives of the Central Committee and the conditions of membership had referred to the clandestine type of organization. The party had since emerged from the underground and it conducted its activities in broad daylight. For the first time its members could vote and elect their leading bodies without fear of the Okhrana. Lenin no less than Martov was anxious that the committees be elected from below and not appointed from above.[3] The Mensheviks, on the other hand, were shaken in their belief in the

---

[1] See the memoirs of F. Mikhailov in Pervaya Russkaya Revolutsia v Peterburge, 1905, vol. i, p. 128; L. Trotsky, Moya Zhizn, vol. i, chapter xiv.

[2] Balalaykin—a satirical character in Saltykov-Shchedrin, a calculating, complacent chatterbox, and a lawyer. This was Lenin's tit-for-tat for the epithet 'slovenly lawyer' Trotsky had thrown at him.

[3] Lenin, Sochinenya, vol. x, pp. 12-21.

revolutionary mission of the middle class, a belief which it was difficult to square with the facts. The Menshevik following in Petersburg had so strongly come under the sway of Trotsky's radicalism that the émigré leaders had to tolerate this. All differences seemed thus to have vanished; and before the year was out the reunion of the two factions, complete with the merger of their Central Committees, was taking place. The fanatics of the schism, so it seemed, had been proven wrong, and the preacher of unity right.[1]

The force of Trotsky's personality and ideas was felt in those days far beyond the Soviet and the Socialist parties. In 1906, when the revolution was already on the wane, Miliukov thus defended himself against attacks from the right: 'Those who now charge our party [the Constitutional Democrats] that it did not then protest . . . against the revolutionary illusions of Trotskyism . . . simply do not understand or remember the mood which then prevailed among the democratic public at the meetings.' Those, Miliukov said, who would have tried in 1905 to protest against the 'illusions of Trotskyism' would have merely brought discredit upon themselves.[2] This is all the more significant as the 'democratic public' Miliukov had in mind, professional people and enlightened businessmen, was not directly within the orbit of Trotsky's activity. Only very rarely did he emerge from the plebeian Soviet to face a bourgeois public; and even then he did so as the Soviet's envoy. In his chronicle of 1905 Trotsky relates how, during the November strike, he appeared at the home of Baroness Uexküll von Hildebrandt to attend an important political gathering. 'The butler waited for my visiting card, but, woe is me, what visiting card shall a man with a cover name produce? . . . In the reception room there appeared first a student, then a radical lecturer, then the editor of a "solid" periodical, and at last the Baroness herself. They apparently expected a more awe inspiring personality to come "from the workers".' Incidentally, in this turbulent year Trotsky looked so very bourgeois and was so immaculately dressed that some of his Socialist friends were shocked.[3] At any rate, the people gathered at the Baroness's

[1] L. Martov, *Istorya Russ. Sots. Dem.* pp. 141–51.
[2] P. Miliukov, *Kak Proshli Vybory vo Vtoroyu Gos. Dumu*, pp. 91–92.
[3] A. Lunacharsky, *Revolutsionnye Siluety*; A. Ziv, op. cit., pp. 50–52.

home missed the thrill of rubbing shoulders with an uncouth revolutionary demagogue. 'I mentioned my name and I was most politely shown in. Drawing back the drapery, I saw a gathering of sixty or seventy persons . . . on one side of the passage—thirty senior military men, among them resplendent Guards officers; on the other side sat the ladies. In the forefront there was a group of black tailcoats', the leading lights of liberalism. Peter Struve, the ex-Marxist, was just urging the Guards officers to defend the Tsar's October Manifesto against attacks from right and left; and as he listened to Struve, Trotsky recalled the words written by Struve himself only seven years before: 'The farther we go to the east in Europe, the more slavish, cowardly and mean is the political conduct of the bourgeoisie.' Then it was Trotsky's turn to address the officers. He told them that the working class, and with it freedom itself, was unarmed. They, the officers, had the keys to the nation's arsenals. It was their duty at the decisive moment to hand these keys to whom they belonged by right, to the people.[1] That senior Guards officers should even have listened to such talk was a measure of the political unsettlement. All the same, his appeal must have sounded to them like a desperate joke. The pyramid of Tsardom could be destroyed, if at all, from its base, not from its top.

From the meetings he hurried to his editorial desks, for he edited and co-edited three papers. The Soviet's *Izvestya* appeared at irregular intervals and was produced with naïve bravado. Each copy was set in the printing shop of another extreme right-wing newspaper, which a Soviet squad raided and requisitioned for the occasion. Apart from this, Trotsky contrived, with the help of Parvus, who had come to Petersburg, to obtain control of a radical Liberal daily *Russkaya Gazeta* (*The Russian Gazette*), which he transformed into a popular organ of militant socialism. Somewhat later he founded, with Parvus and Martov, a great, solid daily *Nachalo* (*The Start*), which was nominally the mouthpiece of Menshevism. In fact, *Nachalo* was mainly Trotsky's paper, for he dictated his terms to the Mensheviks: the paper would advocate his and Parvus's 'permanent revolution'; and it would have no truck with the Constitutional Democrats (Liberals). 'We shall have to agree', so Martov wrote to Axel-

[1] L. Trotsky, *Sochinenya*, vol. ii, book 2, p. 73.

rod, 'to the propaganda of a fairly risky idea, without any counter criticism on our part.'[1] On the contributor's list were the great names of European socialism: Victor Adler, August Bebel, Karl Kautsky, Rosa Luxemburg, Franz Mehring, Klara Zetkin; and it was Trotsky's sweet revenge to open the columns of *Nachalo* to Plekhanov, who had only the year before found it 'morally repugnant' to be Trotsky's neighbour in *Iskra*. Trotsky's papers were much more successful than the Bolshevik *Novaya Zhizn*, edited by Lenin, Gorky, Lunacharsky, and Bogdanov. This is not surprising to anybody who looks through the files and compares them—Trotsky's dailies had far greater verve and pungency.[2] For all their journalistic rivalry, the papers supported one another politically and jointly backed the Soviet.

This flowering of plebeian freedom, with the Soviet and the Socialist parties and press working in the open, was soon to be nipped. The government succeeded in putting down sporadic revolts in the army. The working class began partly to succumb to attrition, and partly to be carried away by eagerness to take up arms. Count Witte reimposed press censorship. The Soviet resisted. 'Defend the free word!' Trotsky appealed. 'To the workers the free word is bread and air. The government fears it as one fears a sharp-edged knife.'[3] The next blow fell on the Soviet itself. On 22 November, Khrustalev-Nosar and a few other leaders were arrested. The government waited to see what the Soviet would do. Once again the Soviet was faced with the familiar dilemma. The Social Revolutionaries pressed for reprisals against the Tsar's ministers. Others preferred to retort by a general strike. The Social Democrats were on principle opposed to terroristic reprisals; and they were wary of calling another general strike. Once again it fell to the exuberant Trotsky to plead for cool-headedness and for a further postponement of

[1] *Pisma Axelroda i Martova*, pp. 145–6.
[2] Lenin himself later acknowledged this. In May 1917, even before Trotsky joined the Bolshevik party, he proposed that Trotsky be appointed Editor-in-Chief of the Bolshevik popular daily; and he recalled the excellent quality of Trotsky's *Russian Gazette* in 1905. Lenin's proposal was, however, rejected. *Krasnaya Letopis*, no. 3 (14), 1923.
[3] *Russkaya Gazeta*, 17 November 1905; L. Trotsky, *Sochinenya*, vol. ii, book 2, pp. 301–3.

the final trial of strength. He submitted a motion proposing that 'the Soviet of Workers' Deputies temporarily elect a new chairman and continue to prepare for an armed rising'. The Soviet accepted Trotsky's recommendation and elected a three-headed Presidium, consisting of Yanovsky (this was Trotsky's cover name), Sverchkov, and Zlydniev. The preparations for the rising which Trotsky had mentioned had so far been less than rudimentary: two delegates had been sent to establish contact with provincial Soviets. The sinews of insurrection were lacking. The government was determined not to leave the Soviet time for further preparation. Soon a police detachment was posted outside the doors of the Free Economic Society, where the Soviet held its sessions.

It was clear that the days of the Soviet were numbered, and henceforward its activity had mainly a demonstrative character. It was designed to impress on the people the principles and methods of revolution. When Trotsky proposed to the Soviet to stop the enforcement of the eight-hour day, he said: 'We have not won the eight-hour day for the working class, but we have succeeded in winning the working class for the eight-hour day.' And, indeed, a short time before the demand for the eight-hour day had seemed unreal to the Russian, and even to the western European, worker. Yet this claim was to head the list of the Russian workers' demands from now until 1917. Similarly, it was Trotsky's fate in 1905 not to win a proletarian insurrection but to win the proletariat for insurrection. On every occasion he explained why a general strike, which some expected miraculously to overthrow Tsardom, could achieve no fundamental change in society unless the strike led to insurrection; and he went on to explain what was needed to ensure the success of insurrection. He would expound this lesson even from the dock; and the events of the next few months and years would help to drive it home. Those who think of a revolution as a cleverly engineered conspiracy and fail to see behind it the long and slow accumulation of grievances, experiences, and tactical ideas in the minds of the people, may think little of such revolutionary pedagogics; they may regard the Soviet's insurrectionary resolutions as empty threats, which in the short run they were. But the test of the Soviet's and of Trotsky's method lay in the future. The revolution of February 1917 was

to put into effect the idea bequeathed from 1905. Its first act
was to be a combination of general strike and armed insurrection, carried to success by the same Petersburg workers
whom Trotsky had addressed in 1905, and by their sons.

The Soviet's last gesture was the proclamation of a financial
boycott of the Tsar. The Soviet called upon the people to stop
payment of taxes; to accept only gold coins, no banknotes; and
to withdraw deposits from the banks.[1] The 'Financial Manifesto', written by Parvus, denounced the corruptness of the
administration, the bankruptcy of its finances, its faked balances,
and above all, its unrepresentative character. 'The fear of
popular control, which would expose to the whole world the
financial insolvency of the government, prompts the government
to shelve the convocation of a popular representation. . . . The
government has never had the confidence of the people and has
received no power from it. At present the government rules over
its own country as over a conquered land.' The Manifesto
declared that the Russian people would not pay the Tsar's
debts, a warning of which the Soviet government was one day
to remind the Tsar's western European creditors. The moral
and political arguments of the Manifesto sounded convincing,
yet as an act of practical policy the boycott merely served to
precipitate the clash which the Soviet had been anxious to
postpone. Both sides saw in it, not without reason, a substitute
for insurrection. The Soviet resorted to it precisely because it
was incapable of armed action. 'There is only one way out . . .
one way to overthrow the government—to deny it . . . its
revenue', the Manifesto declared, in obvious contradiction of
the view so frequently expounded that the 'only way' to overthrow Tsardom was by an armed rising. The government, on
the other hand, might have been hit almost as hard by a strike
of tax-payers as by insurrection. It had to act instantaneously.[2]

[1] The initiative of this boycott came not from the Soviet but from the more
moderate All-Russian Association of Peasants, with which the Soviet closely
co-operated. The 'Financial Manifesto' was signed by the Soviet, the All-Russian
Peasant Association, both factions of the Social Democratic party, the Social
Revolutionary party, and the Polish Socialist Party (P.P.S.).

[2] Seven months later, when, after the defeat of the Socialists, the Tsar decided
to settle accounts with the Liberals and dispersed the second Duma, in which the
Liberals predominated, the latter also called in their famous Viborg Manifesto,

In the afternoon of 3 December, Trotsky presided over a meeting of the Executive which was to prepare the agenda for a plenary session of the Soviet, about to open. He reported on the government's latest strokes: the provincial governors had been given power to declare a state of siege; in some places they had already done so; strikers had been threatened with heavy penalties; the newspapers which had published the 'Financial Manifesto' had been seized; the Minister of the Interior was preparing to re-enforce the ban on the Socialist parties and to imprison their leaders. This time both Mensheviks and Bolsheviks proposed a general strike. In the middle of the debate word was brought that a police raid on the Soviet was imminent. The Executive resolved to go on with its business but to send away a few members who, if the Soviet were to be imprisoned, would continue to act on its behalf. Those so chosen went but came back: the building was already surrounded by Guards, Cossacks, gendarmerie, and police. The Executive then unanimously decided to stay put but to offer no armed resistance against the heavy odds. It continued to deliberate. The trampling of boots and the rattling of sabres came nearer. From the hall on the ground floor, where delegates had assembled for the plenary session, there rose voices of angry protest. From a balcony Trotsky shouted down to the delegates: 'Comrades, offer no resistance. We declare beforehand that only an *agent provocateur* or a policeman will fire a shot here!' He instructed the delegates to break the locks of their revolvers before surrendering them to the police. Then he resumed his chair at the Executive's conference table.

A trade-union spokesman was just declaring his union's readiness to join in the general strike, when a detachment of soldiers and police occupied the corridors. A police officer entered the room where the Executive was sitting and began to read a warrant of arrest. It was now only a question whether the Soviet would carry its own weakness and humiliation with dignity. Resistance was ruled out. But should they surrender meekly, gloomy-faced, without a sign of defiance? Trotsky's pride and his sense of stage effect would not permit him to

for a financial boycott. They did it in almost the same terms in which the Soviet had proclaimed its boycott, and equally without effect. The Viborg Manifesto also called upon the people to refuse recruits to the Tsar's army.

preside over so flat and disheartening a scene. But as he could not afford any serious act of defiance, he could relieve the gloom of the situation only with humour. And so he turned the last scene of this spectacle into a witty burlesque of a bold performance. As the police officer, facing the Executive, began to read the warrant of arrest, Trotsky sharply interrupted him: 'Please do not interfere with the speaker. If you wish to take the floor, you must give your name and I shall ask the meeting whether it wishes to listen to you.'

The perplexed officer, not knowing whether he was being mocked at or whether he should expect armed resistance, waited for the trade-union delegate to end his speech. Then Trotsky gravely asked the Executive whether he should allow the officer to make a statement 'for the sake of information'. The officer read the warrant, and Trotsky proposed that the Executive should acknowledge it and take up the next item on its agenda. Another speaker rose.

'Excuse me', the police officer, disconcerted by this unheard of behaviour, stammered and turned towards Trotsky, as if for help.

'Please do not interfere', Trotsky sharply rebuked him. 'You have had the floor; you have made your statement; we have acknowledged it. Does the meeting wish to have further dealings with the policeman?'

'No!'

'Then, please, leave the hall.'

The officer shuffled his feet, muttered a few words and left. Trotsky called upon the members of the Executive to destroy all documents and not to reveal their names to the police. From the hall below rose the clangour of broken revolver-locks—the delegates were carrying out Trotsky's order.

The police officer re-entered, this time leading a platoon of soldiers. A member of the Executive rose to address the soldiers: The Tsar, he said, was at this very moment breaking the promise of the October Manifesto; and they, the soldiers, were allowing themselves to be used as his tools against the people. The officer, afraid of the effect of the words, hurriedly led the soldiers out into the corridor and shut the door behind them. 'Even through closed doors', the speaker raised his voice, 'the brotherly call of the workers will reach the soldiers.'

At length a strong detachment of police entered, and Trotsky declared 'the meeting of the Executive closed'.

Thus after fifty days ended the epic of the first Soviet in history.[1]

[1] Sverchkov, *Na Zarie Revolutsii*, pp. 163–5; L. Trotsky, *Die Russische Revolution 1905*, pp. 177–9. Some material for this chapter has been derived *inter alia* from V. Voitinsky, *Gody Pobied i Porazhenii*, book 1, pp. 184, 222–3 and *passim*; Garvi, *Vospominanya Sotsial Demokrata*; and S. Yu. Witte, *Vospominanya*, vol. ii.

CHAPTER VI

'Permanent Revolution'

THE liquidation of the Soviet was a political event of the first magnitude; and the Soviet's chief spokesman was an important prisoner of state. Political uncertainty still filled the air. In the prisons, first in Kresty and then in the Peter-Paul fortress, the members of the Soviet were accorded every privilege. Nominally they were kept in isolation; but their cells not being locked, they were free to meet one another, to take walks in the court-yard, to receive books, and under the slightest disguise to engage in intensive political activity.[1]

It was not clear at first whether in its coup against the Soviet the government had not over-reached itself. Petersburg pro-tested through strikes, and Moscow through a general strike, which led to ten days fighting at the barricades. Even after the suppression of the rising in Moscow, the revolution seemed only half defeated. Throughout December and January revolts were flaring up in Siberia, in the Baltic provinces, in the Cau-casus; and punitive expeditions were busy quelling them. In March the elections to the first Duma, boycotted by the Socialists, brought a reverse to the government and striking success to the Constitutional Democrats. It was still doubtful whether the trial of the Soviet would take place at all. The authorities, at any rate, were in no hurry to fix its date. Later it was planned to open the trial on 12 June 1906. In the summer, however, the Tsar recovered confidence, dismissed the semi-Liberal Witte, stopped the talks on the formation of a Constitu-tional Democratic ministry which were in progress, dispersed the Duma, and appointed Stolypin as Prime Minister. The trial became the object of a tug-of-war in the administration; and it was adjourned from month to month till the end of September. The adherents of unmitigated autocracy planned to use the case in order to demonstrate to the Tsar that Witte's weak

[1] The usual prison discipline was so much relaxed that Rosa Luxemburg, herself just released from a prison in Warsaw, was able to pay a 'secret' visit to Parvus and Deutsch in the Peter-Paul fortress. She does not seem to have met Trotsky on this occasion.

policy had been undermining the throne. The quasi-Liberals in the administration were anxious to use the trial for the opposite purpose, and to show that the intrigues of the reactionaries had wrecked the policy of the October Manifesto.

In the meantime the prisoners carefully prepared their defence. At first there were differences over the line of conduct they were to adopt in the dock. On behalf of the Menshevik Central Committee (now about to give up its separate existence) Martov wrote to the prisoners urging them to plead their case with moderation, to base their defence on the October Manifesto, and to demonstrate to the court that the Soviet had acted within limits allowed by that Manifesto. The Soviet should, in particular, refute the charge that it had aimed at armed insurrection. Trotsky indignantly rejected the advice. From his cell he sent through his attorney a reply expressing the 'greatest surprise': 'Not one of the defendants takes this attitude. The programme of the October Manifesto has never been the programme of the Soviet.' The Soviet had met the Tsar's promises with a straight affirmation of its own republican attitude. It was 'a grave political error' on the part of the Central Committee to advise the defendants that they should dissociate themselves from insurrection. All they could and would deny before the Court was that they had engaged in *technical* preparations for a rising; but they must shoulder responsibility for *political* preparation.

The letter, written in a hurry while the attorney was waiting to smuggle it out, was an angry explosion, a retort to an affront. The men of the Soviet, Trotsky insisted, should state their principles, explain their motives, proclaim their objectives; they must use the dock as a political platform rather than defend themselves.[1] In this the Bolshevik Central Committee supported Trotsky; and this was probably why, to quote his old friend Ziv, now again imprisoned with Trotsky, 'his words were full of warm sympathy for the Bolsheviks, to whom he was spiritually akin, and of a hardly suppressed antipathy to the Mensheviks' with whom he was associated.[2] However, Trotsky succeeded in

---

[1] Trotsky's letter to Martov later fell into the hands of the police when Martov was arrested, and it was produced as part of the evidence for the prosecution. The letter is published in L. Trotsky, *Sochinenya*, vol. ii, book 1, pp. 459–60; see also ibid., p. 639, n. 338.   [2] A. Ziv, op. cit., p. 53.

persuading all the defendants to adopt the same defiant attitude, and all endorsed his letter to the Menshevik Central Committee. The only discord was caused by Khrustalev-Nosar, the Soviet's first President, who had behaved ambiguously in the preliminary investigation. The prisoners threatened to brand him publicly, in the dock, as a traitor. Yet despite his former rivalry with Khrustalev-Nosar, Trotsky was anxious to avoid a scandal, which would have lessened the political effect of the trial. He prevailed upon Khrustalev to behave in the dock like all the others and promised him that in return he would be spared the denunciation. Then the chief defendants agreed on their parts in the trial: Khrustalev was to give an account of the Soviet's work under his presidency; Sverchkov was to speak about the Soviet's last days; Knuniants was to describe the attitude of the Social Democratic party, and Avksentiev that of the Social Revolutionaries. Trotsky was to tackle the most dangerous topic: armed insurrection.

Having completed these arrangements, he gave himself to reading and writing. Even the preliminary investigation, conducted by General Ivanov of the gendarmerie, could not divert him: he refused to make any depositions and reserved all that he wanted to say for the public trial. 'Trotsky's prison cell', writes Sverchkov, 'soon became a sort of library. He received all the new books that deserved attention; he read everything; and all through the day, from morning till late night, he was busy with his literary work. "I feel extremely well", he used to say, "I sit and work and am quite sure that nobody can arrest me—in Tsarist Russia this is a rather unusual feeling".'[1] Ziv describes how eagerly Trotsky passed on his books and papers to other prisoners and with what inexhaustible verve he stimulated them intellectually.

A picture of Trotsky taken in his cell some time before the trial shows a man of handsome and cultivated appearance, strikingly 'highbrow'. The face, looking somewhat more regular than it really was, topped by an abundant thatch of black hair and tapering into a little pointed beard, has an air of pensive concentration and self-command. For all its calm, it seems to reflect an inner animation, an intense play of feeling and mood. The thatch of hair, the broad forehead, the raised and strongly

[1] Sverchkov, *Na Zarie Revolutsii*, p. 189.

marked eyebrows, the dark pince-nez, the well-cut moustache and the thrusting chin give to the face a variety of angles emphasizing its inner animation. The prisoner, lean and of average build, is dressed in black. The black suit, the stiff white collar, the white cuffs slightly protruding from the sleeves and the well-polished shoes give the impression of almost studious elegance. This might have been the picture of a prosperous western European *fin-de-siècle* intellectual, just about to attend a somewhat formal reception, rather than that of a revolutionary awaiting trial in the Peter-Paul fortress. Only the austerity of the bare wall and the peephole in the door offer a hint of the real background.

He spent much of his time reading the European classics. 'As I lay on my bunk I absorbed them with the same physical delight with which the gourmet sips choice wine or inhales the fragrant smoke of a fine cigar. . . . It was then that I first truly acquainted myself with the great masters of the French novel in their originals.'[1] This love of the French novel, classical and modern, was to remain with him for life. He had by now mastered French and German and he spoke both languages extremely well, although he used German more easily for economics and politics and preferred French as a literary language. He was now far from those days spent in the prisons of Kherson and Odessa, when he had groped laboriously towards Marx's theories. He was no longer learning Marxism—he was teaching it; and his mind was free to roam at large over the expanses of European literature.

.   .   .   .

In the quietness of his cell he pondered the lessons of the last stormy months; and he set down his conclusions in essays and pamphlets, one of which was to become exceptionally important. Nearly all of his writings of this period are reproduced in his *Works*, except for a study on land rent, which was lost and never saw the light. In his autobiography he describes this as a 'tragic loss' to himself. How far his regret is justified we cannot say. His grasp of economics was sure; but, unlike Lenin or Bukharin, he did not distinguish himself as an abstract economic theorist, and it may be doubted whether he had an original contribution to make to so highly specialized a subject as the

[1] L. Trotsky, *Moya Zhizn*, vol. i, p. 216.

Marxian conception of land rent. Whatever the truth, some of his political writings of this year were of greater weight and originality than any work of his on land rent was likely to be. We may leave aside his *Mr. Struve in Politics*, a brochure, published under the pen-name N. Takhotsky, which gained great popularity. This was another broadside against liberalism, mordantly effective but adding little to a familiar stock of arguments. More important was the *History of the Soviet (Istorya Sovieta Rabochikh Deputatov)*, a work written by several hands and edited by Trotsky. He conceived the idea of it as soon as the doors of the prison had closed behind him; and he contributed a chapter summing up the Soviet's role:

Urban Russia [so he concluded] was too narrow a base for the struggle. The Soviet tried to wage the struggle on a national scale, but it remained above all a Petersburg institution. . . . there is no doubt that in the next upsurge of revolution, such Councils of Workers will be formed all over the country. An All-Russian Soviet of Workers, organized by a national congress . . . will assume the leadership. . . History does not repeat itself. The new Soviet will not have to go through the experiences of these fifty days once again. Yet from these fifty days it will be able to deduce its entire programme of action. . .: revolutionary cooperation with the army, the peasantry, and the plebeian parts of the middle classes; abolition of absolutism; destruction of the military machine of absolutism; part disbandment and part overhaul of the army; abolition of the police and of the bureaucratic apparatus; the eight hour day; the arming of the people, above all, of the workers; the transformation of the Soviets into organs of revolutionary, urban self-government; the formation of Peasant Soviets to be in charge of the agrarian revolution on the spot; elections to the Constituent Assembly. . . . It is easier to formulate such a plan than to carry it out. But if victory is destined for the revolution, the proletariat cannot but assume this role. It will achieve a revolutionary performance, the like of which the world has never seen.

The history of these fifty days will be a pale page in the great book of the proletariat's struggle and victory.[1]

This was indeed the programme for 1917. However, these writings were merely sketches and essays preparatory to his chief work of this period, *Itogi i Perspektivy—Dvizhushchie Sily Revolutsii (The Balance and the Prospects—the Moving Forces of the*

[1] L. Trotsky, *Sochinenya*, vol. ii, book 1, p. 206.

Revolution). As the fundamental statement of 'Trotskyism', this
was to be for decades the object of a fierce controversy.[1] He
wrote it as a long concluding chapter to his book *Nasha Revolutsia* (*Our Revolution*), which was a collection of essays and
chronicles on 1905; and in it he gave a full, almost mathematically succinct formulation of the theory of permanent revolution.
He reviewed recent critical events in the perspective of age-old
trends in Russian history; and then, turning to the international
scene, he defined the place of the Russian Revolution in modern
European history; and he forecast, in broad outline, the impact
of the Russian Revolution upon the world and the world's
impact upon it. Within this framework he explicitly opposed
his conception to the views then current among Marxists. This
was the most radical restatement, if not revision, of the prognosis of Socialist revolution undertaken since Marx's *Communist
Manifesto*, that is since 1847. For this reason alone, it deserves
to be summarized in some detail.

Marxists, we know, generally viewed the Russian upheaval
as a bourgeois revolution, whose purpose it was to overthrow
Tsardom and to clear away its semi-feudal heritage. Only after
the completion of this phase, it was held, could a modern
industrial capitalist society develop fully in Russia; and only
in such a society, after the wealth and the productive resources
of the country had grown and expanded, would revolutionary
socialism rise to power and begin to satisfy the egalitarian
aspirations of the masses. Marxists took it for granted that in the
old capitalist countries of the West the ground for Socialist
revolution was ready. There, in the West, they expected
socialism to win, while the East was still engaged in its bourgeois
revolutions. These were axioms commonly held by western
European Socialists and Russian Mensheviks and Bolsheviks.
The controversy between the latter centred on the question
which social class, the bourgeoisie or the workers, would play
the leading part in the Russian 'bourgeois' revolution.

Trotsky questioned most of these assumptions. He agreed with
the Bolsheviks that the Russian bourgeoisie was incapable of

---

[1] The summary and the quotations are taken from the Moscow (March 1919)
reprint of this work. The author had the original 1906 edition (now a bibliographical
rarity) in his library in Warsaw, which he lost during the Second World War.
The 1919 edition is a faithful reprint of the original, prefaced by a special foreword.

revolutionary leadership, and that the industrial working class was cast for that role. He now went farther and argued that the working class would by its own political supremacy in the revolution be compelled to carry the Russian Revolution from the bourgeois to the Socialist phase, even before the Socialist upheaval had begun in the West. This would be one aspect of the 'permanence' of the revolution—it would be impossible to confine the upheaval to bourgeois limits.

What had destined Russia to become the pioneer of socialism? Why could the Russian middle classes not bring their revolution to a consummation, as the French had done in the eighteenth century? The answer lay in the peculiarities of Russian history. The Russian state, half-Asian, half-European, was based on a slowly evolving, undifferentiated, primitive society. The military pressure of superior European powers, not the impulses coming from Russian society, moulded that state. From its earliest days, when it struggled against Tartar domination and then against Polish-Lithuanian and Swedish invasions, the state exacted from the Russian people the most intense exertions; it absorbed a disproportionately high share of the social wealth produced. It thereby impeded the already slow formation of privileged classes and the even slower growth of productive resources. Yet the state needed a hierarchical organization, and to achieve it it had to stimulate social differentiation. Thus Tsardom curbed and at the same time fostered the development of Russian society. This fact had prompted Miliukov to say that whereas in the West the Estates had created the State, in Russia the State had brought into being the Estates. Trotsky dismissed this as a one-sided view, for 'state-power could not at will manufacture social groups and classes'. Nevertheless, so prodigious had been the rulers' initiative and so sluggish and torpid had been Russian society that in Russia even 'capitalism appeared as the child of the state'.[1] The state, and not private enterprise, had laid the foundations of modern industry. Even Russian thought and opinion appeared as the state's offspring. In modern times, fiscal and military protectionism and European financial assistance secured to Tsardom a degree of modernization which further increased its power over society. The Liberals held that this prodigious preponderance of the state

[1] L. Trotsky, *Itogi i Perspektivy*, p. 16.

made revolution impossible. On the contrary, it made it inevitable.

One outcome of this trend was that Russia entered the twentieth century with an extremely feeble urban middle class. The Russian town itself was the product of the last few decades. Under Peter the Great, the city dwellers were only 3 per cent. of the total population. After the Napoleonic wars they formed 4½ per cent., and even towards the end of the nineteenth century only 13 per cent. The old Russian town, unlike its European counterpart, had been not a centre of industry and commerce but a military administrative unit or a fortress. (Moscow had been the Tsar's village.) The Russian town—like the Asian— did not produce; it merely consumed. It neither accumulated wealth nor evolved a division of labour. Thus were aggravated all the cruel handicaps which Russia's severe climate and enormous spaces had imposed upon the growth of her civilization. In the middle of the nineteenth century, capitalism found in Russia not the urban handicraft from which, in the West, modern industry had sprung, but rural cottage craft. This fact had one striking political consequence, already noted by Parvus: Russia possessed no social class comparable to that concentrated mass of urban craftsmen who had formed the backbone of the French middle class and had made the great French Revolution. Russia's four million craftsmen (*kustari*) were scattered over the country-side.

Even the advance of modern industry did not significantly strengthen the middle class, because Russian industry was, in the main, fostered by foreign investment. In their own countries, the Western bourgeoisie had rallied to the banner of liberalism. In Russia, they were interested mainly in the security of their investments, which seemed best guaranteed by 'strong', that is absolutist, government. Thus, the economic preponderance of the state, the numerical weakness of the middle classes, the predominance of foreign capital in industry, the absence of a middle-class tradition—all combined to make Russian bourgeois liberalism stillborn. Yet modern industry, which did not significantly enhance the middle class, brought the proletariat to the fore. The more belatedly Russian industry expanded, the more readily did it adopt the most advanced forms of organization that had elsewhere been developed slowly and laboriously. The few modern factories that Russia did possess were larger and more concentrated than any western European or even American establishments. Consequently the political strength of the Russian proletariat, its capacity to organize itself and to act *en masse*, was all the more concentrated.

This alignment of the social classes entailed a radical change in the familiar patterns of revolution. European revolutionary history knew three landmarks: 1789, 1848, and 1905. In 1789 the French bourgeoisie, strong and confident, led the struggle against absolutism. True, it was often driven forward against its will by Jacobin plebeians, the *sans culottes*. But these were a shapeless, incoherent mass, lacking a consistent programme of their own. Only sporadically could they oppose themselves to the wealthy bourgeoisie, which, after the brief interval of Robespierre's dictatorship, regained ascendancy. No modern industrial working class was there to challenge its leadership.[1]

By 1848 the centre of bourgeois revolution had shifted to Germany and Austria. But the German middle class had neither the strength nor the self-confidence of the French. The courage which it needed to oppose absolutism was blighted by fear of the rising proletariat. The plebeian mass of 1848 was no longer an angry, confused lower middle class with a pauper-like fringe, but a class of factory workers, groping towards political independence and opposed to the employers even more directly than to the monarchy. However, the working class, already strong enough to inspire fear in the bourgeoisie, was still too feeble and timid to guide the nation. The revolution foundered because it lacked leadership: the bourgeoisie was *already* and the proletariat was *still* too weak to assume it.

Finally, in Russia in 1905 the wheel had turned full circle. The revolution was no longer leaderless. The bourgeoisie was both too feeble and too frightened of the proletariat to direct the war against autocracy. This mission had fallen to the industrial workers, who were much stronger than their German counterparts of 1848, and had avidly assimilated the last word in European socialism.[2]

It followed from this, Trotsky went on, that the revolution,

---

[1] Many years later Trotsky held that this view, which he had accepted from Marx, exaggerated the revolutionary virtues of the French bourgeoisie even in the eighteenth century.   [2] L. Trotsky, *Itogi i Perspektivy*, p. 33.

if it succeeded, would end in the seizure of power by the proletariat. 'Every political party deserving the name aims at
seizing governmental power in order to put the state at the
service of the class whose interests it expresses.'[1] The Mensheviks argued that in backward Russia, 'unripe' for socialism,
the workers must help the bourgeoisie to seize power. Against
this Trotsky boldly declared: 'In a country economically backward, the proletariat can take power earlier than in countries
where capitalism is advanced. . . . The Russian revolution
produces conditions, in which power may . . . pass into the
hands of the proletariat before the politicians of bourgeois
liberalism have had the chance to show their statesman-like
genius to the full.'[2] He brushed aside arguments based on familiar Marxist texts about the sequence of bourgeois and Socialist
revolutions: 'Marxism is above all a method of analysis of social
relations, not of texts.'

His critics were soon to accuse him of wanting Russia to
'jump over' the bourgeois phase of development, and of advocating a policy which would oppose the industrial workers, a
small minority, to the rest of the nation. Trotsky tried to forestall these criticisms. He did not gainsay, he stated, the bourgeois character of the Russian Revolution, in this sense at least,
that its immediate task was to free Russia from the dead weight
of her feudal past, to accomplish that is, what the bourgeoisie
had accomplished in England and France. But he insisted
—and in this he differed from other Socialists—that the revolution would not stop at this. Having uprooted the feudal institutions, it would proceed to break the backbone of capitalism and
to establish a proletarian dictatorship.[3] He did not rule out a
governmental coalition of Socialists and representatives of the
peasantry; but to the latter he assigned the role of junior
partners. The representatives of the workers 'will give content
to the policy of the government and will form a homogeneous
majority in it'.[4]

Was this, then, to be a dictatorship of a minority? More by
implication than explicitly, he envisaged that the revolution
itself would indeed be carried out by the workers alone. It was
in the towns that the old order must be overthrown; and there

---

[1] L. Trotsky, *Itogi i Perspektivy*, p. 34. [2] Ibid., pp. 34–35.
[3] Ibid., pp. 39–40. [4] Ibid., p. 40.

the industrial proletariat would be master. 'Many layers of the toiling mass, especially in the country, will be drawn into the revolution and for the first time obtain political organization only after . . . the urban proletariat has taken the helm of government.'[1] But even though the overthrow of the old order and the seizure of power would be the work of a minority, the revolution could not survive and consolidate itself unless it received the genuine support of the majority, i.e. of the peasants. *'The proletariat in power will appear before the peasantry as its liberator.'*[2] It would, among other things, sanction the seizure of the large estates by the peasants. The French peasant had followed Napoleon, because the latter guaranteed his small-holding against the émigré landlord. For the same reason the Russian peasant would back a proletarian government. That government, therefore, would and would not represent the rule of a minority. The proletarian minority would form its core and in all important matters hold the initiative. But it would rule in the interest, and enjoy the willing support, of an overwhelming majority.

His conception of the peasantry's place in the revolution—in a sense the crux of 'Trotskyism'—was to be the centre of many controversies. The stock accusation levelled against Trotsky is that he 'underrated' the revolutionary potentiality of the Russian peasantry, and denied the possibility of an 'alliance' between it and the proletariat. For this charge no support can be found in his own words. We have seen how emphatically he stated that 'the proletariat in power will appear before the peasantry as its liberator'. In insisting that the Socialists would not merely expropriate the landlords but sanction the seizure of their land by the peasants, he went farther than most Russian Socialists had so far gone. The Mensheviks held that the municipalities should take over the gentry's land. Most Bolsheviks, especially Lenin, advocated, in general terms, nationalization, but not partition of the land.[3] If the 'alliance' with the peasantry is to be understood as the

---

[1] Ibid., p. 41.

[2] Ibid., p. 42.

[3] Of the now known Bolshevik leaders only Stalin pleaded in 1906 that the party should pronounce itself in favour of the sharing out of the large estates among the peasants. J. Stalin, *Sochinenya*, vol. i, pp. 214-35, 236-8. See also I. Deutscher, *Stalin, a Political Biography*, pp. 82-83.

Bolsheviks understood it in and after 1917, then Trotsky certainly stood for it in 1906.

Yet it is true that he did not consider the peasants, any more than other small proprietors or the petty bourgeoisie at large, as an independent revolutionary force. He saw them as an amorphous, scattered mass, with narrow local interests, incapable of co-ordinated national action. It was the peasantry's fate that its rebellions, even in the rare cases when they were successful, led to the rise of new oppressive dynasties or were exploited by other classes. In modern society, the peasants were politically even more helpless than before: 'the history of capitalism is the history of the subordination of the country to the town.'[1] In the town there were only two poles of independent power, actual or potential: the big bourgeoisie, with its concentrated wealth, and the proletariat, with its concentrated capacity to produce wealth. The peasants, despite their far greater numerical strength, had to follow either the one or the other. On the scales of a parliamentary election, the vote of one peasant weighs as much as does the vote of one worker. In revolutionary situations this equality is illusory. A thousand railwaymen on strike are politically more effective than a million scattered villagers. The role of modern social classes is determined not by numbers, but by social function and specific weight. The proletariat must win the support of the peasantry—without this it cannot hold power. But the only way for it to attract the mass of small rural proprietors is to show vigour and determination in the contest for power. The weak are attracted by the strong.

This view, so explicitly stated, marked a radical departure from the then accepted Marxist notions, even though it had been strongly implied in Marx's own writings. (Trotsky's aversion to 'analysis of texts' prevented him from dabbling in helpful quotations.) It was a common Marxist notion that the working class could not and ought not to try to seize power before it had become a majority of the nation. It was also a deep-seated illusion of popular socialism that in modern countries the industrial working class would gradually expand into a majority, as it had done in England.[2] With this illusion Trotsky

[1] L. Trotsky, *Itogi i Perspektivy*, p. 43.
[2] In the foreword to his *Works*, written in 1946 (*Sochinenya*, vol. i, pp. xiv–xv),

broke radically: the revolution, he wrote, would conquer long before the majority of the nation had become transformed into proletarians.[1]

His appraisal of the peasantry was no less sharply opposed to current opinion. The Mensheviks tended to view the small rural proprietor as a prop of reaction. Their hope was in a coalition between the working class and the Liberal bourgeoisie. Lenin, on the contrary, reckoned with the muzhiks' revolutionary energy; but, unlike Trotsky, he would not prejudge its potentialities. He kept his mind open and waited to see whether the peasantry would not form its own revolutionary party, with whom the Socialists would have to deal as with an equal partner. At the beginning of 1905, to the amusement of Plekhanov, Trotsky, and Martov, Lenin approached with intense curiosity and exaggerated hope the enigmatic figure of Gapon. He wondered whether that priest, the son of a Cossack, who had led the workers of the capital to the Winter Palace and thereby helped to open the sluices for the revolution, was not the harbinger of an independent and radical peasant movement.[2] Lenin's formula of a 'democratic dictatorship of the proletariat and the peasantry' seemed broader and more cautious than Trotsky's 'proletarian dictatorship', and better suited for an association of Socialists and agrarian revolutionaries. In 1917 events in Russia were to confirm Trotsky's prognostication. In the twenties, however, the problem was to be posed anew in connexion with Communist policy in China; and nearly half a century after Trotsky had formulated his view, it would be posed over and over again by the revolutions in Asia, in which the relation between the urban and the rural elements would be more intricate and blurred than it was in Russia.

So far we have dealt with the domestic aspect of the revolution. Its international and domestic aspects were, in Trotsky's view, closely interwoven. Although the peasants would by

Stalin stated that in the era of 1905 he 'accepted the thesis familiar among Marxists, according to which one of the chief conditions for the victory of the socialist revolution was that the proletariat should become the majority of the population. Consequently in those countries in which the proletariat did not yet form the majority of the population, because capitalism had not sufficiently developed, the victory of socialism was impossible.'   [1] L. Trotsky, op. cit., p. 55.

[2] Lenin, Sochinenya, vol. viii, pp. 384–8; Trotsky, Sochinenya, vol. ii, book 1, pp. 54–57; see also Parvus on Gapon, Iskra, no. 85 (27 January 1905).

themselves be unable 'to squeeze out the workers',[1] a conflict between the two classes was looming ahead, a conflict in which the proletariat might forfeit the position of acknowledged leader of the nation. As long as the revolution was engaged in breaking the rule and the power of the landlord, it would have the entire peasantry on its side. But after that—'two major features of the proletarian policy, its *collectivism* and its *internationalism*, would meet with [the peasants'] opposition'.[2] Thus, in spite of its initial strength the new régime would discover its weakness as soon as it had carried the revolution, in the country as well as in town, from the bourgeois to the socialist phase. It would then be compelled to seek salvation in international revolution. Russia's industrial poverty and backwardness would anyhow prove formidable obstacles to the building of a Socialist economy; and only with the help of the Socialist West could these obstacles be broken and removed. Finally, the hostility of a Conservative Europe would force the Russian revolution to carry the struggle beyond Russia's frontiers.

Without the direct state support of the European proletariat, the working class of Russia will not be able to remain in power and transform its temporary rule into a stable and prolonged socialist dictatorship. . . .[3]

This will from the very outset impart an international character to the development of the events and open the broadest perspectives: *the working class of Russia, by leading in the political emancipation will rise to a height unknown in history, gather into its hands colossal forces and means and become the initiator of the liquidation of capitalism on a global scale.* . . .[4]

If the Russian proletariat, having temporarily gained, power, does not carry the revolution of its own initiative on to the ground of Europe, then the feudal and bourgeois reaction will force it to do so.[5]

It will be precisely the fear of the proletarian rising which will force the bourgeois parties, voting prodigious sums for military expenditure, solemnly to demonstrate for peace, to dream of international chambers of conciliation and even of the organization of the United States of Europe—all miserable declamation, which can neither do away with the antagonism of the powers, nor with armed conflicts. . . . European war inevitably means European revolution.[6]

---

[1] L. Trotsky, *Itogi i Perspektivy*, p. 42.   [2] Ibid., p. 46.
[3] Ibid., p. 71.   [4] Ibid., p. 73 (Trotsky's italics).
[5] Ibid., p. 74.   [6] Ibid., p. 77.

He went on to denounce the 'propagandist conservatism' of the Socialist parties, which could impede the struggle of the proletariat for power; and he expressed the hope that the Russian Revolution would shake up international socialism, just as the events of 1905 had already stimulated the Austrian and Prussian proletariat to claim universal suffrage by means of general strikes. 'The revolution in the east infects the western proletariat with revolutionary idealism and imparts to it the desire to speak Russian with its enemies.'[1] He concluded his argument as follows:

The Russian proletariat . . . will meet with organized hostility on the part of world reaction and with readiness on the part of the world proletariat to lend the revolution organized assistance. Left to itself, the working class of Russia will inevitably be crushed by the counter-revolution at the moment when the peasantry turns its back upon the proletariat. Nothing will be left to the workers but to link the fate of their own political rule, and consequently the fate of the whole Russian revolution, with that of the socialist revolution in Europe. The Russian proletariat will throw into the scales of the class struggle of the entire capitalist world that colossal state-political power, which the temporary circumstances of the Russian bourgeois revolution will give it. With state power in its hands, with the counter-revolution behind its back, with the European reaction in front of it, it will address to its brothers all over the world the old appeal, which this time will be the call to the last onslaught: Proletarians of all lands, unite![2]

The tenor of Trotsky's argument suggests that he envisaged the European revolution as a single, continuous process. There was thus in his prognostication a fatal admixture of illusion, at least as regards the tempo of the whole process. Here Trotsky was paying his tribute to a belief then commonly accepted by European Socialists, and authoritatively voiced by Karl Kautsky, the intellectual guide of the International, that the European economy and society were already 'ripe' for socialism. Yet, even in 1906, Trotsky, for all the categorical tenor of his forecast, was cautious enough to write that it was impossible to prophesy in what manner the revolution would expand from Russia, whether it would strike out through Poland into Germany and Austria, or whether it would turn eastwards to Asia.[3]

[1] Ibid., p. 80.   [2] Ibid.
[3] Ibid., pp. 74–77.

Not for a moment did Trotsky imagine, however, that the Russian Revolution could survive in isolation for decades. It may therefore be said, as Stalin was to say twenty years later, that he 'underrated' the internal resources and vitality of revolutionary Russia. The miscalculation, obvious in retrospect, is less surprising when one considers that the view expressed by Trotsky in 1906 was to become the common property of all Bolshevik leaders, including Stalin, in the years between 1917 and 1924. Hindsight, naturally, dwells on this particular error so much that the error overshadows the forecast as a whole. True enough, Trotsky did not foresee that Soviet Russia would survive in isolation for decades. But who, apart from him, foresaw, in 1906, the existence of Soviet Russia? Moreover, Trotsky himself, indirectly and unknowingly, provided in advance the clue to his own error—it is found in his appraisal of the Russian peasantry. Its political helplessness and lack of independence best account for the survival of a collectivist régime in a country in which the individualistic peasantry formed the overwhelming majority, and also for the forcible and relatively successful imposition of collectivism upon it.

In apparent contradiction of his own view, Trotsky then stated that the proletarian régime would break down as soon as the muzhiks turned against it. This error, if an error it was, was intimately bound up with his conception of the revolution, as he stated it in 1905–6. It did not occur to him that a proletarian party would in the long run rule and govern an enormous country against the majority of the people. He did not foresee that the revolution would lead to the prolonged rule of a minority. The possibility of such a rule was implicit in his theory; but its actuality would still have appeared to him, as to nearly all his contemporaries, incompatible with socialism. In fact, he did not imagine, in spite of all he had written about Lenin's 'Jacobinism', that the revolution would seek to escape from its isolation and weakness into totalitarianism.

If the trend of his thought is considered as a whole, then it may be said that hardly ever has any political prophecy appeared to be alternately so brilliantly confirmed and so utterly confounded and then in a way confirmed again by the onrush of new historical cataclysms. This is especially true of that part of Trotsky's prognostication in which he spoke about the impulse Russia would give to world revolution. Over the decades events were to throw ever new light on this. In 1917 and after, amid the crumbling of thrones and the thunder of upheaval, his words seemed to be coming true with uncanny accuracy. Then came the reflux of communism in Europe; Bolshevik Russia withdrew within her shell; and Trotsky stood discredited and derided as the prophet of the utterly absurd, of 'the patently impossible and vain'. But then again, in the aftermath of the Second World War, his voice seems posthumously to reverberate in the clash of two worlds. More than ever Russia appears to the West as 'having risen to a height unknown in history, gathered into her hands colossal forces and means, and become the initiator of the liquidation of capitalism on a global scale'. We cannot run too much ahead of our story and consider here whether or to what an extent this is Russia's real role. Nor can we do more here than hint at the contrast between Trotsky's vision and its apparent materialization. He expected the new régime in Russia to become the initiator and inspirer, but not the master, of international revolution; and he saw the 'liquidation of capitalism' beyond Russia as the genuine achievement of the Western working classes rather than as the by-product of a victorious advance of Russian armies.

But no matter how the course of events has swayed and diverged from the route he had mapped out in 1904–6, by the middle of the present century he seemed once again to have grasped the 'main chance of things' correctly. Whether one reads his message with horror or hope, whether one views him as the inspired herald of a new age surpassing all history in achievement and grandeur, or as the oracle of ruin and woe, one cannot but be impressed by the sweep and boldness of his vision. He reconnoitred the future as one who surveys from a towering mountain top a new and immense horizon and points to vast, uncharted landmarks in the distance. True enough, from his coign of vantage, he could not take in the whole landscape below: patches of dense fog enveloped parts of it: and the play of distance and perspective looked different from what is seen in the valley. He misjudged the exact direction of a major road; he saw two or more separate landmarks merged into one; and he grievously overlooked one of the rocky ravines into which one day he himself would slip to his doom.

But his compensation was the unique magnitude of his horizon. Compared with this vision, which Trotsky drew in his cell in the fortress, the political predictions made by his most illustrious and wisest contemporaries, including Lenin and Plekhanov, were timid or muddle-headed.

In *Balance and Prospects* Trotsky reached a peak in his development. The months in prison, in the course of which he pondered and digested recent experience, were for him the transition from early to mature manhood, a transition as sudden and rapid as had been his jumps from childhood to adolescence and from adolescence to adult life. In this brochure of eighty pages was the sum and substance of the man. For the rest of his days, as leader of the revolution, as founder and head of an army, as protagonist of a new International and then as hunted exile, he would defend and elaborate the ideas he had put in a nutshell in 1906. Similarly, Karl Marx spent his whole life developing and drawing conclusions from the ideas he had advanced in the *Communist Manifesto*, his early and brief statement of doctrine.

Trotsky's work might have been for the Russian party what the *Communist Manifesto* had, ever since 1848, been for European socialism: a grand prospectus of revolution and a stirring call to action. Yet the influence of Trotsky's work was almost negligible, despite the controversy it aroused. The reasons for this were in part adventitious, in part inherent in the author's attitude. No sooner had the book appeared, in 1906, than it was seized and confiscated by the police. The few copies that reached readers aroused little interest, even though the author was just then, about the time of the Soviet's trial, very much in the public eye. Most of the book was made up of reprints of old essays; and readers looking for new viewpoints easily missed the one new and important chapter in it.[1] It seems established that Lenin, for instance, never read this work before 1919, although once or twice he referred to it disparagingly on the basis of second-hand quotations.[2] By the time the book went to the printers, the revolution was fizzling out. From a practical standpoint, Socialists were more inclined to weigh the chances of triumphant reaction than to contemplate the vistas of victorious revolution.

---

[1] L. Trotsky, *Permanentnaya Revolutsia*, pp. 39–42.

[2] See Yoffe's farewell letter to Trotsky (16 November 1927) in *The Trotsky Archives* (Harvard).

Thus *Balance and Prospects* appeared either too soon or too late to make a stronger impression than it did. Finally, neither of the two main currents in the party wished to identify itself with the novel and provocative forecast. The Mensheviks had recovered from the radicalism of 1905; they were impatient to shake off Trotsky's influence; and they considered this new epitome of 'Trotskyism' as an exercise in day-dreaming. The Bolsheviks were not in a mood to give serious attention to any prospects of revolution drawn by the spokesman of Menshevism. A lone wolf within his own party, Trotsky was condemned to relative futility just when he might have been most effective. Nor was the accident of his age without effect. He had gained enormous popularity among the rank and file and among non-party workers; but in the eyes of active propagandists and organizers, to whom his doctrine was meant to appeal, he was still too young to be accepted as a prophet.[1]

Despite this lack of response, he was already strongly aware that he was taking his place among the makers of history; and it was with this awareness that, on 19 September 1906, he went into the dock.

. . . .

The trial was full of fight and heat. It did not take place before a military tribunal, as had been expected; and so the shadow of death did not hang over the dock. But the defendants were prepared for long terms of hard labour. The court was surrounded by masses of Cossacks and soldiers. Within the precincts, where a state of siege had been declared, it swarmed with gendarmes with drawn sabres in their hands. Only a hundred persons, among them Trotsky's parents, were admitted to the proceedings. Two score attorneys conducted the defence. In the course of several weeks, 250 witnesses from every walk of life gave evidence on every detail of the Soviet's activity. From the first day the court was flooded by resolutions, signed by scores of thousands of workers, protesting against the trial. 'We, the workers of the Obukhov plant', ran a typical protest, 'declare . . . that the Soviet does not consist of a handful of conspirators but of true representatives of the proletariat of Petersburg . . . and that if our esteemed comrade P. A. Zlydniev is guilty, then we are all guilty, and we confirm this by our own signatures.'[2]

[1] A. Lunacharsky, *Revolutsionnye Siluety*.
[2] L. Trotsky, *Sochinenya*, vol. ii, book 2, pp. 142–3.

The sentiment of the anti-Tsarist public expressed itself in a thousand incidents. 'On the benches of the defendants there constantly appeared newspapers, letters, boxes with sweet-meats, and flowers. No end of flowers! In their buttonholes, in their hands, on their knees, and all over the dock—flowers. The presiding judge has not the courage to remove this fragrant disorder. In the end, even the officers of the gendarmerie and the clerks, altogether "demoralized" by the atmosphere in the hall, carry the flowers from the public to the dock.'[1] At one moment the defendants rose to pay homage to the memory of one of them who had been executed before the trial. The attorneys and the public, too, rose to their feet; and so did the embarrassed officers of the gendarmerie and the police. The aftermath of the revolution was still in the air.

'We have decided to take part in the present extraordinary trial only because we think it necessary . . . to explain publicly the truth about the activity and the significance of the Soviet.' Thus Zlydniev, on behalf of all accused, stated at the opening of the proceedings. The defendants so conducted themselves that they aroused respect, and at times a grudging sympathy, even among their enemies. The police brought against some of the members of the Soviet—Trotsky was not among them— the charge that they had embezzled funds collected from workers. The charge brought forth such a hail of protests from factories and was so effectively exploded in the court that the prosecution itself dismissed it as slanderous. So striking was the evidence that the Soviet had had overwhelming popular sup-port for the general strikes and demonstrations it had called, that the prosecution could not base its case on these activities and concentrated instead on the count of insurrection.[2]

On 4 October Trotsky rose to speak on this subject. He modelled his speech on the pleas which Marx and Lassalle had made when in 1848 they had been confronted with identical charges, but on this occasion he perhaps surpassed his masters. He began with the statement that the issues of republic and

---

[1] L. Trotsky, *Sochinenya*, vol. ii, book 2, p. 141.

[2] A contemporary correspondence from Petersburg in *The Times* stated: 'The remarkable feature about the revolutionary gathering [of October 1905] was its perfect organization. . . . On the other hand, the procession of the "Whites" was a mere rabble of butchers' boys, shopkeepers, beadles, and a few enthusiasts.' *The Times*, 1 November 1905.

insurrection had never figured on the Soviet agenda, so that in strict law the charge was groundless; but that this was so only because the Soviet had taken its own attitude in these matters for granted and had had no need to discuss them. He at once took the bull—the problem of political force—by the horns:

Did the Soviet . . . consider itself justified in using force and repressive measures in certain instances? To this question, posed in this general form, my answer is: Yes. . . . In the conditions created by a political general strike, the essence of which was that it paralyzed the mechanism of government, the old governmental force that had long outlived its day and against which the political strike was directed, proved itself completely incapable of undertaking anything. Even with the barbarous means which alone were at its disposal, it was not in a position to maintain and regulate public order. In the meantime the strike had thrown hundreds of thousands of workers from the factories into the street and had awakened them to public political life. Who could take over the direction of those masses, who could carry discipline into their ranks? Which organ of the old governmental power? The police? The gendarmerie? . . . I find only one answer: nobody, except the Council of Workers' Deputies.'[1]

The Soviet could not but begin to assume quasi-governmental functions. It refrained from coercion, however, and preferred to act by persuasion. The prosecution had produced in its evidence only a few minute, comic rather than tragic, cases of violence. The defence might plead that the Soviet had acted within the limits permitted by the Tsar's own Manifesto; but it preferred frankly to proclaim its democratic, republican conviction. Let the court decide whether the freedom promised in the Manifesto was for monarchists only or for republicans and Socialists as well. 'Let the Manifesto now proclaim to us through the court's verdict: you have denied my reality, but I do exist for you as well as for the whole country.' Otherwise the defendants would be convicted for their beliefs not for their deeds.

Trotsky then went on to prove that, in certain circumstances, insurrection which the court considered illegal must develop from the general strike, which the court held to be legal. Insurrection had in a sense begun with the general strike. The strike had paralysed the existing government and required another

---

[1] L. Trotsky, op. cit., pp. 163–4.

government to step into its place. Something like dual power had come into existence. The prosecution professed to defend the existing order against the Soviet. Yet this order, in so far as it was expressed in the Tsar's Manifesto, had itself been the product of a general strike—it was in response to the October strike that the Tsar had proclaimed it. The legal as well as the real basis under the old order had been shattered. Two governments had in fact existed, each struggling to assert itself, each endeavouring to win the army for itself. Their collision was inevitable. 'Did the workers of Petersburg become aware of this? Yes. Did the proletariat, did the Soviet, believe the open clash of these two powers to be unavoidable? Yes.' And not only they—the middle classes, too, realized this and in many cases demonstrated their sympathy for the Soviet. It was the old government not the Soviet that represented anarchy and bloodshed. It was a requirement of order that the old government be overthrown; and only insurrection could overthrow it.

What was the nature of the insurrection? Trotsky asked. The Russian code, which was a hundred years old, had known only the notion of a conspiracy against the government, staged in secret by a handful of rebels. This had, indeed, been the only form of rising possible in bygone times. The new insurrection was a popular rising, never envisaged by the code. The law was lagging behind the times; and it did not give the prosecution even technical ground for the charge against the Soviet.

And yet our activity was revolutionary! And yet we did prepare ourselves for an armed rising! A rising of the masses is not made, gentlemen the judges. It makes itself of its own accord. It is the result of social relations and conditions and not of a scheme drawn up on paper. A popular insurrection cannot be staged. It can only be foreseen. For reasons that were as little dependent on us as on Tsardom, an open conflict had become inevitable. It came nearer with every day. To prepare for it meant for us to do everything possible to reduce to a minimum the number of victims of this unavoidable conflict.

The Soviet tried to organize the masses and to explain to them the meaning of events. It was not preparing an insurrection; it was preparing itself for an insurrection. True, the masses had no arms. But—'no matter how important weapons may be, it is not in them, gentlemen the judges, that great power resides.

No! Not the ability of the masses to kill others, but their great readiness themselves to die, this secures in the last instance the victory of the popular rising. . . .' For only when the masses show readiness to die on the barricades can they win over the army, on which the old régime relies. The barricade does not play in revolution the part which the fortress plays in regular warfare. It is mainly the physical and moral meeting-ground between people and army. 'It serves the insurrection, because, by hampering the movement of troops it brings these into close contact with the people. Here on the barricade, for the first time in his life, the soldier hears honest, courageous words, a fraternal appeal, the voice of the people's conscience; and, as a consequence of this contact between soldiers and citizens, in the atmosphere of revolutionary enthusiasm, the bonds of the old military discipline snap. . . .'

Having thus defined the place of insurrection in the revolution, he returned to the attack on the government. The rulers, he said, were trying to prolong their domination by means of assassination and pogroms; the hooligans of the Black Hundreds had been taking their cue from the police and gendarmerie; and the Tsar himself had been their protector.[1] Trotsky quoted revelations made in the first Duma by the Liberal Prince Urusov, who had related the following boast of one of the leaders of the gendarmerie: 'We can make a pogrom whenever it suits us, a pogrom of ten people, if we wish, or of ten thousand.'

The prosecution does not believe in all this. It cannot believe, for otherwise it would have to turn the accusation against those whom it now defends, and to acknowledge that the Russian citizen who arms himself with a revolver against the police acts in self-defence. . . . We had no doubt that behind the façade of the Black Hundreds was the powerful fist of the ruling clique. Gentlemen the judges! this sinister fist we see even now in front of us!

The prosecution is asking you to recognize that the Soviet armed the workers for the direct struggle against the existing 'form of

[1] The programme of the Black Hundreds ran:
   '1. The good of the Fatherland lies in the unshakable conservation of Orthodoxy and of the unlimited Russian autocracy. . . .
   '2. The Orthodox Christian Church must have the predominant and dominating position in the state.
   '3. Russian autocracy has sprung from popular reason; it has been blessed by the Church and justified by history.'

government'. If I were asked categorically 'Was this so?', I would answer: Yes! . . . I am prepared to admit this charge, but on one condition only. I do not know whether the prosecution and the court will agree to this condition.

I am asking you: What exactly does the prosecution mean by 'form of government'? Do we live under any form of government at all? The government has long since broken with the nation. . . . What we possess is not a national governmental force but an automaton for mass murder. I can find no other name for the machine of government that cuts into pieces the living flesh of our people. And if you tell me that the pogroms, the arson, the violence . . ., if you tell me that all that has happened in Tver, Rostov, Kursk, Siedlce, . . . if you tell me that Kishinev, Odessa, Bialystok [the places where the pogroms had been staged] represent the form of government of the Russian Empire, then—yes, then I recognize, together with the prosecution, that in October and November we were arming ourselves against the form of government of the Russian Empire.[1]

Thus he faced his judges, addressing them in a sonorous, metallic voice, and casting fleeting glances at the public. There, amid the public, sat his parents; his father staring at him, proud and completely reconciled; his mother quietly weeping. His plea stirred so much emotion that counsel for the defence asked for an adjournment for cooling off; and the court granted the request. During the interval attorneys and the public crowded around the dock to compliment Trotsky; and he tried gently to prepare his mother for a harsh sentence; for she had become naïvely reassured by the respectful commotion around her son. When the proceedings were resumed, the chief prosecutor gleefully declared that the defendant had given him all the evidence required but he also paid homage to Trotsky's honesty and courage.

The cross-examination of witnesses became an entire exposure of the violence and corruption into which government and police had sunk. At one point Trotsky, questioning Ivanov, the general of the gendarmerie who had conducted the investigation, compelled him to say, amid hilarious laughter in court, that a briefcase containing documents had been stolen from him at the headquarters of the political police. It was careless, the general explained, to leave there any personal belongings unattended,

[1] L. Trotsky, *Sochinenya*, vol. ii, book 2, pp. 163–77.

even for a moment—they were invariably stolen. Then, on
13 October, something like a bombshell exploded in the court-
room. One of the defence counsel received a letter from Lopukhin, a recently dismissed director of the police department,
who asked to be called as witness. A semi-Liberal official,
Lopukhin had conducted a special inquiry into the obscure
activities of his own department; and he forwarded to the court
a copy of the report he had submitted to Stolypin, the new
Minister of the Interior. He wished to testify that the year before
Petersburg had escaped a bloody pogrom only thanks to
measures taken by the Soviet. He wished to bear witness that
the leaflets inciting to the pogrom had been printed at the
headquarters of the political police, in the offices of one of its
chiefs who had just testified before the court that he had never
seen them. He further revealed that the political police itself
had organized the gangs of the Black Hundreds, that General
Trepov was actually in command of those gangs; and that the
commandant of the Imperial Court personally submitted to the
Tsar regular reports on these activities. The defence asked that
Witte, the former Prime Minister, Durnovo, the former Minister
of the Interior as well as Lopukhin be summoned to the witness-
stand. The request was refused on the pretext that the cross-
examination had been concluded. To allow the erstwhile chief
of the police department to give evidence for the defendants and
to implicate the Imperial Court would have brought the Tsar's
wrath upon the magistrates. But their refusal to call the witnesses effectively exposed the political character of the trial and
much beside. The defendants and attorneys decided to boycott
further proceedings.

On 2 November the verdict was delivered before an empty
court-room. The members of the Soviet were declared not guilty
on the chief count, that of insurrection. But Trotsky and fourteen others were sentenced to deportation to Siberia for life and
loss of all civil rights.

. . . .

The convicts, dressed in grey prison clothes, started on their
journey at dawn on 5 January 1907. They had been kept in
the dark about the date of their departure and about their
destination; and they were awakened for the journey just after
they had gone to sleep, having spent most of the night at a

'passionate game of chess'. Yet, before departing they had managed to smuggle out a 'Farewell Message' to the workers of Petersburg, thanking them for their solidarity with the Soviet and reaffirming hope in the eventual triumph of the revolution.

The party of deportees, some with their wives and small children, was hustled to the railway station through dark and empty streets, under a strong military escort. The government was still afraid of an attempt to rescue them; and so elaborate were the precautions that the military escort had been brought from Moscow—soldiers of the Petersburg garrison were not thought reliable. At the stations, *en route*, the car with the convicts was surrounded by a dense cordon of gendarmes; and not till very late in the journey were the convicts told the place of their deportation. Apart from this, however, they were treated with respect and consideration. The soldiers openly showed their sympathy; all of them had read the reports of the trial and were relieved to learn that they would escort the workers' delegates to a place of deportation, not of execution. On the way they secretly posted the prisoners' mail; and to this circumstance we owe a vivid description of the journey which Trotsky gave in his letters to Sedova.[1]

The route led from Petersburg through Vologda, Viatka, and Perm, across the Urals, to Tiumen, where the party left the train and the escort was changed. From there they travelled by sleigh northwards towards Tobolsk. The convoy of forty horse-driven sledges was on the move only between sunrise and sunset, so that it covered not more than twenty *versts* at a stretch. The precautions were tightened and the journey was interrupted long before dusk, to prevent any attempt at escape. The country traversed was dotted with deportees' settlements, where the convoy was often greeted with revolutionary songs and red flags. Among the native Siberian peasants rumour and legend ran ahead of the travellers: the unusually strong escort suggested that the deportees were men of great importance, dukes or governors in disgrace, or the deputies of the first dispersed Duma; and the peasants looked on them with reverence and awe.

[1] Trotsky later published these letters in a little book *There and Back*. Our quotations are taken from the German translation which appeared as an appendix in L. Trotsky, *Die Russische Revolution 1905*.

After more than three weeks, the convicts reached Tobolsk, where they were put up for a few days in the local prison. Here they were told that the goal of their journey was the penal colony at Obdorsk, lying in the mountains over the estuary of the river Ob, just on the Polar Circle, nearly 1,000 miles from any railway and 500 from a telegraph station. The route from Tobolsk to Obdorsk led northwards, along the river Ob, through Samarovo and Berezov, across barren, empty, snow- and ice-bound *tundra* and *taiga*, where for hundreds of miles there was no human settlement, except a few scattered Ostyak huts or tents. Horses could still be used on part of the road, but farther on the horse was replaced by the reindeer. Here the finality of his severance from civilization came upon the depor- tee with a shock. From the Tobolsk prison, on 29 January, Trotsky wrote to his wife about the sudden and sharp longing that had overcome him 'for the light of an electric street lamp, for the clangour of a tramway' and—characteristically—'for the loveliest thing the world can offer, the smell of the printing ink of a fresh newspaper'.

So far he had not yet thought of trying to escape, even though before departing from Petersburg he had prudently concealed a false passport and money in the sole of his boot. For one thing, political convicts now refrained from escaping *en route* so as not to get the escort into trouble. For another, he reflected whether, having been so much in the public eye, it was not too risky for him to make the attempt: the escaping deportee, if caught, was automatically punished with three years' hard labour. Enough that when he was writing to Sedova about the place of his deportation, he still expected her to join him there with their baby son, born while he was in prison awaiting trial. He attempted to cheer up Sedova and wrote that Obdorsk had a healthy climate, was inhabited by a thousand people, and that he would have chances of earning a living there. He also urged her to bring or send to Obdorsk books and papers, no end of books and papers. In this mood, bracing himself for a long wait beyond the Polar Circle, not without melancholy, he started out from Tobolsk towards Samarovo and Berezov, the next halting-places.

Galloping at full speed, the convoy traversed a vast area, where typhus was raging and Ostyaks in their huts were dying like flies. On 12 February the convicts were lodged at the prison of Berezov, but allowed to leave their cells in the daytime and to move about. This was the month of snow blizzards in the *tundra*, and the police did not think that anybody would try to get away.

At Berezov a set of favourable circumstances induced Trotsky to change his mind about escape. He met a deportee doctor, who taught him how to simulate sciatica so as to dodge the last lap of the journey and be left behind, under mild surveillance, in the local hospital. The malingering required much will-power; but, if effective, it could not be detected. If he continued the journey and then tried to get away from Obdorsk, he would have added to his road 500 *versts* across the northern desert; and so he made up his mind to apply the lesson the doctor had taught him and to stay behind at Berezov. He found a sympathetic peasant ready to help. He had to choose one of three routes: the Tobolsk road, by which he had come, was in some ways the most convenient, but on it he might easily be caught; the northernmost way across the Urals to Archangel and Finland was difficult as well as dangerous; and so he chose to cross the roadless *tundra* south-westward, across the river Sosva, to a gold-mining settlement in the Urals, which was the terminus of a small single-track railway connected with the Perm-Viatka line. His peasant friend found him a guide, a native Zyrian drunkard, who knew his way in the *tundra* and spoke Russian and the native dialects. They struck a bargain. The guide bought the reindeer and furs needed for the journey; and he was to keep them on completion of the trip.

As the day approached, Trotsky pretended to have recovered from the fit of sciatica. On the evening before the escape, he went to an amateur theatrical performance of a Chekhov play. During the interval, he met the chief of the local police and told him that he was feeling well enough to make the last lap of the journey north. The police officer was well pleased. At midnight, Trotsky, having uneasily put himself into the hands of the drunken guide, was heading southwards.

It took him a week—travelling mostly night and day—to traverse the *tundra* over distances 'which nobody had measured except the archangel Michael'. The guide had an instinctive, animal-like sense of direction and feeling for the *tundra*. Like nearly all Ostyaks and Zyrians he was constantly drunk and falling asleep, to the horror of the passenger who saw the sleigh running into deep snowdrifts and feared pursuit. Himself without food, drink, or sleep, Trotsky kept on thumping and kicking the driver, tearing off his headgear, exposing him to the frost and thus keeping him awake. As they passed by Ostyak huts, which were happily very few and very far between, the driver would stop and disappear; and the passenger would find him either indulging with the Ostyaks and their wives and children in wild bouts of drinking, or lying unconscious on the floor. On the way, the leading reindeer strained its leg, and the others were worn out. The animals had to be left behind and fresh ones bought. This happened again and again, and Trotsky had to join the Ostyaks in a hunt for reindeer.

Despite the discomfort and exasperation, he was happy to be on the move, and he watched with wide eyes the awe-inspiring beauty of the white desert and the ugliness and misery of life in Ostyak huts. Most of the time he fought off sleep; and when they halted in the open waste to make a fire and to melt the snow for tea, he sat by the fire to jot down his observations, which he was later to put into a book. Even the tension of this flight and the terror of the *tundra* could not subdue the inquirer and the man of letters in him. He took notes on the landscape; on the shape of the woods; on the variety of the trails left on the snow by the wolf, the fox, the ermine, the elk, and other beasts; on his conversations with his driver; on the customs and manners of the natives (who liked best to eat fish raw, while it was still fluttering in their hands); on the abject slavery of their women; on hunting for deer; on the behaviour of the hunters and the hunted; and on a thousand other points.

As they approached the Urals, human settlements became frequent, and the inquisitiveness of people encountered embarrassing. He posed alternately as a merchant and as a homebound member of a polar expedition. He had to use his wits to find plausible answers when goods were insistently offered to him for sale and when he ran into someone who had known one or two members of the polar expedition to which he claimed to belong. But nothing untoward happened, and at length he reached Bogoslovsk, the terminus of the single-track railway.

A day later a train carried him westward from Perm through

Viatka and Vologda to Petersburg. 'For the first few minutes', he later recollected, 'the large and almost empty compartment was too crowded and stuffy for me, and I went out on to the front platform, where the wind was blowing and it was dark. A loud cry burst out from me—a cry of joy and freedom.'[1] So flushed was he with joy that he did all that prudence should have counselled him not to do: he was heading for Petersburg, where every police agent knew him; and he cabled to his wife about his arrival, asking her to meet him *en route*. Sedova could hardly believe her eyes: when the cable arrived the newspapers of Petersburg were still carrying reports about the journey of the convicted Soviet leaders to the Polar Circle.

[1] Trotsky, *Moya Zhizn*, vol. i, p. 227.

CHAPTER VII

The Doldrums: 1907–1914

THE year 1907 was the year of the Tsar's revenge. With the *coup* of 3 June autocracy was fully re-established, and Stolypin's reign of terror began. The second Duma was dispersed. A new law disfranchised the bulk of the people; and only after that was a new Duma elected. The Social Democratic deputies to the second Duma were deported to Siberia. The revolutionary parties were crushed, their clubs and newspapers suppressed, and thousands of their members massacred. Courts martial and the gallows dominated the political scene. Even moderate Liberals, who only recently had hoped to come to terms with the Tsar, were victimized and humiliated. Miliukov complained bitterly: 'We were invited to assume office as long as we were thought to have the red forces behind us.... We were respected so long as we were regarded as revolutionaries. But since we have turned out to be a strictly constitutional party, we have been found useless.'

The influence of socialism, so recently still overwhelming, shrank and dwindled. In 1905 everybody seemed in sympathy with socialism; now nearly everybody abjured it. Those who stood by it were a mere handful; even they could not withstand the all-pervading disillusionment and confusion. The Socialists were being driven back into the underground from which they had so hopefully emerged. But how much easier it had been for them before 1905 to band together in small clandestine circles than now, with defeat in their hearts, to re-descend into the underground. They seemed back where they had started, but without the original faith and courage. Some were reluctant to resume the clandestine struggle and hoped to work in the open, within such limits as the régime of 3 June would permit. Others, disdainful of any adjustment to triumphant counter-revolution, made desperate attempts to continue a war *à outrance* from the underground, and most of these boycotted the few social and political institutions which existed precariously in the open. The first attitude, that of the so-called 'liquidators', was prevalent among the Mensheviks, although some

Menshevik leaders, especially Plekhanov and Martov, were convinced of the need for clandestine organization. The 'boycotters' were strong among the Bolsheviks; but they were opposed by Lenin, who endeavoured to combine clandestine and open forms of activity.

In the recovery of Tsardom Trotsky saw a mere interval between two revolutions. He insisted, as much as did Lenin, on the necessity for the movement to rebuild its clandestine organization; and he also urged the underground workers to 'infiltrate' every open institution, from the Duma to the trade unions, in order to preach their views inside. He was therefore opposed to both liquidators and boycotters and went on expounding the idea of permanent revolution with an optimism and ardour uncommon in those years of depression.[1]

Nevertheless, the years between 1907 and 1914 form in his life a chapter singularly devoid of political achievement. 'During the years of reaction', he wrote later, 'the greater part of my work consisted in interpreting the revolution of 1905 and paving the way for the next revolution by means of theoretical research.'[2] He did indeed interpret the revolution of 1905, or rather he repeated his earlier interpretation. But of the new 'theoretical research' there is little evidence in his writings, which consisted of brilliant journalism and literary criticism, but did not include a single significant work on political theory. Yet even in this somewhat apologetic retrospect Trotsky does not claim any practical revolutionary achievement to his credit. In these years, however, Lenin, assisted by his followers, was forging his party, and men like Zinoviev, Kamenev, Bukharin and, later, Stalin were growing to a stature which enabled them to play leading parts within the party in 1917. To the stature which Trotsky had attained in 1904–6 the present period added little or nothing.

Stalin, in the days before he began opposing Trotsky with nothing but preposterous calumny, made a remark which offers a clue to this chapter. Trotsky's strength, Stalin said, reveals itself when the revolution gains momentum and advances; his weakness comes to the fore when the revolution is

---

[1] See his editorial statements in the Viennese *Pravda*, nos. 1, 4, 5; 'Letter to Russian Workers—*Vivos Voco*' in no. 6; and '*Chto-zhe dalshe?*', Supplement to *Pravda*, no. 17.   [2] L. Trotsky, *Moya Zhizn*, vol. i, p. 251.

defeated and must retreat.[1] There is some truth in this. Trotsky's mental and moral constitution was such that he received the strongest impulses from, and best mobilized his resources amid, the strains and stresses of actual upheaval. On a gigantic stage, which dwarfed others, he rose to the giant's stature. Amid the roar and din of battle, his voice attained full power; and when he faced multitudes in revolt, absorbing from them their despair and hope and imparting to them his own enthusiasm and faith, his personality dominated men and, within limits, events. When the revolution was on the wane, however, he was out of his element and his strength sagged. He was equal to herculean, not to lesser, labours.

.   .   .   .

On his return from the far north, Trotsky stopped for a few days in Petersburg, and then, before the police were on his track, crossed into Finland. A new stream of revolutionary émigrés was moving westward, and Finland was their first halting-place. The chief of the police at Helsinki, a Finnish patriot, was only too glad to offer shelter to the Tsar's enemies. Lenin and Martov had already arrived there. They warmly welcomed Trotsky and congratulated him on his behaviour in the dock. His sojourn in Finland lasted a few weeks, during which he prepared for publication a description of his escape from the *tundra*. At the end of April, he was in London to attend a congress of the party.

This was in many respects a strange assembly. Attended by about 350 delegates—nearly ten times as many as in 1903—it was the last congress of the united party. The delegates, although they met on the eve of Stolypin's *coup d'état*, had no clear awareness that the revolution had suffered defeat. On the contrary, the party still seemed to them to be at the zenith of its strength. Its membership was still nominally very large, and not only did Bolsheviks and Mensheviks work together, but even the Polish and the Latvian parties had joined the Russian mother-party—hitherto they had kept aloof so as not to become identified with either of its two factions. The party was, however, so poor that it had to borrow money from a liberal English business man to enable the congress to proceed in a Brotherhood Church in London.

[1] Stalin, *Sochinenya*, vol. vi, pp. 329-31.

The great issues of the revolution—the economic trends, the alignment of the classes, and the historical perspectives—were thrown open to a prolonged and thorough debate, which lasted three weeks. 'The speeches of the leaders lasted for hours . . . it might have been a gathering of academicians. ·. . .'[1] For the first time Trotsky had the opportunity to expound the theory of permanent revolution before a gathering of this sort. He strongly criticized the Mensheviks for their inclination to coalesce with the Constitutional Democrats; and he advocated a bloc of workers and peasants.[2] Rosa Luxemburg, representing the Polish Social Democratic Party, endorsed the theory of permanent revolution. Lenin twice emphatically acknowledged that in advocating an alliance of workers and peasants Trotsky was on common ground with the Bolsheviks. Once again Lenin hoped to win Trotsky over, and once again he failed. For the moment Trotsky was keeping aloof from both factions, and to both he preached unity. 'Here comes', he said, 'Martov . . . and. threatens to raise between the Bolsheviks and the Mensheviks a Marxist wall bristling with guns.' . . . 'We are not afraid . . .', replies the Bolshevik, and threatens to fortify himself behind a deep moat. 'Comrade Martov, you are going to build your wall with paper only, with your polemical literature —you have nothing else to build it with.'[3] In this Trotsky was, of course, wrong: the 'wall' separating the two factions was of much more solid stuff than he imagined, and Martov and Lenin had a prescience of the ultimate irreconcilability of their political methods. 'If you think', Trotsky further pleaded, 'that a schism is unavoidable, wait at least until events, and not merely resolutions, separate you. Do not run ahead of events.'

There was in his attitude towards both wings of the party a certain intellectual superciliousness, for he looked at both through the prism of his theory of permanent revolution. Both Lenin and Martov agreed that the Russian revolution would be merely bourgeois democratic; both were therefore in his eyes wrong, and the views of neither would withstand the test of events.[4] In strict theory, this was true enough; but the

[1] A. Balabanoff, *My Life as a Rebel*, p. 88.
[2] *Pyatyi Syezd RSDRP*, pp. 272–3, 417–18, 420–4.   [3] Ibid., pp. 54–55.
[4] Shortly after the congress, Trotsky wrote in the *Przegląd Socjal-Demokratyczny* (Rosa Luxemburg's Polish paper) that 'while the anti-revolutionary aspects of Menshevism are already revealing themselves fully, the anti-revolutionary features

strictly theoretical viewpoint was not necessarily the most realistic. Whatever the formulas, the party of the revolution was constituting itself under Lenin's inspiration and the potential party of reform under Martov's. With his gaze fixed on wide horizons, Trotsky failed to see this division taking place before his very eyes. His own theory should have prompted him to come closer to the Bolsheviks; but the ties of personal friendship and the dead weight of his old controversy with Lenin held him closer to the Mensheviks.

At the congress in London a new issue brought back the old exacerbation. In committee, delegates discussed the guerilla activities and 'expropriations' in which the Bolshevik fighting-squads had been engaged, especially in the Caucasus. The Mensheviks angrily denounced these activities as a relapse into the old *Narodnik* terrorism, if not outright banditry; and they persuaded the congress, at which Lenin otherwise commanded a majority, to ban them. Throughout this discussion Lenin's attitude was ambiguous. Apparently he still intended to use the fighting squads for a few raids on Russian treasury transports, in order to obtain the money the party needed for its work under the terror of counter-revolution. Throughout the congress, an unknown Caucasian delegate, closely connected with the Bolshevik fighting-squads, Djugashvili-Ivanovich—he had not yet assumed the cover name Stalin—sat in silence, waiting for the result of the controversy and for Lenin's instructions. The records of the congress say nothing about the course of this controversy; only fragmentary reminiscences, written many years after, are available. But there is no doubt that Trotsky was, with Martov, among those who sharply arraigned the Bolsheviks; and some time after the congress he went so far as to carry the denunciation into the columns of the Western European Socialist press. He must have vented his indignation in the lobbies of the congress or in committee. Thus Lenin's earlier acknowledge-ment of the *rapprochement* in their basic views and his renewed attempt to win over Trotsky led to nothing, and towards the end of the congress were succeeded by bitter invective. Trotsky

of Bolshevism strongly threaten to come to light only in the case of a revolutionary victory'. Trotsky hoped, however, that a new revolution would compel both factions to revise their views and would thus bring them closer together, just as the events of 1905 had done. See *Die Russische Revolution 1905*, p. 231.

still cast his vote now for a Bolshevik and now for a Menshevik motion; but on several occasions he burst out against Lenin with ill feeling for which the records offer no explanation.[1]

The quarrel over the fighting-squads was superseded by a wider controversy concerning the character of the movement. The so-called liquidators tried to justify their opposition to clandestine work as part of an endeavour to reform Russian socialism in a European spirit. European Socialist parties, they argued, worked in the open, and so should the Russian organization. The argument appealed to a sentiment which had been strong in all sections of the party because, since the days of the struggle against the *Narodniks*, all Marxists had seen their mission as the 'Europeanization' of Russian socialism. But now each faction gave a different meaning to the term. The liquidators saw the essence of European socialism in its democratic mass organizations, the open work of its growing parliamentary representations, the peaceful bargaining of the trade unions: briefly, in its reformist practice. To the Bolsheviks 'Europeanization' meant what at the beginning it had meant to the party as a whole: the transplantation to Russia of Marxist proletarian socialism, the combined product of German philosophy, French socialism, and English political economy. But they could not see how they could go beyond that and imitate the open and lawful methods of western socialism; the Russian police state, especially under Stolypin, refused to allow even a Liberal party to exist openly, let alone a Socialist. If socialism did no more than what the law allowed, the law dictated by triumphant autocracy, it would in effect efface itself.

Trotsky glorified the underground struggle, its heroism and its martyrdom, with all the romantic zest peculiar to him. But he also responded keenly to the watchword of Europeanization. What he meant by it he never made quite clear. For him it summed up an emotional and cultural attitude rather than a clear-cut political concept. It expressed in a positive form his dislike of the 'dryness and hardness' of the clandestine organization, as Lenin conceived it. He knew that under Tsardom a

---

[1] Shortly after the congress Lenin wrote to Maxim Gorky (who had been present at the congress and tried to reconcile Lenin with Trotsky), that Trotsky behaved 'like a poseur'. Lenin, *Sochinenya*, vol. xxxiv, p. 335. See also *Pyatyi Syezd, RSDRP*, pp. 506, 602, 619, and Medem, op. cit., vol. ii, pp. 187–9.

broadly based, open Labour movement was a castle in the air.
But, yearning for the best of both worlds, he wanted to see the
broad democratic and tolerant spirit of western socialism in-
fused into the Russian underground. He wanted the clandestine
organization to give that scope to the 'self-activity' (*samodeyatelnost*) of the rank and file, which the western Labour parties
seemed to provide. Yet any clandestine movement is of necessity narrow and rigid in comparison with any party which
works in the open. It cannot in truth be broadly based; it
cannot really afford to relax the discipline which its leadership
imposes on the members; it cannot leave to the rank and file
that freedom of initiative and 'self-activity' which may exist
(or merely appear to exist) in a normal party. Lenin had reason
on his side when he insisted that to 'Europeanize' the Russian
party, even in the sense in which Trotsky and not the liquidators wanted it, would have meant wrecking the party.

. . . .

From nobody did the cry for Europeanization come more
naturally than from Trotsky. More than any other émigré he
was a 'European'. Most émigrés lived in their closed circles,
immersed in Russian affairs, unaffected by life in the countries
of their residence. Not so Trotsky. With the adaptability and
mental receptiveness of the wandering Jew—although these are
by no means exclusively Jewish qualities—he felt at home in
most European countries, was passionately absorbed in their
affairs, spoke and wrote in their languages, and participated in
their Labour movements.

In the summer of 1907, after the congress, he went from
London to Berlin, where Sedova with their baby son was waiting
for him. There he was warmly welcomed by the intellectual
élite of German socialism. His fame had gone ahead of him: his
conduct in the Soviet and in the dock had aroused admiration,
and his essays had been translated and published in German
periodicals. Parvus, who had also escaped from Siberia, introduced him to Karl Kautsky, then at the height of his influence
as the spiritual guide of European socialism, the 'Pope' of
Marxism. Trotsky often recollected the exultation of this visit
and the 'other-worldly impression' which the 'white-haired and
bright-eyed' Kautsky made on him. It could not have entered
his mind that one day Kautsky would be the most severe critic

of the October Revolution and the butt for his own devastating attacks. For a few years more, Trotsky, like all Socialists, sat at Kautsky's feet, even though the master's 'dry, angular' mind, and a certain banality and lack of subtlety soon disappointed him. Kautsky's home became his port of call in Berlin, and he took part in the intimate gatherings of the 'Pope's' inner circle. There he met Bebel, the old pioneer who had stood up to Bismarck, and had led German socialism through years of persecution into its seemingly golden age. There he also met Ledebour, Haase, and other leaders. He turned these friendships and contacts to political advantage. In *Neue Zeit*, Kautsky's monthly, and in *Vorwärts*, the influential Socialist daily, he often presented the case of Russian socialism and explained, from his angle, its internal dissensions.[1] The fact that he stood outside the quarrelling Russian factions commended him to the Germans, who could not make head or tail of the intricate Russian controversy and were loth to become involved in it.[2] Trotsky's manner of writing was undogmatic, attractive, European; and he appealed to German readers as no other Russian Socialist did. His German friends, on the other hand, occasionally contributed to his Russian émigré paper, helping to boost it—the German Social Democratic Party was still 'mother, teacher and living example' to all Russian Socialists.

Curiously enough, Trotsky's closest ties were not with the radical wing of German socialism, led by Rosa Luxemburg, Karl Liebknecht, and Franz Mehring, the future founders of the Communist party, but with the men of the centre group, who maintained the appearances of Marxist orthodoxy, but were in fact leading the party to its surrender to the imperialist ambitions of the Hohenzollern empire. This was all the stranger since the German radicals were by no means the counterparts of the Bolsheviks. In most essentials their attitude coincided with

---

[1] In a letter to his followers Lenin once complained that 'Trotsky and Co. write, and the Germans believe. Generally speaking, Trotsky is master at *Vorwärts*.' Lenin, *Sochinenya*, vol. xxxv, p. 11.

[2] This was the attitude of nearly all European Socialists. Jaurès, for instance, warned his staff on *Humanité* not to publish anything from, or about, the Russian party, because otherwise the paper would be swamped by interminable and very obscure statements from the opposed factions. A. Morizet, *Chez Lénine et Trotski*, p. 101.

Trotsky's. They, too, cherished the party's unity; they, too, represented an intellectual and revolutionary brand of Marxism, opposed to the empirical reformism which emanated from the German trade unions. Of all the personalities of European socialism, nobody was in origin, temperament, and political and literary gifts more akin to Trotsky than Rosa Luxemburg— not for nothing was Stalin to denounce her posthumously, in 1932, as a 'Trotskyist'. They found themselves in agreement at the recent congress in London and again at the congress of the International at Stuttgart, where Luxemburg spoke for the anti-militarist left. Like Trotsky, she rejected the general Menshevik conception of the revolution, but viewed with suspicion the work of the Bolsheviks. Like Trotsky, she wanted to see the Russian movement 'Europeanized', while she herself tried to breathe into the German party something of the Russian revolutionary idealism. They sometimes met at Kautsky's home, but they remained aloof from each other, perhaps because of their extraordinary affinity. Agreeing so closely, they may have had little to say to each other. Nor did Karl Liebknecht's passionate and sincere yet unsophisticated idealism attract Trotsky, to his regret in later years. Franz Mehring, whose political temperament was to flare up during the First World War, was now immersed in historical and philosophical work which was a little remote from the issues agitating Trotsky.

For the next seven years, till the outbreak of the First World War, Trotsky settled in Vienna. 'His house in Vienna', writes a Russo-American Socialist who visited him there in 1912, 'was a poor man's house, poorer than that of an ordinary working man. . . . His three rooms in a . . . working-class suburb contained less furniture than was necessary for comfort. His clothes were too cheap to make him appear "decent" in the eyes of a middle-class Viennese. When I visited his house, I found Mrs. Trotsky engaged in housework, while the two light-haired lovely boys were lending not inconsiderable assistance. The only things that cheered the house were loads of books in every corner.'[1] The visitor received perhaps an exaggerated impression of poverty. The Trotskys were better off than most émigrés, even though they lived very modestly and at times, as we shall see, did suffer

[1] See M. J. Olgin's 'Biographical Notes' in the American edition of Trotsky's *Our Revolution*, p. 18.

penury. Throughout these years Trotsky, writing under his old
pen-name Antid Oto, was the Vienna correspondent of
Kievskaya Mysl (*Kievan Thought*), a widely-read radical Liberal
daily; and he contributed frequently to at least half a dozen
Russian, German, and Belgian papers.[1] His wealthy parents,
who were helping to bring up the two daughters of his first
marriage and who several times came abroad to meet him,
almost certainly on occasion opened their purses to him. The
two boys mentioned by the American visitor were Lev or
Lyova, his older son of the second marriage, born in 1906,
while Trotsky was in prison, and Sergei (Seryozha), born in
Vienna in 1908.

By all accounts the family led a quiet and happy existence.
The revolutionary lion was a devoted husband and warm-
hearted father. Anxious to help his wife and to enable her to
pursue her artistic interests and to follow the political life of
the Russian colony, he lent a hand in domestic chores and in the
upbringing of the children. Later, when the boys went to school,
he regularly helped them in their homework, and he found time
for this even in the fever of the war years, after the family had
moved to Paris.[2] Sedova, for her part, resumed in Vienna her
husband's artistic education, which she had begun in Paris
without initial success in 1902. The couple spent many a
day together amid the rich art collections in the Burgschloss
and in Viennese galleries. His interest in the arts was growing
appreciably: on his frequent visits to Paris, London, or Munich
he would steal away from political conventicles to the Louvre,
the Tate Gallery, and other collections; and his writings of this
period, especially his reviews of the annual Viennese exhibitions,
written for *Kievan Thought*, show a slightly more than dilettante
appreciation of trends in European art. While politics and
journalism claimed only part of his time, he also enlarged his
already wide familiarity with the French and the Russian
novel and with German poetry; and this, too, is reflected in his
literary essays of the time.

He settled in Vienna reluctantly, after the German police had

[1] Apart from *Kievskaya Mysl*, he contributed in these years irregularly to the
following papers: *Luch, Den, Odesskie Novosti* (of which his uncle Spentzer was the
publisher), *Borba, Neue Zeit, Vorwärts, Le Peuple* (of Brussels).
[2] A. Rosmer, 'Trotsky during World War I', *The New International*, September–
October 1950.

refused him domicile in Berlin. He was anxious to stay within the orbit of German socialism, and for this Vienna was second best. From Vienna he also watched the clash of German and Slav aspirations in the Balkans. Towards the close of Francis Joseph's rule Vienna, although already somewhat provincial, was still one of Europe's spiritual centres. In politics it prided itself on Austro-Marxism, which had broken the unchallenged domination of clericalism in the most Catholic of empires. In literature it had made, with Arthur Schnitzler, Peter Altenberg, Karl Krauss, and others, its contribution to the hypersensitive, sex- and death-conscious trend of the *fin de siècle*. In the arts, its secession revolted mildly against academic conservatism and bourgeois crudity. There was no lack of solid education and taste in the Viennese intelligentsia and its radical wing, although these virtues were not matched by strength of character or sense of purpose. Perhaps only in psychology did Vienna at that time produce anything epoch-making: Freud's great mind was beginning to dominate the field. For the rest, Court, Parliament, editorial offices, Socialist meetings, literary and artistic groups and cliques, were all reflected in the life and gossip of the cosy Viennese cafés, always astir with intelligent, witty, yet strangely futile conversation.

In *My Life* Trotsky describes this environment with disdainful irony. His writings at that time, however, strongly suggest that he enjoyed the mild effervescence of the Viennese atmosphere. He plunged into local life, joined the Austrian Social Democrats, visited their clubs and meetings, contributed to local Socialist papers, was stirred by local literary and artistic events, and occasionally gave way to the attraction of the cafés. Years later, as the leader of a victorious revolution and the implacable enemy of reformism he drew devastating portraits of the Austro-Marxist leaders. During his stay in Vienna, he was less hard on them and felt gratified by their friendship. He warmly admired Victor Adler, the founding father of the party, in whose home he was as welcome as he was at Kautsky's in Berlin and repeatedly for Russian readers he wrote of Victor Adler with gusto and love.[1] He was attached to Victor's son, Fritz, the rebellious Benjamin of the party and editor of *Kampf*, who would one day kill the Austrian Prime Minister Baron

[1] L. Trotsky, *Sochinenya*, vol. viii, pp. 10 ff.

Stürgkh, in protest against world war.[1] Ties of friendship also bound him to Rudolf Hilferding, the master mind of Austro-Marxism. Just as Trotsky was settling down in the Viennese suburb of Hütteldorf, Hilferding was writing, or completing, his monumental *Finanzkapital*, virtually the only ambitious attempt made since Marx's death to bring the theory of *Das Kapital* up to date. (Hilferding's work was used by Lenin to justify his revolutionary policy, while its author became Minister of Finance in the Weimar republic.) It was Hilferding who introduced Trotsky to Karl Renner, the future Chancellor and President of the Austian republic, to Otto Bauer, foremost Austro-Marxist theorist and expert on national minorities, and future Foreign Minister, and to nearly all the other Austro-Marxist leaders. 'They were well educated people', writes Trotsky, 'who knew about various subjects more than I did. I listened with intense and, one might say, reverent interest to their conversation when I first saw them at the Central Café.'[2]

But Trotsky also grew aware of the difference between his own Marxism and theirs; they were academic, over-sophisticated sceptics, without mettle; and he sensed the politely concealed condescension with which they met his own revolutionary ardour. Behind the thinkers and leaders he saw 'a phalanx of young Austrian politicians, who have joined the party in the firm conviction that an approximate familiarity with Roman law gives a man the inalienable right to direct the fate of the working class'.[3] But he believed that in critical times the bold spirit of socialism would overcome the scepticism of the leaders and the opportunism of the party officials, and that the revolution, when it came, would carry the Austro-Marxists with it, as it would carry the Mensheviks. He obviously mistook his friends for revolutionaries just as they liked to think of him as of one who was at heart a mild reformist.[4]

[1] During the war Trotsky described Friedrich Adler as his 'comrade in ideas and friend' (*Sochinenya*, vol. viii, pp. 33–36). In 1919, Trotsky and Lenin nominated F. Adler Honorary Secretary of the Third International, and they were greatly disappointed when he turned his back on them. Later F. Adler became the secretary of the Second International.   [2] *Moya Zhizn*, vol. i, p. 237.

[3] L. Trotsky, *Sochinenya*, vol. viii, pp. 12–13.

[4] The following incident offers an amusing illustration: towards the end of 1917 when Count Czernin, the Austrian Foreign Minister, was setting out for peace negotiations with Trotsky at Brest Litovsk, he had a talk with Victor Adler. 'Adler said to me in Vienna: "You will certainly get on all right with Trotsky", and when

Fortified by these friendships, Trotsky frequently appeared as the mouthpiece of Russian socialism before the congresses of the German and Austrian parties. He also became a familiar figure at the gatherings of the International, where he met the pioneers: Jaurès and Guesde, Keir Hardie and MacDonald, Vandervelde and Turati. He was spellbound by the personality of Jaurès, and this despite the latter's reformism, by 'the genius-like *naïveté* of Jaurès's enthusiasm' and his 'volcanic moral passion and gift of concentrated anger', and by Jaurès's oratorical genius, more classical, less soaring than his own, yet so much akin to it. At these gatherings, where all the talent of European socialism was assembled, he compared various styles of oratory, noting, for instance, the 'cool, exquisite finish of style and polish of gesture' in Vandervelde, whom he was later to mock as a mediocrity, or analysing the strong oratorical effect of Victor Adler, who 'could never control his [rather weak] voice, wasting it uneconomically, so that towards the end of his speeches he usually coughed and was hoarse'. But it was to Jaurès that, whether in full congress, in committee, or at public meetings, he listened 'each time as if it were the first', as 'he [Jaurès] moved rocks, thundered and exploded but never deafened himself. Like a heavy steel hammer, he could crush a rock or work with infinite precision on the thinnest gold plate.'[1] And once, portraying the great Frenchman, he characteristically remarked: 'Sometimes the man of the Russian black-soil steppe may find in Jaurès merely artificial technical training and pseudo-classical recitation. But in such an appraisal is revealed only the poverty of our own Russian culture.'

The more he steeped himself in this atmosphere of pre-1914 Europe, the more did the sense of the 'poverty and crudity' of Russian culture oppress him and the more emphatically did he insist that it was part of the mission of socialism, and of socialism alone, to transform the Scythian into a 'good European'. He best expressed this idea, with all its strength and weakness, in a superb essay on the Russian intelligentsia which he wrote for *Kievan Thought* in 1912. The editor hesitated long before he published it: even in a radical paper the essay seemed likely to

I asked him why he thought so, he answered: "Well, you and I get on quite well together, you know." ' Count O. Czernin, *In the World War*, p. 234.

[1] L. Trotsky, *Sochinenya*, vol. viii, pp. 13, 19, 30–31.

hurt Russian *amour propre* too strongly. The occasion was a celebrated book by Ivan Razumnik, which extolled the exceptional virtues and the historical role of the Russian intelligentsia. In his criticism of this book Trotsky elaborated some of the views on Russian history he had formulated earlier and tried to explain the peculiar role of the Russian intelligentsia against a wide historical background.

'We are poor', he wrote, 'with the accumulated poverty of over a thousand years. . . . History has shaken us out of her sleeve into a severe environment and scattered us thinly over a vast plain.' Only a Leviathan-like state could defend that plain against Asiatic invasion and withstand the pressure of wealthy and powerful Europe. To feed itself the Leviathan starved the nation, crippled the growth of its social classes and institutions and atrophied its civilization. 'The Russian people was not less heavily oppressed by nobility and Church than were the peoples of the West. But that complex and rounded-off way of life which, on the basis of feudal rule, grew up in Europe—that gothic lacework of feudalism—has not grown on our soil. We lacked the life-matter for it, we could not afford it. . . . A thousand years we have lived in a humble log cabin and filled its crevices with moss—did it become us to dream of vaulting arcs and gothic spires?'

'How miserable', he went on, '. . . was our gentry! Where were its castles, where were its tournaments? Its crusades, its shield bearers, its minstrels and pages? Its chivalrous love?' The Russian gentry was coarse, barbarous, vulgar. Nor did Russia go through the purifying experience of the Reformation; and so she had no inkling of the western burgher's 'human personality, which strove to establish more intimate relations between itself and its God'. In the medieval European town, that 'stone cradle of the third estate', there had grown up a striking diversity of cultural types, and a whole new epoch had been prepared there. 'In the crafts, guilds, municipalities, universities, academic assemblies, elections, processions, fêtes, and disputes there crystallized the precious habits of self-government; there grew the human personality—a bourgeois personality, of course, but still a personality, not a snout which every policeman could kick and punch.' All that the third estate, as it grew, needed to do was to transfer the new human relations and the habits of self-government from the corporations to the nation and the state as a whole. In contrast, the Russian towns, those 'military-feudal excrescences on the body of the Russian countryside', had created no starting-points for bourgeois progress. Under Peter the Great it was the police that sponsored crafts, but no genuine urban culture could grow out of police sponsorship. The misery of Russian bourgeois democracy supplemented the crudeness of the feudal tradition.

The state, however, needed men who were educated and therefore Europeanized; but it was afraid of them. The Tsars gave the intelligentsia compulsory education; but then they kept the ... whip over them. 'No sooner had the young elements of the old estates ... entered the sunlit zone of European ideology than they broke away irresistibly, almost without inner hesitation, from feudalism and inherited orthodoxy.' The Russian intelligentsia were compelled to defend their most elementary rights by the most extreme and wasteful means. 'It became their historical calling ... to use watches for knocking nails into walls.' A Russian had to become a Darwinist in order to justify his decision to marry according to his choice; he had to invoke revolutionary ideas to excuse his craving for education; and he had to have recourse to socialism when all he wanted was a constitution. For all their radicalism, the Russian intelligentsia merely imitated the West, adopting from it ready-made systems, doctrines, and programmes. In a passage which did less than justice to Russian thought and literature of the nineteenth century, Trotsky dismissed these as backwater growths: '. . . the history of our social thought has so far failed to cut its way even with the thin edge into the development of universal human thought. This is a poor consolation for national *amour propre*? . . . Historical truth is not a lady-in-waiting on national pride. . . . Let us rather invest our *amour propre* in the future and not in the past.'

Throughout their severe struggle, the Russian intelligentsia stood alone in the nation, receiving no support from the main social classes. This shaped their character. They 'lived in a terrible moral tension, in concentrated asceticism. . .' They bought moral self-confidence and stability at the price of intellectual conceit and of 'fanaticism in ideas, ruthless self-limitation and self-demarcation, distrust and suspicion and vigilant watching over their own purity. . .', at the price, that is, of an orthodoxy in rebellion opposed to official orthodoxy. Thus they came to develop 'that zeal for the letter, which can sometimes be observed in our intellectuals of the most extreme wing'. It was the misfortune of the intelligentsia that they had always had to act as proxy for undeveloped and passive social forces. Here Trotsky set in a long historical perspective the phenomenon of 'substitutism' about which he had first written in his polemics against Lenin in 1904.[1] He now saw the intelligentsia's 'substitutism' running like a thread through Russian history. First, the leaders of the Decembrist rising of 1825 represented the ideas of an as yet unborn middle class. Then the *Narodniks* tried to speak for a mute and dumb peasantry. Lastly the Marxist intellectuals set themselves up as the spokesmen of a weak, only just awakening industrial working class. To all of them the idea of the class was more important than the class itself. He rounded off this gloomy survey in a more hopeful tone, saying that the revolution of 1905–6 had set in motion the mass of the workers and that henceforward nobody could act as their proxy: this was the end of substitutism.[2]

We shall see later whether or to what extent this optimistic conclusion was justified; substitutism was to reassert itself with unparalleled strength after the revolution, and the idea of the class was then to become for a long time more important than the class itself. Some of the other long trends of Russian history, which Trotsky grasped here with such mastery, were also to come overwhelmingly to the surface after the revolution. What is at this stage of our narrative more relevant is the self-revealing acuteness with which Trotsky contrasted the 'sunlit zone of European ideology', 'the vaulting arcs' and 'the gothic spires and lacework' of western civilization with the barbarous 'log cabin' of Russian history. This contrast was greatly over-drawn, not in historical perspective, where it was broadly true, but in its concluding and contemporary part. The lacework façade of European civilization before 1914 concealed processes of self-destruction and inner decay which were presently to manifest themselves in a succession of world wars, in the paroxysms of Fascism and Nazism and in the impotence and deterioration of the western European Labour movement. On

[1] See Chapter III.   [2] L. Trotsky, *Sochinenya*, vol. xx, pp. 327–42.

the other hand, Trotsky did not do justice to the creative energies with which nineteenth-century and contemporary Russia was boiling over, the energies with which his own personality and activity were merged. He sometimes seemed to view Russia's past and present almost as a vacuum. This was the weakness underlying his call for Europeanization and also the flaw in his attitude towards Bolshevism. It was Lenin's strength that he took Russian reality as it was, while he set out to change it. Lenin's party had its roots deep in Russian soil; and it absorbed all that that soil could yield in revolutionary strength and harshness, in world-shaking courage and in primitive crudity. Bolshevism had its thinkers, its Lenin and Bukharin and others, who drew from European socialism whatever could be transplanted to Russia; but it also had its tough committee-men, its Stalins, who worked in the depths of a semi-European and semi-Asiatic proletariat, and to whom Europeanization meant little.

. . . .

Trotsky did not and could not really abandon the humble Russian 'log cabin'. In October 1908 he began to edit the so-called Viennese *Pravda*. An insignificant paper, published since 1905 by Spilka, a small Ukrainian Menshevik group, *Pravda* was completely run down, and its publishers hoped that Trotsky would put new life into it. The first few issues he edited still bore the imprint of the Ukrainian group; but at the end of 1908, the group disbanded itself and left Trotsky as *Pravda's* sole master. For lack of money, he published it very irregularly— only five issues appeared in the first year of his editorship.[1] But it was less difficult to bring out the paper than to transport it clandestinely to Russia. The editor often appealed to readers for help, complaining that 'several *poods*' of the paper got stuck on the Russian frontier and could not be forwarded because of the lack of fifty roubles; that manuscripts for a new issue had piled up on his desk and he could not send them to the printers; or that *Pravda* was compelled to stop correspondence with readers in Russia because it could not afford the postage.[2] Trotsky's

---

[1] At this time this was the lot of all émigré publications, and most of them appeared even more rarely. N. Popov, *Outline History of the C.P.S.U.*, vol. i, p. 233. Trotsky's *Pravda* is commonly referred to as the Viennese *Pravda*, to distinguish it from the Bolshevik *Pravda* which began to appear much later. The Viennese *Pravda* was at first published in Lvov, in Austrian Galicia, and only in November 1909, with its sixth issue, was it transferred to Vienna. [2] *Pravda*, nos. 3 and 5.

journalistic fees, earned from other papers, went to finance the
little sheet; he sold his books, and his wife trudged to a pawn-
shop so that the few *poods* of *Pravda* should at last get across the
frontier. Or the central committee of the mighty German Social
Democratic Party would lend a thousand roubles; and so some
of the debts would be paid, Mrs. Trotsky would recover a few
of her pawned belongings; and for a couple of months *Pravda*
would come out every fortnight. Then again the intervals between one issue and another began to lengthen, the fortnightly
became a monthly, then almost a quarterly, until its shaky
finances were again temporarily restored by a modest grant
from the Latvian Socialists or from some other well-wishers.
Throughout 1909 Trotsky tried in vain to obtain assistance
from the Russian Central Committee, in which the Bolsheviks
were a majority. Lenin agreed to help, but only on condition
that Trotsky admitted a delegate of the Central Committee as
co-editor. Since Trotsky would not accept this condition, Lenin
forbade his followers to produce *Pravda* at the Bolshevik printing
shop at Geneva otherwise than on strictly commercial terms.[1]
Despite these difficulties and the irregularity of its appearance,
the paper evoked response in Russia and soon its 'wide circulation' was noted in the confidential reports of the *Okhrana's*
agents.[2]

Pravda had a curious team of contributors. A young student
Skobelev, at this time Trotsky's favoured pupil, acted as
the paper's secretary—later Skobelev gained eminence as a
Menshevik parliamentarian in the fourth Duma, and in 1917
he became Minister of Labour in Kerensky's government.
Trotsky's assistant was another Menshevik, Semkovsky, whose
name at this time frequently appeared in inner party controversy; Ryazanov, the future founder of the Marx–Engels
Institute, an untameable rebel bowing to no authority and
standing outside the two factions, was a regular contributor
and Trotsky's close friend. In charge of the paper's contact
with the Russian underground was Uritsky, a former Menshevik,
already renowned for his cool courage in Tsarist prisons; in
1917 Uritsky was among the chief organizers of the October
insurrection, and he then, as special Commissar, dispersed the

[1] Lenin, *Sochinenya*, vol. xxxiv, pp. 348–9.
[2] *Bolsheviki, Dokumenty Okhrannovo Otdelenia*, vol. i, p. 42.

Constituent Assembly. The team included the Menshevik Victor Kopp, one day to make his mark as a subtle and adventurous diplomat: in 1922 he prepared behind the scenes the Russo-German treaty of Rapallo; and in the 1930s he secretly explored for Stalin the chances of agreement with Hitler.

The most original character in this pléiade was Adolphe Yoffe. A young, able but neurotic intellectual of Karaite[1] origin, Yoffe was sharing his time between academic work, contributions to *Pravda*, and psychoanalysis. Through Yoffe, Trotsky met Alfred Adler (whose patient Yoffe was), became interested in psychoanalysis, and reached the conclusion that Marx and Freud had more in common than Marxists were prepared to admit.[2] In Vienna Yoffe struggled desperately with recurrent nervous breakdowns; and the contributions which he produced with painful effort needed much editorial rewriting. Trotsky did his best to befriend him and to boost his self-confidence. In 1917 Yoffe was one of the chief actors in the October insurrection and later in the peace negotiations of Brest Litovsk. (In his private papers Trotsky remarked that the revolution 'healed Yoffe better than psychoanalysis of all his complexes'.)[3] Yoffe was to repay Trotsky's friendship with boundless devotion, and in 1927 he committed suicide in protest against Trotsky's expulsion from the Bolshevik party.

On the whole, *Pravda* was not one of Trotsky's great journalistic ventures. He intended to address himself to 'plain workers' rather than to politically-minded party men, and to 'serve not to lead' his readers.[4] *Pravda*'s plain language and the fact that it preached the unity of the party secured to it a certain popularity but no lasting political influence. Those who state the case for a faction or group usually involve themselves in more or less complicated argument and address the upper and medium layers of their movement rather than the rank and file. Those who say, on the other hand, that, regardless of any differences, the party ought to close its ranks have, as Trotsky had, a simple case, easy to explain and sure of appeal. But more

[1] The Karaites were a sect which abandoned rabbinical Jewry in the middle ages to return to the pure Gospel.

[2] After the revolution Trotsky appealed to Bolshevik scholars to keep an open mind to what was new and revealing in Freud. *Sochinenya*, vol. xxi, pp. 423–32.

[3] *The Trotsky Archives*.

[4] *Pravda*, no. 1.

often than not this appeal is superficial. Their opponents who win the cadres of a party for their more involved argument are likely eventually to obtain the hearing of the rank and file as well; the cadres carry their argument, in simplified form, deeper down. Trotsky's calls for the solidarity of all Socialists were for the moment applauded by many—even the Bolsheviks in Petersburg reprinted his *Pravda*. But the same people who now applauded the call were eventually to disregard it, to follow the one or the other faction, and to leave the preacher of unity isolated. Apart from this, there was in Trotsky's popular posture, in his emphasis on plain talk and his promise to 'serve not to lead', more than a touch of demagogy, for the politician, especially the revolutionary, best serves those who listen to him by leading them.

More than anybody else Trotsky voiced the sentiment, still widespread in the party, which may best be described as a horror of final schism. In January 1910 the leaders of factions met in Paris and for the last time tried to patch up their differences. In both factions there were men determined to bring matters to a head and to part company. But in both the moderates prevailed for the moment. The conciliators who carried the day among the Bolsheviks were Rykov, Sokolnikov, Lozovsky, and Kamenev.[1] On the other side, Trotsky exerted himself for unity and kept in check Martov, who later admitted that he gave way only because the Mensheviks were too weak to risk an immediate break.[2] An agreement was reached; but, even on the face of it, it was too good to be true. Both factions consented to disband their separate organizations and to merge; and both agreed to eliminate the 'extremists' from their midst, the Mensheviks to expel their liquidators and the Bolsheviks their boycotters. Both further agreed to suspend their separate publications and to put their financial resources into a common pool, to be placed under the trusteeship of three German Socialists, Karl Kautsky, Franz Mehring, and Klara Zetkin. Trotsky received all the tributes that on such solemn occasions are paid to the successful matchmaker. The Central Committee formally acknowledged the services his *Pravda* had rendered to the whole party, 'regardless of faction', and it decided to place

---

[1] N. Popov, op. cit., vol. i, p. 248.
[2] Martov, *Spasiteli ili Uprazdniteli*, p. 16.

its authority behind the paper, to pay Trotsky a regular subsidy (150 roubles a month) and to support him in every other
way. Trotsky's Bolshevik brother-in-law, Kamenev, was dele-
gated to serve on *Pravda* as the Central Committee's liaison
officer. The appointment was calculated to smooth co-operation, for Kamenev had sincerely striven to overcome the division
inside the party.

It is easy to imagine the jubilation with which Trotsky
announced all this in *Pravda*.[1] A few weeks later, however, he
had to record that the attempt at reconciliation had broken
down, because—so he himself stated—the Mensheviks had
refused to disband their faction. This could not have greatly
surprised him; he had known all along their utter reluctance
to come to terms with the Bolsheviks, who had in the meantime
suspended their separate publication. This was the occasion
on which Trotsky, the champion of unity, should have spared
the offenders against unity no censure. Yet in *Pravda* he 'suspended judgement' and only mildly hinted at his disapproval of
the Mensheviks' conduct.[2] In vain did Kamenev urge him to
take a firmer attitude. Trotsky resented this as an infringement
of his editorial independence and an attempt to use *Pravda* for
Bolshevik purposes. There followed the inevitable bickerings,
and in no time all the émigré colonies were seething with intrigue.

The Paris conference had resolved to disown the two extreme
wings of the party, the liquidators and the boycotters. The
Mensheviks had undertaken to have no truck with the former,
the Bolsheviks with the latter. Lenin could easily keep his part
of the undertaking. He had, anyhow, expelled the chief boycotters, Bogdanov and Lunacharsky, from his faction. The
Mensheviks, on the other hand, found it almost impossible to
live up to their obligation. The liquidators' attitude was too
common in their ranks for them to dissociate themselves from it
in earnest. If they were to expel those who had turned their
backs on the underground struggle, they would merely have
destroyed their own influence and helped Bolshevism to ascendancy. This they refused to do. The issue then presented itself
in this form. Those who were opposed to clandestine work,
argued the Bolsheviks, had no place in a party staking its future
on that work. The Mensheviks—that is, the anti-liquidators

[1] *Pravda*, no. 10.   [2] *Pravda*, no. 12.

among them—replied that there should be room in the party
for dissenters. The general principle that dissent was permissible
was not questioned by Lenin. He merely argued that this
particular dissent could not be tolerated, because the opponents
of clandestine work could not be effective clandestine workers.
Since, from one angle, this difference could be seen as a conflict between the upholders of discipline and the defenders of the
right to dissent, Trotsky took his stand against the disciplinarians. Having done so, he involved himself in glaring inconsistencies. He, the fighter for unity, connived in the name of
freedom of dissent at the new breach in the party brought about
by the Mensheviks. He, who glorified the underground with
zeal worthy of a Bolshevik, joined hands with those who longed
to rid themselves of the underground as a dangerous embarrassment. Finally, the sworn enemy of bourgeois liberalism allied
himself with those who stood for an alliance with liberalism
against those who were fanatically opposed to such an alliance.

So self-contradictory an attitude brought him nothing but
frustration. Once again to the Bolsheviks he appeared not just
an opponent, but a treacherous enemy, while the Mensheviks,
though delighted to oppose to Lenin a man of Trotsky's radicalism and record, regarded him as an unreliable ally. His long
and close association with Martov made him turn a blind eye
more than once on Menshevik moves which were repugnant to
him. His long and bitter quarrel with Lenin made him seize
captiously on every vulnerable detail of Bolshevik policy. His
disapproval of Leninism he expressed publicly with the usual
wounding sarcasm. His annoyance with the Mensheviks he
vented mostly in private argument or in 'querulous' letters, with
which he bombarded Martov and Axelrod. Consequently, he
appeared in public not quite the same man as he was in private.
The longer this state of affairs lasted, the more did he become
Martov's political prisoner. Martov's correspondence throws
an instructive light on this:

I have answered him [Trotsky] with a more ironical than angry
letter [Martov wrote on one occasion], although I admit that I have
not spared his *amour propre*. I have written him that he can escape
nowhere from the liquidators and ourselves, because it is not his
magnanimity that compels him to defend the right of the liquidators
to remain in the party . . . but the correct calculation that Lenin

wants to devour all independent people, including Trotsky, as well as the liquidators.[1]

The logic of things [Martov wrote to another correspondent] compels Trotsky to follow the Menshevik road, despite all his reasoned pleas for some 'synthesis' between Menshevism and Bolshevism . . . he has not only found himself in 'the camp of the liquidators', but he is compelled to take up there the most 'pugnacious' attitude towards Lenin. His pupils, however, . . . are fretful.[2]

In the summer of 1910 Trotsky's breach with the Central Committee was complete. Kamenev had left *Pravda*, after Trotsky had asked that the Central Committee should replace him by another liaison officer; and the Central Committee withdrew its subsidy.[3] By now the initiative in splitting the united movement had passed from Martov to Lenin; and Trotsky denounced 'the conspiracy of the [Bolshevik] émigré clique against the Russian Social Democratic Party,' adding that 'Lenin's circle, which wants to place itself above the party, will find itself outside it'.[4] He carried the campaign into the German Socialist press, where he wrote that none of the émigré leaders represented the real movement in Russia, which craved for unity and resented their intrigues. This was then, in fact, a common view among the underground workers: none other than Stalin wrote in a similar vein in the Caucasus.[5] Trotsky's articles, nevertheless, caused an uproar among the delegates of the party, who assembled in Copenhagen in October 1910 for a congress of the International. At a meeting of the Russian delegation, Plekhanov, seconded by Lenin, demanded disciplinary action, while Lunacharsky and Ryazanov acted as Trotsky's counsel for the defence. The offender was let off—even his accusers must have found it awkward to penalize him for an opinion expressed in 'fraternal' German papers.

The feud was not without its comic incidents, of which one at least may be related here. Both factions tried to recover the funds which they had deposited with the German trustees; but for some reason neither was able to establish a valid title. In the summer of 1911 Axelrod and Trotsky went to Jena, where a congress of the German Social Democrats was being held, in

---

[1] *Pisma Axelroda i Martova*, p. 230.   [2] Ibid., p. 233.
[3] *Pravda*, no. 20; Lenin, *Sochinenya*, vol. xvi, p. 360.   [4] *Pravda*, no. 21.
[5] Stalin, *Sochinenya*, vol. ii, pp. 146–58; I. Deutscher, *Stalin*, pp. 104–6.

order to approach, on behalf of the Mensheviks, the trustees of the fund.[1] Trotsky certainly hoped to repair *Pravda*'s finances should he succeed in helping the Mensheviks to repair theirs. Kautsky apparently favoured the plan, but the attitude of the other trustees was uncertain; and one of them, Zetkin, was friendly to the Bolsheviks. In great secrecy, Axelrod and Trotsky met Kautsky. 'Only on Tuesday', Axelrod reported to Martov, 'K[autsky] had an opportunity to suggest to me and T[rotsky] that we meet him somewhere for a preliminary private talk. . . . Haase chose as meeting place a restaurant, where one might hope that we would not be detected by other delegates, especially by those close to Zetkin and Luxemburg. . . . The next day, after K[autsky] had talked with Z[etkin] about a joint meeting with us, he and Haase asked me and T[rotsky] not to mention our conversation to Z[etkin]. . . .'[2] Ironically, most of the money deposited had been obtained by the Bolsheviks through the raids and expropriations which Trotsky and the Mensheviks had so indignantly denounced. But the delicate manipulation designed to expropriate the Bolsheviks with the assistance of the senior German trustee, yielded nothing, and the envoys left Germany without the golden fleece.

Early in 1912, the schism was brought to its conclusion. At a conference in Prague Lenin proclaimed the Bolshevik faction to be the Party.[3] The Mensheviks and a few Bolshevik splinter groups coalesced against him under the so-called Organization Committee. In *Pravda* Trotsky denounced Lenin's venture with much sound and fury.[4] His anger rose to the highest pitch in April, when the Bolsheviks began to publish in Petersburg a daily called *Pravda*. This was an outrageous plagiarism, clearly calculated to exploit for the Bolsheviks the goodwill of Trotsky's paper. He thundered against the 'theft' and 'usurpation', committed by 'the circle whose interests are in conflict with the vital needs of the party, the circle which lives and thrives only through

[1] In *My Life* Trotsky relates that he was to address the congress on the persecution of the Finns by the Tsar. During the congress came the news of the assassination of Stolypin in Kiev by Bagrov, an *agent-provocateur*. The Germans were afraid that the appearance of a Russian revolutionary on their platform might provoke diplomatic complications and repressive measures, and so Bebel induced Trotsky to give up his intention of addressing the congress.

[2] *Pisma Axelroda i Martova*, p. 217; Lenin, *Sochinenya*, vol. xviii, pp. 193–4.

[3] Apart from the Bolsheviks, a Menshevik splinter group led by Plekhanov participated in the conference.   [4] *Pravda*, no. 24.

chaos and confusion'. He called upon the editor of the Bolshevik paper to change its name within a given time; and he threatened meaningfully: 'We wait quietly for an answer before we undertake further steps.'[1] He apparently sent a similar ultimatum directly to the Bolshevik editorial offices. He had no inkling that the man who set up the rival paper in Petersburg and issued its first copy was the little-known Bolshevik Joseph Djugashvili, the man who would in the future similarly expropriate him of glories greater than the editorship of *Pravda*—of the titles of the leader of the revolution and the founder of the Red Army.

Yet it would be wrong to blame the plagiarism on to Stalin alone. Lenin wholeheartedly approved it; and in a letter to Petersburg he wrote: 'I advise you to answer Trotsky in the column "Answers to Readers" as follows: "To Trotsky in Vienna: We shall leave your quibbling and pettifogging letters without reply." '[2] One can easily guess how Lenin justified the plagiarism to himself: the Central Committee had subsidized *Pravda*; the title and the goodwill of the paper belonged to the party, not to Trotsky; and since the Bolsheviks were the party, they were entitled to appropriate the paper's name. This was a lame excuse, even though such quarrels over titles occurred in all émigré groups. Trotsky threatened to take further steps; but it seems that he took none, and he ceased to publish his *Pravda*, while the Bolshevik paper under its stolen name embarked on a long and famous career. In 1922, when *Pravda* celebrated its tenth anniversary, Trotsky took part in the celebration and contributed an article in which he did not even hint at the paper's origin.

.   .   .   .

The fact that Socialists could now openly publish dailies in Petersburg (the Mensheviks were publishing *Luch—The Torch*—which counted Trotsky among its contributors) showed a significant change in Russia. The years of reaction were over; the terror had spent itself; the Labour movement was experiencing a new revival; and, willy-nilly, Tsardom had to put up with it. A new generation of revolutionaries was coming of age and flocking into the few openly existing workers' clubs and trade unions and into the clandestine organizations. The new

[1] *Pravda*, no. 25. (From now on all references to *Pravda* are to the Bolshevik paper, unless it is stated otherwise.)   [2] Lenin, *Sochinenya*, vol. xxxv, p. 17.

situation provided the protagonists with new arguments. The liquidators pointed to the government's growing tolerance as proof that it was possible to Europeanize the party and to lead it out of the recesses of the underground. In the years of the terror their argument had sounded unreal; now it was based on facts. Yet the political revival also brought new vigour into the clandestine organization, and the young revolutionaries who were now entering it were not content with that cautious expression of opposition which the police tolerated in the legal clubs and trade unions. The government itself was the more inclined to put up with legal forms of opposition the more it was afraid of the illegal ones. This gave the Bolsheviks a powerful argument: we must, they said, intensify our clandestine efforts even if only to gain more elbow-room for open work.[1]

In these circumstances, Trotsky set out to pursue once again the will-o'-the-wisp of unity. He induced the Organization Committee to convene in Vienna a conference of all Social Democrats for August 1912. He hoped that the rise of the revolutionary temper in Russia would now, as in 1905, help to bring about a reconciliation. This was not to happen. In 1905 the strong tide of revolutionary events could still stop or delay incipient schism. In 1912 the cleavage had become so wide that the new political revival could only widen it further. Moreover, Lenin was now reaping the fruits of his labours: his men led the Social Democratic underground, while Menshevism was a farrago of weak and disconnected groups. The Leninists refused to attend the conference in Vienna; and so Mensheviks, ultra-left Bolsheviks, boycotters, the Jewish Bund, and Trotsky's group came together and formed a confederation, known in the annals of Russian socialism as the August Bloc. Trotsky was that bloc's chief mouthpiece, indefatigable at castigating Lenin's 'disruptive work'. There is no reason to doubt the sincerity of the apologia in which he claimed that he had never intended to turn the conference against the Bolsheviks, and that only Lenin's refusal to attend it or to countenance any attempt to re-establish unity had driven him into his anti-Bolshevik position. This apologia is amply borne out by the private correspondence of the Menshevik leaders; but it also shows how thoroughly Trotsky had misjudged the outcome of a decade of controversy.

[1] F. Dan, *Proiskhozhdenie Bolshevisma*, pp. 440–2.

His Menshevik friends did not share his illusions. They found it tactically convenient to place, once again with his help, the odium of the schism on Lenin; but they were no less determined than Lenin to carry the schism through to the end. The main difference was that while Lenin openly avowed his intention and almost shouted it from the house-tops, Martov, Axelrod, and Dan kept their design to themselves and sought to put it into effect through a subtle tactical game. It is enough to compare Lenin's utterances with the confidential correspondence of the Menshevik leaders, to see how strongly from their opposed angles they agreed on this one point that the split was both inevitable and desirable; and how they ridiculed, almost in the same terms, Trotsky's efforts to avert or to reverse it.[1]

.   .   .   .

The August Bloc left Trotsky galled and upset, despite, or perhaps because of, the 'pugnacity' he had displayed on its behalf. When, therefore, in September 1912 the editor of *Kievan Thought* asked him to go as the paper's correspondent to the Balkans, he eagerly seized this opportunity of getting away from émigré politics and changing from an actor playing an uncongenial part into an observer watching a storm centre of world politics. Early in October he left Vienna; and in a cab on the way to the station he learned of the outbreak of the first Balkan war, in which the southern Slavs joined hands against the Turkish empire.

From Vienna he had watched the Balkans and established connexions with Balkan Socialists. Two years before, in July 1910, he went to Sofia to expose and denounce a Pan-Slav congress taking place there under Miliukov's auspices. He addressed there a convention of the Bulgarian *Tesniaki* ('die-hards' of socialism), which assembled simultaneously with the Pan-Slav demonstration. Kolarov, the future Stalinist president of Bulgaria, introduced Trotsky to the congress and to crowds

[1] Trotsky was at this time on very friendly terms with the 'ultra-left' Bolshevik splinter groups, the boycotters and 'god-seekers'. In the summer of 1911 he lectured at their party school at Bologna, which Lunacharsky had set up with Gorky's help. A vivid description of the school is contained in a report by an *agent-provocateur* to the Okhrana. The report says *inter alia* that the lecturers (Lunacharsky, Menzhinsky, Kollontai, Pokrovsky) behaved towards their pupils, clandestine workers from Russia, in a haughty and patronizing manner. Trotsky, exceptionally, entertained friendly and private relations with his pupils. *Bolsheviki. Dokumenty Okhrannovo Otdelenia*, vol. i, p. 40.

in streets and squares as the legendary hero of the Petersburg
Soviet; and Trotsky was enthusiastically acclaimed. He warned
the southern Slavs that Tsarist diplomacy was trying to use
them as pawns, and that the Russian Liberals were fostering
Pan-Slavism because they were anxious to find common ground
with Tsardom in foreign policy, while surrendering to it at
home.[1] After that Trotsky often went on short trips to Belgrade
and Sofia and kept in close touch with events there. As early as
January 1909 he wrote in *Kievan Thought* that the Balkans were
the Pandora's box of Europe.[2]

The Pandora's box had now begun to release its horrors; and
the sight of them shook Trotsky. He had speculated abstractly
on the problems of war; but now as he saw the castle in Belgrade
floodlit by Austrian searchlights from across the frontier, as he
watched the long queues of called-up reservists and learned that
many of his friends, politicians, editors, university lecturers, were
already in the front line, the first to kill and to die, a sense of
tragedy overcame him, a 'feeling of helplessness before fate . . .
and a pain for the human locusts carried to their destruction'.[3]
'The abstract, humanitarian, moralist view of history is barren
—I know this very well. But this chaotic mass of material acquisi-
tions, of habits, customs, and prejudices, which we call civilization, has hypnotized us all, giving us the false impression that
we have already achieved the main thing. Now comes the war
and shows us that we have not even crawled out on our bellies
from the barbarous period of our history.'[4]

This sense of tragedy coloured all his Balkan correspondence, which was in the grand style of journalism, characteristic
of the Liberal-radical press of pre-revolutionary Russia. Each
article was a considerable essay, remarkable for the solidity
of its background information, for the wealth of impression and
local colour, for the excellence of its portraiture and analysis,
and, last but not least, for imaginative and vivid language.
Collected in his *Works*, these essays are still an invaluable
chronicle of the Balkans before 1914. The essayist was also a

---

[1] L. Trotsky, *Sochinenya*, vol. ii, book 1, pp. 207–23; vol. vi, pp. 34, 46.

[2] 'Only a single state', Trotsky wrote then, 'of all Balkan nationalities, built on a
democratic, federative basis—on the pattern of Switzerland or of the North
American republic—can bring international peace to the Balkans and create
conditions for a powerful development of productive forces.' Ibid., vol. vi, p. 10.

[3] Ibid., p. 66.   [4] Ibid., p. 141.

full-blooded journalist, keen to see things for himself, to interview people in all walks of life, and to supply his readers with
hot topical matter. He loved the excitement and the drudgery
of news gathering, and he mingled so freely with his colleagues
from the European press—he worked in close partnership with
the correspondents of the *Frankfurter Zeitung* and the *Daily
Telegraph*—that for a time the ambitious politician and the
tribune of the revolution seemed to disappear behind the newspaper man.[1] No sooner had he arrived in Belgrade than he
interviewed nearly every member of the Serbian government
and, with much wit and artistry, wrote character-sketches of
them, showing how the personalities reflected recent history
and the mentality of a small peasant nation. He delved into
problems of supply, military training, and tactics, and revealed
the atrocities and the primitive cruelty of the war. He visited
and described with the same eagerness churches in Sofia where
thanksgiving services were held for victories invented by propagandists; hospitals where he talked to wounded soldiers; dirty
and overcrowded prisoners' cages where he learned about the
experiences of Turkish infantrymen; comfortable hotels which
served as prisoners' cages for Turkish officers; fashionable cafés
in the spuriously European centres of the Balkan capitals; and
wretched, almost Asiatic, suburbs—nests of destitution, horror,
and degradation.

   He had first approached the war of the southern Slavs against
the Turkish empire with a certain sympathy, for he found the
memory of Turkish oppression even more alive in the Balkans
than was the memory of serfdom in Russia.[2] The Slav revolt
in some respects reminded him of the Italian *Irredenta* of 1859.
But he feared that the grievances of the Slavs would be abused
by the great powers, especially by the Tsar, and that they would
be used as pretexts for European war. Paraphrasing one of
Bismarck's sayings, he wrote: 'If the leading Balkan parties . . .
see no way of settling the fate of the Balkans other than by a
new European intervention . . . then their political plans are
truly not worth the bones of a single infantryman of the Kursk
province. This may sound cruel, but only thus can an honest,
democratic politician pose this tragic problem.'[3] The Balkan

---

[1] Ibid., pp. 283–92.
[2] Ibid., pp. 142–3, 187.   [3] Ibid., p. 144.

peasant leaders, who had in their youth imbibed the Russian revolutionary influence, were now paradoxically setting their hopes on the Tsar. This alone was enough to cool and to damp Trotsky's sympathy for their cause. The local contrasts of luxury and hunger, the corruption of the rulers, the needless atrocities inflicted on Turkish soldiers and civilians, the orgies of chauvinism, the bluff of the propagandists and the follies of the censorship evoked in Trotsky anger and disgust. He defended the weak and the defeated, the Turks.

The Bulgarian censorship pounced upon him, confiscated his articles and barred him from visiting the front. Curiously enough, the chief censor was a radical poet, Petko Todorov, who only two years before had, together with Trotsky, addressed in Sofia the meetings against Pan-Slavism. In an 'Open Letter to the Censor' Trotsky retorted with a scathing exposure of the sophisms and excuses with which military censorship is usually justified, and with an eloquent plea for freedom of information. The Letter, full of fire and thunder a little out of proportion to the object of the attack, made a considerable stir.[1] A more worthy object of attack presented itself soon. When Miliukov, as apostle of Pan-Slavism, arrived in Sofia, he flattered the Bulgarians and kept conveniently silent about their atrocities. Trotsky wrote another 'Open Letter' to Miliukov, which, when it appeared in a Petersburg daily,[2] opened a controversy which for many months filled the columns of the Russian press. Miliukov questioned the truthfulness of Trotsky's reports on atrocities; and Russian correspondents of Pan-Slav leanings joined in the affray. Trotsky, however, produced documentary evidence, collected by himself and the correspondents of the *Daily Telegraph* and *Frankfurter Zeitung*. These acrimonious exchanges were still in full swing when the whole situation suddenly changed: the first Balkan war ended with Slav victory; the victors, Serbs and Bulgarians, fell out over the spoils; official and Liberal Russian sympathies went to the Serbs; and the Bulgarians changed overnight from glorified heroes into atrocious villains, even in Miliukov's own paper.

Trotsky conducted part of this campaign from Vienna, where he also summed up the bearing of the first Balkan war upon

---

[1] L. Trotsky, *Sochinenya*, pp. 263–73.
[2] *Luch*, 13 January 1913 and *Sochinenya*, vol. vi, pp. 273–92.

European politics. Through the Balkan prism he saw the alignment of the great powers as it was to appear in 1914; and he saw it with great clarity, dimmed only by the wishful belief that the French, Austrian, and German Socialists, the latter with their 'eighty-six dailies and millions of readers', would defend to the end 'the cause of culture and peace against the onslaught of chauvinist barbarism'.[1]

Back in Vienna, he was soon again engrossed by the party cabal, protesting in private letters against the undisguised relish of his Menshevik friends at their separation from the Bolsheviks and against the ascendancy of the liquidators in the August Bloc. He quietly resigned from one Menshevik paper and growled against another, to which he continued to contribute. He was too much attached to the Mensheviks to part company and too restive to stay with them. 'Trotsky', Martov sneered in a private letter, 'while he was in the Balkans missed the evolution of the entire [August] Bloc'; the Mensheviks had in the meantime finished with talk of unity and with that 'empty, verbal conciliationism' which had been in vogue in the dubious hey-day of the Bloc. 'I think', Martov added, and he repeated this advice right and left, 'that we ought to show him [Trotsky] our "teeth" (of course, in the softest and politest manner).'[2]

It was therefore without regret that Trotsky again left Vienna to watch the second Balkan war. This time Serbia and Greece defeated Bulgaria, and Trotsky, the supposed enemy of the Bulgarians, turned into their defender. He described the plunder and violence of which the new victors were guilty; he visited the territories they annexed, and depicted the political unsettlement, the human misery, and the ethnographical nonsense entailed by hostilities 'conducted in the manner of the Thirty Years War' and by the shifting of frontiers and populations. He wrote a study of Romania, a classic of descriptive reporting, reprinted many times after 1917. 'Whereas Bulgaria and Serbia', he summed up, 'emerged from Turkish domination as primitive peasant democracies, without any survivals of serfdom and feudalism, Romania, in spite of decades of spurious constitutionalism, even now keeps its peasantry in the grip of

---

[1] L. Trotsky, *Sochinenya*, vol. vi, p. 302.
[2] *Pisma Axelroda i Martova*, pp. 262 ff. and 274.

strictly feudal relations.'¹ Romania was the 'jackal' in this war, and without having fired a shot, shared in the victors' spoils and annexed southern Dobrudja. Trotsky toured the province while its rural areas were afflicted by an epidemic of cholera and by a plundering *soldateska*, to the total indifference of the new Romanian rulers. He described how whole villages were dying out from lack of food and medicine; and how doctors, belonging to landed families, examined—from afar through binoculars—the cholera-stricken peasants, not deigning to approach them.

His descriptions of these scenes were oddly shot through with intimate flashes of a peculiarly Russian nostalgia. He travelled in a cab over land very similar to his native steppe. The landscape of the Dobrudja swept by breezes from the Black Sea, the burial mounds scattered over the steppe, the heat, and the sleepy pace of the journey brought back memories of his childhood at Gromokla and Yanovka and the picture of his recently deceased mother.

The road is so Russian, dusty like our Kherson road. The hens flee from under the horses' hoofs in a somewhat Russian way, and around the necks of little Russian horses are tied Russian harness ropes; even the back of Kozlenko [the cabman] is Russian. . . . Oh, how Russian his back is: you may travel round the world and you will not find such a back. . . . It is growing dusky. There is a smell of grass and road dust, Kozlenko's back darkens, and it is calm all around. Holding on to each other, we doze off. Phrrr!! Kozlenko stops his horses, patiently waits and thoughtfully whistles at them. Quiet. The blood itches in the feet, and it seems that we are travelling for our holidays from the station Novyi Bug to the village Yanovka.²

His homesickness became even more nagging when he visited Russian settlements scattered over the Dobrudja. The settlements were inhabited by Skoptsy. It was with members of this strange sect, the 'holy eunuchs', that he had travelled on barges down the Lena river during his first deportation to Siberia in 1901. The colonies and orchards of the Skoptsy in Dobrudja shone with cleanliness and neatness; but, Trotsky noted, 'somehow it is boring here, lonesome and dull. Something is lacking. Life is lacking; children are lacking; mothers are lacking.

¹ L. Trotsky, *Sochinenya*, vol. vi, p. 348.   ² Ibid., pp. 415–20.

Faces are bloated, and, despite honest looks, unpleasant.' And he copied with approval a remark made by a 'doctor friend', who was his guide through the Dobrudja: 'Watching the life of the Skoptsy you become convinced . . . that sex is a social principle, the source of altruism and of every sort of human nobility.'[1]

The 'doctor friend' and guide was Christian Rakovsky, whom Trotsky had met many times before in western Europe and in the Balkans. Their friendship now acquired an intimacy which was to outlast war, revolution, triumph and defeat, exile, and even purges—this was perhaps the only lasting and intimate friendship in Trotsky's life. Six or seven years older than Trotsky, Rakovsky was to play in the Russian Revolution a role reminiscent of that played by Anacharsis Cloots in the French. Like Cloots, he was an aristocrat, a thinker, and a citizen of the world; and, also like Cloots, he adopted the country of the revolution as his own and sided with the radical wing in the revolution. Even now, in 1913, he had behind him an astonishing career. The scion of a great Bulgarian landed family of northern Dobrudja, he had become a Romanian citizen when his native land was annexed by Romania in 1878. At the age of fifteen he was, as a Socialist, expelled and barred from all schools in Bulgaria. His family sent him abroad to study medicine. He graduated at the University of Montpellier; and his doctorial thesis on 'The Causes of Crime and Degeneration' earned him high repute in the medical profession. Then he studied law at another French university. In 1893, when he was twenty, he represented the Bulgarian Socialists at the congress of the International in Zürich, where he came under Plekhanov's influence and was befriended by Jules Guesde, the eminent French Marxist, and by Rosa Luxemburg. In the next year he engaged in Socialist activity in Berlin, which was still living in the aftermath of Bismarck's draconian anti-Socialist laws, and he was expelled from Germany. Thereafter he appeared at every important Labour gathering on the Continent. In 1905 he returned to Romania. As a defender of the peasants he drew upon himself the landlords' hatred, and was persecuted and finally expelled on the ground that he was a Bulgarian citizen, although he had in the meantime served as medical officer in

[1] Loc. cit.

the Romanian army. For five years the Socialist party and the
trade unions waged a campaign for his return. The government refused to admit him, denouncing him alternately as
an agent of the Russian General Staff and as a dangerous
anti-Tsarist conspirator.

In exile Rakovsky published several books, one, *Russia in the
East*, exposing Tsarist expansion in Asia, and another, *The
Rumania of the Boyars*. In his spare time, the pamphleteer, propagandist, and doctor devoted himself to historical research, the
fruit of which was *Metternich and his Age*. Writing with equal ease
in Bulgarian, French, Russian, German, and Romanian, he
contributed to political, medical, and historical periodicals in
all these languages. Repeatedly he returned to Bucharest, but
each time the expulsion order was re-enforced despite stormy
parliamentary protests and street demonstrations. Once the
French government, prompted by Jaurès, intervened to release
him from a Balkan jail, for he was also the Balkan correspondent
of Jaurès's *Humanité*. Just before the first Balkan war he was
allowed to return to Bucharest; and he became the acknowledged leader of the Romanian Socialist party, editor of its
daily, expounder of the idea of a Balkan federation, and the
most effective mouthpiece of anti-militarism in the Balkans.
At the same time he managed his family estate in the Dobrudja,
where he freed his peasants from feudal servitude and served
them as doctor. Constantly on the move between parliament,
party headquarters, and editorial offices in Bucharest and his
native estate in the country, constantly struggling against some
injustice, great or small, he would also follow the plough, often
in the tailcoat in which he had just arrived from the capital.
It was while thus inspecting his fields, the tails of his coat
flapping in the wind, in the intervals between talks with his
peasants and visits to patients, that he initiated Trotsky into the
intricacies of Romania's economics and politics.

During this trip Trotsky also entered into friendship with
Dobrodjanu Gerea, the old founder of Romanian socialism,
from whom Rakovsky had just taken over the leadership of the
party. Gerea was an enchanting and picturesque character.
A Russian Jew—his original name was Katz—one of the early
Narodniks, he had escaped from Russia and settled in Romania,
where he discovered for the Romanians their own history and

became their most important historian and literary critic and the inspirer of Romania's so-called literary renaissance. A whole generation of Romanian intellectuals learned to think politically from his book *Neo-Serfdom*; and his pupils later led the Conservative and Liberal parties as well as the Socialist. Dobrodjanu Gerea kept a restaurant at the railway station of Ploesti, and this was a place of pilgrimage for Romanian men of letters and politicians. At the counter of that restaurant Trotsky spent many an hour, picking the brains of the eccentric old sage.[1]

.   .   .   .

It was towards the end of January or the beginning of February 1913, during Trotsky's short stay in Vienna between the two Balkan wars, that Stalin's figure flitted past like a shadow on a screen. Curiously enough, Trotsky described the incident in detail only in the last year of his life.[2] One day he visited the Menshevik Skobelev, his former assistant on *Pravda*, who had just been elected a deputy to the Duma. They were sitting by a *samovar* and talking when suddenly, without knocking at the door, there entered from another room a man of middle height, haggard, with a swarthy greyish face, showing marks of smallpox. The stranger, as if surprised by Trotsky's presence, stopped a moment at the door and gave a guttural growl, which might have been taken for a greeting. Then, with an empty glass in his hand, he went to the *samovar*, filled the glass with tea, and went out without saying a word. Skobelev explained that this was a Caucasian, Djugashvili, who had just become a member of the Bolshevik Central Committee and seemed to be acquiring some importance in it. Trotsky, so he himself asserted, retained a vivid memory of this first glimpse of his future adversary and of the perturbing impression Stalin then made on him. He noticed the Caucasian's 'dim but not commonplace' appearance, 'a morose concentration' in his face, and an expression of set hostility in his 'yellow' eyes. It was his silence and the weird look of the man that engraved the casual scene on Trotsky's

---

[1] L. Trotsky, *Sochinenya*, vol. vi, pp. 386–402.

[2] This description of the meeting between Stalin and Trotsky is based on Trotsky's own memoir (written on 22 September 1939), which I found in the *Archives* at Harvard. In my *Stalin* I wrote mistakenly that 'neither Trotsky nor Stalin has described their meeting in Vienna'. Trotsky, at any rate, did not describe it before the last year of his life.

memory, enabling him to describe it with a retrospective shudder twenty-seven years later.

On internal evidence, Trotsky's description seems truthful, and not necessarily coloured by after-knowledge. The haggard, grim, inwardly concentrated and somewhat uncouth Bolshevik appears true to character: this was the Stalin of those days, after years of clandestine work, of hiding among Tartar oil-workers at Baku, and after repeated imprisonments, deportations, and escapes. Nor does Trotsky's impression of the set hostility in Stalin's looks seem unfounded; that hostility reflected the attitude of the Bolshevik Committee man towards the inspirer of the August Bloc. Stalin had seen Trotsky before, at the party congress in the Brotherhood Church in London, although Trotsky had not noticed him then. He had certainly remembered Trotsky's agitation against the Bolshevik raids and expropriations, with which Stalin had been closely concerned; and even in 1907, in his report on the congress, Stalin had already written of Trotsky's 'beautiful uselessness'. Trotsky did not know who edited the first issue of the Bolshevik paper which appropriated the name of his *Pravda*. Stalin knew. Only a fortnight or so before this silent meeting he had described Trotsky in the *Social Democrat* as a 'noisy champion with faked muscles', and under these words he had placed, for the first time, the signature Stalin.[1]

The rough growl with which he had met Trotsky came as if from the depth of the Russian log cabin.

[1] Stalin, *Sochinenya*, vol. vii, pp. 271–84; see also chapter iv in Deutscher, op. cit.

CHAPTER VIII

War and the International

THE outbreak of the First World War brought to an abrupt end the golden age of European Liberal capitalism, parliamentarianism, and reformist socialism which had flourished together in nearly half a century of peace, interrupted only by minor wars in the colonies and on the Balkan fringe. Two generations of Europeans had grown up in the optimistic belief that man had progressed far enough to secure ascendancy over nature and to change and perfect his social environment through argument, conciliation, and the majority vote. They had also been inclined to view war as a relic of a barbarous past, to which mankind would surely not revert. The accumulation of wealth in Europe as a whole had been so impressive and so rapid that it appeared to guarantee growing prosperity to all classes of society and to rule out violent social conflict.

Nowhere were these illusions more deeply seated than in the Labour movement, especially in the Second International. The International had inherited its ideology, its watchwords, and its symbols from the revolutionary periods of the past century, from the upheavals of 1848, from the Paris Commune of 1871, and from the underground struggle of German socialism against Bismarck. The watchwords and symbols spoke of the workers' international solidarity and of their irreconcilable class struggle, culminating in the overthrow of bourgeois government. The practical work of the Socialist parties had long since ceased to have much in common with these traditions. Irreconcilable class struggle had given way to peaceful bargaining and parliamentary reformism. The more successful these methods, the closer grew the connexion between the formerly outlawed Socialist parties and trade unions on the one hand and governments and associations of employers on the other; and the more effectively did national interests and viewpoints prevail over the inherited watchwords of internationalism. Up to 1914 the Socialist parties still managed, on the whole, to explain and justify their reformist work in customary revolutionary terms. Their leaders continued to profess Marxism, internationalism, and anti-militarism until the first day of war, when the International crumbled.

Of the great European nations, Russia was the only one that had participated but little in the peaceful progress of the preceding era. Her economic advance, indubitable though it had been, was insignificant in comparison with the accumulation of wealth in western Europe. It had, at any rate, been insufficient to implant in the nation habits of peaceful bargaining and compromise and to foster belief in a gradual progress from which all classes would benefit. Parliamentarianism, and all the institutions for social conciliation and arbitration which usually cluster around it, had taken no roots in Russian soil. Class struggle, in its most violent and undisguised form, had been raging from one end of the empire to the other; and Tsardom had not left the workers and peasants even the illusion that it was allowing them any influence on the nation's destinies. In the Socialist International, the Russian party had been almost the only one to treat the revolutionary traditions and watchwords with passionate seriousness and not as a matter of mere decorum.

In 1914 the Russian émigrés, with few exceptions, watched with horror the cataclysm engulfing the International; and they could hardly believe their eyes when they saw the leaders of European socialism throwing to the winds all their solemn anti-militarist resolutions and internationalist oaths and calling their working classes to fight for their emperors and to hate and kill the 'enemy'. At first, most Russian émigrés—Bolsheviks, Mensheviks, and Social Revolutionaries alike—denounced this conduct as a betrayal of socialism. Later many of them had second thoughts, but many went even farther: the slaughter of the next few years, in which millions of people laid down their lives to wrest a few yards of land from the enemy, taught them to despise and hate the humanitarian façades and shams of the European body politic. They concluded that if civilized governments in pursuit of their national power-politics found it possible to exterminate millions of people and to maim scores of millions, then it was surely the Socialists' duty to shrink from no sacrifice in the struggle for a new social order that would free mankind from such folly. The old order was giving them a lesson in ruthlessness. The 'Gothic lace-work' of European civilization

had been torn to pieces and was being trampled into the mud
and blood of the trenches.

.   .   .   .

The outbreak of war found Trotsky in Vienna—he had just
returned from Brussels where, together with Martov and Plekhanov, he had made a last appeal to the Bureau of the International asking it to intervene in the internal feud of the Russian
party. In the morning of 3 August he went to the editorial
offices of the Viennese *Arbeiterzeitung*. The news of the
assassination of Jaurès by a French chauvinist had just reached
Vienna. The diplomatic chancelleries were exchanging the last
notes, designed to shift the blame for the war on to the enemy.
General mobilization was on foot. On his way to the Socialist
editorial offices, Trotsky watched vast crowds carried away by
warlike hysteria and demonstrating in the fashionable centre
of the city. At the *Arbeiterzeitung* he found confusion. Some
editors were ready to support war. His friend Friedrich Adler
spoke with disgust about the rising flood of chauvinism. On
Adler's desk lay a pile of xenophobe pamphlets and next to it
another pile of jubilee badges prepared for a congress of the
Socialist International convened to meet in Vienna on 15
August—the International was to celebrate the twenty-fifth
anniversary of its foundation. The congress was now cancelled,
and the treasurer of the Austrian party was lamenting the
20,000 crowns he had wasted on preparations. The old Victor
Adler despised the chauvinist mood invading his own entourage, but he was too sceptical to resist. He took Trotsky to
the chief of the political police to inquire how, in view of the
expected state of war between Austro-Hungary and Russia,
he proposed to treat the Russian émigrés. The chief of the police
answered that he was preparing to intern them. A few hours
later, Trotsky and his family boarded a train for Zürich.

Neutral Switzerland became the refuge of Russian revolutionaries who had lived in Germany and Austria. To Zürich
went Karl Radek, expelled from Germany for anti-militarist
propaganda; Bukharin, who had been detained for a short time
in Vienna; while Lenin, still jailed by the Austrians in Galicia,
was to arrive a little later. The country's neutrality allowed the
Swiss Socialist party to view with tolerance and even friendliness
the internationalist propaganda of the Russians. In a workers'

H

educational association Trotsky found an eager audience for his denunciations of the war and of the Socialists who supported it. 'With Trotsky's arrival in Zürich', recollects a well-known Swiss writer, 'life returned to the Labour movement, or at least to one sector of it. He brought with him the belief . . . that from this war would arise revolution. . . . With Trotsky these were not merely words but his innermost conviction.'[1] So strongly did he sway his new audience that almost at once he was elected delegate to a national convention of the Socialist party of Switzerland. It gave the leaders of the party some trouble to explain to the rank and file that it was impolitic to give voting rights at the congress to a foreigner and a citizen of a belligerent country.

During this stay in Zürich, which lasted only a little more than two months, Trotsky wrote *The War and the International*, the first extensive statement of anti-war policy by a Russian Socialist. Its polemical edge was turned primarily against the German Social Democrats, who were arguing that in fighting Tsardom, the 'gendarme of Europe', Hohenzollern Germany was pursuing a progressive historical mission. 'In our struggle against Tsardom', Trotsky retorted, 'in which we know no truce, we have not sought and are not seeking assistance from the militarism of the Habsburgs or the Hohenzollerns. . . . We have owed a lot to the German Social Democratic Party. We have all gone through its school and learned from its successes and mistakes. It was for us not one of the parties of the International but *the* party.' All the keener was the indignation with which he now repudiated the attitude of the German Social Democrats. It was the Socialists' duty, he insisted, to stand for peace, but not for a peace that would mean a return to the *status quo* or a new balance between the imperialist powers. The Socialists' objective must be a democratic peace, without annexation and indemnities, and one allowing for the self-determination of the subject nations. Only a rising of the belligerent peoples against their rulers could achieve such a peace. This part of his argument anticipated by more than three years President Wilson's Fourteen Points; and Trotsky's pamphlet, when it appeared in the United States, had a direct influence on Wilson. Yet, 'self-determination of the nations',

[1] F. Brupbacher, *60 Jahre Ketzer*, pp. 188–9.

as Trotsky advocated it, had little in common with its Wilsonian interpretation. Its purpose was not to set up new nation-states— Trotsky, we know, had long since considered the nation-state an anachronism. The small and oppressed nations should be enabled to obtain independence in order that they might, of their free will, join in the building of an international Socialist body politic. 'In the present historical conditions', he wrote, 'the proletariat is not interested in defending an anachronistic national "Fatherland", which has become the main impediment to economic advance, but in the creation of a new, more power-ful and stable fatherland, the republican United States of Europe, as the foundation for the United States of the World. To the imperialist blind alley of capitalism the proletariat can oppose only the socialist organization of world economy as the practical programme of the day.'[1] This bold conclusion seemed unreal to many. Trotsky relates that Radek criticized it there and then on the ground that the 'productive forces' of the world, or even of Europe, had not developed sufficiently to allow of their organization on an international Socialist basis. Lenin, on his arrival in Switzerland, criticized the phrase 'the United States of Europe', because it suggested to him that Trotsky envisaged the Russian Revolution only as part of a simultaneous Europe-wide insurrection. To this controversy we shall return.

In November 1914 the pamphlet was brought out in a German translation and with the help of Swiss Socialists dispatched to Germany. German anti-militarists who distributed it were prosecuted, and Trotsky himself was indicted *in absentia* for *lèse majesté* and sentenced to several months of prison by a German court—he learned this from reports in French news-papers. The German Social Democrats insinuated that he had written his pamphlet in the interest of Russia and her allies. But, as he had not hesitated to criticize the allied Socialists who supported the war, they in their turn charged him with white-washing the German 'social-patriots'.[2]

Late in November Trotsky left Switzerland for France. *Kievan Thought* appointed him correspondent in Paris, and he eagerly seized the opportunity of watching the war from this

---

[1] *War and the International* was first published in Russian serially in the Parisian *Golos*, in November 1914, beginning with no. 59.

[2] *Golos*, no. 63, 25 November 1914.

excellent vantage-point. He was also anxious to join Martov, who was then editing in a spirit of undiluted opposition to war a Russian paper in Paris, *Golos* (*The Voice*). He had last seen Martov in Brussels, in the middle of July, where they went together to obtain from the Executive of the International a verdict against Lenin's schismatic activities; and jointly with Plekhanov they had then composed a manifesto to Russian Socialists. How remote and irrelevant all this seemed only a few months later! The leaders of the International, whom, as the highest authorities in socialism, they had solicited to intervene against Lenin, were now branded as 'social-chauvinists and traitors' by Martov and Trotsky as well as by Lenin. Plekhanov had in the meantime patriotically extolled the war on the ground that the Hohenzollerns and the Habsburgs, not the Romanovs, were the arch-enemies of progress and socialism. It seemed that the old divisions had been effaced and super-seded by new ones. Lenin, who had never abandoned a secret yearning for political reunion with Martov, the friend of his youth, stated: 'The Parisian *Golos* is at present the best socialist newspaper in Europe. The more often and the more strongly I dissented from Martov, the more categorically must I say that he is now doing exactly what a social democrat ought to do.'[1] The founder of Menshevism warmly reciprocated: he welcomed the appearance of Lenin's *Social Democrat* and agreed that the old controversies had lost all significance.[2] Events were to show that this was not so and that a reunion was, after all, impossible. But at the moment Trotsky rejoiced at its prospect.

In Paris he divided his time between work for Martov's paper and *Kievan Thought* and contacts with anti-militarist groups in the French Socialist party and trade unions. Almost from the day of his arrival he had to defend himself against charges of pro-Germanism, which emanated mostly from Alexinsky, a former Bolshevik deputy to the Duma, now a violent anti-Bolshevik and supporter of war. (The same ex-Bolshevik was in 1917 to spread the accusation that Lenin was a German spy.) A curious circumstance gave colour to the insinuations: a man bearing the name Nicholas Trotsky stood at the head of an Austrian-sponsored Union for the Liberation of the Ukraine,

[1] Lenin, *Sochinenya*, vol. xxi, p. 21, and *Golos*, no. 38, 27 October 1914.
[2] *Golos*, no. 52, 12 November 1914.

the prototype of the Ukrainian agencies that Germany was later to launch. It was easy to attribute the pro-Austrian and pro-German statements of the one Trotsky to the other, even after the author of *War and the International*, convicted in his absence by a German court, had publicly explained the confusion.[1]

Golos continued to appear for only six or seven weeks after Trotsky's arrival in Paris. Harassed by the censorship it ceased publication in the middle of January 1915. In these few weeks Trotsky gave even more definite expression to his views. The future, he wrote, held out only one set of alternatives: 'permanent war or proletarian revolution'. The war was 'a blind rebellion' of Europe's outgrown productive forces against the tight and constraining framework of the capitalist nation-states. Capitalist imperialism could break down the national barriers only by force; it was therefore incapable of breaking them down for good; and as long as it ruled the world it would plunge mankind into war after war, slaughter on slaughter, and drive civilization to its doom. Socialist reformism had no future, for it had become an integral element of the old order and an accomplice in its crimes. Those who were hoping to rebuild the old International, imagining that its leaders could by a mutual amnesty wipe out their betrayal of internationalism, were impeding the rebirth of the Labour movement.[2]

In one of the last issues of *Golos* he carried the argument even farther, saying that the struggle against 'the chauvinist falsifiers of Marxism' was only the negative side of the task ahead. The positive, constructive side was 'to gather the forces of the Third International'. This trend of thought ran parallel to Lenin's and was almost certainly inspired by it, for Lenin had formulated the same idea a little earlier.[3]

Martov had at first eagerly concurred in these views. But even before *Golos* had ceased publication, he was beset by doubts and second thoughts. The émigré Mensheviks who had, like himself, been opposed to the war, were reluctant to draw such sweeping conclusions. They held that the Socialist parties, in

[1] Ibid., nos. 62 and 63, 24 and 25 November 1914. Incidentally, in 1903–4, Leon Trotsky used to sign his writings *N.* Trotsky.

[2] Ibid., no. 66, 28 November 1914; no. 79, 13 December 1914.

[3] Ibid., no. 100, 8 January 1915; Lenin, *Sochinenya*, vol. xxi, p. 24.

supporting the war, had committed a grave error; but that they could still expunge it; and that the working classes, quite as much as their leaders, had been carried away by the social-patriotic mood. A new, 'purified' International had no chance of rallying the working classes; it would be a sect incapable of superseding the old organization. Some Mensheviks were opposed to war from pacifist rather than revolutionary conviction. Most were opposed to the Tsar, who on behalf of their nation conducted the war, rather than to war itself. And, inside Russia, some Mensheviks had committed themselves to a more patriotic attitude. All this could not but influence Martov. He was torn between his own conviction and the pull that the party he had founded exercised on him. He slid backwards and forwards, tried to patch up differences, and escaped from his dilemmas into the soothing atmosphere of the Parisian cafés.

Before the year 1914 was out, the pre-war divisions began to reimpose themselves on the recent 'solidarity of the internationalists'. Lenin insisted that his party as a whole had remained true to internationalism, while those of the Mensheviks who did so, Martov and Axelrod, were in discord with their own followers. Martov soon confided to Axelrod that Trotsky, too, was charging him, Martov, with Machiavellian tactics and with grinding the Menshevik axe. In reply Martov resorted to a well-tested stratagem: he tried to 'frighten' Trotsky (as Martov himself put it), telling him that if he were to break with the Mensheviks he would place himself at the mercy of the Bolsheviks and 'deliver himself into the hands of Grisha Zinoviev', now Lenin's chief assistant in Switzerland. But the bogy was not as effective as it used to be; and Martov related that he had to approach Trotsky with smooth diplomacy and to treat him 'like a little china statuette'.[1]

Trotsky, although as yet unwilling 'to deliver himself into the hands of Grisha Zinoviev', was nevertheless anxious to disentangle himself at last from the old alignment, dating back to the August Bloc. On 14 February 1915 he published a statement in *Nashe Slovo* (*Our Word*), the paper that had replaced *Golos*, in which for the first time he recounted publicly the inner story of his disagreements with the Mensheviks, revealing that even

[1] *Pisma Axelroda i Martova*, p. 309. Martov wrote this letter to Axelrod on 9 January 1915.

two years before he had refused to contribute to their papers and
to speak for them at the Bureau of the Socialist International;
and that he was now refusing to represent them at a planned
conference of allied Socialists in London. This repudiation of the
August Bloc was Trotsky's first and decisive step on the road
that was to lead him into the Bolshevik party.[1]

Other ties of old political connexions and friendship were
snapping as well. The most painful to Trotsky personally was
his break with Parvus, who had just declared his solidarity with
the official German Socialist leaders in support of the war and
was, in addition, engaged in vast commercial operations in the
Balkans to his own and the German government's profit. The
metamorphosis of this Marxist writer, who had so brilliantly
analysed the obsolescence of the nation-state and expounded
internationalism, into a 'Hohenzollern socialist' and a vulgar
war-profiteer, was indeed one of the most startling changes that
men were undergoing in those days. To Trotsky this was a
severe blow: his and Parvus's names had been coupled in the
joint authorship of the 'permanent revolution'; and since 1904
Parvus had participated in most of Trotsky's journalistic and
political ventures. On Parvus Trotsky must have fixed his fondest
expectations, hoping that alongside Rosa Luxemburg and Karl
Liebknecht, he would defy the chauvinism triumphant in the
German party.

More in grief than in anger, Trotsky wrote 'An Obituary on a
Living Friend', in which, even across the gulf now yawning
between them, he paid sad homage to Parvus's wasted greatness.

To turn away for a moment from the figure which now appears
under so well merited a pseudonym in the Balkans, the author of
these lines considers it a matter of personal honour to render what is
due to the man to whom he has been indebted for his ideas and
intellectual development more than to any other person of the older
generation of European social democrats. . . . Even now, I see less
reason than ever to renounce that diagnosis and prognosis, the lion's
share of which was contributed by Parvus.

Trotsky generously recalled how much he and others had

[1] *Nashe Slovo*, no. 13, 14 February 1915; *Pisma Axelroda i Martova*, pp. 315–17.
The occasion of Trotsky's statement was a speech which Larin, still a Menshevik,
made at a national convention of the Swedish Socialist party. Larin had referred to
Trotsky, Plekhanov, and Axelrod as the three leaders of the so-called Organizational Committee.

learned from Parvus and how proud they had been of him. He acknowledged that Parvus had taught him, among other things, 'to express plain thoughts in plain words'. But—'Parvus is no longer. A political Falstaff is now roaming the Balkans, and he slanders his own deceased double.'[1] When presently Parvus set up at Copenhagen a 'sociological institute', suspected of being a German propagandist agency, Trotsky publicly warned Socialists against entering into any contact with it.[2] When Parvus sent an apologia, in the form of a Letter to the Editor, Trotsky first intended to publish it, but then changed his mind.[3] Once for all he put an end to relations with his former friend; and when, after the revolution, Parvus tried to approach him and to offer his services to the Soviet government, Trotsky left these approaches without an answer. Even so, the shadow of this association was to haunt him more than once: in July 1917, the 'month of the great slander', and again during his struggle against Stalin in the years of the great slander.[4]

Nashe Slovo began to appear on 29 January 1915. This was a modest sheet of two, rarely four, pages abundantly strewn with white spaces marking the censor's deletions, and yet packed with news and comment. The paper was constantly in danger of being killed by the censor and by its own poverty. Editors and contributors received no salaries or fees. Wages of the compositors and printers were usually many months in arrears; but the half-starved workers, political émigrés like the editors, went on producing the daily without a murmur. Every now and then collections were made in shabby émigré centres such as the Russian Library in the Avenue des Gobelins, the Club of the Russian Émigrés in Montmartre, or the Library of Jewish Workers in the rue Ferdinand Duval. The donations were in *centimes* and *sous* rather than francs, and the money went to pay

[1] *Nashe Slovo*, no. 15, 14 February 1915.
[2] Ibid., no. 208, 5 October 1915. Yet, when Alexinsky used Trotsky's warning to brand Parvus as a German *agent-provocateur*, Trotsky wrote a letter to *Humanité*, explaining that he had charged Parvus with being a social-patriot, but he did not believe him to be an *agent-provocateur*. Ibid.
[3] Martov revealed this when he himself resigned from *Nashe Slovo*. Martov, 'Letter to the Editor', *Nashe Slovo*, no. 235, 9 November 1915.
[4] Rich, and enjoying great influence in the Weimar Republic, Parvus nevertheless felt frustrated and repeated his advances to the Bolsheviks, until Lenin curtly dismissed him, saying that 'the Soviets certainly need clever brains, but above all clean hands'. M. Beer, *Fifty Years of International Socialism*, p. 197.

for the meagre supply of paper. Yet, *Nashe Slovo* had a remarkable circle of contributors, nearly every one of whom was to inscribe his name prominently in the annals of the revolution; and as a journalistic venture it was much superior to the Viennese *Pravda*, and much more influential. If a Parisian journalist or politician had been told that this obscure Russian daily was politically weightier than all the French boulevard press, he would have taken this as a joke. Yet in less than three years the ideas expounded in *Nashe Slovo* would resound from Petrograd and Brest Litovsk throughout the world.

The chief organizer of the paper was Antonov-Ovseenko, a Menshevik of long standing and a former officer in the Tsarist army, who had rebelled in 1905 at the head of his detachment, had been sentenced to death, but escaped and joined in the clandestine struggle. In October 1917 he was to lead the Red Guards in the attack on the Winter Palace, arrest Kerensky's ministers, and thus bring the Bolshevik insurrection to success. Small, lean, short-sighted, of mercurial temper and imagination, the future Commissar now used his inventiveness to secure, against all odds, the existence of the paper. He 'showed a tenacity and an optimism which astonished even Trotsky, who was by no means devoid of these qualities'.[1] This was one of the new ties of friendship which were replacing the old ones in Trotsky's life: between 1923 and 1925 Antonov-Ovseenko was to be one of the leaders of the Trotskyist opposition.

It was apparently Antonov-Ovseenko who invited Trotsky and Martov to be joint editors of *Nashe Slovo*. Trotsky at first refused, suspecting that the paper was meant to serve a narrowly Menshevik purpose.[2] But eventually he assumed the co-editorship and, in constant controversy with Martov, so strongly impressed his own outlook on *Nashe Slovo* that the paper came to be considered his personal domain. Lunacharsky, the God-seeking Bolshevik, who had broken away from Lenin and who was to become the revolution's great Commissar of Education, worked for the daily and sometimes acted as peacemaker between Trotsky and Martov. Ryazanov, who had also come from Vienna to Paris, was one of the pillars of *Nashe Slovo*. Lozovsky, the future chief of the Red trade unions' International,

[1] A. Rosmer, *Le Mouvement ouvrier pendant la guerre*, pp. 244–9.
[2] *Pisma Axelroda i Martova*, p. 319.

now leader of a small trade union of Jewish hat-makers in Paris, surveyed French political and syndicalist developments. Manuilsky, the Bolshevik boycotter, future chief of the Stalinist Comintern and Foreign Minister of the Ukraine, contributed under the pen-name *Bezrabotnyi*—the Jobless. His only 'job' at the moment was that of the *gérant* of *Nashe Slovo*, the figure-head editor, legally responsible to the authorities. He regaled the editorial staff with witty anecdotes, which he composed and narrated with the *élan* of a first-rate comedian. Angelica Balabanov, the half-Russian, half-Italian Socialist, exposed in *Nashe Slovo* her old friend and protégé Mussolini, whom she had once lifted from the gutter to prominence in the Italian party and who was now urging neutral Italy to join in the war. Balabanov also translated into many languages, but especially into Italian, Trotsky's more important articles, helping thereby to keep the bulk of the Italian Socialist party in opposition to war. The editorial team further included men like Sokolnikov, later one of the chief organizers of the October insurrection, signatory to the peace of Brest Litovsk, Commissar of Finance, and diplomat; Pokrovsky the historian, and a few eminent Polish Socialists.

Of the outside contributors Chicherin, correspondent in London, should be mentioned first. Descendant of one of the first families of the Russian aristocracy, former Secretary of a Tsarist Embassy, he had thrown away his diplomatic career to cultivate in obscurity the great passions of his life: revolution, music, and history. For years he was a familiar figure in Paris at the Montparnasse branch of the French Socialist party. He used to appear there before midnight, wrapped in a vast Spanish cloak, the pockets of which were bulging with an incredible number of books, pamphlets, and periodicals: and there for many an hour of the night he would develop his ideas in leisurely fashion to those who would listen, supporting his arguments with quotations from his pocket reference library. These bat-like habits and this taste for keen but unhurried argument he was to retain as Foreign Secretary of the Soviet republic. In Paris, Chicherin was still a Menshevik, but he was too aloof and wayward to involve himself in émigré politics, and so nobody even guessed the talents hidden in him. The war had caught him in London. In a memoir, which does not seem to

have been published, Trotsky says that Chicherin's correspondence from London was written in a vaguely social-patriotic
spirit, but was so uncommonly subtle and original that he,
Trotsky, was glad to have it in the paper.[1] Later in the war
Chicherin was interned in Britain as an anti-war propagandist.

From Sweden and Denmark Alexandra Kollontai and Moissei
Uritsky, both former Mensheviks, disgusted with 'social-patriotism' and rapidly evolving towards Bolshevism, contributed
more or less regularly. Kollontai was to be Commissar of Social
Welfare in Lenin's first government, while Uritsky—he had
worked for the Viennese *Pravda* too—was to become one of the
foremost Bolshevik leaders in 1917. The list of contributors
included Theodore Rothstein, the Anglo-Russian historian of
Chartism and future Soviet Ambassador in Persia; Radek,
Rakovsky, and Maisky the future Soviet Ambassador in
London. Rarely has any paper had so brilliant a galaxy of
contributors.

The members of the editorial team were at one in their
opposition to war and 'social-patriotism'; but, apart from this,
they represented various shades of opinion. The editorial conferences, which took place every morning in the printing shop,
developed into lively disputes which in their turn were reflected in the columns of the paper. As is usual in cases in which
outward agreement conceals differences in frame of mind and
approach, the controversies were involved and seemingly
irrelevant; and often they degenerated into bitter wrangling.
We might well ignore these wranglings were it not for the fact
that they manifested the re-alignment of groups and individuals
who were soon to come forward as leaders of great parties and
mass movements. Next to Lenin's *Social Democrat*, Trotsky's
paper was at this juncture the most important laboratory of the
revolution. The issue passionately debated in it concerned the
demarcation line that was to be drawn between the internationalists and the social-patriots. Where, how firmly, with
what degree of finality should it be drawn? In their attempts to
answer this question groups and individuals either drew closer
to, or drifted away from, one another, until eventually some of
those who at first seemed of one mind found themselves on
different sides of that line.

[1] *The Trotsky Archives.*

Broadly speaking, three groups tried to influence *Nashe Slovo*. Martov exerted himself to reconcile his loyalties to Socialist internationalism and to Menshevism; and gradually he transferred his old distrust of Bolshevism to the single-minded 'angular' internationalism which Lenin preached. At the other extreme were the prodigal sons of Bolshevism, Manuilsky and Lozovsky, and to a lesser extent Lunacharsky, whom the impulse of war was driving back towards Lenin. Trotsky held an intermediate position; he tried to curb the pro-Bolshevik group and also to persuade Martov that he should dissociate himself from Menshevik social-patriots. 'The editorial conferences', Lunacharsky relates, 'dragged on in long debates, in the course of which Martov evaded with amazing elasticity of mind and almost sophistic slyness a clear answer. . . . Trotsky often attacked him very angrily.'[1] In the first issue of the paper Martov had, in fact, denounced some of his followers;[2] but after a few weeks he argued that it was wrong to charge the 'social-patriots' with treason to socialism.[3] The pro-Bolshevik group then indignantly turned against Martov; but Trotsky, for all his anger in debate, still shrank from a break with him.

Nevertheless, recent events and the continued débâcle of European socialism impelled him to review in his thoughts past controversies, and, as he himself put it, 'to see Lenin in a new light'. This revision, in all its gradualism and minute twists and turns can be followed through his writings in *Nashe Slovo*. In July 1915 he admitted, for instance, that the pre-war divisions in the Russian party had a close bearing on the current controversy, and that the Bolsheviks formed the core of the internationalist sector in Russian socialism. But he was still afraid that they were out to dominate the non-Bolshevik internationalists.[4] Martov protested against this and similar statements, refused to bear responsibility for the direction Trotsky was giving to the paper, and threatened to resign. At the same time, Lenin subjected Trotsky to relentless criticism, saying that Trotsky's internationalism was purely verbal, for it did not prevent him from co-operating with Menshevik social-patriots.

[1] A. Lunacharsky, *Revolutsionnye Siluety*, pp. 23–26, 68.
[2] *Nashe Slovo*, no. 1, 29 January 1915. Martov repudiated there the Menshevik periodical *Nasha Zarya*, published in Petrograd.
[3] Ibid., no. 31, 5 March 1915.
[4] Ibid., no. 146, 23 July 1915.

In the middle of this dispute there occurred the one great event of those days in which Trotsky played a central part. On 5 September 1915 there assembled at Zimmerwald, a little village in the Swiss mountains outside Berne, an international conference of Socialists, the first to take place since the outbreak of war. The initiative came from Italian Socialists who had had no intention of convening the gathering in defiance of the pre-war International. Earlier in the year an Italian Socialist deputy, Ordino Morgari, went to Paris to request the president of the International, the Belgian Socialist Vandervelde, to convene a session of the Executive. 'As long as German soldiers are billeted in the homes of Belgian workers', Vandervelde replied, 'there can be no talk of convening the Executive.' 'Is the International then a hostage in the hands of the Entente?' asked Morgari. 'Yes, a hostage!' replied Vandervelde. Morgari then asked for a conference at least of the Socialist parties of neutral countries. When Vandervelde rejected this suggestion too, the Italian deputy approached Martov, Trotsky, and Swiss Socialists with the proposal to convene a conference independently of the old International. Thus came into being the movement which was to become the forerunner of the Third International.[1]

Thirty-eight delegates from eleven countries, belligerent and neutral, assembled at Zimmerwald to reassert their international solidarity.[2] The German delegation was headed by several influential deputies of the Reichstag and brought greetings from the imprisoned Karl Liebknecht. The French delegation was less impressive, for the anti-militarist groups in the French party were weak and only a few syndicalist leaders arrived. Lenin represented the Bolsheviks, Axelrod the Mensheviks. Rakovsky and Kolarov came from the Balkans, and there were Polish, Swiss, Dutch, Italian, and other delegates. In normal times a gathering of this sort would not have been considered very representative; but in the days when it was a crime for

[1] Trotsky described the preliminaries to the Zimmerwald conference in *Nashe Slovo*, no. 109, 10 May 1916.

[2] Before the opening of the conference the Russians met to discuss their representation. *Nashe Slovo* sent three delegates: Martov, Trotsky, and Manuilsky, representing the three attitudes among the editorial staff. Lenin questioned their credentials and Martov and Manuilsky resigned in favour of Trotsky. The conference admitted Trotsky and accorded him full voting rights, but only against Lenin's protests. Trotsky related this with mild resentment in *Nashe Slovo*, no. 212, 9 October 1915.

citizens of belligerent countries to be in contact with one another, the mere fact that well-known labour leaders 'shook hands across the barbed wire and bleeding trenches' was an unheard-off challenge to all warring governments.

The participants in the conference were, however, less united in purpose than their resolutions implied. The majority were pacifists, eager to reassert their faith, but not inclined to go farther. A minority, grouped around Lenin, who for the first time now came forward as the protagonist of an international and not merely of a Russian trend in socialism, urged the conference to adopt a defeatist attitude towards all warring governments, to call upon the peoples to 'turn the imperialist war into civil war', and to proclaim the need of a new International. This the majority refused to do. On most points Trotsky was in agreement with the minority, although he would not endorse Lenin's revolutionary defeatism. (It was, he wrote, in the interest of socialism that the war should end 'without victors and vanquished'.) He held, moreover, that these differences should be transcended so as to enable the conference unanimously to condemn the war. In this everybody concurred, and Trotsky was asked to draw up a statement of principles, which was soon to become famous as the Zimmerwald Manifesto. In it he stirringly described the plight of embattled Europe, placing the responsibility on the capitalist order, the governments, and the self-betrayed Socialist parties; and he called upon the working people to recover from their intoxication with chauvinism and to put an end to the slaughter. Rousing though it was, the Manifesto was vague in its conclusions. It did not call for civil war that would put an end to the imperialist war; and it did not envisage the new International. The conference adopted the Manifesto unanimously, but Lenin's group placed its reservations on record. Finally, an international committee was elected which, although it was not yet nominally opposed to the second International, was nevertheless to become the nucleus of the third.

Only good luck enabled Trotsky safely to return to France. On the frontier his luggage was opened for examination, and in it he carried all the Zimmerwald documents. An inspector picked them up, but seeing on top of them a sheet of paper with a conspicuous, patriotic inscription *Vive le Tsar!*, he did not bother to examine them further. At Zimmerwald during the sessions, while he had been covering sheets of paper with doodles, Trotsky had copied those words from an article by Gustave Hervé, the French semi-anarchist turned patriot. In Paris the censorship suppressed reports of the conference. 'All the same, the conference has taken place; and this is a momentous fact, Mr. Censor', Trotsky wrote in *Nashe Slovo*. 'The French press has written more than once that Karl Liebknecht has saved Germany's honour. The Zimmerwald conference has saved the honour of Europe.' 'An obtuse professor', Trotsky went on, 'had written in *Journal des Debats* that the conference had no significance and that it gave comfort to Germany; an equally obtuse professor across the Rhine had written that it was of no significance and that it gave comfort to the Entente. If the conference was so impotent and insignificant, why have your superiors banned every mention of it? And why, despite all the banning, have you yourselves had to begin to discuss it? You shall still discuss it, gentlemen. . . . No force will delete it from the political life of Europe.'[1] The article was more than usually mutilated by the censor, the white gaps taking more space than the printed matter.

Almost since the beginning of his stay in Paris, Trotsky, at first jointly with Martov and then alone, kept in touch with small French anti-militarist groups, mainly syndicalist, headed by Bourderon and Merrheim, as well as with Alfred Rosmer and Pierre Monatte, who were later to found the French Communist party. Trotsky attended regularly the weekly meetings of these groups, which were closely watched by the police. He gave them the benefit of his political experience, and explained to them the background of the war and the developments in foreign Labour movements; he inspired their policy and brought them into the Zimmerwald movement. He thus acted as godfather to the French Communist party, with which he was to maintain close ties in later years.

In addition to these activities he kept up his correspondence for *Kievan Thought*, which earned him his livelihood. *Kievan Thought* supported the war, and so in his articles he had to tack about cautiously to avoid a breach with the paper. The Kievan editor was only too glad to publish the Paris correspondent's denunciations of German imperialism, but his criticisms of the

[1] *Nashe Slovo*, no. 218, 19 October 1915.

Entente were unwelcome. Trotsky could tell his readers in Russia only half the truth as he saw it, that half which somehow fitted in with official Russian policy. He tried on occasion to tell it in such a manner that the shrewd reader should guess the suppressed half of the story. To the author of the Zimmerwald Manifesto this was a most embarrassing position; and so he confined himself more and more to reportage and strictly military surveys.

The man who from Zimmerwald had defied the mighty of the world and whose Manifesto resounded throughout Europe did not spurn the chores of journalism. He travelled to the south of France and to the Channel ports to gather impressions and to gauge the moods behind the fighting lines. As he had done during the Balkan wars, he visited the hospitals to talk to the wounded, and mingled with French and British soldiers in the cafés and market places of small French towns. With never-flagging curiosity he listened to the harrowing tales of wartime refugees, Belgian, French, and Serbian, and filled his notebooks with their stories. Back in Paris, he would read some twenty European newspapers a day at the Café Rotonde, where Martov could be found at almost any time of the day. From the Rotonde he rushed to a library to study serious military periodicals and literature, French, English, Italian, German, Austrian, and Swiss. In these journeys and studies he found relaxation and refreshment; and they also prepared him for a great job ahead. As the experience of a Captain of the Hampshire Grenadiers had not been useless to Gibbon as historian of the Roman Empire, so the experience of a conscientious military correspondent would one day be of use to the founder of the Red Army.

His military correspondence, reprinted in his *Works*, has been altogether forgotten since his political eclipse; yet, together with his writings of the years of the civil war, it should have earned him a place in the history of military thought. Like nearly all Marxists who seriously delve into military matters, he was greatly influenced by Clausewitz's classical strategic conceptions. Amateur though he was, he had this advantage over contemporary military experts, Clausewitzian and anti-Clausewitzian, that he saw behind the clash of arms a contest of economic powers and political régimes; and that he had a shrewder eye for the morale of the embattled nations.

Almost from the first weeks of hostilities he forecast, against prevailing expert opinion, the prolonged and bloody stalemate of trench warfare, and ridiculed the hopes which Clausewitz's German epigones were placing on the offensive power of their army.[1] He did not share, however, the characteristically French illusions of a purely defensive strategy and a war of attrition. He pointed out that their conception of defence would impel the French repeatedly to undertake the most costly and futile offensives, and that a war of attrition would be more, not less, bloody than ordinary warfare. He explained the military stalemate as the result of an equilibrium between the economic resources of the hostile coalitions. This approach, which we can only baldly summarize here, enabled him over the first three years of the war to forecast with rare accuracy the course of successive military operations. With the prospect of a relentless strategic deadlock he connected the vistas of revolution, for he expected that the stalemate of trench warfare would drag on almost indefinitely, sap the foundations of the old society, and drive the peoples to despair and revolt. Sometimes, it is true, he expected a development of strategy and technology which would break the stalemate, but not before very late in the war; and he came close to adumbrating the invention of the tank.[2] Yet, on the whole, the nightmare, for so long only too real, of the self-perpetuating mutual slaughter of equally balanced forces overshadowed his military thinking; and it would still do so even in the last year of the war, when, as we shall see later, it would cause him to make important errors of judgement.

Even while he was surveying with detachment the course of hostilities and eagerly absorbing military theories, his mind was gripped by the tragedy of Europe, bleeding and distraught.

[1] L. Trotsky, *Sochinenya*, vol. ix, pp. 7–15.

[2] On one occasion he forecast that after the war the military leaders would forget or neglect this new weapon which would decide the outcome of the war. He thus came very near to predicting the neglect of the tank by the British and French General Staffs on the eve of World War II. Ibid., p. 190. In a sarcastic aside he dismissed in advance the illusion of a Maginot Line as it was beginning to emerge from the French experience in World War I. 'The triumph of the French [in defence] is so evident that not only military experts bow to it, but also . . . pacifists. One of them . . . has reached the happy conclusion that war can be eliminated altogether if the boundaries of states are reinforced by continuous trenches and demarcated by a powerful electric current. Poor, scrofulous pacifist who seeks a shelter in the trenches.' Loc. cit.

This preoccupation with the 'human factor' in war lifts his military writings far above the professional level. For example, his essay 'Barbed Wire and Scissors' is a technical study of trench warfare and, at the same time, an intuitive and imaginative reconstruction of its psychological impact on the huge armies involved in it. It is almost incredible that the author of this essay had never even seen a trench—so intimately did he penetrate its strange atmosphere, foreshadowing much of what writers like Remarque, Zweig, Hasek, Sherriff, Barbusse, Gläser, and others were to write after the war in autobiographical novels and plays.

If the fate of Trotsky's writings, we repeat, and the extent to which they are read or ignored had not been so inseparably bound up with his political fortunes and with the sympathies and antipathies that his mere name evokes, he would have had his niche in literature on the strength of these writings alone. This is especially true of his descriptive pieces. In these he usually narrates the adventures of a single soldier, revealing through them some significant aspect of the war. In 'The Seventh Infantry Regiment in the Belgian Epic', for instance, which he wrote at Calais in February 1915, he describes the experiences of De Baer, a student of law at the University of Louvain, in whom he focuses the whole drama of invaded and occupied Belgium. He follows the young lawyer from the outbreak of the war through the confusion of mobilization, through battles, retreats, encirclements, and escapes, through a sequence of strange yet quite normal scenes, in which we see and feel the elemental upsurge of patriotism in the invaded people, their sufferings, their unwitting, often accidental heroism, a heroism in which the tragic and the comic are intertwined, and, above all, the boundless absurdity of war. The student De Baer goes through appalling torments in the trenches; then he is detailed to a court martial to act as defending counsel for fellow soldiers; he returns to the trenches and unknowingly distinguishes himself in battle and is decorated with much pomp and solemnity. After that, almost alone of his encircled company, he survives without a scratch, and loses only his spectacles in the fray. Sent to a hospital in France, he is found to be too short-sighted to be a soldier, and is released. Thrown out by the military machine in a foreign country, he finds no employment; and, when the author meets him, he is starving and in rags. Because of its great realistic simplicity, the story reads like a modernized fragment of *War and Peace*. The author makes no propaganda; his hero is no proletarian; the patriotic feelings of the invaded Belgians, in seeming contradiction with the writer's political views, are described with such warm sympathy that the story might fit excellently into a patriotic anthology of Belgian martyrdom; all the more effectively does he expose the absurdity of war.

'From a Notebook of a Serb' is written in a similar vein. There the epic of another small nation, first flattered, then exploited, and then trampled on by the great powers, is brought into focus in the adventures of Todor Todorovich, a Serbian peasant from the Austrian-ruled Banat who has deserted from the Austrian army. Todor Todorovich plods alongside the retreating Serbian army, through burning villages and ice-bound mountains. Frequently he is in danger of being shot either as a deserter and Serbian traitor by the Austrians or as an Austrian spy by the Serbs. Each time he has a tragi-comic escape and trudges on to stare at scenes of Dantesque horror, until he becomes almost a symbol of man, forlorn amid the primordial savagery which has burst through the thin crust of civilization.[1]

In other essays such as 'The Psychological Puzzles of War' Trotsky tried to feel himself into the condition in which the European mind would emerge from the holocaust. He guessed that the man of the trenches would not easily adjust himself to 'normal' society:

. . . the present disaster will, in the course of years, decades, and centuries, emit a sanguinary radiation, in the light of which future generations will view their own fate, just as Europe has hitherto sensed the radiation of the great French Revolution and of the Napoleonic wars. Yet how small were those events . . . in comparison with what we are performing or experiencing now, and especially with what we are heading for. The human mind tends to banality; only slowly and reluctantly does it clamber up to the height of these colossal events . . . it strives unwittingly to belittle for itself their

[1] Op. cit., pp. 87–112. 'Where is the modern Swift to place before bourgeois Europe his satirical mirror?' Trotsky asked in *Nashe Slovo* (16 Mày 1916), describing satirically how the embassies, general staffs, and academies of Germany and France tried to exploit, each for its own patriotic purposes, an anniversary of Cervantes.

import so that it can more easily assimilate them. . . . It is not our mind that masters the great events; on the contrary the events, arising from a combination, interplay, and concatenation of great objective historical forces, compel our sluggish, lazy mind, waddlingly and limpingly to adjust itself. About this fact, so hurtful to our megalomania, our second nature, there cries out, in the merged thunder of all the guns and weapons, the present fate of the civilized nations.[1]

.   .   .   .

Towards the turn of the year 1915 the cleavage in the Zimmerwald movement became accentuated. The minority, led by Lenin, was more and more emphatically dissociating itself from the pacifist Socialists and from those 'centrists' who tried to hold a middle position. The controversy grew in bitterness as the belligerent governments, supported by the 'social-patriots', proceeded to repress the Zimmerwald movement, to imprison its leaders and adherents or to send them to the trenches. Among the Russian émigrés feelings were incensed by the conduct of the Menshevik deputies in the Duma—the Bolshevik deputies had already been tried and deported to Siberia. The leader of the Menshevik deputies, the Georgian Chkheidze, had spoken in the Duma about Zimmerwald, defending it in so ambiguous and half-hearted a manner that the defence amounted to repudiation. Lenin at once denounced Chkheidze and insisted that every Russian member of the Zimmerwald movement should do the same.

The bitterness was aggravated when, in Russia, Vera Zasulich and Potresov, like Plekhanov, came out in support of the war. To Trotsky this was a new blow and disillusionment. He had first embroiled himself with Lenin from devotion to the veterans of the party; and although he had in the meantime outgrown the veterans and had had his differences with them, his devotion to them had remained undiminished. Now he saw all of them, with the partial exception of the émigré Axelrod, 'deserting the cause'. With Chkheidze, too, he had been politically associated before the war: it was to Chkheidze that in 1913 he had written in a letter about that 'master squabbler Lenin . . . that professional exploiter of the backwardness

[1] L. Trotsky, *Sochinenya*, vol. ix, pp. 244–8. These words were written in September 1915.

of the Russian labour movement . . . '.[1] Now Trotsky still tried to find mitigating circumstances for Chkheidze's behaviour; but with Vera Zasulich he broke with a heavy heart as he had broken with Parvus.[2] More than once he had to ask himself what had caused the old guard to abandon their principles, and whether Lenin had not been right all along in spurning them and going his way.

In his autobiography Trotsky describes his evolution towards Bolshevism as a process in which of his own accord he was drawing closer and closer to Lenin, and he does no justice to the influence which some of his contributors had on him. The truth which emerges from the pages of *Nashe Slovo* is that he was prodded and pushed that way by the pro-Bolsheviks on his staff, who, although they were men of much smaller stature, were quicker in grasping the trend of the realignment and urged him to abandon his old loyalties and to draw conclusions from the new situation.[3]

One ought not to and one need not (wrote one of them) share the sectarian narrow-mindedness of [Lenin's group] . . . but it cannot be denied that . . . in Russia, in the thick of political action, so-called Leninism is freeing itself from its sectarian features . . . and that the workers' groups connected with *Social Democrat* (Lenin's paper) are now in Russia the only active and consistently internationalist force. . . . For those internationalists who belong to no faction there is no way out but to merge with the Leninists, which in most cases means joining the Leninist organization. . . . There exists, of course, the danger that through such a merger we shall forfeit some valuable features . . . but the spirit of the class struggle, which lives not in literary laboratories but in the dust and tension of mass political strife, will brace itself and boldly develop.[4]

Another writer, himself a former Menshevik, tried to explain why the founding fathers of Russian socialism had turned into

[1] This letter to Chkheidze was found in the archives of the Russian police in 1921. Olminsky, who was in charge of the party archives, wrote to Trotsky asking him whether the letter should be published. Trotsky advised against publication, saying that it was impolitic to revive old controversies, especially as he did not think that he was always wrong in what he had written against the Bolsheviks. See Trotsky's letter to Olminsky of 6 December 1921 in the *Trotsky Archives*.

[2] *Nashe Slovo*, no. 58, 9 March 1916.

[3] When Trotsky was writing his autobiography, in 1929, most of his former pro-Bolshevik contributors to *Nashe Slovo* had sided with Stalin against him.

[4] *Nashe Slovo*, no. 15, 19 January 1916.

'social-patriotic opportunists'. They had begun their political
and literary careers with a critique of the voluntarist Utopias of
the *Narodniks*; and this left a lasting impression on their outlook.
In their polemics against the *Narodniks* they had concentrated
so exclusively on 'objective conditions', on what was and what
was not historically possible in Russia, that they became the
slaves of their own determinism. The Mensheviks had indubitable merits in analysing the social conditions of Russia and in
attempting to Europeanize the movement (merits, the writer
added, which Trotsky's *Pravda* shared with them). But they completely neglected to cultivate the revolutionary will, which
changes the social conditions within which it works. The principle of will and action was as much essential to the Marxist
doctrine as was its determinism; and this principle, so the writer
concluded, was embodied in Lenin's group. That was why the
Mensheviks had floated with the tide of events to their social-
patriotic débâcle, while the Bolsheviks had the strength to
resist the tide.[1]

Manuilsky and Lozovsky, especially the former, argued along
the same lines. Still refusing to accept Leninism as the 'ready
made and rounded off form of the new internationalist ideology',
still criticizing its 'national narrow-mindedness and angular
crudity', Manuilsky, nevertheless, insisted that Bolshevism,
because of its emphasis on will and action, had legitimately
become the core of the Russian revolutionary movement.
'History', he wrote, 'has placed the Russian working class in
a position more favourable for revolutionary initiative than that
in which the western proletariat has found itself. . . . It has imposed higher duties and obligations on us than on European
labour.' All the more urgent was it to find a common language
with Lenin's group. Discreetly, Manuilsky criticized Trotsky,
without mentioning him by name, for his attempts to excuse
the ambiguous conduct of Chkheidze and of the other Menshevik deputies.[2]

Quite perceptibly these influences worked on Trotsky. If
a distaste for the 'sectarian' and distinctly Russian side of

---

[1] The author of this article was K. Zalewski, a Polish Socialist, who had before
the war sided with the Menshevik liquidators. *Nashe Slovo*, nos. 35, 36, 11 and 12
February 1916.

[2] *Nashe Slovo*, nos. 75–78, 29 March–1 April 1916. In the same issues Trotsky
went on defending Chkheidze in unsigned editorials.

Bolshevism lingered on in a man like Manuilsky, it was all the stronger in Trotsky. But he, too, preached close co-operation with 'the very active and influential group of Leninists', although he was still afraid of remaining tête-à-tête with it.[1] When he made the *rapprochement* with the Bolsheviks a principle of editorial policy, Martov, after many 'ultimatums and counter-ulti-matums', at last resentfully resigned from *Nashe Slovo*.[2] Thus snapped another old friendship, and thus Trotsky made another step towards Lenin and the Third International.

However, neither Trotsky nor even Lenin had yet made up his mind to secede at once, come what might, from the Second Inter-national. In the spring of 1916 the leaders of that International, alarmed by the response which the Zimmerwald movement had evoked, at last convened at the Hague a session of their Inter-national Bureau. In *Nashe Slovo*, Lozovsky urged the Russian Socialists to boycott the conference or to attend it only in order to declare demonstratively that they would not rejoin the pre-war organization. In a reply which is of considerable interest to the historian of the Third International, Trotsky pleaded for a more cautious attitude: '. . . it is possible that we, the left, may be in a position not to attend The Hague conference, if we have the masses behind us. We might then go there only in order to make a demonstration . . . as Lozovsky, pre-judging the issue, one-sidedly counsels us to do. But it is also possible that the alignment inside the labour movement may compel us to take up for a time the position of a left wing in *their* [i.e. the Second] International.'[3] He recalled that the Zimmerwald movement had not arisen as an explicit attempt to set up a new Inter-national. Trotsky's attitude in this matter was a shade less definite than Lenin's. At the end of April 1916 Lenin carried with him the second conference of the Zimmerwald movement, which assembled at Kienthal, in Switzerland. Trotsky did not attend—this time the French authorities did not permit him to cross the frontier. But in defiance of the raging censorship, he stated in *Nashe Slovo* his solidarity with the Kienthal resolutions.[4]

---

[1] Ibid., no. 89, 14 April 1916.   [2] Ibid., no. 93, 19 April 1916.
[3] Ibid., no. 97, 23 April 1916. In support of his attitude Trotsky quoted *The Communist*, a Bolshevik paper, edited by Bukharin, which had expressed a similar view.
[4] Ibid., nos. 111, 115, 12 and 17 May 1916. See also issue of 2 September 1916.

Differences on broader issues still separated Trotsky from Lenin. There was, first, the disagreement over revolutionary defeatism. 'The revolution is not interested in any further accumulation of defeats', Trotsky wrote, while Lenin expounded the view that Russia's military defeat would favour revolution. On the face of it, two extremely opposed views seem to clash here; and so the Stalinist historians present the story. Actually the difference was one of propagandist emphasis, not of policy. Both Lenin and Trotsky urged Socialists to turn the war into a revolution and to spread their ideas and views among workers and in the armed forces, even if this should weaken their country militarily. Both agreed that the fear of national defeat should not deflect the Socialist from doing his duty. For all the provocative emphasis which Lenin gave to his defeatism, he did not ask his followers to engage, or to encourage others to engage, in sabotage, desertion, or other strictly defeatist activities. He merely argued that although revolutionary agitation would weaken Russia's military strength, Russian Socialists were bound in duty and honour to take this risk in the hope that German revolutionaries would do the same so that in the end all the imperialist governments would be vanquished by the joint efforts of the internationalists. The defeat of any one country would thus prove only an incident in the revolution's advance from country to country. Trotsky, and with him many of Lenin's own followers, refused to tie the fortunes of revolution so exclusively to defeat.[1] It was enough, Trotsky argued, to preach and prepare revolution, no matter what the military situation. Each attitude had, from the viewpoint of those who held it, its advantages and disadvantages. Trotsky's non-defeatism did not in advance expose the internationalist to the charge that he was giving aid and comfort to the enemy. Lenin's attitude, for all its obvious tactical inconvenience, was better calculated to make the revolutionary immune from warlike patriotism and to erect an insurmountable barrier between him and his adversaries. In 1917 these two shades of opposition to war merged without controversy or friction in the policy of the Bolshevik party.

Another controversy concerned the 'United States of Europe'. Although this has come to be regarded as a hallmark of Trotskyism, Lenin had included it in his own theses on Socialist war

[1] *Nashe Slovo*, no. 68, 21 March 1916; *Sotsial-Demokrat*, no. 50.

policy as early as September 1914.[1] 'The United States of Europe' epitomized the unshakeable hope of both Lenin and Trotsky that at the end of the war the whole of Europe would be engulfed by proletarian revolution. Lenin, nevertheless, raised objections to the manner in which Trotsky advanced the idea, because at one moment Trotsky seemed to imply that revolution could break out in Russia only simultaneously with a European upheaval. Such a view, Lenin pointed out, might be an excuse for quietism and might lead the Socialists of any country to wait passively until 'the others begin'. Or it might contain the pacifist illusion that the United States of Europe could be erected on a capitalist, instead of a Socialist, foundation. The revolution, Lenin wrote, might well develop and succeed in Russia before it did so in the rest of Europe, because 'the unevenness of economic and political development is an ineluctable law of capitalism'. For this criticism Trotsky had given some grounds when, carried away by the grandiose vista of a unified Socialist continent, he had argued that the war 'breaking up the nation-state, was also destroying the national basis for revolution'.[2] If the whole trend of Trotsky's reasoning is kept in mind, the interpretation which Lenin gave to these words appears incorrect, since Trotsky had argued all along that the Russian revolution would be the first to conquer and that it would then stimulate revolutions elsewhere.

To Lenin's criticism Trotsky replied: 'That no country should in its struggle idly wait for the others to begin is a basic idea which it is useful to repeat. . . . Without waiting for the others we have to begin the struggle on our national ground, fully confident that our initiative would give a fillip . . . to other countries.'[3] He went on to develop an argument which contained the seeds of a controversy not with Lenin but with Lenin's successor. It was true, Trotsky wrote, that capitalism had developed 'unevenly'; and so the revolution was likely to win in a single country first. Yet 'the unevenness of the development is itself uneven.' Some European countries had advanced, economically and culturally, more than others; but Europe, as a whole, had progressed further than Africa or Asia and was riper for Socialist revolution. There was, therefore, no

---

[1] Lenin, *Sochinenya*, vol. xxi, p. 4.   [2] *Nashe Slovo*, no. 23, 24 February 1915.
[3] Ibid., no. 87, 12 April 1916.

need to contemplate the prospects of a revolution permanently
or for long isolated in a single country. There was no need to
fall into 'that national revolutionary Messianic mood which
prompts one to see one's own nation-state as destined to lead
mankind to socialism. If a victorious social revolution were
really conceivable within the boundaries of a single . . . nation,
then this Messianic attitude . . . would have its relative historic
justification.' 'To fight for the preservation of the national base
for social revolution by methods which threaten to cut the
international ties of the proletariat, means to sap the foundations of the revolution. *The revolution must begin on a national basis
but, in view of the economic and military-political interdependence of the
European states, it cannot be concluded on that basis.*'[1]

With this attitude Lenin had no quarrel. What strikes us now
about Trotsky's words is his prescience, negatively expressed,
of the 'national revolutionary Messianic mood', which views
'its own nation-state as destined to lead mankind to socialism'.
Of this mood Stalin, in his later years, was to become the
exponent.[2]

.   .   .   .

The second year of Trotsky's stay in Paris was drawing to a
close when, on 15 September 1916, the French police banned
Nashe Slovo. The next day Trotsky himself was ordered to leave
the country. Socialist deputies protested to the Prime Minister,
Aristide Briand, and obtained a delay in the enforcement of the
order. Legally there was no ground for the expulsion. *Nashe
Slovo* had not been able to say more than the censorship had
allowed it to say; and although Trotsky had often wrangled
with and poked fun at the censor, he had scrupulously complied
with his directions. Nor did the French government take a
grave view of Trotsky's contacts with the still feeble French
anti-war groups. But the Tsarist Embassy intrigued against the
revolutionary émigrés, and the French complied, willy-nilly,

---

[1] Loc. cit.

[2] Trotsky took it for granted, of course, that the prospect of a capitalist United
States of Europe was Utopian. German imperialism, he wrote, was striving to
unify the old continent under its domination; but even if it succeeded, it would
merely produce a compulsory military alliance and customs union, 'a parody of the
United States of Europe, written in fire and by the sword of German militarism'.
Only Socialist revolution could bring about a voluntary union of the peoples.
Nashe Slovo, no. 29, 4 February 1916.

with the wishes of their allies. An accident assisted the embassy's intrigue. A mutiny, partly provoked by a secret agent of the Russian police, had broken out among Russian soldiers disembarked at Marseilles; and it was claimed that the mutineers had acted under the influence of *Nashe Slovo*. Trotsky feared that the French intended to extradite him to Russia. For six weeks he tried in vain to obtain permission to enter Switzerland or Italy or to travel through England to Scandinavia until, on 30 October, he was detained by two police agents and deported to the Spanish frontier.

Before the expulsion he addressed an 'Open Letter' to Jules Guesde, the pioneer of French Marxism who had become Minister of War:

Is it possible for an honest socialist not to fight against you? In an epoch when bourgeois society—whose mortal enemy you, Jules Guesde, once were—has disclosed its true nature through and through, you have transformed the Socialist Party into a docile chorus accompanying the coryphaei of capitalist banditry. . . . The socialism of Babeuf, Saint-Simon, Fourier, Blanqui, the Commune, Jaurés, and Jules Guesde—yes, of Jules Guesde, too—has finally found its Albert Thomas to deliberate with the Tsar on the surest way of seizing Constantinople. . . . Step down, Jules Guesde, from your military automobile, get out of the cage, where the capitalist state has shut you up, and look around a little. Perhaps fate will for once, and for the last time, have pity on your sorry old age, and you will hear the muted sound of approaching events. We await them; we summon them; we prepare them.[1]

He entered Spain, hoping to proceed from there to Italy and Switzerland—his Italian friends were still trying to obtain the entry permits. But while the French had compelled him to cross the Spanish border, they had warned the Spanish police that a 'dangerous anarchist' had sneaked into their country. He stayed for a day at San Sebastian, and with rueful irony contemplated in his hotel a picture 'La Muerte del Pecador' ('The Death of a Sinner') hung over his bed. From there he went to Madrid, and, in expectation of news from Italy, loitered for ten days, mingling with gay and noisy crowds, watching picturesque ceremonies and taking notes. He knew no Spanish and had no acquaintance

---

[1] Quoted by Alfred Rosmer in 'Trotsky during World War I' in *The New International*, September–October 1950.

in Madrid, except a French Socialist who worked there as manager of the Spanish branch of a French insurance company. The day of 7 November—next year on this very day he would lead the Bolshevik insurrection—he spent at the Prado and jotted in his note-book reflections on the 'eternal' element in Spanish classical paintings, contrasting it with the less majestic but more intimate and subtle appeal of French impressionistic art.

Two days later, while he was attending a sporting event, he was spotted by a police agent and arrested. Fearing that the Spanish police might put him on board a ship bound for Russia, he dispatched cables and letters of protest right and left. In a letter to the Spanish Minister of Home Affairs he explained, with the usual flourish and irony, that he knew no Spanish, had met not a single Spanish citizen, had published not a single line in Spain, and had only visited museums and churches. The only reason for his arrest, given to him by the chief of the police of Madrid, was that his 'views were a little too advanced for Spain'. The Socialist and republican press began to clamour for his release. After three days he was ordered to proceed under escort to Cadiz. There he was allowed to remain at large, under mild, almost farcical police surveillance, to await the arrival of the first boat in which he could leave the country.[1]

At Cadiz Trotsky spent six weeks, bombarding the Spanish government with protests and killing time in the company of a police agent at an ancient library, where, in a quietness such that 'one could hear the bookworm eating his way through the folios', he pored over old French and English books, took notes and copied excerpts on Spanish revolutions and counter-revolutions, on their effect on bullfights, on the failures of Spanish liberalism and on the intrigues of the great powers in the Peninsula.[2] At last a boat bound for Cuba came in. He

---

[1] In the Madrid prison he made long entries in his diary, describing humorously the prison, its administration, its inmates, and his own wranglings with his jailors. One of the inmates was a 'Thieves' King', who had 'operated' in half the world and was treated with reverence by the prisoners and the guards. The 'King' wanted to learn from Trotsky what chances Canada offered to an enterprising thief—surely, a multilingual pacifist and anarchist should be able to tell that. ' "Canada?" I answered hesitatingly, "you know, there are many farmers there, and a young bourgeoisie, who, like the Swiss, should have a strongly developed sense of property!" '

[2] After a visit to the old harbour of Cadiz, where he had watched a brutal brawl,

refused to board it, and, after new protests and a few anxious
moments, was allowed to stay until the arrival of a ship bound
for the United States. His Italian friends now wrote him that
they hoped soon to obtain the Italian and Swiss visas. 'When
I am already at Cadiz', he remarked, 'the whole of Europe
becomes hospitable to me.' On 20 December he was allowed to
leave, again under police escort, for Barcelona whither his wife
and two sons had arrived from Paris. From Barcelona he sailed
with his family on a ramshackle Spanish ship, crowded with
well-to-do deserters and destitute 'undesirables' from all
European countries. The neutral flag of the ship at least offered
some protection from German submarines. On the last day of
the year, the ship passed Gibraltar.

'This is the last time', Trotsky wrote to Alfred Rosmer, 'that
I cast a glance on that old *canaille* Europe.'

.   .   .   .

On a cold, rainy Sunday morning, 13 January 1917, he
disembarked in New York harbour. The colony of Russian
Socialists enthusiastically welcomed the author of the Zimmerwald Manifesto; and there was no end to greetings and ova-
tions.[1]

Trotsky 'looked haggard; he had grown older; and there was
fatigue in his face', says the Russo-American Communist
M. Olgin, who had visited him in Vienna five years before.
'His conversation hinged around the collapse of international
socialism.' This was also the theme of the lectures which,
shortly after his arrival, he delivered to Russian, Finnish,
Latvian, German, and Jewish Socialists in New York, Philadelphia, and other cities.

With his family he settled in a lodging rented (for 18 dollars
a month) in the Bronx, 164th Street. The cheap apartment
offered the family unaccustomed luxuries: for the first time in
his life, the future leader of the revolution had a telephone in his
home. Various American writers have given highly coloured
descriptions of Trotsky's life in New York: one remembered him
as a starving tailor, another as a dish-washer in a restaurant,
and still another as a film actor. Trotsky denied these stories;
and the memoirs of people like Ziv and Olgin who were at the

he noted in his diary: 'Gigantic screwjacks will be needed in order to raise the
culture of the masses.'   [1] A. Ziv, op. cit., pp. 68–69.

time close to him, offer no foundation for them. He earned his
living from journalism and lecturing.[1]

The Russian émigrés published in New York a daily, *Novyi
Mir* (*New World*), edited by Bukharin, Kollontai, and Volo-
darsky. Of this paper Trotsky at once became the mainstay.
This was his first close association with any Bolshevik circle.
Bukharin had lived in Vienna while Trotsky was editing his
Pravda there, but the bitterness of factional strife had separated
them. Now they drew together in a friendship which was to
dissolve, though not entirely, only eight years later, after
Bukharin had become Stalin's partner. Kollontai had from a
Menshevik become one of Lenin's most fanatical adherents.
Volodarsky, a Russo-American who described himself as 'an
American worker by origin and way of life' was also strongly
attracted by Bolshevism—he was to bring something of the
American *élan* and organization into the Bolshevik revolution.
With this group, though not yet with the Bolshevik party,
Trotsky identified himself.

During his sojourn in the States, which lasted little more than
two months, he had only a slender chance to acquaint himself
with American life, and he had, as he himself put it, 'only a peep
into the foundry in which the fate of men is to be forged'. He
was fascinated by New York and impressed by the statistical
evidence of American wealth, which had grown rapidly since
the war. But his mind and heart were with that 'old *canaille*
Europe': 'It is a fact', he said at a meeting, 'that the economic
life of Europe is being shattered to its very foundations, while
American wealth is growing. As I look enviously at New York—
I who have not ceased to feel like a European—I wonder
anxiously: "Will Europe be able to stand all this? Will it not
decay and become little better than a graveyard? And will not
the world's economic and cultural centres of gravity shift to
America?" '[2] Now and through the rest of his life he dreamt
about the great and original contribution which the United
States would make to Marxism and socialism, a contribution
surpassing in scale and momentum the one it had made and

[1] An amusing 'memoir' which appeared in the *New York Herald Tribune* (14
February 1932), depicts Trotsky as acting the part of a station-master in a film 'My
Official Wife'. As an actor, says the writer, Trotsky, was a 'washout', without
personality and sex appeal, a 'shy, retiring man' who never talked about politics or
socialism.   [2] L. Trotsky, *Moya Zhizn*, vol. i, p. 308.

was making to the development of capitalism. For the time
being, however, the American Socialist sects appeared to him
narrow, timid, ludicrously parochial, and led by a quaint
Socialist variety of Babbitt, who 'supplements his commercial
activities with dull Sunday meditations on the future of humanity'. A 'Babbitt of Babbitts', so he described, for instance, Hillquit, that 'ideal socialist spokesman for successful dentists'.
The only exception was Eugene Debs, the pioneer and martyr,
who, although a poor Marxist, had in him the 'quenchless
inner flame of his socialist idealism. . . . Whenever we met, he
embraced and kissed me. . . .'[1]

.   .   .   .

Before the middle of March 1917 came the first confused
news about 'disturbances' in the Russian capital. Because of a
break in communications the telegraph agencies still reported
mere 'bread riots'. But already on 13 March Trotsky was writing in *Novyi Mir*: 'We are the witnesses of the beginning of the
second Russian revolution. Let us hope that many of us will
be its participants.' A fever of excitement took hold of the
Russian colony; and meeting followed upon meeting. 'At all
those meetings', wrote Dr. Ziv, now a Menshevik and a 'social-
patriot', 'Trotsky's speech was the main event and the natural
climax. Meetings were sometimes delayed for hours because
Trotsky was taking part in many gatherings convened simultaneously . . . but the public patiently waited for him, thirsting
for the words that would throw a light on the momentous event
that had occurred in Russia.'[2] From the beginning, so Ziv
relates resentfully, Trotsky assailed the Provisional Government
of Prince Lvov, which had just constituted itself. Was it not a
shame, he exclaimed at the meetings, that the first Foreign
Minister of the revolution should be Miliukov, who had called
the Red Flag a red rag, and its first Minister of War should be
Guchkov, who had kowtowed to Stolypin? Kerensky, the only
man of the left in this government, was merely its hostage.
'What has happened to Trotsky? What does he want?' Ziv's
friends asked in amazement.

How Trotsky received the revolution and what he expected
from it can be seen from his writings in *Novyi Mir*. Within the
fortnight that passed between the first news of the 'bread riots'

[1] Ibid., vol. i, p. 313.   [2] A. Ziv, op. cit., p. 80.

in Petrograd and his departure from New York, he stated fully and clearly the main ideas he was to expound in the course of the year. When the composition of Prince Lvov's government became known and when that government called for a return to order, he wrote: 'The powerful avalanche of the revolution is in full swing, and no human force will stem it.' The Liberals were afraid that the popular movement which had given them power would swamp them. So they were calling for an end to the revolution 'as if its iron broom had already cleared to the end all the reactionary litter that had over the centuries piled up' around the Tsar's throne. 'The nation will now rise, layer after layer, all those who have been oppressed, disinherited, deceived. ... At the head of the popular masses of Russia the revolutionary proletariat will carry out its historical work: it will expel monarchist reaction from wherever it tries to shelter; and it will stretch out its hand to the proletariat of Germany and of the whole of Europe. It is necessary to liquidate not only Tsardom but the war as well.'[1]

He accused the first government of the revolution of inheriting from Tsardom its imperialism and its designs on the Balkans and the Dardanelles; and he greeted hopefully the emergence of the Soviet of Petrograd as the potential government bound to assert itself against the old administration, now headed by the Cadets (Constitutional Democrats). When it became evident that the Soviet, guided by the Mensheviks and presided over by Chkheidze, had given its support to Prince Lvov's government and endorsed its foreign policy, Trotsky vehemently attacked Chkheidze, whom he had so recently defended from the Bolsheviks, and Kerensky, that 'young lawyer of Saratov . . . who has no great weight on the scales of revolution'. The Mensheviks and the Social Revolutionaries were evoking the patriotism of the peasantry to justify their support of the war. But, Trotsky wrote, it was not the alleged patriotism of the peasantry but its hunger for land that was of real importance. Tsardom, the landlords, and the bourgeoisie had done their best to divert the peasantry from agrarian revolution to imperialist war. It was the task of socialism to lead the peasants back from war to agrarian revolution. 'The landlords' land and not Constantinople', thus the soldier–proletarian will say to the soldier–

[1] L. Trotsky, *Sochinenya*, vol. iii, part 1, pp. 5–7.

peasant.[1] In an essay written for *Zukunft*, an American-Jewish Socialist monthly, Trotsky made this point even more explicit: 'The peasant masses will rise in the villages and, not waiting for a decision of the Constituent Assembly, they will begin to expel the big landlords from their estates. All efforts to put an end to class warfare . . . will lead to nothing. The philistine thinks that it is the revolutionaries who make a revolution and who can call it off at any point as they wish.'[2]

Thus, separated by an ocean and a continent from the scene of events, through the haze of confused and contradictory reports, he firmly grasped the direction in which things were moving, formulated the problems of the revolution, and un-hesitatingly pointed to those whom he now considered to be its enemies, even if only yesterday they had been his friends. The question which he still had to answer was: Which was the real party of the revolution, *his* party?

Having drawn with so much foresight and precision the image of the revolution, he threw over that image, however, a veil of dream and fantasy. He fondly cherished his hope for the insur-rection of the European proletariat, and he saw the Petrograd rising as a mere prelude to it. This hope underlay all his ideas; it was to give him wings in his ascendancy; and its frustration was subsequently to break and crush him. Through the pages of *Novyi Mir* we can watch Trotsky in the first of his many wrestlings with illusion. Just before he left New York he tried to answer critics who fervently held that Russia, even while she was governed by Prince Lvov, must be defended against invasion by the Kaiser's troops. Trotsky, even now, persisted in opposition to war:

'The Russian revolution [so he answered the critics] represents an infinitely greater danger to the Hohenzollern than do the appetites and designs of imperialist Russia. The sooner the revolution throws off the chauvinist mask, which the Guchkovs and Miliukovs have forced upon her, and the sooner she reveals her true proletarian face, the more powerful will be the response she meets in Germany and the less will be the Hohenzollern's desire and capacity to strangle the Russian revolution, the more will he have of his own domestic trouble.

'But what will happen [the critic asks] if the German proletariat fails to rise? What are you going to do then?

[1] Op. cit., pp. 17–20.   [2] Op. cit., pp. 27–28.

I

'You suppose, then, that the Russian revolution can take place without affecting Germany . . .? But this is altogether improbable.

'Still, what if this were nevertheless to be the case?

'Really, we need not rack our brains over so implausible a supposition. The war has transformed the whole of Europe into a powder magazine of social revolution. The Russian proletariat is now throwing a flaming torch into that powder magazine. To suppose that this will cause no explosion is to think against the laws of historical logic and psychology. Yet if the improbable were to happen, if the conservative, social-patriotic organization were to prevent the German working class from rising against its ruling classes in the nearest future, then, of course, the Russian working class would defend the revolution arms in hand . . . and wage war against the Hohenzollern, and call upon the fraternal German proletariat to rise against the common enemy. . . . The task would be to defend not the fatherland but the revolution and to carry it to other countries.'[1]

Thus, every time he tried to answer the question: 'What happens if there is no revolution in Germany?' he actually dodged it. He seemed to be getting away from his dream only to plunge back into it, and to throw away his hope only in order to embrace it again. He saw no prospect, no hope, no life beyond European revolution.

.   .   .   .

On 27 March Trotsky, his family, and a small group of other émigrés, having the day before been given a boisterous farewell by a multilingual gathering of Socialists, sailed from New York on board the Norwegian ship *Christianiafjord*. For the first time in his life he travelled 'respectably', having obtained without difficulty all the necessary documents, the Russian entry permit and the British transit visa; and he expected plain sailing. All the greater was the surprise, when, on 3 April, the *Christiania-fjord* dropped anchor at Halifax, Nova Scotia, and the British naval police forcibly removed him and his family from the ship, carried him away to a camp for German prisoners of war at Amherst, and placed his wife and children under close surveillance. The other Russian émigrés who had accompanied him were also prevented from continuing the voyage. They had all refused to tell the British interrogating officer what were

[1] Op. cit., pp. 17–20.

their political views and what they intended to do in Russia. This, they claimed, was no business of the British naval police.

From the camp, Trotsky cabled protests to the Russian government and to the British Prime Minister; but his messages, confiscated on the spot, never reached their destination. All the same, the internment became a political scandal. The Menshevik Executive of the Petrograd Soviet demanded Trotsky's release: 'The revolutionary democracy of Russia', it stated, 'impatiently awaits the return of its fighters for freedom and calls to its banners those who, by their lifelong efforts, have prepared the overthrow of Tsardom. Yet, the English authorities allow some émigrés to pass and hold up others. . . . The English government thereby intervenes intolerably in Russia's domestic affairs and insults the Russian revolution by robbing her of her most faithful sons.' Meetings of protest were held all over Russia; and Miliukov, the Foreign Minister, asked the British Ambassador that Trotsky be released. Two days later, however, he cancelled the request, knowing full well that he had nothing to expect from Trotsky but enmity.[1] Meanwhile, as the internment dragged on for nearly a month, Trotsky raged, protested, and hurled insults at the camp administration. There were at Amherst 800 German prisoners, sailors of sunken submarines. Trotsky addressed them, explaining to them the ideas of Zimmerwald, and telling them of the fight against the Kaiser and the war, which Karl Liebknecht had been waging in Germany. The camp resounded with his speeches, and life in it changed into a 'perpetual meeting'.[2] On the insistence of the German officers, the commandant of the camp forbade Trotsky to address the prisoners. 'Thus', Trotsky mocked, 'the English colonel immediately sided with Hohenzollern patriotism.' More than 500 sailors signed a protest against the ban. Finally, after much bungling and intrigue, Miliukov was compelled to renew the demand for Trotsky's release. On 29 April Trotsky left Amherst, followed to the gates of the camp by cheering German sailors and by the sounds of the *Internationale* played by their orchestra.

[1] Sir George Buchanan, *My Mission to Russia*, vol. ii, p. 121; Trotsky, *Sochinenya*, vol. iii, book 1, pp. 35 ff.

[2] Trotsky described his experience in a brochure *V Plenu u Anglichan* which he published immediately after his return to Petrograd (*Sochinenya*, vol. iii).

After a sea voyage of nearly three weeks, on 17 May (4 May in the old Russian calendar) he travelled by train across Finland to Petrograd. By the same train, and in the same compartment, went Vandervelde, the president of the Second International, and De Man, another eminent Belgian Socialist, both intent on infusing a warlike and patriotic spirit into their Russian comrades. Trotsky and Vandervelde have given two different accounts of this meeting, the former claiming that he refused to talk with the 'social patriots', the latter describing their long, polite, but rather unfriendly conversation.[1] Whatever the truth, the gulf between the Second and the Third Internationals ran for a few hours across that railway compartment.

At the Russian frontier a delegation of internationalists from Petrograd waited to welcome Trotsky. The Bolshevik Central Committee also greeted him, but not without reserve: the Bolshevik delegate who came to the frontier was not one of the party's well-known leaders. In Petrograd a crowd, demonstrating with red banners, carried Trotsky on its shoulders from the train; and to that crowd he made at once his call for a new revolution.

[1] Trotsky, *Moya Zhizn*, vol. ii, pp. 5–6. E. Vandervelde, *Souvenirs d'un Militant Socialiste*, p. 230.

CHAPTER IX

Trotsky in the October Revolution

TROTSKY arrived in Petrograd on 4 May. The revolution was then ten weeks old; and during those weeks events had thronged so thick and fast that the capital presented a dream-like picture even to the man who had cherished the memory of its streets and crowds ever since 1905.[1] The revolution had begun where it had stopped in 1905; but it had already left its recent starting-point far behind. The Tsar and his ministers were still prisoners of state, but to most of their former subjects they were like ghosts of a remote past. The age-old splendours, terrors, and fetishes of the monarchy seemed to have vanished with last winter's snow.

Lenin, who had returned exactly a month before Trotsky, described the Russia he found as the freest country in the world.[2] Her freedom, to be sure, was only that of expression; but of this the people availed themselves to the full, as if hoping to discover through passionate debate a new mode of existence, since the old had led to the brink of the abyss. That tense search for new principles, new forms, and a new content of social life, a search in which the mass of the humbled and the downtrodden participated with impressive dignity, characterized the moral climate of Petrograd in this spring of 1917. No authority and no truth was taken for granted. Only a vague belief prevailed that good was what promoted the revolution and helped to right the wrongs of the oppressed. The social character of the upheaval was reflected even in the city's appearance. The streets and squares in the fashionable centre were constantly crowded with dwellers from suburban slums. Multitudes of workers and soldiers attended the meetings, which took place day and night there and in the factories and barracks on the outskirts. The red flag, until recently the forbidden standard of rebellion, dominated the neo-classical architecture of the buildings on the Neva. The predominance of the worker and the soldier in the revolution could be guessed from every casual scene and incident in

---

[1] Trotsky, *Moya Zhizn*, vol. ii, p. 7.   [2] Lenin, *Sochinenya*, vol. xxiv, p. 4.

the street. The newcomer had only to glance at the capital to see how incongruous it was that Prince Lvov should still be the revolution's first minister.

Trotsky had hardly deposited his family and its few belongings in a lodging-house when he made for the Smolny Institute, the seat of the Petrograd Soviet.[1] Its Executive, the successor to the body of which he had been the presiding spirit in 1905, was just in session. The man who now presided was Chkheidze, his former associate whom he had just attacked in *Novyi Mir*. Chkheidze rose to welcome Trotsky, but the welcome was lukewarm.[2] A moment of embarrassment followed. The Mensheviks and Social Revolutionaries, who were in a majority, did not know whether the newcomer was their friend or their foe—from a friend of long standing he seemed to have turned into a foe. The Bolshevik members of the Executive pointed out that the leader of the Soviet of 1905 ought to be invited to take a seat on the Executive of the present Soviet. The Mensheviks and Social Revolutionaries consulted each other in perplexed whispers. They agreed to admit Trotsky as an associate member, without the right to vote. He wished for nothing more: what mattered to him was not the right to vote, but the opportunity to make himself heard from the chief platform of the revolution.

Nevertheless, the cool reception could not but irk him. Angelica Balabanov, the secretary of the Zimmerwald movement, wrote that he even suspected that the party leaders had not pressed energetically enough for his release from British internment, because they had not been eager to see him on the scene. 'Both Mensheviks and Bolsheviks regarded him with rancour and distrust . . . partly out of fear of competition. . . .'[3] Whatever the truth, the fact was that between February and May the political alignments had become defined; the parties and groups had formed their ranks and clarified their attitudes, and the leaders had assumed their roles and taken up their positions. In 1905 Trotsky had been the first of the émigrés to return. Now he was the last. And no appropriate vacancy seemed to be open for a man of his gifts and ambition.

[1] From now on 'the Soviet' (in the singular) denotes the Soviet of Petrograd, unless it is stated otherwise.

[2] L. Trotsky, *Moya Zhizn*, loc. cit.; N. Sukhanov, *Zapiski o Revolutsii*, vol. iii, pp. 440–1.

[3] A. Balabanoff, *My Life as a Rebel*, p. 176.

The moment was such that all parties, except the Bolsheviks, had reason to fear any new and incalculable influence. For the first time, the régime that sprang from the February insurrection had lost its unstable balance; and it was trying to regain that balance through delicate combinations and manœuvres. Prince Lvov's first government had ceased to exist. In that government only the gentry and the upper middle class had been represented, the former by the Conservatives who followed Guchkov, the latter by Miliukov's Cadets. The Mensheviks and Social Revolutionaries, who dominated the Soviet, had pledged their support to the government but had not joined it. Yet the government could not have existed a single day without the backing of the Soviet, the *de facto* power created by the revolution. The point had now been reached where the moderate Socialist parties in the Soviet could no longer support the government without joining it.

The parties which had formed Prince Lvov's first government strove to limit the revolution to the overthrow of Tsar Nicholas II and to save, if possible, the monarchy; to continue the war, and to restore the social and military discipline without which it could not be continued.[1] The workers and soldiers who followed the Soviets hoped, on the contrary, for a 'deepening' of the revolution and for an early 'democratic peace without annexations and indemnities'. The moderate Socialists tried to reconcile the conflicting policies and demands. Inevitably they involved themselves in blatant contradictions. They tried to assist the government in prosecuting the war and at the same time to soothe the popular longing for peace. They told their followers that the government had discarded the Tsar's rapacious war aims—Russian domination over the Balkans, the conquest of Galicia and Constantinople—and that it was seeking to achieve a just and democratic peace.[2] Prince Lvov tried to put into operation the old administrative machinery inherited from Tsardom, while the workers and soldiers regarded the Soviets as the real administration. The Mensheviks and Social Revolutionaries hoped that the new system of government would

[1] P. Miliukov, *Istorya Russkoi Revolutsii*, vol. i, book 1, pp. 54–76 and *passim*.

[2] 'Miliukov . . . held that the acquisition of Constantinople was a matter of vital moment for Russia', wrote Sir George Buchanan the British Ambassador in Russia in *My Mission to Russia*, vol. ii, p. 108.

incorporate both the old administration and the Soviets. The government exerted itself to re-establish discipline in the war-weary and revolutionized army, in which the soldiers refused to obey their officers and listened only to their own elected committees. The moderate Socialists pledged themselves to help the government in restoring discipline; yet they called upon the soldiers to defend their newly won rights embodied in the Soviet's famous Order No. 1 against Tsarist generals and officers. The government wished to create security for landed property, while the peasantry clamoured for a sharing out of the gentry's estates. The Mensheviks and Social Revolutionaries tried to postpone the solution of this vital problem until the convocation of the Constituent Assembly, which in its turn was indefinitely postponed.[1]

It was inevitable that this tall structure, built of equivocation and delusion, should one day crumble over the heads of those who erected it. The first tremor shook it in April. Guchkov, unable to restore military discipline, resigned from the Ministry of War. Soon afterwards Miliukov had to resign from the Ministry of Foreign Affairs. He had declared in a note to Russia's western allies that the new government would faith-fully pursue the war aims of its Tsarist predecessor. This pro-voked such an outburst of popular indignation that Prince Lvov's first government could no longer carry on.

The ruthless logic of revolution began to show itself. Within two months the revolution had discredited and used up its first government and the parties that had formed it. Only a short time before, in the last days of the Tsarist régime, Doumergue, the future President of the French Chamber, on a state visit to Petrograd, had urged the Cadet leaders to compose patiently their differences with the Tsar. 'At the very word "patience" Miliukov and Maklakov jumped up: "Enough of patience! We have exhausted all our patience! Anyhow, if we do not act soon, the masses will not listen to us any longer. . . ." '[2] These words were to become one of the revolution's favourite refrains; and now they recoiled upon Miliukov. The moderate Socialist major-ity of the Soviet had no intention of unseating him. But when

    [1] Miliukov, op. cit., vol. i, book 1, pp. 101–15, 125–38 and *passim*; L. Trotsky, *The History of the Russian Revolution*, vol. i, chapters xi–xiii.
    [2] M. Paléologue, *La Russie des Tsars pendant la Grande Guerre*, vol. iii, p. 188.

he openly pledged government and country to the pursuit of the Tsarist war aims, the Mensheviks and Social Revolutionaries jumped up: 'Enough of patience! We have exhausted all our patience! And, anyhow, if we do not act soon, the masses will not listen to us any longer.' The masses would not have listened to them any longer if they had left the whole business of government to the leaders of those classes that had used the February Revolution but not made it.

The first coalition between the Cadets and the moderate Socialists thus came into being. When Trotsky appeared at the session of the Soviet Executive, the new partners were just sharing out the governmental seats. There were to be 'ten capitalist and six socialist ministers'. The Cadets were the senior partners; and so the programme of the new government was in essentials indistinguishable from that of its predecessor. The six Socialist ministers could only dilute it to make it more palatable to the Soviet. Kerensky, who had a connexion with the Social Revolutionary party, succeeded Guchkov as Minister of War. Tseretelli, the most eminent Menshevik leader of this period, a former deputy and hard-labour convict, became Minister of Posts and Telegraphs. Chernov, chief of the Social Revolutionaries and a participant in the Zimmerwald conference, was appointed Minister of Agriculture. Skobelev, Trotsky's former pupil and editorial assistant, was Minister of Labour.

On 5 May, the day after Trotsky's arrival, the Socialist ministers stood before the Soviet, asking it to support the coalition. When Trotsky appeared he was greeted with loud applause, and Skobelev addressed him as 'dear and beloved teacher'. From the floor Trotsky was asked to state his view on the day's event. He 'was visibly nervous over the début, under the . . . stare of an unknown mass and the hostile glances . . . of "social traitors" '.[2] Cautiously he felt his way. He began by extolling the grandeur of the revolution, and he so described the impression it had made upon the world that by implication he at once reduced that day's event to modest proportions. If only, he said, they could see and gauge, as he had done abroad, the impact of the revolution upon the world, they would know that Russia 'had opened a new epoch, an epoch of blood and iron, a struggle no longer of nation against nation, but of the suffering and

---

[1] N. Sukhanov, op. cit., vol. iii, pp. 440–2.

oppressed classes against their rulers'.[1] These words jarred on the ears of the Socialist ministers, who had committed themselves to continuing the war and calming the raging elements of revolution. 'I cannot conceal', Trotsky went on, 'that I disagree with much that is going on here. I consider this participation in the Ministry to be dangerous. . . . The coalition government will not save us from the existing dualism of power; it will merely transfer that dualism into the Ministry itself.' This was indistinguishable from what the Bolsheviks were saying—they, too, dwelt on the division of power between the Soviets and the government. As if wary of hurting his old friends, Trotsky then struck a more conciliatory note: 'The revolution will not perish from a coalition Ministry. But we must remember three commands: distrust the bourgeoisie; control our own leaders; and rely on our own revolutionary strength. . . .' He spoke in the first person plural—'we must', 'our strength'—as if to identify himself, in his manner, with his former comrades. But in the matter of his speech he was irreconcilable: 'I think that our next move will be to transfer the whole power into the hands of the Soviets. Only a single power can save Russia.' This again sounded like Lenin's slogan. He concluded a long and brilliant argument with the exclamation 'Long live the Russian revolution, the prologue to world revolution', and the audience was captivated if not by his ideas then by the sincerity and eloquence with which he expounded them.[2]

One after another the ministers rose to reply. Chernov promised that the Socialists would make their influence felt in the government, but for this they needed the Soviet's wholehearted support. Tseretelli dwelt on the dangers to which the Soviets would be exposed if they refused to share power with the bourgeoisie. Skobelev admonished his 'dear teacher': in the middle of a revolution 'cool reason was needed as much as a warm heart'. The Soviet voted confidence in the new ministry. Only the extreme left minority voted against it.

The political group which greeted Trotsky as its proper chief was the Inter-Borough Organization, the *Mezhrayonka* as it was briefly called. He had inspired this group from abroad since its formation in 1913 and contributed to its publications. The group did not aspire to form a party. It was a temporary association

[1] L. Trotsky, *Sochinenya*, vol. iii, book 1, pp. 45–46. [2] Sukhanov, loc. cit.

of neither-Bolsheviks-nor-Mensheviks, who persisted in opposition to war, Prince Lvov, and the 'social patriots'. Its influence
was confined to a few working-class districts in Petrograd only;
and even there it was swamped by the rapid growth of Bolshevism. To this small group adhered, however, men who had
in the past been eminent either as Mensheviks or as Bolsheviks
and who were presently to rise again. Most of them, Lunacharsky, Ryazanov, Manuilsky, Pokrovsky, Yoffe, Uritsky, Volodarsky, had written for Trotsky's papers. A few others, like
Karakhan and Yureniev, later became leading Soviet diplomats.
Together they formed a brilliant political *élite*, but their organization was too weak and narrow to serve as a base for independent action. When Trotsky arrived, the group was discussing
its future and contemplating a merger with the Bolsheviks and
other Left groups. At public meetings its agitators were insistently asked in what they differed from the Bolsheviks and why
they did not join hands with them. To this question they had,
in truth, no satisfactory answer. Their separation from the
Bolsheviks had resulted from the long and involved feud in the
old party; it reflected past not present differences.[1]

On 7 May the Bolsheviks and the Inter-Borough Organization arranged a special welcome for Trotsky; and on 10 May
they met to consider the proposed merger. Lenin arrived,
accompanied by Zinoviev and Kamenev; and here Trotsky
saw him for the first time since their not very friendly meeting
at Zimmerwald. Of this conference we have only a fragmentary
but informative record in Lenin's private notes. Trotsky
repeated what he had said at the reception in his honour: he
had abandoned his old attitude and no longer stood for unity
between Bolsheviks and Mensheviks. Only those who had
completely broken with social patriotism should now unite
under the flag of a new International. Then he apparently asked
whether Lenin still held that the Russian Revolution was merely
bourgeois in character and that its outcome would be 'a
democratic dictatorship of the proletariat and the peasantry',
not proletarian dictatorship.[2] It seems that he was not clearly
aware of the radical re-orientation which Lenin had just carried

[1] Sukhanov, op. cit., vol. iv, p. 365; Trotsky, *Sochinenya*, vol. iii, book 1, p. 47;
See also Yureniev's report in *6 Syezd RSDRP*.
[2] *Leninskii Sbornik*, vol. iv, pp. 300–3.

through in the Bolshevik party. Lenin had spent the month before Trotsky's arrival in an intense controversy with the right wing of his party, headed by Kamenev; and he had persuaded the party to abandon the 'old Bolshevik' view on the prospects of the revolution. It may be assumed that this was explained to Trotsky there and then. If nobody else, then his brother-in-law Kamenev must have told him that Lenin's Bolshevik opponents, indeed Kamenev himself, had reproached Lenin with having taken over lock, stock, and barrel the theory of 'permanent revolution', and with having abandoned Bolshevism for Trotskyism.

In truth, the roads of Lenin and Trotsky, so long divergent, had now met. Each of them had reached certain conclusions to which the other had come much earlier and which he had long and bitterly contested. But neither had consciously adopted the other's point of view. From different starting-points and through different processes their minds had moved towards their present meeting. We have seen how the events of the war had gradually driven Trotsky to take the view that the breach in the Labour movement could not be healed; that it was wrong and even pernicious to try to heal it; and that it was the duty of the revolutionary internationalists to form new parties. Long before the war, Lenin had arrived at this conclusion, but only for the Russian party. The war had induced him to generalize it and to apply it to the international Labour movement. In Lenin's reasonings and instinctive reactions his Russian experience was the primary factor, although it alone did not determine his attitude. Trotsky had, on the contrary, proceeded from the international generalization to the application of the principle to Russia. Whatever the processes by which they arrived at the common conclusion, the practical implications were the same.

A similar difference in approach and identity in conclusion can be seen in their evaluation of prospects. In 1905–6 Trotsky had foreseen the combination of anti-feudal and anti-capitalist revolutions in Russia and had described the Russian upheaval as a prelude to international socialist revolution. Lenin had then refused to see in Russia the pioneer of collectivist socialism. He deduced the character and the prospects of the revolution from Russia's historic stage of development and from her social structure, in which the individualistic peasantry was the largest element. During the war, however, he came to reckon with Socialist revolution in the advanced European countries and to place the Russian Revolution in this international perspective. What now seemed decisive to him was not that Russia was not ripe for socialism, but that she was part of Europe which he thought to be ripe for it. Consequently, he no longer saw any reason why the Russian Revolution should confine itself to its so-called bourgeois objectives. The experience of the February régime further demonstrated to him that it would be impossible to break the power of the landlords without breaking and eventually dispossessing the capitalist class as well; and this meant 'proletarian dictatorship'.[1]

Although the old differences between Lenin and Trotsky had evaporated, the position of the two men was very different. Lenin was the recognized leader of a great party, which, even though a minority in the Soviets, had already become the rallying ground for all proletarian opposition to the February régime. Trotsky and his friends were a pleiade of brilliant generals without an army. As an individual, Trotsky could make his voice heard from the platforms of the revolution; but only a massive and well-disciplined party could now transform words into lasting deeds. Each side needed the other, though in different degrees. Nothing suited Lenin better than to be able to introduce the pleiade of gifted propagandists, agitators, tacticians, and orators, headed by Trotsky, into the 'general staff' of his party. But he was proud of the party he had built and aware of the advantages it held. He was determined that Trotsky and Trotsky's friends should join *his* party. Inside it, he was willing to accord them every democratic right, to share with them his influence, and, as the record shows, to allow himself to be outvoted on important occasions. But he was not prepared to scrap his party and to merge it with minor groups into a new body. To do so he would have had either to indulge in make-believe or to pay a needless tribute to the vanity of others.

At the meeting of 10 May he asked Trotsky and Trotsky's friends to join the Bolshevik party immediately. He offered them positions on the leading bodies and on the editorial staff of *Pravda*.[2] He put no conditions to them. He did not ask Trotsky

---

[1] Lenin, *Sochinenya*, vol. xxiv, pp. 214–16, 274–5, 276–9, and *passim*.
[2] Even earlier, Lenin had proposed to the Bolshevik Central Committee that

to renounce anything of his past; he did not even mention past controversies. He himself had put these out of his mind and expected Trotsky to do likewise—so anxious was he to join hands with anybody who could promote the common cause. At this time he even hoped for a reunion with Martov, who had detached himself from the Mensheviks, remained faithful to the programme of Zimmerwald, and opposed the coalition government.[1]

Trotsky would have had to be much more free from pride than he was to accept Lenin's proposals immediately. He also had to consider objections raised by some of his associates who spoke about the lack of democracy in Lenin's party and the 'sectarian practices' of the Bolshevik committees and conventicles. Trotsky, who had so long criticized Lenin's party in the same terms, now saw little substance in these misgivings. In his reply to Lenin he dwelt on the recent change in the Bolshevik party, which, he said, 'had acquired an internationalist outlook' and become 'de-bolshevized'. Politically, he was therefore in complete agreement with Lenin; and he also accepted most of Lenin's technical proposals for immediate co-operation. But, precisely because the Bolshevik party had changed so strikingly and to such advantage, he and his friends should not be asked to call themselves Bolsheviks. 'I cannot describe myself as a Bolshevik. It is undesirable to stick to the old labels.'[2] They ought to join hands in a new party, with a new name, at a joint congress of their organizations. Trotsky must have been aware that at such a congress, the Bolsheviks would in any case enjoy an absolute preponderance; and so the whole difference reduced itself to the 'label'. This was too slight a matter to justify him and his associates in clinging to their political isolation. But for the moment the issue was shelved.

When about this time Lenin was asked what, despite their complete agreement, still kept him and Trotsky apart, he

Trotsky be invited to edit the party's popular daily, but this proposal had been rejected by the Committee. *Krasnaya Letopis*, no. 3, 1923.

[1] Lunacharsky (*Revolutsionnye Siluety*, p. 69) writes: 'In May and June of 1917 Lenin desired an alliance with Martov.' Lunacharsky himself hoped even much later that Martov might yet become the leader of a right wing within the Bolshevik party and he expressed this hope in his book, which was published in 1923. Ibid., p. 70.

[2] *Leninskii Sbornik*, vol. iv, loc. cit.

replied: 'Now don't you know? Ambition, ambition, ambition.'[1]
For Trotsky to declare himself a Bolshevik was a tacit surrender,
not to the Lenin of the present, but to the Lenin of the past;
and at this he balked. Yet the surrender was in part inevitable,
for it was the Lenin of the past, the émigré, who had been the
master architect of what turned out to be *the* party of revolution.
On the other hand, the present programme of the party embodied what used to be Trotsky's rather than Lenin's point of
view. For this Trotsky received no recognition and no acknowledgement. Much as this may have hurt Trotsky, Lenin was
almost certainly unaware of it; and it was practically impossible
for him to make the acknowledgement in any form, even if he
had been willing to make it. A revolutionary party, in the middle
of a revolution, has no time for fine scruples over the copyright
of political ideas. Later in the year, Lenin unstintingly paid
tribute to Trotsky, saying that since he had broken with the
Mensheviks there was no better Bolshevik.[2] Trotsky on his part
had far too much political sense not to see that it would be
laughable to insist at this time on his superior foresight. For him,
too, the practical politics of the revolution were infinitely more
important than old theoretical prognostications. His hesitancy
was merely the last flicker of his opposition to Lenin.

For the moment he remained a political free-lance. Looking
round for contacts he stopped at the editorial offices of Maxim
Gorky's *Novaya Zhizn* (*New Life*). He and Gorky had known and
admired each other for a long time past. The differences in their
ages, temperaments, and modes of thinking were such as to
preclude intimate friendship; but they had occasionally co-
operated, especially when Gorky moved away from Lenin. At
present Gorky stood half-way between Bolsheviks and Mensheviks; and in his great daily he remonstrated with both and
preached revolutionary morals to both. He hoped for Trotsky's
accession, believing that like himself Trotsky would try to
conciliate the adversaries in the Socialist camp. Trotsky's first
utterances in Petrograd had caused him forebodings, and his
contributors whispered that 'Trotsky was even worse than
Lenin'. Nevertheless, Gorky arranged a meeting between his
editorial staff and Trotsky. At once it became clear that they

[1] Balabanoff, op. cit., pp. 175–6.
[2] Trotsky, *The Stalin School of Falsification*, p. 105.

were at cross purposes. Apart from this, Gorky's influence was strictly literary. His paper, for all its journalistic merits, had no serious ties with the bodies of opinion and the organizations that mattered in the revolution. In Marxist politics, the great novelist was childishly naïve. Yet with the lack of modesty characteristic of a famous self-made man, he assumed the posture of political oracle. Nothing would have been more incongruous than that Trotsky should associate himself with Gorky, let alone accept him as a political guide. Trotsky was in search of a firm framework of organization, of a solid anchorage in the realities of the revolution; and this Gorky could not offer him. Their exchange of views was rather sour, and Trotsky concluded it by saying that nothing was left to him but to join hands with Lenin.[1]

In the meantime he founded *Vperyod* (*Forward*), the paper of the Inter-Borough Organization. *Vperyod*, although it had many brilliant contributors, was not successful. At this time only such papers gained wide currency as could rely on strong financial backing or on the disinterested services of a widely ramified organization. *Vperyod* had neither. It began as a weekly; but it came from the presses irregularly; altogether only sixteen issues appeared before the Inter-Borough Organization joined the Bolshevik party.

It was through the spoken rather than the written word that Trotsky made his impact on the political life in the capital. He addressed, usually with Lunacharsky, innumerable meetings. Within only two or three weeks of his arrival, both he and Lunacharsky had gained enormous popularity as the most eloquent agitators of the Soviet Left.[2] The naval base of Kronstadt, situated just outside the capital, was his favourite stumping-ground; and Kronstadt proved extremely important in his further political fortunes. The navy was in utter rebellion. The base formed a sort of red republic bowing to no authority. The sailors violently resisted attempts to reimpose discipline on them. The ministry appointed commissars, some of whom had been discredited by their association with the old régime and even with the Black Hundred gangs. The sailors refused to admit them on board ship and manhandled some of them. Trotsky

---

[1] Sukhanov, op. cit., vol. iv, p. 191; Trotsky, *History of the Russian Revolution*, vol. i, pp. 486–7.   [2] Sukhanov, op. cit., vol. iv, pp. 164–7.

urged the sailors to keep their tempers and to refrain from vengeance; but he also did his best to kindle their revolutionary ardour.[1]

Towards the end of May the Socialist ministers indicted the sailors before the Soviet, and Trotsky came out to defend them. He did not condone their excesses, but he pleaded that these could have been avoided if the government had not appointed as commissars discredited and hated men. 'Our socialist ministers', he exclaimed, 'refuse to fight against the danger of the Black Hundreds. Instead, they declare war on the sailors and soldiers of Kronstadt. Yet should reaction rise and should a counter-revolutionary general try to throw a noose around the neck of the revolution, your Black Hundred commissars will soap the rope for all of us, while the Kronstadt sailors will come and fight and die with us.'[1] This phrase was much quoted later when the sailors of Kronstadt actually defended Kerensky's government against General Kornilov's mutiny. Trotsky also wrote for the sailors the fiery manifesto in which they appealed against the Ministry of War to the country—this was Kerensky's first setback since he had become Minister of War. Henceforward the sailors faithfully followed Trotsky, guarded him, almost idolized him, and obeyed him whether he called them to action or exhorted them to curb their tempers.[2]

In these days, too, he established his platform in the Cirque Moderne, where almost every night he addressed enormous crowds. The amphitheatre was so densely packed that Trotsky was usually shuffled towards the platform over the heads of the audience, and from his elevation he would catch the excited eyes of the daughters of his first marriage, who attended the meetings. He spoke on the topics of the day and the aims of the revolution with his usual piercing logic; but he also absorbed the spirit of the crowd, its harsh sense of justice, its desire to see things in sharp and clear outline, its suspense, and its great expectations. Later he recollected how at the mere sight of the multitude words and arguments he had prepared well in advance receded and dispersed in his mind and other words and arguments, unexpected by himself but meeting a need in his listeners, rushed up as if from his subconscious. He then listened

[1] Trotsky, *Sochinenya*, vol. iii, book 1, pp. 52 ff.
[2] F. F. Raskolnikov, *Kronstadt i Piter v 1917 godu*, p. 77.

to his own voice as to that of a stranger, trying to keep pace with the tumultuous rush of his own ideas and phrases and afraid lest like a sleepwalker he might suddenly wake and break down. Here his politics ceased to be the distillation of individual reflection or of debates in small circles of professional politicians. He merged emotionally with the warm dark human mass in front of him, and became its medium. He became so identified with the Cirque Moderne that when he went back to the Tauride Palace or the Smolny Institute, where the Soviet sat, and assailed his opponents or argued with them, they shouted at him: 'This is not your Cirque Moderne', or 'At the Cirque Moderne you speak differently.'[1]

. . . .

At the beginning of June the first All-Russian Congress of the Soviets assembled in Petrograd; and it was in session for three weeks. For the first time the parties and their leaders confronted one another in a national forum, the only national elected body then existing in Russia. The moderate Socialists commanded about five-sixths of the votes. They were led by civilian intellectuals, but in their ranks military uniforms and peasant *rubakhas* were most conspicuous. On the extreme left, among the 120 members of the opposition, workers from the great industrial centres were predominant. The Congress reflected a division between the military and rural elements of the provinces and the proletarian elements of the cities. A few days before, a municipal election in Petrograd had revealed a significant shift. The Cadets, dominant in the government, had suffered a crushing defeat in their 'safest' boroughs. The Mensheviks had polled half the votes. The working-class suburbs had solidly voted for the Bolsheviks. The Mensheviks came to the Congress as the hopeful victors of the day. The Bolsheviks brought with them a new confidence in their future victory.[2]

The spokesmen of the Left opposition used against the majority the latter's own success. Prince Lvov and the Cadets, they said, had a negligible following. The moderate Socialists represented the nation's overwhelming majority. Why then did they content themselves with the roles of ministerial hewers of wood and drawers of water for the Cadets? Why did they

---

[1] Trotsky, *Moya Zhizn*, vol. ii, pp. 15–16; John Reed, *Ten Days that Shook the World*, p. 17. [2] Sukhanov, op. cit., vol. iv, pp. 204–5.

not form their own government, as they were democratically entitled and in honour bound to do? This was the tenor of Lenin's speech.[1] This was also Trotsky's main theme.[2] Although his argument was in parts more trenchant than Lenin's, he appealed to the majority in a more friendly tone, invoking common interests and destinies. He tried to open the eyes of the Mensheviks and Social Revolutionaries to their own humiliating position and to persuade them to break up their partnership with the bourgeois parties. It was, he said, no use trying to turn the government into a chamber of conciliation between social classes. 'A chamber of conciliation cannot exercise power in a revolutionary epoch.' Prince Lvov and his friends represented classes accustomed to rule and dominate; and the Socialist ministers, with their sense of inferiority, all too easily allowed themselves to be browbeaten. He made, however, a few friendly references to Peshekhonov, the least known of the Socialist ministers, which brought him applause from the benches of the majority. And he argued that a government consisting only of such Peshekhonovs would be 'a serious step forward'. 'You see, comrades, that in this issue I am starting not from the angle of any faction or party, but from a broader view. . . .' He agreed with the Socialist ministers that the working classes should be disciplined; but they could not be disciplined by a capitalist ministry and for the sake of capitalist policies. This was the source of all the agitation on the extreme Left, about which the majority complained.

'The so-called Left agitators', he pleaded, 'prepare the future of the Russian revolution. I venture to say that we, with our work, do not undermine your authority—we are an indispensable element in preparing the future.' 'Comrades, I am not hoping to convince you to-day, for this would be too bold a hope. What I would like to achieve to-day is to make you aware that if we oppose you, we do so not from any hostile . . . motives of a selfish faction, but because, together with you, we are suffering all the pangs and agonies of the revolution. We see solutions different from those which you see, and we are firmly convinced

[1] Lenin, *Sochinenya*, vol. xxv, pp. 3–14.
[2] *Pervyi Vseros. Syezd Sovietov*, vol. i, pp. 142–9. The summary of Trotsky's speech is based on this source—in later reprints the friendly references to the Mensheviks were retouched.

that while you are consolidating the present of the revolution, we prepare its future for you.'[1] At this stage, Lenin no longer granted his adversaries the credit Trotsky still gave them, although he agreed with Trotsky that a 'Ministry of twelve Peshekhonovs' would be an advance upon the present coalition.

These debates were exacerbated by the 'Grimm incident'. Grimm was a Swiss parliamentarian, a Socialist, and a pacifist, who had taken part in the Zimmerwald conference. There he had belonged to the 'centre' and disagreed with Lenin's revolutionary tactics. Later he helped to arrange Lenin's journey from Switzerland to Russia, via Germany. In May Grimm conveyed to leaders of the ruling parties in Petrograd a message from the German government sounding Russia on the possibility of peace. The Russian government expelled him as a German agent, but it did not reveal its reasons.

Grimm was not, strictly speaking, a German agent. As a pacifist of not much sophistication, he found it quite natural to try and act the role of a peace-maker. Not well versed in the intricacies of Russian revolutionary politics, he could not see why Russian Socialists, whether those who, like the Bolsheviks and Trotsky, clamoured for peace or those who, like the Mensheviks, merely kept on promising an early peace, should object to his action.[2] Lenin and Trotsky were not informed about his doings. The fact, however, that the government had denounced Grimm as a German agent was at once used to discredit the Russian participants of the Zimmerwald movement. Miliukov made a speech in which he was reported to have branded Lenin and Trotsky, too, as German agents. Trotsky rose in Congress to defend Grimm. He did not believe that the government was right in expelling Grimm, and he saw in the incident Miliukov's sinister intrigue. Referring to Miliukov's charges against himself and Lenin, he said, turning to the journalists' bench: 'From this platform of revolutionary democracy, I am appealing to the honest Russian press with the request that they should reproduce my words: As long as Miliukov does not withdraw his charges, he is branded as a dishonest slanderer.'[3]

'Trotsky's statement', so Gorky's paper reported the scene, 'made with *élan* and dignity, met with the unanimous applause

---

[1] *Pervyi Vseros. Syezd Sovietov*, vol. i, p. 149.   [2] Balabanoff, op. cit., p. 178.
[3] *Pervyi Vseros. Syezd Sovietov*, p. 158.

of the whole assembly. The whole Congress, without difference of faction, stormily acclaimed Trotsky for several minutes.'[1] On the next day Miliukov declared that he had not described Lenin or Trotsky as German agents—he had merely said that the government ought to imprison them for their subversive activity.[2]

This was the last occasion on which the Congress so unanimously acclaimed Trotsky. As the debates went on, the gulf between the parties became fixed. Tempers rose during a controversy over the last Duma. That Duma had been elected in 1912 on a very limited franchise; it had functioned as the Tsar's consultative assembly, not as a real parliament; and its great majority had consisted of the Tsar's underlings. The Cadets pressed for the revival of the Duma, which they hoped to use as a quasi-parliamentary base for their government. The Mensheviks and Social Revolutionaries laid before the Soviet a vague resolution, which Martov wittily paraphrased as follows: 'The Duma no longer exists, but a warning is hereby issued against any attempts to put it out of existence.'[3] Lunacharsky moved that the Duma should be buried as a relic of a shameful past. Trotsky seconded him with a scathing speech. When at one of the next sittings he rose again and as usual began his address with the word 'Comrades', he was interrupted by an outcry: 'What sort of comrades are we to you?' and 'Stop calling us comrades!' He stopped, and he moved closer to the Bolsheviks.[4]

The main issue which occupied the Congress was the condition of the army. Since the overthrow of Tsardom the Russian fronts had been inactive. Pressed by the western allies, the government and the General Staff were preparing a new offensive for which they were anxious to obtain the Soviets' approval. The General Staff was also pressing for a revision of the famous Order No. 1, the Magna Charta of the soldiers' freedom. In this debate Trotsky made his chief speech, in which he warned the government that after the prodigious losses the army had suffered and after the disruption of its supply services by inefficiency, profiteering, and corruption, the army was incapable of further fighting. The offensive would end in disaster; the attempt to reimpose the old discipline would lead

[1] *Novaya Zhizn*, 6 June 1917.   [2] *Rech*, 7 June 1917.
[3] *Pervyi Vseros. Syezd Sovietov*, pp. 295–8.   [4] Ibid., p. 352.

nowhere. 'Fortunately for Russia's whole history, our revolutionary army has done away with the old outlook of the Russian army, the outlook of the locust . . . when hundreds of thousands used to die passively . . . without ever being aware of the purpose of their sacrifice. . . . Let this historical period which we have left behind be damned! What we now value is not the elemental, unconscious heroism of the mass, but a heroism which refracts itself through every individual consciousness.'[1] At present the army had no idea to fight for. 'I repeat, that in this same army, as it has emerged from the revolution . . . there exist and there will exist ideas, watchwords, purposes capable of rallying it and of imparting to this our army unity and enthusiasm. . . . The army of the great French revolution consciously responded to calls for an offensive. What is the crux of the matter? It is this: no such purpose that would rally the army exists now. . . . Every thinking soldier asks himself: for every five drops of blood which I am going to shed today will not one drop only be shed in the interest of the Russian revolution, and four in the interest of the French Stock Exchange and of English imperialism?'[2] If only Russia disentangled herself from the imperialist alignments, if only the power of the old ruling classes was destroyed and a new democratic government established by the Soviets, then 'we should be able to summon all European peoples and tell them that now a citadel of revolution has risen on the map of Europe'.[3]

He then resumed his ever-recurring dialogue with the sceptic who did not believe that 'the revolution would spread and that the Russian revolutionary army and Russian democracy would find allies in Europe': 'My answer is that history has given no guarantee to us, to the Russian revolution, that we shall not be crushed altogether, that our revolutionary will is not going to be strangled by a coalition of world capital, that world imperialism will not crucify us.' The Russian Revolution represented so great a danger to the propertied classes of all countries that they would try to destroy it and to transform Russia into a colony of European or, what was more probable, of American capital. But this trial of strength was still ahead, and the Soviets were in duty bound to be ready for it. 'If . . . [revolutionary] Germany does not rise, or if she rises too feebly, then we shall move

[1] *Pervyi Vseros. Syezd Sovietov*, p. 353.   [2] Ibid., p. 354.   [3] Ibid., pp. 356 ff.

our regiments . . . not in order to defend ourselves but in order
to undertake a revolutionary offensive.' At this point the powerful peroration was interrupted by an anonymous voice from
the floor: 'It will be too late, then'. Before the year was out, the
anonymous voice was proved right. But in the Trotsky who
addressed the Congress the features can be clearly discerned of
the man who was not only to confront, without any armed
strength behind him, the diplomacy of the Hohenzollerns and
the Habsburgs, but also to create the Red Army.

At this Congress he had his last clash with Plekhanov. They
addressed each other frigidly as 'Citizens', not 'Comrades'.
Plekhanov had reached the extreme of his warlike mood, and
even the Mensheviks were so embarrassed by his chauvinist
outbursts that they kept aloof from him. But the Congress paid
a warm tribute to Plekhanov's past merits, only to be treated by
him to a hackneyed patriotic sermon. Trotsky aggressively
reproached him for this, and Plekhanov replied haughtily,
comparing himself now with Danton and now with Lassalle and
contrasting the disheartened and dejected armies of the Russian
Revolution with the armies of Cromwell and of the Jacobins,
whose 'spirits soared when they drank the sap of revolution'.
Little did the sick veteran imagine that it was his younger and
much snubbed opponent who was destined for the role of the
Russian Danton, destined to make the Russian armies 'drink
the sap of revolution'.

Through the greater part of the proceedings, the majority
treated lightly the Bolsheviks and their associates. When
Tseretelli, pleading for the coalition government, challenged
the delegates to say whether there was a single party in Russia
prepared alone to shoulder responsibility for government, Lenin
interrupted from the floor to say that his party was prepared
for that. The majority drowned Lenin's words in hilarious
laughter. The delegates from the provinces were not aware that
in Petrograd the opposition's influence was already growing
like an avalanche. Lenin was eager to impress them and to show
them that Petrograd demanded an end to the coalition and the
formation of a Socialist ministry, that is of a ministry consisting
only of the moderate Socialists. Despite his statement from the
floor of the Congress, which was a declaration of principle, not of
immediate purpose, Lenin did not yet aim at the overthrow

of the government. Still less did he favour a coalition between the moderate Socialists and his own party. As long as the Bolsheviks were a minority in the Soviets, he urged his followers not to play at seizing power but 'patiently to explain their attitude to the masses', until they gained the majority. This was the crux of his Soviet constitutionalism. In the meantime, the Bolshevik slogan was not 'Down with the government', but 'Down with the ten capitalist ministers!' Overcoming the forebodings in his own Central Committee, Lenin was in great secrecy preparing a monster demonstration under this slogan for 10 June. Trotsky, dispelling his friends' misgivings, induced the Inter-Borough Organization to join in the demonstration. But on 9 June, when *Pravda* made an open call to the workers and the garrison, the Executive of the Congress banned the demonstration.

Neither Lenin nor Trotsky wished to defy the ban. They decided to submit to the decision of the majority, to cancel the demonstration, and to explain their attitude in a special manifesto. This was an anxious moment. Would the workers and soldiers take note of the cancellation? If so, would they not misunderstand the party's attitude? Would their urge for action not be chilled? Lenin drafted an explanatory statement, but as his followers and he himself were not pleased with it he gladly adopted another text, submitted by Trotsky; and this was read out at the Congress in the name of the entire opposition. Trotsky, not yet a member of the party, also composed for the Bolshevik Central Committee a manifesto on the subject.[1]

On 10 June Petrograd remained calm. But the leaders of the Soviet majority decided to call another monster demonstration on 18 June, hoping to turn it into a manifestation in favour of their policies. On the appointed day, 500,000 workers and soldiers marched past the stands on which the Congress had assembled *in corpore*. To the dismay of the moderate Socialists, all the banners in the procession had Bolshevik slogans inscribed on them: 'Down with the ten capitalist ministers!', 'Down with the war!', and 'All power to the Soviets!' The march-past was concluded peacefully. There were no riots and no clashes, but for the first time the anti-Bolshevik parties

[1] Lenin, *Sochinenya*, vol. xxv, pp. 60–61; Trotsky, *Sochinenya*, vol. iii, book 1, p. 137; and *Lénine*, pp. 66–69.

gauged the impression which Bolshevik policies and slogans had made on the masses.

In this early period of his activity—it was only the second month after his return—Trotsky's personality had already acquired a fresh and immense lustre. Lunacharsky writes that 'under the influence of Trotsky's dazzling success, and of the enormous scope of his personality many people who were close to Trotsky were even inclined to see in him the genuine first leader of the Russian revolution. Uritsky . . . said once to me and, it seems, to Manuilsky: "Well, the great revolution has come, and you see that, although Lenin has so much wisdom, he begins to grow dim beside the genius of Trotsky."' This opinion, Lunacharsky goes on, was incorrect, not because it exaggerated Trotsky's gifts and his power, but because the scope of Lenin's political genius had not yet revealed itself. 'It is true that in this period . . . Lenin was dimmed a little. He did not speak publicly very often and he did not write very much. He directed mainly the work of organization in the Bolshevik camp, while Trotsky thundered at the meetings.' In 1917, how-ever, the revolution was made as much at mass meetings as within the narrower compass of the party.[1]

.   .   .   .

For the beginning of July the Bolsheviks convened the sixth national congress of their party. This was to be the occasion on which the Inter-Borough Organization was to join their ranks. There was no longer any talk about changing the party's 'label'. For a time the majority of the Inter-Borough Organiza-tion resisted; and on its behalf Yureniev still warned members against 'the bad organizational manners' of the Bolsheviks and their inclination to work through narrow secretive caucuses. Trotsky headed the minority which was impatient for the merger. He pleaded that with their emergence from the twilight of clandestinity and the awakening of the broad popular move-ment, the Bolsheviks had largely rid themselves of their old habits, and that what was left of these would best be overcome in a common, openly working party. Assisted by Lunacharsky, he converted the majority to this view.[2] But before the merger had taken place, the country was shaken by the crisis of the July days.

---

[1] Lunacharsky, op. cit., pp. 25–28.
[2] Trotsky, *Sochinenya*, vol. iii, book 1, pp. 145–9.

This was one of those violent convulsions which occur unexpectedly in every revolution, upset the plans of all leaders,
accelerate the rhythm of events, and press the polarization of
hostile forces to the utter limit. The patience of the garrison and
of the working population of Petrograd was exhausted. Bread
queues grew interminably. Money, of which ten times more
than before the war was in circulation, was depreciated.
Profiteering was rampant. The masses saw that since the revolution the conditions of their daily existence had become worse,
and they felt that they had been cheated. On top of all this came
the costly offensive, now in progress. But there was still a
discrepancy between the mood of the capital and that of the
provinces. Petrograd clamoured for immediate change and for
the resignation of Prince Lvov's second government. In the
provinces, however, the February régime was by no means
discredited.

Trotsky and Lenin, as they surveyed the balance of strength
in the country as a whole, knew that the hour had not yet come
for them to strike. But their following in the capital, seething
with restlessness, began to view with distrust their tactics. The
Anarchists denounced the waiting game and the treachery of
the Bolsheviks, as the Bolsheviks had denounced the hesitations
and the treachery of the Mensheviks and Social Revolutionaries.
Finally, a number of regiments confronted Bolshevik headquarters with an accomplished fact and called an armed demonstration for 3 July. The sailors of Kronstadt and the civilian
workers in the capital, stirred by rank-and-file Bolshevik
agitators, eagerly responded to the call. As in most such situations, when a risky political initiative springs directly from the
impulsive anger of the masses, the purpose of the initiative was
not clear. Those who called the demonstration did not know
whether they were out to overthrow the government or merely
to demonstrate in a peaceful manner. Bolshevik headquarters
made an attempt to cancel the demonstration as they had done
on 10 June. But this time popular passion could not be dammed.[1]

Lenin then tried to place his party at the head of the move-

---

[1] Trotsky, *History of the Russian Revolution*, vol. ii, chapters i–iii; Zinoviev,
Sochinenya, vol. xv, p. 41; Lenin, *Sochinenya*, vol. xxv, pp. 142–3. Stalin, who was very
active in the opening phase of the July events, gave a full account of them to the
sixth Congress of the party. Stalin, *Sochinenya*, vol. iii, pp. 156–68. (His account is
summarized in Deutscher, *Stalin*, pp. 148–9.) Raskolnikov, op. cit., pp. 116 ff.

ment in order to keep the movement within the limits of a
peaceful demonstration, the purpose of which would be once
again to urge the moderate Socialists to form their own Ministry based on the Soviets. With this demand enormous crowds
appeared in the centre of the city, filling the streets, marching,
and holding meetings in the course of two days and nights.
Bolshevik speakers, including Lenin, addressed them, inveighing
against the ruling coalition but also appealing for calm and
discipline.

The greatest and the angriest crowd besieged the Tauride
Palace, where the central Executive of the Soviets had its offices.
The crowd sent delegations to the Palace to declare that they
would not disperse until the moderate Socialists broke up their
coalition with the Cadets. Some Mensheviks and Social Revolutionaries were convinced that Lenin had staged the spectacle
and intended it as an armed insurrection. True, for leaders of an
insurrection, the Bolsheviks behaved strangely: they harangued
the masses, restraining them and warning them against acts of
violence. There were, nevertheless, some appearances of pre-
meditated Bolshevik action. It was known that Bolshevik
rankers had led the agitation, and the sailors of Kronstadt were
most prominent in the commotion.[1] The moderate Socialists
sat in the besieged Palace in terror of their lives. They appealed
to military headquarters for help. As almost the entire garrison
was on the side of the Bolsheviks, reliable detachments were
called from the front. While the Mensheviks and Social Revolutionaries waited to be rescued, word came that the crowd
outside had seized Chernov, the Minister of Agriculture, and
was about to lynch him. Trotsky, who had spent the whole night
and the morning in the Palace, now pleading with the demonstrators outside and now with the Executive inside, rushed out
to the scene of the riot.

[1] Thirty-five years after the event, R. Abramovich, the Menshevik leader wrote:
'The anti-war mood began to rise feverishly after the ill-starred June offensive. The
hostile reaction to this attempt to revive a war which in the mind of the masses was
already dead was so strong that my own feeling at the time was that already during
the July days the Bolsheviks could have seized power by means of their semi-coup,
if Lenin and his friends had shown greater determination.' (*Sotsialisticheskii Vestnik*,
March 1952: 'The Tragedy of a Belated Revolution'.) During the events, however,
and afterwards, Abramovich charged the Bolsheviks with outright conspiracy to
seize power. Trotsky, *History of the Russian Revolution*, vol. ii, p. 39.

What followed has been described many times, but nowhere as vividly as in Sukhanov's *Notes on the Revolution*:

As far as the eye could see, the crowd was raging. Around one car, a group of sailors with quite ugly faces behaved in an exceptionally rowdy manner. On a back seat in that car sat Chernov who had quite visibly lost control of himself. The whole of Kronstadt knew Trotsky and seemed to trust him. But the crowd failed to calm down when Trotsky began his speech. If a provocative shot had at this moment been fired anywhere in the neighbourhood, a terrible bloodbath would have followed: they would have torn to pieces all of us, including Trotsky. Excited, with difficulty finding his words, . . . Trotsky just managed to compel the attention of those who stood nearest to him. [He began by extolling the revolutionary virtues of Kronstadt in a manner which seemed to Sukhanov to smack of unworthy flattery.] 'You have come here, you, red men of Kronstadt, as soon as you heard about the danger threatening the revolution. . . . Long live red Kronstadt, the glory and the pride of the revolution!'

But they listened to Trotsky in a sullen mood. When he tried to talk to them about Chernov, the people surrounding the car were again in a fury.

'You have come here to state your will [Trotsky went on] and to show the Soviet that the working class does not wish to see the bourgeoisie in power. But why should you harm your own cause? Why should you obscure and blot your record by mean violence over random individuals? . . . Every one of you has shown his devotion to the revolution. Every one of you is prepared to lay down his head for the revolution. I know this. . . . Give me your hand, comrade! . . . Give me a hand, my brother. . . .'

Trotsky stretched down his arm to a sailor who was violently protesting against his words. The sailor grasped a rifle in one hand and withdrew the other from Trotsky. It seemed to me that he must have listened to Trotsky more than once at Kronstadt, and that he was now really under the impression that Trotsky had betrayed the cause.[1]

Finally, Trotsky defied the crowd and asked those who wanted violence to be done to Chernov openly to raise their hands. Not a hand went up. Amid silence, he took Chernov, half-

---

[1] Sukhanov, op. cit., vol. iv, pp. 423–5. See also V. Chernov, *The Great Russian Revolution*, pp. 422–6. Trotsky later claimed that those who had seized Chernov were *agent-provocateurs* who had nothing in common with the sailors. (*Sochinenya*, vol. iii, book 1, pp. 193 ff.) On internal evidence, Sukhanov's version appears more credible, and it is shared by Raskolnikov, the leader of Kronstadt (op. cit., pp. 128–30).

fainting by now, by the arm and led him into the Palace. Trotsky's own face, as he returned with his rescued enemy, was of a deadly pallor and covered with cold perspiration.

In various parts of the city minor disturbances and affrays occurred, which could easily have led to profuse bloodshed had it not been for the restraining influence of the Bolsheviks. At length the demonstrators became tired and their energy sagged. They were on the point of dispersing when the troops from the front arrived. A violent reaction set in at once. Secret and half-secret right-wing organizations, which had hitherto lain low, descended upon the streets. After a few clashes, the pro-Bolshevik crowds, craving for sleep and rest, dispersed. Just then the papers broke the news of the collapse of the offensive on the front. This added fuel to the anti-Bolshevik reaction. The right-wing parties, the generals, and the officers' leagues blamed the Bolsheviks; it was their agitation, they said, that had destroyed the army's morale and prepared the defeat.[1]

This charge alone would have been enough to bring a storm on the heads of the Bolshevik party. Added to it was another, even more inflammatory, accusation. A popular right-wing newspaper published 'documents' alleging that Lenin had been in the pay of the German General Staff; and writs were issued for the arrest of Lenin, Zinoviev, and Kamenev. The documents could be recognized at a glance as a clumsy fabrication. The witness who produced them, a certain Yermolenko, turned out to be a former stool-pigeon, now in the service of military counter-intelligence.[2] But at first the impression made by the accusation was devastating. Appearances spoke against Lenin; and for the moment appearances were decisive. The non-political citizen, no initiate in the history and habits of revolutionary parties, asked: Did Lenin not in fact return via *Germany*,

[1] A week before these events, on 28 June, Trotsky wrote in *Vperyod*: 'And if after three years of war and four months of revolution not all the soldiers are persuaded by the evasively cautious resolution of the Congress [of the Soviets, which approved the offensive] or by the cheap oratorical fanfaronade of semi-socialist semi-ministers, then the 'loyal' press can always resort to a tested device: it can call "society" to a crusade against the revolutionary socialists at large and the Bolsheviks in particular.'

[2] A detailed account and analysis of this affair will be given in my *Life of Lenin*. Kerensky's version is in *Crucifixion of Liberty*, pp. 285–94 and its refutation is in M. N. Pokrovsky, *Oktyabr'skaya Revolutsia*, pp. 115–36. See also Trotsky, *History*, vol. ii, pp. 96–123.

by agreement with the German government? Did he not
agitate against the war? Did he not foment upheaval? It was no
use replying that Lenin had resolved to travel through Germany
only after all other routes, via France and England, had been
denied to him, and that many of his Menshevik adversaries had
returned together with him, or somewhat later, by the same
route.[1] It was no use pointing out that Lenin hoped that the
revolution would destroy the Hohenzollerns and the Habsburgs
as it had destroyed the Romanovs. In the stampede which
followed the July days such subtleties were overlooked. The
upper classes were mad with fear and hatred of revolution. The
middle classes were blind with despair. The General Staff needed
a face-saving explanation of the latest military disaster. And the
moderate Socialists felt the earth opening beneath their feet.
The need for a scapegoat and a spectacular sin-offering was
overwhelming.

In the middle of this turmoil Trotsky saw Lenin. 'They have
chosen this moment to shoot us all', Lenin said.[2] He reckoned
with the probability of a successful counter-revolution; he
believed that the Soviets, emasculated by the Mensheviks and
Social Revolutionaries, had played out their role; and he was
preparing his party for a return to clandestinity. After a little
hesitation, he made up his mind that he would not allow himself
to be imprisoned but would go into hiding, together with Zinoviev. Trotsky took a less grave view and Lenin's decision seemed
to him unfortunate. Such behaviour was altogether against the
grain of Trotsky's own habits. He thought that Lenin had nothing to hide, that, on the contrary, he had every interest in
laying his record before the public, and that in this way he could
serve his cause better than by flight, which would merely add
to any adverse appearances by which people might judge him.[3]
Kamenev shared Trotsky's feelings and decided to submit to
imprisonment. But Lenin stuck to his decision. He did not expect
to be given a fair trial by a government which heaped false
accusations on him and circulated faked documents in the press.

[1] During the official investigation on the July days it was ascertained that about
500 Russian émigrés had returned from Switzerland via Germany. Of these 400
were anti-Bolsheviks and 'social patriots'. Pokrovsky, op. cit., p. 123.
[2] Trotsky, Lénine, p. 69.
[3] See Trotsky's deposition which he later made in prison. Sochinenya, vol. iii,
book 1, p. 193 passim; History, vol. ii, pp. 240–1.

The atmosphere was tense. The Bolshevik party was virtually ostracized. *Pravda* had been banned and its offices demolished. Bolshevik headquarters in several districts had been wrecked. Nothing was easier for the thugs of the old Okhrana, who were still entrenched in the police, or for fanatics of the counter-revolution than to assassinate a hated leader of the revolution on the way to or from prison. Lenin was too well aware of his importance to the party to take this risk, and, disregarding all conventional considerations, went into hiding.[1]

In public attacks, Trotsky's name was most often coupled with Lenin's, but no writ of arrest was issued against him. There were obvious reasons: he was not nominally a member of the Bolshevik party; the circumstances of his return to Russia were so different from those in which Lenin had travelled that it was not easy to tack on to him the label of German agent; and the incident with Chernov, the political enemy whom he had so courageously rescued, was still fresh in everybody's mind. But he was not spared for long. *Ryech*, Miliukov's paper, published a story that before his departure from New York Trotsky had received 10,000 dollars from German-Americans, which he was to use for defeatist agitation in Russia. In less respectable newspapers the German General Staff figured as the source of the money. Trotsky at once replied with an Open Letter which appeared in Gorky's paper and deflated Miliukov's revelations with much comic effect. He remarked ironically that the German-Americans or the German General Staff apparently considered the overthrow of a régime in an enemy country an extremely cheap affair, costing only 10,000 dollars. He attacked the sources from which the story emanated, saying that it had come from Sir George Buchanan, the British Ambassador. The Ambassador denied the charge, but this did not prevent Miliukov from claiming that he had the story from that source. Then Trotsky related what had really happened before his departure from New York: Russian, American, Latvian, Jewish, Finnish, and German-American Socialists arranged a farewell meeting for him and three other Russian émigrés who were

---

[1] This step embarrassed quite a few of Lenin's followers. Only much later, when during the German revolution Rosa Luxemburg and Karl Liebknecht were assassinated in such a way, did Lenin's behaviour acquire full justification in the eyes of those who were at first uneasy about it.

about to leave with him. A collection was made on the spot which yielded 310 dollars to which the German-American part of the audience contributed 100. The sum was handed to Trotsky, and he divided it equally among the returning émigrés. The meeting and the collection were reported in American newspapers. He concluded with a good-humoured 'confession' which, as he knew, would discredit him in the eyes of the bourgeois public even more than being in the pay of the German General Staff: never in his life, he wrote, had he at one time possessed 10,000 dollars or even one-tenth of that sum.[1]

In another Open Letter he related the story of his friendship and break with Parvus, since this connexion was also brought up against him. He exposed Alexinsky, the former Bolshevik deputy turned renegade, as chief inspirer of the calumny. Alexinsky, he wrote, had been expelled as a slanderer from all journalistic organizations in Paris, and the Mensheviks had, on moral grounds, refused to admit him to the Petrograd Soviet. And this was the man now promoted to be the guardian of patriotic morality.[2]

This attempt at involving Trotsky having failed, intrigue was started from the opposite angle. The press was full of stories alleging that Trotsky had broken with Lenin, the German agent. On 10 July, four days after Lenin had gone into hiding, Trotsky therefore addressed the following Open Letter to the Provisional Government:

Citizen Ministers—I understand that you have decreed the arrest . . . of Comrades Lenin, Zinoviev, Kamenev, but that the writ of arrest does not concern me. I therefore think it necessary to bring these facts to your attention: 1. I share in principle the attitude of Lenin, Zinoviev, and Kamenev, and I have expounded it in the journal *Vperyod* and in all my public speeches. 2. My attitude towards the events of 3 and 4 July was uniform with that of the above-mentioned Comrades.[3]

He gave an account of those events and explained that the fact that he did not belong to the Bolshevik organization was due to outdated and now meaningless differences.

You can have no logical grounds for exempting me from the effect of the decree by dint of which Lenin, Zinoviev, and Kamenev are

---

[1] Trotsky, *Sochinenya*, vol. iii, book 1, pp. 150–4.   [2] Ibid., pp. 155–9.
[3] Ibid., pp. 165–6.

subject to arrest. . . . You can have no reason to doubt that I am just as irreconcilable an opponent of the general policy of the Provisional Government as the above-mentioned Comrades. My exemption only underlines more graphically the counter-revolutionary and wanton character of the action you have taken against them.[1]

For two or three days, while the terror against the Bolsheviks was at its peak, Trotsky did not appear at the Soviet. He spent the nights at the home of Larin, the former Menshevik who was about to join the Bolsheviks. But after the publication of the 'Open Letter to the Provisional Government' Trotsky, full of fight and defiance, reappeared in the limelight. He defended Lenin and the Bolshevik party in the Soviet, on the Executive of the Soviets, and on the Executive of the peasant Soviets. Everywhere he spoke amid continuous uproar. 'Lenin', he exclaimed, 'has fought for the revolution thirty years. I have fought against the oppression of the popular masses twenty years. We cannot but hate German militarism. Only he who does not know what a revolutionary is can say otherwise. . . . Do not allow anybody in this hall to say that we are German mercenaries, for this is the voice . . . of villainy.'[2] He warned the Mensheviks, who were washing their hands of the affair, that this would be their own undoing. Chernov, the 'social patriot', had already been compelled to resign from the ministry, because he had participated in the Zimmerwald movement. The counter-revolution had chosen the Bolsheviks as its first targets; the moderate socialists would be its next victims.

Even in those days of hysteria and panic he was listened to with attention and respect. His appeals, however, had little or no effect. The moderate Socialists knew that it was preposterous to accuse Lenin and Zinoviev of being German agents; but they were convinced that the Bolshevik agitation against the war had gone too far; and they suspected that in the July days Lenin, or perhaps Lenin and Trotsky, had attempted to seize power;

[1] Loc. cit. At the same time Trotsky wrote a letter to Gorky. Gorky, who had been Lenin's close friend, behaved (in contrast to Martov, who defended Lenin) rather vaguely. Trotsky intended to urge him to come out strongly in Lenin's defence and to remind him of Zola's role in the Dreyfus affair. The letter, which Trotsky did not post, is reprinted in *Sochinenya*, vol. iii, book 1, pp. 346–7.
[2] Sukhanov, op. cit., vol. v, pp. 52, 59–62.

K

and they refused to lift a finger for Lenin's rehabilitation. Only Martov defended the honour of his old adversary.[1]

Trotsky remained at large for another fortnight. The ministry was embarrassed by his challenge. It had no ground to order his arrest, unless it declared as lawless the principles which guided the Soviet as a whole, including its moderate majority, for it was in terms of those principles that Trotsky had framed his own activity. The ministry could not, on the other hand, allow him to remain at large and make a mockery of its action against the Bolsheviks. On the night of 23 July Trotsky and Lunacharsky were arrested and transferred to the Kresty prison. Sukhanov describes the impression which this made in Petrograd. The next day, Sukhanov himself addressed a Menshevik meeting at the Cirque Moderne. 'My announcement about the arrest of Trotsky and Lunacharsky . . . was met with such a storm of indignation that for nearly a quarter of an hour it was impossible to go on with the meeting. Shouts were heard that the whole crowd, numbering many thousands, should at once march and express its protest to the authorities. It was with difficulty that Martov contrived to reduce the affair to an improvised resolution of protest.'[2]

Thus in the middle of a revolution in which his former friends and a former pupil had risen to power, Trotsky found himself in the same prison in which the Tsarist government had locked him up in 1905. The conditions inside the prison were worse now. The cells were extremely overcrowded: the rounding up of suspects continued, and large batches were brought in daily. Criminal and political offenders were herded together, whereas under the old régime the political offenders had enjoyed the privilege of separation. All were kept on a near-starvation diet. The criminals were incited against the 'German agents', robbed them of their food and manhandled them. Prosecutors, examiners, and jailers were the same as under the Tsar. The contrast between the pretensions of the new rulers and the inside aspect of the judicial machinery was striking; and, as Trotsky watched

---

[1] Among the many versions of the July events one claimed that there had been a plan for the dictatorship of a triumvirate, consisting of Lenin, Trotsky, and Lunacharsky. How widely this version was believed can be judged from the circumstance that even Sukhanov was inclined to take it at face value. Sukhanov, op. cit., vol. iv, p. 511.

[2] Ibid., vol. v, p. 121.

it, he reflected that Lenin was not so mistaken when he decided to take refuge. Yet in this wild chaos, in which even the life of the prisoner was sometimes in peril, there was, just as under the old régime, still enough latitude for the prisoners' political and literary activity. With such debaters as Kamenev, Lunacharsky, Antonov-Ovseenko, and Krylenko, political debate flourished. Among the inmates were also Dybenko and Raskolnikov, the leaders of Kronstadt. Here were assembled nearly all the chief actors of the October insurrection and nearly the whole first Bolshevik Commissariat of War.

Trotsky himself took to the pen, and once again a cataract of his articles and pamphlets found its way to the outside world. Some of these, including a detailed description of life in the prison, appeared, under the pen-name P. Tanas, in Bolshevik papers, and others in Gorky's daily. In another of his 'Open Letters to the Provisional Government' Trotsky covered the legal proceedings with ridicule. He revealed that he was charged with having returned to Russia, together with Lenin, via Germany and with having been a member of the Bolshevik Central Committee. These charges testified to the wantonness and the lazy indolence of the prosecution.[1] It was, incidentally, only some weeks after Trotsky's arrest that the Inter-Borough Organization finally joined the Bolshevik party and Trotsky became a member of the Bolshevik Central Committee. His exposure of the proceedings had the effect of causing his prosecutor's dismissal. But the proceedings went on. 'The Dreyfus case and the Beyliss case are nothing compared with this deliberate attempt at moral assassination', Trotsky protested to Zarudny, the Minister of Justice who, by a strange freak, had been counsel for the defence in the Soviet's trial in 1906.[2]

As the weeks passed, events unexpectedly took a turn at once more hopeful and more menacing to the prosecuted men and their cause. The reaction against the July 'insurrection' was broadening into an impetuous movement against all the institutions and conditions which had their origin in the February Revolution: against the Soviets, the army committees, the land committees, the factory committees, and similar bodies which had wittingly and unwittingly disputed the authority of the old

---

[1] *Novaya Zhizn*, 30 July 1917.
[2] Trotsky, *Sochinenya*, vol. iii, book 1, p. 203; Raskolnikov, op. cit., pp. 170–9.

administrative machine. The reaction now hit the moderate
Socialists. The leaders of the right-wing argued, not without
reason, that the Bolsheviks were only the most consistent
advocates of a state of affairs to the defence of which the
moderate Socialists were in varying degrees also committed.[1]
The Bolshevik cry 'All power to the Soviets!' would not die
down as long as the Soviets were in existence; and the Mensheviks and Social Revolutionaries had a stake in their existence.
If the Bolsheviks did their utmost to stir up the opposition of
soldier against officer, the moderate Socialists, the initial mouthpieces of that opposition, had a vested interest at least in pre-
venting the officers' corps from regaining its old status. The
leaders of the middle classes had hitherto hoped to tame the
revolution with the hands of the moderate Socialists; they now
cast around for a military dictator capable of taming or crushing
the moderate Socialists as well as the Bolsheviks. Only thus did
the right wing, which now included former Liberals, hope to
bring to an end what they regarded as the most shameful chapter
in Russian history.

The July days had shown that if any strength was left in
anti-Bolshevik Russia that strength resided in the officers' corps.
The picture of the moderate Soviet leaders, besieged in the
Tauride Palace, trembling for their lives and praying to be
rescued from Bolshevik crowds by loyal troops was not forgotten. Yet such was the illogical mechanism of the February
régime that the real relationship of power was now more than
ever masked by the political façade. Immediately after the July
days, a second coalition government was formed with Kerensky
as Premier, in which the moderate socialists assumed nominal
leadership. In their heyday they had been the junior partners
in the coalition; and only after their weakness had been so
devastatingly revealed did they assume the role of senior partners, at least in appearance. This paradox could not last.

The Conservative and anti-revolutionary forces rested their
hopes on General Kornilov, whom Kerensky had appointed
Commander-in-Chief. Feted and acclaimed by the upper and
middle classes, Kornilov began to feel and behave like a man of
Providence. His attitude towards Kerensky became ambiguous

[1] Miliukov, op. cit., vol. i, book 2, pp. 58–72; A. I. Denikin, *Ocherki Russkoi
Smuty*, vol. i, book 2, pp. 232–8.

and then provocative. Finally, on 24 August, he openly declared war on the government and ordered his troops to march on the capital. Confident of victory, he boasted in advance of the clean sweep he was going to make of the revolution.

Trotsky and his friends in Kresty received the news with mixed feelings. Kerensky kept them behind the bars, and if Kornilov were to win they would be delivered as virtual hostages to the victorious *soldateska*. They had no doubt that they would be slaughtered; and this was certainly not a figment of panicky imaginations. But the situation also offered new hope. The moderate Socialists could not save themselves from Kornilov without the help of the Bolsheviks, just as in the July days they could not save themselves from the Bolsheviks without the help of the generals. Soon the government itself was pressing rifles into the hands of the Red Guards, whom it had just disarmed. It begged the Bolshevik agitators, on whose destructive influence it had blamed all military disasters, to bring that influence to bear on Kornilov's troops and persuade them to disobey and desert their commanders. And, finally, Kerensky implored the sailors of Kronstadt, the villains of July, to rally to his defence.

A scene of almost whimsical fantasy took place in Trotsky's cell. The sailors of Kronstadt sent a delegation to ask him whether they ought to respond to Kerensky's call and defend Kerensky against Kornilov or whether they should try to settle accounts with both Kornilov and Kerensky. To the hot-headed sailors the latter course certainly appealed more. Trotsky argued with them, reminding them how in May he had defended them in the Soviet and had said that if a counter-revolutionary general were to try to throw a noose around the neck of the revolution then 'the sailors of Kronstadt would come and fight and die with us'. They must now honour this pledge and postpone the reckoning with Kerensky, which could not be far off anyhow. The sailors took his advice. While this was going on, the prosecution mechanically continued its job. The examination dragged on and Trotsky had to answer questions about his connexions with the German General Staff and the Bolsheviks. Antonov-Ovseenko and Krylenko, against whom no charges were brought after six weeks of imprisonment, threatened a hunger strike, but Trotsky tried to dissuade them. At length he decided to take no further part in the farce of interrogation. He refused to answer the examiner's questions and gave his reasons in a letter to the Central Executive of the Soviets. Three days later, on 4 September, he was released on bail.

Straight from the prison he went to the Smolny Institute to participate in a session of the Committee for Struggle against Counter-revolution, which had, with Kerensky's blessing, been formed by the Soviet. This body was to be the prototype of the Military Revolutionary Committee which led the October insurrection.

Kornilov was defeated not by force of arms, but by Bolshevik agitation. His troops deserted him, without firing a shot. From Kornilov's defeat started a new chain of events leading straight to the October insurrection. Just as the abortive revolution of 3–4 July had swung the balance in favour of counter-revolution, so this abortive counter-revolution had swung it much more powerfully in the opposite direction. The second coalition government broke down. The Cadet ministers resigned, because they did not favour Kerensky's action against Kornilov. The Socialist ministers withdrew, because they suspected Kerensky of having previously intrigued with Kornilov against the Soviet and encouraged his ambitions. For a month Kerensky, incapable of piecing together the broken fragments of the coalition, ruled through a so-called Directorate, a small and quite unrepresentative committee.

In the Soviet Trotsky and Kamenev asked for an investigation of the events that led to Kornilov's coup and of Kerensky's role in the preliminaries. With increased insistence they pressed the moderate Socialists to part company at last with the Cadets, many of whom had backed Kornilov. After the Kornilov affair the argument in favour of a purely Socialist government sounded irrefutable. When the Mensheviks and Social Revolutionaries still continued their attempts to revive the coalition, their followers deserted them *en masse*. Within a few days the moderate majority in the Soviet disintegrated. On 9 September Trotsky made one of his rousing speeches, demanding an unequivocal rehabilitation of himself and the Bolshevik leaders. He asked for the government's long-overdue report on the July events, and he tabled a motion of no confidence in the Menshevik 'Presidium' of the Soviet. To everybody's immense surprise, the motion was carried. For the first time the Bolsheviks obtained for their proposal a majority vote in the Soviet. The revolution had set up a new landmark.[1]

As they were losing ground in the Soviet, the Mensheviks and their associates made an attempt to rally outside the Soviet. For 14 September they convened the so-called Democratic Conference. This was not in any sense an elected assembly. Its composition was so devised as to secure in advance an anti-Bolshevik majority. A haphazard assortment of delegations from various non-political institutions, such as co-operatives and pre-revolutionary *Zemstvos*, was to pronounce on all the burning political issues. Such was the paradox of the situation that, regardless of what was to happen later, at this stage it was the Bolsheviks who appeared to stand firmly by the principle of representative and elected government, while the moderate Socialists sought to negate that principle. The Soviets, elected in the factories and barracks, did not represent the bourgeoisie; but they fully represented the working classes, the army, and important sections of the peasantry. Their authority and popular appeal were in part due to the absence of any truly national parliamentary institutions. To create such institutions, so it might seem, was a vital interest of the anti-Bolshevik parties. Yet the coalition governments kept on postponing the promised elections to the Constituent Assembly, and the Bolsheviks clamoured for the elections. In their own minds they were not yet clear about the future relationship between a Constituent Assembly and the Soviets. They did not foresee that by investing all power in the Soviets they would make a Constituent Assembly impossible; and that they themselves would convoke it only in order to disperse it. The moderate Socialists, on the other hand, complied with the repeated postponement of elections in deference to the wishes of the Cadets, who feared that a national poll now taken would produce too radical a legislature.[2] In the meantime the moderate Socialists tried to concoct a substitute

[1] At the same sitting, Trotsky proposed the election of a new Presidium on the basis of proportional representation. This brought an angry comment from Lenin, who argued that the Mensheviks and Social Revolutionaries had not adopted proportionate representation when they were the majority—why should the Bolsheviks accord them this privilege? However, Trotsky's conciliatory gesture met with a rebuff from the Mensheviks too: they refused to sit with the Bolsheviks in the Presidium.

[2] Miliukov, op. cit., vol. i, book 2, pp. 91–2.

for a parliament in the form of the Democratic Conference and
the so-called pre-Parliament which issued from it.

The Conference offered a spectacle of disarray in the ruling
groups. The moderate Socialists came forward with bitter
recriminations against the Cadets. Kerensky's own supporters
openly aired their distrust of him, saying that his role in the
Kornilov affair had been ambiguous and that he had tried
to place himself above the parties that had sent him to the
government and to establish his personal rule. Kerensky
attempted to refute the charges and to persuade the conference
of the need to revive the governmental coalition. But his performance was so grotesquely melodramatic that he filled his
friends with despair and achieved none of his objectives. It was
on this occasion that Trotsky for the first time appeared as the
chief Bolshevik spokesman. The impression of his speech is thus
described by the Menshevik chronicler of the revolution:[1]

This was undoubtedly one of this amazing orator's most brilliant
speeches, and I cannot suppress the desire to adorn the pages of my
book with an almost full reproduction of this magnificent oration.
If in the future my book finds a reader as Lamartine's not very
imaginative book still finds readers today, let that reader judge from
this page the oratorical art and the political thought of our days.
He will draw the conclusion that mankind has not lived in vain this
last century and a half, and that the heroes of our revolution relegate
far to the background the famous leaders of 1789.

The audience at the Alexandrinsky theatre was electrified at the
very sound of Trotsky's name. . . . Trotsky had prepared himself
well. Standing on the stage a few steps behind him, I saw on the
pulpit in front of him a closely written sheet, with underlined phrases,
footnotes, and arrows drawn with a blue pencil. . . . He spoke quite
plainly, without any rhetorical art (though he can rise to its heights
whenever he needs to), without the slightest posturing or trickery.
This time he talked with the audience, sometimes advancing towards
it a step or two and then leaning his elbow on the pulpit. The
metallic clarity of speech and the polish of the phrase, which are so
characteristic of Trotsky, were not there in this performance.

We need not summarize this speech, which reproduced the
main lines of Bolshevik policy; only a few points illustrating
his polemical manner will suffice. 'Comrades and Citizens,' he
began very quietly, 'the socialist ministers have just spoken to

[1] Sukhanov, op. cit., vol. v, pp. 125-6. See also Chernov, op. cit., pp. 306-7.

you. Ministers are supposed to appear before representative
bodies to give an account of their work. Our ministers have
preferred to give us advice rather than an account. For the
advice we are grateful, but we still demand an account. Not
advice, but an account, Citizen Ministers', the speaker repeats
very quietly, tapping the pulpit. Summing up the preceding
debate, he remarked that not a single speaker had defended
Kerensky, and so the Prime Minister stood condemned by his
own friends and followers. This struck the opposing camp at its
most vulnerable point, and an angry tumult rose from the floor.
One of the issues most hotly debated was a recent decree
reintroducing the death penalty. 'You may curse me if I ever
sign a single death sentence', Kerensky, anxious to appease his
own resentful followers, exclaimed at the conference. To this
Trotsky retorted: 'If the death penalty is necessary, how can
Kerensky take it upon himself to say that he will make no use
of it? If he thinks that he can commit himself in front of the
whole of democratic opinion and say that he will not apply the
death penalty, then I tell you that he is turning its reintroduction
into an act of lightmindedness which transcends the limits of
criminality.'

The supporters of the coalition had said that the whole Cadet
party should not be blamed for Kornilov's mutiny; and that
the Bolsheviks who protested when their party was denounced as
responsible for the July days, should be the last to blame the
Cadets wholesale. 'In this comparison', Trotsky replied, 'there is
one small inaccuracy. When the Bolsheviks were charged with
… having brought about or provoked the movement of 3–5 July,
there was no question of your inviting them into the Ministry—
they were being invited to the Kresty prison. There is, comrades,
a certain difference here. . . . We say: if in connexion with the
Kornilov movement you want to drag the Cadets to prison,
then, please, do not act indiscriminately. Examine the case of
every Cadet individually, examine it from every possible angle!'
The hostile audience was convulsed with laughter; and even
the most pompous among the ministers and the leaders on the
platform could not suppress a giggle. But this note of jollity was
quickly silenced by one of grim gravity. Trotsky urged that the
Red Guards be armed. 'What for? What for?' the cry came
from the Menshevik benches. 'Firstly, in order that we may

build up a genuine rampart against counter-revolution', he answered, 'against a new and more powerful Kornilov movement. Secondly, if a government of genuine dictatorship by the revolutionary democracy is established, if that new government offers an honest peace and its offer is rejected, then, I am telling you this on behalf of our party . . ., the armed workers of Petrograd and of the whole of Russia will defend the land of revolution from the troops of imperialism with a heroism such as Russian history has never known.' He concluded by denouncing the unrepresentative character of the Conference; and he led the Bolshevik delegates out of the assembly.[1]

Even after this exodus, the Conference failed to meet Kerensky's expectations. It ended, as it had begun, in confusion. A slight majority voted for a new coalition; but then a solid majority emphatically decided against any accommodation with the Cadets, the only partners available for a coalition. When, on 21 September, Kerensky, disregarding the view of his own pseudo-parliament, did set up a new government with the Cadets, the government was in the air from the outset. This was the fifth cabinet formed in seven months. The life-span which Trotsky and Lenin were to leave to it was one month.

In the Soviets, the Bolsheviks went from strength to strength. At the beginning of September they had a majority in Petrograd, Moscow, and other industrial cities. They confidently expected to emerge as the dominant party at the forthcoming national Congress of Soviets. The body entitled to convene the Congress was the Central Executive of the Soviets, which had been elected in June and was still controlled by the moderate Socialists. The latter did their best to postpone what for them was a leap in the dark, and the Bolsheviks pressed, of course, for early convocation. Trotsky pleaded with the moderate leaders and threatened them: 'Do not play with this Congress. The local Soviets, those of Petrograd and Moscow in the first instance, demand it; and if you do not convene it in a constitutional manner, it will be convened in a revolutionary manner.'[2]

On 23 September the Petrograd Soviet elected Trotsky as its President. As he mounted the dais, 'a hurricane of applause went up . . . everything changed in the Soviet!' In contrast to the disheartened assembly of the July days, 'this was now once

---

[1] Trotsky, *Sochinenya*, vol. iii, book 1, pp. 287–93.   [2] Ibid., p. 320.

again a revolutionary army. . . . This was now Trotsky's guard, ready at a wink from him to storm the coalition, the Winter Palace and all the fortresses of the bourgeoisie. . . . The only question was whither Trotsky would lead them.'[1] In his presidential address, he recalled 1905 and expressed the hope that this time he would lead the Soviet towards a different destiny. He gave a solemn and emphatic pledge, on which later events were to throw a melancholy shadow: 'We are all party men, and more than once we shall clash with one another. But we shall conduct the work of the Petrograd Soviet in a spirit of lawfulness and of full freedom for all parties. The hand of the Presidium will never lend itself to the suppression of a minority.'[2] On behalf of the new Soviet he sounded the first summons to the second revolution, calling for Kerensky's resignation and the transfer of governmental power to the Congress of Soviets. He argued against the Mensheviks and Social Revolutionaries as trenchantly as ever, but without ill feeling, without a trace of the craving for revenge which might have been expected from a leader of a party so recently proscribed.[3]

Despite Lenin's objections, all parties were represented in the new Presidium of the Soviet in proportion to their strength.[4] Was this display of scrupulous respect for the rights of the minority merely a tactical stratagem, designed to deceive the minority's vigilance? Hardly so. Sukhanov relates that three years later, after the Bolsheviks had banned all the parties of the opposition, he reminded Trotsky of his pledge not to lend himself to the suppression of any minority. Trotsky lapsed into silence, reflected for a while, and then said wistfully: 'Those were good days.'[5] They were indeed. The revolution was still taking seriously its own assurance that it would widen and make real the freedoms which bourgeois democracy only promised or which it granted with a niggardly hand.

Trotsky now referred to himself in public without inhibition as a Bolshevik. He accepted the label he had so long considered as little better than a slur. While in prison he had been elected to the Central Committee of the party. In the seven weeks that

---

[1] Sukhanov, op. cit., vol. vi, pp. 188 ff.
[2] Loc. cit.   [3] Ibid., p. 194.
[4] Even a group like Gorky's which was too small to claim representation, was allocated seats.   [5] Sukhanov, ibid., p. 190.

passed between his release and the October insurrection, his
name became not merely identified with Bolshevism, but to the
outside world it came to symbolize the aspirations of Bolshevism
even more strongly than did the name of Lenin, who had withdrawn from the public eye.[1] These were weeks so charged with
history that they crowded from men's minds the events of
preceding months and years. Trotsky's feud with Lenin for
nearly fifteen years seemed insignificant in comparison with
the things he would do in fifteen minutes for the Bolshevik party
nowadays. Yet in the inner circle of the party there were,
naturally, men from whose memories nothing could efface the
past feud. They viewed his sudden ascendancy in the party with
well-concealed pique. They had to acknowledge the proud
courage with which he had stood by their party in recent
adversity, when he was not yet a member of it. Nor could they
deny that in Lenin's absence none of them could speak for the
party with Trotsky's firmness, clarity, and authority; and that
not even Lenin could act as its mouthpiece with comparable
brilliance.

Trotsky's ascendancy in the party was therefore undisputed.
But it is enough to scan the records of the Central Committee
to glimpse the feelings below the surface. Earlier in the year
Lenin had tried in vain to prevail upon his colleagues to accord
Trotsky a prominent role in the direction of the Bolshevik press.
As late as 4 August the Central Committee elected a chief
editorial board for Bolshevik newspapers. The board consisted
of Stalin, Sokolnikov, and Miliutin. A proposal that Trotsky,
when released from prison, should join the board was defeated
by eleven votes to ten.[2] On 6 September, however, two days
after his release, when he first appeared at the Central Committee, he was appointed unopposed as one of the party's chief
editors.[3] The Central Committee was now composed of twenty-
one regular and eight deputy members. Some of these had been
familiar figures in the émigré colonies, and some had come from
the Inter-Borough Organization. Others, like Miliutin, Nogin,
Rykov, Sverdlov, Stalin, and Shaumian were home-bred com-

---

[1] Jacques Sadoul, later an ardent Stalinist, wrote at the time: 'Trotsky dominates the insurrection, being its soul of steel, while Lenin remains rather its theo-
retician.' *Notes sur la Révolution*, p. 76.

[2] *Protokoly Tsentralnovo Komiteta*, p. 5.   [3] Ibid., p. 56.

mittee men, who had known almost no life outside their austere, clandestine party, who felt that they had been the real moles of revolution, and who looked with instinctive distrust upon the former émigrés, especially the one who was the most proud, colourful, and eloquent of all. But this antagonism was suppressed almost to the depth of the unconscious.

In the Central Committee Trotsky at first behaved with the discretion and tact of a newcomer. On the day of his first appearance there, differences between the old Bolsheviks came to light which bore directly upon the party's fundamental attitude. These were the preliminaries to the great controversy over the insurrection: from his refuge, Lenin had just posed the problem before the Central Committee. Zinoviev, who shared Lenin's hiding place, had already applied to the Committee for permission to come into the open and dissociate himself from Lenin. The Committee had refused permission; but it was uneasy about the continued concealment of its two leaders; and it allowed Kamenev to negotiate with the moderate Socialists an arrangement which would make it possible for both of them to come into the open. In this prelude to the controversy over insurrection and for some time later, Trotsky said little or nothing, although he held strong views.

Lenin was already prodding his party to insurrection. In his letters to the Central Committee he dwelt on the change in the mood of the Soviets, the rising tide of peasant revolt, and the impatience of the army, to urge that the party should at once pass from revolutionary declarations and promises to armed action. He was confident that if the party seized the opportunity it would gain the support of an immense majority of the people. But history offered a fleeting opportunity only: if the Bolsheviks missed it, another Kornilov would soon be ready with a *pronunciamento* and crush the Soviets and the revolution. In view of this danger, Lenin wrote, no constitutional niceties, not even the niceties of Soviet constitutionalism, deserved attention. The party ought to stage the insurrection in its own name and on its own responsibility. It need not necessarily start in Petrograd: the beginning might be made in Moscow or even in Finland, and from there the insurgent movements could later converge upon the capital.[1] On 15 September the Central Committee

[1] Lenin, *Sochinenya*, vol. xxvi, pp. 1-9.

debated these proposals for the first time. Kamenev came out in categorical opposition and asked the Committee to warn all organizations against any move of an insurrectionist character. The Committee did not accept Kamenev's advice, nor did it accept Lenin's proposals.[1]

In the meantime Trotsky was approaching the problem from his new point of vantage as President of the Petrograd Soviet. He agreed with Lenin on the chances and the urgency of insurrection. But he disagreed with him over method, especially over the idea that the party should stage the insurrection in its own name and on its own responsibility. He took less seriously than Lenin the threat of an immediate counter-revolution.[2] Unlike Lenin, he was confident that the pressure of the Bolshevik majority in the Soviets would not allow the old Central Executive to delay much longer the All-Russian Congress. He reasoned that since the Bolsheviks had conducted their whole agitation under the slogan 'all power to the Soviets', they should stage the rising in such a manner that it would appear to everyone as the direct conclusion of this agitation. The rising should therefore be timed to coincide with, or slightly precede, the Congress of the Soviets, in whose hands the insurgents should then lay the power seized. Furthermore, he wanted the insurrection to be conducted in the name of the Petrograd Soviet and through its machinery, all the components of which were in Bolshevik hands, and of the whole of which he was in personal command. The rising would then appear to the world not as the business of one party only but as a much broader undertaking.[3]

It would be a mistake to read into this difference any deeper conflict over principles, and to deduce from it that, while Trotsky wished to seize power for the Soviets, Lenin aimed at placing power in the hands of his party alone. Both were in a sense Soviet constitutionalists. Lenin, too, envisaged that the insurgents would convene an All-Russian Congress of the Soviets and place power in its hands. He refused to let insurrection wait until the Congress convened, because he was convinced that the Menshevik Executive would delay the Congress to

---

[1] *Protokoly Tsen. Kom.*, p. 65.
[2] This difference can be traced back to the July days. Raskolnikov, op. cit., p. 171; Trotsky, *History*, vol. ii, pp. 315–19.   [3] Ibid., vol. iii, chapters v and vi.

the Greek Calends, and thus the insurrection would never take place as it would be forestalled by a successful counter-revolution. But he, too, saw the Congress of the Soviets as the constitutional source of power. Trotsky, on the other hand, took it for granted that the Bolsheviks, constituting a majority in the Soviets, would actually be the ruling party. Neither of them at this stage saw any conflict between Soviet constitutionalism and a Bolshevik dictatorship, just as, *mutatis mutandis*, no British democrat sees any conflict between parliamentary rule and the cabinet system based on the majority party.

The difference between Lenin and Trotsky centred on a much narrower issue: namely, on whether the rising itself ought to be conceived in terms of Soviet constitutionalism. The tactical risk inherent in Trotsky's attitude was that it imposed certain delays upon the whole plan of action. The political disadvantage of Lenin's approach was that it was likely to narrow the popular appeal of insurrection. Lenin concentrated exclusively on the end to be attained. Trotsky paid more regard to its political context, to the moods of the masses, and to the need to win over the hesitant elements, who might respond to the Soviet's but not to the party's call. The one in hiding had the bare and changeable realities of power before his eyes. The other weighed, in addition, the moral and political imponderables; and he did so with the confidence that comes from being at the centre of events and dominating them.

This difference was incidental to the main controversy between the adherents and the opponents of insurrection. Zinoviev and Kamenev held that Lenin and Trotsky were plunging the party and the revolution into a suicidal adventure. This was one of the greatest and most stirring arguments that had ever rent a party, an argument the basic pros and cons of which were to reappear, in different combinations, in innumerable future controversies; an argument about which, regardless of its immediate conclusion, history has perhaps not yet said its last word. After the event, it is easy and natural to say that the advocates of the insurrection were right, and its opponents wrong. In truth, each side presented its case in such a way that the rights were strangely blended with the wrongs and the realistic assessment of historical prospects was offset by momentous errors. Lenin and Trotsky assessed Russia's national situation and the balance of the forces inside the country with penetrating clear-sightedness. They detected the illusion in the appearance of strength with which the Kerensky régime was endowed by the mere fact of its existence; and they based their optimism about the outcome of the insurrection on an almost mathematically accurate survey of the forces arrayed against each other. Against this optimism, Zinoviev and Kamenev placed on record this warning: 'Before history, before the international proletariat, before the Russian revolution and Russian working class, we have no right to stake the whole future on the card of an armed uprising. . . . There are historical situations when an oppressed class must recognize that it is better to go forward to defeat than to give up without battle. Does the Russian working class find itself at present in such a situation? No, and a thousand times no!!!'[1]

Zinoviev and Kamenev saw nothing ahead but débâcle; and for the rest of their tragic lives they were to burn with shame whenever they were reminded of these words. But the advocates of the rising, in the first instance Lenin and Trotsky, based their arguments not merely and not even mainly on their view of the balance of strength inside Russia. Even more emphatically they pointed to the imminence of European revolution, to which the Russian insurrection would be the prelude, as Trotsky had maintained since 1905–6. In the motion which Lenin submitted to the Central Committee on 10 October, he put first among the motives for insurrection: 'the international position of the Russian revolution (the revolt in the German navy, which is an extreme manifestation of the growth throughout Europe of the world socialist revolution).'[2] He repeated this in almost every subsequent statement, public and private. 'The ripening and inevitability of world socialist revolution can be under no doubt.'[3] 'We stand on the threshold of world proletarian revolution.'[4] 'We shall be genuine traitors to the International', he wrote in a letter to party members, 'if, at such a moment, under such propitious conditions, we answer such a summons from the German revolutionaries [i.e. the revolt in the German navy]

---

[1] *Protokoly Tsen. Kom.*, pp. 102–8. The English version of this statement is in Lenin, *Collected Works*, vol. xxi, book 2, pp. 328–32.

[2] Lenin, *Sochinenya*, vol. xxvi, p. 162.

[3] Ibid., p. 21.   [4] Ibid., p. 55.

only by verbal resolutions.'[1] 'The international situation', he argued on another occasion, 'gives us a number of objective data showing that if we act now we shall have on our side the whole of proletarian Europe.'[2] This belief governed not only Trotsky's but also Lenin's entire view of the situation, and Lenin insisted that a Soviet government ought to be prepared to wage a revolutionary war to help the German proletariat in its rising.

Zinoviev and Kamenev, on the other hand, said: 'If we should come to the conclusion . . . that it is necessary to wage a revolutionary war, the masses of the soldiers will rush away from us.' This was a precise anticipation of the developments which led to the peace of Brest Litovsk. 'And here we come', they argued further, 'to the second assertion—that the majority of the international proletariat is, allegedly, already with us. Unfortunately, this is not so. The revolt in the German navy has immense symptomatic significance. . . . But it is a far cry from that to any sort of active support of the proletarian revolution in Russia, which is challenging the entire bourgeois world. It is extremely harmful to overestimate [our] forces.'

Thus those who were supreme realists when summing up the Russian situation became illusionists when they turned towards the broader international scene; and those who saw Russia only dimly through a mist of timid scepticism became then the realists. To be sure, the advocates of insurrection embodied the energy and the indomitable courage of the revolution, while their opponents voiced the revolution's faint doubt of itself. Yet it may be wondered whether Lenin and Trotsky would have acted as they did, or whether they would have acted with the same determination, if they had taken a soberer view of international revolution and foreseen that in the course of decades their example would not be imitated in any other country. A speculative question of this sort cannot be answered. The fact was that the whole dynamic of Russian history was impelling them, their party, and their country towards this revolution, and that they needed a world-embracing hope to accomplish the world-shaking deed. History produced the great illusion and planted and cultivated it in the brains of the most soberly realistic leaders when she needed the motive power of

[1] Ibid., pp. 154–5.   [2] Ibid., p. 164.

illusion to further her own work. In the same way she once inspired the leaders of the French Revolution with a belief in the imminence of a universal republic of the peoples.

.   .   .   .

While the controversy was unresolved in the Central Committee, the party was naturally incapable of initiative. Towards the end of September Kerensky opened the pre-Parliament, the new substitute for an elected assembly. The Bolsheviks had to decide whether they would participate. The question was related to that of the insurrection. Those who were opposed to the rising and those who hesitated were for participation: they wished the Bolshevik party to act as a regular opposition in the pre-Parliament, despite the fact that this body could not claim to be a national representation. The advocates of the insurrection held that the time for their party to act as an opposition had passed—otherwise they would not have contemplated the immediate overthrow of the existing government. They argued that as long as the Bolsheviks were a minority in the Soviets they could only urge the moderate majority to transfer all power to the Soviets; they themselves could not effect the transfer. But having become the majority, they had to effect it, if they were not to prove themselves mere phrasemongers. By their presence in the pre-Parliament they would merely give the latter the appearance of a real parliament and divert their own energy from direct action.

In this debate, Trotsky and Stalin—this was the first time they appeared together—spoke in unison for a boycott of the pre-parliament. Kamenev and Rykov pleaded for participation. The Bolshevik delegates, who had arrived from all over the country for the opening of the pre-Parliament, voted by a majority for participation. Lenin pressed for a revision of this attitude. In a letter to the Central Committee he wrote: 'Trotsky has spoken for the boycott—bravo, comrade Trotsky! The boycott has been defeated inside the group of the Bolshevik delegates. . . . We are still for the boycott.'[1] The incident showed that the party was mentally not yet in a condition to lead in an insurrection.

It was with evident relief that Lenin penned the words: 'Trotsky has spoken for the boycott—bravo, comrade Trotsky!'

He viewed Trotsky's attitude in the matter of insurrection with uneasiness, and even suspicion. He wondered whether, by insisting that the rising should be linked with the Congress of the Soviets, Trotsky was not biding his time and delaying action until it would be too late. If this had been the case, then Trotsky would have been, from Lenin's viewpoint, an even more dangerous opponent than Kamenev and Zinoviev, whose attitude had at least the negative merit that it was unequivocal and that it flatly contradicted the whole trend of Bolshevik policy. Trotsky's attitude, on the contrary, seemed to follow from the party's policy and therefore carried more conviction with the Bolsheviks; the Central Committee was in fact inclined to adopt it. In his letters, Lenin therefore sometimes controverted Trotsky's view almost as strongly as Zinoviev's and Kamenev's, without, however, mentioning Trotsky by name. To wait for the rising until the Congress of the Soviets, he wrote, was just as treasonable as to wait for Kerensky to convoke the Constituent Assembly, as Zinoviev and Kamenev wanted to do.

Much later Trotsky excused Lenin's behaviour: 'If it were not', he wrote, 'for this Leninist anxiety, this pressure, this criticism, this tense and passionate revolutionary distrust, the party might not have straightened its front at the decisive moment, because the resistance at the top was very strong. . . .'[1] It may be added that it was natural that Lenin's 'tense and passionate revolutionary distrust' should include Trotsky himself, the lover of words and gestures, the 'empty bell' and 'Balalaykin' of the past, the former Menshevik helpmeet, who had only just become a Bolshevik and was now by the fortuitous circumstance of Lenin's absence placed at the head of the party. True enough, he had behaved with impressive dignity and courage in the July days. But Lenin had never doubted Trotsky's dignity and personal courage, not even in the days of their most bitter quarrelling. Martov, too, had bravely defended Lenin in July. Yet it was one thing to defend a comrade, even an opponent, baited by counter-revolutionaries, but quite another to lead in a revolution. Would Trotsky be equal to that? Would he know when to pass from tirades to deeds? Up to the moment of the rising, and even during it, doubt was gnawing at Lenin's mind.

[1] See *Uroki Oktyabrya* in *Sochinenya*, vol. iii, book 2, pp. xlviii–xlix.

In the meantime Trotsky was working on the preliminaries to the insurrection. He was doing this with so much psychological subtlety and tactical acumen that although he made his moves in broad daylight, neither friend nor foe could be sure what he was aiming at. He did not try to impose from outside a scheme of insurrection upon the course of events. He developed the insurrection out of the situations as they arose. He was therefore able to justify each step he took by some urgent and in a sense real need of the moment, which ostensibly had nothing to do with insurrection. Everything he did had an aspect of innocence; and although his moves were connected with one another in a single design, their connexion, too, was perfectly camouflaged. Not a single one of the trained political and military observers who watched the scene for the government, the General Staff, the allied embassies and military missions, saw through the camouflage. And even Lenin was in part misled by it.

By the beginning of October the crisis had reached a new height. Economic chaos was mounting. The provisioning of the cities broke down. Over wide stretches of the country peasants were seizing the gentry's estates and burning the mansions. The army suffered fresh defeats. The German navy was active in the Gulf of Finland. For a moment Petrograd itself seemed exposed to German attack. Government departments and military and business circles mooted the evacuation of the capital and the transfer of the government to Moscow. A reversal of attitudes took place, for which parallels can be found in the annals of war and revolution. Some of those who longed for a counter-revolution but were themselves too weak to bring it about, came to contemplate with pleasure, despite their habitual profession of patriotism, the prospect that an invading enemy might do the job for them. Rodzianko, the ex-President of the Duma, was imprudent enough to state publicly that he would rejoice if the German army re-established law and order in Petrograd. Dismay spread in the working class and in the 'defeatist' Soviet. On 6 October, in the presence of delegates from all regiments stationed in the capital, Trotsky addressed the soldiers' section of the Soviet and presented the following resolution: 'If the Provisional Government is incapable of defending Petrograd, then it ought either to conclude peace or to make room for another government. The transfer of the government to Moscow would be a desertion from a responsible battle position.'[1] The resolution was carried without a single dissentient vote. The garrison gave notice of its interest in organizing the defence of the city, if need be without and even against the government.

On the next day Trotsky sounded the alarm from the platform of the pre-Parliament: 'The idea of surrendering the revolutionary capital to German troops', he said, 'was a natural link in a general policy designed to promote . . . counter-revolutionary conspiracy.'[2] A flood of abuse broke loose against the speaker, but this was the last time he addressed the pre-Parliament—on Lenin's insistent promptings, the party had, after all, decided to boycott the assembly. Overcoming the tumult, Trotsky announced the Bolshevik exodus: 'With this government of treason to the people and with this Council of counter-revolutionary connivance we have nothing in common. . . . In withdrawing from the Council, we summon the workers, soldiers, and peasants of all Russia to be on their guard and to be courageous. Petrograd is in danger! The revolution is in danger! The people is in danger!' From now on almost every day the insurgents took a long stride towards their goal.

Both sides, Kerensky and his General Staff on the one hand, Trotsky and the Soviet on the other, were engaged in a series of manœuvres designed to set the stage for civil war; but both pretended to act in the broader interest of national defence. Kerensky was preparing a redistribution of troops, ostensibly designed to strengthen the front. In the process the most revolutionary regiments were to be sent out of Petrograd, as a prelude to a showdown with the Soviet. Trotsky had to frustrate Kerensky's plan and to prevent the departure of the pro-Bolshevik regiments. He did so on the ground that the depletion of the garrison would expose the capital to German invasion, which was not untrue. The government had in the meantime denied that it proposed to evacuate Petrograd. But mistrust of its intentions had been aroused; and when it became known that Kerensky was bent on reshuffling the troops the suspicion was confirmed and strengthened. On 9 October the Soviet was in a state of extraordinary agitation. Trotsky urged its plenary session

---

[1] Trotsky, *Sochinenya*, vol. iii, book 1, p. 321.　　[2] Ibid., pp. 321–3.

and its sections to intervene in the matter of the redistribution
of troops. Since the Soviet had already assumed responsibility
for the defence of Petrograd, it could not look on idly at the
dismantling of the garrison. Trotsky did not yet explicitly propose that the Soviet should veto Kerensky's plan—the first step
he proposed was that the Soviet should find out what was the
significance of the plan and that it should 'keep a check' on
the condition of the garrison. Implicitly, however, he had
already posed the question who was to be the master of the
garrison.[1]

On the same day, the Military Revolutionary Committee
was formed at a session of the Executive of the Soviet. This
committee, eventually the supreme organ of insurrection,
appeared at the time only to assume on behalf of the Soviet the
responsibility for the city's defence. The proposal for setting it
up was made by one Lazimir, a boy of eighteen, a Left Social
Revolutionary, who had no premonition of the consequences.
The Menshevik members of the Executive were opposed to the
idea, but, when it was pointed out to them that this Committee
would be a replica and a continuation of a body they themselves
had formed at the time of Kornilov's coup, they had no effective
answer. In its Menshevik period, the Soviet had, indeed,
repeatedly vetoed moves contemplated by the government—
the practice was inherent in the 'dual power' of the February
régime—and these precedents, when they were now cited,
disarmed the opposition. Trotsky *ex officio* headed the Military
Revolutionary Committee. The task of the Committee was to
establish the size of the garrison needed for the defence of the
capital; to keep in touch with the commands of the northern
front, the Baltic fleet, the Finnish garrison, &c.; to assess the
man-power and the stocks of munitions available; to work out
a plan of defence; and to maintain discipline in the civilian
population. Among the members of the Committee there were,
apart from its youthful and uncomprehending initiator, Podvoisky, Antonov-Ovseenko, and Lashevich, the future operational commanders of the insurrection. The Committee split
into seven sections, which were to be in charge of defence,
supplies, liaison, information, workers' militias, and so on.
Again in conformity with precedents, the Committee appointed

[1] Trotsky, *Sochinenya*, vol. iii, book i, pp. 324 ff.

commissars who were to represent it with all detachments of the garrison.[1]

While, partly by design and partly by the spur of great events and trivial accidents, Trotsky was forging the machinery of insurrection, the Central Committee of the party had not yet taken any final decision. On 3 October it listened to the report of an envoy from Moscow, Lomov-Oppokov, who spoke for insurrection and demanded an end to irresolution. 'It was decided', says the record of the Central Committee, 'not to discuss this report' but to ask Lenin to come to Petrograd and to put his arguments before the Central Committee.[2] On 7 October a Bureau was appointed to 'collect information on the struggle against counter-revolution'. Its members were Trotsky, Sverdlov, and Bubnov.[3] Only on 10 October, the day after the formation of the Military Revolutionary Committee, did that historic session take place at which Lenin was present and at which, after grave debate, the leaders of the party took by ten votes to two the decision in favour of the rising. At this session, also, the first Political Bureau was elected —Lenin, Zinoviev, Kamenev, Trotsky, Stalin, Sokolnikov, and Bubnov—to offer the party day-to-day guidance on the insurrection.[4] But the next day Zinoviev and Kamenev appealed to the lower grades of the organization against the decision of the Central Committee, and the party's attitude was again in flux. In any case, the newly-elected Politbureau was incapable of offering guidance. Lenin returned to his refuge in Finland. Zinoviev and Kamenev were opposed to the rising. Stalin was almost completely absorbed by editorial work. Sokolnikov's views were a shade more cautious than Trotsky's. Lenin, however, still distrustful of Trotsky's plan, urged the party to take on itself alone the initiative of armed action. All members of the Politbureau who were not in principle opposed to such action preferred the rising to be conducted through the Soviet.

During the following week, Trotsky, assisted by the most effective agitators, Lunacharsky, Kollontai, and Volodarsky, was mustering the forces of the revolution. On 10 October he addressed a city conference of factory committees. On 11 and

---

[1] See the memoirs of the participants given on the third anniversary of the insurrection in *Proletarskaya Revolutsia*, no. 10, 1922.

[2] *Protokoly Tsen. Kom.*, p. 87.   [3] Ibid., p. 94.   [4] Ibid., pp. 98–101.

12 October he called upon a conference of northern Russian Soviets to be ready for great events. 'Our government', he stated, 'may flee from Petrograd. But the revolutionary people will not leave the city—it will defend it to the end.'[1] At the same time he did his utmost to force the hands of the Menshevik Central Executive and to compel it to convene the second Congress of the Soviets. On 13 October, over the heads of that Executive and on behalf of the Soviets of northern Russia, he sent out a radio message 'To All, To All, To All', calling all Soviets and the army to send delegates to the Congress. 'At the famous Cirque Moderne', writes Sukhanov, 'where Trotsky, Lunacharsky, and Volodarsky took the platform, there were endless queues and crowds, whom the enormous amphitheatre could not contain. . . . Trotsky, breaking away from his work at the revolutionary headquarters, ran from the Obukhovsky to the Trubochnyi, from the Putilovsky to the Baltiisky [the largest industrial plants], from the Manege to the barracks; and it seemed that he spoke everywhere simultaneously. Every worker and soldier of Petrograd knew him and listened to him. His influence on the masses and the leaders alike was overwhelming. He was the central figure of those days, and the chief hero of this remarkable chapter of history.'[2]

On 16 October the regiments of the garrison declared that they would disobey Kerensky's marching orders and remain in Petrograd. This was, as Trotsky later put it, the silent rising which in advance decided the outcome of the contest.[3] Until now Trotsky himself had been somewhat uneasy about the risk he had taken by linking the insurrection with the Congress of the Soviets. Now he was reassured: in the short run, Kerensky would not be able to alter the balance of strength in his favour. On the same day, Trotsky signed an order to the arsenals that 5,000 rifles be issued to the civilian Red Guards. This was a way of checking whether the writ of the Military Revolutionary Committee ran in the garrison. It did.

During this 'silent rising', the Central Committee met once again in the presence of important local Bolshevik leaders.[4]

[1] Trotsky, *Sochinenya*, vol. iii, book 2, p. 5.
[2] Sukhanov, op. cit., vol. vii, pp. 44, 76.
[3] Trotsky, *Sochinenya*, vol. iii, book 2, p. 1.
[4] *Protokoly Tsen. Kom.*, pp. 110–25.

Lenin who had arrived, heavily disguised, moved that the conference should confirm the decision on insurrection, and that the Central Committee should at once issue a call to action. The representative of the Petrograd Committee spoke about apathy in the masses, but declared that the call for insurrection, if it came from the Soviet, not from the party, would stir up the masses and meet with response. Krylenko, leader of the party's military branch, on which the execution of Lenin's plan entirely depended, declared that only a minority of the branch was for insurrection, but even this minority favoured initiative by the Soviet, not by the party. Volodarsky spoke in the same vein. Zinoviev and Kamenev emphatically restated their objections to armed action in any form. Stalin reproached them with lack of faith in European revolution, and remarked that while the party leaders were engaged in confused argument, the Soviet was already 'on the road to insurrection'. Miliutin, for Moscow, spoke ambiguously. Sokolnikov held that the rising ought to be started only after the opening of the Congress of the Soviets. From all sides there came anxious voices about the apathy and the weariness of the masses. Lenin recapitulated his arguments, but he made a concession to the adherents of Trotsky's plan and submitted that 'the Central Committee *and* the Soviet should in due time indicate the right moment and the practical methods of attack'.[1] Tentatively 20 October was fixed as the day of action.

The Central Committee had fixed this date because it was the eve of the expected opening of the Congress. Only three or four days were left for preparations. Yet no sooner had the Central Committee confirmed its decision on insurrection than Zinoviev and Kamenev made a vigorous attempt to frustrate it. They denounced the plan, this time not within the Bolshevik caucus but in the pages of Gorky's newspaper. Thus, from the men supposed to act as members of the General Staff of the insurrection, the outside world received a warning about what was pending. Lenin, beside himself with indignation, demanded

[1] Loc. cit., and Lenin, *Sochinenya*, vol. xxvi, p. 165. At this session a 'Military Centre' was appointed, consisting of Sverdlov, Stalin, Bubnov, Uritsky, and Dzerzhinsky. It was to 'become part of the Military Revolutionary Committee of the Soviet', i.e. to serve under Trotsky. On his membership of this 'Centre', which throughout the rising never acted as a separate body, Stalin and the Stalinist historians later based the claim that Stalin had been the actual leader of the rising.

the immediate expulsion from the party of the two 'strike-breakers of the revolution'. His demand fell on deaf ears. In the Bolshevik newspaper Stalin tried to reconcile the adversaries, although this was a matter in which reconciliation was impossible: an insurrection either is or is not made.[1]

Trotsky utilized even the confusion among the Bolshevik leaders to further his plan. On 17 October he received with well concealed relief the news that the Menshevik Central Executive had again postponed the Congress of the Soviets for a few days. This gave him a little more time for the last preparations. But the other camp might also have benefited from the delay; and Zinoviev's and Kamenev's disclosures threatened to arouse its vigilance. On 18 October two embarrassing questions were put to Trotsky in the Soviet, one about the widespread rumours on insurrection, and the other about his order to the arsenals for the issue of rifles to Red Guards. His answer was a masterpiece of diplomatic camouflage: 'The decisions of the Petrograd Soviet are published', he said. 'The Soviet is an elected institution, every deputy is responsible to the workers and soldiers who have elected him. This revolutionary parliament . . . can have no decisions which are unknown to the workers. We conceal nothing. I declare on behalf of the Soviet: we have not decided on any armed action.' This was literally true: the *Soviet* had decided nothing of the sort. As its President he was expected to give an account only of the Soviet's work. He was under no obligation to make a public confession of a confidential decision taken by a private body such as the Central Committee of the party.

But he did not stop at this denial, which might have confounded friends as well as foes. Nor did he tie his hands. 'If the course of events', he added, 'compels the Soviet to decide on armed action, then the workers and the soldiers will come out in response to its appeal like one man.' He admitted that he had ordered rifles for the Red Guards, but he covered himself by the familiar precedent: the Menshevik Soviet had done the same. 'The Petrograd Soviet', he added defiantly, 'will go on organizing and arming workers' guards. . . . We must be ready. We have entered a period of more acute struggle. We must be constantly prepared for attack by the counter-revolution.

[1] *Protokoly Tsen. Kom.*, pp. 127–9.

But to the first counter-revolutionary attempt to break up the Congress of the Soviets, to the first attempt of an attack on us, we shall retort with a counter-attack which will be merciless and which we shall press to the very end.'[1] Thus he stirred the militancy of the insurgents and of their friends while he was obfuscating their enemies. With meticulous care he brought to the fore the defensive aspect of the insurgents' activity, and kept the offensive aspect in the background. On the spot Kamenev rose to declare his complete solidarity with Trotsky, and Zinoviev did the same in a letter to the editor of *Rabochyi Put*. The two opponents of the rising hoped thereby to tie down their party to a strictly defensive attitude, and so to make it renounce insurrection in a roundabout way. But their demonstrative expression of solidarity with Trotsky had a quite different effect. The anti-Bolshevik parties, seeing that the known opponents of the coup declared their agreement with Trotsky, assumed that he was also in agreement with them. 'There will be no insurrection, then', the Mensheviks and Social Revolutionaries consoled themselves.

Immediately after this incident, Trotsky had a secret meeting with Lenin, the only one, it seems, that they had in these weeks. He wondered whether Lenin had not misunderstood his statement and the appearance of agreement between himself and Zinoviev and Kamenev; and he was anxious to dispel Lenin's misapprehension.[2] But on this point his fears were groundless. Lenin had just written to the Central Committee: 'Kamenev's trick at the session of the Petrograd Soviet is something simply mean. He, you see, is in full agreement with Trotsky. But is it difficult to understand that Trotsky could not and should not have said more than he did in the face of enemies.'[3] At this meeting, Trotsky wrote later, Lenin was 'more calm and confident, I would say, less suspicious. . . . All the same, now and again he shook his head and asked: "And will they not forestall us? Will they not catch us napping?" I argued that from now on everything would develop almost automatically.'[4]

Lenin was not quite reassured. That his reiterated demand for the immediate expulsion of Zinoviev and Kamenev met with

[1] Trotsky, *Sochinenya*, vol. iii, book 2, pp. 31–32.
[2] Trotsky, *Lénine*, p. 86.
[3] Lenin, *Sochinenya*, vol. xxvi, p. 192.   [4] Trotsky, *Lénine*, loc. cit.

no response from Trotsky and the Central Committee as a whole made him bristle with suspicion again. Zinoviev's and Kamenev's indiscretion would be regarded as treacherous by any party in similar circumstances. And so Lenin saw in the consideration shown to them by the Central Committee a sign of the latter's irresolute attitude in the matter of insurrection.[1]

The preliminaries to the rising came to a close when the Soviet instructed the garrison to carry out only such official orders as were endorsed by the Military Revolutionary Committee or its commissars. On 21 October Trotsky conveyed this instruction to a general meeting of regimental committees; and he appealed to the Cossacks, the former praetorian guards of the Tsars, to stand by the revolution. The regimental committees adopted Trotsky's resolution, which stated *inter alia*:

Endorsing all political decisions of the Petrograd Soviet, the garrison declares: the time for words has passed. The country is on the brink of doom. The army demands peace, the peasants demand land, the workers demand employment and bread. The coalition government is against the people, an instrument in the hands of the people's enemies. The time for words has passed. The All-Russian Congress of Soviets ought to take power in its hands and secure peace, land, and bread to the people. . . . The Petrograd garrison solemnly

[1] Characteristic of the relations inside the Bolshevik party at the time is the fact that not a single voice in the Central Committee supported Lenin's demand. Kamenev had of his own accord announced his resignation from the Committee. Lenin, nevertheless demanded his and Zinoviev's expulsion as an exemplary punishment not for their dissent but for the unheard-of breach of discipline they had committed. The record of the sitting of the Central Committee of 20 October makes instructive reading. Dzerzhinsky expressed the opinion that Kamenev should be advised to withdraw from political activity; but he did not advocate expulsion. It was not worth while bothering, he added, about Zinoviev, who was in hiding anyhow. Stalin and Miliutin advised shelving the question until a plenary session of the Central Committee. Stalin had in the party's paper defended the motives of Zinoviev and Kamenev, and he himself now came under fire. Uritsky was for postponing the matter. Sverdlov spoke strongly against Kamenev, but held that the Central Committee had no right to expel anybody. Trotsky was for accepting Kamenev's resignation, but not for expulsion. He attacked Stalin's editorial conduct, saying that the ambiguous attitude of the party's paper created 'an intolerable situation'. Yoffe spoke in the same vein. Stalin once again defended Zinoviev and Kamenev, saying that they should remain on the Central Committee: 'Expulsion from the party is no remedy—unity must be preserved.' Kamenev's resignation was accepted by five votes to three. Then Stalin announced that he was resigning as editor of the party's paper. But this was not accepted. It is quite impossible to square this and many similar episodes with the view that monolithic or totalitarian uniformity had reigned in the Bolshevik party ever since its inception. *Protokoly Tsen. Kom.*, pp. 127-9.

pledges itself to put at the disposal of the All-Russian Congress all its forces, to the last man, to fight for these demands. Rely on us. . . . We are at our posts, ready to conquer or die.[1]

Events showed that this last assurance was more solemn than true. The civilian workers were in fact 'ready to conquer or die'; but the garrison supported the Soviet because it was confident in an easy victory over Kerensky, a victory which was expected to end the war. Whatever its motives, the fact was that the garrison placed itself under the orders of the Soviet.

Inevitably this gave rise to a conflict between the regular military command and the Military Revolutionary Committee. Even now, Trotsky did not claim on behalf of that Committee that it was superseding the military command. Commissars of the Committee were attached to the General Staff, ostensibly in order to co-ordinate activities and eliminate friction; and on the very day of the rising Trotsky inspired reports that the negotiations were proceeding satisfactorily.[2] At the same time as he made these military preparations, Trotsky put the Red Guards and the civilian organizations on the alert. On 22 October he addressed a monster meeting at the *Narodnyi Dom* (People's House). 'Around me', the eyewitness whom we have often quoted describes the scene, 'the crowds were in an almost ecstatic mood.' Trotsky asked them to repeat after him the words of an oath. 'A numberless multitude lifted up their hands. Trotsky hammered out the words: "Let this your vote be your oath with all your might and power of sacrifice to support the Soviet, which has taken on itself the great burden of bringing the victory of the revolution to completion and of giving the people land, bread, and peace." The numberless multitude keep their hands up. They agree. They take the oath. . . . Trotsky has finished. Somebody else is taking the platform. But it is not worth while to wait and look any more.'[3]

The theatrical quality of Trotsky's appearances and the almost poetic loftiness of his speech did no less than his *ruses de guerre* to mislead the anti-Bolshevik leaders. The latter were too well accustomed to the bright fireworks of his oratory to suspect that this time it was real fire. Trotsky seemed to them, and not only to them, too voluble for a commander of a successful

[1] Trotsky, *Sochinenya*, vol. iii, book 2, p. 37.
[2] Trotsky, *Lénine*, p. 87.   [3] Sukhanov, op. cit., vol. vii, p. 91.

insurrection. Yet in this revolution words, great idealistic words, were in fact more effective than regiments and divisions, and inspired tirades did the work of pitched battles. Up to a certain moment they relieved the revolution of the need to fight battles at all. The revolution worked mainly through its titanic power of persuasion, and it seemed to have vested the greater part of that power in a single person.

By 23 October the Military Revolutionary Committee had a detailed plan of operations in hand. It was as simple as it was carefully laid. It provided for a rapid occupation by picked detachments of all strategic positions in the capital. Liaison between insurgent headquarters and the garrison functioned infallibly. The picked units were ready for the signal. As the members of the Military Revolutionary Committee surveyed for the last time the disposition of forces, they were confident that they could knock the government over by a slight push— so overwhelming was the superiority of the forces arrayed behind the Soviet. Only one important position was uncertain: the Peter-Paul fortress on the Neva, the garrison of which was reported to stand for Kerensky or at least to waver. Antonov-Ovseenko prepared a plan to assault the fortress, the only important engagement which was expected. Trotsky, however, decided to try to storm it with words. In the afternoon of the 23rd, accompanied by a non-Bolshevik commander of the Soviet guard, he went on a lorry into what was supposed to be the enemy's camp. He addressed the garrison of the fortress and induced it to repeat after him the oath of allegiance to the Soviet.[1]

All that Trotsky was now waiting for was provocation from Kerensky, which would allow him to launch the insurrection as a defensive operation. He had no doubt that Kerensky was bound to give the provocation—he himself had provoked him sufficiently into giving it.[2] And indeed, on the 23rd, Kerensky

[1] *Proletarskaya Revolutsia*, no. 10, 1922; Sukhanov, op. cit., vol. vii, p. 113.

[2] There can be no doubt, however, that Kerensky had always regarded the Soviets as an embarrassment to be got rid of. He did so even when Bolshevik influence in the Soviets was slight and when he himself owed his position entirely to the Soviets. As early as 27 March (9 April in the new calendar) Sir George Buchanan noted in his diary: 'Kerensky, with whom I had a long conversation yesterday, does not favour the idea of taking strong measures at present either against the Soviet or the Socialist propaganda in the army. On my telling him that the government would never be masters of the situation as long as they allowed

attempted to strike a blow from the vacuum in which he and his government were suspended. He banned *Rabochyi Put* (*Workers' Road*), under which title *Pravda* had appeared since the July days, and he ordered the closing of its editorial offices and printing-press. A working girl and a man from the press rushed to the Military Revolutionary Committee, saying that they were prepared to break the seals on the premises of *Rabochyi Put* and to go on producing the paper if the Committee gave them an effective military escort. This suggestion, breathlessly made by an unknown working girl, came to Trotsky like a flash. 'A piece of official sealing wax', he wrote later, 'on the door of the Bolshevik editorial room as a military measure—that was not much. But what a superb signal for battle!'[1] On the spot he signed an order sending a company of riflemen and a few platoons of sappers to guard the Bolshevik offices and printing-press. The order was carried out instantaneously.

This was a tentative gambit. It was made on the dawn of 24 October. Next morning the papers were full of reports about Kerensky's plan to suppress the Soviet and the Bolshevik party. The Military Revolutionary Committee was working out the last details of the rising, which, as was now clear, could not be delayed a single day. The Smolny Institute, hitherto guarded with insouciant slackness, was rapidly transformed into a fortress, bristling with cannon and machine-guns. In the early morning, the Central Committee of the party met for the last time before the decisive event. All members present in Petrograd had arrived, with the exception of Lenin and Zinoviev, who had not yet come into the open, and Stalin who was unaccountably absent.[2] Kamenev, who had resigned from the Committee to oppose the insurrection, placed himself at the service of the insurgents once the action had started; and he displayed surprising initiative. It was he who proposed, *inter alia*, that no member of the Committee should leave Smolny during the day. On Trotsky's initiative, each was given a specific assignment in liaison and organization. Dzerzhinsky kept in touch with the posts and telegraphs; Bubnov with the railwaymen; Nogin and Lomov with Moscow. Sverdlov was to watch the movements

---

themselves to be dictated to by a rival organization, he said that the Soviet would die a natural death. . . .' Sir George Buchanan, *My Mission to Russia*, vol. ii, p. 11.

[1] Trotsky, *History*, vol. iii, p. 205. [2] *Protokoly Tsen. Kom.*, pp. 141-3.

of the Provisional Government, while Miliutin was to take charge of the city's food supplies. Kamenev and Berzin were to win over the Left Social Revolutionaries, who were breaking away from their mother party. Finally, Trotsky proposed that, in case the Bolsheviks were routed at the Smolny, the headquarters of the insurrection should move to the Peter-Paul fortress, the garrison of which he had just won over for the cause.[1]

While this was taking place, Kerensky addressed the pre-Parliament and indulged in belated threats. He announced that he had ordered the prosecution of the entire Military Revolutionary Committee, a new search for Lenin, the arrest of Trotsky and other Bolshevik leaders released on bail, and that he was taking action against the sailors of Kronstadt.[2] Trotsky convened an extraordinary session of the Petrograd Soviet and reported on the steps just taken by the Military Revolutionary Committee. Even now he did not proclaim the rising:

We are not afraid to shoulder responsibility for maintaining revolutionary order in the city. . . . Our principle is—all power to the Soviets. . . . At the forthcoming sessions of the All-Russian Congress of the Soviets, this principle ought to be put into effect. Whether this will lead to an insurrection or to any other form of action depends not only and not so much on the Soviets as on those who, in defiance of the people's unanimous will, still hold governmental power. [He reported the incident with *Rabochyi Put* and asked:] Is this an insurrection? We have a semi-government in which the people has no confidence and which has no confidence in itself, because it is dead within. This semi-government only awaits the sweep of history's broom. . . .

He announced that he had countermanded Kerensky's action against the Kronstadt sailors and ordered the cruiser *Aurora* to lie in readiness on the Neva:

To-morrow the Congress of the Soviets opens. It is the task of the

[1] Loc. cit., Kamenev proposed that reserve headquarters be established on board the cruiser *Aurora*, with the crew and the radio station of which he kept liaison.

[2] The day before, Major General Sir Alfred Knox, the British Military Attaché, knew about the plan. 'To-day Bagratuni told me', runs an entry in his note-book, 'that Kerensky had decided to arrest Trotsky and the members of the Military Revolutionary Committee. . . . I asked if we were strong enough to carry out this programme, and Bagratuni said we were. Podryelov said: "We can take the risk." ' *With the Russian Army*, vol. ii, p. 705.

garrison and of the proletariat to put at its disposal the power they have gathered, a power on which any governmental provocation will founder. It is our task to carry this power, undiminished and unimpaired, to the Congress. If the illusory government makes a hazardous attempt to revive its own corpse, the popular masses will strike a decisive counter-blow. And the blow will be the more powerful the stronger the attack. If the government tries to use the twenty-four or forty-eight hours still left to it in order to stab the revolution, then we declare that the vanguard of the revolution will meet attack with attack and iron with steel.[1]

When a delegation from the city council approached him to inquire about the Soviet's intentions, he answered cryptically that the Soviet was prepared to co-ordinate the defence of the revolutionary order with the city council; and, tongue in cheek, he invited the council to participate in the Military Revolutionary Committee.

Late in the evening the Menshevik Central Executive called a meeting of the delegates who had assembled for the Congress. For the last time Dan spoke on behalf of the old leadership of the Soviets. He warned the delegates against bloodshed. 'The counter-revolution is only waiting for the Bolsheviks to begin riots and massacres—this will be the end of the revolution. . . . The masses are sick and exhausted. They have no interest in the revolution. . . . It is inadmissible . . . that the Petrograd garrison should not submit to the orders of the Staff. . . . All power to the Soviets means death. . . . We are not afraid of bayonets. . . . The old Executive will defend the revolution with its body. . . .'[2] Amid uproar and cries of derision, Dan promised immediate peace negotiations and land reform, thereby unwittingly admitting that the Bolsheviks had all along been right in their demands. ('Russia' he declared, 'could no longer afford to wage the war.') From the floor came cries: 'Too late!'

Then Trotsky mounted the tribune, borne on a wave of roaring applause . . . a rising house, thunderous. His thin, pointed face was positively Mephistophelian in its expression of malicious irony.

'Dan's tactics proved that the masses—the great, dull, indifferent masses—are absolutely with him!' (Titanic mirth.) He turned towards the Chairman, dramatically. 'When we spoke of giving the land to the peasants you were against it. We told the peasants, "If they don't

---

[1] Trotsky, *Sochinenya*, vol. iii, book 2, pp. 51–53.
[2] John Reed, *Ten Days that Shook the World*, pp. 58–60.

L

give it to you, take it yourselves!" and the peasants followed our
advice. And now you advocate what we did six months ago. . . .
The time may come when Dan will say that the flower of the revolution participated in the rising of the July days. . . . No. The history
of the last seven months shows that the masses have left the Mensheviks. . . . Dan tells you that you have no right to make an insurrection. Insurrection is the right of all revolutionaries! When the
downtrodden masses revolt it is their right. . . . If you maintain
complete confidence, there will be no civil war. Our enemies will
surrender at once and you will take the place which is legitimately
yours, that of the masters of the Russian land.'[1]

Dan, deceived by the vague manner in which Trotsky still
spoke about the rising, and perhaps also hoping that the Bolsheviks might not obtain a majority at the Congress, rushed off
to Kerensky to assure him that there would be no Bolshevik
coup and to implore him to refrain from repressive action.[2]

The rising was already in progress. Trotsky issued his famous
Order No. 1: 'The Petrograd Soviet is in imminent danger.
Last night the counter-revolutionary conspirators tried to call
the Junkers and the shock battalions into Petrograd. You are
hereby ordered to prepare your regiment for action. Await
further orders. All procrastination and hesitation will be
regarded as treason to the revolution.' The firmness of his tone
inspired the insurgents with confidence. During the night of
24–25 October Red Guards and regular regiments occupied
with lightning speed, almost noiselessly, the Tauride Palace,
the post-offices and the railway stations, the national bank, the
telephone exchanges, the power-stations, and other strategic
points. While the movement which overthrew Tsardom in
February lasted nearly a week, the overthrow of Kerensky's
government took a few hours only. In the morning of 25
October Kerensky had already escaped from the capital in the
car of a foreign embassy. His Ministers were vainly waiting for
him in the Winter Palace, when at noon they were already
besieged there, just as the Tsarist government had been in the
final phase of the February Revolution. Without bloodshed, the
Bolsheviks had become the masters of the capital.[3] By mid-day

---

[1] Loc. cit.   [2] Kerensky, *Iz Daleka*, pp. 197–8; *Crucifixion of Liberty*, p. 346.
[3] Major-General Sir Alfred Knox, a most hostile observer of the Bolshevik
success, gives the total number of the casualties as 'about ten'. *With the Russian Army*,
vol. ii, p. 711.

Trotsky reported to the Petrograd Soviet, almost stunned with incredulity, on further developments: some Ministers had been placed under arrest; the pre-Parliament had been disbanded; the whole city was under control. The enemy now held only the Winter Palace, which Antonov-Ovseenko was preparing to storm.

On the evening of the 24th Lenin, still heavily disguised, arrived in the Smolny. Reports in the newspapers about friendly negotiations between the General Staff and the Military Revolutionary Committee had stirred his mistrust afresh. He still suspected that the rising was being bungled. As he made his way stealthily from the Vyborg suburb, where he had been hiding for the last few days, to the Smolny, he did not realize that the city he walked through was virtually in his party's hands. He bombarded Trotsky and the other leaders with questions: Were they really on the point of coming to terms with the General Staff? And why was the city so calm?[1] But as he listened to the answers, as he watched the tense staff work in the room of the Military Revolutionary Committee, the reports coming in ceaselessly and the instructions going out, as he eyed the leaders of the rising themselves, almost exhausted, unshaven, dirty, with eyes inflamed from sleeplessness, yet confident and composed, he realized that they had crossed the Rubicon without him, and his suspicion melted away. Somewhat shyly and apologetically, he remarked that the rising could, of course, be conducted in their manner as well—the main thing was that it should succeed.

He behaved like a commander-in-chief who, watching the decisive battle from afar and knowing that the operational commander has ideas at variance with his, is inclined to exaggerate the importance of the difference and fears that without his intervention things might go wrong; who then rushes to the battlefield while the battle is in progress and then, without a trace of offended vanity, reconciles himself to the course of action taken and acknowledges his junior's achievement. Although Trotsky had been in charge of the operation and had conducted it entirely according to his own lights, Lenin's influence was a decisive factor in the success. Trotsky had more than any single man moulded the mind of the broad

[1] *Proletarskaya Revolutsia*, no. 10, 1922.

mass of workers and soldiers, on whose attitude the issue depended. But the active insurgents had come from the cadres and the ranks of the Bolshevik party; and on their minds, Lenin, the founder and unrivalled leader of the party, had even from his hiding-place exercised by far the greater influence. Without his sustained and stubborn promptings, without his alarming warnings, they might not have followed Trotsky's orders and instructions as they did. He had inspired them with the idea of the rising before they carried out Trotsky's scheme of the rising. But it was only when he actually saw the insurrection in progress that Lenin finally and unreservedly acknowledged in Trotsky his monumental partner in the monumental game.

On the evening of 25 October, the two men were resting on the floor of a dark and empty room adjoining the great hall of Smolny, where the Congress of the Soviets was about to open. The night before, Trotsky had fainted from fatigue, and now he tried to get a little sleep. But sleep would not come. Ceaseless telephone calls in the next room roused him. Assistants and messengers knocked at the doors. One message reported a hitch in the attack on the Winter Palace; and Trotsky ordered the cruiser *Aurora* into action: Let them bombard the Winter Palace with blanks—this should be enough to bring about the government's surrender. He went back to lie on the floor by Lenin's side. There were fleeting moments of somnolence, new messages, rapid whispers along the floor. Soon they would have to go to the large and brightly lit hall and face the Congress. They would, of course, declare that the Congress was the only source of power, that the land belonged to the peasants, and they would offer immediate peace to Russia and the world; and tomorrow they would present the new government to the world. The thought that he or any of his comrades, the professional revolutionaries, should assume titles of ministers seemed incongruous to Lenin. Shreds of historical reminiscences—as always, reminiscences from the great French Revolution—floated through Trotsky's somnolent mind: perhaps they would call themselves *Commissaires*, People's Commissars—a Council of People's Commissars?[1]

The Congress opened to the accompaniment of the *Aurora's*

[1] Trotsky proposed these titles at a session of the Central Committee next day. *Moya Zhizn*, vol. ii, pp. 48-49, 59-60.

bombardment of the Winter Palace—with blanks. The Bolsheviks alone commanded a majority of nearly two-thirds; with the Left Social Revolutionaries they had about three-quarters of the votes. Fourteen Bolsheviks, seven Social Revolutionaries, Right and Left, three Mensheviks, and one representative of Gorky's group, took their seats at the table of the new 'Presidium'. The defeated parties at once raised an outcry against the rising and the storming of the Winter Palace. In the name of the most irreconcilable group of Mensheviks, Khinchuk, Stalin's future Ambassador in Berlin, declared that they were leaving the Congress. Amid cries: 'Deserters! Go to Kornilov!' the group left the hall. The Mensheviks of the Centre and of the Left stayed behind and demanded the formation of a coalition government of Bolsheviks, Mensheviks, and Social Revolutionaries. When the Bolsheviks rejected this demand, these groups, too, declared a boycott of the Congress and of its decisions. As Trotsky watched their exodus, led by Martov and Abramovich, his mind may have flashed back to the scene at the second congress of the party, in 1903, when Martov declared a boycott of the Bolshevik Central Committee. He himself was then among the boycotters. How similar in a way these two scenes appeared: the leading men were the same, the 'soft' and the 'hard' ones; most of the recriminations of 1903 echoed in the declaration Martov had just made: even the words 'conspiracy', 'usurpation', and 'state of siege' came back. But how different was the scale of the spectacle and the intensity of the struggle. And how different was his own place in it, after all the years of side-slipping and straying, from which he had returned to Lenin.

As Trotsky rose to answer Martov, while the latter was still standing opposite him on the platform, he could find in himself no softness, no lenity, not even charity for the vanquished—only gravity, exasperation, and angry contempt. 'The rising of popular masses', he began, 'needs no justification. What has taken place is an insurrection not a conspiracy. We have hardened the revolutionary energy of the workers and soldiers of Petrograd. We have openly steeled the will of the masses for a rising, not a conspiracy. . . .' Politically this was true, although militarily the insurrection had in fact been conducted like a conspiracy, and could not have been conducted otherwise.

'Our rising', he went on, 'has been victorious. Now they tell us: Renounce your victory, yield, make a compromise. With whom? With whom, I am asking, shall we make this compromise? With those miserable little groups that have left or with those that make these proposals? But we have seen them in their full stature. Nobody in the whole of Russia follows them any more, and is it with them as with equal partners that the millions of workers and peasants . . . should conclude an agreement? . . . You are miserable, isolated individuals. You are bankrupt. You have played out your role. Go where you belong: to the dustheap of history!'[1] This *Vae Victis!* pierced the ears of Martov and of his followers as they made their way out of the hall, through the serried ranks of soldiers and workers, who indignantly reminded them of all the misdeeds of the Provisional Government, of the people's hunger and cold, of the senseless and bloody offensives, of the July days, of the proscription of the Bolsheviks, and of the peasants' craving for land. Pent-up emotion burst from the victors.

Nemesis stalked the halls of the Smolny. She was only beginning her work.

. . . .

Never before had any body of men seizing power assumed so prodigious a burden of commitments as that which the Bolshevik leaders shouldered when they read out to the Congress their first hastily scribbled decrees. They promised to give the people Peace, Land, and Bread. The distance from promise to fulfilment was immeasurable. The peace was to be just and democratic. It was to admit no annexations or indemnities, none of the injuries and insults which victors impose upon vanquished. Lenin and Trotsky had said over and over again that such a peace could not be expected from the absolutist or even the bourgeois parliamentary governments—it could only be achieved by proletarian revolutions in the belligerent countries. Yet the armies of the Hohenzollerns and Habsburgs stood on lands wrested from the Russian empire; and as long as they had not renounced their emperors and their rulers and had not disavowed their rapacious ambitions, the Bolsheviks were in a sense committed to go on waging war, the revolutionary war for a just peace. But they were also, and in the popular mind even

[1] Sukhanov, op. cit., vol. vii, pp. 202–4. John Reed, op. cit., p. 79.

more strongly, committed to achieve an *immediate* peace, which could be neither just nor democratic. This was their first dilemma. Its solution would be dictated to them by weary peasant–soldiers, who were all the more eager to turn their guns into ploughs now that all the land to plough was at last theirs. But the tenuous peace, attained under their pressure, would not avert from Russia the long ordeal of foreign intervention and civil war.

The Bolsheviks shared the land among the peasants, or, rather, they sanctioned the share-out accomplished by the peasantry itself. No great country can go through an agrarian revolution of this scale and momentum without its entire economy being shaken and weakened, if only temporarily. The old links between town and country were loosened or broken; the old channels of exchange shrank and became clogged; the old obsolete and inadequate yet automatic, and in its way effective, manner of running the body politic was rendered impossible. In the most favourable circumstances, even without a civil war, it would have taken time before new links, new channels, and a new way of managing the nation's existence replaced the old ones. Before that happened, so elementary a process as the flow of food from country to town, the pre-condition of modern civilization, was bound to be disrupted. The demands for land and bread were not quite compatible. After the large estates had been split, less, not more, bread was available to urban workers. To the peasants the agrarian revolution was a boon at first. It not only gave them land— it relieved them of the burdens of age-old servitude and debt. But to the nation as a whole the prospect looked less promising. Rural Russia was now broken up into 25,000,000 smallholdings, most of which were tiny and worked with ante-diluvian tools. The Bolshevik leaders knew that in the long run this spelt economic and social stagnation. They had to encourage and then to sanction the share-out of the land, because this was preferable to the old semi-feudal system of tenure, and because otherwise they would have suffered the fate of their predecessors in government. But they were from the beginning broadly committed to foster collective ownership in land, to regroup and merge the 25,000,000 smallholdings into relatively few large, modern, and efficient farms. They could not say when, how, or by means of what industrial resources they would be able to do this. They only knew that they had embarked upon a complex, paradoxical, and dangerous course: they had made one agrarian revolution with the avowed purpose of undoing it by means of another.

'Bread' means to the industrial worker and the city dweller at large the growth and the development of industry. To the Russian worker in 1917 it also implied the elimination from industry of private ownership and control. In the theoretical conception of socialism, which the leaders of the revolution had imbibed from early youth, national and ultimately international ownership and central planning of production and distribution held a crucial place. Russia's industry, as the Bolsheviks found it, even if it had not been further destroyed through civil war, was too small and poor to serve as a basis for socialism. It provided only a starting-point for evolution towards socialism. Despite the fact that they had proclaimed the Socialist purpose of their revolution, the Bolsheviks could ill afford an attempt to bring Russian industry under public ownership or management at once. The resources, the administrators, the technicians, and the techniques needed were not available. They hoped to be able to seek an unhurried solution of the problem by trial and error. They were at first as reluctant to dispossess the industrialists and merchants as they had been eager to dispossess the landlords.

But in the course of 1917 a state of affairs had spontaneously come to prevail, under which the owners of factories had already been more than half dispossessed. Just as in the barracks the elective soldiers' committees had deprived the commissioned officers of all authority and function, even before they tore off their epaulettes, so in the factories and mines the elected works committees had appropriated most of the rights and privileges of owners and managers, even before the latter were dispossessed or dismissed. The duality of power which, from February to October, ran through Russia's system of government ran also through Russian industry, even after October. The popular instinct was a mixture of anarchism and socialism. In part naturally and in part because of the prevalent chaos, it tended to destroy the national coherence of industry, without which there could be no evolution towards socialism. Each works committee tended to become a closed community and a law unto itself. Not only the capitalists but also the nation itself was in danger of being expropriated of its industrial resources.

Such a state of affairs forced the hands of the Bolsheviks. The revolutionary government, which seized power on behalf of the working class, could not re-establish the authority of the old industrialists, even if for economic reasons it had wanted to do so. It was compelled to put an end to the dual power in industry in the same way as it put an end to it elsewhere—by destroying the old power. Only after that could it strive to overcome the centrifugal trends in the nation's economy. The half-dispossessed bourgeoisie, knowing that it could expect nothing good from the revolution, could not help defending itself by the only means at its immediate disposal: economic resistance and sabotage. This again impelled the Bolsheviks to press dispossession through to the end. When the economic and political struggle culminated in civil war, all these trends became focused in the sudden and premature nationalization of all industry, which was decreed in June 1918. The revolution was permanent, according to the forecast of the chief character of this book. More firmly than other Bolsheviks, Trotsky had reckoned with this prospect. But its realization meant that from the outset the Russian Revolution had to build on extremely shaky economic foundations. The result was that over the years now this and now that part of the structure was bound to collapse over the heads of the Russian people or to be pulled down in panicky haste.

The Bolsheviks, nevertheless, believed that they were capable of fulfilling the three great and simple promises—Peace, Land, Bread—to which they owed their victory. They ardently believed that the bleeding and maimed peoples of Europe would very soon follow the Russian example and help the Russian revolution to solve its staggering problems. Russia would then enter the international Socialist community, within which the wealth and civilization of western Europe would outweigh Russian poverty and backwardness, just as the many millions of enlightened German, French, and perhaps also British proletarians would outweigh, if not outnumber, the millions of benighted muzhiks. Russia had opened to the West the road of Socialist revolution; and now the West would tow

Russia along that road, helping her to obtain access to the blessings of real civilization. Each phrase uttered by the Bolsheviks breathed this passionate, almost Messianic, belief. The dazzling blaze of this great vision brightened in their eyes even the darkest aspects of the legacy they were taking over.

Similar hope glowed through their ideas on their intended system of government. Theirs was to be a state without a standing army, without police, without bureaucracy. For the first time in history, the business of government was to cease to be the professional secret and privilege of small groups of people, elevated above society. It was to become the daily concern of the ordinary citizen. After the July days, while he was hunted as a German spy and expected to be assassinated at any moment, Lenin wrote his *State and Revolution*, a sort of political testament, in which he revived the half-forgotten Marxist idea about the withering away of the state, the idea of a government which in a classless society would cease to be government, because it would administer 'things' instead of governing human beings and so would no longer wield the instruments of coercion (prisons, courts, &c.). To be sure, this was the ideal state of the future, not the Russian state of 1917. But the Soviet republic, as it emerged from the revolution, was to be directly related to the ideal. Trotsky's conception of the state was less crystallized than Lenin's, though this did not prevent him from accepting Lenin's view when he became familiar with it. In their ideas on the Soviet republic, which were of more immediate consequence, there was no difference between them.

In the Soviets the propertied classes were not represented: they were to be disfranchised in the way in which old ruling classes are disfranchised in any revolution. (This did not necessarily imply that they should also be deprived of freedom of expression.) The Soviets were to combine legislative and executive powers, and the government was to be responsible to them. The electors were entitled to revoke, to change their deputies at any time, not merely during periodic polls; and the Soviets could at any time depose the government through a vote of no confidence. The existence of opposition and the continued contest of parties within the Soviets were taken for granted. That the ruling party alone should be entitled to form public opinion did not yet enter anybody's mind. Of course, the Soviet republic was to be a 'proletarian dictatorship'. By this was meant the social and political preponderance of the working class; but the means by which this preponderance was to be established were not fixed in advance. The Bolsheviks, and Socialists of other schools as well, were wont to describe the parliamentary democracies of the West as 'bourgeois dictatorships', in the sense that they embodied the social preponderance of the bourgeoisie, not that they were actually ruled in a dictatorial manner. The Bolsheviks at first described their own system of government as a dictatorship in that broad sense, expecting in all sincerity that by comparison with the bourgeois democracies the republic of the Soviets would bring to the vast majority of the nation more, not less, liberty; more, not less, freedom of expression and association.

The plebeian democracy of the Soviets did not at first think of itself as a monolithic or totalitarian state, because its leaders were confident that the bulk of the Russian people shared their aspirations. It did not soon occur to them to consider what they would do if this hopeful assumption proved wrong. They took it for granted that if they came in conflict with the majority of the nation, then they, their party, and their revolution would be doomed, and that all that would be left to them would be to perish with honour. But in 1917 this danger seemed to them no more real than the threat of a cosmic catastrophe.

How did the Russian people view the Bolsheviks and their objectives? A mere handful participated directly in the October insurrection—'hardly more', says Trotsky, 'than 25,000 or 30,000 at the most'.[1] In this sense, the revolution was the work of a tiny minority, unlike the February insurrection during which the great, overflowing, unguided energy of the masses had swept away the monarchy. But in the last fortnight before the October rising, in Petrograd alone 'hundreds of thousands of workers and soldiers took direct action, defensive in form but aggressive in essence'.[2] Many more facilitated the Bolshevik victory through their friendly attitude, active and passive; and many others did so by adopting all possible shades of neutrality. The second Congress of the Soviets represented about 20,000,000 electors, perhaps rather fewer. Of these the great majority voted for the Bolsheviks. Even in the elections to the Constituent

---

[1] Trotsky, *History of the Russian Revolution*, vol. iii, p. 290. [2] Loc. cit.

Assembly, held after the revolution, nearly 10,000,000 votes were cast for the Bolsheviks alone without their Left Social Revolutionary associates. These 10,000,000 included the bulk of the urban working class, proletarianized elements of the peasantry, and a very large section of the army—at any rate the most energetic elements in the nation, on whose continued active support the revolution depended for its survival. But the electorate represented by the Constituent Assembly was nearly twice as large as that represented in the Soviets; and in the poll for the Assembly the Bolsheviks obtained only a large minority of the votes.

Rural Russia, vast, illiterate, boiling over with revolt and revenge, had little grasp of the involved disputes between the urban parties. It would be futile to try to put the attitude of that Russia into a clear-cut formula: it was confused, changeable, self-contradictory. Nothing characterizes that attitude better than the following scene described by historians: In one rural area a large body of peasants concluded a meeting with a religious vow that they would no longer wait for any land reform; that they would at once seize the land and smoke out the landlords; and that they would consider as their mortal enemy anybody trying to dissuade them. They would not rest, the peasants proceeded to swear, until the government concluded an immediate peace and released their sons from the army and until 'that criminal and German spy' Lenin had received exemplary punishment. In the election to the Constituent Assembly, peasants like these undoubtedly cast their votes for a Social Revolutionary. But they did so because they attributed to the Social Revolutionaries, the party which had had its roots in the country, the firm intention of carrying out the programme to which the Bolsheviks alone were determined to give effect. That is why each of these two parties, the only broad movements left after the débâcle of the Cadets and the Mensheviks, could claim, each with some reason, to enjoy the peasantry's support. 'Do not the peasants abhor Lenin, the German spy?' the Social Revolutionary said with self-confidence. 'But do they not declare those who, like you, delay the dispossession of the landlords and prolong the war as their mortal enemies?' the Bolshevik retorted triumphantly.

The abhorrence in which many peasants held the Bolsheviks

was due to the fact that the Bolsheviks were the avowed enemies of property. This feeling, however, was largely dispelled as soon as the Bolsheviks appeared in the countryside as the ruling party, and proclaimed the end of the war, and sanctioned or regulated the share-out of the land. In the civil war, the peasants further discovered that, by and large, only the Red Army stood between them and the return of the landlord. As the only effective opponents of restoration and defenders of the agrarian revolution, the Bolsheviks did in fact enjoy the support of the nation's overwhelming majority. But in the countryside this support was often reluctant, and it changed into its opposite when the figure of the returning landlord had ceased to cast its shadow and when Bolshevik squads went on rummaging the villages for food. Even at the height of Bolshevik popularity only the urban proletarian minority whole-heartedly identified itself with the cause of the revolution. It was to that minority that the Bolsheviks appealed in every predicament. To it they preached their transcendent ideals. From its ranks they drew the new administrators, commanders, and leaders.

The Russian working class of 1917 was one of history's wonders. Small in numbers, young, inexperienced, uneducated, it was rich in political passion, generosity, idealism, and rare heroic qualities. It had the gift of dreaming great dreams about the future and for dying a stoic death in battle. With its semi-illiterate thoughts it embraced the idea of the republic of the philosophers, not its Platonic version in which an oligarchy of pundits rules the herd, but the idea of a republic wealthy and wise enough to make of every citizen a philosopher and a worker. From the depth of its misery, the Russian working class set out to build that republic.

But side by side with the dreamer and the hero there lived in the Russian worker the slave; the lazy, cursing, squalid slave, bearing the stigmata of his past. The leaders of the revolution addressed themselves to the dreamer and the hero, but the slave rudely reminded them of his presence. During the civil war, and still more after it, Trotsky in his military speeches repeatedly complained that the Russian Communist and Red Army man would sacrifice his life for the sake of the revolution sooner than clean his rifle or polish his boots. This paradox reflected the lack in the Russian people of those innumerable small habits

of self-disciplined and civilized life on which socialism had hoped
to base itself. Such was the human material with which the
Bolsheviks set out to build their new state, the proletarian
democracy, in which 'every cook' should be able to perform the
business of government. And this was perhaps the gravest of all
the grave contradictions with which the revolution had to
contend.

History gave the Bolshevik leaders a first warning of this
problem almost immediately after she had given them her most
gracious smile; and she did so with that malignant taste for
anti-climax which she so often exhibits. The grotesque sequel
to the October insurrection, a sequel to which historians rarely
give attention, was a prodigious, truly elemental orgy of mass
drunkenness with which the freed underdog celebrated his
victory. The orgy lasted many weeks and at one time threatened
to bring the revolution to a standstill and to paralyze it. Drunkenness reached its height just when the new government was
confronted with the boycott of the entire civil service and with
the first stirrings of civil war, when the government had no
administrative organs of its own and when its fate depended
entirely on the vigilance, discipline, and energy of its supporters. The orgy was also of some importance in the events
which set the stage for the peace of Brest Litovsk, for in the
course of it much of the old Russian army dissolved into nothing-
ness. Contemporary sources abound in descriptions of these
strange saturnalia. A most striking account is found in the
memoirs of Antonov-Ovseenko, who at the time was one of the
two chief Commissars of the Army and commander of the Petrograd garrison:

The garrison, which began completely to disintegrate, gave me
personally much more trouble than did the adherents of the Constituent Assembly. . . . A wild and unexampled orgy spread over
Petrograd; and until now it has not been plausibly explained whether
or not this was due to any surreptitious provocation. Now here and
now there, crowds of ruffians appeared, mostly soldiers, broke into
wine cellars and sometimes pillaged wine shops. The few soldiers
who had preserved discipline and the Red Guards were worn out
by guard duty. Exhortations were of no avail.

The cellars of the Winter Palace [the former residence of the Tsar]
presented the most awkward problem. . . . The Preobrazhensky

regiment, which had hitherto kept its discipline, got completely drunk while it was doing guard duty at the Palace. The Pavlovsky regiment, our revolutionary rampart, did not withstand the temptation either. Mixed guards, picked from different detachments were then sent there; They, too, got drunk. Members of the [regimental] committees [i.e. the revolutionary leaders of the garrison] were then assigned to do guard duty. These, too, succumbed. Men of the armoured brigades were ordered to disperse the crowds—they paraded a little to and fro, and then began to sway suspiciously on their feet.

At dusk the mad bacchanals would spread. 'Let us finish off these Tsarist remnants!' This gay slogan took hold of the crowd. We tried to stop them by walling up the entrances. The crowd penetrated through the windows, forced out the bars and grabbed the stocks. An attempt was made to flood the cellars with water. The fire brigades sent to do this themselves got drunk.

Only the sailors from Helsingfors managed to render the cellars of the Winter Palace harmless. This was in its way a titanic struggle. The sailors stood firm, because they were bound by a severe comradely vow: 'Death to anyone who breaks the oath'; and, although they themselves were at other times magnificent tipplers, they came off with flying colours. . . .

This was not yet the end of the struggle. The whole city was infected by the drinking madness. At last the Council of the People's Commissars appointed a special commissar, endowed him with emergency powers, and gave him a strong escort. But the commissar, too, proved unreliable. . . . A bitter struggle was in progress at the Vassilevsky Island. The Finnish regiment, led by men with anarcho-syndicalist leanings, declared a state of siege on the island and announced that they would blow up the wine cellars and shoot plunderers at sight. Only after an intense effort was this alcoholic lunacy overcome. . . .[1]

Trotsky again and again addressed the Soviet on this matter, for the first time on 29 October, four days after the rising, and for the last time on 2 December. 'Vodka is just as much a political factor as the word', he said. 'The revolutionary word awakens the people and enthuses it to fight against its oppressors; vodka . . . puts the people to sleep again. . . .'[2] More than anybody Trotsky had appealed to the dreamer and the hero in the working man and had spread before his eyes the grand

[1] Antonov-Ovseenko, *Zapiski o Grazhdanskoi Voinie*, vol. i, pp. 19–20.
[2] Trotsky, *Sochinenya*, vol. iii, book 2, pp. 139–40.

324 THE PROPHET ARMED

vision of socialism. Now this vision seemed blurred by alcoholic vapours. At length the Council of the People's Commissars ordered the contents of the wine cellars to be pumped into the waters of the Neva.

In the course of the orgy, the great Petrograd garrison, which had played so important a role in the revolutions of February and October, ultimately disintegrated and ceased to exist. After Petrograd came the provinces' turn. 'Comrade Berzin [a well-known member of the Central Committee] reports his great difficulties', Antonov-Ovseenko notes further in his memoirs. 'He also notices mass consignments of spirits and wine on the railways. . . . Echelons of soldiers break into the wagons and get drunk. Detachments disintegrate. Plunder goes on. . . .'[1]

Under this grotesque omen, which seemed to mock at its high and noble aspirations, the Soviet republic started its first year.

[1] Antonov-Ovseenko, op. cit., vol. i, p. 31. A vivid description of the orgy and of its tragi-comic consequences by a foreign, pro-Bolshevik eye-witness is in Bessie Beatty, *The Red Heart of Russia*, pp. 329–34.

CHAPTER X

The People's Commissar

The first Soviet Government was in its composition purely Bolshevik. It was out of the question that the parties which had refused to acknowledge the Congress of the Soviets as the only constitutional source of power, and had then declared a boycott on the Congress, should join the government. Only one non-Bolshevik group, the Left Social Revolutionaries, who had broken away from their mother-party, were inclined to share with the Bolsheviks the responsibilities of government. To them Lenin offered seats in the Council of the People's Commissars. But the Left Social Revolutionaries still hoped to mediate between the Bolsheviks and their adversaries and, in order not to spoil the chance of this, they preferred to stay outside the government.[1]

Trotsky relates that, when the composition of the government was first discussed, Lenin proposed that Trotsky should be placed at its head, since he had led the insurrection of which this government was born. Out of deference to Lenin's political seniority, Trotsky refused.[2] This version has never been denied by any source; and it is indirectly confirmed by what Lunacharsky, a member of this government, related to Sukhanov, his intimate friend. Lenin, Lunacharsky said, was reluctant to preside over the Council of the People's Commissars or even to join it; he preferred to give undivided attention to the management of the party's affairs. But those Bolshevik leaders who had been opposed to the insurrection and those who had vacillated, including Lunacharsky himself, saw in this an attempt by Lenin to evade his responsibilities and insisted that he should preside over the government. Lenin was the last man to shrink from the consequences of his actions, and he agreed to head the *Sovnarkom*.[3]

He then proposed that Trotsky be appointed Commissar of Home Affairs.[4] This Commissariat was to direct the struggle against the counter-revolution, and a firm hand was needed there. Trotsky objected to this appointment, too, partly be-

---

[1] John Reed, op. cit., p. 116.   [2] Trotsky, *Moya Zhizn*, vol. ii.
[3] Sukhanov, op. cit., vol. vii, p. 266. *Sovnarkom*, abbreviation for the Council of the People's Commissars.   [4] Trotsky, op. cit., vol. ii, pp. 62–63.

cause he had been tired by the exertions of the last months and partly because he feared that in this office his Jewish origin might be a liability: the counter-revolution would whip up anti-Semitic feeling and turn it against the Bolsheviks. This consideration seemed irrelevant to Lenin. But Sverdlov, another Jew among the Bolshevik leaders, shared Trotsky's apprehension, and Lenin gave way.

This was a curious episode. In the Socialist parties and the Soviets, racial prejudice had never made itself felt; if it had, it would not have been countenanced. Jews, Poles, and Georgians had been prominent in all radical and revolutionary movements for the simple reason that they had been members of oppressed minorities. There were even more Jews among the Mensheviks and Social Revolutionaries than among the Bolsheviks. Despite his origin, Trotsky had been the leader of the insurrection. But, so far, the revolution had been an urban affair, and Russia's most advanced city its main scene. Now the Bolsheviks had to feel themselves into new roles, those of the rulers of rural Russia, which was still wrapped up in Greek Orthodoxy, distrust of the cities, and racial prejudice. In a few months Trotsky would call the sons of that Russia to defend the revolution on a dozen fronts; and his origin would not handicap him. But in those few months the Soviet régime had acquired some sense of stability and so could defy inveterate prejudice. On the day after the insurrection, Trotsky may have felt that it would be imprudent for the victors to offer too strong a provocation.

It is possible, however, that he had other and unavowable motives. The job of the revolution's chief policeman may not have suited his inclinations and tastes. True, he would presently be among the strongest advocates of repressive measures against incipient counter-revolution; and he would not shun the Red Terror when the time for it came. But it was one thing to justify and even direct the red terror in a civil war, in an atmosphere of high drama; and it was quite another to accept the office of chief policeman on the very day of the revolution. This may have seemed to him too flat a sequel. The internationalist may have been unattracted by an office in which he would have had to turn his mind mainly to domestic preoccupations.

Whatever the truth, he readily agreed to become the revolution's first Foreign Secretary. It was on Sverdlov's initiative that he was invited to assume this office. Next to the leadership of the government this was the most important appointment. Trotsky himself played it down. The revolution, he said, had no need for diplomacy: 'I shall publish a few revolutionary proclamations and then close shop.' There was a little affectation in his assumption of the back seat. Sverdlov proposed his appointment on the ground that he was the right man 'to confront Europe' on behalf of the revolution; and this assignment was as important as it was congenial to Trotsky. It is true, however, that he did not intend to 'confront Europe' in the manner of the conventional diplomat.[1]

The government was formed, but few believed it would last. To the anti-Bolsheviks, and to many Bolsheviks as well, the insurrection and its outcome looked quite unreal. Most of them expected a bloody suppression. The day after the formation of the government, the capital was astir with rumours that Lenin and Trotsky had already fled.[2] From Gatchina, less than twenty miles south-west of Petrograd, Kerensky self-confidently announced his imminent return at the head of General Krasnov's loyal Cossacks. The Commissar for Foreign Affairs, resuming his functions as chief of the Military Revolutionary Committee, had to gather an armed force in order to stop the advance of Kerensky's troops. This proved to be more difficult in some respects than it had been to make the insurrection. The garrison was in no fighting mood. It had gladly helped Trotsky to overthrow Kerensky when the latter threatened to send the rebellious regiments to the front. But when Trotsky ordered these same regiments to leave their barracks and to take up positions on the heights outside the capital, it was with much grumbling and discontent that they carried out his order. They did not expect any fighting, and when suddenly they found themselves under fire, their hearts sank. The Red Guards of the civilian workers were the only militant force available. But, like any such militia, while they acted with self-reliance and boldness as long as they moved within the walls of their city—where they were familiar with every street, passage, and recess—they were little suited to meet an enemy in the open field.[3]

---

[1] Trotsky, loc. cit.; *Proletarskaya Revolutsia*, nr. 10, 1922.
[2] Sadoul, *Notes sur la Révolution*, p. 63.
[3] Trotsky, *Sochinenya*, vol. iii, book 2, pp. 86–90.

At this moment Kerensky might have re-entered Petrograd if he had mustered a few reliable and disciplined detachments, though it is doubtful whether he would have been able to re-assert his authority. But, like the troops which Trotsky sent against him, his Cossacks were by no means prepared to shed their blood. They had been told that their job was to suppress a revolt staged by a handful of German spies; and they were surprised to find the regiments of the capital and the Red Guards arrayed against them. For a moment the fate of a great country, indeed the fate of the world, depended on the encounter of a few small dispirited brigades. That side which could evoke a flicker of spirit in its troops and act with the more purpose and speed was bound to win. Victory lay in a very narrow margin of superiority, as it sometimes does even when numerous, well-equipped, tenaciously fighting but equally strong armies are locked in battle.

Trotsky was confident that words of persuasion rather than bullets would disperse Krasnov's Cossacks.[1] But, before Bolshevik propagandists could approach the Cossacks, guns had to shake their self-assurance. At this stage already Trotsky had to look round for experienced and skilled commanders. On the day after the insurrection, he and Lenin turned for help to the regular officers, hitherto the target of Bolshevik attacks. But the officers who were persuaded to appear at the Smolny cautiously refused co-operation. Only a few desperados and careerists were ready to serve under the 'illegitimate' government. One of these, Colonel Muraviev, was chosen to command in the battle on the Pulkovo Heights; and subsequently he played a conspicuous part in the first phase of the civil war. A braggart, posing as a Left Social Revolutionary, he seems to have been moved less by sympathy with the Bolsheviks than by a grudge against Kerensky. Trotsky first received him with suspicion. But the Colonel was mettlesome, resourceful, and eager to win a prize in a seemingly hopeless assignment; and so Trotsky was captivated by his initiative and courage. Colonel Valden, another officer of this small group, commanded the artillery, which decided the outcome of the Pulkovo battle in favour of the Bolsheviks.

The employment of these officers aroused much indignation in the Soviet. Bolsheviks and Left Social Revolutionaries were

[1] Sadoul, op. cit., pp. 68–69.

horrified to see, as they thought, the fate of the revolution placed in the hands of disreputable climbers—Muraviev was said to have been especially zealous in the suppression of the Bolsheviks in July. Boycotted by the entire officer corps, the Bolsheviks could not, however, afford to scrutinize too closely the credentials of those few who were willing to serve. In the party's military branch there were men skilled in the arts of insurrection, but almost none competent in regular warfare. The garrison was in complete chaos; and Trotsky was incapable even of tracing the stocks of ammunition and food in its possession. At that moment he was ready to employ the devil himself, provided he could keep a pistol at the devil's head and watch the way he went. In these improvisations one may discern in miniature the main elements of Trotsky's military policy in the civil war.

On 28 October Trotsky arrived at the head of the Red Guards at Gatchina, where a battle was fought for the approaches to the capital. At Gatchina Kerensky's troops suffered their first reverse; and Trotsky hoped to bring back the former Premier as the Soviet's prisoner. But Kerensky escaped him.[1]

While the fighting outside Petrograd was still on, inside the city the cadets of the officers' schools staged a revolt. They had some initial success, and among the prisoners they captured was Antonov-Ovseenko, the Commissar of War. Speaking to the Soviet on the steps taken to suppress this revolt, Trotsky declared among other things:

The prisoners we have taken are hostages in our hands. If our enemies happen to take prisoners from us, let them know that we shall exchange each worker and peasant for five military cadets. . . . We have shown them to-day that our hesitations have come to an end. We do not joke when the fundamental interests of the workers and peasants are at stake. We know how the landlords and capitalists have fought . . ., how they have treated insurgent soldiers, workers

[1] Sukhanov, op. cit., vol. vii, p. 305. The atmosphere which prevailed in the Soviet is well conveyed by a scene described by John Reed (op. cit., pp. 178–9): Trotsky was reporting on the progress of the fighting. 'The cruisers *Oleg, Aurora,* and *Respublika*', he said, 'are anchored in the Neva, their guns trained on the approaches to the city. . . .'

'Why aren't you out there, with the Red Guards?' shouted a rough voice.

'I'm going now!' answered Trotsky and left the platform. The rough plebeian anger of the masses did not spare even the leaders of the revolution and often dictated their steps.

and peasants, how much blood they have shed, how much life they have destroyed. . . .[1]

These words, liable to be taken as a signal for indiscriminate executions, provoked angry protests.[2] During a later sitting, Trotsky took advantage of a question put to him from the floor to explain what he meant. It was a matter of course, he said, that the life of prisoners was inviolable 'for humanitarian reasons and because the living are worth more to us than the dead'. He had previously referred to the 'exchange', not the shooting of prisoners.[3] The incident, nevertheless, gave a foretaste of the ferocity of the civil war. At the same session, reporting on the difficulties of supplying the Red Guards, Trotsky announced that the Soviet would not respect the sanctity of private property: 'The organizations of workers and soldiers can obtain from the Military Revolutionary Committee authorization for requisitions.' He also reported that the government was preparing a decree which would give it power to ban newspapers backing the other side in the civil war.

On 31 October Kerensky's Cossacks surrendered at Pulkovo. Their commander General Krasnov was taken prisoner, but Kerensky escaped once again. From the battlefield Trotsky reported victory in an eloquent message to the Soviet. He released Krasnov on parole, which did not prevent the general from taking up arms against the Soviets soon afterwards. At the same time, after protracted and bloody fighting, the Bolsheviks obtained control in Moscow. The ascendancy of the Soviets was reported from most other cities as well. Lenin's government was no longer isolated in Petrograd, and some time was to elapse before the civil war flared up for good.

The first armed threat to Lenin's government had hardly been warded off when that government was in danger of being undone by the scruples and second thoughts of its own members. The moderate Bolsheviks were anxious to reconcile the Mensheviks and Social Revolutionaries and to invite them to participate in the government. The leaders of the railwaymen's union threatened to stop traffic on the railways if a coalition government of all Socialist parties was not formed. On 29 October

[1] Trotsky, op. cit., vol. iii, book 2, p. 71.
[2] Lozovsky, for instance, reproached Trotsky with 'imitating the methods of Hindenburg'.   [3] Loc. cit.

the Bolshevik Central Committee, in the absence of Lenin, Trotsky, and Stalin, resolved to open negotiations.[1] The Mensheviks and Social Revolutionaries then put forward the following conditions for their entry into the coalition: the new government was to be responsible not to the Soviets but to 'the broad circles of revolutionary democracy'; it was to disarm the Bolshevik detachments; and Lenin and Trotsky were to be debarred from it.[2] These conditions amounted to a demand that the Bolsheviks should declare the October Revolution null and void; that they should disarm themselves in the face of their enemies; and that they themselves should ostracize the inspirer and the leader of the insurrection. Addressed by parties defeated in a revolution to victors seeking reconciliation, these were bold demands. The Bolshevik negotiators, Kamenev, Ryazanov, and Sokolnikov, especially the former two, stood on the right wing of their party and desired nothing more than to be able to return to the party with a practicable compromise which it would be hard for Lenin and Trotsky to reject. So anxious were the Bolshevik negotiators to meet the Mensheviks and Social Revolutionaries half-way that, while the battle at Pulkovo was still undecided, they signed a joint appeal for a cease-fire, an appeal implicitly directed against their own party and the government. Yet even the most moderate Bolsheviks could not accept the Menshevik terms. They could not return to their party with the advice that it should commit suicide.

Straight from the Pulkovo battle, Trotsky rushed to a conference which the Central Committee held with the Petrograd committee and the leaders of the military branch in order to take a decision on the negotiations. He was the first to assail Kamenev and Ryazanov. 'There was no need for us to stage the rising', he said, 'if we were not to obtain a majority in the government. . . . We ought to obtain three-quarters of all the seats.' He added that Lenin must in any circumstances continue to preside over the government.[3] Lenin went even farther and asked that the negotiations be broken off. At the other extreme Ryazanov (and Lunacharsky) was inclined to agree to the exclusion of Lenin and Trotsky from the government, saying that the party should insist on principles,

[1] *Protokoly Tsen. Kom.*, pp. 144–7.
[2] Ibid., p. 156.   [3] Ibid., p. 149.

not on personalities. The conference decided to carry on the negotiations, but only on conditions guaranteeing the party's preponderance in the proposed coalition.

This controversy was a prolongation of that which had preceded the insurrection. On the face of it, all Bolsheviks agreed that the Soviets should form the constitutional basis and framework of government. All seemed to agree also on the advisability of a coalition with any party or group prepared to endorse this principle. On 2 November the Central Committee solemnly reiterated that the Bolsheviks were still willing to form a government with the parties which had declared a boycott on the Soviets, provided that those parties retraced their steps and accepted Soviet constitutionalism. The Mensheviks and Social Revolutionaries could not agree to this without disavowing everything they had done since February. If the terms the Mensheviks had laid down were an implicit demand that the Bolsheviks should commit political suicide, then Lenin's party, in its turn, invited its would-be partners to commit an act of moral self-effacement. Lenin had no doubt that they would not agree and so he saw no use in further parleying. At best, he said, this could only serve as a *ruse de guerre*, designed to confound Kerensky's supporters while the struggle against Kerensky lasted.

Neither Lenin nor Trotsky saw any reason why their party should not form an administration consisting solely of its own members. There was nothing, they argued, to prevent the Soviet majority from shouldering exclusive responsibility. In no democratic system can the minority claim the right to participate in the government. What is vital for the minority is that it should be unhampered in its activity as an opposition, on the understanding that that activity remains within a constitutional framework accepted by both government and opposition. No such commonly accepted framework existed after the October revolution. One party had proclaimed a new constitutional principle, which was inherently unconstitutional in the view of nearly all other parties. Emphatically denying the sovereignty of the Soviets, the Mensheviks and their associates could not even become a loyal opposition within the Soviets (even though some groups of them occasionally tried to do so). Still less could they become the Bolsheviks' partners. The opposed parties were all Socialist in name; yet all that connected them now were fading reminiscences of a common past.

The large and influential body of Bolshevik leaders who still sought to bridge the gulf, was in part moved by these reminiscences. Many of the Bolshevik conciliators also felt that their party had driven into a blind alley and that to get out it ought to grasp the helping hands of its adversaries. Kamenev, Rykov, Zinoviev, and others argued in alarm that Petrograd was without food supplies, that the Bolsheviks could not rule the country if the railways were stopped, and that they had no chance of surviving a protracted civil war. Lenin and Trotsky, ardently supported by Sverdlov and Dzerzhinsky, did not deny the risks and dangers; but they believed that they could hold their ground if they acted with determination. To sue for coalition was to show weakness; and, anyhow, the would-be partners had stretched out hands not to help but to strangle.

On 2 November the issue was discussed by the Central Executive of the Soviets; and the Bolshevik 'conciliators', together with anti-Bolshevik members, voted against their own party. This open split was most embarrassing; all the more so as the 'conciliators' were headed by Kamenev who, despite his recent quarrel with the party, had been elected Chairman of the Central Executive of the Soviets, an office equivalent to that of President of the republic. Briefly, the Bolshevik President openly asked for the dismissal of the Bolshevik government and for its replacement by a coalition. Kamenev had behind him most important members of the government itself: Rykov, Commissar of Interior; Miliutin, Commissar of Agriculture; Nogin, Commissar of Industry and Trade; Lunacharsky, Commissar of Education; Teodorovich, Commissar of Supplies; and outside the government Zinoviev, Lozovsky, Ryazanov, and Yureniev, to mention only the most influential.

There could be no graver crisis in both government and party. The rule that the members of a party should act in office on the party's instructions and be bound by its discipline was generally accepted not only by the Bolsheviks but by most Russian and indeed European parties, although the rule was more often honoured in the breach than in the observance. Lenin and Trotsky set out to enforce observance. They persuaded the Central Committee to reaffirm its view: 'To yield to ultimatums and threats from a minority in the Soviets would amount to a complete renunciation [by us] not only of government based on the Soviets but of the democratic attitude. Such yielding would testify to the majority's fear of using its majority; it would amount to submission to anarchy; and it would encourage any minority to confront us with ever-new ultimatums.'[1] On 3 November the majority of the Central Committee presented the 'conciliators' with its own 'ultimatum' demanding disciplined behaviour and threatening to convoke an emergency Congress of the party, which would be asked either to endorse the 'conciliators' ' policy or to expel them.[2] The 'conciliators' replied with collective resignation from the Central Committee and the government. They justified their step in strongly worded protests against the party's insistence on a purely Bolshevik government. Such a government, Nogin declared on their behalf, 'can be kept in power only by means of political terror'. It would lead to an 'irresponsible régime'; and it would 'eliminate the mass organizations of the proletariat from leadership in political life'.[3]

As in Trotsky's controversy with Lenin in 1904 and as in recent debates on insurrection, so here the wrongs and the rights of the issue were inextricably confused. From the Bolshevik viewpoint, the considerations which Lenin and Trotsky adduced to justify their policy were irrefutable. The negotiations for a broad coalition were futile. The Mensheviks and the Right Social Revolutionaries were trying in a roundabout way to wrest power from the Bolsheviks, not to share it with them. For all his anxiety to bring about agreement with the Mensheviks, Kamenev could not accept their terms. At the same session of the Central Executive of the Soviets where he virtually demanded the resignation of Lenin's government, he also declared that without Lenin and Trotsky the party would be 'decapitated'.[4] The other side insisted on the 'decapitation' because it could not eliminate the Bolsheviks from power without first breaking their self-reliance. Nothing was better calculated to achieve this than the demand that the Bolshevik party should allow outsiders to dictate whom it was to delegate to the government and to insist that it should disavow its two chiefs.

---

[1] *Protokoly Tsen. Kom.*, p. 161.   [2] Ibid., pp. 162–4.
[3] Ibid., pp. 169–70.   [4] Ibid., p. 166.

As in October, so now, Lenin did not question the right of Kamenev and his friends to dissent. But he denied them the right to act against the party's declared policy beyond the confines of the party. When they demonstratively left office, he branded them once again as 'deserters'. Kamenev and his friends eventually surrendered, as they had done in October. Their roles had been played out when it became clear that neither of the opposed parties was in a mood for conciliation. Zinoviev was the first to change sides and to declare that the Mensheviks had made a compromise impossible.[1] In words foreshadowing his future and more tragic surrenders, he appealed to his friends: 'We remain with the party; we prefer to err with the millions of workers and to die with them than to stand aside in this decisive, historical moment.' Within a few days the 'conciliators' were routed. Kamenev was deposed from his high office on the Executive of the Soviets; and at a session of the Executive Trotsky sponsored Sverdlov as Kamenev's successor. The only positive outcome of the negotiations was that the Left Social Revolutionaries, resentful at the attitude of the anti-Bolshevik parties, joined Lenin's government.

Yet Lenin's and Trotsky's opponents in the party were not quite as wrong as they presently professed. Their forecast that 'a purely Bolshevik government could be maintained only by means of political terror' and that it would result in an 'irresponsible régime', was eventually to come true. For the moment, Lenin and Trotsky repudiated this forecast with sincere indignation, reiterating the assurance that the Soviets could overthrow the government by a simple majority vote.[2] But history was to justify the warning though, when it was made, no basis for it was apparent. Lenin, Trotsky and the other Bolshevik leaders undoubtedly had every intention of governing the country in a spirit of genuine responsibility to the Soviet electorate. But the fact that their party alone was to embrace Soviet constitutionalism wholeheartedly could not but lead them to identify the policies of their party with Soviet constitutionalism, then to substitute the party's wishes and desires for the principles of that constitutionalism, and in the end to abandon those principles altogether. To put it more broadly, the circumstance that the Bolsheviks were *the* party of the revolution impelled them

[1] Ibid., p. 177.   [2] Ibid., pp. 171-5.

first to identify the revolution with themselves, and then to reduce the revolution to being exclusively an affair of their party.
Eleven years later Bukharin, surveying the sequence of events
that led to the perversion of Soviet democracy and to Stalin's
ascendancy, traced back these 'disasters' to a 'single mistake':
the identification of the party with the state.[1] The force of circumstances began to drive the party on to this road in the first
week of the revolution; and the moderate Bolsheviks expressed
an instinctive dread of the road. Nobody imagined the length,
the direction, or the tragic character of the journey.

Next to Lenin, Trotsky was the most outspoken and tenacious
advocate of an exclusively or predominantly Bolshevik government. He had proudly sent the Mensheviks and the Social
Revolutionaries to the 'dustheap of history'; and he was in no
mood to recall them as partners and allies. Yet neither he nor
any of his colleagues intended to suppress these parties. When,
on the day after the Menshevik exodus from the Congress of the
Soviets, Martov returned to intercede with the Bolsheviks for
the arrested Socialist ministers, as he had in July interceded
with these ministers for the arrested Bolsheviks, the Bolsheviks
softened. Trotsky released the ministers from prison, placing
them first under house arrest and then freeing them altogether.
This was at any rate more generous than the treatment the
ministers had so recently meted out to himself and Lenin.[2] In
the Soviets the Bolsheviks kept the doors wide open for the return of the Mensheviks and Social Revolutionaries; and on the
Central Executive they kept vacant a number of seats proportionate to their adversaries' strength at the Congress. Both
Lenin and Trotsky, even though they had no desire to share the
government with the Mensheviks and Social Revolutionaries,
wished to see them fairly represented in the 'proletarian parliament' and its agencies.

Trotsky opposed the Bolshevik 'conciliators' without showing
any sign of hesitation. Yet we have reliable testimony to his
inner misgivings. Sadoul relates that three days after the insurrection Trotsky confided to him his worry about the Mensheviks, who were likely by their pretensions and obstructiveness

[1] This is quoted from Bukharin's conversation with Kamenev in 1928, of which
The Trotsky Archives contain the fullest summary.
[2] Sukhanov, op. cit., vol. vii, p. 243.

to compel the Bolsheviks to treat them roughly and so to widen the gulf between the parties. This, Trotsky said, caused him more anxiety than the advance of Krasnov's Cossacks and the reports about the formation of White Guards.[1] Somewhat later he expressed to Sadoul his hope that, after the Bolsheviks had carried out the most essential points of their programme, they would invite the Mensheviks to join the government.

The talks about coalition came to an abrupt end on 3 November, when Martov and Abramovich declared that they would engage in no negotiations as long as the arrests then taking place continued and the newspapers just banned were not allowed to reappear.[2] The Bolsheviks had arrested a few right-wing politicians and banned some newspapers which had openly called for armed resistance. In the Soviet Trotsky thus justified these measures: 'The demand to stop all repression at the time of civil war amounts to a demand that we stop the civil war. . . . Our adversaries have not proposed peace to us. . . . In conditions of civil war it is legitimate to ban hostile papers.'[3] He emphatically assured the Soviet that the government had no intention of setting up its own press monopoly. It was, however, in duty bound to destroy the press monopoly of the propertied classes, as every Socialist party had promised to do. The printing presses and the paper-mills would be nationalized; and then the government would allocate printing facilities and paper to all parties and groups in proportion to their strength in elections. Thus genuine freedom of the press would be established for the first time in history. The capacity of people to spread their views would depend on their real influence in social and political life, not on their financial resources.[4]

A month after the revolution, the first White Guards, under the command of Kornilov, Kaledin, Alexeev, and Denikin,

---

[1] Sadoul, op. cit., pp. 68–69.   [2] *Protokoly Tsen. Kom.*, p. 174.

[3] Trotsky, *Sochinenya*, vol. iii, book, 2 pp. 104–5.

[4] Some time later Trotsky addressed the Grenadier Regiment on the same subject. 'What do the advocates of the bourgeoisie mean by the freedom of the press? The same as they mean by freedom of trade. Every man who has some capital has the right, because he has the means, to open a factory, a shop, a brothel, or a newspaper, according to his personal tastes. . . . But do the millions of peasants, workers, and soldiers enjoy freedom of the press? They do not have the essential condition of freedom, the means, the actual and genuine means of publishing a newspaper.' On this occasion, too, he defended the principle of proportional allocation of newsprint and other facilities to the political parties. Ibid., pp. 125–7.

moved into action on the Don; and the Cossacks of Orenburg
rose under their *Ataman* Dutov. The White generals did not
even pretend to fight for the restoration of Kerensky's government. They aimed frankly either at the restoration of Tsardom
or at their own dictatorship. Simultaneously with this opening
of actual civil war in remote provinces, the Cadets and some
Right Social Revolutionaries staged a semi-insurrection in the
capital. On 28 November Trotsky announced that the Cadet
party was outlawed. The Central Committee of that party, he
said, was the political headquarters of the White Guards; and
it directed the recruiting of officers for Kornilov and Kaledin.[1]
The Cadets would therefore be barred from the Constituent
Assembly which the government was about to convene. 'We
have made', Trotsky added, 'a modest beginning. We have
arrested the chiefs of the Cadets and ordered that a watch be
kept on their followers in the provinces. At the time of the French
Revolution, the Jacobins guillotined men more honest than
these for obstructing the people's will. We have executed nobody
and we have no intention of doing so. But there are moments of
popular anger, and the Cadets themselves have been looking for
trouble.'[2]

The words 'we have made a modest beginning' had an
ominous ring. Having accomplished a revolution, the Bolsheviks
could not renounce revolutionary terror; and the terror has its
own momentum. Every revolutionary party at first imagines
that its task is simple: it has to suppress a 'handful' of tyrants or
exploiters. It is true that usually the tyrants and exploiters form
an insignificant minority. But the old ruling class has not lived
in isolation from the rest of society. In the course of its long
domination it has surrounded itself by a network of institutions
embracing groups and individuals of many classes; and it has
brought to life many attachments and loyalties which even a
revolution does not destroy altogether. The anatomy of society
is never so simple that it is possible surgically to separate one of
the limbs from the rest of the body. Every social class is connected with its immediate neighbour by many almost impercep-

---

[1] That this was literally true can be seen from as authoritative a source as
Denikin who describes in great detail the connexions between the White Guards
and the headquarters of the Cadets. *Ocherki Russkoi Smuty*, vol. ii, pp. 35, 186–94.
[2] Trotsky, *Sochinenya*, vol. iii, book 2, p. 138.

tible gradations. The aristocracy shades off into the upper middle class; the latter into the lower layers of the bourgeoisie; the lower middle class branches off into the working class; and the proletariat, especially in Russia, is bound by innumerable filiations to the peasantry. The political parties are similarly interconnected. The revolution cannot deal a blow at the party most hostile and dangerous to it without forcing not only that party but its immediate neighbour to answer with a counter-blow. The revolution therefore treats its enemy's immediate neighbour as its enemy. When it hits this secondary enemy, the latter's neighbour, too, is aroused and drawn into the struggle. The process goes on like a chain reaction until the party of the revolution arouses against itself and suppresses all the parties which until recently crowded the political scene.

The generals who led the White Guards were monarchists *tout court*. They had been brought up to be the servants of Tsarist absolutism; and they viewed the revolution in all its phases, Bolshevik and pre-Bolshevik, with bitter hatred and a yearning for revenge. The Cadets had been constitutional monarchists. Under the Tsar, the main body of the defenders of absolutism and the main body of the constitutional monarchists had confronted one another in hostility and mutual contempt. But the two parties had also overlapped. Since the downfall of the monarchy their disagreements had become largely irrelevant—they all aimed at the overthrow of the 'socialist republic'. After the October Revolution, they finally sank their differences and fought under the same banner. But a large section of the constitutional monarchists was closely connected with the semi-Socialist republicans, who had been the pillars of the February régime. Within the Menshevik and Social Revolutionary parties all shades of opinion, from bourgeois republicanism to quasi-revolutionary socialism, could be found; and in their extreme left wings these parties overlapped with the Bolsheviks. If it had been possible for the Bolsheviks to isolate the White Guards, their most active and dangerous enemies, as the sole targets for attack, the revolution and the civil war might have developed in a different way. The natural alliance between the constitutional monarchists and the White Guards made this impossible. To deprive the White Guards of their political supply services, the Bolsheviks were compelled to outlaw the Cadets.

The main body of the Mensheviks and Social Revolutionaries would never have dreamt of defending Kornilov, Denikin, or Kolchak. But they could not remain indifferent when the Cadets were declared 'enemies of the people', if only because their own right wing had lived with the Cadets in a sort of political symbiosis, hatching common political plans and plots. A Left Menshevik like Martov would hardly have stood up for the Cadets alone. But he was well aware that after the Cadets, the scourge of the revolution would chastise the right wing of the Social Revolutionaries and of his own party; and this he was anxious to avert.

Trotsky's assurance that the Bolsheviks had no intention of installing the guillotine testified to his awareness that the terror might run away with the revolution. The anxiety to prevent this was widespread among the Bolsheviks. On the day after the rising they abolished the death penalty; and Lenin was alone in protesting.[1] But even Lenin, when he argued against the moderate Bolsheviks, said: 'In Paris, they [the Jacobins] used the guillotine, while we only take away the food cards of those who fail to obtain them from the trade unions.'[2] The party as a whole tried, in part instinctively and in part consciously, to avoid the slope, slippery with blood, down which the Jacobins had rushed. Having, of necessity, put one foot on the top of the slope the party resisted the downward pull hard and long. The government outlawed the Cadets, but not the right wing of the Social Revolutionaries, who had taken part in the semi-insurrection of 28 November. It decreed elections to the Constituent Assembly, and it was still half-unaware of the inevitable conflict between government by Soviets and a Constituent Assembly. Towards the end of November, Bukharin still urged the Central Committee to postpone the settling of accounts with the Cadets till the opening of the Constituent Assembly. Invoking precedents from French and English history, he proposed that the Cadets be expelled from the Constituent Assembly, and that the rump Assembly should then declare itself a revolutionary Convention. He hoped that in the Assembly the Bolsheviks and Left Social Revolutionaries would command an overwhelming majority, and that this would give the revolution the advantage

[1] Trotsky, *Lénine*, pp. 116–17.
[2] Trotsky, *The Stalin School of Falsification*, p. 110.

of formal legitimacy. Trotsky broadly supported Bukharin's plan of action. Stalin alone seems to have had, at this stage, a clearer idea of the trend of events, probably because he did not believe that the Bolsheviks and the Social Revolutionaries commanded a majority in the country. Bukharin's proposal, he declared, had come too late; the suppression of the Cadets had already begun and could not be delayed. He expected a split in the Assembly and a struggle between two rival assemblies. As yet nobody mooted the dispersal of the Constituante. In the records of even the most confidential discussions not a trace can be found of any suggestion for the suppression of other parties.[1]

. . . . . , ...

It was little more than two months since Trotsky had joined the Bolshevik party, and his leading position in its inner councils was firmly established. The first Politbureau, elected before the insurrection, never came to life. It was replaced by a smaller body, 'the Bureau of the Central Committee', an Executive in permanent session, which consisted of four men: Lenin, Trotsky, Stalin, and Sverdlov.[2] When the coalition with the Left Social Revolutionaries was consummated, the Council of the People's Commissars elected an inner cabinet in which the Bolsheviks were represented by the same men, with the exception of Sverdlov who held no office in the government. Lenin and Trotsky were generally recognized as the party's chief policy-makers and supreme authorities in matters of doctrine. Stalin and Sverdlov were the chief organizers.

The relationship between Lenin and Trotsky was one of mutual confidence, cordiality, and respect, though not of personal intimacy. Their common struggle against the moderate Bolsheviks, before and especially after the insurrection, the hatred with which their enemies honoured both of them, demanding the exclusion of both from any coalition government, their agreement on all major issues—all this bound the two men with the strongest of ties. Underneath this concord there was still a discord in temperament and habit. Lenin's manner was unassuming and almost impersonal, even in the exercise of power. He mistrusted the colourful gesture and word. For about two decades he had been surrounded by many devoted followers, whom he had led by the sheer strength of his intellec

[1] *Protokoly Tsen. Kom.*, pp. 180–91.   [2] Ibid., p. 189.

M

and character. He had acquired a mastery in judging the merits
and the faults of his colleagues and subordinates and in handling them with the greatest advantage to the party. Blunt and
even ruthless in serious controversy, he was otherwise reserved,
tactful, and careful to spare his followers' susceptibilities and
weaknesses, and open-minded to their ideas and suggestions.

Trotsky's volcanic passion and his mighty language stirred
the souls of the people in a way in which Lenin's incisive didactic
prose never did. Now, when they were once again united in
a common cause, Lenin listened to Trotsky's overflowing tirades
with approval and even with admiration, but also with something of that uneasiness with which the muzhik listened to
urban grandiloquence. The contrast in their temperaments extended to other qualities as well. The many years of political
free-lancing had left their traces on Trotsky. He did not possess
the habits of free and easy teamwork which make the strength
of a real leader of men. Lunacharsky, even when he still
looked up to Trotsky with intense admiration, dwelt emphatically on this feature, saying that Trotsky had never succeeded
in organizing any stable group of followers.[1] He was imperious
and wrapped up in himself. It is all the more remarkable that
in the next few years he proved himself so great and brilliant
an administrator. His administrative achievement, however,
was due not to his management of men but to the clarity and
precision of his schemes, to his drive and will-power, and to his
systematic method of work. The capacity for systematic work,
in which he surpassed Lenin, was rare in a country where
people attached little value to time or to steady effort. His
present close partnership with Lenin was based on certain
personal adjustments as well as on common purpose. With indubitable sincerity he acknowledged Lenin's leadership. He did
so without a hint of sycophancy and without renouncing his
own independence, but with distinct remorse for his past mistake in underrating Lenin as a revolutionary and leader. Lenin,
on his part, did his best to make Trotsky feel in the party as if he
had always been in it and of it. In the course of the six years of
their partnership, years which brought a number of new disputes, Lenin made not a single allusion to their past controversies, except to say privately that in some respects Trotsky had

[1] Lunacharsky, *Politicheskye Siluety*, pp. 25–30.

been right and to warn the party, in his will, that it ought not to hold his non-Bolshevik past against Trotsky.

The two other men in the 'Bureau of the Central Committee' were of quite different stuff. Sverdlov was Stalin's actual predecessor as the party's General Secretary—nominally the office had not yet been created. Like Stalin, he had spent all his political life in the underground. He had the same gift for organization, the same flair for handling men, the same empirical mind, and the same firmness of character.[1] More happy than Stalin in his role of organizer, cherishing no ambition to shine as an authority in matters of doctrine, Sverdlov possessed, however, if one may judge from his few writings and speeches, an intellect broader, more cultivated and flexible than Stalin's; and he was vastly more articulate.[2] It was he who, in Lenin's absence, had introduced Trotsky to the inner life of the party, had made him *au fait* with its military organization and facilitated Trotsky's co-operation with the various grades of the Bolshevik caucus. Sverdlov, we know, had also proposed Trotsky's appointment as Commissar of Foreign Affairs. While Trotsky's relations with Sverdlov were those of an easy comradeship, his first closer contacts with Stalin were quite different. He himself wrote later that he was hardly aware of Stalin's existence until after the October Revolution.[3] Yet Stalin had been the editor of the party's paper and one of the most important members of the Central Committee. If it was true that Trotsky overlooked him, as it were, this would point not so much to the unimportance of Stalin's role, which Trotsky was out to prove, as to Trotsky's own lack of interest in the personal influences that were at work in the party he had joined. Stalin was not a spectacular personality. Reserved, inarticulate, at times vulgar, he did not catch Trotsky's eye, because Trotsky was inclined to look in other people for the qualities which distinguished himself. With more excuse he repeated a mistake he had once made about Lenin: Stalin's 'greyness' concealed from him Stalin's strength. He continued to treat his future rival with an unintentional yet all the more hurtful haughtiness, even after Stalin

[1] Sadoul mentions that the Bolsheviks nicknamed Sverdlov '*la ferme gueule*', op. cit., p. 266.

[2] This emerges clearly from Sverdlov's private correspondence published in *Pechat i Revolutsia*, vol. ii, 1924.

[3] Trotsky, *Stalin*, pp. 242–3 and *passim*.

had become his colleague in the smallest group which managed the party's and the government's affairs. It is hardly surprising that Stalin's pride was stung.

Personal feelings and barely incipient jealousies were as yet of no importance. Amid the turmoil and the raptures of these months, the Bolshevik leaders lived as if in an ecstatic dream which might suddenly and tragically fade. They held on to, and tried to consolidate, positions of power in which for the time being there seemed to be no power at all; but they half-expected that in the process they themselves might go under and that the revolution would then roll over their dead bodies to ultimate triumph. 'If we both are killed by the White Guards', Lenin once said to Trotsky, 'do you think that Sverdlov and Bukharin will be able to carry on?'[1] In the meantime they were issuing proclamations, decrees, and laws, more for the historical record than for immediate execution. If the worst came to the worst, they thought and said, they would at least bequeath to their successors a set of ideas, a restatement of revolutionary policy, which would inspire others as the message of the Commune of Paris had inspired two generations of Socialists. In this seemingly impractical manner, the Bolshevik leaders were actually laying the foundations of the Soviet republic.

The external circumstances in which they carried out this task conformed to the idealistic purpose. It would be an understatement to say that the founders of the new state had around them none of the paraphernalia and nothing of the pomp of power. They did not possess even the simple facilities for work which could be found in the most modest of business offices. At the Smolny a typewriter was a rarity, stenographers a myth, and the telephone a delightful technical amenity. The new rulers wrote their momentous proclamations and decrees with their own hands. They ran to one another's offices through a maze of corridors. They lunched and supped at the Smolny's canteen on thin cabbage soup and black bread. And most of them lived and slept in their tiny offices, amid the endless tumult, the comings and goings of messengers and agitators, the trampling of soldiers' boots, the alarums, the panics, the enthusiasms, the *Tohu-wabohu* of dying and nascent worlds. Their offices were already guarded by volunteers from the Red

[1] Trotsky, *Moya Zhizn*, vol. ii, p. 60.

Guards; but they were always accessible to the humblest worker, sailor, and journalist. To this circumstance we owe innumerable descriptions of the Trotsky of the Smolny period. Here is a typical impression, given by an American journalist:

During the first days of the Bolshevik revolt, I used to go every morning to Smolny to get the latest news. Trotsky and his pretty little wife, who hardly ever spoke anything but French [to foreign journalists], lived in one room on the top floor. The room was partitioned off like a poor artist's attic studio. In one end were two cots and a cheap little dresser and in the other a desk and two or three cheap wooden chairs. . . . Trotsky occupied this office all the time he was Minister of Foreign Affairs and many dignitaries found it necessary to call upon him there. . . . every little difficulty under the sun was brought to Trotsky. He worked hard and was often on the verge of a nervous breakdown: he became irritable and flew into rages.[1]

Before the insurrection Trotsky had lived as a sub-tenant in a middle-class block of flats, where he and his family were surrounded by intense hatred. 'Trotsky appears tired, nervous . . .', writes Sadoul. 'Since 20 October he has not been in his home. His wife, nice, small, militant, fresh, vivacious and charming, says that their neighbours threatened to kill her husband. . . . Is it not amusing to think that this pitiless dictator, this master of all the Russias, dare not sleep in his home for fear of the broom of his concierge?'[2]

[1] Louise Bryant, *Six Red Months in Russia*, p. 145.
[2] Sadoul, op. cit., p. 94.

CHAPTER XI

The Drama of Brest Litovsk

'THIS government would consider it the greatest crime against humanity if the war were to be continued solely in order to decide which of the strong and wealthy nations should dominate the weak ones. . . . This government solemnly declares its resolution to conclude at once a peace . . . equally just to all nations and nationalities without exception.'[1] In these words Lenin's peace decree, adopted on 26 October by the Congress of the Soviets, formulated the essence of Bolshevik foreign policy. Only that peace would be just that allowed all occupied and subject peoples, whether in Europe or on other continents, to determine their own fate in free votes, taking place after the withdrawal of all occupation armies. Having put forward this bold peace aim, which could be attained only through the overthrow of all colonial empires, Lenin cautiously added that the Soviets were prepared to join in peace talks even if their programme was not accepted—they were willing to consider any alternative terms. For itself, the Bolshevik government stood for open covenants openly arrived at; and it would therefore publish and declare null and void the secret imperialist treaties concluded by previous Russian governments. This message, as Lenin explained to the Congress, appealed to the governments as well as the peoples of the belligerent countries. Implicitly, it called on the peoples to rise against the existing governments, and expressly it urged those governments to arrange an immediate armistice. The central dilemma of Bolshevik foreign policy and the germ of the Brest Litovsk tragedy were contained in this double appeal.

War-weary Russia received the decree on peace with a gasp of relief. The governments and the patriotic opinion of France and Britain replied with an outcry of indignation. The allied ambassadors and the heads of allied military missions in Russia had been more or less aware of Russia's incapacity to wage war.[2]

[1] Lenin, *Sochinenya*, vol. xxvi, p. 218.
[2] M. Paléologue, *La Russie des Tsars*, vol. iii, pp. 265, 280, and *passim*, Sir George Buchanan, *My Mission to Russia*, vol. ii, p. 228 and *passim*. As early as on 1 April 1917, i.e. before Lenin's arrival in Russia, Paléologue watched a parade in which

The Bolshevik peace propaganda, as an American observer put it, 'was indeed urgent and active, but . . . it was much the case of a man blowing with his breath in the same direction with a full grown natural tornado'.[1] Yet in their desire to avert Russia's 'defection', the allied envoys almost persuaded themselves that the tornado would die down if only the Bolsheviks stopped blowing. Almost from the beginning of the February Revolution the British and the French ambassadors urged Prince Lvov, Miliukov, and Kerensky to suppress Lenin's party.[2] The heads of their military missions hopefully encouraged Kornilov to stage his coup against Kerensky and the Menshevik Soviets.[3] Two days before the October insurrection, the British Ambassador in quite undiplomatic language pressed the Russian Ministers for Trotsky's immediate arrest.[4] Now when the Bolsheviks were in power, their revolutionary appeals, their disregard of diplomatic form, and their threat to publish and declare null and void the secret treaties and to withdraw Russia from the war, brought the hostility of the allies to a head. Their envoys were so bewildered by the upheaval they had witnessed and at such a loss to account for it that they were inclined to accept any crime story purporting to offer an explanation. They were half-convinced that Lenin and Trotsky were in fact Germany's bought agents and that it was German officers who had so efficiently and smoothly directed the October insurrection.[5] One consolation was left—that the Bolsheviks would soon be overthrown; and that it was the duty of the allied powers to speed up that moment.[6]

only the least revolutionized troops took part, and he noted in his diary that even these most loyal detachments were completely unwilling to fight. Even earlier, in March 1917, Paléologue sent a report to Ribot, the French Foreign Minister, which he concluded with the following significant sentence: 'In the present phase of the revolution Russia can make neither peace nor war.' Thus the French Ambassador anticipated Trotsky's formula by nearly a year.

[1] W. Hard, *Raymond Robins' Own Story*, p. 29. Later, when they were in exile, most leaders of the anti-Bolshevik parties agreed with this view.

[2] Paléologue, op. cit., vol. iii, pp. 245–7, and *passim*. Buchanan, op. cit., vol. ii, p. 11, 119 and *passim*.

[3] Major General Sir Alfred Knox, *With the Russian Army 1914–1917*, vol. ii, p. 692; A. Kerensky, *The Crucifixion of Liberty*, pp. 295–319.   [4] Buchanan, ibid., p. 203.

[5] Sir George Buchanan wrote in his diary: 'Information has now reached me, though I am unable to vouch for its accuracy, to the effect that there are six of their officers [i.e. German officers] attached to Lenin's staff in the Smolny Institute.' Ibid., p. 232; Knox, op. cit., vol. ii, p. 718.

[6] Sadoul claims that it was under the inspiration of allied diplomatic circles that

Despite their revolutionary appeals, the Bolsheviks were anxious to enter into diplomatic contact with the allies. No sooner had they routed Kerensky's troops than Trotsky suggested the resumption of normal relations to the British and the French.[1] The Bolsheviks, and Trotsky more than others, reckoned with the possibility that the Germans might, by dictating unacceptable peace terms, force Russia back into the war and into the Entente. Trotsky's suggestion fell on deaf ears. The allied embassies ignored him. Only the Belgian Minister paid him a reconnoitring visit in that little partitioned room in the Smolny. Trotsky's manner, as he was explaining his government's peace aims to the incredulous envoy, was 'a little firm, a a little haughty', but courteous. The Belgian Minister went away impressed by Trotsky's personality and by his sincerity, but also convinced that the revolution's Foreign Secretary was an ideologue and dreamer, not to be taken seriously; and thus he described him to colleagues.[2]

Not only the foreign embassies but also the staff of the Russian Ministry of Foreign Affairs met Trotsky with a boycott. It was only a week after his appointment, the week taken up by the fighting against Kerensky's troops, that he first appeared at the ministry, accompanied by Markin, a sailor from Kronstadt. He was eager above all to get hold of the secret treaties and the diplomatic correspondence of his predecessors. But the offices and the corridors of the ministry were deserted—there was not a soul to answer his questions. At length, his sailor friend found the permanent head of the ministry, Count Tatishchev, descendant of a long line of diplomats. The Count declared that the employees of the ministry had failed to come to work. Trotsky threateningly ordered him to assemble at once the whole staff, and in no time a crowd of officials came to report. Trotsky briefly introduced himself as their new chief, told them that no force on earth could undo the revolution and that those of them who wanted honestly to serve the new government could do so. But the officials refused to hand over the secret documents and the keys to the safes containing them. Trotsky left the ministry. A little later his sailor friend returned and ordered Tatishchev and

the Mensheviks made the exclusion of Lenin and Trotsky a condition for the formation of a coalition government, op. cit., p. 74.

[1] Sadoul, op. cit., p. 77.   [2] Ibid., pp. 77–80.

the heads of the departments to follow him to the Smolny—where he placed them under arrest. Two days later the Count conducted Trotsky over the ministry, opened all safes, and sorted out and handed over the secret treaties and the diplomatic correspondence. To the alarm of the diplomatic chancelleries, the treaties soon began to appear in print. They confirmed all too clearly the Bolshevik accusations: Russia had been fighting the war in order to conquer Galicia and Constantinople and to dominate the Balkans.[1]

On 7 November, Lenin, Stalin, and Krylenko ordered General Dukhonin, Kerensky's last Chief of Staff, to propose an immediate cease fire to the German command. Trotsky addressed his first formal message to the allied ambassadors, asking them to consider the decree on peace, which he enclosed, as a formal proposal for the immediate opening of peace negotiations. 'Accept, Mr. Ambassador', he concluded, 'assurances of the Soviet Government's profound respect for the people of your country, which cannot but strive for peace, as do all the other peoples, exhausted and bled white by the unparalleled slaughter.'[2] On the same day he reviewed for the first time the diplomatic scene at the Central Executive of the Soviets. 'The routine-ridden mind of bourgeois Europe', startled by the decree on peace, treated it as a statement of party policy rather than an act of statesmanship. The first reaction of the Germans was ambivalent: as Germans they rejoiced at the offer of peace; as Conservatives they were afraid of the revolution which was making the offer. Official Britain was unmistakably hostile. The French were war-weary, but 'the *petite bourgeoisie* of France considers us as a government allied to the German Kaiser'. Italy responded enthusiastically; the United States tolerantly. Far from lumping together all shades of foreign opinion, Trotsky drew careful and precise distinctions between them. Then he announced the publication of the secret treaties. He granted that the central powers would try to benefit from the disclosures, but the Soviets had to give an example to others, especially the German working class, of how to treat the secret bargains and compacts of their ruling classes. He hoped that when the German Social Democrats obtained access to the diplomatic safes of their governments and published their secret treaties, the world would

[1] Trotsky, *Sochinenya*, vol. iii, book 2, pp. 97–99.   [2] Ibid., p. 157.

see that 'German imperialism, in its cynicism and banditry, was
in no way inferior to the banditry of the allies'.[1] 'The peoples of
Europe', thus he inaugurated the publication of the secret
treaties on the next day, 'have paid with numberless sacrifices
and universal impoverishment for the right to know this truth.
The elimination of secret diplomacy is the very first condition
for an honest, popular, truly democratic foreign policy.'[2]

The allied ambassadors held a conference at which they decided to ignore Trotsky's message and to advise their governments to leave it unanswered on the ground that the Soviet
régime was illegitimate. The allied governments accepted the
advice and decided to establish formal relations only with the
Supreme Command of the Russian army, that is with General
Dukhonin, who had his headquarters at Moghilev. By this act
they elevated, as it were, Army Headquarters to the status of a
rival government. They also warned Dukhonin against any
parleying for a cease fire; and they clearly hinted that if Russia
withdrew from the war, they would retaliate by a Japanese
attack on Siberia.[3] Trotsky at once protested against these moves
and threatened to arrest any allied diplomats who might try to
leave Petrograd in order to attach themselves to anti-Bolshevik
forces in the provinces; and he appealed to the neutral diplomats to use their influence for peace. On the same day, General
Dukhonin, who had in any case refused to carry out the cease
fire order, was deposed—he was brutally murdered later by his
own soldiers when they learned that he was bent on continuing
the war. The Bolshevik Krylenko, who had been an ensign in
the Tsarist army and one of the leaders of the party's military
branch, was appointed Commander in Chief.

The relations between Russia and the Entente at once
assumed the bitterness which foreshadowed the wars of intervention. It could not have been otherwise. Given the determination
of the allied powers to continue the war, their ambassadors
could not but use their influence against a government which
threatened to withdraw Russia from the war. This alone inevitably led to their interference in Russia's domestic affairs.
The fundamental hostility of the old school of diplomats and

---

[1] Trotsky, *Sochinenya*, vol. iii, book 2, p. 161.   [2] Ibid., pp. 164–5.
[3] J. Noulens, *Mon Ambassade en Russie Soviétique*, vol. i, p. 145; John W.
Wheeler-Bennett, *The Forgotten Peace*, p. 71.

soldiers towards the revolution gave to that interference an unscrupulous and spiteful appearance. In the circumstances the allied embassies and military missions tended from the beginning to become participants in the Russian civil war.[1] Trotsky tried to counteract this trend and to prevent the British, the French, and the Americans from committing themselves irrevocably. With Lenin's consent he did what he could to impress on them that it was in their interest that Russia should not feel completely abandoned and driven to sign any peace with Germany, regardless of terms. To this consideration the Entente paid little or no attention. Its ambassadors maintained unofficial contacts with Trotsky through junior members of their staffs, Captain Sadoul of the French military mission and Bruce Lockhart of the British Embassy. It was to these officials, and to Colonel Robins of the American Red Cross, that Trotsky made his proposals and protests; and through them he kept the allies informed about the preliminary armistice talks. Each of the allied officials in touch with him was converted to Trotsky's view and hopefully went to convert his superiors; but nothing came of it. 'We persist in denying that the earth turns,' so Sadoul, at this time still an unrepentant 'social patriot', wrote to Albert Thomas, one of the chief exponents of French 'social patriotism', 'we go on claiming that the Bolshevik government does not exist.' Bruce Lockhart was reprimanded from London for treating Trotsky as seriously as if he were 'another Talleyrand'.[2]

On 14 November the German High Command agreed to negotiate an armistice. Krylenko ordered the cease fire and 'fraternization on the fronts', hoping that through contact with the Russian troops the German army would become infected with revolution. On the same day Trotsky notified the western powers:

Ensign Krylenko, the Supreme Commander of the armies of the republic, has proposed delaying the opening of the armistice talks for five days until 18 November/1 December so that it may once

[1] In the Second World War the western powers, confronted by the defection of France, also intervened in French domestic affairs. While Russia's withdrawal from the war in 1917–18 was inspired by revolutionary elements, it was under Conservative, right-wing leadership that France withdrew in 1940. A comparative study of allied policy in these two cases would reveal striking similarities and differences. It would also show more clearly to what extent the anti-Bolshevik policy of the Entente was a reaction against the defection of an ally and to what extent it was prompted by class antagonism.

[2] Sadoul, op. cit., p. 127; Lockhart, *Memoirs of a British Agent*, pp. 197, 226–31.

again be proposed to the allied governments to define their attitude.
. . . We, the Council of the People's Commissars, put this question
to the governments of our allies . . . we are asking them in the face of
their own peoples, in the face of the whole world: do they agree to
join us in the peace talks on 1 December? We . . . appeal to the
allied peoples and above all to their working masses: do they agree
to drag on this senseless and purposeless slaughter and to rush
blindly towards the doom of European civilization? . . . The answer
should be given now, in deeds not words. The Russian army and
the Russian people neither can nor will wait any longer. . . .
If the allied peoples do not send their representatives, we alone
shall negotiate with the Germans. We desire a universal peace, but
if the bourgeoisie of the allied countries compels us to conclude a
separate peace, the responsibility for this will rest totally on the
bourgeoisie. Finally, we appeal to the soldiers of the allied countries
to act and not to lose a single hour: Down with the winter campaign!
Down with the war![1]

In a report to the Petrograd Soviet, Trotsky added: 'We shall in
no case allow the principles of universal peace, proclaimed by the
Russian revolution, to be distorted. . . . Under popular pressure,
the German and Austrian governments have already agreed to
place themselves in the dock. You may rest assured that the
prosecutor, in the person of the Russian revolutionary peace
delegation, will be equal to his task and in due time pronounce
the thunderous accusation of the diplomacy of all imperialists.'[2]

Such was the unprecedented style which he introduced into
diplomacy. Even as Foreign Secretary he remained the revolution's chief agitator. He staked almost everything on the potential or actual antagonism between the rulers and the ruled; and
he spoke to the former so that the latter might hear him. But,
since he did not exclude the possibility of an understanding with
the existing governments, he combined his revolutionary
appeals with extremely flexible and subtle diplomacy. Irreconcilable and mordantly aggressive when confronted with hostility, he responded to any conciliatory gesture with tact and
politeness. When General Judson, head of the American military mission, breaking the allied boycott, paid him a visit and
expressed the hope that the allies would use no more threats
against the Soviets, Trotsky answered that he had no desire to
quarrel over bygones, that he was satisfied with the general's

[1] Trotsky, *Sochinenya*, vol. iii, book 2, pp. 173–5.   [2] Ibid., p. 179.

declaration; and he repeated the assurance that he would conduct the peace negotiations openly and publicly so that the allies
could watch them closely and join in later, if they so desired.[1] But
when General Niessel, head of the French military mission, who
had been accustomed to talk down to Russian ministers and
generals in their palatial offices—France had been Russia's chief
creditor and political inspirer—appeared in the 'poor artist's
attic' at the Smolny, confident that here he could afford to speak
even more haughtily, Trotsky quite unceremoniously turned
him out. He ordered the French Embassy to close down its
press bureau, which published bulletins offensive to the Soviet
government.[2] When Noulens, the French Ambassador, came to
the Smolny to smoothe out the conflict, Trotsky was all politeness and helpfulness. His first business with the British was to
demand the immediate release of Chicherin, the former correspondent of *Nashe Slovo*, and of other Russian revolutionaries
imprisoned in Britain for anti-war propaganda. When the
British continued to keep Chicherin in jail, he notified them
that until his demand was satisfied no British citizen would be
allowed to leave Russia.[3] With firmness and dignity quite unknown to recent Russian governments, Trotsky insisted on
Russia's equality with other powers, and answered insult with
insult, although even his insults took the form of reasoned and
persuasive argument.

On 19 November the armistice delegations met, and the
Germans at once proposed a preliminary truce of one month.
The Soviet delegation refused this and asked instead for the
prolongation of the cease fire for one week only so as to give the
western powers time to consider the situation. Once again
Trotsky turned to the allied embassies; and once again he met
with icy silence. Yet he instructed the Soviet negotiators to
sign no truce unless the central powers undertook not to transfer
any troops from the Russian to the western fronts, and—this was
a quite extraordinary condition—unless they expressly allowed
the Soviets to conduct revolutionary agitation among German

[1] Ibid., p. 185.   [2] Noulens, op. cit., vol. ii, p. 27.
[3] 'There is, after all', the British Ambassador noted in his diary, 'something in
Trotsky's argument that, if we claim the right to arrest Russians for making
pacifist propaganda in a country bent on continuing the war, he has an equal right
to arrest British subjects who are conducting war propaganda in a country bent on
peace.' Buchanan, op. cit., vol. ii, p. 228.

and Austrian troops. General Hoffmann, German Supreme Commander on the Russian front, rejected both demands. For a moment it seemed that the negotiations were breaking down and that Russia was back in the war. Facing once again his old audience at the Cirque Moderne, Trotsky declared that the Soviets would go on demanding an armistice on all fronts. 'But if we are compelled alone to sign the armistice, then we shall tell Germany that the transfer of troops from the Russian to other fronts is impermissible, because we are proposing an honest armistice and because England and France must not be crushed. . . . And if, because of these open, direct and honest statements the Kaiser refuses to sign a peace . . . the peoples will see who is right, and . . . we shall feel like victors not like vanquished, for there are victories other than the military ones . . . If France and Germany . . . do not join us in the peace talks, their peoples will drive their governments to join us, they will drive them with sticks.'[1]

On the same day, 3 December, he reported to the All-Russian Congress of Peasant Soviets: 'There was another point giving rise to serious conflict: the condition that no troops must be transferred to the western front. General Hoffmann declared that this was inacceptable. The problem of peace was on a knife edge. In the course of the night we instructed our delegates: make no concession. Oh, I shall never forget that night! Then Germany made the concession and committed herself not to transfer any troops, except those already under way. . . . We have our representatives with the staffs of the German army who will watch whether these terms are observed.' Displaying a map showing German troop movements in the two months preceding the revolution, he went on: 'While Kerensky was still in office and dragged on the war, the German General Staff could well afford to switch troops. . . . Now, thanks to us, the allies are in a more advantageous position.'[2] The German command no doubt treated this condition as make-believe and had no intention of observing it; but events were to show that Trotsky's words were not an empty boast.[3]

[1] Trotsky, *Sochinenya*, vol. iii, book 2, pp. 185–9.
[2] Ibid., p. 199.
[3] Mr. Wheeler-Bennett, in his excellent history of the Brest Litovsk peace, written from the Entente's viewpoint, thus sums up its results: 'But a victor's peace must be enforced. A million troops immobilized in the east was the price of German

So far all the great issues arising from the armistice had been left open. The Bolsheviks and the Left Social Revolutionaries had made up their minds in favour of separate peace talks, but not of a separate peace. And even those who, like Lenin, already inclined towards a separate peace were not yet prepared to have it at any price. The main purpose of the Soviet government was to gain time, to proclaim loudly its peace aims amid the sudden stillness on the front; to gauge the intensity of the revolutionary ferment in Europe; and to test the attitude of allied and enemy governments.

The Bolsheviks had no doubt about the proximity of social upheaval in Europe. But they began to wonder whether the road to peace would lead through revolution or whether, on the contrary, the road to revolution did not lead through peace. In the first case, the war would be brought to an end by revolutionary governments. In the second, the Russian Revolution would have to come to terms for the time being with capitalist rulers. Only time could show which way events were moving and to what extent the revolutionary impulse from Russia determined or failed to determine their direction. So far the soundings had produced no clear results. The German and the Austrian working classes were unmistakably restless; but it could not be said whether this pointed to the enemy's immediate collapse or towards a crisis in a more remote future. The peace delegations of the central powers had shown a surprising readiness to yield. Their attitude might reflect the desperate position of the central powers; but it might also conceal a trap. On the other hand, the hostility of the Entente seemed to relax for a moment. While still refusing to recognize the Soviets, the allied powers, at the beginning of December, consented to exchange certain diplomatic privileges which are usually granted to recognized governments. Soviet diplomatic couriers were allowed to move between Russia and western Europe; diplomatic passports were mutually recognized; Chicherin was at last released and returned to Russia; and Trotsky exchanged diplomatic visits with some western envoys. Was the Entente perhaps changing its mind about peace? In *Pravda*, Trotsky wishfully commented on these

aggrandizement, and half that number might well have turned the scale in the early stages of the battle of giants which was raging in the west.' Op. cit., p. 327.

events as 'symptoms pointing to the possibility of a general armistice and universal peace'.[1]

That he should have drawn such far-fetched conclusions from what were, after all, details of the diplomatic game, must be explained by a basic mistake in his reading of the strategic prospects. Early in the war, when governments and general staffs were taking an early conclusion of hostilities for granted, he had rightly forecast the protracted stalemate of trench warfare.[2] He had been inclined to believe that neither camp could break the stalemate resulting from the equilibrium of opposed forces. The events of more than three years had so strikingly confirmed this forecast that he clung to it even now, when the premiss for it was about to vanish. The United States had entered the war. But this did not cause Trotsky to modify his view; and after the revolution, as before, he reiterated that neither of the hostile camps could hope to win. From this rigid assumption it seemed logical to conclude that at length the belligerent governments might realize the futility of further fighting, acknowledge the deadlock, and agree to open peace negotiations. This was the reasoning which made him jump to a conclusion about the possibility of an imminent 'general armistice and universal peace'.

At the same time, however, the Bolsheviks feared that the Entente might conclude a separate peace with Germany and Austria and strike jointly at the Russian Revolution. More than anybody, Lenin voiced this apprehension in public and private. The inner story of the war, when it was revealed, showed that this was not quite groundless. Germany and Austria had repeatedly and secretly, jointly and separately put out peace feelers to their enemies in the West.[3] In the ruling classes of France and Britain the fear of revolution was mounting; and the possibility of an accommodation between the Entente and the central powers, an accommodation prompted by that fear, could not be ruled out in advance. This was a potential threat only; but it was enough to drive Lenin to the conclusion that only separate peace in the East could forestall separate peace in the West.

---

[1] Trotsky, *Sochinenya*, vol. iii, book 2, pp. 210–11.
[2] See Chapter viii, p. 229.
[3] D. Lloyd George, *War Memoirs*, vol. ii, chapter lxx; Richard von Kühlmann, *Erinnerungen*, pp. 475–87.

To sum up, the Bolsheviks were enmeshed in the following intertwined dilemmas: They had to resolve whether they could wait for peace until the revolution had spread; or whether they would try to spread the revolution by concluding peace? If the road to European revolution were to lead through peace, would it be universal or separate peace? And if the terms of a separate peace were to prove so onerous and humiliating as to be unacceptable, could they wage a revolutionary war against Germany? If driven to war, could they, as a matter of principle, accept assistance from the Entente? And would the Entente be willing to grant them assistance? If not, should they strive for separate peace at any price? Or was there perhaps some way of escaping these dilemmas?

On 8 December, the day before the inauguration of the actual peace talks at Brest Litovsk, Trotsky addressed a joint session of the government, the Central Executive of the Soviets, the Soviet and town council of Petrograd, and leaders of trade unions. This was one of his most remarkable speeches, not only because of its rhetorical excellence and its soaring revolutionary humanitarian ethos, but also because it vibrated with his own mental wrestlings:

Truly this war has demonstrated man's power and resilience, which enables him to endure unheard of sufferings. But it has also shown how much barbarity is still preserved in contemporary man. . . . He, king of nature, has descended into the trench-cave, and there, peeping out through narrow holes, as from a prison cell, he is lurking for his fellow man, his future prey. . . . So low has mankind fallen. . . . One is oppressed by a feeling of shame for man, his flesh, his spirit, his blood, when one thinks that people who have gone through so many phases of civilization—Christianity, absolutism, and parliamentary democracy—people who have imbibed the ideas of socialism, kill each other like miserable slaves under the whip of the ruling classes. Should the war have this outcome only that people return to their mangers, to pick the miserable crumbs thrown from the tables of the propertied classes, should this war finish with the triumph of imperialism, then mankind would prove itself unworthy of its own sufferings and of its own prodigious mental effort, which it has sustained over thousands of years. But this will not happen—it cannot happen.

Having risen in the land of Europe's former gendarme, the Russian people declares that it desires to speak to its brothers under arms . . .

not in the language of guns, but in that of international solidarity of the toilers. . . . This fact cannot be eliminated from the mind of the popular masses . . . of all countries. Sooner or later they will hear our voice, they will come to us and stretch out a helpful hand. But even if . . . the enemies of the people were to conquer us and we were to perish . . . our memory would still pass from generation to generation and awaken posterity to a new struggle. To be sure, our position would have been much easier if the peoples of Europe had risen together with us, if we had to parley not with General Hoffmann and Count Czernin but with Karl Liebknecht, Klara Zetkin, and Rosa Luxemburg. This has not happened. And we cannot be blamed for that. Our brothers in Germany cannot accuse us of having communed with the Kaiser, their sworn enemy, behind their backs. We are talking to him as to an enemy—we do not soften our irreconcilable hostility to the tyrant.

The truce has brought a pause in hostilities. The booming of guns has been silenced, and everybody is anxiously waiting to hear in what voice the Soviet government will talk with the Hohenzollerns and Habsburgs. You must support us in this that we should talk with them as with freedom's enemies . . . and that not a single atom of freedom should be sacrificed to imperialism. Only then will the genuine meaning of our strivings penetrate deeply into the consciousness of the German and Austrian peoples.

This appeal was followed by a curious passage in which he was thinking aloud before his large audience and gave free rein to his hesitation and indecision. 'If the voice of the German working class . . . does not exercise a powerful and decisive influence . . . peace will be impossible', he stated abruptly. Then came a second thought: 'But if it should turn out that we had been mistaken, if this dead silence were to reign in Europe much longer, if this silence were to give the Kaiser the chance to attack us and to dictate terms insulting to the revolutionary dignity of our country, then I do not know whether—with this disrupted economy and universal chaos entailed by war and internal convulsions—whether we could go on fighting.' As if feeling that his audience was stunned by his cry of despair, he turned abruptly and exclaimed: 'Yes, we could.' This brought forth stormy applause. Spurred on by the response, he added: 'For our life, for our revolutionary honour, we would fight to the last drop of our blood.' Here the verbatim report records 'a new outburst of applause'. The audience, which consisted of the leading groups of the two governmental parties, thus demonstrated its emotional opposition to separate peace.

'The weary and the old ones', Trotsky continued, 'would step aside . . . and we would create a powerful army of soldiers and Red Guards, strong with revolutionary enthusiasm. . . . We have not overthrown the Tsar and the bourgeoisie in order to kneel down before the German Kaiser.' If the Germans were to offer an unjust and undemocratic peace, then 'we should present these terms to the Constituent Assembly and we should say to it: make up your mind. If the Constituent Assembly accepts such terms, the Bolshevik party will step aside and say: Look for another party willing to sign such terms. We, the Bolsheviks, and I hope the Left Social Revolutionaries too, would summon all peoples to a holy war against the militarists of all countries.' It hardly entered his mind that one day the Left Social Revolutionaries would rise against the Bolsheviks with the cry for this 'holy war,' and that he himself would then suppress them. 'If in view of the economic chaos', he concluded, 'we should not be able to fight . . . the struggle would not be at an end: it would only be postponed, as it was in 1905, when Tsardom crushed us but we lived to fight another day. That is why we have joined in the peace negotiations without pessimism and without black thoughts. . . .'[1] His speech worked up his audience into an exalted state similar to that in which before the insurrection the crowds of Petrograd repeated after him the words of the revolutionary oath.

The negotiations at Brest Litovsk began on 9 December. The representatives of the central powers let it be known that they 'agreed to conclude immediately a general peace, without annexations and indemnities'.[2] Yoffe, who headed the Soviet delegation, asked for another pause of ten days to give the western powers once again time to change their minds. During the pause, only the commissions of the peace conference were in session, and their work proceeded with strange smoothness. The real negotiations were not to begin till 27 December, when Trotsky arrived. In the meantime the Council of the People's Commissars took a number of demonstrative steps. It intensified its propaganda against German imperialism; and Trotsky,

---

[1] Trotsky, *Sochinenya*, vol. iii, book 2, pp. 211-17.
[2] *Mirnye Peregovory v Brest Litovske*, p. 9.

assisted by Karl Radek who had just arrived in Russia, edited *Die Fackel* (*The Torch*), which was distributed in the German trenches. On 13 December the government allocated two million roubles for revolutionary propaganda abroad, and it publicized the fact. On the 19th it started the demobilization of the Russian army. It also freed German and Austrian prisoners of war from compulsory labour, allowing them to leave the camps and to organize and work as free citizens. It declared null and void the Russo-British treaty of 1907, under which Persia had been partitioned between the two powers; and on 23 December it ordered Russian troops to evacuate northern Persia. Finally, Trotsky instructed Yoffe to demand that the peace negotiations be transferred from Brest Litovsk to Stockholm, or any other place in a neutral country.

Exactly two months after the insurrection, on 24 or 25 December, Trotsky set out for Brest Litovsk. On the way, especially in the area of the front, he was greeted by delegations from local Soviets and trade unions which urged him to speed up the negotiations and to return with a peace treaty. He was astounded to find that the trenches on the Russian side of the front were almost empty: the soldiers who had manned them had dispersed. A German liaison officer who conducted him across the front noticed the fact and reported to his superiors that Trotsky 'grew ever more and more depressed'.[1] He did indeed become acutely and painfully aware that it was without any armed strength behind him that he would have to confront the enemy. He was all the more determined to wield his 'weapons of criticism'. With him travelled Karl Radek, whose luggage bags were packed with revolutionary pamphlets and leaflets, and as soon as their train stopped at Brest Litovsk, Radek, before the eyes of the diplomats and officers assembled on the platform to greet them, began to distribute the pamphlets among German soldiers. A Polish Jew, nominally an Austro-Hungarian subject, Radek had gained fame as a radical, sharp-witted pamphleteer in the German Social Democratic party. His appearance at Brest, as a member of the Russian delegation, could not but scandalize the German and Austrian diplomats. It was intended to demonstrate that the revolution championed the cause of a class, not of a nation, and that the mere notion of an 'enemy national'

[1] Count Ottokar Czernin, *In the World War*, p. 232.

was alien to it. Trotsky had asked Radek to accompany him, because, as he told Sadoul, 'he had confidence in his very lively intelligence and political loyalty and was convinced that the intransigence and *élan* of this energetic, passionate man would act as a tonic for the Yoffes, Kamenevs, and other softer Russian delegates'.[1]

The scene of the meeting was desolate and grim. The town of Brest Litovsk had early in the war been burnt and razed to the ground by retreating Russian troops. Only the old military fortress was intact; and in it was the general headquarters of the eastern German armies. The peace delegations were housed in drab blocks and huts within the compound. The officers' mess served as the conference hall. The place had the air of a Prussian barrack transferred to the Polish-Ukrainian plain. Enclosed by barbed wire, surrounded by sentries, amid the routine bustle of a military establishment, the Russian delegates might have felt like inmates of an internment camp. The Germans had insisted that the negotiations should be held there, partly for their own convenience and partly in order to humble the Soviet envoys. But they had also put on several layers of velvet glove. Before Trotsky's arrival, the delegations had supped. and dined together; had been received by Prince Leopold of Bavaria, the nominal Commander in Chief; and had exchanged various other courtesies. It was ironical that those who exchanged the courtesies were, on the one hand, titled members of the German and Austrian aristocracies, and, on the other, professional agitators, recent convicts, among them a Left Social Revolutionary woman-terrorist, Bitsenko, who had assassinated a Tsarist Minister of War and had served a sentence of forced labour. The insinuating sociability of the Germans and Austrians did not fail to disconcert even the leading Bolshevik delegates. Yoffe, Kamenev, Pokrovsky, Karakhan, seasoned and well educated revolutionaries, showed at the conference table something of the awkwardness natural in novices to diplomacy. Throughout the first phase of the parleys, when Yoffe acted as chief Soviet delegate, the conference was completely dominated by Kühlmann, the German Foreign Minister.

Trotsky arrived dissatisfied with this state of affairs. On Lenin's insistence, he had undertaken this mission in order to

[1] Sadoul, op. cit., p. 176.

give quite a different aspect to the conference. At the outset, he frigidly rejected an invitation to meet Prince Leopold, and he put a stop to all hobnobbing. 'With Trotsky's appearance here', General Hoffmann remarked, 'the easy social intercourse outside the conference hall has ceased. Trotsky has requested that the delegations be served their meals at their quarters and has generally forbidden any private contact and entertainment.'[1] 'The wind seems to blow in a very different direction than it did until now', Czernin, the Austrian Foreign Minister, noted in his diary.[2] A diplomat of the other side had only to approach Trotsky with jovial flattery or a gesture of familiarity to make him stiffen and bristle. Appearances had to conform to the realities: he had come to negotiate with enemies, not with friends.

The first session, at which he replaced Yoffe as chief of the Russian delegation, was held on 27 December. Kühlmann opened it with a statement that the principle to which the central powers had agreed—'peace without annexations and indemnities'—had been intended for a general peace only. As the western powers had refused to join in the negotiations and only a separate peace was on the agenda, Germany and her allies were no longer bound by that principle.[3] He rejected the Soviet demand for negotiations in a neutral country; and he assailed Soviet propaganda against German imperialism, which, he said, raised doubts whether the Soviets sincerely desired peace; but he wound up on a conciliatory tone. Then General Hoffmann, a pile of Soviet proclamations to German soldiers in front of him, repeated the protest on behalf of the German Supreme Command. The Austrian, Turkish, and Bulgarian diplomats spoke in the same vein. Trotsky, taking the measure of his adversaries, listened with a faintly ironical smile; and, without answering the charges, asked for a day's break.

Among his adversaries three figures stood out. Kühlmann, a Bavarian Catholic and traditionalist, one of the shrewdest diplomats of Imperial Germany, was not devoid of personal charm, some open-mindedness, and courage. Earlier than the Kaiser's other servants, he had come to reckon with Germany's defeat in a war on two fronts; and he was anxious to obtain in

---

[1] *Die Aufzeichnungen des Generalmajors Max Hoffmann*, vol. ii, pp. 206–7.
[2] Czernin, op. cit., p. 232.   [3] *Mirnye Peregovory*, p. 45.

the East a peace profitable to his government but not too obviously imposed on Russia. Perhaps alone among Germany's rulers, he realized that a dictated peace would amount to a defeat for Germany: it would forewarn other nations what they had to expect from German victory and would stiffen their resistance. The Supreme Command bitterly opposed Kühlmann's policy. In the eyes of Hindenburg and Ludendorff he was little better than a traitor; and they did their utmost to discredit him. He was therefore compelled to defend himself behind the scenes against the military, while he was engaged in his open duel with Trotsky. Both the military and he appealed to the Kaiser as supreme arbiter. The Kaiser backed now his diplomat and now his generals, but at heart he was with the latter, allowing them to overrule his civilian government. Kühlmann had enough character not only to defy Ludendorff, but to disregard, on one occasion, the Kaiser's blunt order to break off the negotiations. His differences with the military, nevertheless, concerned the manner rather than the matter: he was at one with them in wishing to secure for Germany the Polish and Baltic lands conquered from Russia. But he was anxious to obtain the appearance of Russian consent; and the weakness of his position, as it revealed itself later, was that he could not obtain it. He also wished to disguise the German annexation of those lands as their liberation. The generals had neither the time nor the patience for such subtleties.

General Hoffmann was supposed to be the Supreme Command's eye, ear, and strong arm at the conference table. It was his business to bring the talks to a speedy conclusion and to release the eastern armies of the central powers for the last, all-out offensive in the West. Every now and then he voiced his irritation and impatience with Kühlmann's method. But more sophisticated than his superiors and more in touch with the impact of the revolution, he could not gainsay that Kühlmann's method had its merits. He sometimes yielded to Kühlmann and then brought Ludendorff's thunders upon his own head.[1]

Count Czernin, the Austrian Foreign Minister, acted Kühlmann's brilliant second. Even more acutely than his German

---

[1] Trotsky mistakenly treated Hoffmann as the authentic voice of the German Supreme Command, and this may have contributed to his underrating later the German readiness to renew hostilities against Russia.

colleague, he was aware of the catastrophe which hung over
the central powers. From the secret treaties which Trotsky
had published, he knew that the allies had marked down the
Austro-Hungarian empire for dismemberment. With starvation
in Vienna and revolt among the subject nations, the empire had
begun to crumble already; only by draining strength from
Germany did it prolong its days. Czernin was therefore in a real
panic whenever it seemed to him that Hoffmann's blunt intervention lessened the chances of peace. At first he threatened his
German colleagues with separate negotiations, but, as his
government was becoming every day more dependent on
German help, he abandoned the threat. He still tried to act the
soft-spoken mediator although he was more than a little frightened by the 'clever and very dangerous adversary [as he described
Trotsky] . . . exceptionally gifted, with a swiftness and adroitness
in retort which I have rarely seen'.[1] In his spare hours, Czernin
read memoirs on the French Revolution, trying to find a historical yardstick for the 'dangerous adversary'; and he wondered
whether a Russian Charlotte Corday was not already lurking
for Trotsky.

Czernin, it seems, was alone in indulging in such meditations
and looking for historical parallels. His colleagues at first viewed
Trotsky and the other Russian delegates as petty adventurers,
obscure upstarts or, at best, quixotic creatures, whom a quirk
of destiny had thrown on the stage to act a very brief, grotesque
episode in the world's drama, in which they, the great servants
of two illustrious dynasties, were among the chief characters.
They were sure that they would buy the Russian delegates with
small favours; but they wanted first to put them in their places.
This they tried to do at their first meeting with Trotsky; and
they adopted the same tactics at the next session. They set
against the Soviet delegation the Ukrainians, who claimed to
represent independent Ukraine and denied Petrograd's right to
speak for all the Russias.

Such was the interplay of interests, personalities, and ambitions into which Trotsky wedged himself, when, on 28 December,
he addressed the conference for the first time. He brushed aside
the Ukrainian intrigue. The Soviets, he declared, had no objection
to the Ukraine's participation in the parleys; they had proclaimed

[1] Czernin, op. cit., pp. 234-5.

the right of all nationalities to self-determination; and they meant to respect that right. Nor did he question the credentials of the Ukrainian delegates, who represented the *Rada*—a provincial replica or rather parody of the Kerensky régime. Kühlmann once again tried to provoke an open quarrel between the Russians and the Ukrainians, which would have allowed him to become the *tertius gaudens*, but once again Trotsky avoided the pitfall. Turning to the charges and protests of the previous day, he refused to make any apology for the revolutionary propaganda which the Soviets conducted among German troops. He had come in order to discuss peace terms, Trotsky said, not in order to limit his government's freedom to express its views. The Soviets raised no objection to the counter-revolutionary propaganda which the Germans spread among Russian citizens. The revolution was so confident of its case and of the appeal of its ideals that it welcomed an open argument. This gave the Germans no ground to question Russia's desire for peace. It was Germany's sincerity that must be doubted, especially when the German delegation declared that it was no longer bound by the principle of a peace without annexations and indemnities. 'We, on our part, think it necessary to state that the principles of a democratic peace which we have proclaimed have not, in our eyes, become null and void after ten days . . . For us they are the only conceivable basis for the co-existence and co-operation of peoples.'

He renewed the protest against holding the conference in the artificial isolation of the Brest fortress. The German Chancellor had told the Reichstag that in a neutral country the conference would be exposed to allied machinations. 'The job of protecting the Russian government from hostile machinations', Trotsky remarked, 'belongs exclusively to the Russian government.' 'We are confronted by an ultimatum: either parleys at Brest Litovsk or no parleys at all', an ultimatum prompted by the German sense of power and conviction of Russia's weakness. 'We neither can deny nor intend to try to deny that our country has been weakened by the policy of its recent ruling classes. But the place of a country in the world is determined not only by the present condition of its technical apparatus, but also by the potentialities inherent in it.' He was not going to measure the economic strength of Germany, whose population was starving, by the

present state of Germany's food stocks. The central powers
tended to base the peace not 'on agreement between the peoples,
but on the so-called war map. This tendency is equally pernicious to the German and to the Russian peoples, because the
war maps change and the peoples remain.' Yet—'we stay here,
at Brest Litovsk, in order not to leave unexplored a single chance
of peace . . . in order to learn, here at the headquarters of the
eastern front, clearly and precisely whether a peace . . . is now
possible without violence towards the Poles, Lithuanians, Lat-
vians, Estonians, Armenians, and other peoples, to whom the
Russian revolution has guaranteed the full right of self-determination'. But the conference could continue on one condition
only, namely that the negotiations should be held in public
throughout; and Trotsky refused to engage in private talks, for
which Kühlmann had asked, believing that Trotsky's defiant
statement was merely meant as face-saving.[1]

Two days later the delegations discussed a German draft of
the peace treaty. At the outset a little incident seemed to transfer the sedate diplomats of the central powers into the atmosphere of a Shavian comedy. A preamble to the treaty contained
the respectable cliché that the contracting parties desired to
live in peace and friendship. The authors of the draft could not
expect this to give rise to objections. They were mistaken.
'I would take the liberty', Trotsky said, 'to propose that the
second phrase [about friendship between the contracting pow-
ers] be deleted. Its thoroughly conventional, ornamental style
does not correspond, so it seems, to the dry business-like sense
of the document.'[2] Half-amused and half-scandalized, the professional diplomats could not see the point: Was Trotsky
speaking seriously? And how could he dismiss so lofty a statement as ornamental and conventional? 'But such declarations',
Trotsky pertly went on, 'copied from one diplomatic document
into another, have never yet characterized the real relations
between states'; he could only hope that more serious factors
would shape these relations in the future. For a moment the
diplomats felt as if they had been told that their emperors and
they themselves were naked. What were those 'more serious
factors'? And what formula would Trotsky propose? He could
give them his formula, Trotsky said, but they would not accept

[1] *Mirnye Peregovory*, pp. 52–60.   [2] Ibid., p. 66.

it anyhow. The comic wrangle went on for a while, and the words about friendship disappeared from the draft.

Then followed a dramatic argument, centred on the principle of self-determination and dealing with the fate of the nations situated between Russia and Germany. The argument, mainly between Trotsky and Kühlmann, occupied many sessions and took the form of a conflict between two interpretations of self-determination. Both sides pursued the argument in the tone of a seemingly dispassionate, academic debate on legal, sociological, and historical themes; but behind these themes loomed the realities of war and revolution, occupation and annexation. Convinced that Trotsky was merely seeking to dress up Russia's surrender, Kühlmann seemed anxious to provide Trotsky, and himself even more, with decorous formulas, and to present the German annexation of Poland and the Baltic States as self-determination for these. To his perplexity, Trotsky thrust aside all attempts at face-saving and insisted on the facts of annexation. Kühlmann made his case with a systematic, relentless, yet subtle logic, the only defect of which was that it summed up the wisdom of a Conservative statesman in the face of the ungovernable phenomenon of revolution. Trotsky stood before the conference as the embodiment of that phenomenon, endowed with a logic even more relentless and subtle and with a quick and deadly wit from which there was no escape. He himself obviously revelled in his own wry and sardonic humour which made General Hoffmann growl and sent him into a huff, while the rest of the delegates quivered with suppressed laughter. Trotsky once begged the general to remember that the differences in their views were due to deeper discrepancies in their outlooks: he, the head of the Russian delegation, was still under the prison sentence which a German court had passed on him for anti-war propaganda. The general suddenly saw himself in the role of a jail-bird's partner, and, feeling as if all his medals had been torn off his chest, he withdrew from the exchange. When Kühlmann asked him whether he had anything more to say, Hoffmann angrily snapped back: 'No, enough.'

Almost every paragraph in the draft treaty contained the statement of a noble principle and also its negation. One of the first clauses provided for the evacuation of the occupied territories. This did not prevent Kühlmann from declaring that

Germany intended to occupy the territories seized from Russia until a general peace, and indefinitely even after it. Kühlmann also argued that Poland and the other German-occupied countries had achieved self-determination, because the Germans had installed native governments everywhere. No country, Trotsky retorted, can determine its fate while it is held by foreign troops—'as a preliminary foreign troops must clear out of the territories in question'. Politely, and without calling anyone names, yet unmistakably, he made it clear that what the Germans had installed were puppet administrations.

As the argument became involved and apparently abstract, Trotsky switched from Russian to German. Kühlmann was in his element with juridical-diplomatic formulas and imprudently provoked further debate. 'When, according to the Chairman of the Russian delegation', he asked, 'does a nation come into existence as a single entity?' If it cannot come into existence under foreign occupation, then when and how does the moment of birth arise? Grateful for the new opportunity to restate his case, Trotsky began to answer the puzzling question by the method of elimination. What is certain is that no nation is independent as long as it is occupied and possesses only an administration whose title to govern rests on the presence of foreign troops. The final criterion is the will of the people, freely and democratically expressed in a referendum. Finland, evacuated by Russian troops, was a case in point. In the Ukraine 'the process of self-determination was still in progress'. But, Kühlmann pointed out, a government so created meant a break in legal continuity; and to the Conservative way of thinking legal continuity is alpha and omega. Trotsky reminded the German Minister, that any occupying power breaks legal continuity and does so without the justification with which a revolution does it. Kühlmann adroitly retorted that, if revolution claims for itself no basis in law, then it is based solely on force and accomplished fact. This seemed to knock the bottom out of Trotsky's argument: if he admitted the point, he had no ground for protest against the accomplished facts of German annexation. The crux of Trotsky's answer lay in the distinction which he drew between a force emerging from inside a nation to determine its fate and an outside force imposing its will.

The controversy had thus developed into a clash of *Weltan-*

schaungen, a contest of opposed moral and historical philosophies. Every phase of this contest was reported and misreported
all over the world. The occupied nations whose future was at
stake listened with bated breath. At one point Kamenev prompted Trotsky to explain that in denying so forcefully Germany's
right to keep these nations in subjection, he was not claiming
that right for Russia, as any traditionalist Russian diplomat
would have done. 'We undertake the obligation', Trotsky declared, 'not to coerce these countries directly or indirectly into
accepting this or that form of government, not to infringe their
independence by any customs or military conventions. . . . And
I should like to know whether the German and the Austro-
Hungarian delegations are in a position to make statements to
the same effect. . .?'

This brought the debate back to the burning issues. Kühlmann answered that the governments of the German-occupied
countries had the right to conclude any agreement they wished;
they were even entitled to cede territory to the occupying
powers. On Kühlmann's part this was an act of self-exposure,
into which Trotsky had skilfully enticed him. 'The assertion of
the Chairman of the German delegation', said Trotsky, clinch-
ing the argument, 'that these people [the puppet governments]
are entitled to conclude pacts and agreements and to cede
territories is a full and categorical denial of the principle of self-
determination.' The central powers had not invited the governments of the occupied countries to Brest; and this alone revealed that they treated them as dependencies with no will of
their own. 'In the conventional language which we use in such
cases this is described, not as self-determination of the peoples,
but by quite a different expression . . . annexation. . . .'[1]

Trotsky had undoubtedly out-argued his adversary. Yet the
argument was somewhat inconclusive, and precisely because
of its subtlety it had less effect upon German opinion than
Trotsky was inclined to believe. It could not, at any rate,
greatly appeal to the German workers and soldiers whom he
was out to revolutionize; and therein consisted the weakness of
this part of his performance. Only when General Hoffmann,
eager to clothe himself in the spoils of Achilles, intervened, did
the debate become at once more popular and, from the Bolshevik

[1] *Mirnye Peregovory*, pp. 84–85; Kühlmann, op. cit., pp. 524–32.

standpoint, politically fruitful. 'The Russian delegation', the general, freeing himself from Kühlmann's restraints, burst out, 'has spoken as if it represented a victorious invader of our country. I should like to remind its members that the facts point to the contrary: victorious German troops are on Russian soil. I should further like to say that the Russian delegation demands that we should recognize the right to self-determination in a form and on a scale which its own government does not recognize. . . . The German Supreme Command thinks it necessary to repudiate its interference in the affairs of the occupied areas.' Hoffmann refused to enter into any discussion on evacuation.

This was Trotsky's field day. Ironically he asked Hoffmann whether he represented the Supreme Command only or the German government; and the allusion was received with a great deal of *Schadenfreude* by Kühlmann and Czernin. If, as the general claimed, the most important fact was where whose troops stood, then the Russians, who held Austrian and Turkish territory, should talk with the Austrians and the Turks in a tone different from the one they used with the Germans; but they were not going to do so. Trotsky welcomed Hoffmann's brutal remarks about Bolshevik domestic policy, for he himself had invited his adversaries to speak on this without inhibition. 'The General was quite right when he said that our government based itself on force. In history hitherto we have known no government dispensing with force. . . . I must, however, categorically protest against the completely untrue statement that we have outlawed all those who do not think as we do. I should be very happy to know that the Social Democratic press in Germany enjoys the freedom which our adversaries and the counter-revolutionary press enjoy in our country.' (At this stage this comparison did in fact still work in favour of the Soviets.) 'What in our conduct strikes and antagonizes other governments is the fact that we place under arrest not workers who come out on strike but capitalists who declare lock-outs on workers, that we do not shoot peasants demanding land, but arrest the landlords and the officers who try to shoot the peasants.'[1] He pointed to a contradiction between Kühlmann's and Hoffmann's arguments. The former had claimed that the German-occupied lands already had more or less independent governments, while

---

[1] *Mirnye Peregovory*, p. 102.

the latter tried to justify indefinite German occupation by the fact that they had no administration of their own. Yet from their different arguments both the general and the *Staats-sekretar* drew the same conclusion, which went to show that 'legal philosophy had quite a subordinate place in their decisions on the fate of living peoples'.[1]

The effect of this exposure was devastating. Hoffmann noted in his diary: 'My speech actually made a smaller impression than I expected.'[2] Kühlmann lost his temper and regretted that he had allowed himself to be tempted into open diplomacy.[3] Later he tried to efface the aftertaste of Hoffmann's intervention and to excuse the latter's 'soldierly bluntness'. The excuse, Trotsky remarked, confirmed that the differences between the military and the civilians in the enemy camp were a matter of form, not of substance. 'As for ourselves, members of the Russian delegation, our record is there to show that we do not belong to the diplomatic school. We ought rather to be considered as soldiers of the revolution. We prefer—I shall admit this frankly —statements which are definite and clear in every respect.'[4]

On 5 January, Trotsky asked for a break in the conference so that he might acquaint his government with the German demands. The conference had already lasted nearly a month. Much time had been gained; and now party and government had to take a decision. As he travelled back to Petrograd, Trotsky stared again at the Russian trenches, the very emptiness of which seemed to cry out for peace. But now he knew better than ever that the price of peace was Russia's and the revolution's utter prostration and discredit. At Brest, reading the German and Austrian Socialist newspapers, he had been shocked to see that some of these treated the peace conference as a prearranged spectacle, the outcome of which was in no doubt. Some German Socialists believed that the Bolsheviks were in fact the Kaiser's agents, and even those who did not doubt Lenin's and Trotsky's integrity viewed their policy as a 'psychological puzzle'. The desire to lift the stigma from the

---

[1] In an aside, Trotsky turned to Kühlmann, who had quoted in his support a decision of the Supreme Court of the United States after the War of Independence. Herr *Staatssekretar*, Trotsky said, would have been truer to character if he drew inspiration from the jurisdiction of George III rather than from that of George Washington.　　　　[2] Hoffmann, op. cit., vol. ii, p. 209.
[3] *Mirnye Peregovory*, pp. 100–4.　　　　[4] Ibid., pp. 133–4.

party was among the most important motives which guided Trotsky's conduct at the conference table.[1] It now seemed as if his efforts had not been quite fruitless. Peace demonstrations and strikes had at last begun in the enemy countries; and from Berlin and Vienna came loud protests against Hoffmann's attempt to dictate terms. The Soviets, so Trotsky concluded, must not accept these terms. They must go on biding their time and try to establish between themselves and the central powers a state which would be neither war nor peace. With this conclusion he reached the Smolny, where he had been eagerly and tensely awaited.

His return coincided with the conflict between the Soviet government and the Constituent Assembly, at last convoked. Against the expectations of the Bolsheviks and their associates, the Right Social Revolutionaries commanded a majority. The Bolsheviks and the Left Social Revolutionaries decided to disperse the Assembly; and they did so after the latter had refused to ratify Lenin's decrees on land, peace, and the transfer of power to the Soviets. The dispersal was at first justified by the specious argument that the elections had been held under an obsolete law, so construed under Kerensky as to give undue weight to the well-to-do minority of the peasantry. The paradox which made it possible for the Bolsheviks to emerge as the majority in the Soviets and remain a minority in the Assembly has been discussed in a previous chapter. The real reason for the dispersal was that the rule of the Assembly was incompatible with the rule of the Soviets. Either the Assembly or the October Revolution had to be undone. Trotsky was wholeheartedly for the dispersal, and he repeatedly defended the deed in speech and writing, assuming unqualified moral responsibility for it.[2] Since 1905–6 he had stood for proletarian dictatorship in Soviet form, and when he had to choose between that dictatorship and parliamentarianism he knew no hesitation. In the event itself, however, he played no role. The Assembly was dispersed on 6 January before his return to Petrograd. When he arrived, on the 7th, he and Lenin had a moment of anxiety

---

[1] See Trotsky's preface to *Mirnye Peregovory v Brest Litovske*.
[2] See the chapter on the Constituent Assembly in *The Defence of Terrorism*, pp. 41–45. Also *Tretii Vseross. Syezd Sovietov*, pp. 17, 69–70.

because the adherents of the Assembly seemed on the point of organizing a strong popular protest against the dispersal. But the protest fizzled out inconsequentially—only much later, during the civil war, was a 'movement for the Constituante' started on the Volga.[1]

On 8 January, two days after the dispersal of the Assembly, the Central Committee was completely absorbed in the debate on war and peace; and in order to sound the party's mood it conducted the debate in the presence of Bolshevik delegates who had arrived from the provinces for the third Congress of Soviets. Trotsky reported on his mission and presented his conclusion: neither war nor peace. Lenin urged the acceptance of the German terms. Bukharin spoke for 'revolutionary war' against the Hohenzollerns and Habsburgs. The vote brought striking success to the adherents of revolutionary war, the Left Communists as they were called. Lenin's motion for immediate peace received only fifteen votes. Trotsky's resolution obtained sixteen. Thirty-two votes were cast in favour of Bukharin's call for war.[2] Since outsiders had taken part, however, the vote was not binding on the Central Committee.

The whole Bolshevik party was soon rent between those who advocated peace and those who stood for war. The latter had behind them a large but confused majority and they were powerfully reinforced by the Left Social Revolutionaries, none of whom favoured peace. But the war faction was not sure of its case. It was stronger in voicing opposition to the peace than in urging resumption of hostilities.

At the next session of the Central Committee, on 11 January, the war faction bitterly attacked Lenin. Dzerzhinsky reproached him with timidly surrendering the whole programme of the revolution, as Zinoviev and Kamenev had surrendered it in October. To accept the Kaiser's *Diktat*, Bukharin argued, would

[1] Antonov-Ovseenko describes this incident almost humorously. Lenin had received a report that the Right Social Revolutionaries were leading a demonstration 100,000 strong to the Tauride Palace. Trotsky's wife had seen the demonstrators and estimated their number at 20,000. Lenin and Trotsky nervously ordered Antonov-Ovseenko to disperse the demonstration if need be. Antonov led a regiment to the Tauride Palace but found nobody to disperse. 'The adherents of the Assembly had come, had made a glorious noise, and had disappeared like Chinese shadows. There had been no more than 5,000 demonstrators in all.' Antonov-Ovseenko, *Zapiski o Grazhdanskoi Voinie*, vol. i, pp. 18–19.

[2] *Protokoly Tsen. Kom.*, p. 200.

be to stab in the back the German and Austrian proletariat—
in Vienna a general strike against the war was just in progress.
In Uritsky's view, Lenin approached the problem 'from a
narrow Russian and not from an international standpoint', an
error of which he had been guilty in the past. On behalf of the
Petrograd organization, Kossior repudiated Lenin's attitude.
The most determined advocates of peace were Zinoviev, Stalin,
and Sokolnikov. As in October, so now, Zinoviev saw no ground
for expecting revolution in the West; he held that Trotsky had
wasted time at Brest; and he warned the Central Committee
that Germany would later dictate even more onerous terms.
More cautiously, Stalin expressed the same view. Sokolnikov,
arguing that the salvation of the Russian Revolution was the
overriding consideration, foreshadowed in a curious epigram a
distant future change in the party's outlook. 'History clearly
shows', he said, 'that the salt of the earth is gradually shifting
eastwards. In the eighteenth century, France was the salt of the
earth, and in the nineteenth—Germany. Now it is Russia.'[1]

Lenin was sceptical about the outcome of the general strike
in Austria, to which Trotsky and the war faction attached so
much importance; and he drew a graphic picture of Russia's
military impotence. He admitted that what he advocated was
a 'shameful' peace, implying the betrayal of Poland. But he was
convinced that, if his government refused that peace and tried
to wage war, it would be wiped out and another government
would accept even worse terms. He disavowed, however, the
cruder arguments of Stalin and Zinoviev about the sacred
egoism of the Russian Revolution. He did not ignore the revolutionary potentialities of the West, but he believed that the peace
would hasten their development. The West was merely pregnant with revolution, while the Russian Revolution was already 'a healthy and loudly crying infant' whose life must be
safeguarded.

For the time being, Trotsky's formula provided a meeting
point for the opposed factions, although each at heart accepted
only that part of the formula that suited its purpose. The war
faction adopted it because it made peace impossible, while
Lenin and his group saw in it a means of keeping the war faction
at bay. Lenin was willing to let Trotsky try his hand once again

[1] *Protokoly Tsen. Kom.*, p. 206.

and play for time, especially as Trotsky was doing his best to
impress the Left Communists with the unreality of revolutionary
war. On Lenin's proposal, against Zinoviev's solitary vote, the
Central Committee authorized Trotsky to delay by every possible means the signature of the peace. Trotsky then submitted
his own resolution: 'We interrupt the war and do not sign the
peace—we demobilize the army.' Nine members voted for this,
seven against. Thus the party formally authorized Trotsky to
pursue his policy at Brest.[1]

During this interval Trotsky also presented his report to the
third Congress of Soviets. The mood of the Congress was so
overwhelmingly in favour of war that Lenin kept in the background. Even Trotsky spoke more emphatically about his
opposition to peace than about his opposition to war. 'The great
speech of the evening', writes a British eye-witness, 'was made
by Trotsky, whose report . . . was listened to with rapt attention.
All eyes were upon him, for he was at the zenith of his influence
. . . the man who incorporated the revolutionary will of Russia,
speaking to the outer world. . . . When Trotsky had ended his
great speech, the immense assembly of Russian workmen,
soldiers and peasants rose and . . . solemnly sang the *Internationale*. The outburst [was] as spontaneous as it was soul-stirring
to those who, like the writer, witnessed it. . . .'[2] The Congress
unanimously approved Trotsky's report, but it took no decision
and left the government a free hand.

Before Trotsky set out on his return journey to Brest, he made
a private arrangement with Lenin which, in one point, modified
essentially the decisions of the Central Committee and of the
government. He promised that in certain circumstances he would
abandon his own policy in favour of Lenin's. His tactics made
sense as long as the Germans were willing to allow him to evade
the choice between war and peace. What would happen, Lenin
anxiously asked, if they chose to resume hostilities? Lenin was
rightly convinced that this was bound to happen. Trotsky
treated this danger lightly, but he agreed to sign the peace if
Lenin's fears proved justified. That he and Lenin should have
found it permissible so to depart from the formal decision of the
Central Committee and of the government was due to the

[1] *Protokoly Tsen. Kom.*, pp. 199–207.
[2] M. Philips Price, *My Reminiscences of the Russian Revolution*, pp. 224–5.

ambiguity of that decision: the vote for 'neither war nor peace' had made no provision for the contingency which was uppermost in Lenin's mind. But their private arrangement, too, was ambiguous, as it turned out later. Lenin was under the impression that Trotsky had promised to sign the peace as soon as he was confronted with an ultimatum or a threat of a renewed German offensive. Trotsky held that he had obliged himself to accept the peace terms only after the Germans had actually launched a new offensive; and that even then he had committed himself to accept such terms only as the Central powers had so far offered, not the even worse terms which they dictated later.

By the middle of January Trotsky was back at the conference table in Brest. In the meantime the strikes and peace demonstrations in Austria and Germany had been suppressed or had come to a standstill; and his adversaries met him with new self-confidence. In vain did he, discarding formality, ask that German and Austrian Socialists be invited to Brest.[1] In vain did he ask for permission for himself to go to Vienna to contact Victor Adler, who had protested in the Austrian parliament against General Hoffmann's conduct at Brest. He was allowed, however, to pay a brief visit to Warsaw, where he was warmly acclaimed for his defence of Poland's independence.

Ukraine and Poland came to the fore in this part of the discussions. Behind the scenes Kühlmann and Czernin prepared a separate peace with the Ukrainian *Rada*. At the same time the Bolsheviks strenuously fostered a Soviet revolution in the Ukraine: the *Rada*'s writ still ran in Kiev, but Kharkov was already under a Soviet government; and a representative of the latter accompanied Trotsky on his return to Brest. Among the Ukrainian parties a curious reversal of attitudes occurred. Those who, under the Tsar and Kerensky, had stood for union or federation with Russia were now bent on separation. The Bolsheviks who had encouraged separatism now called for federation. Separatists became federalists and vice versa, not from motives of Ukrainian or Russian patriotism, but because they desired to separate from, or to federate with, the system of government prevalent in Russia. From this reversal of atti-

---

[1] The German government had just refused the Social Democratic leaders permission to go to Stockholm, whence they had intended to get in touch with the leaders of the Russian Revolution.

tudes the central powers hoped to benefit. By appearing as the protectors of Ukrainian separatism, they hoped to lay hands on the Ukraine's food and raw materials, of which they stood in desperate need; and also to turn the argument about self-determination against Russia. The *Rada*, weak, lacking self-confidence, on the verge of collapse, tried to lean on the central powers, despite the oath of loyalty it had sworn to the Entente. The *Rada*'s delegation consisted of very young, half-baked politicians—'*Bürschchen*', to quote Kühlmann[1]—who had just emerged from the backwoods and were intoxicated by the roles assigned to them in the great diplomatic game.

Even at this stage, Trotsky did not object to the *Rada*'s participation, but he served notice that Russia would recognize no separate agreements between it and the central powers. He also warned Kühlmann and Czernin that they overrated the strength of Ukrainian separatism. Then Lubinsky, the *Rada*'s delegate, launched a violent attack against Trotsky and the Soviet government, accusing them of trampling on the rights of the Ukraine and forcibly installing their own government in Kharkov and Kiev. 'Trotsky was so upset that it was painful to see', Czernin noted in his diary. 'Unusually pale, he stared fixedly in front of him. . . . Heavy drops of sweat trickled down his forehead. Evidently he felt deeply the disgrace of being abused by his fellow citizens in the presence of the enemy.'[2] Trotsky later denied that he was so greatly embarrassed, but Czernin's account seems credible. Trotsky certainly realized that his adversaries had succeeded up to a point in confusing the issue of self-determination. At heart he may have wondered whether the *Rada*'s spokesman was not justified in claiming that the Ukrainian Soviets were not representative of the Ukrainian people.[3] Not that Trotsky himself would have scrupled greatly about imposing Soviet rule on the Ukraine: the revolution could not be consolidated in Russia without its being extended to the Ukraine, which was wedged in deeply between northern and southern Russia. But here for the first time the interest of

---

[1] *Erinnerungen*, p. 531. [2] Czernin, op. cit., p. 246.

[3] This is inferred from a private message from Trotsky to Lenin, found in the *Trotsky Archives* at Harvard and written towards the end of the civil war. In that message Trotsky bluntly stated that the Soviet administration in the Ukraine had from the beginning been based on people sent from Russia and not on local elements. He then asked for a radical break with this method of government.

the revolution clashed with the principle of self-determination; and Trotsky could no longer evoke that principle with quite the same clear conscience with which he had evoked it hitherto.

He returned to the attack with the question of Poland, and asked why Poland was not yet represented at Brest. Kühlmann made the appearance of a Polish delegation dependent on Russia's prior recognition of the existing Polish administration. 'We have been asked again', Trotsky said, 'whether or not we acknowledge Poland's independence. . . . The question so posed is ambiguous. Do we acknowledge Ireland's independence? Our government does . . . but for the time being Ireland is still occupied by the British. We recognize that every human being has the right to food . . . which is not the same as recognizing the hungry man as sated.'[1] The recognition of Poland's right to independence did not imply the admission that she was independent under German-Austrian tutelage. Then Radek came forward with a telling indictment of German-Austrian domination of his native country: he spoke of the forced deportation of hundreds of thousands of Polish labourers to Germany; the appalling conditions in which this had taken place; political oppression; the imprisonment or internment of Polish political leaders of all parties, including the internment of Radek's old adversary Pilsudski, then commander of a Polish legion which had fought on Germany's and Austria's side, and Poland's future dictator.

In the middle of these exchanges, on 21 January, Trotsky received a message from Lenin about the downfall of the *Rada* and proclamation of the Soviet government all over the Ukraine.[2] He himself got in touch with Kiev, checked the facts, and notified the central powers that he no longer recognized the *Rada*'s right to be represented at the conference.

These were his last days at Brest. The mutual charges and recriminations had reached a point where the negotiations became barren and could not be much prolonged. In the intervals between the sessions he refreshed himself by writing *From February to Brest Litovsk*, one of his minor classics, a preliminary sketch for the monumental *History of the Russian Revolution* which he was to produce fifteen years later during his exile on Prinkipo Island. At last he sent a letter to Lenin in which he wrote: 'We

---

[1] *Mirnye Peregovory*, p. 162.   [2] Lenin, *Sochinenya*, vol. xxvi, p. 464.

shall declare that we end [the negotiations] but do not sign a peace. They will be unable to make an offensive against us. If they attack us, our position will be no worse than now. . . . We must have your decision. We can still drag on negotiations for one or two or three or four days. Afterward they must be broken off.'[1] Events did not allow him to wait for any new decision from Petrograd; and the vote taken before his departure had in any case given him enough latitude for the action he contemplated. Count Czernin still offered his services as mediator and even visited Trotsky in his lodging, warning him about the imminence of a new German offensive and begging him to state his final terms. Trotsky replied that he was prepared to bow to force, but would not give the Germans a testimonial of good moral conduct. Let them, if they so desired, annex foreign countries, but let them not expect the Russian Revolution to exonerate or embellish their acts of violence.

On the last day before the break, the central powers produced a *fait accompli*: they signed a separate peace with the *Rada*. 'We have officially informed the other side about the downfall of the *Rada*', Trotsky remonstrated. 'Nevertheless, the negotiations with a non-existing government continued. We then proposed to the Austro-Hungarian delegation—we did it in a private talk but in quite a formal manner—that they should send a representative to the Ukraine who would see for himself the *Rada*'s collapse . . . but we have been told that the signature of the treaty could not be delayed.'[2] General Hoffmann noted in his diary that Trotsky said that they were concluding a peace with a government whose territory extended no farther than its rooms at Brest Litovsk. Kühlmann self-righteously declared that German reports, 'the reliability of which was subject to no doubt, sharply contradicted this communication'.[3] This did not prevent General Hoffmann from remarking in his diary that 'according to reports that lay before me . . . there was unfortunately ground for regarding Trotsky's statement as not unfounded'.[4] The separate peace with the Ukraine served the central powers merely as a pretext for spreading their control to the Ukraine; and so in their eyes the credentials of their

---

[1] Trotsky confirmed to Mr. Wheeler-Bennett the authenticity of this letter. See *The Forgotten Peace*, pp. 185–6.   [2] *Mirnye Peregovory*, pp. 178–81.
[3] Ibid., p. 182.   [4] Hoffmann, op. cit., vol. ii, p. 213.

Ukrainian partners were irrelevant. It was precisely for this reason that Trotsky felt that he could not go on with the negotiations, for to do so would have meant to connive at the *coup* and at all that it entailed: the overthrow of the Ukrainian Soviets and the separation of the Ukraine.

On the next day, at a sub-commission, took place the famous scene at which General Hoffmann displayed a great map showing the full extent of the proposed German annexations. As Trotsky had said that he was 'prepared to bow to force' but would not help the Germans to keep up appearances, the general evidently believed that a blunt statement of German claims might be the short-cut to peace. When, on the same day, 28 January/10 February, the political commission reassembled, Trotsky rose to make his final statement:

The task of the sub-commission . . . was to say to what extent the frontier proposed by the opposite side was capable of securing, be it in the slightest degree, the self-determination of the Russian people. We have heard the reports of our representatives and . . . the time for decision has come. The peoples wait with impatience for the results of the peace talks at Brest Litovsk. They ask when this unparalleled self-annihilation of mankind, provoked by the selfishness and lust for power of the ruling classes, is going to end? If either of the two camps has ever fought this war in self-defence, this has long since ceased to be true. When Great Britain seizes African colonies, Baghdad, and Jerusalem, she is not waging a defensive war. When Germany occupies Serbia, Belgium, Poland, Lithuania, and Rumania and seizes the Monsoon Islands, this is not a defensive war either. This is a struggle for the partitioning of the world. Now this is clear, clearer than ever.

We do not want to take part any longer in this purely imperialist war, in which the claims of the possessing classes are openly paid for in human blood. . . .

In expectation of the approaching hour when the working classes of all countries seize power . . . we are withdrawing our army and our people from the war. Our soldier, the tiller of the land, should go back to his land to till it this spring, the land which the revolution has taken from the landlord and given to the peasant. Our soldier, the worker, should return to the factory bench to turn out not tools of destruction but tools of construction and to build, together with the tiller of the land, a new socialist economy.

As they listened to these impassioned words, the delegates of the central powers were still ready to applaud Trotsky with a 'well roared, lion'. This, they hoped even now, was Trotsky's final roar, after which would come the whimper of surrender. Only gradually did the import of his statement dawn upon them, and then they became breathlessly aware that they were witnessing an act which in its tragic pathos, was unique in history.[1]

We are withdrawing from the war [Trotsky went on]. We announce this to all peoples and governments. We are issuing an order for the full demobilization of our army. . . . At the same time we declare that the terms proposed to us by the governments of Germany and Austro-Hungary are in fundamental conflict with the interest of all peoples. They are repudiated by the toiling masses of all countries, including the Austro-Hungarian and the German peoples. The peoples of Poland, Ukraine, Lithuania, Kurland, and Estonia feel in them the violence inflicted upon their aspirations. To the Russian people these terms are a permanent threat. The popular masses of the whole world, guided by political consciousness or moral instinct, repudiate them. . . . We refuse to endorse terms which German and Austro-Hungarian imperialism is writing with the sword on the flesh of living nations. We cannot put the signature of the Russian revolution under a peace treaty which brings oppression, woe, and misfortune to millions of human beings.[2]

'When the echoes of Trotsky's powerful voice died away', writes the historian of Brest Litovsk, 'no one spoke. The whole conference sat speechless, dumbfounded before the audacity of this *coup de théâtre*. The amazed silence was shattered by an ejaculation of Hoffmann: "*Unerhört*", he exclaimed, scandalized. The spell was broken. Kühlmann said something about the necessity of calling a plenary session of the conference, but this Trotsky refused, saying that there remained nothing to discuss. With that the Bolsheviks left the room, and in gloomy silence, still scarcely believing what they had heard and wholly at a loss as to what to make of it, the delegates of the Central Powers dispersed.'[3]

However, before the delegations had dispersed, something

[1] On the next day, Krüge, the chief German legal expert, told Yoffe that he had looked for historical precedents and found only one—in the remote antiquity of the wars between Persia and Greece. See Yoffe's memoir appended to *Mirnye Peregovory*, p. 262.
[2] *Mirnye Peregovory*, pp. 207–8.   [3] Wheeler-Bennett, op. cit., pp. 227–8.

happened, the full significance of which Trotsky missed—something which confirmed Lenin's worst fears. Kühlmann declared that in view of what had taken place, hostilities would be resumed, because Russia's demobilization was of no legal consequence—only her rejection of the peace mattered. Trotsky treated this as an empty threat; he did not believe, he replied, that the German and Austrian peoples would allow their governments to continue a war so obviously devoid of any defensive pretext. Kühlmann himself gave Trotsky some reason for dismissing the threat when he inquired whether the Soviet government was at least prepared to enter into legal and commercial relations with the central powers and in what way they could keep in touch with Russia. Instead of answering the query, as, from his own standpoint he ought to have done—this might have entailed a commitment by the central powers to respect the state of 'neither war nor peace'—Trotsky haughtily refused to discuss it.

He stayed on at Brest for another day and got wind of a quarrel between Hoffmann, who insisted on the resumption of hostilities, and the civilian diplomats, who preferred to accept the state of neither war nor peace. On the spot the civilians seemed to have carried the day. Trotsky was therefore returning to Petrograd confident and proud of his achievement. At this moment, the man stands before our eyes in all his strength and weakness. 'Single-handed, with nothing behind him save a country in chaos and a régime scarce established, [he] . . . who a year before had been an inconspicuous journalist exiled in New York, [had fought] successfully the united diplomatic talent of half Europe.'[1] He had given mankind the first great lesson in genuinely open diplomacy. But at the same time he allowed himself to be carried away by his optimism. He underrated his enemy and even refused to listen to his warning. Great artist that he was, he was so wrapped up in himself and in his ideal and so fascinated by the formidable appeal of his own work that he lightly overlooked its deficiencies. While Trotsky was still on his way to Petrograd, General Hoffmann, backed by Ludendorff, Hindenburg, and the Kaiser, was already issuing marching orders to the German troops.

The German offensive began on 17 February, and it met with

[1] Wheeler-Bennett, op. cit., p. 166.

no resistance.[1] 'This is the most comic war I have ever experienced', Hoffmann wrote, 'It is waged almost exclusively in trains and cars. One puts on the train a handful of infantry-men with machine guns and one gun, and one rushes to the next railway station. One seizes that station, arrests the Bolsheviks, entrains another detachment and travels farther.'[2] When the news of the offensive reached Smolny, the Central Committee of the party, after eight votes, failed to agree on a way out of the situation. The Committee was equally divided between the adherents of peace and the advocates of war. Trotsky's single vote could resolve the deadlock. Indeed, during this and the next day, 17 and 18 February, he and he alone could make the momentous decision. But he refused to join either faction.

His position was extraordinarily complex. He had so behaved and spoken that many identified him with the war faction; and politically and morally he did in fact stand closer to it than to Lenin's faction. But he had also made the private promise to Lenin that he would support peace, if and when the Germans resumed military operations. He still refused to believe that this moment had arrived. On 17 February he voted with the adherents of war against Lenin's proposal for an immediate request for new peace negotiations. He then voted with the peace faction against revolutionary war. And finally he submitted his own motion, advising the government to hold up new negotiations until the military and political results of the German offensive had become clear. As the war faction voted with him, his motion was passed by a majority of one vote, his own. Lenin then posed the question whether peace should be concluded if it turned out that the German offensive was a fact and if no revolutionary opposition to it developed in Germany and Austria. The Central Committee answered the question in the affirmative.[3]

Early next morning, Trotsky opened a session of the Central Committee with a survey of the latest events. Prince Leopold of Bavaria had just broadcast to the world that Germany was defending all nations, including her western enemies, from the infection of Bolshevism. German divisions from the western front were reported to have appeared in Russia. German aviation

[1] From now on all dates are given according to the European calendar, which was adopted in Russia on 14 February 1918.
[2] Hoffmann, op. cit., vol. i, p. 187. [3] *Protokoly Tsen. Kom.*, pp. 226–9.

was active over Dvinsk. An attack on Revel was anticipated. All this pointed towards a full-scale offensive, but the facts were not yet established. Prince Leopold's broadcast indicated a possibility of collusion between Germany and the Entente, but no more than a possibility. Lenin urgently renewed his proposal for an immediate approach to Germany. 'We must act', he said, 'we have no time to lose. It is either war, revolutionary war, or peace.' Trotsky, wondering whether 'the offensive might not bring about a serious explosion in Germany', still held that it was too early to sue for peace. Once again Lenin's proposal was rejected by the majority of one vote.

Between the morning and the evening of this day, 18 February, a dramatic change occurred. When Trotsky opened the evening session of the Central Committee, he reported that the Germans had already seized Dvinsk and that there were widespread rumours of an imminent offensive in the Ukraine. Still hesitant, he proposed to sound the central powers about their demands but not to request peace negotiations. 'People will not understand this', Lenin answered, 'If there is war we should not have demobilized'. This was 'joking with war', which might lead to the collapse of the revolution. 'We are writing papers and in the meantime they [the Germans] are seizing rolling stock. . . . History will say that you have delivered the revolution [to the enemy]. We could have signed a peace which was not at all dangerous to the revolution.' Sverdlov and Stalin spoke in the same vein. 'If they open a hurricane fire for five minutes', Stalin said, 'we shall not be left with a single soldier on the front. . . . I disagree with Trotsky. To pose the question as he does is all right in literature.' Yet Zinoviev, the most extreme advocate of peace, now had his qualms. Lenin was for peace even if it entailed the loss of the Ukraine, but Zinoviev would not go as far as that.[1]

Thrice Trotsky spoke against suing for peace, and thrice he proposed only tentative soundings. But when Lenin once again presented his motion, Trotsky to everybody's surprise voted not

---

[1] Of this session two records are available. According to one, Zinoviev argued for peace, saying that the Bismarck tradition of co-operation with Russia was not yet dead in Germany and that the Germans had just as vital an interest in the peace as the Russians. It is curious to see how many of the future *leitmotifs* of Soviet foreign policy appear fleetingly and inchoately in these hurried debates. *Protokoly Tsen. Kom.*, p. 242.

for his own proposal, but for Lenin's. With the majority of one vote the peace faction won. The new majority asked Trotsky and Lenin to frame the message to the enemy governments. Later that night the Central Committees of the two ruling parties, the Bolshevik and the Left Social Revolutionary, met; and at this meeting the war faction once again had the upper hand. But in the government the Bolsheviks outvoted their partners; and on the next day, 19 February, the government formally sued for peace.

Four days of suspense and panic passed before the German answer reached Petrograd. In the meantime nobody could say whether or on what terms the central powers would agree to reopen negotiations. Their armies were on the move. Petrograd was exposed. A committee of revolutionary defence was formed in the city, and Trotsky headed it. Even while they were suing for peace, the Soviets had to prepare for war. Trotsky turned to the allied embassies and military missions to inquire whether, if the Soviets re-entered the war, the western governments would help them. He had made such soundings before, but without effect.[1] But this time the British and the French seemed more responsive. Three days after he had sent off the request for peace, Trotsky reported to the Central Committee (in Lenin's absence) an Anglo-French suggestion for military co-operation. To his mortification, the Central Committee rejected this out of hand and so repudiated his action. Both factions turned against him: the adherents of peace—because they feared lest the acceptance of allied help compromise the chances of separate peace; and the adherents of war—because the same motives of revolutionary morality, by which they were actuated in opposing a compact with Germany, militated also against co-operation with 'the Anglo-French imperialists'. Trotsky then declared that he was resigning from the Commissariat of Foreign Affairs. He could not stay in office if the party did not see that a Socialist government

[1] Colonel Robins relates that in January Trotsky proposed that American officers should go to the front and help to stop the leakage of Russian goods to Germany and to remove stocks of raw materials to the interior of the country. Trotsky then said that even if they signed a separate peace, the Soviets had no interest in strengthening Germany. Hard, *Raymond Robins' Own Story*, pp. 64–65. 'The Allied and American Governments', this is Robins's comment, 'rather than admit the existence of Trotsky, let the Germans do all the grabbing of Russian raw materials on the Russian frontier.' Ibid., pp. 70–71.

had the right to accept assistance from bourgeois powers, provided it maintained complete independence.[1] Eventually he converted the Central Committee to his view, and Lenin firmly supported him.

The German answer, when it at last arrived, came as a shock. It allowed the Soviets only forty-eight hours for a reply and only three days for negotiations. The terms were much worse than those offered at Brest: Russia was to carry out complete demobilization; to cede Latvia and Estonia; and to evacuate the Ukraine and Finland. When, on 23 February, the Central Committee met, it had less than a day to make up its mind. It was again on Trotsky's single vote that the outcome hung. He had yielded to Lenin on the point that a new request for peace be made, but he was not committed to accept the new, much harsher, terms. He did not agree with Lenin that the Soviets were utterly incapable of defending themselves. On the contrary, more distinctly than hitherto, he now leaned towards the war faction. 'Lenin's arguments', he said, 'are far from convincing. If only we had unanimity in our midst we could shoulder the task of organizing the defence, we could cope with this. We would not act a bad role even if we were compelled to give up Petrograd and Moscow. We would keep the whole world in tension. If we sign this German ultimatum to-day, we may be confronted by another to-morrow. . . . We may gain peace but we shall lose the support of the advanced elements of the proletariat. We shall, in any case, lead the proletariat to disintegration.'[2]

And yet, despite his forebodings about the peace, despite his confidence in the capacity of the Soviets to defend themselves, he once again ensured, by his single vote, the ascendancy of the peace faction.

His puzzling conduct cannot be explained without a closer look at the alignment of the groups, their arguments and motives. Lenin strove to obtain for the Soviets a 'respite', which would enable them to put their house into some order and to build up a new army. He was prepared to pay almost any price for the respite, to withdraw from the Ukraine and the Baltic lands and to discharge any indemnity. He did not accept this 'shameful' peace as final. He, too, held that revolutionary war

[1] *Protokoly Tsen. Kom.*, pp. 243-6.   [2] Ibid., p. 248.

was inescapable; and more than once he recalled the peace of Tilsit which Napoleon had dictated to Prussia in 1807 and which the progressive Prussian statesmen, von Stein and Gneisenau, had used to modernize their country and army and to prepare revenge. He was following their example; and he also hoped that during the respite revolution might mature in Germany and renounce and annul the Kaiser's conquests.

Against this the war faction argued that the central powers would not permit Lenin so to use the respite: they would cut off Russia from the grain and coal of the Ukraine and the petrol of the Caucasus; they would bring under their control half the Russian population; they would sponsor and support counter-revolutionary movements and throttle the revolution. Nor would the Soviets be able to build up a new army during any respite. They had to create their armed strength in the very process of the fighting; and only so could they create it. True, the Soviets might be forced to evacuate Petrograd and even Moscow; but they had enough space into which to retreat and gather strength. Even if the people were to prove as unwilling to fight for the revolution as they were to fight for the old régime—and the leaders of the war faction refused to take this for granted—then every German advance, with all the accompanying terror and pillage, would shake the people from weariness and torpor, force them to resist, and finally generate a broad and truly popular enthusiasm for revolutionary war. On the tide of this enthusiasm a new and formidable army would rise. The revolution, unshamed by sordid surrender, would achieve its renaissance; it would stir the souls of the working classes abroad; and it would finally dispel the nightmare of imperialism.

Each faction was convinced that the policy proposed by the other was pernicious, and the debates were charged with emotional tension. Trotsky, it seems, was alone in holding that much could be said from a realistic standpoint for and against each of the proposed courses of action, and that neither was inadmissible on grounds of principle and revolutionary morality.

It has since become the historian's commonplace, a commonplace which after the event Trotsky himself did much to establish, that Lenin's policy had all the merits of realism and that the war faction represented an utterly quixotic aspect of

Bolshevism. This view does not do full justice to the leaders of the war faction. It is true that Lenin's political originality and courage rose in those days to the height of genius and that events—the crumbling of the Hohenzollern and Habsburg dynasties and the annulment of the treaty of Brest before the end of the year—vindicated him. It is also true that the war faction often acted under confused emotional impulses and presented no consistent policy. But at their best its leaders argued their case very strongly and realistically; and much of their argument, too, was confirmed by events. The 'respite' which Lenin obtained was, in truth, half-illusory. After the signing of the peace, the Kaiser's government did all it could to strangle the Soviets. It could not, however, do more than its involvement in the gigantic struggle on the western front allowed it to do. Without a separate peace in the West it could not have done much more even if the Soviets had not accepted the *Diktat* of Brest. Bukharin and Radek, when they argued against Russia's surrender, pointed to this circumstance as to one which severely restricted Germany's freedom of action. In this respect the inner story of the war, when it was revealed, proved their judgement to have been more correct than Lenin's. The occupation of the Ukraine and of parts of southern Russia alone tied down a million German and Austrian troops. If Russia had refused to sign the peace, the Germans might, at the most, have tried to seize Petrograd. They could hardly have risked a march on Moscow.[1] If they had seized both Petrograd and Moscow, the Soviets, whose chief strength lay in the two capitals, would have found themselves in an extremely dangerous, perhaps fatal, crisis. But this was not the point at issue between Lenin and the war faction, for Lenin, too, repeatedly stated, with curious confidence, that the loss of the one or the two capitals would not be a mortal blow to the revolution.[2]

The other argument advanced by the leaders of the war faction that the Soviets would have to build up a new army on the battlefields, in the process of the fighting, and not in the

---

[1] Ludendorff states that a deep German offensive was 'out of the question'—only 'a short energetic thrust' had been planned. *Meine Kriegserinnerungen*, p. 447.

[2] Stalin alone held that the surrender of any capital would mean the decay, the 'rotting' of the revolution; and in this, as an advocate of peace, he was in a way more consistent than Lenin. *Protokoly Tsen. Kom.*, p. 248.

barracks during a calm respite, was, paradoxically, realistic. This was how the Red Army was eventually built up; and Bukharin's and Radek's speeches at the seventh congress of the party anticipated on this point the military policy which Trotsky and Lenin were to adopt and pursue in the coming years.[1] Precisely because Russia was so extremely war weary, she could not raise a new army in relatively calm times. Only severe shocks and the ineluctable necessity to fight, and to fight at once, could stimulate the energies hidden in the Soviet régime and bring them into play. Only thus could it happen that a nation which had under the Tsar, Prince Lvov, and Kerensky been too exhausted to fight, went on fighting under Lenin and Trotsky in civil wars and wars of intervention for nearly three years.

The weakness of the war faction lay not so much in its case as in its lack of leadership. Its chiefs were Bukharin, Dzerzhinsky, Radek, Yoffe, Uritsky, Kollontai, Lomov-Oppokov, Bubnov, Pyatakov, Smirnov, and Ryazanov. All were eminent members of the party. Some of them had great intellectual gifts and were brilliant spokesmen and pamphleteers. Others were courageous men of action. Yet none of them possessed the indomitable will, the moral authority, the political and strategic talents, the tactical flexibility, and the administrative capacity required of a leader in a revolutionary war. As long as the war faction had no such leader, it represented merely a state of mind, a moral ferment, a literary cry of despair, not a policy, even though at first a majority of the party was drawn into the ferment and echoed the cry of despair. The leadership of the war faction was vacant, and the faction cast inviting glances at Trotsky. Incidentally, in their ranks were many of his old friends who had joined the Bolshevik party together with him. On the face of it, there was little to prevent him from responding to their expectations. Although he held that Lenin's policy, like that of the adherents of war, had its justification, he did not conceal his inner revulsion against it. All the more astounding was it that at the most critical moments he threw the weight of his influence behind Lenin.

He shrank from assuming the leadership of the war faction because he realized that this would have transformed at a

[1] *Sedmoi Syezd RKP*, pp. 32–50, 69–73 and *passim*.

stroke the cleavage among the Bolsheviks into an irretrievable split and, probably, into a bloody conflict. He and Lenin would have confronted each other as the leaders of hostile parties, divided not over ordinary differences but over a matter of life and death. Lenin had already warned the Central Committee that if they outvoted him once again in the matter of peace, he would resign from the Committee and the government and appeal against them to the rank and file.[1] At this time Trotsky was Lenin's only possible successor as the chief of the government. But as chief of a government committed to wage a most dangerous war in desperate conditions, he would have had to suppress the opposition to war, and almost certainly to take repressive action against Lenin. Both factions, aware of these implications, refrained from uttering plain threats. But the unspoken threats were there—in the undertones of the debate. It was in order to stop the party drifting towards a civil war in its own ranks that at the crucial moments Trotsky cast his vote for Lenin.[2]

Some analogy to the situation which was likely to arise if Trotsky had acted otherwise may be found in the three-cornered struggle which developed between the Commune of Paris, Danton and Robespierre during the French Revolution. In 1793 the Commune (and Anacharsis Cloots) stood, as Bukharin and the Left Communists were to do, for war against all the anti-revolutionary governments of Europe. Danton advocated

---

[1] *Protokoly Tsen. Kom.*, pp. 247–8.

[2] Twenty years later, during the purge trials, Bukharin was charged with having attempted at the time of the Brest crisis to stage a coup against Lenin and to arrest him. This version, designed to make credible the charge about Bukharin's plot against Stalin, must be dismissed. But the leaders of the war faction must have considered at one point what they would do if they obtained a majority in the Central Committee. They would then have had to form a government without Lenin and, if Lenin persisted in opposing war, they might have had to arrest him. In 1923 Zinoviev claimed that Bukharin and Radek seriously discussed this with the Left Social Revolutionaries. Radek denied the allegation, saying that they had only joked about Lenin's arrest. Col. Robins, a completely disinterested witness, who kept in close touch with the Bolshevik leaders, described, as early as in 1920, a scene between Radek and Lenin, in which Radek is alleged to have said that if there were 500 courageous men in Petrograd, they would imprison Lenin and make possible a revolutionary war. Lenin replied that he would first imprison his interlocutor (Hard, *Raymond Robins' Own Story*, p. 94). If any serious conspiracy against Lenin had been afoot, Radek would hardly have hastened to give Lenin advance notice of it. But although this dialogue was in fact jocular, the logic of the situation gave it a serious undertone.

war against Prussia and agreement with England, where he hoped that Fox would replace Pitt in office. Robespierre urged the Convention to wage war against England; and he strove for an agreement with Prussia. Danton and Robespierre joined hands against the Commune, but, after they suppressed it they fell out. The guillotine settled their controversy.

Trotsky, who so often looked at the Russian Revolution through the prism of the French, must have been aware of this analogy. He may have remembered Engels's remarkable letter to Victor Adler, explaining all the 'pulsations' of the French Revolution by the fortunes of war and the disagreements engendered by it.[1] He must have seen himself as acting a role potentially reminiscent of Danton's, while Lenin's part was similar to Robespierre's. It was as if the shadow of the guillotine had for a moment interposed itself between him and Lenin. This is not to say that, if the conflict had developed, Trotsky, like Danton, would necessarily have played a losing game; or that Lenin was, like Robespierre, inclined to settle by the guillotine an inner party controversy. Here the analogy ceases to apply. It was evident that the war party, if it won, would be driven to suppress its opponents—otherwise it could not cope with its task. A peaceable solution of the crisis in the party was possible only under the rule of the adherents of peace, who could better afford to tolerate opposition. This consideration was decisive in Trotsky's eyes. In order to banish the shadow of the guillotine he made an extraordinary sacrifice of principle and personal ambition.

To Lenin's threat of resignation he replied, addressing himself more to the advocates of war than to Lenin: 'We cannot wage revolutionary war with a split in the party. . . . Under these conditions our party is not in a position to wage war, especially as those who stand for war do not want to accept the material means for waging it [i.e. assistance from the western powers].'[2] 'I shall not take upon myself the responsibility of voting for war.' Later he added: 'There is a lot of subjectivism in Lenin's attitude. I am not sure that he is right, but I do not want to do anything that would interfere with the party's unity. On the contrary, I shall help as much as I can. But I

[1] K. Marx and F. Engels, *Selected Correspondence*, pp. 457–8.
[2] *Protokoly Tsen. Kom.*, p. 248.

cannot stay in office and bear personal responsibility for the conduct of foreign affairs.'[1]

The leaders of the war faction did not share Trotsky's fears. Dzerzhinsky, already the head of *Cheka*,[2] held that the party was strong enough to stand the split and Lenin's resignation. Lomov-Oppokov, leader of the Bolsheviks in Moscow, appealed to Trotsky not to let himself be 'intimidated' by Lenin's ultimatums—they could take power without Lenin.[3] In the course of the debate, however, the gravity and urgency of Trotsky's argument so impressed some of the advocates of war, Dzerzhinsky and Yoffe, that they retraced their steps. Lenin obtained seven votes for peace. This was still a minority of the Central Committee. But as Trotsky and three leaders of the war faction abstained, and only four voted against Lenin, the peace terms were accepted. The three leaders of the war faction who abstained, Yoffe, Dzerzhinsky, and Krestinsky, issued a solemn statement saying that they could not contemplate 'a war to be fought simultaneously against German imperialism, the Russian bourgeoisie, and a section of the proletariat headed by Lenin'; and that a split would be such an unmitigated disaster that the worst peace was preferable.[4] But the irreconcilable adherents of war, Bukharin, Uritsky, Lomov, Bubnov (and Pyatakov and Smirnov, who were present at the session) denounced the decision in favour of peace as a minority opinion; and in protest against it they resigned from all responsible offices in party and government. In vain did Lenin try to dissuade them from taking this step. Trotsky, having brought about the defeat of the Left Communists, now showed them his sympathy and affection, and wistfully remarked that he would have voted differently had he known that they were going to resign.[5]

The peace faction had won, but its conscience was troubled. No sooner had the Central Committee, on 23 February, decided to accept the German terms than it voted unanimously to

[1] *Protokoly Tsen. Kom.*, p. 251.

[2] *Cheka*—Extraordinary Commission for Struggle against the Counter-revolution, the predecessor of G.P.U.   [3] Ibid., p. 250.   [4] Ibid., p. 253.

[5] At the same session, a curious scene took place. Lenin assured his defeated opponents that they had every right to conduct an agitation against the peace. Against this Stalin remarked that since they had been so undisciplined as to resign from their posts, the leaders of the war faction automatically placed themselves outside the party. Both Lenin and Trotsky strongly protested against Stalin's statement, and Stalin had to withdraw it. Ibid., pp. 254–5.

start immediate preparations for future war. When it came to the appointment of a new delegation for Brest Litovsk, a tragi-comic scene took place: every member of the Committee dodged the dubious honour; none, not even the most ardent advocate of peace, was eager to place his signature under the treaty. Sokolnikov, who eventually headed the new delegation, threatened to resign from the Central Committee when his candidature was proposed; and only Lenin's good-tempered persuasion induced him to yield.[1] This matter having been settled, Trotsky asked—amid Stalin's sneers, for which Stalin later apologized—that the Central Committee take cognizance of his resignation from the Commissariat of Foreign Affairs, which was already virtually under Chicherin's management. The Central Committee appealed to Trotsky to stay in office until the peace was signed. He only agreed not to make public his resignation until then and declared that he would not appear any more in any governmental institution. Prompted by Lenin, the Committee obliged him to attend at least those sessions of the government at which foreign affairs were not under debate.[2]

After all the recent exertions, triumphs, and frustrations Trotsky's nerves were frayed. It looked as if his performance at Brest had been wholly wasted; and this was indeed what many thought and said. Not without reason, he was blamed for having lulled the party into false security by his repeated assurances that the Germans would not dare to attack. Overnight the idol became almost a culprit. 'On the evening of 27 February', writes M. Philips Price, 'the Central Soviet Executive met at the Tauride Palace, and Trotsky addressed them. . . . He had disappeared for some days, and no one seemed to know what had happened to him. That night, however, he came to the Palace . . . hurled the darts of eloquent scorn against the Imperialisms of the central powers and of the allies, upon whose altar the Russian Revolution was being sacrificed. When he had finished, he retired again. Rumour had it that he was so overcome with mortification that he broke down and wept.'[3]

. . . .

On 3 March Sokolnikov, making it abundantly clear that the

---

[1] Ibid., pp. 259–66. [2] Ibid., p. 268.
[3] M. Philips Price, op. cit., p. 251. See also I. Steinberg, *Als ich Volkskommissar war*, pp. 208–13.

Soviets were acting under duress, signed the treaty of Brest
Litovsk. In less than a fortnight, the Germans seized Kiev and
vast parts of the Ukraine, the Austrians entered Odessa, and
the Turks Trebizond. In the Ukraine the occupying powers
crushed the Soviets and reinstalled the *Rada*, only to overpower
shortly thereafter the *Rada* too, and to place *Hetman* Skoropadsky at the head of their puppet administration. The momentary
victors showered upon Lenin's government demands and ultimatums, each more humiliating than the preceding. Most
galling was the ultimatum demanding that the Soviets sign an
immediate peace with 'independent Ukraine'. In the Ukraine
the people, especially the peasants, were putting up a desperate
resistance to the occupying forces and their Ukrainian tools. By
signing a separate treaty with the latter, the Soviets could not
but appear to disavow the whole Ukrainian resistance. At the
Central Committee Trotsky demanded the rejection of the
German ultimatum. Lenin, always with the idea of future revenge in his mind, was determined to drain the cup of humiliation. But at every German provocation the opposition to peace
rose again in the party and in the Soviets. The treaty of Brest
had not yet been ratified and ratification was still uncertain.

On 6 March an emergency congress of the party met at the
Tauride Palace to decide whether to recommend ratification to
the forthcoming Congress of the Soviets. The proceedings were
held in strict secrecy, and the records were published only in
1925. The atmosphere was heavy with dejection. The delegates
from the provinces found that, in expectation of a German
attack, governmental offices were preparing to evacuate Petrograd, a move from which Kerensky's government had shrunk.
The Commissars were already 'sitting on their bags and cases'
—only Trotsky was to stay behind to organize the defence. The
delegates reported a general slump in the party's popularity.[1]
Only recently the clamour for peace had been so powerful as to
destroy the February régime and to lift the Bolsheviks to power.
But now, when the peace had come, the party responsible for
it was the first to be blamed.

At the congress, Trotsky's activity was inevitably the pivot of

---

[1] 'The local organizations', says the official record, 'were weak and disorganized,
and the congress reflected the condition of our entire party, of the entire working
class, of the whole of Russia.' *Sedmoi Syezd RKP*, pp. 4–5.

debate. In a most incisive speech Lenin urged ratification of the peace. The main burden of his argument was against the war faction, but he also castigated Trotsky's 'great mistake' and wishful belief that the Germans would not attack, the belief which had underlain 'neither war nor peace'.[1] The war faction jumped to Trotsky's defence. 'Even the chauvinist German press', Radek said, 'had to admit that the proletariat of Germany was against Hindenburg and for Trotsky. Our policy at Brest Litovsk has not failed; it has not been an illusion but a policy of revolutionary realism.'[2] It was much better for the Soviets to have concluded peace only after the German offensive, because nobody could doubt that they acted under external compulsion. But then Radek voiced the war faction's disappointment with Trotsky: 'One may reproach Trotsky only for this, that having achieved so much at Brest he then joined the other side. . . . For this we have a right to reproach him; and we do so.'[3]

Trotsky once again, and more explicitly, justified his behaviour. Bukharin, Radek, and their friends, he said, saw in war the only salvation and so they were 'obliged, infringing upon formal party considerations, to pose the issue on a knife-edge. . . . With a weak country behind us, with a passive peasantry, with a sombre mood in the proletariat, we were further threatened by a split in our own ranks. . . . Very much was at stake on my vote. . . . I could not assume responsibility for the split. I had thought that we ought to retreat [before the German army] rather than sign peace for the sake of an illusory respite. But I could not take upon myself the responsibility for the leadership of the party. . . .'[4]

This, as far as the records show, was the only time he openly stated that he had shrunk from superseding Lenin as the leader of the party. 'The danger of the split', he added, 'will have neither disappeared nor lessened if European revolution is further delayed.'[5] He admitted that he had misjudged German intentions, but he reminded Lenin that they had both agreed on breaking off the negotiations. He had, he said, a profound respect for Lenin's policy, but not for the manner in which Lenin's faction was putting its case before the country. They fostered apathy and defeatism, which were demoralizing the working

[1] Ibid., p. 22.   [2] Ibid., p. 71.   [3] Ibid., p. 72.   [4] Ibid., p. 83.   [5] Ibid., p. 84.

class, and amid which it was extremely difficult to build up the new army they all wanted. He did not urge the congress to refuse ratification; but there ought to be a limit to surrenders: they must not give in to Lenin and sign a treaty with Germany's Ukrainian puppets.[1] And here he made a remark hinting at a most ominous contingency. If, he said, the party was so powerless that it had to let down the Ukrainian workers and peasants, then it might be its duty to declare: '. . . *we have come before our time*, we withdraw into the underground, and we let Chernov, Guchkov, and Miliukov settle accounts with . . . the Ukraine. . . . But I think that even if we should be compelled so to withdraw, we must still act as a revolutionary party and fight for every position to the last drop of our blood.'[2] This was his strongest intimation so far that the Russian Revolution might have been a false spring; and to Marxist ears his words carried the grimmest connotation: Marx and Engels had repeatedly written about the tragic fate which overtakes revolutionaries who 'come before their time'.[3] Finally, recalling Dzerzhinsky's, Yoffe's, Krestinsky's, and his own 'great act of self-restraint' and his 'sacrifice of the Ego' on the altar of Bolshevik unity, he told Lenin that there were as many dangers as opportunities in Lenin's policy, and that the peace faction might be 'sacrificing life's only end for the sake of mere living'.[4]

Lenin once again used the threat of resignation: he would resign, he said, if the congress limited his freedom of action with regard to the Ukraine. There is, he pleaded, no treason in the behaviour of soldiers who refuse to come to the rescue of surrounded comrades in arms, when they know that they are too weak to rescue those surrounded and that they themselves will perish in the attempt. Such was the position of the Soviets in relation to the Ukraine. This time a large majority agreed with Lenin.

[1] 'Lenin knows no limit to surrender and retreat, even though Trotsky tries to catch him by his coat-tails and stop him', Ryazanov said in the debate. *Sedmoi Syezd RKP*, p. 9.   [2] Ibid., p. 85.
[3] 'The worst thing that can befall a leader of an extreme party is to be compelled to take over a Government in an epoch when the movement is not yet ripe for the domination of the class which he represents and for the realization of the measures which that domination would imply . . . he necessarily finds himself in a dilemma. What he *can* do is in contrast to all his previous actions, to all his principles and to the present interests of his party; what he *ought* to do cannot be achieved. . . . Whoever puts himself in this awkward position is irrevocably lost.' Engels, *The Peasant War in Germany*, pp. 135–6.   [4] *Sedmoi Syezd RKP*, p. 86.

THE DRAMA OF BREST LITOVSK

Trotsky, nevertheless, tabled an amendment to Lenin's motion affirming that peace was 'necessary'—he proposed to replace 'necessary' by 'permissible'. From the platform of the congress, he could not fully explain why, after all he had done to promote Lenin's policy, he vacillated again. Behind the scenes he and Lenin, in perfect concord, were sounding the Entente once again on whether they would get assistance if they refused to ratify the peace. In expectation of the answer Lenin was even delaying the Congress of the Soviets which was to vote on ratification. He very nearly committed himself with President Wilson to renouncing the treaty of Brest if the President gave a binding promise of help.[1] At the congress of the party, Lenin cryptically remarked that the situation was changing so rapidly that in two days he himself might speak against ratification.[2] Trotsky was therefore anxious that the congress should not frame its resolution in terms which were too rigid. Lenin, however, did not at heart expect any encouraging answer from the Entente; and once again he was right. He had agreed, on Trotsky's prompting, to make the soundings in order to have a clear conscience in the matter. But in the meantime he wished the congress to approve peace without qualification. This the congress did.

In the debate Trotsky had recalled his 'great act of self-restraint' and his 'suppression of the Ego'. These words bring to mind the remark of a friend of his early youth: 'Trotsky's entire behaviour is dominated by his Ego, but his Ego is dominated by the revolution.'[3] This trait of the boy of eighteen was still there in the great and famous man of thirty-eight. His conduct during this drama testified to his subordination of personal ambition and inclination to the interests of the party. But now, when Lenin's triumph was complete, Trotsky's Ego chafed; and from the platform of this grim congress it cried out for compensation. The great debate over peace was followed by a grotesque wrangle over Trotsky's faults and merits. His friends and followers, Krestinsky, Yoffe, and Ryazanov, tabled a formal motion justifying his policy at Brest. It was, from every point of view, preposterous to press such a motion at this moment.

---

[1] Hard, *Raymond Robins' Own Story*, pp. 135-9; Wheeler-Bennett, *The Forgotten Peace*, pp. 290-301.

[2] *Sedmoi Syezd RKP*, p. 140.   [3] See Chapter II, p. 35.

The congress had just decided that peace was an absolute necessity, and it should not have been expected to give now its retrospective blessing to 'neither war nor peace'. The circumstance that Trotsky's defenders came from the war faction made this demonstration appear a last sally from a defeated minority. The congress had been in no mood to rebuff Trotsky for what he had done at Brest; it preferred to let bygones be bygones. But, having been expressly asked to declare itself, it could not but administer a rebuff. It rejected the motion; and this wounded Trotsky's pride and ambition. He exclaimed that he had become the man most hated by the imperialists of the central powers, the man blamed for the continuation of war, and now, wittingly or unwittingly, the party had lent its authority to the enemy's charges against him. He therefore resigned from all responsible offices with which the party had entrusted him.

By this time Trotsky's appointment as Commissar of War was either mooted or decided upon in the inner councils of the party; and the congress was anxious to give him at least partial satisfaction. Amid much uproar and confusion, several resolutions were tabled and many votes were taken, the result of which was not clear. During this undignified wrangle, Lenin kept silent. In the name of Lenin's faction, Zinoviev assured Trotsky that the whole party warmly appreciated his brilliant efforts from Brest to arouse the German working class and considered this part of his work as 'fully correct'. But Trotsky ought to appreciate that the party had changed its attitude, and that it was pointless to argue over the formula 'neither war nor peace'. The congress first adopted Zinoviev's resolution. Then it voted for Radek's motion which contradicted it, and then it passed still another text which contradicted Radek's. 'It is an event unheard of in history', Trotsky complained, 'that in the face of the enemy a party should repudiate the policy of its representatives.' In pique he submitted an ironical resolution roundly condemning his own policy. The congress, of course, rejected it, and he withdrew from the fray. When it came to the election of the Central Committee, he and Lenin obtained the highest number of votes. Abandoning his policy, the party nevertheless gave him its unreserved confidence.

. . . .

Four crowded months had passed since the Soviets had

ratified the peace. The Council of the People's Commissars had
moved from Petrograd and had installed itself at the Kremlin
in Moscow. The allied diplomatic missions had also left Petrograd; but in protest against the peace they went to Vologda,
a small provincial town. Trotsky had become Commissar of
War and had begun to 'arm the revolution'. The Japanese had
attacked Siberia and occupied Vladivostok. The Germans had
suppressed the Finnish revolution and forced the Russian navy
to withdraw from the Bay of Finland. They had also occupied
the whole of the Ukraine, the Crimea, and the coasts of the
Black and the Azov Seas. The British and the French had
landed at Murmansk. The Czech Legion had risen against the
Soviets. Encouraged by foreign interventions, the Russian anti-
revolutionary forces had resumed the life-and-death struggle,
subordinating to it all principles and scruples. Many of those
who had only recently accused the Bolsheviks of being German
agents, Miliukov and his followers in the first instance, had
come to rely on German assistance in their fight against the
Bolsheviks.[1] Hunger had visited Moscow and the cities of
northern Russia, cut off from their granaries. Lenin had decreed
wholesale nationalization of industry and called on the Committees of Poor Peasants to requisition food from wealthier
farmers in order to feed the urban workers. Several real risings
and several phantom conspiracies had been suppressed.

Never yet had any peace brought so much suffering and
humiliation as the 'peace' of Brest had brought to Russia. But
Lenin nursed his 'child'—the revolution—through all these
trials and disappointments. He would not renounce the treaty
of Brest, although in more than one respect he disregarded its
stipulations. He had not ceased to call on the German and
Austrian workers to rise in revolt. He had, despite the clause
about Russia's disarmament, authorized the formation of the
Red Army. But in no circumstances did he permit his followers
to rise in arms against Germany. He had recalled to Moscow
the Bolsheviks who had directed the Ukrainian Soviets and who
had been tempted to strike from the underground at the
occupying power.[2] All over the Ukraine, the German war
machine crushed anti-German guerillas. Russian Red Guards

---

[1] Denikin, *Ocherki Russkoi Smuty*, vol. iii, pp. 72–90.
[2] Antonov-Ovseenko, *Zapiski o Grazhdanskoi Voinie*, vol. i, pp. 294–5.

watched their agony from across the frontier and yearned to go
to their rescue; but Lenin held the Red Guards unyieldingly
in check.

Trotsky had long since given up his opposition to the peace.
He had accepted the party's final decision and its consequences.
Cabinet solidarity and party discipline alike obliged him to
stand by Lenin's policy. He did so with complete loyalty and
devotion, although he must have paid for that loyalty with many
an inner conflict and many moments of acute anguish. The
Bolshevik war faction, leaderless and confused, had lapsed into
silence. All the more loudly and impatiently did the Left Social
Revolutionaries voice their opposition to the peace. In March,
immediately after the ratification, they had withdrawn from
the Council of the People's Commissars. They still sat in nearly
all departments of the government, including the *Cheka*, and in
the executive organs of the Soviets. But, exasperated by all that
had happened, they could not for long remain half in opposition
to the government and half responsible for it.

Such was the situation when the fifth Congress of the Soviets
assembled in Moscow at the beginning of July 1918. The Left
Social Revolutionaries resolved to bring matters to a head and
to break with the Bolsheviks. The outcry against the peace went
up once more. Delegates from the Ukraine mounted the platform to describe the desperate struggle of the Ukrainian guerillas
and to beg for help. The leaders of the Left Social Revolutionaries, Kamkov and Spiridonova, denounced the 'Bolshevik
betrayal' and clamoured for a war of liberation.

Both Kamkov and Spiridonova were great revolutionaries of
the old *Narodnik* type. They had fought bomb in hand against
Tsardom and had paid for their courage with many years of
solitary confinement and hard labour. They spoke with the
authority of heroes and martyrs rather than that of leaders and
politicians. They refused to weigh pros and cons. They demanded
from the victorious revolution the heroism and the martyrdom
to which they themselves had risen. The Bolsheviks as a body
were far removed from such unreasoning ardour. Yet Spiridonova's and Kamkov's appeals still struck a chord in many a
Bolshevik, and certainly in Trotsky. When, at the Congress,
Kamkov walked across the platform towards the diplomatic
box where Count Mirbach, the German Ambassador, was

listening to the debates and, pointing at the Ambassador, poured out his detestation of the Kaiser and of German imperialism, the Congress applauded his courage. At heart Trotsky must have done the same. Kamkov was, after all, only repeating what he himself had done at Brest; and from the lips of Kamkov and Spiridonova the echoes of his own voice seemed to come back to him. It was only a few months since he had publicly, solemnly, and confidently vowed that the Bolsheviks would defend the honour of the revolution 'to the last drop of blood', and expressed the hope that the Left Social Revolutionaries would do likewise. It was an even shorter time since he had begged his comrades rather to declare that they had come before their time and go under in unequal struggle than wash their hands of the fate of the Ukraine. He had in the meantime followed Lenin, hoping that this might be the way to save the revolution. But at heart he could not condemn those who did not do so.

He was therefore acting a grimly paradoxical part when, on 4 July, he asked the Congress to authorize an emergency order which, as Commissar of War, he was about to issue.[1] The order was designed to impose severe discipline on Russian partisan detachments which threatened to disrupt the peace by self-willed attacks on German troops. The text ran as follows: 'These are my orders: all agitators who, after the publication of this order, continue to urge insubordination to the Soviet government are to be arrested, brought to Moscow, and tried by the Extraordinary Tribunal. All agents of foreign imperialism who call for offensive action [against Germany] and offer armed resistance to Soviet authorities are to be shot.'

He argued the need for this order with perfect logic. He was not going to discuss, he said, which was the right policy: peace or war. On this the previous Congress of Soviets, constitutionally the supreme authority in the state, had spoken the last word. What he was arguing was that nobody had the right to arrogate to himself the functions of the government and take war into his own hands. The agitation against peace, conducted among Red Guards and partisans, had assumed dangerous forms. Commissars who had stood for peace had been assassinated; commissions of inquiry sent from Moscow had been fired

[1] Trotsky, *Kak Vooruzhalas Revolutsia*, vol. i, pp. 266–74.

at; his friend Rakovsky, who at one time headed the delegation negotiating with the *Rada*, had been threatened with bombs. 'You understand, comrades, that there can be no joking in such matters. As the person at present responsible for the conduct of the Red Army. . . .'

At this moment, Kamkov interrupted him with the cry: 'Kerensky!' 'You think yourself the new Napoleon', another Left Social Revolutionary shouted. 'Kerensky!' Trotsky replied, 'Kerensky obeyed the bourgeois classes, and I here am responsible to you, representatives of Russian workers and peasants. If you pass censure upon me and adopt a different decision, one with which I may or may not agree, then, as a soldier of the revolution, I shall submit to your decision and carry it out.' He thus made it clear that he was acting in solidarity with the government of which he was a member rather than from fundamental disagreement with the opposition. But he also warned the opposition that at this stage the disruption of peace could only benefit either the Entente or the extreme German militarists who were not satisfied even with the Brest *Diktat*. Despite their bitter attacks on him, he still addressed the Left Social Revolutionaries with mild persuasiveness, not accusing them yet of any responsibility for incitement to war.[1] When Spiridonova scolded him for his 'militarist, Bonapartist style', he replied half-apologetically: 'I myself, comrades, am by no means a lover of military style. I have been accustomed to use the publicist's language, which I prefer to any other style. But every sort of activity has its consequences, even stylistic ones. As the People's Commissar of War who has to stop hooligans shooting our representatives, I am not a publicist, and I cannot express myself in that lyrical tone in which comrade Spiridonova has spoken here.'

By now Spiridonova, too, had abandoned the 'lyrical tone'. The small, frail woman mounted the platform to accuse Lenin and Trotsky of treason and to threaten them. 'I shall grasp in my hand the revolver and the bomb, as I once used to do', she exclaimed. This was advance notice of an insurrection which

---

[1] Only towards the end of the debate did Trotsky accuse the Left Social Revolutionaries, but even then he made it clear that his accusations were directed against individuals, not against the party as a whole. In truth, the party as a whole was engaged in a desperate attempt to disrupt the peace. Op. cit., p. 275.

was only two days off. Sadoul has left a graphic description of the scene and of the different ways in which Lenin and Trotsky reacted to the threat:

Lenin rises. His strange, faun-like face is, as always, calm and mocking. He has not ceased and will not cease to laugh under the insults, attacks, and direct threats showered upon him. In these tragic circumstances, when he knows what is at stake, his work, his idea, his life, this vast laughter, broad and sincere, which some find out of place, gives me the impression of extraordinary strength. Every now and then . . . a sharper affront just for a second manages to freeze this laughter, which is so insulting and exasperating to the adversary. . . .

By Lenin's side, Trotsky, too, tries to laugh. But anger, emotion, agitation change his laughter into a painful grimace. Then his animated, expressive face becomes extinguished . . . and disappears under a Mephistophelian, terrifying mask. He does not have the master's sovereign will, his cool head, his absolute self-control. Yet he is . . . less implacable.[1]

It was, of course, easier for Lenin so self-confidently to face his opponents: he had all the time been firmly convinced that peace was the revolution's only salvation. The contortion of Trotsky's face reflected the conflict in his mind.

These tumultuous debates were interrupted on 6 July by the assassination of Count Mirbach, the German Ambassador. The assassins, two Left Social Revolutionaries, high officials of the *Cheka*, Blumkin and Andreev, acted on Spiridonova's order, hoping to provoke war between Germany and Russia.[2] Immediately afterwards the Left Social Revolutionaries staged their insurrection against the Bolsheviks. They succeeded in arresting Dzerzhinsky and other chiefs of the *Cheka*, who had gone without any guard to the insurgents' headquarters; and they occupied the Posts and Telegraphs and announced to the country the overthrow of Lenin's government. But they had no

---

[1] Sadoul, *Notes sur la révolution Russe*, p. 396.

[2] Blumkin later repented his deed, joined the Bolshevik party, won distinction in the civil war, and rejoined the *Cheka*. In the 1920s he was in sympathy with the Trotskyist opposition, but, on Trotsky's advice, continued to serve with the G.P.U. When Trotsky was an exile on Prinkipo Island, Blumkin secretly visited him there and returned to Moscow with a message from Trotsky to the opposition. Before he managed to deliver the message, however, he was arrested and shot. (*The Trotsky Archives*, Harvard.)

leadership and no plan of action; and after two days of skir-
mishing they surrendered.

On 9 July the Congress of the Soviets reassembled and Trotsky
reported the suppression of the rising. He said that the government had been surprised by the attack. It had denuded the
capital of the few reliable detachments it had possessed, sending
them to fight against the Czechoslovak Legion in the east. For
its own security the government had relied mainly on that same
Red Guard, consisting of Left Social Revolutionaries, which
staged the rising. All that Trotsky could oppose to the insurgents
was a Latvian rifle regiment commanded by Vatzetis, a former
Colonel of the General Staff, who was presently to become
Commander-in-Chief of the Red Army; and a detachment of
revolutionized Austro-Hungarian prisoners of war, led by Bela
Kun, the future founder of the Communist party of Hungary.
But the rising had an almost farcical character, from the
military if not from the political viewpoint. The insurgents were
a band of brave but undisciplined partisans. They failed to
co-ordinate their attacks; and eventually they yielded more to
Bolshevik persuasion than to force. Trotsky, who was just then
disciplining the Red Guards and guerillas into a centralized
Red Army, used the rising as an object lesson demonstrating
the correctness of his military policy. Even now he spoke of the
insurgents half-pityingly saying that he and others had defended
them in the government as 'children who had run amok'; but
he added that there could be 'no room for such children'.[1] The
leaders of the rising were arrested; but they were amnestied a
few months later. Only some of those who had abused positions
of trust inside the *Cheka* were executed.

Thus, with Trotsky hurling back the stubborn echo of his
own passionate protests against the peace, ended the great controversy over Brest Litovsk.

[1] Trotsky, *Kak Vooruzhalas Revolutsia*, vol. i, pp. 276 ff.

CHAPTER XII

Arming the Republic

'WAR is an instrument of Policy; it must necessarily bear its character, it must measure with its scale: the conduct of War, in its great features, is therefore Policy itself, which takes up the sword in place of the pen, but does not on that account cease to think according to its own laws.' This Clausewitzian phrase described war between nations, in which the identity of strategy and politics is often obscured and far from obvious. In civil war it is direct and undisguised. It is the laws of politics that dominate every phase, dictate to the belligerents nine-tenths of their moves, and produce the final verdict on the battlefields. When in the middle of March 1918 Trotsky was appointed Commissar of War and President of the Supreme War Council, he did not even put down his pen to take up his sword—he used both.

He undertook to conjure an army out of an apparent void. The armed forces of the old régime had vanished. On the Don and in the Northern Caucasus a few pro-Bolshevik detachments of the old army still confronted the first White Guards. But they too were militarily so worthless that the government preferred to disband them rather than try to salvage them for the new army: so strong was its fear that the remnants of the old army might infect the new with anarchic vices. Thus the once gigantic military power was completely scrapped; all that survived of it and was still battleworthy was a single division of Latvian riflemen, commanded by Colonel Vatzetis. Apart from this there were the workers' Red Guards and bands of partisans inspired by enthusiasm and sometimes not lacking self-discipline, but with little or no training or organization. Their numbers were far from impressive. In October 1917 the Red Guards of Petrograd had no more than 4,000 and those of Moscow no more than 3,000 fully trained and armed members.[1] Since October their numerical strength had not grown appreciably. From such slender beginnings sprang into being the Red Army which, after two and a half years, had five million men under arms.

[1] *Pyat Let Vlasti Sovietov*, pp. 154–5.

Numbers alone give only a faint idea of the difficulties. The greatest obstacles were moral and political. When he set out to found the Red Army, Trotsky seemed to be burning all that he had worshipped and worshipping all that he had burned. The Bolsheviks had denounced militarism and encouraged the soldier to revolt against discipline and to see in the officer his enemy. They had done this not from enmity towards the army as such, but because they had seen in that army the tool of hostile interests. So overwhelmingly successful had their agitation been that it rebounded upon them. They were therefore compelled to break down the frame of mind which they themselves had built up before they could create the army which was a condition of their self-preservation. The popular mood was compounded of various strains: pacifist abhorrence of war; conviction that the revolution could rely on Red Guards and partisans and needed no regular army; and belief that it was the inalienable right of soldiers to elect their commanders and soldiers' committees. When Trotsky first came forward to say that soldiers' committees could not lead regiments into battle and that an army needed centralization and formal discipline, his words sounded like a profanation of a revolutionary taboo.

Moreover, all the machinery of government had broken down so completely that the attempt to create a new army seemed hopelessly unreal. Trotsky took over his department from an ineffective Collegium of three Commissars—Podvoysky, Antonov-Ovseenko, and Dybenko. Since November he had nominally headed the 'All-Russian Collegium for the Administration of the War Department Affairs'; but the Brest crisis had prevented him from giving much attention to this office. This Collegium prepared the decree of 15 January 1918 about the creation of an army of volunteers. Like most laws and ordinances of this period, this too was a statement of principle, on which the government was as yet unable to act. There were no administrative agencies to recruit the men, to put them into barracks, to clothe and feed them. There were no officers and sergeants to train the recruits. Only in April, a month after he had assumed his new office, did Trotsky begin to form regional and local offices of his Commissariat, i.e. recruiting centres; but still there was a gulf between decree and execution. All that had been achieved five months after the October insurrection was that in a few cities several hundred members of the Red Guards had begun to train for positions of command.

The first pronouncements which Trotsky made in his new office contained the main elements of his military policy.[1] He appealed primarily to the members of the party and of the Soviets: only with their support could he hope to carry out his task. He impressed upon them the need for the revolution to pass from its first, destructive, to its next, constructive, phase; and his text was: 'Work, Discipline, and Order will save the Soviet Republic.' It was in the military field that the transition had to be made first, for on it depended the revolution's survival. He did not opportunistically decry the first destructive phase, which, he said, had brought 'the great awakening of the personality in Russia'. Therein lay the historical significance and greatness of the first phase of the revolution. But the 'awakened personality', reacting against its former suppression, revealed its self-centred and anti-social features: 'Yesterday the man of the mass was still a nobody, a slave of the Tsar, of the gentry, of the bureaucracy, an appendage to the ... machine ... a beast of burden. ... Having freed himself, he is now most acutely aware of his own identity and begins to think of himself as of ... the centre of the world.'[2] It was the party's duty to inure the awakened personality to a new, conscious social discipline. For this the party itself must overcome its own anti-militarist bias: too many of its members still viewed any army as an instrument of counter-revolution. It was not yet the immediate task to create a fully fledged army; it was rather to gather a nucleus for it. The government decreed universal obligatory military training, in principle; but only volunteers would be immediately drafted and trained. The party must also overcome the crude bias in favour of elected commanders and soldiers' committees, for these were not of the essence of revolutionary democracy. The democratic principle required that the government should be elected and controlled by the masses, not that the masses should arrogate its functions and deprive it of the powers of appointment. The Red Army must use the services of the former Tsarist officers. In matters of defence, courage, revolutionary

---

[1] See his speech of 19 March to the Moscow Soviet, his statement of 21 March, and his speech of 28 March at the Moscow conference of the party. *Kak Vooruzhalas Revolutsia*, vol. i.   [2] Ibid., p. 39.

enthusiasm, and readiness for sacrifice were not enough. 'As industry needs engineers, as farming needs qualified agronomists, so military specialists are indispensable to defence.'[1]

While those who had made the revolution were utterly reluctant to take orders from the generals and colonels of the old régime, the generals and colonels were not less reluctant to place their skill and experience at the disposal of the Bolsheviks. There were only a few exceptions. The first military man of stature who volunteered for service was General Bonch-Bruevich, former commander of the northern front, who was won over by his brother, a well-known Bolshevik writer. Trotsky entrusted the general with organizing the General Staff, a task which had been quite beyond the ensign Krylenko, the Commander-in-Chief appointed in the first days of the revolution. But very few officers followed Bonch-Bruevich. Those who did so approached their task with all the mental habits of the regular soldier, accustomed to work within the rigid and well-ordered framework of a normal army and ill at ease in the climate of revolution. Radek describes Trotsky's first conferences with these officers in April 1918. In the course of many days the officers put forward and discussed their ideas, while Trotsky listened in silence. All sorts of schemes for galvanizing the old army were advanced; and none took account of the recent psychological upheavals. Then Trotsky outlined his scheme for recruiting volunteers. The only answer he obtained was an embarrassed silence and a shrugging of shoulders. The officers attributed the collapse of the old army to lack of discipline, and they were sure that there would be no discipline in an army of volunteers. Trotsky's project struck them as the fancy of a revolutionary dilettante.[2]

But in Trotsky's scheme of things politics dictated the military course of action. He had to enlist the enthusiasts of the revolution first, for only they would serve with complete self-discipline and could be counted upon later to impose discipline upon others. Even the drafting of volunteers was no easy matter. Adventurers and pot-hunters flocked to the recruiting centres, and they had to be carefully eliminated. Only in the late summer of 1918 did Trotsky proceed to experiment with conscription; he called up a small number of industrial workers in

---

[1] *Kak Vooruzhalas Revolutsia*, vol. i., p. 29.　[2] K. Radek, *Portrety i Pamflety*, pp. 31–32.

Petrograd and Moscow. When the first 10,000 workers had been drafted, this was hailed as a feat. Gradually more were recruited although, as conscription widened, the workers' reluctance to enrol began to show itself. But persuasion and appeals to class solidarity were, for the most part, effective. Only when the proletarian core of the army had been firmly established, did Trotsky begin to call up the peasants, first the poor and then the *serednyaks* (the middle peasants). These often deserted *en masse* and their morale fluctuated violently with the ups and downs of the civil war.[1]

As armies were lost and raised periodically with the frequent and sudden contraction and expansion of Soviet-held territory, the process had to be repeated in various provinces at different times. Until very late in the civil war, the Red Army had therefore little uniform outlook. Various stages in its organization constantly overlapped. Hardened and well-disciplined divisions fought side by side with units which were little better than a half-armed rabble. This increased the instability and nervousness peculiar to a revolutionary army, formed amid universal unsettlement. If, in spite of this, and in spite of a chronic shortage of munitions, uniforms, and boots, and also in spite of hunger and epidemics, the Red Army stood the test, this was due to the fact that it was set up in a number of concentric and gradually widening rings, each from a different social stratum and each representing a different degree of loyalty to the revolution. In every division and regiment the inner core of Bolsheviks carried with it the proletarian elements, and through them also the doubtful and shaky peasant mass.

On 22 April 1918 Trotsky laid his scheme before the Central Executive of the Soviets.[2] When he came to his point about the

---

[1] The *kulaks* were, like the urban bourgeoisie, drafted only for auxiliary services and labour detachments. Conscientious objectors, who refused service on religious grounds, were granted exemption.

[2] The decree which Trotsky laid before the Executive began as follows: 'Socialism has as one of its basic tasks to free mankind from militarism and from the barbarism of bloody contests between peoples. The goal of socialism is general disarmament, permanent peace, and fraternal co-operation of all the peoples inhabiting the earth.' *Kak Vooruzhalas Revolutsia*, vol. i, pp. 123-4. On this occasion the Executive also approved the text of the Red Army oath written by Trotsky:

'I, a son of the toiling people and a citizen of the Soviet Republic, assume the title of a soldier of the Workers' and Peasants' Army.

'Before the working classes of Russia and of the whole world I undertake to bear this title with honour, to learn conscientiously to wield arms. . . .

employment of officers, the Mensheviks raised an outcry. 'Thus the Napoleons make their appearance!' Dan exclaimed. Martov accused Trotsky of paving the way for a new Kornilov. These charges carried little conviction when they came from a party which had all but delivered the revolution to Kornilov.[1] More serious were the objections of the Left Social Revolutionaries, to whom this was no mere debating point. But the most persistent and influential opposition arose within the Bolshevik party itself. This opposition was actuated by the most diverse motives. Most of the Left Communists, who had opposed the peace of Brest, repudiated Trotsky's policy in the name of the revolution's libertarian spirit. They refused to countenance a centralized standing army, let alone one officered by Tsarist generals and colonels. Led by I. N. Smirnov, Bukharin, Pyatakov, and Bubnov, the Left Communists came out against Trotsky as frankly and bitterly as they had come out against Lenin in the controversy over Brest; they saw in their present opposition a continuation of their previous struggle: they refused to accept any compromise with forces of the old régime, whether in foreign or in domestic policy.

The other element in the opposition was formed by men who belonged to the inner Bolshevik hierarchy. As a rule these men stood for centralized authority and strict discipline and they viewed the Left Communists as irresponsible trouble-makers. They were not fundamentally opposed to Trotsky's idea of the new army; but they viewed with suspicion his solicitations of the former officers' corps. They suspected, not quite without reason, that the officers would enlist in order to betray the Red Army from within; and some were jealous for newly-acquired positions of power which they were now being asked to share in the

'I undertake to observe revolutionary discipline strictly and unflaggingly. . . .

'I undertake to abstain and to restrain other comrades from deeds which might harm and lower the dignity of a citizen of the Soviet Republic, and to direct all my actions and thoughts towards the great goal of the emancipation of all working people.

'I undertake to come forward on the first call of the Workers' and Peasants' Government to defend the Soviet Republic . . . in the struggle for the Russian Soviet Republic and for the cause of socialism and of the brotherhood of the peoples I shall spare neither my own strength nor my own life.

'If by evil design I should depart from this my solemn promise, let general contempt be my lot and let the severe hand of the revolutionary law punish me.' Ibid., p. 125.   [1] Ibid., p. 117.

army with erstwhile enemies. The jealousy and the suspicion were blended into a strong sentiment, which found expression in the Central Committee of the party. Even those Bolsheviks who agreed that the officers should be employed did so with strong mental reservations; and every now and then they gave vent to suppressed feeling. They opposed Trotsky's policy deviously, attacking it not in principle but in detail and execution.

These two trends of opposition overlapped and formed an ambiguous alliance. They enlisted the support of the commissars and commanders of the Red Guards and partisan groups, ordinary workers and non-commissioned officers, who had distinguished themselves in the first weeks of the upheaval, were surrounded by a halo of heroism, and bitterly resented subordination to Tsarist generals or any other military authority.

Implied in the immediate issue was a wider question concerning the attitude of the new state towards the positive values of the pre-revolutionary civilization and towards the intelligentsia which represented the sum total of the ideas, knowledge, and higher skills bequeathed by the old order. In the military field this question was most acute; but it was of vital significance to every aspect of Soviet life. Among Bolsheviks and ordinary workers there was an intense dislike of the professional men who had enjoyed freedom and privileges while the revolutionaries had spent their best years in banishment and prison. They were stunned when they were told that the revolution should restore the Tsar's 'flunkeys' and the 'bourgeois philistines' to respectability and influence. Yet this was what the revolution was beginning to do, because it could not wreak vengeance upon the intelligentsia without shattering the basis of its own future. Without its doctors, scientists, research workers, and technicians, of which it had none too many, and without its writers and artists, the nation would have sunk finally to the level of primitive barbarism, to which it was anyhow dangerously close. The disputes over the 'specialists' were therefore implicitly a struggle over the level of civilization from which the 'building of socialism' was to begin. Trotsky repeatedly posed the issue in this wider context, and not merely as a matter of military expediency. He argued that the 'cultural heritage' of which the revolution had taken possession must be saved, cultivated, and developed; and as long as the revolution had to defend itself,

military skill and knowledge must be considered as part of that
heritage. His exhortations to this effect make up many pages in
the volumes of his military writings and they belong to the
cultural as well as to the military history of the Soviet régime.

The combination of the groups opposed to Trotsky's policy
was all the more formidable as Lenin for a long time reserved
judgement on the employment of the officers, although he himself most emphatically insisted on a considerate and tactful
treatment of the civilian 'specialists'. The military branch of the
party, on whose co-operation so much depended, was firmly
against Trotsky's policy. The conflict came into the open when
Lashevich, the leader of that branch, a member of the Central
Committee and Zinoviev's close friend, publicly boasted that
the party would use the old generals only to 'squeeze them like
lemons and then throw them away'. Zinoviev spoke in the
same manner, as if setting out to wound the officers' self-respect
and to obstruct Trotsky's attempts to enlist them.[1] A General
Novitsky who had of his own accord declared his readiness to
serve under the Bolsheviks wrote an open letter to Trotsky, in
which he refused co-operation, saying that he had no desire to
be 'squeezed and thrown away like a lemon'. Trotsky countered
this with an emphatic repudiation of the attacks on the officers:
'Those former generals', he wrote, 'who work conscientiously
in the present difficult conditions, deserve, even if they are of
a conservative outlook, infinitely more respect from the working
class than pseudo-socialists who engage in intrigue. . . .'[2]

Trotsky was not merely anxious to reassure the officers. He
was sincerely indignant about Zinoviev's and Lashevich's crude
and offensive language. Even after the civil war, when the need
to employ the old officers was less pressing, he continued to
demand that they should be treated with consideration. He
held that they should be employed even after a new officers'
corps had been raised up, because no civilized and rationally
governed society can waste men of skill, knowledge, and merit.
He also spoke from his own faith in the moral greatness of the
revolution by which even men of conservative upbringing must

[1] A. F. Ilin-Zhenevskii, *Bolsheviki u Vlasti*, pp. 87–89.
[2] Trotsky, *Kak Vooruzhalas Revolutsia*, vol. i, p. 135; Ilin-Zhenevskii, op. cit., pp.
89–90. Trotsky's words were ostensibly directed against the non-Bolshevik opposition, but they actually aimed at Zinoviev and Lashevich. He explicitly repudiated
the talk about 'squeezing them like a lemon'.

be impressed; and he bitterly reproached with pusillanimity those Bolsheviks who thought that once a man had been a Tsarist officer he must for ever remain insensitive to the appeal of socialism.

He himself strove to impress upon the officers the moral grandeur of the revolution, obscured by its miseries. Some of his pleadings with the officers therefore belong among the most stirring apologias for the revolution. This, for instance, is a passage from an inaugural address he gave at the Military Academy in 1918. The address was devoted largely to the Academy's curriculum, but it also contained words the like of which had hardly ever resounded within the walls of a Military Academy:

People unaccustomed to the revolution and its psychology . . . may, of course, view with some horror . . . that riotous, self-willed, and violent anarchy which appeared on the surface of revolutionary events. Yet in that riotous anarchy, even in its most negative manifestations, when the soldier, the slave of yesterday, all of a sudden found himself in a first-class railway carriage and tore off the velvet upholstery to make puttees for himself, even in such a destructive act there manifested itself the awakening of the personality. The ill-treated, down-trodden Russian peasant, accustomed to be slapped in the face and abused with the worst curses, all of a sudden found himself, perhaps for the first time in his life, in a first-class carriage; he saw the velvet upholstery; in his own boots he had stinking rags; he tore off the velvet, saying that he, too, had the right to something good. After two or three days, after a month, after a year—no, after a month, he has understood the ugliness of his behaviour. But his awakened personality . . . the human personality will remain alive in him for ever. Our task is to adjust this personality to the community, to induce it to feel itself not a number, not a slave, as it had felt before, and not merely an Ivanov or a Petrov, but Ivanov the Personality.[1]

Supremely self-confident in his own intellectual power, Trotsky often castigated the generals he had enlisted for their attachment to routine, narrowness, and sometimes ignorance. For all his insistence on the need to employ the old officers, he showed the utmost vigour and initiative in educating former N.C.O.s and ordinary workers into a new officers' corps. He appealed to the N.C.O.s as the future 'unbreakable cadre of the

[1] Trotsky, op. cit., p. 165.

officers' corps of the Soviet Republic', telling them that in the Russian Revolution as in the French, it was they who carried the marshal's batons in their knapsacks.[1] By the end of the civil war, the 'Tsarist' officers made up only one-third of the commanding staffs—two-thirds had been promoted from the ranks; and among those so promoted were many of the future marshals of the Second World War. But in 1918 more than three-quarters of the commanding and administrative staffs of the Red Army consisted of officers of the old régime; and in the highest commands the proportion was even greater.[2]

Among the officers there were, of course, traitors and would-be traitors. Some waited for an opportunity to join the White Guards; others deployed their troops so as to expose them to loss and defeat; still others passed important secrets to enemy headquarters. Soon after he became Commissar of War, Trotsky appeared as chief witness in the trial of Admiral Shchastny, whom he charged with sabotage. The admiral was condemned to death on the strength of Trotsky's deposition. The trial was designed to implant in the mind of the nascent army the idea, taken for granted in any established army, that certain actions must be regarded and punished as treason; and it was meant to intimidate the officers who were in sympathy with the White Guards. In civil war any penalty milder than death rarely has a deterrent effect. The fear of prison does not deter the would-be traitor, because he hopes in any case for the victory of the other side which will free him, honour him, and reward him; or he may hope at least for an amnesty after the end of the civil war. Trotsky's orders of the day bristled with dire threats to the agents of the White Guards. But even the threat of capital punishment was no grave deterrent to officers in the fighting lines. Trotsky then ordered that a register of their families be kept so that the would-be traitor should know that if he went over to the enemy, his wife and children would stay behind as hostages. This was a cruel measure, and Trotsky employed all his dramatic eloquence to make the threat as awe-inspiring as possible. He justified it on the ground that without it the revolution would be defeated and the classes that stood for the

[1] Trotsky, *Kak Vooruzhalas Revolutsia*, vol. i, pp. 174–85.
[2] Trotsky, *Stalin*, p. 279. See also *Voprosy Istorii*, no. 2, 1952; Yu. P. Petrov, 'Voennye Komissary.'

revolution be exposed to the vengeance of the White Guards. Amid the panics, the intense suspicions, and the violent passions of civil war, there were many innocent victims; and all too often Trotsky had to remind his over-zealous subordinates that the purpose of the terror was not to destroy potential enemies but to compel them to serve the revolutionary state.

He placed the commissar by the officer's side. For this, as for many other institutions, precedents could be found in the French Revolution, and Kerensky had already appointed commissars with the army. But hitherto the commissars had been attached only to the highest commands, and their role had been vague. Trotsky placed them at every level of the military ladder, from company commander to Commander-in-Chief. He also tried clearly to define the duties and responsibilities of commander and commissar. The former was responsible for military training and the conduct of operations, the latter for the commander's loyal behaviour and the morale of the troops.[1] No military order was valid unless it was signed by both. But no matter how clearly duties were assigned in theory, military authority was split. Rivalry and jealousy were inevitable. The officer resented the commissar's control; the commissar refused to reconcile himself to an arrangement which placed a colonel or a general under him politically and above him militarily. Trotsky tried to keep the balance between the two hierarchies. He sometimes appeared to the commissars as the protector of the officers and to the officers as the chief instigator of the commissars; and as he acted without regard for persons, he made many enemies. But he gained many devoted adherents among the officers, who were grateful to him for their rehabilitation, and also among the commissars, who held that the Red Army owed its political cohesion and power to his scheme. On the whole the system worked, though not without friction; and no alternative to it could be devised. Under the uncontrolled leadership of the former officers the Red Army would have collapsed politically. Under the command of Bolshevik dilettantes it would have been doomed on the battlefields. And nobody paid the effectiveness of this system a fuller, though reluctant, tribute than Denikin, its victim: 'The Soviet Govern-

---

[1] See the speech which Trotsky gave at the first congress of commissars in Moscow, in June 1918. *Kak Vooruzhalas Revolutsia*, vol. i, pp. 130 ff.

ment may be proud of the artfulness with which it has enslaved
the will and the brains of the Russian generals and officers and
made of them its unwilling but obedient tool. . . .'[1]

The task still to be accomplished was to centralize the Red
Army and to establish single command. Trotsky went on to
disband the Red Guards and the partisan detachments. The
incorporation of partisan units proved unsatisfactory, because
it infected the regular detachments with the 'guerilla spirit'.
In the end Trotsky demanded the complete disbandment of
partisan units and threatened with severe punishment commanders and commissars willing to incorporate such units. He
insisted on the organization of the entire army into uniformly
constituted divisions and regiments. This led to innumerable
conflicts with guerillas, especially with the anarchist partisan
army led by Makhno.[2] But even in divisions which were led by
Bolsheviks often only lip service was paid to centralization and
uniform organization. To many a Bolshevik the enforcement of
centralization was all the more odious when it entailed subordination to a 'Tsarist' general. The Left Communists continued
frankly to voice their opposition. A less open but all the more effective focus of the opposition was in the Tenth Army, which, under
Voroshilov's command, stood at Tsaritsyn, the future Stalingrad.

.   .   .   .

In the middle of 1918 the Soviet republic was still virtually
without an army. If foreign intervention had developed then
on its later scale, or if the White Guards had been ready, the
position of the Soviets would have been desperate. But the
course of events somehow favoured the Bolsheviks: it imparted
approximately the same rhythm and tempo to the efforts of both
camps to gather and marshal their armed strength. Like the
Red Army, the White Guards were only beginning to form.
The German advance was confined to the southern fringe, and
the troops of the Entente landed only at the remote outposts of

[1] Denikin, *Ocherki Russkoi Smuty*, vol. iii, p. 146.
[2] Several vain attempts were made to achieve reconciliation with Makhno's
partisans. In the course of one such attempt Trotsky publicly stated that the accusation that Makhno had collaborated with the White Guards was false, but he
emphatically denounced the conduct of Makhno's partisans on military and political
grounds. In the end, Budienny's cavalry dispersed and destroyed Makhno's detachments. See *Kak Vooruzhalas Revolutsia*, vol. ii, book 2, pp. 210–12, 216–17; and P.
Arschinoff, *Geschichte der Machno-Bewegung*.

Murmansk, Archangel, and Vladivostok. In central Russia the Bolsheviks consolidated their power in comparative safety. This circumstance accounted in part for the relatively slow progress they had so far made in the military field. It needed an imminent and mortal threat to speed up the process. That threat came suddenly from the Czechoslovak Legion, formed earlier in the war by prisoners of war eager to fight against Austro-Hungary.

Under the treaty of Brest the Soviet government was obliged to disarm the Legion. The disarming was carried out so reluctantly and perfunctorily that the Legion remained in possession of most of its arms. The British and the French at first proposed to evacuate the Legion from a Russian harbour; and to this the Soviet government agreed. Subsequently, however, the Entente failed to supply the ships and resolved to leave the Legion in Russia, where it might be used against either the Bolsheviks or the Germans, or against both. Trotsky guaranteed the Legion full security; and he offered its members the right to settle and work in Russia, if they so desired. While the Legion was aimlessly shifted across the Urals and Siberia, it was aroused by a rumour that the Bolsheviks were about to extradite it to the Germans. The Legion took up arms. In the military vacuum of Asian Russia, it rapidly occupied a vast area, overthrew the Soviets and made common cause with Kolchak's White Guards.[1]

When the Czechs seized Samara on the Volga, Trotsky ordered the first compulsory call-up of workers. From Moscow he hastily dispatched the conscripts against the Czechs. Most of them had had almost no preliminary training and were armed only *en route*. During the Czech advance the Left Social Revolutionaries rose against the Bolsheviks. The latter, we know, had at their disposal in Moscow only the Lettish troops commanded by Vatzetis and a detachment of revolutionized prisoners of war under Bela Kun. After the suppression of the rising in Moscow, the Lettish troops, too, were sent to fight the Czechs. The situation on the Volga was aggravated by the alleged treason of Muraviev, the colonel who had defeated

---

[1] '. . . I succeeded in securing Trotsky's good-will, and but for the folly of the French I am convinced that the Czechs would have been safely evacuated without incident', writes R. H. Bruce Lockhart, op. cit., pp. 272, 285.

Kerensky's attempt to recapture Petrograd, who had then distinguished himself fighting in the south and who had been appointed commander of the eastern front. Muraviev was, or claimed to be, in sympathy with the Left Social Revolutionaries; and the Bolsheviks accused him of collusion with the Czechs and Kolchak. According to one version, he committed suicide after he had been unmasked; according to another, he was executed. In the meantime the Czechs seized Ufa, Simbirsk, and Ekaterinburg.

In Ekaterinburg the Bolsheviks had kept in internment the Tsar and his family: they had intended to let a revolutionary tribunal try the Tsar, as Charles I and Louis XVI had been tried; and Trotsky had chosen for himself the role of the Tsar's Chief Prosecutor. But the advance of the Czechs and of Kolchak had so surprised the Bolsheviks on the spot that, so they claimed, they had no time to arrange for the safe evacuation of the Tsar and his family. They feared that the Tsar might be rescued by the Whites and rally all the forces of the counter-revolution, hitherto divided because of the lack of any unifying authority. Remembering perhaps Marat's dictum: 'Woe to the revolution which has not enough courage to behead the symbol of the *ancien régime*', the Bolsheviks, before their hasty withdrawal, executed the Tsar and his whole family. The official Bolshevik version claims that the execution was decided upon by the local Bolsheviks but approved after the event by Moscow. There are reasons to doubt the veracity of this version. It seems that the local Bolsheviks first asked the Politbureau for a decision, that Trotsky still counselled evacuation so that the Tsar might be placed in the dock; but that the Politbureau refused to take any risk and ordered the execution. Thus the world was deprived of the spectacle of a most dramatic trial, in which Trotsky and the Tsar would have faced each other.

The advance of the Czechs and of the White Guards continued. On 6 August the Red Army withdrew in panicky haste from Kazan, the last important town on the eastern bank of the upper Volga. If the Czechs succeeded in crossing the river at this point, they could surge across the open plain towards Moscow; and they would have found no obstacle in their way.

The Central Executive of the Soviets declared the Republic in danger. Trotsky ordered the first compulsory call-up of commissioned and non-commissioned officers, and stern measures against easy-going or privilege-seeking Communists in the army.[1] Two days after the fall of Kazan, he himself left for the front in the train which was to serve as his abode and mobile headquarters during two and a half years. In an order of the day issued before his departure, he wrote:

Leaving for the Czechoslovak front, I send my greetings to all those . . . who honestly and bravely defend the freedom and independence of the working class. . . .

Honour and glory to the valiant fighters!

At the same time I am issuing this warning: no quarter will be given to the enemies of the people, the agents of foreign imperialism, the mercenaries of the bourgeoisie. In the train of the People's Commissar for War, where this order is being written, a Military Revolutionary Tribunal is in session . . . [which] has unlimited powers within the zone of this railway line. A state of siege is proclaimed over this zone. Comrade Kamenshchikov, whom I have charged with the defence of the Moscow-Kazan line, has ordered concentration camps to be set up at Murom, Arzamas, and Svyazhsk. . . . I am warning responsible Soviet officials in all regions of military operation that we shall be doubly exacting towards them. The Soviet Republic will punish its sluggish and criminal servants no less severely than its enemies. . . . The Republic is in peril! Woe to those who directly or indirectly aggravate the peril.[2]

Trotsky arrived at Svyazhsk, a little town on the western bank of the Volga, opposite Kazan. This was the most advanced position of the Reds, after their retreat across the river. He found the front in a state of virtual collapse: mass desertion from the ranks, prostration among commanders and commissars. From his train, which stood within the reach of enemy fire, he descended into panic-stricken crowds of soldiers, poured out on them torrents of passionate eloquence, rallied them and, on occasion, personally led them back to the fighting line. At an especially critical moment, his own escort joined in the battle, leaving him almost alone on his train. The local commissars proposed that he should move to a safer place on a steamboat on the Volga; but fearing the effect this might have on the troops, he refused. On a ramshackle torpedo boat he went with

---

[1] Trotsky, *Kak Vooruzhalas Revolutsia*, vol. i, pp. 174–85.   [2] Ibid., p. 233.

sailors of Kronstadt, who had brought over a tiny flotilla to the Volga, on an adventurous night raid to Kazan. Most of the flotilla was destroyed but it managed to silence the enemy batteries on the banks of the river; and Trotsky returned safely to his base.

The forces engaged in this fighting were extremely small.[1] As at the opening of every civil war, so here the fortunes of a great revolution swayed on minute scales. In a battle of this sort the leader is constantly before the eyes of the men: his faith, his presence of mind, and his courage may work wonders. He has to establish his military authority also by personal example, which the leader of a normal army is rarely expected to give. In such a battle, on the other hand, the local commanders are constantly before his eyes; and the reputation which they gain on the spot helps them to undreamt-of promotion and fame. From Svyazhsk dated Trotsky's friendship for Vatzetis, whom he presently promoted to Commander-in-Chief of the Red Army. There, too, the young Tukhachevsky caught his eye. There the ties of comradeship with Raskolnikov, the commander of the Kronstadt sailors, and with the commissars I. N. Smirnov and Arkadi Rosengoltz grew close. At Svyazhsk he also conceived a high regard for V. Mezhlauk's organizing ability, and throughout the civil war he promoted Mezhlauk, who later became his enemy and vice-Premier under Stalin. These men— the veterans of the Fifth Army—remained close to Trotsky during the civil war; and they formed something like a counterpart to the Tsaritsyn group, whom Stalin befriended.

Lavish in praise for those who distinguished themselves by courage and talent, Trotsky dealt implacably with those who failed in their duties. He brought before a court martial the commander and the commissar of a regiment—the commissar's name was Panteleev—who at the height of the battle had taken themselves and their men away from the front line. Both the commander and the commissar were shot. 'The soldiers of the Red Army . . .', Trotsky commented on the event, 'are neither cowards nor scoundrels. They want to fight for the freedom of the working class. If they retreat or fight poorly, commanders

---

[1] Even after their victory, when their ranks grew considerably, the Reds numbered only 25,000 men. When Trotsky arrived their strength must have been much smaller.

and commissars are guilty. I issue this warning: if any detachment retreats without orders, the first to be shot will be the
commissar, the next the commander. . . . Cowards, scoundrels,
and traitors will not escape the bullet—for this I vouch before
the whole Red Army.'[1]

Trotsky's unpublished correspondence with Lenin shows what
meticulous attention he gave to the details of battle. In one
message he insistently demands reinforcements; in another he
asks that disciplined Communists 'ready to die' be sent to the
Volga—'light-weight agitators are not needed here'. In still
another message he asks for a supply of pistols and for a good
military band. Eager to appeal to the soldiers' imagination and
pride, he asked that the popular satirical poet Demian Bednyi
be sent to the front and that the government should establish
medals for bravery. The shyness which, after the abolition of all
medals, the Bolsheviks felt about this last proposal can be
guessed from the fact that Trotsky repeated it three times with
increasing impatience. The correspondence also reveals a curious
instance of Trotsky's ruthlessness. On 17 August Lenin communicated to him that the Red Cross, supported by the French
and American Consuls, asked for permission to transport food
from Nizhnii Novgorod, which was held by the Bolsheviks, to
Samara which was occupied by the Whites. Lenin saw no
objection to the expedition. But Trotsky refused to allow the
Red Cross to move across the fighting lines. 'Fools and charla-
tans', he answered Lenin, would start talking about the possibility of conciliation with the Whites. He did not, he added, wish
the Red Cross to witness the bombardment ('the burning and
the scorching') of the 'bourgeois quarters' of Kazan. Before the
bombardment, however, he issued a public warning to the working people of Kazan: 'Our artillerymen . . . will do their utmost
to avoid damaging the dwellings and living quarters of the poor.
But in a savage battle accidents may occur. We warn you about
the imminent danger. . . . Remove your children from the town
. . . seek refuge on Soviet territory—we offer fraternal hospitality to all toiling and needy people.'[2]

On 10 September the Reds stormed and seized Kazan. Two

[1] Trotsky, *Kak Vooruzhalas Revolutsia*, vol. i, p. 235.
[2] Ibid., p. 244: Lenin's message about the Red Cross was published in *Leninskii Sbornik*, vol. xviii, p. 186; Trotsky's answer is in *The Archives*.

days later Tukhachevsky captured Simbirsk and announced this
in a laconic message to Trotsky: 'Order carried out. Simbirsk
taken.' At the beginning of October the whole of the Volga
region was again under Soviet rule.

This victory had an electrifying effect, especially because it
coincided with a grave political crisis. In Moscow, a Social
Revolutionary, F. Kaplan, had just made an attempt on Lenin's
life. Another Social Revolutionary assassinated Uritsky in Petrograd. In retaliation, the Bolsheviks proclaimed the Red Terror
and ordered the shooting of hostages. During these events
Trotsky was recalled to Moscow. He found Lenin recovering
from his wound; and, having reassured Lenin and the Executive of the Soviets about the prospects of the campaign, he
returned to the front. About the same time the Right Social
Revolutionaries tried to reassemble the dispersed Constituent Assembly and to form a rival government at Samara,
under the protection of the Czechs and Kolchak. The Social
Revolutionaries wielded considerable influence among the
Volga peasants; and even a mere symbolic revival of the Constituent Assembly threatened to embarrass the Bolsheviks. By
recapturing the Volga region, the Red Army eliminated this
threat. The movement for the Constituante, cut off from its
peasant following, was reduced to impotence. The Social Revolutionaries found themselves at the mercy of Kolchak, who
presently proclaimed himself dictator ('Supreme Ruler'), dispersed the rump Assembly, executed some of its leaders, and
compelled others to seek refuge in Soviet territory. Thus the
adherents of the Assembly were crushed between the mill-
stones of the Soviets and the White Guards.[1]

Finally, the victory on the Volga gave a powerful stimulus to
the growth of the Red Army. Peril had shaken the Soviets from
complacent indolence; victory gave them confidence in their
own strength. The work of preliminary organization carried on
in the Commissariat of War began to yield results: commanding
staffs had been set up; recruiting centres were functioning; a
rough framework for an army was ready.

At the end of September Trotsky returned to Moscow and
reorganized the Supreme War Council into the Revolutionary
War Council of the Republic. The body had to decide on

[1] V. Tchernov, *Mes Tribulations en Russie.*

matters of military policy.[1] Under it were the Revolutionary War Councils of fourteen armies, each Council consisting of the commander of the army and two or three commissars. Trotsky himself presided over the War Council of the Republic. His deputy, who managed the Council's day-to-day work while Trotsky was inspecting the fronts, was E. M. Sklyansky. Trotsky himself paid generous tribute to the talents, energy, and industry of his deputy, describing him as the Carnot of the Russian Revolution. The histories of the civil war written during the Stalin era hardly ever mention Sklyansky, even though he had not been involved in the struggle between Trotsky and Stalin and died in 1925. But Lenin's published correspondence and, even more, the unpublished records leave no doubt about Sklyansky's crucial role in the conduct of military affairs. His was one of the extraordinary careers of the time. As a young graduate of the medical faculty of Kiev, he had been drafted before the revolution into the army as a doctor and soon became prominent in the clandestine military organization of the Bolsheviks. Trotsky met him only in the autumn of 1917; and he was so impressed by Sklyansky's 'great creative *élan* combined with concentrated attention to detail' that he appointed him as his deputy.[2]

The other members of the Council were Vatzetis, who had just been appointed Commander-in-Chief; I. N. Smirnov and A. Rosengoltz, the commissars who had served with Vatzetis on the Volga; Raskolnikov who commanded the Red flotilla at Kazan; and Muralov and Yureniev. Thus the victors of Kazan were now placed at the head of military affairs.

With their help Trotsky set out to overhaul and centralize the southern front. It was in the south that the White Guards now had their main strongholds. The strongest Bolshevik force in the south was Voroshilov's Tenth Army. But Voroshilov was refusing to overhaul his troops according to Trotsky's uniform pattern. The conflict had been brewing for some time. Stalin had spent most of the summer at Voroshilov's headquarters at Tsaritsyn and had lent his support to Voroshilov. Somewhat

---

[1] The Revolutionary War Council should not be confused with the Council of Workers' and Peasants' Defence (where Lenin presided, with Trotsky as his deputy), which co-ordinated military and civilian policies.

[2] Trotsky, *Sochinenya*, vol. viii, pp. 272–81.

later, in September, Stalin acted as chief political commissar to
the whole southern front; and there was constant friction between the front and headquarters in Moscow. Trotsky was resolved to put an end to this. At the beginning of October, he
appointed Sytin, a general of the old army, as commander of
the southern front; and he demanded subordination from
Voroshilov. He also appointed a new Revolutionary War
Council for the southern front, on which Shlyapnikov, a prominent Bolshevik, replaced Stalin as chief commissar. Trotsky
accompanied these appointments by a threat: 'Commanders
and commissars who dare to infringe on rules of discipline, will,
regardless of past merit, be immediately committed to trial
before the Revolutionary Military Tribunal of the southern
front.'[1] At the same time, Trotsky proposed the appointment of
Stalin to the War Council of the Republic, hoping either to
appease him or to tie his hands—Stalin had already repeatedly
protested to Lenin against Trotsky's handling of the southern
front.

Stalin returned to Moscow, and a superficial reconciliation
between the adversaries took place. But Voroshilov, confident
in Stalin's protection, continued to defy higher authority and
ignored the orders of the new commander. Soon afterwards
Stalin returned to Tsaritsyn. But as the conflict was getting
worse, Lenin diplomatically recalled him to Moscow, and
Trotsky set out to inspect the front. The story of Trotsky's visit
to Tsaritsyn has been described many times by Trotsky himself
and others. He threatened to court martial Voroshilov. In a
public order of the day, he castigated his command for putting
its own ambitions above the interests of the entire front.[2] Confronted with the threat, Voroshilov promised obedience; and
Trotsky took no further action, except that he placed a man
whom he trusted, Okulov, in the command of the Tenth Army
in order to keep Voroshilov in check.[3] He gave further publicity
to the conflict when, on the first anniversary of the revolution, he
reported on the military situation to a Congress of Soviets and
spared no black paint in depicting the condition of the Tenth

[1] Trotsky, *Kak Vooruzhalas Revolutsia*, vol. i, pp. 347–8.
[2] See Trotsky's order of the day dated Tsaritsyn, 5 November 1918, *Kak Vooruzhalas Revolutsia*, vol. i, pp. 250–1.
[3] Trotsky's message to Lenin of 14 December 1918 in *The Trotsky Archives*.

Army. The Tsaritsyn group did not forgive Trotsky this humiliation.[1]

Trotsky spent the rest of the autumn and the beginning of the
winter at the southern front. In the meantime, his opponents
in Moscow, especially Stalin and Zinoviev, worked against
him and tried, not without some success, to influence Lenin.
Trotsky later recounted that, while he was at the front, Menzhinsky, the future chief of the G.P.U., warned him about the
'intrigue'. Menzhinsky said that Stalin tried to persuade Lenin
that Trotsky was gathering around him elements hostile to
Lenin. Trotsky frankly put the question to Lenin; and he relates
that Lenin, embarrassed, did not deny the fact of the intrigue,
but assured Trotsky of his complete confidence in Trotsky's
loyalty. All the same, Lenin refused to become involved in the
quarrel and exerted himself to compose it. Some time later he
suggested that Okulov, the man whom Trotsky had left at
Tsaritsyn to keep an eye on Voroshilov, should be recalled.
Trotsky refused and this time brought matters to a head: he
asked that Voroshilov be deposed from his command and transferred to the Ukraine, and that new commissars should be
appointed to the Tenth Army. Lenin yielded, and Voroshilov
had to go.

The Tsaritsyn group sought to revenge itself. It whispered
that Trotsky was the friend of Tsarist generals and the persecu-
tor of Bolsheviks in the army. The accusation found its way into
the columns of *Pravda*, which was under Bukharin's editorship.
On 25 December 1918 *Pravda* published a scathing attack on
Trotsky by a member of Voroshilov's staff.[2] This coincided with
a new attempt of the Left Communists to achieve a revision of
military policy. Having failed in their opposition to the employment of officers, the Left Communists shifted their ground and
demanded that the commissars should hold all commanding
posts and that the officers should serve under them as mere
consultants. The whispering campaign against Trotsky became

---

[1] In the anniversary report, mainly devoted to argument against the critics of
centralization, Trotsky gave a deliberately exaggerated account of the Red Army's
strength, saying that *The Times* of London, which estimated the army's establishment at half a million men, greatly underrated it. In truth, the establishment was
still only 350,000 men. *Kak Vooruzhalas Revolutsia*, vol. i, pp. 332–41; *Pyat Let Vlasti
Sovietov*, p. 156.

[2] The article bore the title: 'It 's High Time!' and was signed by Kamensky.

even deadlier: it was said that he delivered Communists and commissars to the firing squad. The accusation was brought before the Politbureau and the Central Committee by Smilga and Lashevich, two members of the Committee, who held important political posts in the army. (Lashevich, it will be remembered, had been in conflict with Trotsky because of the speech about 'squeezing the officers like lemons'.) The cases of the commissar Panteleev, who had been court martialled and shot at Svyazhsk, and of two other commissars, Zalutsky and Bakaev, who were said to have narrowly escaped execution, were brought to the notice of the Central Committee.

Trotsky replied to these charges in a confidential letter to the Committee.[1] He made no apology for the shooting of Panteleev, who had been court martialled for plain desertion; but he added that as far as he knew this was the only case of the sort which had occurred. More recently there was a misunderstanding in connexion with his order that the commissars should keep a register of officers' families in order that officers should know that if they committed treason their relatives might be victimized. On one occasion several officers went over to the White Guards; and it turned out that the commissars had not bothered to keep a register of their families. Trotsky then wrote that Communists guilty of such neglect deserved to be shot. Smilga and Lashevich apparently thought that it was at them that Trotsky had aimed his threat. Trotsky explained that this was preposterous. Smilga and Lashevich knew that he valued them as the best commissars in the army. He had uttered the threat 'as a general remark', aimed at nobody in particular.

On internal evidence, Trotsky's explanation seems to be true. His opponents did not support their charges by any specific instances, except the case of Panteleev. Nevertheless, Trotsky's orders were full of such blood-curdling threats; and although he may have uttered them merely to discipline his subordinates, they blotted his reputation; and the charges connected with them were levelled against him by Stalin's followers long after the civil war.

Trotsky asked the Central Committee to define its attitude towards his military policy and to remonstrate with *Pravda* for

---

[1] The letter bears no date but from inner evidence it is clear that it was written towards the end of December 1918. It has not been published. *The Trotsky Archives.*

having printed the accusation without prior investigation. He himself replied in *Pravda* with an attack on 'conceited, semi-educated party quacks', who spread distrust and hostility towards the officers. 'The general public knows almost every case of treason . . . but even in narrower party circles all too little is known about those professional officers who have honestly and willingly given their lives for the cause of the Russia of workers and peasants.'[1] The public should, of course, be informed about the instances of treason; but it should also know how often entire regiments perished because they were commanded by amateurs incapable of understanding an order or reading a map. He firmly rejected the new proposals that the officers should be mere consultants to the commissars. The idea was militarily worthless; and it was 'calculated to satisfy vindictive cravings'. The purpose of the Red Terror was not to exterminate or to degrade the intelligentsia, but at the most to intimidate it and so to induce it to serve the workers' state.

He took up this subject in a 'Letter to a Friend', which appeared in *Voennoe Delo (Military Affairs)* in February 1919.[2] The letter reveals the bitterness of the controversy. He wrote with scorn about the 'new Soviet bureaucrat', 'trembling over his job', who looked with envy and hatred at anybody superior to him in education or skill. Unwilling to learn, he would never see the cause of his failings in himself, but was always on the look-out for a scapegoat, and always ready to cry treason. Conservative, sluggish, and resenting any reminder that he ought to learn, this bureaucrat was already a baleful 'ballast' in the new state. 'This is the genuine menace to the cause of communist revolution. These are the genuine accomplices of counter-revolution, even though they are not guilty of any conspiracy.' The revolution would be an absurdity if its only result were to be that a few thousand workers should get government jobs and become rulers. 'Our revolution will fully justify itself only when every toiling man and woman feels that his or her life has become easier, freer, cleaner, and more dignified. This has not yet been achieved. A difficult road lies between us and this our essential and only goal.'[2]

This in a nutshell is the *leitmotif* of Trotsky's later struggle

[1] *Pravda*, 31 December 1918; *Kak Vooruzhalas Revolutsia*, vol. i, pp. 154–61.
[2] Trotsky, op. cit., vol. i, pp. 170–2.

against Stalin; and it first appears as early as one year after the October insurrection.

. . . .

In November 1918 the Austro-Hungarian and German empires crumbled under the impact of defeat and revolution. The treaty of Brest was annulled. The armies of the central powers withdrew from Russia and the Ukraine, leaving a military vacuum. Into this vacuum Trotsky was anxious to move the Red Army. But the bulk of the army was tied down by Kolchak in the Urals and by Denikin and Krasnov in southern Russia and on the Don. On the western and south-western fronts the situation was much the same as it had been on other fronts shortly after the revolution: the Bolsheviks there could rely only on Red Guards and partisan units. Even these were desperately short of ammunition; their guns rusted because lubricants could not be obtained; and their horses died for lack of fodder. The railways carried military transport at only a mile an hour. The rigours of the Bolshevik rural policy—the requisitioning of food—adversely affected the temper of the troops.[1]

In such circumstances Lenin was not very anxious to press on with the occupation of the Ukraine. He attached more importance to clearing the Don and the northern Caucasus of anti-Bolshevik forces. Trotsky was inclined to give priority to the occupation of the Ukraine. He expected allied expeditionary forces to land on the coast of the Black Sea; and, by bringing the Ukraine under Soviet control, he wanted to keep them as far from Moscow as possible. In the meantime, Kolchak's Guards had struck once again and seized Ufa and Perm. Fearing that Kolchak, Denikin, and Krasnov might effect a juncture on the Volga, Lenin warned Trotsky not to allow himself 'to be carried away' by his Ukrainian plans at the expense of other fronts. Soon, however, Kolchak's advance was stopped; and the danger which was uppermost in Lenin's mind did not arise. On the other hand, the French landed at Odessa and Nikolaev, as Trotsky had feared. The Bolshevik guerrillas in the Ukraine proved, after all, strong enough to defeat Petlura, to seize

---

[1] This description is based on the messages exchanged between Lenin and Trotsky in November, December, and January. Throughout this time Trotsky alarmed Moscow about the conditions prevailing in the Ukraine, and he urged an easing of the party's policy towards the peasants. *The Trotsky Archives.*

Kharkov, and to carry the revolution into most of the country. But in the meantime Denikin was gathering strength in the steppe of the northern Caucasus.

With the beginning of the winter a lull set in in the fighting; and for a moment it seemed that the lull might end in a formal armistice. The French intervention was collapsing. Stirred by Bolshevik agitation, the French garrison of Odessa revolted; and some time afterwards the whole French expeditionary force was withdrawn from Russia, to the disappointment of the White Guards. But Clemenceau and Foch did not give up the policy of intervention. In opposition to them, President Wilson proposed an armistice between the warring Russian parties and governments and a conference on Prinkipo Island. The Soviet government accepted the proposal. On 24 January 1919 Lenin cabled Trotsky: 'I am sorry but you will have to go to Wilson.'[1] He urged Trotsky to seize a few more cities so as to strengthen his bargaining position at the Prinkipo conference, which indicates that he seriously contemplated the armistice. Trotsky agreed to speed up military operations, but refused the diplomatic assignment, perhaps because of the still fresh and bitter aftertaste of Brest; and he proposed that Chicherin and Rakovsky be sent. The incident had no sequel. The chiefs of the White Guards, encouraged by the French, refused to meet the Bolsheviks, and so President Wilson's attempt at mediation foundered.

The new campaigning season was approaching, but even now, a year after Trotsky had become Commissar of War, his military policy had not yet received the party's blessing—he carried it out as if on his own responsibility. His opponents feverishly prepared to challenge his policy at the forthcoming eighth congress of the party, convened for March. Lenin stood at least as firmly as Trotsky for centralization and strict discipline, but he had not yet made up his mind on the employment of officers. Treason occurred all too frequently; and the opposition made the most of it. Shortly before the congress Lenin suggested to Trotsky the wholesale dismissal of the officers and the appointment of Lashevich, who had been a sergeant in the Tsarist army, as Commander-in-Chief. He was intensely surprised when Trotsky told him that more than 30,000 officers were already serving with the Red Army. Only now did Lenin realize the

[1] *The Trotsky Archives.*

magnitude of the problem and admit that, in comparison with
the number of the officers employed, the instances of treason were
few. He agreed at last that it was impossible to dismiss the
officers; and he publicly spoke with admiration of the originality with which Trotsky was 'building communism' with the
bricks left over from the destroyed edifice of the old order.[1]

Assured of Lenin's support, Trotsky confidently looked forward to the debate. The opposition marshalled its adherents
in the army and brought to the congress as many of them as
could be elected. However, before the congress opened, Kolchak
launched a new full-scale offensive. Once again the eastern
front was convulsed. It seemed preposterous that at such a
moment the head of the War Department should waste time
defending his policy in prolonged debate, and that hosts of
commissars should leave the fighting line to attend the congress.
The Central Committee therefore decided that Trotsky should
at once leave for the eastern front and that the military delegates should return to the front. The opposition protested,
saying that Trotsky was using the emergency to silence its
adherents and to evade a critical scrutiny of his policy. The
Central Committee then reversed its decision and allowed the
military delegates of the opposition to stay in Moscow. But
Trotsky himself and his adherents from the army immediately
departed for the front. He left behind 'Theses' explaining the
main aspects of his policy; and on his behalf Sokolnikov presented these to the congress.

The main debate on military affairs took place in secret
sessions of the military section of the congress. The records are
not available, but the broad lines of the debate and its outcome

---

[1] Lenin, *Sobranie Sochineniy* (First edition, 1920–6), vol. xvi, p. 73. The fact
that a year after the controversy had begun, Lenin had not been aware of the
scale on which officers had been drafted, shows that, absorbed in the conduct of
political and economic affairs, he took only a remote and general interest in the
direction of military affairs. Under the fresh impression of what Trotsky had
revealed to him, he thus argued with Gorky, whom he was trying to win back for
Bolshevism: 'Show me another man able to organize almost a model army within
a single year and win the respect of military experts. We have such a man. We have
everything. And we shall work wonders.' M. Gorky, *Lénine et le Paysan Russe*,
pp. 95–96. Gorky wrote this after Lenin's death, when the campaign against Trotsky was already in full swing. In a later edition, published after Trotsky's expulsion,
Gorky toned down the eulogistic words about Trotsky in a way which only confirms the authenticity of his own first version. See Gorky, *Days with Lenin*, pp. 56–
57. Lenin's eulogy of Trotsky is omitted from later editions of Lenin's works.

are clear from the papers of the Politbureau and from messages exchanged between Trotsky, Zinoviev, and Stalin.[1] The Left Communists and Voroshilov subjected Trotsky to severe criticism; and even the charges about his shooting of commissars were brought up again. Lenin made a strong plea in defence of Trotsky and left to attend to other business. The debate was then conducted by Zinoviev and Stalin. The defeat of the opposition was a foregone conclusion after Lenin's intervention. Both Zinoviev and Stalin were careful to give the impression that their views were identical with Lenin's; but they supported Trotsky's policy rather half-heartedly; and they made a few minor concessions to the opposition which were just enough to sully Trotsky's triumph. The opposition mustered about one-third of the votes; and it may be that the concessions helped to reduce its strength, as Zinoviev later reported to the Politbureau. In a public vote the congress fully approved Trotsky's activity and adopted his 'Theses'. But the approval was qualified by an instruction, passed in secret by the military section, which demanded that Trotsky pay more attention to Communist opinion in the army, hold regular monthly meetings with the important commissars, and so on. Thus, while the general public learned that the party had fully endorsed Trotsky's policy, his opponents in the Bolshevik hierarchy had the satisfaction that not all the charges against him had been unequivocally dismissed. Something of the accusation that he was the enemy of the party man in uniform had indeed stuck to Trotsky.[2]

Trotsky first learned that the congress had fully approved his policy from a telegram, signed by Stalin, which reached him at the front on 22 or 23 of March. Soon afterwards he received a message from the Central Committee, written by Zinoviev, who informed him about the concessions made to the opposition and urged him to treat this as a 'warning'. Trotsky refused to accept the 'warning'. He replied in writing that he could not recall commissars from the front every month to hold conferences with them. The 'warning' was in any case dictated by 'a shameful, crude, plebeian bias', which permeated all of

[1] *The Trotsky Archives.* Also *Vosmoi Syezd RKP*, pp. 337–8.
[2] In later controversy Trotsky dwelt on the public vote of the congress, while Stalinist sources spoke about the rebuff which the congress had administered to him in secret. Both versions are true, but each gives a different part of the truth.

Voroshilov's attacks. He reproached himself for having treated Voroshilov too leniently, for 'every discontent in the army is armed discontent'. Even in the civilian Bolshevik organization, he wrote, the margin of permissible controversy was narrow, from the moment when the party had passed from debate to action. The margin must be even narrower in the army; he must exact formal discipline. With much warmth he then recounted some of his conflicts with commanders and commissars, whom he had had to arrest and punish for breaches of discipline, but who, he hoped, would realize the need for this and would face him without bitterness in the future. Finally, he demanded a formal inquiry into the charges about the shooting of commissars.[1] He implied that Lenin and Zinoviev were not fully aware of the appalling conditions at the front. The attitude of the opposition resulted from weariness and strained nerves; and he was afraid that the party leadership, too, might succumb to this mood.

For the moment the matter was closed. The Left Communists, defeated at the congress, could not repeat their challenge. Their resentment still simmered; but in the subsequent crises of the civil war the need for discipline, centralization, and expert military leadership was generally accepted as a matter of course. However, the opposition in the party hierarchy, led by Stalin and Zinoviev, was as strong as ever—it merely shifted its ground from the issues hitherto debated to strategy and operational plans.

.   .   .   .

The strategy of the civil war was determined by the fact that the Red Army fought on fronts with a circumference of more than 5,000 miles. Even a numerous, well-equipped, and superbly trained army could not hold all these fronts simultaneously. The war consisted of a series of deep thrusts by the White Guards now from this and now from that part of the outer fringe into the interior and of corresponding, even deeper, Red counter-thrusts. After the defeat of the Czech Legion, three major campaigns formed the climaxes of the civil war in 1919: Kolchak's offensive, undertaken from Siberian bases, towards the Volga and Moscow, in the spring; Denikin's advance from

---

[1] A commission of inquiry was formed, but apart from the notorious case of Panteleev, no evidence was brought to support the charges. It seems that the commission's verdict was made public, but I have not been able to trace it.

the south, also aiming at Moscow, in the summer; and Yudenich's attempt to capture Petrograd, in the autumn. Had all
these offensives converged simultaneously on the centres of
Soviet power, the counter-revolution might have won. But the
White Guards operated on 'external lines'; and they were
separated from each other by thousands of miles. Each White
Army grew up independently and at a different pace; and the
commander of each was eager to win laurels exclusively for
himself. The Red Army, on the contrary, benefited from operating on 'internal lines'. It shifted its strength from one front to
another to secure local superiority. Its operations were eventually planned and its resources controlled from a single centre.
But it was natural that the fixing of strategic priorities should
give rise to friction and controversy, especially as almost every
decision involved a choice between political as well as strategic
alternatives.

In March and April Kolchak's troops once again advanced
on a broad front towards the Volga and renewed the threat to
Moscow so narrowly averted in the previous summer. The Red
Army in the east was depleted: its best troops had been sent
against Denikin in the south. Trotsky spent two months on the
eastern front, during which he stiffened the retreating army
and prepared the counter-thrust. This time he could view the
prospects with greater confidence than during the campaign
against the Czechs. He already had more than half a million
men under arms; and as the trade unions called up 50 per cent.
of their members, the army's establishment rose to one and a
half million men before the close of this campaign.[1] Towards
the end of April the commander of the eastern front, S. Kamenev, a former colonel of the Tsarist General Staff, carried out a
bold outflanking manœuvre against Kolchak's southern flank
and struck at the over-extended lines. Soon the White troops
began to fall back in disorder towards the Urals.

At this point a controversy ensued between Vatzetis, the
Commander-in-Chief, and Kamenev, the commander of the
front. The latter was eager to exploit his victory and to pursue
Kolchak into Siberia. He was confident that he could inflict a
final defeat on Kolchak even though with only a part of his
forces, which were again to be depleted in order to strengthen

[1] *Pyat Let Vlasti Sovietov*, pp. 156–7.

the southern front. Vatzetis, however, vetoed Kamenev's plan. He supposed that Kolchak had strong reserves in Siberia, and, considering the risk of a deep pursuit to be too great, he ordered Kamenev to stop at the Urals. Trotsky backed the Commander-in-Chief. He, too, feared that the eastern armies might march into a trap set for them by Kolchak.[1] At the moment Trotsky was also more eager to clear European Russia of the White Guards than to extend Soviet rule to Siberia. New commitments also appeared: Hungary and Bavaria had just been proclaimed Soviet republics, and Lenin urged the Red Army to establish liaison with Soviet Hungary, even though Polish troops in eastern Galicia barred access to Hungary.[2] For all these reasons Trotsky was anxious to reduce the commitments on the eastern front. As Kamenev would not give up his plan to pursue Kolchak, Trotsky removed him from the command. But now the commissars of the eastern front, Lashevich, Smilga, and Gusev, declared their solidarity with the removed commander and asked that he should be reinstated and given a free hand. The commissars had Stalin's ear, then Lenin's; and they achieved a reversal of Trotsky's and Vatzetis's decision. Kamenev pressed the pursuit beyond the Urals and presently crushed Kolchak, who, it turned out, had no strategic reserve in Siberia. Thus Trotsky's opponents scored a notable advantage.

Trotsky had in the meantime gone to the southern front, and there he spent most of the summer. Just as Kolchak's retreat was beginning, Denikin had advanced into the Ukraine, meeting only negligible resistance. The Ukraine, having only recently and superficially come under Soviet control, had no regular army. Red Guards and partisan bands roamed the country, looting and spreading anarchy. Makhno's anarchist detachments held part of the country under their sway. The Left Communists, defeated in Russia, had found refuge on the Ukrainian front which, being in an early phase of revolutionary ferment, was congenial ground to them. Trotsky himself had placed Antonov-Ovseenko, Podvoysky, and Bubnov in charge of military affairs in the Ukraine: but Bubnov was one of the leaders of the Left Communists and Antonov-Ovseenko was also inclined to give free

[1] Trotsky, *Sochinenya*, vol. xvii, book 2, p. 587.
[2] See messages exchanged between Vatzetis and Lenin on 21, 22 April 1919. *The Trotsky Archives*.

rein to Red Guards and partisans. At first Trotsky proposed firm action, and suggested to Moscow that the three commissars be removed from the Ukraine and replaced by convinced disciplinarians. He even complained about the 'softness' of his friend Rakovsky, who headed the Soviet Ukrainian government; and he asked that either S. Kamenev or Voroshilov should be appointed commander of the Ukrainian front, with a categorical assignment to subdue the guerrillas.[1]

From Moscow no reply came at first. The longer Trotsky stayed in the Ukraine, however, the more he felt himself overwhelmed by the prevalent chaos. He came to think that the military disorder could not be overcome before the economic and political condition of the country had become more normal. He could not, he reported to Moscow, centralize and discipline troops whom he was unable to feed, clothe, and arm. 'Neither agitation nor repression can make battleworthy a barefoot, naked, hungry, lice-ridden army.'[2] He asked for supplies from Russia, but in vain. In addition, the Ukrainian peasantry showed utter hostility towards the Soviets; and the Bolshevik leaders on the spot were half-resigned to defeat. The reshuffling of commanders he himself had proposed could not remedy these conditions. In the meantime Lenin began to urge him with increasing impatience to carry out the proposed change in the Ukrainian command.

At the beginning of July Trotsky returned to Moscow. This was the lowest point in his fortunes during the civil war. He admitted that he had misjudged the position on the eastern front when he opposed the pursuit of Kolchak. Now he had to answer strictures on his management of the Ukrainian front. In addition, the Commander-in-Chief whom he had promoted and backed had become the victim of scathing attacks. Stalin pressed for Vatzetis's dismissal and even charged him with treason. He proposed that Kamenev, the victor over Kolchak, whom Trotsky had so recently demoted, should be appointed Commander-in-Chief. Stalin himself, incidentally, had just successfully directed the defence of Petrograd against Yudenich;

[1] Trotsky believed that Voroshilov had in the meantime become a convinced adherent of his policy (cable of 17 May sent from Kharkov to the Central Committee. *The Trotsky Archives*). Now it was Lenin who denounced Voroshilov for 'pilfering' army stocks, &c. (Lenin's cable to Trotsky of 2 June).

[2] Message of 1 July 1919.

and he walked in the fresh glory of that victory. On 3 July the Central Committee resolved to act on Stalin's advice: Vatzetis was dismissed with honours, and Kamenev was appointed Commander-in-Chief. Trotsky resisted the change and sulked; but Kamenev's 'success on the eastern front', as he himself wrote later, 'bribed Lenin and broke down my resistance'.[1] This reverse was bitter enough, but yet another followed. The Central Committee also decided to overhaul the Revolutionary War Council of the Republic. Trotsky was to remain its Chairman, but his friends (Smirnov, Rosengoltz, Raskolnikov) were removed, and their places were taken by Smilga and Gusev, the commissars who had defended the new Commander-in-Chief against Trotsky and whose candidatures Stalin favoured.

The double reproof was so hurtful to Trotsky that he resigned on the spot from the Politbureau, the Commissariat of War, and the Council of War. But the Politbureau could not permit the conflict to come into the open. No matter with what Trotsky may have been taunted in the inner councils of the Kremlin, to the country he remained the leader of the October insurrection, the founder of the army, the artisan of its victories. His resignation in the middle of a new emergency would have dismayed the army and the party. And Lenin, at any rate, was genuinely anxious that his government should not forfeit Trotsky's services. On Lenin's proposal, the Politbureau rejected Trotsky's resignation, and it adopted unanimously a resolution solemnly assuring Trotsky of its deep respect and complete confidence and urging him to continue his 'extremely difficult, dangerous and important' work on the southern front. It was also on this occasion that Lenin, obviously perturbed by the incident, handed to Trotsky as a token of his confidence an endorsement in blank of any order which Trotsky might issue.[2] On these terms Trotsky stayed in office.

Another tug-of-war arose at once over the campaign against Denikin; and in this, too, Trotsky's adversaries worsted him. By this time Denikin had seized Tsaritsyn, the coal basin of the Donetz, and Kharkov. The anti-Bolshevik front spread from the

[1] Trotsky, *Stalin*, p. 313.

[2] The endorsement, under Lenin's official stamp, runs as follows: 'Knowing the stern character of Comrade Trotsky's orders, I am so convinced, so absolutely convinced, of the correctness, expediency, and necessity for the success of the cause of Comrade Trotsky's order that I endorse it without reservation.' *The Archives*.

Volga and the Don to the western steppe of the Ukraine. Its eastern sector between the Volga and the Don was held by the Don Cossacks, while the White Guards proper advanced on the central and western sectors. The question to resolve was at which sector the Red Army should direct a counterstroke. The new Commander-in-Chief proposed to direct it at the eastern sector, along the Don valley, towards Tsaritsyn and Denikin's bases in the northern Caucasus. On strictly military grounds this was a sound plan. It was designed to outflank Denikin's forces and to cut them off from their main bases. It was also calculated to separate Denikin's army from Kolchak's so that even if Kolchak were to regain the initiative and advance once again, he could not join hands with Denikin. The offensive was to be carried out by Red armies withdrawn from the Urals; and it was easier to throw these armies against Denikin's eastern flank than to shift them farther to the west.

To this scheme Trotsky objected. Denikin, he argued, was weakened by a dissension between the White Guards proper and the Don Cossacks. The White Guards consisted mainly of Russian officers impatient to overthrow the Bolsheviks in Moscow and Petrograd. The Cossacks, indulging in particularism, wished merely to keep the Bolsheviks out of their *stanitsas*, and were reluctant to stick out their necks beyond the Don valley. Denikin's plans for an offensive on Moscow left them lukewarm. Trotsky held that if the Red Army were to throw its main force into the Don valley, it would arouse the Cossacks, force them into a bitter fight, and thus unwittingly help to close the breach in the enemy's camp. Even after an initial success, the Red Army would have to advance across land with poor communications and amid a hostile population. In the meantime, Denikin would strike at the weak central sector, for there was the shortest route to Moscow. Trotsky proposed that the main force of the Red Army should be shifted to the central sector, with Kharkov and the Donetz Basin as its chief objectives. In an advance along this line the Reds could split Denikin's army, separate the Cossacks from the White Guards and neutralize them. The attackers would enjoy the advantage of operating in a highly industrialized area, the population of which favoured the Soviets; and they would also have at their disposal a dense network of roads and railways.

P

The social and political lie of the land should therefore determine the direction of the offensive. Kamenev's plan, though correct from an abstract strategic standpoint, failed to make allowance for the close interplay of politics and strategy in civil war.

When the controversy between the Commissar of War and the Commander-in-Chief was brought before the Politbureau, the arguments of the Commander-in-Chief carried the day. The Politbureau authorized the main offensive on the eastern sector.

This continuous succession of personal reverses for Trotsky had a strange sequel. In a somewhat sullen mood Trotsky returned to the southern front. He had hardly arrived at his field headquarters at Kozlov before he received an enigmatic message, bearing the signatures of Dzerzhinsky, Krestinsky, Lenin, and Sklyansky, informing him that the Commander-in-Chief (i.e. Vatzetis) had been charged with treason and imprisoned. The message did not specify the charges—it merely stated that they were based on depositions made by another arrested officer. The blow was deadly. It originated with Stalin who had already denounced Vatzetis as a traitor and it was unmistakably aimed at Trotsky. We do not know exactly how Trotsky reacted to this blow. Almost certainly he strongly defended the imprisoned man and personally vouched for his integrity, for this is how he acted in similar cases, when less important officers were implicated.[1] Enough that after a few days Vatzetis was released and rehabilitated. Trotsky himself later gave two versions of the charges: according to one, Vatzetis had not shown enough vigilance in dealing with counter-revolutionary officers in his entourage: according to the other, he nourished hopes of a future Napoleonic career.[2] Neither lack of vigilance nor a privately cherished ambition amounted to treason or justified the imprisonment; and, after his release, Vatzetis continued to hold high posts in the army

[1] Earlier in the year, for instance, Trotsky categorically protested against the arrest of General Zagin, who, he wrote, had done more to help the Soviets than those who kept him behind bars. The arbitrary treatment of such men had a disastrous effect on the officers' morale, Trotsky wrote; he asked for the General's release and personally vouched for him until his conviction in court should take place. *The Trotsky Archives* (correspondence of January 1919).

[2] Trotsky, *Stalin*, pp. 310–16.

until late in the Stalin era. His arrest in 1919 was therefore intended to add humiliation to the setbacks Trotsky had already suffered.

These were weeks of exceptional tension between Trotsky and Lenin, as their correspondence testifies. In part this was due to the disagreement over strategy and in part to the fact, connected with it, that Trotsky's assignment to hold the Ukraine against Denikin was a Sisyphean labour. Lenin also suspected that Trotsky was seeking to discredit the new Commander-in-Chief in the eyes of the officers on the southern front. From the south Trotsky reported that Yegoriev, the commander of the front, took a highly critical view of Kamenev's plan for the offensive; and that he carried out Kamenev's orders without conviction. Regardless of the rights and wrongs of the issue, Trotsky wrote, this was an abnormal state of affairs; and he proposed the appointment of a new commander of the front who would share the views of the Commander-in-Chief. This proposal, which actually testified to Trotsky's loyalty, stirred suspicion in the Kremlin. The Politbureau changed the commander of the front, but also detailed to the Ukraine Smilga and Lashevich, who were at loggerheads with Trotsky; and, further, it meaningfully reminded Trotsky that he ought to do all he could to strengthen the authority of the new Commander-in-Chief. Against the insinuation Trotsky vigorously protested. Repeatedly he expostulated with Lenin and the Politbureau for their 'unbusinesslike' replies to his messages. Lenin, in his turn, showered upon him admonitions and reproaches: why had he so little achievement to report? Where were the offensives that were to be mounted in the Ukraine?

In truth the unsettlement prevalent in the Ukraine afforded Trotsky little or no scope for military action. The Red Army had invested its main strength in the eastern sector of the front; and the Ukraine, which formed the central and western sectors, was left to fend for itself. Trotsky ceaselessly alarmed Moscow about the insufficiency of the Ukrainian forces, still utterly disorganized; and he demanded reinforcements and supplies. The Politbureau almost certainly suspected that Trotsky made these demands in order to achieve by a roundabout way a revision of Kamenev's operational plan and a different distribution of the troops.

A glimpse of the situation on the spot may be gained from an angrily aggressive message which Trotsky addressed to the Politbureau on 11 August. The Red Army men in the Ukraine, he wrote, were starving. Half of them had neither boots nor underwear, and very few had coats. It was no better with rifles and ammunition. Everybody was armed except the soldiers. The *kulaks* had vast stocks of weapons bought from deserters. Hungry and unarmed, the Red Army man lost confidence when he came face to face with the well-fed village usurer. The *kulaks* must be taken severely to task and disarmed. Two or three thousand well-equipped and reliable communists could stiffen the front; but Moscow refused to dispatch them. The Ukrainian Bolsheviks were in a defeatist mood. They held that it might not be a bad idea to let the Ukraine experience White rule for a short time—this would cure the people of illusions and turn them back towards the Bolsheviks. He assured the Politbureau that he firmly resisted this mood. But the Ukrainian divisions needed a respite, a chance 'to wash, to dress, and to prepare for the offensive'.[1]

Denikin, however, did not allow them the respite. A fortnight later he seized Kiev and nearly the whole of the Ukraine; and he pressed at the Red Army's weak centre, towards Voronezh and Kursk, along the shortest line to Moscow.

At this moment Trotsky demanded a revision of the operational plan. He urged that the reserves of the Supreme Command be shifted from the eastern sector towards Voronezh and Kursk. Over and over again he repeated this demand; and over and over again the Politbureau and the General Staff rejected it. Meanwhile the Red Army failed to make any decisive progress on the Don, and Denikin seized Kursk, Voronezh, and Orel. Only when the threat to Moscow became imminent, at the beginning of October, did the Commander-in-Chief change his mind and begin to mass reserves on the central sector. But by now Denikin's forces had broken through towards Tula, the last important town in front of Moscow. And simultaneously, Yudenich, armed by the British and supported by the British Navy, rapidly advanced from Estonia towards Petrograd and reached the outskirts of the city.

If it were not for the extreme gravity of the situation, Trotsky

[1] *The Trotsky Archives.*

might have rejoiced at the completeness with which events had vindicated him and converted all his opponents to his view. Now even Stalin pressed for the final abandonment of Kamenev's operational plan, and sparing Kamenev no insult, he repeated word by word Trotsky's arguments.[1]

At this moment of general depression Trotsky's optimism and energy knew no bounds. He was convinced that the regrouping of forces at last undertaken would soon yield results. The front was virtually overhauled, the reserves built up; and, with communication lines so radically shortened, abundant supplies reached the troops. The enemy was over-extended; and the power of the Red Army was like a compressed spring ready for the recoil. Trotsky confidently assessed the material and moral resources the Soviets could still marshal. Like no other member of the Politbureau, he had constantly stared at the inferno of the civil war. He was haunted by the image of half-naked soldiers trembling in the frost and of the wounded dying *en masse* for lack of medical attention. He had also fully gauged the army's nervous instability. But at moments of mortal peril he believed in the army's capacity for sudden bursts of enthusiasm, in its readiness for sacrifice, and in the spirited initiative of its commanders and men, which triumphed over the chaos into which the revolution seemed periodically to dissolve.

He now rose to his full height not merely as the chief manager and organizer of the army but as its inspirer, as the prophet of an idea. He boldly tapped the hidden moral resources of the revolution. The quality of his appeal may be gauged, for instance, from an address he gave at a congress of the Comsomol, the Communist Youth, which met just when Moscow and Petrograd had come within reach of the White Guards. He spoke to juveniles about the duties they had to perform 'within the shrinking area left to the Red Army'. They should assist in the mobilization; they should help to maintain liaison between units in combat; they should steal through the enemy's lines to reconnoitre his dispositions; and so on. But before they went on

[1] It is on this basis that latter-day Soviet historians attribute to Stalin the authorship of Trotsky's scheme for the offensive. But Stalin's letter to Lenin in which he urged a concentration of striking-power on the central sector is dated 15 October 1919 (see Stalin, *Sochinenya*, vol. iv, pp. 275–7) while Trotsky wrote his memorandum on this issue in September. Trotsky, *Sochinenya*, vol. xvii, book 2, pp. 556–9; Voroshilov, *Stalin i Krasnaya Armia*, pp. 21–22.

their perilous assignments, they ought to know the place they occupied in the affairs of the world. Lucidly, simply, without a trace of condescension, he surveyed the international scene. They should also see their own role against the background of world history, in the long perspective of mankind's slow, painfully slow, yet inspiring progress 'from the dark animal realm' to undreamt-of summits of civilization, towards which socialism was leading them. He turned his listeners' minds back to primitive man, who 'hobbling and limping, wandered through sleepy forests and who, gripped by superstition, created for himself little gods and tsars and princes'. Then man 'replaced the many gods by one God and the many little tsars and princes by one Tsar'. 'But he has not stopped at this. He has renounced tsars and gods and has made an attempt to become free master of his own life. . . . We are participants in this unprecedented historic attempt.' 'These hundreds of thousands of years of man's development and struggle would be a mockery if we were not to attain . . . a new society, in which all human relations will be based on . . . co-operation and man will be man's brother, not his enemy.' He then spoke about 'history's enormous furnace', in which the Russian national character was remoulded and freed from its langour and sluggishness. 'This furnace is cruel . . . tongues of flame lick and scorch us, but [they also] . . . steel our national character.' 'Happy is he', Trotsky exclaimed, 'who in his mind and heart feels the electrical current of our great epoch.'[1]

It was in the grimmest of moods that the Politbureau met on 15 October. At Orel the battle still swayed; and on its outcome hung Moscow's fate. There seemed to be little hope for Petrograd's defence. Under so gloomy an aspect did the situation present itself to Lenin that he proposed to abandon Petrograd and to gather all available strength around Moscow. He reckoned even with the possibility of Moscow's fall and with a Bolshevik withdrawal to the Urals.

Against this proposal Trotsky vigorously protested: Petrograd, the cradle of the revolution, must not be abandoned to the White Guards. The surrender of that city might have a disastrous effect on the rest of the country. He proposed that he himself should go to Petrograd to take charge of its defence.

[1] Trotsky, *Pokolenie Oktyabrya*, pp. 157-67.

He submitted to the Politbureau a series of emergency decrees aiming at total mobilization: Let them disband the multiple and now useless government departments and agencies in Moscow and call everybody to arms. He would rush reinforcements to Petrograd from the dead ends of the front, from the coast of the White Sea and the Polish marches.

This time his habitual antagonist supported him. Stalin, too, demanded the defence of both capitals.[1] In their attitude there was that concord which may unite enemies on a sinking ship when they are bent on rescuing it. While Trotsky volunteered to go to Petrograd, Stalin replaced him on the southern front. The Politbureau adopted the decrees submitted by Trotsky; and it elected a commission of four (Lenin, Trotsky, Kamenev, Krestinsky) which was to give effect to them. It also authorized Trotsky to leave for Petrograd, but it still reserved judgement on his plan to defend the city.

On 16 October, in his train *en route* to Petrograd, Trotsky dictated his reflections on the situation. He mocked at Churchill's recent proclamation of the anti-Soviet crusade of fourteen nations. These, he wrote, were nothing but 'fourteen geographic notions'—Kolchak and Denikin would have been happier to be succoured by fourteen Anglo-French divisions. The loud rejoicing of the bourgeois West over the imminent downfall of the Soviets was premature. Even if the Red Army were not to succeed in halting Yudenich outside Petrograd, it would crush him within the walls of the city. He sketched something like a plan for a battle inside Petrograd, which curiously resembles the tactics of the battle of Stalingrad in the Second World War.

Having broken through this gigantic city, the White Guards would get lost in this labyrinth of stone, where every house will present them with an enigma, a threat or a deadly danger. From where should they expect a blow? From a window? From a loft? From a cellar? From behind a corner? From everywhere! . . . We can surround some streets with barbed wire, leave other streets open and transform them into traps. All that is needed is that a few thousand people should be firmly resolved not to surrender. . . . Two or three days of such street fighting would transform the

---

[1] This is based on Trotsky's own account. From the records it does not appear that Stalin was present at this session of the Politbureau. On 15 October he sent a letter to Lenin from the southern front. He probably communicated his opinion before his departure.

invaders into a frightened and terrified flock of cowards, surrendering in groups or individually to unarmed passers-by and women. . . . But street fighting causes accidental casualties and it results in the destruction of cultural values. This is one of the reasons why the field command is obliged to take every step not to allow the enemy to approach Petrograd.[1]

In Petrograd bad news awaited him: Yudenich had seized Krasnoe Selo, at the approaches to the city. The defences had been depleted by a transfer of troops to the southern front and disorganized by treason among high staff officers. Zinoviev, chief of the 'Commune of the North', was in a mood of prostration; and his irresolution infected his subordinates. But from Moscow came Lenin's notification that the Politbureau had approved Trotsky's plan and authorized him to wage the battle, if need be, inside the city. Lenin still prudently insisted that he should prepare for a retreat, evacuate official documents and arrange for the blowing up of power-stations and for the scuttling of the Baltic fleet. Trotsky replied with a confident report; and as if to give to his confidence a peculiarly defiant twist, he inquired whether he would be allowed to pursue Yudenich into Estonia, Yudenich's jumping-off ground.[2]

He addressed once again the Petrograd Soviet he had led in 1905 and 1917. He described frankly the threatening disaster and, calling for a supreme effort, he gave vent to his personal feeling for the city:

In these dark, cold, hungry, anxious, bad autumn days Petrograd presents to us again the grand picture of rallying self-confidence, enthusiasm, and heroism. The city which has suffered so much, which has burned with so strong an inward flame and has braved so many dangers, the city which has never spared itself, which has

[1] Trotsky, *Sochinenya*, vol. xvii, book 2, pp. 266–7.
[2] This question led to a long exchange between Lenin, Trotsky, and Chicherin. The Commissar of Foreign Affairs, fearing international complications, strongly protested against pursuit into Estonia. Trotsky then contented himself with a mere threat that the Red Army would cross the frontier if the Estonian government failed to disarm the White Guards retreating into its territory. The attitude of the Baltic states gave the Politbureau and Trotsky some anxiety. Trotsky publicly threatened the Finnish government that he would let loose Bashkirian divisions upon Helsinki if the Finns made any move against Petrograd. The governments of the Entente secretly urged the Baltic governments to join in Yudenich's offensive; but impressed by Trotsky's threats the Baltic states adopted an attitude of wait and see.

inflicted on itself so much devastation, this beautiful Red Petrograd remains what it has been—the torch of revolution. . . .[1]

Of the effect of Trotsky's intervention we have many eye-witness accounts. The following comes from Lashevich, who at this time was, as we know, anything but friendly towards Trotsky and himself played an eminent role in these events:

Like fresh reinforcements arriving . . . Trotsky's presence on the spot at once showed itself: proper discipline was restored and the military and administrative agencies rose to their task. Whoever was inefficient was demoted. The higher and the middle commanding personnel were changed. Trotsky's orders, clear and precise, sparing nobody and exacting from everybody the utmost exertion and accurate, rapid execution of combat orders, at once showed that there was a firm directing hand. . . . The inward rallying had begun. The staffs got into working order. Liaison, hitherto defective, became satisfactory. The supply departments began to function without a hitch. Desertion from the front was radically reduced. In all detachments field tribunals were in session. . . . Everybody began to realize that only one road was left—forward. All avenues of retreat had been cut. Trotsky penetrated into every detail, applying to every item of business his seething, restless energy and his amazing perseverance.[2]

For a few days Yudenich's advance continued. The appearance of British tanks on the outskirts of the city caused a panic. On horseback Trotsky gathered terror-stricken and retreating men and led them back into the fighting-line. In a spurt of improvisation factories, working within the range of Yudenich's artillery, began to turn out tank-like vehicles; and the panic was over. Regular troops, hastily formed Red Guards, even detachments of women, fought back, as Yudenich put it, with 'heroic madness'. A week after Trotsky's arrival, the defenders passed to the offensive. On the second anniversary of the revolution, which was also his fortieth birthday, Trotsky was back in Moscow to report victory to the Central Executive of the Soviets.

The last act of the civil war had begun. On the southern front, too, the White Guards were reeling back and disintegrating.[3] The Red Army pressed forwards towards Kharkov, Kiev,

[1] Trotsky, *Sochinenya*, vol. xvii, book 2, p. 287.
[2] *Borba za Petrograd*, pp. 52–53.
[3] The reasons for the collapse of the White armies have by nobody been stated more bluntly and truthfully than by Denikin himself: 'The liberation by ourselves of enormous areas should have brought about . . . a rising of all elements hostile to

and Poltava. In Siberia Kolchak was utterly defeated. So rapidly did the tide turn that only three weeks after that critical session at which defeat had stared the Politbureau full in the face, Red Moscow gloried in triumph. At the ceremonial anniversary session of the Executive of the Soviets, Trotsky was acclaimed as father of victory and awarded the Order of the Red Banner.[1]

He was now at the summit of his political and military achievement. He had led a revolution, he had founded a great army and had guided it to victory. He had won the adoration of the broad mass of the revolution's well-wishers and the grudging admiration as well as the unforgiving hatred of its enemies. Like other Bolshevik leaders, he hoped that the horrors and terrors of the civil war were over and that the era of peaceful Socialist reconstruction was about to begin. In this he expected to play a part as pre-eminent as the one he had played in military affairs. In December 1919, at the seventh Congress of the Soviets, he drew up a balance-sheet of the civil war; for, although the fighting was still on, its outcome was in no doubt.[2] He paid a high-minded tribute to those who had borne the crushing burden of the last years. He eulogized the commissars,

Soviet power. . . . The question was only whether the popular masses had lived down Bolshevism . . . ? Will the people go with us . . . ? Life has given an answer which was at first indefinite and then negative.' Denikin, *Ocherki Russkoi Smuty*, vol. v, p. 118. 'The troops of the army of the south did not avoid the general malady and they blotted their reputation by pogroms of Jews. . . . The inner sores festered in the atmosphere of hatred. The pogroms brought suffering to the Jewish people, but they also affected the spirit of the troops, warped their mind and destroyed discipline. . . .' Ibid., p. 146. And this is how Wrangel drew the moral balance of the campaign: 'The Volunteer Army has discredited itself by pillage and violence. Here we have lost everything. We cannot even try to march once again along the same roads, under the same flag.' Ibid., p. 263. Writing about corruption in his army, Denikin goes on to say: 'This feast at a time of pestilence aroused anger and disgust in outside observers. . . .' And finally: 'English munitions and Kuban bread still reached us from our supply bases, but the moral bases had already been destroyed.' Ibid., p. 314.

[1] The same Order was awarded to the city of Petrograd and to Stalin, who did not even attend the ceremony. Trotsky later recounted that those present were surprised by the honour bestowed upon Stalin and that nobody applauded it. Be that as it may, Trotsky was certainly annoyed, for soon afterwards he wrote: 'Petrograd has been awarded the Order of the Red Banner. And it is Petrograd which has really and honestly deserved it. When rewards are given to individuals, mistakes and accidental privileges are always possible. But when the distinction goes to Petrograd there is no mistake and no bias.' *Sochinenya*, vol. xvii, book 2, p. 310.   [2] Ibid., pp. 325-55.

whose enemy he had been supposed to be: 'In our commissars
. . . we have a new communist order of Samurais, the members
of which have enjoyed no caste privileges and could die and
teach others to die for the cause of the working class.' He
praised lavishly the commanders of the victorious armies, those
who had been Tsarist generals and those who had risen from
the ranks and had in civilian life been metal-workers or barbers.
With especial warmth he spoke of the achievements of three
army commanders: Frunze, the worker, Tukhachevsky, the
Guard officer, and Sokolnikov, the revolutionary journalist.
Then he outlined the prospect of the abolition of the standing
army and of its transformation into a democratic militia
inspired by the Socialist ideal, the militia of which Jaurès had
once dreamt.[1] He had a few friendly words even for the Mensheviks who had, in the last emergency, rallied to the defence
of the Soviets and were present at this congress. 'We appreciate
very highly', he said, 'the fact that other parties, too, parties
belonging to the opposition . . . have mobilized a certain
number of their workers for the army. They have been received
there as brothers.' A few months earlier he had threatened the
Mensheviks that they would be 'crushed to dust' if they ob-
structed defence. But now he addressed himself to Martov, who
had congratulated the Bolsheviks on their military and diplomatic successes. He expressed 'real joy . . . without any *arrière
pensée* and without a trace of irony', because 'Martov has spoken
about *our* army and *our* international struggle—he has used the
word *we*, and in so doing he has added political and moral
strength to our cause.'

Like other Bolsheviks, Trotsky looked forward to appeasement
in domestic policy, which would allow the parties at least of the
Socialist opposition to resume open activity. The curtailment of
the powers of the *Cheka* and the abolition of the death penalty
in January 1920 were intended as first steps in that direction.
But these sanguine hopes were not to materialize.

The horrors of war had not yet receded into the past.[2]

[1] See 'Note on Trotsky's Military Writings', pp. 477 ff.
[2] Material for this and the next chapter has been drawn, *inter alia*, from
Bubnov, Kamenev, Eideman, *Grazhdanskaya Voina*, vols. i–iii; Kakurin, *Kak
Srazhalas Revolutsia*, vols. i–ii; and Frunze, *Sobranie Sochineniy*, vols. i–iii.

CHAPTER XIII

Revolution and Conquest

THROUGHOUT these years the leaders of Bolshevism anxiously watched for the omens of revolution in Europe. Every phase in the social and political struggles of Europe reacted directly upon the course of the civil war. The downfall of the Hohenzollerns and Habsburgs allowed the Soviets to regain ground lost under the Peace of Brest Litovsk. But soon afterwards the victorious Entente proclaimed the blockade of Russia and this was followed by the 'crusade of fourteen nations'. The mere threat of Allied intervention profoundly affected the situation in Russia. Since the revolution the old ruling classes had been in a state of utter depression, terrified by the abyss which separated them from the mass of the people. They lacked organization and faith in their own cause; they were divided against themselves; they were incapable of producing any plan of action.[1] The promise of intervention put courage into their hearts. It was only after the promise had been made, after British, French, and American liaison officers had appeared at the headquarters of the White generals and the first foreign cargoes of guns and munitions had reached Russian shores that the ranks of the White Guards began to swell and the civil war flared up in earnest. The Bolsheviks thought that only intense revolutionary ferment abroad could paralyse the intervention. They were compelled to carry the struggle into the enemy's camp; and they were all the more inclined to do so as they had persistently predicted that Europe's ruling classes would not reconcile themselves to the Russian Revolution and that for its self-preservation the revolution would be forced to assail the European capitalist order, which was anyhow about to crumble under the blows of the European working classes. Half of this prediction had come true: the ruling classes of the Entente had declared war on Bolshevism; and there were moments when

[1] One of the first leaders of the White Guards, General Kaledin, said before he committed suicide early in 1918: 'Our situation is hopeless. The population not only does not support us—it is definitely hostile. We have no strength, and resistance is useless.' Denikin, op. cit., vol. ii, p. 220.

the other half, too, foreshadowing the rising of the European proletariat, seemed close to fulfilment.

Since November 1918 Germany and most of central Europe had been in the throes of upheaval. In Berlin, Vienna, and Warsaw councils of workers' deputies existed side by side with Social Democratic governments. The Bolsheviks, who looked at things through the prism of their own recent experience, saw in this an exact reproduction of that 'dual régime' which had, in Russia, sprung from the February Revolution. They spoke about the 'German February'; and they expected a rapid disintegration of the dual régime, an ascendancy of the Councils of Workers' Deputies, a 'German October'.

It was an extremely simple-minded notion that history could so precisely and so rapidly repeat itself in country after country. But the mechanics of all the classical popular revolutions have very many features in common. Each begins with a partial collapse of the established system of government; each passes through the transitory phase of a dual régime; and in each the conservative, moderate, and conciliatory parties, at loggerheads with one another, successively exhaust and discredit themselves. It was this broad succession of phases that the Bolsheviks expected to recur in other countries. What was wrong in their expectations was not merely the calendar of revolutionary events but the fundamental assumption that European capitalism was at the end of its tether. They grossly underrated its staying power, its adaptability, and the hold it had on the loyalty of the working classes. The revolutionary ferment in Europe was strong enough for a minority of the working class to be determined to follow in Bolshevik footsteps. The majority exerted themselves to wrest reforms from their governments and propertied classes. But even when they exhibited sympathy for the Russian Revolution, they were in no mood to embark upon the road of revolution and civil war at home and to sacrifice in the process the standards of living, the personal security, the reforms they had already attained, and those which they hoped to attain.

The historic tragedy of Bolshevism in its heroic period was its refusal not merely to reconcile itself to this fact but even to make full allowance for it. The Bolshevik leaders viewed the relative conservatism of European labour as the deceptive

surface of politics, beneath which pulsated all the revolutionary
instincts of the proletariat. What was needed was to break
through the thin crust and to release the hidden anti-capitalist
energies. This picture of the world resulted from something
more than an error of political judgement. It reflected the
psychological incapacity of early Bolshevism to acknowledge its
own isolation in the world, an incapacity which was common to
all leaders of the revolution, but which was in nobody as strong
and as complete as in Trotsky. An instinctive horror of the
revolution's isolation permeated the whole of his being, his
brain and his heart. None of the Bolshevik leaders had as yet
even the faintest premonition of 'socialism in one country'. But
to Trotsky the isolation of Bolshevism was already a nightmare
too terrible to contemplate, for it meant that the first and so far
the only attempt to build socialism would have to be undertaken
in the worst possible conditions, without the advantages of an
intensive international division of labour, without the fertilizing
influence of old and complex cultural traditions, in an environment of such staggering material and cultural poverty, primi-
tiveness, and crudity as would tend to mar or warp the very
striving for socialism. Sooner or later this horror of isolation was
bound to clash with reality; and the clash was to compel Bolshevism to wrestle convulsively with its own mental image of
the world.

After Brest, when this dilemma had first upset his inner
confidence, Trotsky found a sort of escape in the herculean
exertions of the civil war. For the time being his horror of
isolation found inverted expression in violent bursts of confidence in the imminent expansion of the revolution. In January
1919, when the streets of Berlin were littered with barricades,
he wrote: 'It is no longer the spectre of communism that is
haunting Europe . . .—communism in flesh and blood is now
stalking the continent.'[1] It was the ideas and the hopes of the
bourgeoisie that had assumed an air of utter unreality in his
eyes. He saw something ghost-like in the appearance in Europe
of President Wilson, 'that Tartuffe brought up on a Quaker
fasting diet, who roams bleeding Europe as the supreme representative of morality, the Messiah of the American dollar, and
punishes and pardons the nations and settles their fate'. Europe

[1] Trotsky, *Sochinenya*, vol. xiii, pp. 6–14.

could not fail to see that its only salvation was a continent-wide federation of Soviet republics; and once Germany had acceded to that federation 'Soviet Italy and Soviet France will join a month earlier or a month later'.[1]

In the first week of March 1919 a significant event occurred within the walls of the Kremlin. In an old, imperial court of justice, Lenin opened a meeting of about two score of delegates from various foreign Left Socialist groups. The arrival of those delegates was in a sense the first breach in the blockade. Most of them had had to steal across frontiers: some of the expected delegates had been prevented by their governments from leaving their countries; others had been arrested *en route*. Having for a long time been completely cut off from the West, the Bolsheviks listened eagerly to what the delegates reported on the state of affairs abroad. The reports were confused and contradictory; but on balance they seemed to justify the expectation of early revolution.

The purpose of the conference was not quite clear. It was either to proclaim the foundation of the Third International or to make preliminary arrangements for this. The Bolsheviks were inclined to form the new International there and then, but they waited to hear the opinion of foreign delegates. The most important of these, the Germans, held that the groups represented at the conference were, apart from the Russian party, too weak to constitute themselves as a fully fledged International. However, an Austrian delegate who, after an adventurous journey, arrived in the middle of the debate, gave a startling description of Europe seething with revolution; and he passionately called on the conference to raise at once the banner of the new International. The conference responded: it constituted itself as the foundation congress of the Communist International. Thus, fathered by wish, mothered by confusion, and assisted by accident, the great institution came into being.

Its birth coincided with the ebbing away of revolution in Europe. The January rising in Berlin had been crushed; its reluctant leaders Rosa Luxemburg and Karl Liebknecht had been assassinated. This was a turning-point in European history, for none of the waves of revolution that came in the following

[1] Loc. cit.

years equalled in impetus and impact the wave of 1918. The
Bolshevik leaders failed to recognize the turning-point for what
it was. The defeat of the January rising in Berlin seemed to
them an episodic reverse, very much like their own setback in
July 1917, to be followed by an aggravation of social strife.
Greeting the foreign delegates in the Kremlin, Lenin told them:
'Not only in Russia, but even in the most advanced capitalist
countries of Europe as, for instance, in Germany, civil war has
become a fact. . . . Revolution has begun and is gaining strength
in all countries. . . . The Soviet system has won not merely in
backward Russia, but even in Germany, the most developed
country of Europe, and also in England, the oldest capitalist
country.'[1] Lenin was given to this illusion not less than Trotsky,
although Trotsky, with his foible for indulging in breath-taking
predictions, made the blunder appear even more egregious.

It is doubtful whether Lenin and Trotsky would have founded
the International at this stage if they had had a clearer perception of the condition of Europe. They would, in any case,
have gone on advocating the idea of the new International, as
they had done since 1914. But it is a far cry from advancing an
idea to imagining that it has become reality. In the period of
Zimmerwald and Kienthal both Trotsky and Lenin had contemplated the new International not as a body representing
a revolutionary minority and competing with the old 'social
patriotic' International, but as an organization leading the
majority of workers and replacing the old International.
Trotsky had explicitly argued that, if they remained in a
minority, the revolutionary Marxists might have to return to
the old International and act as its left wing.[2] Nothing had been
further from his thoughts or Lenin's than the intention of giving
an assortment of small political sects the high-sounding label
of the International.

And yet this was what they did in March 1919. Most of the
delegates who constituted themselves the founding fathers of the
Comintern represented small Marxist or pacifist sects nesting
in the nooks and crannies of the European Labour movements.
This might not have mattered in a truly revolutionary situation,
for, in such a situation the extreme 'sect' as a rule, rises rapidly
to influence and leadership. The Bolsheviks were not quite

---

[1] Lenin, *Sochinenya*, vol. xxviii, pp. 433-4.   [2] See above, p. 235.

aware of the weakness of their foreign associates; but even if they had been aware of it they could still hope that with the progress of international revolution these associates would gain strength, as it had been gained by the Bolsheviks, who had themselves been little more than a 'sect' early in 1917. The hope seemed all the more justified as the Second International had fallen into such disrepute that it appeared to be dead beyond resurrection. The workers' widespread opposition to the old International sprang, however, not from any positive revolutionary attitude, but from a revulsion against war and social patriotism. The Bolsheviks, naturally, confused the motives. Even so, their expectations were not altogether groundless: within a year the new International did, in fact, gain a formidable hold on the European Labour movement.

Trotsky made only a brief appearance at the founding congress. Kolchak's spring offensive had just begun and Trotsky, interrupting an inspection of the battlefields, came to the conference hall straight from his train, in full uniform, bringing with him a breath of the civil war. The delegates who had known him as the spokesman of Zimmerwald eyed with thrilled curiosity the passionate anti-militarist transfigured into the leader of an army.[1] He gave the conference a hurried explanation of the main lines of his military policy and then presented a manifesto he had written to introduce the new International to the world. The manifesto began with a rapid incisive survey of the changes which capitalism had recently undergone. The war had brought the twilight of *laissez faire*. The state now tended to dominate economic life. Which state would dominate it, the bourgeois or the proletarian? This was the question. The reformists and social patriots evaded the issue and preached conciliation. 'If these preachings were to find acceptance among the working classes, capitalist development in new, much more concentrated and monstrous forms, would be restored on the bones of several generations, with the inevitable prospect of new world war. Luckily for mankind, this is impossible.'[2] Socialism, if it won in Europe, would also free the colonial nations, and assist them with its technology, organization, and spiritual influence so as to speed up their transition to an organized Socialist economy.

[1] Arthur Ransome, *Six Weeks in Russia*, p. 143.
[2] Trotsky, *Sochinenya*, vol. xiii, pp. 38–49.

'Colonial slaves of Africa and Asia! The hour of proletarian dictatorship in Europe will strike for you as the hour of your own emancipation.' From earlier classical statements of Marxist policy, the manifesto differed mainly in its emphasis on proletarian dictatorship, on the role of a revolutionary party, and in its aggressive opposition to bourgeois democracy. But if these were differences of emphasis rather than principle the idea of an alliance between Socialist revolution in the West and the colonial peoples of the East was quite new; it bore the hallmark of the Third International. Nevertheless, the manifesto was addressed primarily to Europe:

The whole bourgeois world charges the communists with the destruction of freedom and political democracy. The charge is untrue. Assuming power, the proletariat only discovers the full impossibility of the application of . . . bourgeois democracy, and it creates the conditions and the forms of a new and higher workers' democracy. . . . The wailings of the bourgeois world against civil war and Red Terror are the most prodigious hypocrisy known in history. . . . There would have been no civil war if cliques of exploiters, who had brought mankind to the brink of perdition, had not resisted every step forward made by the toilers, if they had not organized conspiracies and assassinations and called in armed assistance from outside. . . . Never artificially provoking civil war, the Communist Parties strive to shorten as much as possible the duration of such war . . ., to diminish the number of its victims and, above all, to secure victory to the working class.

Far from forming a group of conspirators or from renouncing the patrimony of European socialism, the International prided itself on inheriting 'the heroic efforts and the martyrdom of a long line of revolutionary generations from Babeuf to Karl Liebknecht and Rosa Luxemburg'.[1]

Not a month passed from the issue of this manifesto before revolution had gained important footholds in central Europe: Hungary and Bavaria were proclaimed Soviet republics. Bolshevik hopes soared: from Munich and Budapest the revolution would surely spread at once to Berlin and Vienna. The news reached Trotsky while he was mounting an offensive in the foothills of the Urals; and there, on the marches of Asia, he greeted the promise of the revolution's salvation coming from

[1] Trotsky, *Sochinenya*, vol. xiii, pp. 38–49.

the West. In 'Reflections on the Course of the Proletarian Revolution', written under the fresh impression of these events, he remarked: 'Once the Church used to say: *Ex Oriente Lux*. . . . In our epoch, indeed, the revolution has begun in the east'; but 'the revolution which we live through is a proletarian one, and the proletariat is strongest, most organized, most enlightened in the old capitalist countries'. Yet he had a foreboding about the strange course of events. Hungary had been the most backward land in the Austro-Hungarian empire. Bavaria was the most retrograde province of Germany. In both countries the peasants, not the workers, predominated; and both had traditionally been regarded as ramparts of reaction. Why was it that the revolution obtained footholds there and not in the centres of proletarian socialism?

He answered his own question, saying that although the proletariat was weak in the backward countries, the ruling classes there were weaker still. 'History has moved along the line of least resistance. The revolutionary epoch has made its incursion through the least barricaded gates.' The suggestive metaphor suggested more than Trotsky himself intended. He had no doubt that the revolution would advance to the heart of the fortress: 'To-day Moscow is the centre of the Third International. To-morrow—this is our profound conviction—the centre will shift westwards, to Berlin, Paris, London. The Russian proletariat has welcomed with joy the envoys of the world's working classes within the walls of the Kremlin. With even greater joy will it send its own envoys to the second congress of the Communist International to one of the western European capitals. An international congress in Berlin or in Paris will mean the full triumph of proletarian revolution in Europe and consequently all over the world. . . . What happiness it is to live and fight in such times!'[1]

Barely three months later the great prospects and hopes had gone with the wind. Soviet Bavaria had succumbed to the troops of General Hoffmann, Trotsky's adversary at Brest. White Terror reigned over the ruins of Soviet Hungary. The workers of Berlin and Vienna viewed with apathy the suppression of the two Communes. Germany and Austria, indeed the whole of Europe, seemed to be finding a new conservative

Op. cit., pp. 14-30.

balance under the Peace of Versailles, just concluded. These
events coincided with the worst predicament of the civil war:
British and French intervention reached its height, and Denikin
seized the Ukraine and advanced towards Moscow.

This was a strange moment in the history of Bolshevism. Not
only did the anti-Soviet intervention gather strength and
momentarily meet with little or no effective counteraction from
the western working classes. Not only had the revolution lost its
footholds in central Europe. Even in Russia it stood in the gravest
danger of forfeiting the relatively wealthy and civilized western
and central provinces and of having to draw back into the
wastes of the east, for only there did the course of the war favour
the Red Army. But while fortune frowned upon the Bolsheviks
from the West, it enticed them with new opportunities in the
East. Not only did the wild mountain ranges of the Urals offer
hospitality and security to the Soviets. Beyond the Urals and
Siberia, Asia stirred in rebellion against the bourgeois West.
In India these were the days of Amritsar, when Gandhi's
campaign of civil disobedience all but transformed itself into
a nation-wide anti-British rising. This concatenation of events
set in motion Trotsky's political imagination and impelled it
in a curious direction.

On 5 August 1919 Trotsky sent from the front a secret memorandum to the Central Committee, urging a radical 'reorientation' in international affairs. He argued that the revolution had
been thrown back eastward and—eastward it must face. He still
assumed that the delay in European revolution would last from
one to five years only; and he did not believe that Denikin would
consolidate his hold on the Ukraine. Yet for the time being, he
wrote, the Red Army could play only a minor part in Europe,
whether as an offensive or a defensive force. But the gates to
Asia were open before it! There the Red Army would have to
contend only with Japanese forces which were too small for
Siberian spaces and which would be hampered by American
jealousy of Japanese expansion.[1] The weight of the Soviet
régime in Asia was such that the Bolsheviks were in a position

[1] Trotsky remarked that the United States was so frightened of Japanese
domination in Siberia that the 'Washington wretches' (although they were still
using Kolchak as their agent) might yet resolve to back the Soviets against Japan.
Some time later Lenin similarly set store by the rivalry between America and Japan.
Lenin, *Sochinenva*, vol. xxxi, pp. 433–40.

not merely to wait there for new developments in Europe, but to embark upon an intense activity in the east.

In a tone of disillusionment with the recently formed International, Trotsky suggested that a body directing the revolution in Asia might soon be of much greater importance than the Executive of the Comintern. The Red Army might find the road to India much shorter and easier than the road to Soviet Hungary. A 'serious military man' had suggested to him a plan for the formation of an expeditionary cavalry corps to be used in India. Trotsky repeated that the revolution's road to Paris and London might lead through Kabul, Calcutta, and Bombay. With the utmost urgency he made the following proposals: an industrial base should be built up in the Urals to make the Soviets independent of the strategically vulnerable Donetz Basin; a revolutionary academy should be opened in the Urals or in Turkestan; political and military staffs should be set up to direct the struggle in Asia; technicians, planners, linguists, and other specialists should be mobilized for this work, particularly from the Ukrainian Communists, who, having lost the Ukraine, should now help the revolution to establish itself in Siberia.[1]

These proposals bore little relation to what could and had to be done immediately to ward off a military débâcle. Together with this memorandum Trotsky forwarded two other messages with detailed proposals for the overhaul of the southern front. To these, it may be surmised, the Politbureau immediately devoted closer attention than to the suggested 'Asian reorientation'.[2] Nor was this train of thought firmly rooted in Trotsky's own mind. It came as an impetuous reflex of his own brain in response to an exceptional set of circumstances; and the reflex ran counter to the principal, European, direction of his thought. It is, nevertheless, instructive as a pointer towards the future. In milder form the circumstances which gave rise to these suggestions—Russia's severance from the West and the abeyance of revolution in Europe—would persist after the end of intervention and civil war; and the reaction to them would follow broadly the lines suggested by Trotsky. The centres of

[1] *The Trotsky Archives.*
[2] The influence of Trotsky's ideas may, of course, be traced in the work of the second congress of the Comintern and in the congress of the eastern peoples at Baku which took place a year later.

Soviet power would shift eastwards, to the Urals and beyond.
Only Stalin, not Trotsky, was to become the chief agent and
executor of this momentous shift, which could not but entail an
'orientalization' of the revolution's mental and political climate,
an orientalization to which Trotsky was not assimilable. The
road of the revolution to Peking and Shanghai, if not to Calcutta
and Bombay, was to prove shorter than that to Paris and London and certainly easier than the road to Berlin or even to
Budapest. It is a tribute to the fertility of Trotsky's mind that
in a single side-flash it opened vistas upon the future which far
surpassed the comprehension of most contemporaries.

Before the year 1919 was out, the Bolsheviks again hopefully
faced west. The Ukraine and the southern provinces of European Russia were again under their control. The White Armies
awaited the *coup de grâce*. The opposition of western European
labour was at last seriously hampering British and French
intervention. Only relations with Poland were in suspense.
Poland was egged on by France to act as the spearhead of the
anti-Soviet crusade. But Pilsudski, who already ruled Poland
but not yet as dictator, adopted an ambiguous attitude. He
cherished the ambition of conquering the Ukraine, where the
Polish landed gentry had possessed vast domains, and setting
up a Polish-Ukrainian federation under Polish aegis. But he
hung fire as long as the Bolshevik forces were engaged against
the White Guards, for he knew that Denikin's or Yudenich's
victory would mean an end to Poland's independence. In strict
secrecy from the French, who were arming and equipping his
army, he concluded an informal cease-fire with the Bolsheviks.
For a moment it seemed that the cease-fire would lead to an
armistice and peace. In November 1919 the Politbureau
deliberated over the terms of a settlement proposed by the
Poles. It found the terms acceptable, and it commissioned
Trotsky and Chicherin to work out the details.[1]
So confident were the Bolshevik leaders in the approach of
peace that they put on a peace footing those of their armies
which were not engaged in combat and transformed them into
labour armies. On 16 January 1920 the Entente lifted the block-

[1] See the excerpts from the records of the Politbureau, session of 14 November
1919, in *The Trotsky Archives*.

ade from Russia; and immediately the Central Executive of the Soviets decreed the reforms already mentioned—the abolition of the death penalty and the curtailment of the *Cheka*'s powers. A few days later, however, on 22 January, Trotsky communicated to the Politbureau his apprehension that Pilsudski was preparing for war.[1] With Lenin's encouragement, he proceeded to strengthen the Red Armies on the Polish front.[2]

At the beginning of March the Poles struck. From the Urals, where he had been inspecting the labour armies, Trotsky rushed to Moscow. The peace reforms were stopped or annulled. The country was once again in a warlike spirit.

In view of what happened later, it ought to be underlined that at this juncture Trotsky stood for a policy of the strong arm towards Poland. For many months Chicherin had in vain addressed secret peace offers to Warsaw, urging a settlement of frontier disputes extremely favourable to Poland. Pilsudski ignored the advances and kept Polish opinion in the dark about them. Chicherin continued to make conciliatory proposals even after the beginning of the Polish offensive. His policy, however, aroused opposition within the Commissariat of Foreign Affairs, especially from Litvinov, his deputy. Trotsky intervened and firmly sided with Litvinov. He urged the Politbureau to stop the overtures. Pilsudski saw in them merely signs of Soviet weakness; and, as they had been made secretly, they failed to move Polish opinion towards peace. Trotsky demanded a return to open diplomacy which should enable the Polish people to see who was responsible for the outbreak of hostilities. Pilsudski settled this controversy, for shortly thereafter he found a pretext for breaking off negotiations, invaded the Ukraine, and seized Kiev. On 1 May 1920 Trotsky appealed to the Red Army to inflict upon the invader a blow 'which would resound in the streets of Warsaw and throughout the world'.

The Polish invasion stirred Russia deeply. For the first time the Bolsheviks now called for national not for civil war. To be sure, to them this was a struggle against 'Polish landlords and capitalists', a civil war in the guise of national war. But whatever their motives, the conflict let loose patriotic instincts and chauvinist emotions beyond their control. To the Conservative

[1] Trotsky's message to Zinoviev, Lenin, and Krestinsky in *The Archives*.
[2] Messages from the second half of February in *The Archives*.

elements in Russia this was a war against a hereditary enemy, with whose re-emergence as an independent nation they could not reconcile themselves—a truly Russian war, even though waged by Bolshevik internationalists. To the Greek Orthodox this was a fight against a people incorrigible in its loyalty to Roman Catholicism, a Christian crusade even though led by godless Communists. Some of those Conservative elements had at heart been in sympathy with the White Guards. But now that the White Guards had gone down in ruin, they were on the look-out for a pretext which would allow them to climb on the Soviet band-wagon without loss of patriotic and Greek Orthodox 'face'. The Polish invasion provided it. General Brusilov, Commander-in-Chief under the old régime, headed the movement of conversion. He placed himself at Trotsky's services and called upon all good Russians to follow in his footsteps. Thus, in addition to its revolutionary overtones, the war acquired its nationalist undertones. Pilsudski's troops did much to whip up the anti-Polish sentiment. Their behaviour in occupied Ukraine was overbearing; they began to establish the Polish landlords on their former domains; and they marked their victories by the shooting of prisoners of war and by pogroms.

To be carried on a tide of national unity was for the Bolsheviks a novel and embarrassing experience. Trotsky exerted himself to assert the party's internationalist outlook. He welcomed Brusilov's demonstration of solidarity with the Red Army; but he publicly repudiated Brusilov's chauvinist and anti-Catholic tone.[1] When the rumour spread that Brusilov would lead the Red armies against the Poles, Trotsky denied this and emphasized that the Polish front was under the command of Tukhachevsky and Yegorov, whose loyalty to the internationalist idea of the revolution had been tested in the civil war. At the height of hostilities, he publicly ordered the closing down of *Voennoe Delo* (*Military Affairs*), the periodical of the General Staff, because in an article on Pilsudski it had used language 'insulting the national dignity of the Polish people'. He further ordered an inquiry into the matter, so that the culprits 'should never again be entrusted with any work enabling them to influence the mind of the Red Army'.[2] (The incident has re-

---

[1] Trotsky, *Sochinenya* vol. xvii, book 2, pp. 407–8.
[2] *Kak Vooruzhalas Revolutsia*, vol. ii, book 2, p. 153.

mained something of a noble curiosity in an age when during war 'civilized' statesmen and men of letters brand without scruple the national character of an enemy as Hun-like, beast-like, or subhuman.) On his visits to the front, he kept in check the angry passion aroused in the army by reports about Polish shootings of prisoners of war. Even an enemy, he argued at meetings of front-line soldiers, must not be slandered. He emphatically forbade retaliation on Polish prisoners: 'Let the hand be cut off of any Red Army man who lifts his knife on a prisoner of war, on the disarmed, the sick and wounded', he wrote in an order of the day. Ruthless in battle, the Red Army man must show magnanimity towards the captive and helpless enemy.[1]

Pilsudski's victory in the Ukraine was short-lived. A few weeks of Polish occupation were enough to arouse the Ukrainian peasantry against the invaders. Tukhachevsky's armies on the northern sector of the front and Yegorov's on the southern were reinforced by divisions released from fighting against Denikin and Kolchak. The Red Army, although poorly equipped, was now at the peak of its strength—before the end of the campaign it had five million men under colours. On 12 June the Bolsheviks recaptured Kiev; and presently Pilsudski's troops retreated in panic towards the boundaries of ethnographic Poland.

At this point important political issues intervened to complicate the conduct of the war. Some of these concerned Russia's relations with Britain; others bore on her attitude towards Poland; and the two sets of problems were at some points interconnected.

The opposition of British Labour to intervention and the defeat of the White Guards had weakened the interventionist party, led by Winston Churchill. The government was divided against itself, the Prime Minister (Lloyd George) being inclined to withdraw from intervention and to resume trade with Russia. At the end of May 1920 a Soviet trade mission, headed by Krasin, left Moscow for London. In the meantime, however, the interventionist party was momentarily strengthened by Pilsudski's victories. The Politbureau was under the impression that the British government, like the French, wholeheartedly backed Pilsudski. The Commissariat of Foreign Affairs and the

[1] Trotsky, *Sochinenya*, vol. xvii, book 2, pp. 403–5.

Comintern tried to hit back at British positions in Asia, especially
in Persia and Afghanistan, as Trotsky had suggested in the
previous year. But before long British official policy wavered
again: Labour's opposition to intervention had risen to a high
pitch; and the Red Army's pursuit of the Poles had in any case
exposed once more the futility of intervention. On 11 July Lord
Curzon, the British Foreign Secretary, offered his government's
mediation between the Soviets and Poland and also between the
Soviets and that remnant of Denikin's army which, under
Baron Wrangel, had entrenched itself in the Crimea.

Throughout June and July the Politbureau and the Commissariat of Foreign Affairs tried to grasp the trend of British
policy. Trotsky repeatedly intervened in the debate and found
himself in opposition to the majority view. Of this controversy
there is a vivid account in Trotsky's confidential messages to
Chicherin, Lenin, and other members of the Politbureau, and
in Lenin's laconic remarks, in his own handwriting, found in
The Trotsky Archives. In a memorandum of 4 June, Trotsky
insistently urged the adoption of a conciliatory attitude towards
Britain. He argued that British policy by no means followed a
single line set on intervention, and that it was in the Soviet
interest to keep it fluctuating. Soviet attempts to stage anti-
British revolts in the Middle East, let alone a Soviet expedition
to the Middle East, would tend to consolidate British policy in
extreme hostility towards the Soviets. Last August he himself
had set great store by the revolutionary movements in Asia;
but now, in the light of fresh information, he argued that in the
Middle East, at any rate, these movements lacked inherent
strength.[1] The Bolsheviks ought to further revolutionary propaganda and clandestine organization, but avoid any steps
which might involve them in risky military commitments. At
best they could use the threat of revolution in the Middle East
as a bargaining counter in diplomatic exchanges with Britain.
But they ought to use every opportunity to impress the British
with their desire to reach agreement over the East.

On the margin of this document Lenin remarked with some
irony that Trotsky, like Krasin, was mistaken about British

[1] Trotsky added that even in Soviet Azerbaijan, in the Caucasus, which had a
numerous industrial working class and old ties with Russia, the Soviet régime did
not stand on its own feet.

policy: its line was firmly set; it was 'absolutely clear' that England helped and would continue to help both the Poles and Wrangel.[1]

In July, after Lord Curzon's offer of mediation, the issue was once again under discussion. Lenin communicated the offer to Trotsky, who was at the front. On the same day, 13 July, Trotsky replied in two messages, urging the Politbureau and Chicherin to accept British mediation between Russia and Poland, and to aim at an armistice which would lead to peace with the Entente as well as with Poland.[2] He once again advised the Politbureau to pay more careful attention to divergent trends in British opinion and policy.[3]

The Politbureau rejected Trotsky's proposals and, of course, the British offer. Oddly enough, it asked Trotsky to administer the rebuff to Lord Curzon. Actuated by the principle of Cabinet solidarity, he did so. In a scintillating sarcastic manifesto, from which nobody could even remotely guess his mental reservations, he explained that the British government, with its record of intervention, was a party to the conflict and could not aspire to render service as an impartial conciliator.[4]

This difference, after all, concerned only diplomatic tactics. But it was connected with another and fundamental controversy. Rejecting Curzon's proposal, Lenin demanded 'a furious speeding up of the offensive on Poland'. To this, too, Trotsky was opposed. By now the Red Army had reconquered all Ukrainian and Byelorussian lands and stood roughly along a line which Lord Curzon, when he still reckoned with Denikin's victory, had proposed as the frontier between Russia and Poland. At this line Trotsky intended to halt the Red Army and to make a public offer of peace. Lenin and the majority of the Politbureau were bent on continuing the pursuit of the Poles into Warsaw and beyond.

Once again the interplay of politics and strategy dominated the dispute. There was a military risk in Trotsky's proposal.

---

[1] A resolution of the Politbureau, also dated 4 June, shows that the Politbureau believed that Pilsudski acted in collusion with the German government as well.

[2] Trotsky was, however, against any mediation in the conflict between the Soviets and Wrangel, which was a domestic Russian affair.

[3] *Inter alia* Trotsky asked that Theodore Rothstein, the eminent Russo-British Marxist, should be consulted about the state of British opinion.

[4] Trotsky, *Sochinenya*, vol. xvii, book 2, pp. 426 ff.

Pilsudski was not likely to accept the 'Curzon line' as a frontier
and he might have used the respite of an armistice to prepare
a come-back. Trotsky was willing to take this risk. He set his
mind on the political and moral advantages of the course of
action he advocated and on the dangers which would attend
Lenin's policy. He held that a straightforward public peace
offer, making it clear that the Soviets had no designs on Poland's
independence and coveted no truly Polish territory, would
favourably impress the Polish people. If Pilsudski accepted the
offer, well and good. If not, the Polish people and the world
would know whom to blame for the continuation of war.
Trotsky argued that the Red Army's advance towards Warsaw,
without a preliminary offer of peace, would destroy the Russian
Revolution's goodwill with the Polish people and play into
Pilsudski's hands. For nearly a century and a half the greater
part of Poland had been subjugated by the Tsars. It was less
than two years since the Poles had regained independence,
solemnly guaranteed to them by the Russian Revolution. A
Russian army invading Polish soil, even though under provocation from Pilsudski and even though marching under the Red
Flag, would seem to them the direct successor to those Tsarist
armies which had kept them, their fathers, and their fore-
fathers in bondage. The Poles would then defend their native
soil tooth and nail.[1]

Lenin did not share these scruples and forebodings. It was
Pilsudski who had, deliberately and conspicuously, played the
aggressor's part, while Lenin had made every effort to avert
the war. Now, when the fortunes of battle favoured the Red
Army, it was, in Lenin's view, its right and duty to grasp the
fruits of victory—no victorious soundly led army stops halfway
in the pursuit of an almost routed enemy; and no moral,
political, or strategic principle forbids an army to invade the
aggressor's territory in the course of a pursuit.

Nor was this all. Lenin believed that the workers and peasants
of Poland would greet the invaders as their liberators. All the
Bolshevik leaders, including Trotsky, had only a dim idea of the
facts of the situation: they had as a result of the blockade lost

[1] The feelings of the small Baltic nations were similar. Throughout the year
Trotsky urged the Politbureau to conclude peace with all of them. This was done
(*The Trotsky Archives*).

contact with Poland as completely as if that country had been many thousands of miles away. They knew that there had been Soviets in Poland, in which the communists had wielded a very strong influence; and they believed them to be still in existence. Their information was more than a year out of date. In the meantime, in Poland as in the rest of central Europe, the tide had turned: Pilsudski had dispersed the Soviets and severely suppressed the Communist party.[1] A group of eminent Polish Socialists, who had joined the Bolsheviks, lived in Moscow; and to them the Politbureau turned for advice. They were strangely divided: Radek, Markhlevsky, and (it seems) Dzerzhinsky, who had belonged to the internationalist wing of Polish socialism and had not believed in the resurrection of Poland as a nation-state, now warned the Politbureau that the Red Army's invasion would be foiled by a powerful upsurge of Polish patriotic sentiment. It was in part as an effect of this warning that Trotsky adopted his attitude. Lenin appears to have been more impressed by a report of Lapinsky, who had come from the more patriotic wing of Polish socialism, and who greatly exaggerated the strength of Polish communism. Swept by optimism, believing that the Red Army's advance would be a signal for the outbreak of revolution in Poland, Lenin swayed the Politbureau. Even Stalin, who had soberly dismissed the idea of a march on Warsaw, changed sides; and Trotsky was alone in opposing it.

Lenin played for even higher stakes. Poland was the bridge between Russia and Germany; and across it Lenin hoped to establish contact with Germany. He imagined that Germany, too, was in intense revolutionary ferment. There was some fire behind the smoke of illusion. In March 1920 a section of the German army carried out a *coup d'état* in Berlin, with the intention of crushing the parliamentary régime and establishing a military dictatorship. Within two days, the coup, the so-called Kapp *Putsch*, was undone by a general strike of the German workers. This was a signal demonstration of the strength of German Labour. The initiative for the strike had come from the trade unions, not from the communists; but shortly thereafter German communism was vigorously making headway,

[1] In 1920 even Trotsky still spoke about the significance of the Polish Soviets, assuming that they were still in existence. See his *Sochinenya*, vol. xv, p. 301.

although it still failed to carry the bulk óf the working class. Enough that Lenin mooted the idea that the appearance of the Red Army at Germany's frontier might stimulate and intensify the processes of revolution. He intended to 'probe Europe with the bayonet of the Red Army'. At a session of the Revolutionary War Council, which took place at the height of the offensive, he passed a note to Sklyansky, saying that 'Warsaw must be taken within three to five days at any cost'. He insistently inquired whether the Red Army, which had already entered the Pomeranian 'corridor', could cut that corridor so as to deny the Poles access to Danzig. Danzig was the port through which Poland received munitions from the West; but it was also a point of contact with Germany.[1]

Despite his premonition of disaster, Trotsky submitted to the decision of the majority. He stayed in office, issued the marching orders, and carried on with routine jobs—only his visits to the front seem to have ceased. As the offensives progressed, a Revolutionary War Council of Poland was appointed, virtually a Provisional Government, headed by those Polish Bolsheviks who had been opposed to the venture. The farther the Red Army advanced, the more uneasy were the Council's reports to Moscow. The Polish workers and peasants met the invaders as conquerors, not liberators. But now the Red Army was irresistibly carried forward by its own impetus, extending its lines of communication and exhausting itself. A dangerous gap also arose between the northern armies, which, under Tukhachevsky, were approaching Warsaw, and the southern ones, which, under Yegorov and Budienny, had veered south-westwards towards Lvov. The chief political commissar to the southern armies, appointed on Trotsky's insistence,[2] was Stalin, who was keen on emulating Tukhachevsky and on getting Lvov as his prize while Tukhachevsky was entering Warsaw. Into this gap in the centre Pilsudski would presently spring to strike at Tukhachevsky's flank and rear. For a moment the gap worried Lenin;[3] and the General Staff began, somewhat late in the day, to urge the commanders of the southern armies to close it.

---

[1] The note is in *The Trotsky Archives*.

[2] Trotsky's message to the Central Committee of 11 May 1920. *The Archives*.

[3] *The Trotsky Archives* contain an undated note from Lenin to Sklyansky, in which Lenin expressed his misgivings.

But the Red Army still rolled on; and Moscow was all exultation.

At this stage of the campaign, from the middle of July to 7 August, the second congress of the Communist International was in session in Petrograd and Moscow. During the past year the European Labour movements had swung towards the International: leaders of great and old Socialist parties now almost humbly knocked at its doors. The congress discussed the terms of membership, the famous '21 Points', formulated by Lenin and Zinoviev, the tasks of the Communist parties, the fate of the colonial nations, and so on. But the debates were dominated by the thrilling expectation of the military *denouement* in Poland which would give a new and mighty impulse to European revolution. In front of a large war map Lenin daily gave the foreign delegates his optimistic comment on Tukhachevsky's advance.

At the beginning of the congress, Trotsky made a brief appearance in order to endorse the '21 Points' in the debate. He came back just before the end of the congress—the Red Army now stood at the very gates of Warsaw—to present the Manifesto he had written on behalf of the International. The delegates greeted him with a tributary roar of applause. In a crescendo of resounding phrases and images he surveyed the international scene in the first year of the Versailles Peace. He angrily denounced the 'Babylon' of decaying capitalism and tore the 'mask of democracy' from its face. 'German parliamentary democracy', he stated, 'is nothing but a void between two dictatorships.'[1] The delegates listened to him in breathless suspense; and the magic of his words and images was heightened as the battle, of which they thought him to be the inspirer, mounted to its climax. Yet Trotsky refrained from boasting, and in the manifesto he made no reference to the Red Army's victories. The delegates did not even notice his reticence. They could not guess what tense apprehension was hidden behind his self-confident appearance and resounding language. In this assembly, where even the most prudent men were carried away by joyous excitement, he alone refused to celebrate the victory, as the architect of which he was being acclaimed.[2]

[1] Trotsky, *Pyat Let Kominterna*, p. 89.
[2] Addressing the party cells of the Military Academy and of other schools,

A week later the battle of the Vistula began. It lasted only three days. It did not change the course of history, as its contemporaries believed—it only delayed it by a quarter of a century. But at the end of the battle the Red Army was in full retreat. While the battle was at its height, the Politbureau asked Trotsky to go to the front and try to retrieve the situation. He refused. He did not deceive himself, he replied, that he could now stave off defeat by any brisk personal intervention on the spot.[1]

For the moment the débâcle seemed even worse than it was, because Wrangel's Guards, seeing the Red Army tied down by the Poles, had broken out of the Crimea and invaded the Caucasus. Two days after the battle of the Vistula, on 19 August, Trotsky and Stalin jointly reported to the Politbureau on the military situation; and the Politbureau, apparently acknowledging defeat in Poland, resolved to give first priority to the campaign against Wrangel. Both Stalin and Trotsky were put in charge of a new mobilization of party members. Most of those mobilized were to be sent to the Crimea; and the bulk of Budienny's cavalry was to be diverted from the Polish front. Stalin was also instructed to work out measures to be taken in case of Wrangel's further advance. However, Wrangel's troops, although excellently equipped, were too weak in numbers and too disheartened to create a serious threat. They soon withdrew into the Crimea, hoping to hold out behind the fortified narrow neck of the Perekop Isthmus. After an epic and savage battle, directed by Frunze and Stalin, the Red Army broke through the Isthmus and drove Wrangel into the sea. This was the epilogue of the civil war.[2]

On 12 October the Soviets signed a provisional peace with Poland. But for a time war was still in the air. In Poland the ruling parties were divided. The Peasant Party—its leader Witos headed the government—pressed for peace, while

---

Trotsky said soon after the war that he did not believe for a moment that the Red Army would seize Warsaw—he did not even expect it to advance as far as it did. On this and other occasions he spoke quite frankly about the disagreements over the march on Warsaw, and his version was not contradicted from any source. (*Kak Vooruzhalas Revolutsia*, vol. iii, book 1, p. 91.)

[1] Trotsky's message to the Politbureau of 17 August. (*The Trotsky Archives.*) The battle lasted from 14 to 17 August.

[2] *The Trotsky Archives.*

Pilsudski's military party did its utmost to disrupt the parleys with Russia.[1] In Moscow, too, views were divided. The majority of the Politbureau favoured a renewal of hostilities. Some of those who did so expected that Pilsudski would not keep the peace anyhow; others craved for revenge. The General Staff discussed a new offensive. Tukhachevsky was confident that next time he would hold his victory parade in Warsaw. Trotsky relates that Lenin was at first inclined towards war, but only half-heartedly. At any rate, Trotsky insisted on peace and on the loyal observance of the provisional treaty with Poland; and once again he found himself in danger of being outvoted and reduced to dutiful execution of a policy he abhorred. From this he at last shrank. He declared that the differences went so deep that this time he would not feel bound by any majority decision or by Politbureau solidarity, and that, if outvoted, he would appeal to the party against its leadership. He used a threat similar to that which Lenin had, with overwhelming effect, used in the controversy over Brest; and he, too, achieved his purpose. In comparison with that controversy the roles were indeed curiously reversed. But the sequel was in a way similar, for now Lenin deserted the war faction and shifted his influence to back Trotsky. Peace was saved.[2]

The differences had gone deep. Yet it is doubtful whether any single Bolshevik leader, including Trotsky, was or could be aware of their full historic import, on which only the events of the middle of this century have thrown back a sharp, illuminating light.

It had been a canon of Marxist politics that revolution cannot and must not be carried on the point of bayonets into foreign countries. The canon was based on the experience of the French Revolution which had found its fulfilment and also its undoing in Napoleonic conquest. The canon also followed from the fundamental attitude of Marxism which looked to the working classes of all nations as to the sovereign agents of socialism and certainly did not expect socialism to be imposed upon peoples from outside. The Bolsheviks, and Trotsky, had often said that the Red Army might intervene in a neighbouring country, but

---

[1] An authoritative description of this tug-of-war was given by J. Dabski, the chief of the Polish peace delegation at Riga, in his memoirs.

[2] Trotsky, *Moya Zhizn*, vol. ii, pp. 193–4.

only as the ally and auxiliary of actual popular revolution, not as an independent, decisive agent. In this auxiliary role Lenin wished the Red Army to help the Soviet revolution in Hungary, for instance. In this role, too, the Red Army or the Red Guards had sporadically intervened in Finland and Latvia to assist actual Soviet revolutions which enjoyed popular backing and which were defeated primarily by foreign, mostly German, intervention. In none of these instances did the Red Army carry the revolution abroad. In the Polish war the Bolsheviks went a step farther. Even now Lenin had not become plainly converted to revolution by conquest. He saw the Polish working classes in potential revolt; and he expected that the Red Army's advance would act as a catalyst. But this was not the same as assisting an actual revolution. Whatever Lenin's private beliefs and motives, the Polish war was Bolshevism's first important essay in revolution by conquest. True, the Politbureau embarked on it in the heat of war, under abundant provocation, without grasping all the implications of its own decision. But this is the way in which great fateful turns in history occur: those who initiate them are often unconscious of what it is they initiate. This in particular is the manner in which revolutionary parties begin to throw over-board their hallowed principles and to transform their own character. If the Red Army had seized Warsaw, it would have proceeded to act as the chief agent of social upheaval, as a substitute, as it were, for the Polish working class. It will be remembered that in his youthful writings Trotsky had berated Lenin for 'substitutism', i.e. for a propensity to see in the party a *locum tenens* of the working class.[1] And here was indeed an instance of that substitutism, projected on the international scene, except that an army rather than a party was to act as proxy for a foreign proletariat.

This was all the more strange as in the course of two decades Lenin had fervently inculcated into his disciples and followers an almost dogmatic respect for the right of every nation, but more especially of Poland, to full self-determination. He had parted with comrades and friends who had been less dogmatic about this. He had filled reams with incisive argument against those Poles—Rosa Luxemburg, Radek, and Dzerzhinsky—who, as internationalists, had refused to promote the idea of a

Polish nation-state, while Poland was still partitioned. Now Lenin himself appeared to obliterate his own efforts and to absolve the violation of any nation's independence, if committed in the name of revolution.

Lenin grew aware of the incongruity of his role. He admitted his error.[1] He spoke out against carrying the revolution abroad on the point of bayonets. He joined hands with Trotsky in striving for peace. The great revolutionary prevailed in him over the revolutionary gambler.

However, the 'error' was neither fortuitous nor inconsequential. It had had its origin in the Bolshevik horror of isolation in the world, a horror shared by all leaders of the party but affecting their actions differently. The march on Warsaw had been a desperate attempt to break out of that isolation. Although it had failed it was to have a deep influence on the party's outlook. The idea of revolution by conquest had been injected into the Bolshevik mind; and it went on to ferment and fester. Some Bolsheviks, reflecting on the experience, naturally reached the conclusion that it was not the attempt itself to carry revolution abroad by force of arms but merely its failure that was deplorable. If only the Red Army had captured Warsaw, it could have established a proletarian dictatorship there, whether the Polish workers liked it or not. It was a petty bourgeois prejudice that only that revolution rested on solid foundations which corresponded to the wishes and desires of the people. The main thing was to be better armed and better prepared for the next venture of this kind.[2]

We shall discuss in the next chapter the domestic experiences of the Bolsheviks which fed and reinforced this trend of thought. Here it is enough to say that the trend showed itself in the attitude of those members of the Politbureau who favoured a renewal of hostilities with Poland. Yet the old Bolsheviks could develop such views only privately and tentatively. They were not in a

[1] Klara Zetkin, *Reminiscences of Lenin*, pp. 19–21.

[2] The party historian N. Popov writes: 'Trotsky was opposed to the advance on Warsaw, not because he considered our forces insufficient . . . but because of a Social-Democratic prejudice that it was wrong to carry revolution into a country from the outside. For these same reasons Trotsky was opposed to the Red Army aiding the rebels in Georgia in February 1921. Trotsky's anti-Bolshevik, Kautskyist reasoning was emphatically rejected by the Central Committee, both in July 1920 in the case of Poland and in February 1921 in the case of . . . Georgia.' (*Outline History of the C.P.S.U.*, vol. ii, p. 101.)

position to state them in a more formal manner or elevate them
to a principle. It was in the nature of such views that they did
not lend themselves to public statement; and the Marxist
tradition could not be openly flouted. That tradition was so
much alive in all Bolshevik leaders that it inhibited the working
of their own minds and prevented them from pursuing the new
line of thought to its conclusion. Even three decades later Stalin
would never admit that he favoured revolution by conquest,
even though he had already practised it on a vast scale. How
much more difficult was it for Bolsheviks to admit the fact even
to themselves in 1920!

Yet an idea which is in the air soon finds a mouthpiece.
Shortly after the Polish war, Tukhachevsky came forward as
the advocate of revolution by conquest. He had not lived down
the defeat on the Vistula, the only setback—and what a setback—he had suffered since his meteoric rise. He had come to
Bolshevism only in 1918 as a young officer, and now, at the age
of twenty-six, he was the most brilliant and famous general of
the Red Army. He was unquestionably devoted to the Soviets,
but he was the revolution's soldier, not a revolutionary. He was
not inhibited by the party's traditions; and he drew his inspiration from Napoleon rather than from Marx. He did not understand why the Bolsheviks should go on mouthing anathemas
against carrying revolution on the point of bayonets. He expounded his views in essays and lectures at the Military
Academy and argued that it was both possible and legitimate
for the Red Army to impose revolution on a capitalist country
'from without'.[1] Somewhat later he even proposed the formation
of an international General Staff of the Red Army, which would
direct revolutionary military activities in all countries. Intellectually impulsive, original, and courageous, he openly attacked the party's taboo. But he presented his case in so extreme
a form that it did not gain much support. Other leaders of the
civil war were inclined to accept his argument, properly diluted.
There was, at any rate, a logical link between Tukhachevsky's
view and their insistence that the Red Army should adopt an
expressly offensive military doctrine.[2]

Trotsky struggled against this new mood. In the aftermath of

---

[1] M. Tukhachevsky, *Voina Klasov*, see, in particular, his essay 'Revolution from
Without', pp. 50–60.   [2] See the 'Note on Trotsky's Military Writings'.

the Polish war, he warned against the temptation to carry revolution abroad by force of arms. The warning runs indeed like a red thread through his writings and speeches of this period.[1] His rational opposition to revolution by conquest was in a sense merely the obverse side of his almost irrational belief in the craving of the western working classes for revolution and in their ability to make it. He was so unshakably confident that the proletarians of Europe and America were already impelled by their own circumstances to follow in the footsteps of Bolshevism that he was firmly convinced of the absolute harm latent in any attempt to make the revolution for them or to probe and prod them with bayonets. He saw the world pregnant with socialism; he believed that the pregnancy could not last long; and he feared that impatient tampering with it would result in abortion. The solidarity which the Russian Revolution owed to the working classes of other countries, he maintained, should express itself mainly in helping them to understand and interpret their own social and political experience and their own tasks, not in trying to solve those tasks for them. In one controversy he angrily remarked of anyone who thought of replacing revolution abroad by the Red Army's operations that 'it were better for him that a millstone were hanged about his neck and he cast into the sea'.[2]

Yet such was the strength of the new Bolshevik proclivity that it could not be altogether suppressed. It soon manifested itself again in the Red Army's invasion of Georgia.

Up to February 1921 Georgia had been ruled by a Menshevik government, with which the Soviets had signed a treaty during the Polish war. Nearly the whole of the Caucasus was already under Soviet control; and Menshevik Georgia was a thorn in its flesh. The claim of the Georgian Mensheviks to independent nationhood was rather spurious: before the October Revolution they themselves had ardently advocated Georgia's unity with Russia and had asked only for a degree of local autonomy. Their present separatism was a convenient pretext. The mere existence of Menshevik Georgia made it more difficult for the Bolsheviks to consolidate their régime in the rest of the Caucasus; and the Bolsheviks had not forgotten that the Georgian

[1] *Kak Vooruzhalas Revolutsia*, vol. iii, book 2, pp. 114, 124, 142-3, 206, 225-7 and *passim*.   [2] Trotsky, op. cit., p. 225.

Mensheviks had meekly submitted to the successive occupation of their country by the Germans and then by the British, and had severely suppressed the Georgian Bolsheviks. Nevertheless the Soviet government had solemnly committed itself to respect Georgia's independence, and it had recognized the Menshevik government. The Politbureau hoped that Georgia would eventually find the pull of the Soviet Caucasus irresistible, that its Menshevik rulers would not be able to govern the country in opposition to all its neighbours, and that the scene would thus be set for their overthrow by native revolutionary forces. Consequently, the Politbureau was inclined to wait patiently until the experiment had run its course.

Trotsky was therefore greatly surprised when, in the middle of February 1921, during an inspection in the Urals, he learned that the Red Army had marched into Georgia. He was on the point of leaving for Moscow to attend a session of the Central Committee; and before his departure he got in touch with Sklyansky and inquired who had issued the marching orders and why. It turned out that the invasion was a bolt from the blue to the Commander-in-Chief as well. Trotsky suspected that the adventure had been irresponsibly staged behind the back of the General Staff and of the Politbureau; and he intended 'to raise the matter in full session of the Central Committee' and to bring to book the presumed adventurer.[1] But the marching orders had been issued, with the Politbureau's approval, by the Revolutionary War Council of the Caucasus, on which Ordjonikidze, Stalin's friend and himself a Georgian, served as chief commissar. The Politbureau had considered the matter in Trotsky's absence. Stalin and Ordjonikidze had reported that a Bolshevik insurrection had, with strong popular backing, broken out in Georgia; that the outcome was in no doubt; and that the Red Army would merely shorten the struggle. The Politbureau, which naturally treated Stalin and Ordjonikidze as experts on Georgian affairs, accepted their advice.

The rising in Georgia did not, however, enjoy the popular backing claimed for it; and it took the Red Army a fortnight of heavy fighting to enter Tiflis, the Georgian capital. Like the other small border nations, the Georgians had long memories of

[1] *The Trotsky Archives.*

Tsarist oppression. The forcible re-annexation aroused fierce resentment. The grievance rankled long after, and it was indirectly reflected in the opposition of Georgian Bolsheviks to Moscow's centralizing policies. This was to become one of the major points at issue between Stalin and Trotsky in the last year of Lenin's leadership. For the time being, however, Trotsky accepted the accomplished fact. The invasion could not be called off. It was only possible to try to soften its shock. This Lenin was doing of his own accord. He warned Ordjonikidze and the other Caucasian commissars 'to behave with especial respect towards the sovereign organs of Georgia and to show special attentiveness and caution in dealing with the Georgian population'. He asked to be informed of any offence against his instruction and of the slightest instances of friction with the Georgians. He further urged Ordjonikidze to strive for a reconciliation with the Mensheviks, even with Jordania, the head of the Menshevik government, who had not been absolutely hostile towards the Soviet régime.[1] There was little else that Trotsky himself could do or could wish to be done at the moment. Lenin's injunctions, however, produced little effect, because the invaders, having violated Georgia's sovereignty wholesale, were in no mood to respect it in detail. But it took time before this became clear.

Trotsky went on to disclaim and denounce in general the idea of revolution by conquest. But he did not feel justified in discussing publicly the specific differences over Georgia and once again flouting the Politbureau's collective responsibility. Moreover, when the Social Democratic leaders of the West, Kautsky, MacDonald, Henderson, and others, raised an outcry for the evacuation of Georgia by the Red Army, Trotsky rejoined with a *tu quoque*: he wrote a pamphlet in which he devoted only a brief passage to the invasion. He reasserted the right of the Red Army to assist a fully fledged revolution abroad; but he evaded the question whether such a revolution had occurred in Georgia. Instead, he concentrated on an acute exposure of the inconsistencies in the attitude of the Social Democratic critics towards the Russian Revolution, the fate of the colonial peoples, &c.[2] With all his fiery temperament he defended the Soviets, right or wrong, against their enemies and lukewarm friends. In

[1] Lenin, *Sochinenya*, vol. xxxii, p. 137.   [2] Trotsky, *Between Red and White.*

the eyes of the world he therefore bore a major share of responsibility for the invasion of Georgia.

In the Politbureau's behaviour over Poland and Georgia Trotsky saw mistakes, into which the party had blundered as if in a fit of absent-mindedness. He set his face against both 'mistakes', but he saw no inner connexion and no deeper significance in them. Up to a point he was right, because the party as a whole had entered the road of revolutionary conquest neither consciously nor deliberately. The invasion of Georgia was its only successful step on that road, and there was no lack of mitigating circumstances. Georgia had, after all, been part of Russia: it could not survive as a little 'bourgeois island' in the Soviet Caucasus. Yet there was an inner connexion between the Polish and the Georgian ventures, for both marked the initiation of a new current in Bolshevism.

The revolutionary cycle, which the First World War had set in motion, was coming to a close. At the beginning of that cycle Bolshevism had risen on the crest of a genuine revolution; towards its end Bolshevism began to spread revolution by conquest. A long interval, lasting nearly a quarter of a century, separates this cycle of revolution from the next, which the Second World War set in motion. During the interval Bolshevism did not expand. When the next cycle opened, it started where the first had ended, with revolution by conquest. It is a commonplace in military history that there exists a continuity between the closing phase of one war and the opening phase of the next: the weapons and the ideas on warfare invented or formed towards the end of one armed conflict dominate the first stage of the next conflict. A similar continuity may be seen to exist between the two cycles of revolution. In 1945–6 and partly even in 1939–40 Stalin began where he, and in a sense he and Lenin, had left off in 1920–1. Trotsky did not live to witness the momentous chapter which Stalin's revolutionary conquest has since written in modern history. His attitude towards the early symptoms of the trend was inconclusive. He was for revolution and against conquest; but when revolution led to conquest and conquest promoted revolution, he was confronted with a dilemma which, from his viewpoint, admitted no satisfactory solution. He did not press his opposition to revolutionary conquest to the point of an open breach. On the other hand, he left behind this suggestive half-warning, half-curse: 'He who wants to carry revolution abroad on the point of bayonets, it were better for him that a millstone were hanged about his neck. . . .'

Note

A SUMMARY of Trotsky's military activities cannot be concluded without a reference to his military writings. As founder and leader of an army, he remained a man of letters with the urge to give form and expression to his experiences and ideas, even in the smoke of battle. The many volumes of his military essays, speeches, and orders are distinguished by such contrasting qualities as romantic *élan*, and practical realism and at times by an almost philosophical depth.

Radek relates that Trotsky, when he became Commissar of War, had read only a few books on military affairs: Jaurès's *L'Armée Nouvelle*, a large *History of War* by Schulz, an Austrian Socialist, and Franz Mehring's writings on Frederick the Great. Radek undoubtedly belittles Trotsky's theoretical preparation in order to emphasize all the more strongly his achievement. During the Balkan wars and in the first years of the World War Trotsky had studied current military literature. He was certainly familiar, as Lenin was, with the work of Clausewitz, whom he quoted and in whose spirit he often approached his own problems. But Radek is right in holding that Trotsky was most strongly impressed by Jaurès's *L'Armée Nouvelle*, the work of a great historian and democratic Socialist, not a military expert.

Jaurès tried to reconcile two aspects of his own policy: his struggle against the reactionary French officers' corps, whose influence on domestic politics had shown itself in the Dreyfus affair; and his patriotic desire to see the French Republic armed and ready for defence. He conceived a reform of the army which, he hoped, would fit in with the economic and political reforms which were to transform bourgeois France into a 'social republic'. He advocated the replacement of the standing army by militias. The standing army, confined and trained within the rigid framework of the barracks, in artificial isolation from and latent opposition to civilian society, had been the officers' corps' main source of political strength. Militias were to be set up on the basis of productive units, factories, and village communities; the militiamen were to receive their training locally and were to continue to live and work as normal citizens, devoting themselves part-time or intermittently to the art and craft of war. The militias should therefore be so organically integrated into the civilian community that no ambitious general or military clique could use them as a political instrument.[1]

Trotsky borrowed Jaurès's idea but put it in a different context. Jaurès believed that it would be possible to democratize the army into a militia system even under the capitalist system. To Trotsky this belief was a reformist illusion. The virtual or actual opposition of a standing army to civilian society reflected, in his view, the clash between the interests of the propertied classes, which that army defended in the last instance, and those of the working classes. Only after the interest of the working classes had become paramount, he argued, could the army become submerged in the people and identified with it. The abolition of the standing army fitted the state which was to wither away gradually, as the proletarian state was expected to do.

Nevertheless, Trotsky built the Red Army as a standing army. The militia system, he argued, could be fully effective only against the background of a highly industrialized, organized, and civilized society. The Russian environment dictated to the Red Army the principles of its organization, which were very much the same as those that had underlain the structure of the Tsarist army. The difference between the two armies lay in their political and social outlook, not in their strictly military features.

Trotsky excused this as a temporary necessity and insisted that party and government should commit themselves to the militia system as their ultimate objective. He argued the case in the 'Theses' which he submitted to the eighth party congress in March 1919 and which, in his absence, Sokolnikov defended before the congress.[2] He looked forward to the time when men would receive their military training not in barracks but in conditions closely approximating to the workaday life of workers and peasants. The transition could not begin in earnest before a revival of industry; but even now, Trotsky insisted, a barracks must be made to resemble a military and general school, not a mere drilling-place. In the Red Army the commanding staffs were appointed, not elected; but Trotsky envisaged a return to the elective principle in the future. The eighth congress adopted Trotsky's 'Theses', and the ninth endorsed them again.

The programme aroused considerable criticism towards the end of the civil war, when Trotsky made the first attempt to put it into effect. The old professional officers were surprised that he, who had so severely centralized the army and extirpated the guerrilla spirit,

---

[1] Poles apart from Jaurès's conception is the idea of a wholly professional army, to be used as a decisive weapon in civil war, the idea expounded by General de Gaulle in *Vers l'Armée de Metier* before 1939.

[2] Trotsky, *Kak Vooruzhalas Revolutsia*, vol. i, pp. 185–95.

should advocate a military organization which in their eyes looked suspiciously like the old Red Guards. They could not seriously entertain the idea that an army could be trained, disciplined, and inured to collective action otherwise than in the barracks. One of Trotsky's critics was General Svechin, the author of a standard work on strategy and professor at the Military Academy. Against this critic Trotsky defended 'the dreamer Jaurès':

If Professor Svechin thinks that the Communist Party has taken power in order to replace the three-coloured [Tsarist] barracks by a red one, he is gravely mistaken. . . . The objection that under a militia system the command would not enjoy proper authority strikes one with its political blindness. Has perhaps the authority of the present leadership of the Red Army been established in the barracks? . . . That authority is based not on the salutary hypnosis of the barracks but on the appeal of the Soviet régime and of the Communist Party. Professor Svechin has simply overlooked the revolution and the enormous spiritual upheaval it has brought about. . . . To him the ignorant, drunken mercenary, syphilis-ridden and numbed by Catholicism, who served in Wallenstein's camp, the artisan-apprentice of Paris, who, led by journalists and lawyers, destroyed the Bastille, the Saxon worker and member of the Social Democratic Party of 1914–18, and the Russian proletarian who first in world history took power—all these are to him approximately the same cannon fodder to be delicately processed in the barracks. Is this not a mockery of history?

The development of the communist order will run parallel to the growth in the spiritual stature of the broadest popular masses. What the party has so far given mainly to advanced workers, the new society will increasingly give to the people as a whole. . . . For its members the party has hitherto in a sense 'replaced' the barracks: it has given them the necessary inner solidarity, made them capable of self-sacrifice and collective struggle. Communist society will be able to do this on an incomparably vaster scale. . . . The spirit of co-operation in the broadest sense is the spirit of collectivism. It can be fostered not merely in the barracks, but in a well-arranged school, especially one which combines education with physical labour; it can be fostered by the co-operative principle of labour; it can be fostered by broad and purposeful sporting activities. If the militias are based on the natural, occupational-productive groupings of the new society, the village communes, the municipal collectives, industrial associations . . . inwardly unified by school, sports association, and circumstances of labour, then the militia will be much richer in the 'corporate' spirit, in a spirit of much higher quality, than are barracks-bred regiments.[1]

The idea of the militias was also criticized in the party, and a demand arose for the revision of the resolutions adopted in its favour. At a congress of army commissars at the end of 1920 Smilga made a convincing case against the militias. He argued that under this system most regiments and divisions would consist almost exclusively of muzhiks; the industrial, proletarian units would be very few and isolated from the rest of the army. This might spell danger to the proletarian dictatorship. It was vital for the Bolsheviks to distribute the proletarian elements over the whole army; but this was incompatible with the territorial-productive principle of organization. On military grounds, Smilga argued, the militias would also be inadequate. With defective and sparse railways, Russia would not be able at the outbreak of war to mobilize in time and concentrate the militias at strategic points. Under this system, Russia might not be able to fight before an invader had reached the Volga. Militias were defensive in character. Jaurès had been prejudiced in their favour because he had started from an unrealistic distinction between defensive and offensive warfare. For their success militias required: a very high degree of industrialization; a numerous, technically advanced, and relatively educated working class; and a dense network of communication lines. It followed that Russia could not dispense with a standing army.[2]

Trotsky acknowledged the validity of much of this criticism, but he continued to point to the militias as the ultimate goal of military policy. In 1921 he set up three militia divisions—in Petrograd, in Moscow, and in the Urals—by way of experiment. But he himself urged caution. This was a time of much trouble and popular discontent. 'If the workers of the Urals were to starve', he said, 'the experiment would break down.' 'One cannot say in the abstract which system is preferable, one should not try to solve this like a mathematical problem. It is necessary to work this out as a political and social task, in accordance with prevailing circumstances.'[3] In later years, however, nearly three-quarters of the Red Army was reorganized into territorial units, and only one-quarter remained on the footing of a standing army. The experiment went farther than Russia could afford. In the middle 1930s, under the threat of the Second World War, the whole Red Army was overhauled and restored as a standing army. The reasons for this counter-reform,

[1] Trotsky, op. cit., vol. ii, book 1, pp. 115-21.
[2] I. Smilga, *Ocherednye Voprosy Stroitelstva Krasnoi Armii*, pp. 8-12.
[3] Trotsky, op. cit., vol. iii, book 1, p. 12.

carried out by Stalin and Tukhachevsky, were those which Smilga had stated in 1920. The counter-reform also harmonized with the general authoritarian trend of the time.

The problem of military doctrine occupies an important place in Trotsky's writings. He himself claimed no originality in this field. But he brought to the discussion of the issues a broad view of history and a freshness of approach which, if they were not enough to make a new philosophy of war, did much to guard the Red Army from pitfalls of one-sided doctrines. He had to contend against the old generals on the one hand, and against young revolutionary officers on the other. To the former he spoke as an innovator, attacking their conservative habits of thought. To the latter he appeared almost as an advocate of military orthodoxy.

He was the presiding spirit of Moscow's Military Academy, where the old generals were professors and lecturers. He strove to modernize the Academy's curriculum, to free it from pedantry, and to bring it close to the fresh experiences of warfare. Once, for instance, he expostulated with the writers of the Academy for their lifeless pseudo-historical style and urged them to emulate French military writers who, he said, knew how to combine historical research with an interest in contemporary warfare and in its sociological background. The academicians viewed the civil war rather contemptuously, as a bastard of grand strategy. Trotsky retorted irritably:

It is said among you that in the present civil or small war . . . military science has no role, in any case. I am telling you, Messieurs the military specialists, that this is an altogether ignorant statement. . . . Civil war, with its highly mobile and elastic fronts, affords enormous scope to genuine initiative and military art. The task is just the same here as elsewhere: To obtain the maximum result through a minimum expenditure of strength. . . . It was precisely the last [world] war . . . that offered relatively little scope to strategic art. After the gigantic front from the Belgian coast to Switzerland had become fixed, the war became automatic. Strategic art was reduced to a minimum; everything was staked on mutual attrition. Our war, on the contrary, has been full of mobility and manœuvre which allowed the greatest talents to reveal themselves. . . . [1]

While the old generals refused to learn the lessons of the civil war, the young ones were often reluctant to learn anything else. Their ambition was to construct a brand-new 'proletarian military

[1] Trotsky, op. cit., vol. iii, book 1, p. 156.

doctrine'. That doctrine, they held, should meet the needs of the
revolutionary class and suit its mentality: It must disdain defence
and static warfare and favour mobility and the offensive. Only
decaying classes, retreating in all fields, favoured the defensive
attitude. The 'proletarian style of warfare' appealed to commanders
who had risen from the ranks. Its most gifted expounders were
Tukhachevsky and Frunze, while Voroshilov and Budienny also
counted among its adherents. With Tukhachevsky the offensive
doctrine logically supplemented 'revolution from without'; and in
advocating both he remained within the Napoleonic tradition. But
being of a more modern outlook than his colleagues, he saw the future
offensive warfare as conducted by means of mass formations of tanks
and armoured vehicles co-operating with air forces. (He was also
the originator of parachute troops, whom he intended to use far
behind the enemy lines, in areas engulfed by civil war.)

Trotsky's polemic against this school of thought is perhaps the
most instructive part of his military writings. He dismissed 'proletarian strategy', just as in another field he disavowed 'proletarian
culture' and 'proletarian literature'. 'War bases itself on many
sciences', he wrote, 'but war itself is no science—it is a practical art,
a skill . . . a savage and bloody art. . . . To try to formulate a new
military doctrine with the help of Marxism is like trying to create
with the help of Marxism a new theory of architecture or a new
veterinary text-book.'[1] He protested, often with biting derision,
against the treatment of Marxist dialectics as the philosopher's
stone; and he demanded respect for a certain continuity of experience
and cultural tradition. He saw in the 'proletarian' innovations a
cover for intellectual crudity and conceit. He constantly drew the
attention of his military audiences to the barbarous poverty,
uncouthness, and dirt of the Red Army, to be mitigated only by
hard work and attention to detail, from which the Russian only too
frequently sought to escape into the realm of abstract doctrine.

The adherents of the 'proletarian doctrine of the offensive'
theorized from their own experience in the civil war, in which rapid
manœuvre predominated. Trotsky replied that the Red Army had
learned manœuvrability, allegedly the exclusive virtue of a rising
social class, from the White Guards, just as the latter had borrowed
methods of propaganda from the Red Army. Whites and Reds had
become mutually assimilated in military matters: 'Fighting one
another over a long time, enemies come to learn from one another.'[2]

[1] From a speech to the military delegates at the eleventh party congress. Op.
cit., vol. iii, book 2, p. 244.
[2] Trotsky, op. cit., vol. ii, book 1, pp. 61–62.

Trotsky himself had issued his famous order 'Proletarians, to horse!', the signal for the formation of Budienny's cavalry corps, only at the height of Denikin's offensive when the White cavalry, led by Mamontov, threatened to disrupt the Bolshevik interior by its deep and swift raids behind Bolshevik lines.[1]

But the high mobility peculiar to the civil war reflected (according to Trotsky) the primitive conditions in which the war was fought over vast, sparsely populated areas. He drew an analogy between the American Civil War and the Russian. In both, the opposed forces operated over thinly populated continents, with extremely poor lines of communication and means of transport. In both, cavalry had exceptionally wide scope. In both, the Whites were the traditional horsemen; and the armies both of the Northern States and of the Soviets had to wrest the initiative and form their own cavalries. It did not follow that high mobility was the 'style' of civil war at large. On the Scheldte, the Seine, or the Thames civil war would be fought much more statically than in steppes or prairies.[2]

The civil war had been fought in Russia in quasi-Napoleonic style, because of the country's low level of civilization. But it was foolish and unhistorical, Trotsky argued, to try to adopt the Napoleonic offensive doctrine for the Red Army, as Tukhachevsky tried to do. Trotsky sharply contrasted the position of revolutionary France in Europe with that of revolutionary Russia. At the beginning of the nineteenth century France was the most civilized and technically advanced nation on the Continent—this enabled Napoleon to pursue the offensive strategy. Russia was technically one of the most backward nations in Europe; Napoleonic strategy would bear no relation whatever to her social and military potentialities. He pointed out that the French General Staff, especially Foch, had in vain cultivated the Napoleonic strategy—France's position in

[1] Trotsky at first viewed Budienny's plan for a cavalry corps with reluctance, in part because the typical cavalryman was the reactionary Cossack, and in part because, thinking characteristically in terms of western technique, Trotsky was inclined to assume that the day of the horseman had gone. When he finally changed his mind, he wrote in September 1919: 'This most conservative service, largely withering away, has suddenly, as it were, revived. It has become the most important means of defence and offence in the hands of the most conservative and decaying classes. We must wrest this weapon from their hands and make it our own.' Op. cit., vol. ii, book 1, pp. 287–8. Budienny had a justified grievance against Trotsky for his initial, contemptuous dismissal of the idea.

[2] To illustrate his reasoning Trotsky discussed the hypothetical problem of defence which 'proletarian Britain' would have to solve if confronted by a threat of invasion. He sketched an imaginative picture of that defence: fortified shores; defence of the beaches; trenches, bunkers, barbed wire, and road blocks along the roads leading to the interior of the island, &c., a picture strangely familiar in Britain in 1940–1. Op. cit., vol. iii, book 2, p. 268.

Europe could not and did not allow for its application in 1914–18. And Trotsky poked fun at the brand-new 'proletarian doctrine' which on a closer view was merely a plagiarism of French pre-1914 text-books.

Attempts to define the 'essence' of warfare in general and of proletarian warfare in particular were, according to Trotsky, meta-physical doctrine-mongering.[1] He himself argued the need for a certain eclecticism in military theory. 'In practical arts', he approv-ingly quoted Clausewitz, 'one should not drive the flowers and the foliage of theory too high—one should rather keep them close to the soil of experience.' He spoke with qualified respect about the empirical methods of the English imperialists, 'who think in cen-turies and continents' and slightingly about the German epigones of Clausewitz. None of the 'national' doctrines of war offered or could offer any 'final truth' about war. Each school of thought merely reflected temporary conditions of national existence. The English doctrine of balance of power and naval supremacy; the cautious military thought of Bismarck's Germany, which went hand in hand with diplomatic aggressiveness; the exclusively offensive doctrine of latter-day German imperialism, which, carried away by its own momentum, threw all caution to the winds; the Bonapartist offensive doctrine of pre-1914 France (and, one might add, the reaction from it in the form of the Maginot mood before 1940); all these doctrines merely isolate and exaggerate certain moments and aspects of military experience. The Marxist way of thinking is averse to military doctrinairism of any sort. 'Only the traitor re-nounces attack; only the simpleton reduces all strategy to attack.'[2]

Scattered in these essays and speeches are noteworthy suggestions and anticipations, thrown out in the course of argument, of which only a few can be adduced here. Thus, discussing the strategy of a second world war, nearly twenty years before its outbreak, Trotsky remarked that it would greatly differ from that of the first, both in western Europe and in Russia. In western Europe, trench warfare would become less prominent or would disappear altogether. In Russia, on the contrary, there would be more position fighting than

[1] 'If we check the inventory of the 'eternal truths' of military science, we obtain not much more than a few logical axioms and Euclidean postulates. Defend your flank; secure your lines of communications and retreat; strike at the enemy's least defended point; and so on, and so on. Such principles . . . may well be applied even to matters very remote from the art of warfare. The donkey that steals oats from a hole in a torn sack ('the enemy's least defended point') and vigilantly turns its croup in the direction opposite to that from which danger threatens, certainly behaves according to the eternal principles of military science.' Op. cit., vol. iii, book 2, essay on 'Military Doctrine and Pseudo-Military Doctrinairism'.
[2] Ibid., p. 222.

there was in the civil war.[1] In a polemic against Frunze and Voro-shilov he argued that if Russia were attacked from the west by a technically stronger capitalist power, the Red Army's task in the first phase of hostilities would be not to attack but to behave defen-sively, because Russia would be slower in mobilization, and the defensive operations should give her time to complete it. It was therefore absolutely wrong to inculcate in the army the notion about the attacker's invariable moral superiority. 'Having space and numbers on our side, we may calmly and confidently mark the line at which mobilization, secured by our stubborn defence, will allow us to gather sufficient striking-power to pass to the counter-offensive.'[2] The Red Army may be forced to retreat, but the depth of the retreat should be dictated solely by the needs of mobilization.

If [however] I am the first to attack and my attack is not suffici-ently supported by mobilization and I am compelled to retreat, then I lose tempo and I may lose it irretrievably. If, on the con-trary, my plan envisages a preliminary retreat, if the plan is clear to the senior commanding staffs, if the latter have confidence in the near future and convey this confidence downwards, if their confidence does not founder on the prejudice that one ought invariably to be the first to attack—then I have every chance of regaining tempo and winning.[3]

Trotsky found, of course, no use for Tukhachevsky's International General Staff. The time, he maintained, for the setting up of such a staff would come only when, in the process of genuine revolution abroad, new Red armies would come into being. But he himself insisted on the need for rules and regulations of civil war, in which the experiences of the revolutions and risings in various countries would be utilized and evaluated; and he drew up a conspectus for such rules and regulations.

In the aftermath of the civil war, the educational problems of the army, the technological complications of warfare and its ever closer connexion with politics occupied Trotsky. 'In the education of our Red commanding officer', he said, 'the development of his capacity for a synthetic evaluation of the co-operation and mutual interaction of all kinds of modern weapons ought to go hand in hand with the acquisition of a correct social-political orientation. . . .'[4] At the Military Academy he urged the commanding staffs to learn foreign languages, to get out of their national shell, to broaden their horizon and to 'participate in mankind's world-wide experi-ence'.

[1] Ibid., p. 268.   [2] Ibid., p. 256.   [3] Loc. cit.   [4] Op. cit., vol. i, p. xi.

CHAPTER XIV

Defeat in Victory

AT the very pinnacle of power Trotsky, like the protagonist of a classical tragedy, stumbled. He acted against his own principle and in disregard of a most solemn moral commitment. Circumstances, the preservation of the revolution, and his own pride drove him into this predicament. Placed as he was he could hardly have avoided it. His steps followed almost inevitably from all that he had done before; and only one step now separated the sublime from the sinister—even his denial of principle was still dictated by principle. Yet in acting as he did he shattered the ground on which he stood.

Towards the end of the civil war he initiated courses of action which he and the Bolshevik party could carry through only against the resistance of the social classes which had made or supported the revolution. The Bolsheviks had denounced bourgeois democracy as a sham concealing the inequality of the social classes and the predominance of the bourgeoisie. But they had pledged themselves to uphold proletarian democracy, guaranteeing freedom of expression and organization to the working class and the poor peasantry. No Bolshevik leader had repeated that pledge so often and so ardently as Trotsky. None repudiated it now as plainly. The paradox is all the more striking because at the same time he was unaffectedly opposed to carrying revolution abroad on the bayonet's point. Such opposition was consistent with the principle of proletarian democracy. If the working class of any country was to be its own master, then it was preposterous and even criminal to try to impose on it any social order 'from without'. But this argument applied *a fortiori* to the Russian working class: it, too, should have been master in its own country. Yet the policies which Trotsky now framed were incompatible with that *samodeyatelnost*, that political self-determination of the working class, which he had indefatigably preached for twenty years and which he was to preach again during the seventeen years of his open struggle against Stalin.

He promoted the new policies at first with Lenin's consent.

But as he proceeded, he found Lenin and most of the Bolsheviks arrayed against him and invoking the principle of proletarian democracy. His own ideas now bore the clear hallmark of that 'substitutism', which he himself had once denounced as the chief vice of Bolshevism, indeed, as the hereditary vice of Russian revolutionary politics. For, in his view, the party, informed by the proper understanding of the 'tasks of the epoch' and of its own 'historic mission', was to substitute that understanding and that mission for the wishes and strivings of the broad social forces which it had led in the revolution. Thus Trotsky now began to resemble that caricature of Lenin which he himself had once drawn.[1]

What accounted for this extraordinary transformation? What was it that made the armed and victorious prophet of revolution contradict the tenor of his own prophecy? Before an answer can be attempted, the economic and social condition of Russia must be briefly surveyed, for it was to that plane that the drama had now shifted.

. . . .

From the end of 1919 Trotsky devoted only a minor part of his attention to military affairs. The issue of the civil war was no longer in doubt; and in the latter part of 1920 he kept somewhat aloof from the conduct of military policy because of his differences with the Politbureau over the Polish war. But even earlier he had become absorbed in the problems of economic reconstruction. He entered this new field with the impetuous self-confidence which success at the Commissariat of War had given him; and he was inclined to apply there the methods and solutions which he had worked out and tested in the military field. On 16 December 1919 he submitted to the Central Committee a set of propositions ('Theses') on the economic transition from war to peace. Among the measures which he proposed, militarization of labour was the most essential. He had written this paper only for the members of the Central Committee, hoping to start a discussion in their closed circle. By mistake Bukharin at once published the paper in *Pravda*. The indiscretion gave rise to an extremely tense public controversy which lasted until the spring of 1921.[2]

The years of world war, revolution, civil war, and intervention

[1] See above, pp. 90-7.   [2] Trotsky, *Sochinenya*, vol. xv, pp. 10-14, 36.

had resulted in the utter ruin of Russia's economy and the disintegration of her social fabric. From a ruined economy the Bolsheviks had had to wrest the means of civil war. In 1919, the Red Army had already used up all stocks of munitions and other supplies. The industries under Soviet control could not replace them by more than a fraction. Normally southern Russia supplied fuel, iron, steel, and raw materials to the industries of central and northern Russia. But southern Russia, occupied first by the Germans and then by Denikin, was only intermittently and during brief spells under Soviet control. When at last, at the end of 1919, the Bolsheviks returned there for good, they found that the coal-mines of the Donetz valley were flooded and the other industries destroyed. Deprived of fuel and raw materials, the industrial centres of the rest of the country were paralysed. Even towards the end of 1920, the coal-mines produced less than one-tenth and the iron- and steel-works less than one-twentieth of their pre-war output. The production of consumer goods was about one-quarter of normal. The disaster was made even worse by the destruction of transport. All over the country railway tracks and bridges had been blown up. Rolling stock had not been renewed, and it had only rarely been kept in proper repair, since 1914. Inexorably transport was coming to a standstill. (This, incidentally, was one of the contributory causes of the Red Army's defeat in Poland. The Soviets had enlisted five million men, but of these less than 300,000 were actually engaged in the last stages of the Polish campaign. As the armies rolled onward, the railways were less and less capable of carrying reinforcements and supplies over the lengthening distances.) Farming, too, was ruined. For six years the peasants had not been able to renew their equipment. Retreating and advancing armies trampled their fields and requisitioned their horses. However, because of its technically primitive character, farming was more resilient than industry. The muzhik worked with the wooden *sokha*, which he was able to make or repair by himself.

The Bolsheviks strove to exercise the strictest control over scarce resources; and out of this striving grew their War Communism. They nationalized all industry. They prohibited private trade. They dispatched workers' detachments to the countryside to requisition food for the army and the town-dwellers. The government was incapable of collecting normal taxes; it possessed no machinery for doing so. To cover government expenses, the printing-presses produced banknotes day and night. Money became so worthless that wages and salaries had to be paid in kind. The meagre food ration formed the basic wage. The worker was also paid with part of his own produce, a pair of shoes or a few pieces of clothing, which he usually bartered away for food.

This set of desperate shifts and expedients looked to the party like an unexpectedly rapid realization of its own programme. Socialization of industry would have been carried out more slowly and cautiously if there had been no civil war; but it was, in any case, one of the major purposes of the revolution. The requisitioning of food, the prohibition of private trade, the payment of wages in kind, the insignificance of money, the government's aspiration to control the economic resources of the nation, all this looked, superficially, like the abolition of that market economy which was the breeding-ground of capitalism. The fully grown Communist economy about which Marxist text-books had speculated, was to have been a natural economy, in which socially planned production and distribution should take the place of production for the market and of distribution through the medium of money. The Bolshevik was therefore inclined to see the essential features of fully fledged communism embodied in the war economy of 1919–20. He was confirmed in this inclination by the stern egalitarianism which his party preached and practised and which gave to war communism a romantic and heroic aspect.

In truth, war communism was a tragic travesty of the Marxist vision of the society of the future. That society was to have as its background highly developed and organized productive resources and a superabundance of goods and services. It was to organize and develop the social wealth which capitalism at its best produced only fitfully and could not rationally control, distribute, and promote. Communism was to abolish economic inequality once for all by levelling up the standards of living. War communism had, on the contrary, resulted from social disintegration, from the destruction and disorganization of productive resources, from an unparalleled scarcity of goods and services. It did indeed try to abolish inequality; but of necessity it did so by levelling down the standards of living and making poverty universal.[1]

The system could not work for long. The requisitioning of food and the prohibition of private trade for the time being helped the government to tide over the direst emergencies. But in the longer run these policies aggravated and accelerated the shrinkage and disintegration of the economy. The peasant began to till only as much of his land as was necessary to keep his family alive. He refused to produce the surplus for which the requisitioning squads were on the look-out. When the countryside refuses to produce food for the town, even the rudiments of urban civilization go to pieces. The cities of Russia became depopulated. Workers went to the countryside to escape famine. Those who stayed behind fainted at the factory benches, produced very little, and often stole what they produced to barter it for food. The old, normal market had indeed been abolished. But its bastard, the black market, despoiled the country, revengefully perverting and degrading human relations. This could go on for another year or so; but, inevitably the end would be the breakdown of all government and the dissolution of society.

Such was the situation to which Trotsky bent his mind towards the end of 1919. To cope with it one of two courses of action had to be taken. The government could stop the requisitioning of food from the peasant and introduce an agricultural tax, in kind or money. Having paid his taxes, the peasant could then be permitted to dispose of his crop as he pleased, to consume it, sell it, or barter it. This would have induced him to grow the surpluses for urban consumption. With the flow of food from country to town restored, the activity of the state-owned industries could be expected to revive. This indeed would have been the only real solution. But a reform of this kind implied the revival of private trade; and it could not but explode the whole edifice of war communism, in the erection of which the Bolsheviks took so much pride.

The alternative was to look for a solution within the vicious circle of war communism. If the government was to go on requisitioning food and enforcing the ban on trade, it had to

[1] The reader will find a detailed and instructive account of war communism in E. H. Carr, *The Bolshevik Revolution*, vol. ii.

increase the pressure on the peasantry first in making it produce more food and then in requisitioning the food. It might also offer special rewards to food growers—clothing, footwear, agricultural implements. It could not do so, however, before the famished workers had repaired and set in motion the destroyed and dilapidated industrial plant and begun to turn out the goods for which the peasantry craved. The government was therefore compelled to press for more industrial production. Unable to offer incentives to the workers, it had to apply more force to them as well as to the peasants. It was a sure sign of the Utopian character of war communism that it went on ignoring realities until it drove itself into an impasse and could maintain itself only by ever-increasing doses of violence.

Trotsky did not at first go beyond the framework of accepted policy. He was preoccupied with the means by which the dispersed working class could be reassembled and brought back to industry. There were the workers who had fled to the countryside; there were those who in search of food had abandoned skilled jobs for unskilled ones; and there were those *declassés* who were completely engulfed in the black market and lost to industry. How could they all be brought back to a normal environment and reintegrated into the nation's productive apparatus? As they could not be attracted by a promise of better living, so Trotsky concluded, they must be recruited to the factories in the same way as soldiers. Thus, empirically, Trotsky arrived at the idea of militarization of labour. The revolution had loudly proclaimed the duty of every citizen to work and declared that 'he who does not work shall not eat'. The time had now come, Trotsky argued, to enforce that duty. The revolution had sent hundreds of thousands to die on the battlefields. Surely it had the moral right to send people into workshops and mines, where the new battle for survival must be waged.

In those 'Theses' which *Pravda* published prematurely on 17 December 1919, Trotsky characteristically linked this scheme with the military reform he envisaged, the transition of the army to the militia system. He proposed that the machinery for military mobilization should be employed for the mobilization of civilian labour. It is strange how his aspiration to carry out a most democratic reform in the army was combined with his attempt to introduce this extreme form of compulsion of labour. The army was to become permeated with the spirit of civilian citizenship. Its detachments were to be organized on the basis of productive units. On the other hand, civilian labour was to be subjected to military discipline; and the military administration was to supply manpower to industrial units. The Commissariat of War was to assume the functions of the Commissariat of Labour.[1]

Lenin wholeheartedly supported Trotsky's policy. He clung to war communism, which could be made to work, if at all, only on condition that the measures proposed by Trotsky were successful. Nor did Lenin object to the assumption by the Commissariat of War of the responsibility for the supply of industrial labour. Lenin had had to build up the civilian branches of his administration from scratch; and, after the years of civil war, most of them were still in a rudimentary stage. The Commissariat of War had absorbed the best men; it had had first claim on the government's resources; it was directed by the most clear-headed administrator. Its machinery, formidable and highly efficient, was the most solid part of Lenin's administration, its real hub. It seemed a matter of administrative convenience to switch the Commissariat to civilian work.

No sooner had these proposals become known than they let loose an avalanche of protests. At conferences of party members, administrators, and trade unionists, Trotsky was shouted down as the 'new Arakcheev', the imitator of that ill-famed general and Minister of War who, under Alexander I and Nicholas I, had set up military farming colonies and ruled them with a rod of iron. *Arakcheevshchina* had ever since been the by-word for grotesque flights of military-bureaucratic fancy over the field of economic and social policies. The cry of protest rose in the Bolshevik newspapers. It came from Trotsky's old associates, Ryazanov and Larin, from the eminent Bolsheviks Rykov, Miliutin, Nogin, Goltzman, and from others. Weariness of civil war and impatience with the architect of victory mingled in these protests. As usually happens in a time of reaction from the tensions and sacrifices of war, people were willing to cover with

[1] On 27 December 1919 it was announced that the government had formed a Commission on Labour Duty, over which Trotsky presided.

laurels the man responsible for victory. But they were even more
eager to get rid of the rigours of wartime discipline; and they
looked for guidance to men who were of less fiery temperament
and less splendid talents, but who were willing to pursue milder
courses of action. Old, battle-hardened Bolsheviks were heard
to declare that they had had enough of the army's impositions,
that the Commissariat of War had long enough kept the country
under terror and sucked its blood, and that they would not
countenance Trotsky's new ambitions.

Matters came to a head on 12 January 1920, when Lenin and
Trotsky appeared before the Bolshevik leaders of the trade
unions and urged them to accept militarization. Trotsky
defended his own record. If his Commissariat, he said, had
'pillaged' the country and exacted severe discipline, it had done
so to win the war. It was a disgrace and a 'sin against the spirit
of the revolution' that this should now be held against him, and
that the working class should be incited against the army. His
opponents were complacent about the country's economic
condition. The newspapers concealed the real state of affairs.
'It is necessary to state openly and frankly in the hearing of the
whole country, that our economic condition is a hundred times
worse than our military situation ever was. . . . Just as we once
issued the order "Proletarians, to horse!", so now we must raise
the cry "Proletarians, back to the factory bench! Proletarians,
back to production!" '[1] The nation's labour force continued
to shrink and degenerate. It could not be saved, reconstituted,
and rehabilitated without the application of coercive measures.
Lenin spoke in the same vein. Yet the conference almost unanimously rejected the resolution which he and Trotsky jointly
submitted. Of more than three score Bolshevik leaders only two
men voted for it. Never before had Trotsky or Lenin met with so
striking a rebuff.

Trotsky's strictures on the complacency of his critics were not
unjustified. The critics did not and could not propose any
practical alternative. They, too, clung to war communism and
disavowed only the conclusion Trotsky had drawn from it. He
had little difficulty therefore in exposing their inconsistency.
Yet there was a certain realism and valuable scruple in their
very lack of consistency. Trotsky's opponents refused to believe

[1] Trotsky, op. cit., pp. 27–52.

that the wheels of the economy could be set in motion by word of military command, and they were convinced that it was wrong for a workers' state to act as a press gang towards its own working class.[1]

In the meantime the first labour army came into being, not by the militarization of civilian labour but by the transformation of a regular army into a labour force. The initiative came from the Revolutionary War Council of the Third Army, which was stationed in the Urals. After its victory over Kolchak, that army frittered away its time and energy in idleness. It could not release and send home its men, primarily because of the lack of transport. Its Revolutionary War Council proposed that meanwhile the army should be employed in timber felling, farming, and other work. Lenin and Trotsky welcomed the suggestion, which gave them a chance to put their policy into effect virtually without opposition: the trade unions did not object to the productive employment of idle regiments.[2]

Trotsky hoped to use this experiment as a starting-point for the conscription and direction of civilian labour. Nothing could be simpler than that the army, before releasing its men, should take a census of their productive skills, mark every soldier's trade in his service-book, and then direct him straight from the demobilization point to the working place where he was wanted. Trotsky planned to combine the soldier's service-book with the worker's labour-book, a device which should also facilitate the formation of militias on the basis of productive units. This was an imaginative idea. Its flaw was that the released soldier, anxious to reunite with his family or to look for a better living, was likely to abandon the working place to which he had been directed. Trotsky drew blueprints for the organization of communal feeding-centres to attract workers; but such schemes could not be put into effect amid the famines and disorders of the time. He displayed astounding originality and inventiveness, but his imagination worked feverishly in a vacuum; and his ideas were out of joint with reality.

After the army of the Urals, the armies of the Caucasus and of the Ukraine were put to work in mines, forests, and fields. Trotsky headed the entire organization. General Bonch-Bruevich

[1] This controversy filled the pages of *Ekonomicheskaya Zhizn* and *Pravda* throughout January 1920. [2] *The Trotsky Archives*.

was his Chief of Staff; Pyatakov was his representative in the Urals; and Stalin was chief commissar of the Ukrainian labour army. The organization maintained military discipline; and each labour army regularly reported its successes and failures on the 'fronts'. (It was Trotsky who first systematically applied military terms, symbols, and metaphors to civilian economic matters and thus introduced a fresh, vivid style in the Russian language, a style which later became ossified into a bureaucratic mannerism and spread to other languages.) Views about the economic efficiency of the labour armies were divided—it could, at any rate, not have been lower than that of civilian labour at the time. The Bolsheviks acclaimed the labour armies, especially after Trotsky had gone to some length to mollify the trade unions and had appealed to the labour armies for friendly co-operation with them.

He brought to this work his moral passion and theatrical *élan*, which led him, however, to exaggerate the significance of what he did and to cast a false glamour over what were at best sad expedients. This, for instance, is how he wrote in one of his Orders to the Labour Armies:

Display untiring energy in your work, as if you were on the march or in battle. . . . Commanders and commissars are responsible for their detachments at work as in battle. . . . The political departments must cultivate the spirit of the worker in the soldier and preserve the soldier in the worker. . . . A deserter from labour is as contemptible and despicable as a deserter from the battlefield. Severe punishment to both! . . . Begin and complete your work, wherever possible, to the sound of socialist hymns and songs. Your work is not slave labour but high service to the socialist fatherland.[1]

On 8 February he departed with his staff for the Urals, on the first inspection of the labour armies. In *En Route*, the paper published on his train, he thus addressed his staff:

The old capitalist organization of labour has been destroyed irrevocably and for ever. The new socialist organization is only beginning to take shape. We must become conscious, self-sacrificing builders of the socialist economy. Only on this road shall we find a way out, salvation, warmth, and contentment. We must begin from the foundations. . . . Our train is proceeding to the northern

---

[1] *Pravda*, 16 January 1920.

Urals, where we shall devote all our strength to the organization
of labour in which the Ural workers, the Ural peasants, and the
Red Army men . . . will participate hand in hand. Bread for the
starving! Fuel for the freezing! This is the slogan of our team this
time.[1]

He had just written these words when, in the middle of the
night, he was shaken by a violent concussion. His train became
derailed in a severe snowstorm. Throughout the night and the
whole of the next day the train lay in snowdrifts almost within
sight of a small station. Not a soul came to inquire what had
happened. The station-masters had ceased to signal the passage
of trains; even the train of the President of the Supreme War
Council had passed through unnoticed. Despite the threat of
court martial, nobody bothered to clear away the snowdrifts
from the tracks. The accident unexpectedly revealed to Trotsky
the void which grew around governmental policies and plans.
A fathomless apathy shrouded the people. Trotsky raged,
conducted an investigation on the spot, and ordered a military
tribunal into action. But he could not help reflecting that
repression alone could not remedy the people's numb insensi-
bility. His forebodings grew darker during his sojourn in the
countryside of the Urals. He became acutely aware that the
nation's energy and vitality was drying up at its very source—
on the farmstead.

He now searched for remedies beyond war communism.
He returned to Moscow with the conclusion that a measure of
economic freedom should be restored to the peasantry. In clear
and precise terms he outlined the reform which alone could lead
the nation out of the impasse. There must be an end to the
requisitioning of crops. The peasant must be encouraged to
grow and sell surpluses and to make a profit on them. The
government and the party were not aware of the magnitude of
the disaster, because the last forcible collection had yielded more
food than the previous one. This, he argued, was because after
the retreat of the White Guards, the requisitions had been
carried out over a much wider area than before. 'In general,
however, the food reserves are in danger of drying up, and
against this no improvement in the requisitioning machinery

[1] Trotsky, *Sochinenya*, vol. xv, pp. 324-5.

can help.' That way lay further disruption, further shrink-age of the labour force and final economic and political degra-dation.[1]

At the Central Committee his arguments carried no convic-tion. Lenin was not prepared to stop the requisitions. The reform Trotsky proposed looked to him like a leap in the dark. The government, he held, had already shown too much haste in preparing the transition to peace: Trotsky himself had just warned the Central Committee that Poland was about to attack. It seemed safer to stick to an established policy rather than tamper with the army's food supplies, which had, after all, been secured by the requisitions. Nor was that all. Lenin and the Central Committee had not yet lived down the illusions of war communism. They still hoped that the system, having rendered valuable service in war, would be even more useful in peace. Trotsky proposed to throw the economy back on to the treacher-ous tides of a free market. This was what the Mensheviks demanded. Did Trotsky agree with them? had he become a free trader? he was asked.[2] He was told that the party had ad-vanced towards an organized and controlled economy and that it would not allow itself to be dragged back.

The Central Committee rejected his proposals. Only more than a year later, after the failure of war communism had been demonstrated with tragic conclusiveness, did Lenin take up the same proposals and put them into effect as the New Economic Policy (N.E.P.). This was then and still is hailed as a stroke of Lenin's genius, a rare feat of courageous, undogmatic statesmanship. In the light of the facts it seems that the feat was at least overpraised; and that when Trotsky later re-proached Lenin and the Central Committee for initiating the most important changes in economic policy when these were overdue by a year or two, the stricture was not quite

---

[1] Trotsky, *Sochinenya*, vol. xvii, book 2, pp. 543-4. It is not clear, however, whether Trotsky was aware that his proposals, if accepted, would necessarily lead to the winding up of the policies of war communism, including those he himself advocated. In later years he argued that he had stood for militarization of labour only in the context of war communism. At the tenth congress of the party, however, when N.E.P. was introduced, he insisted that his labour policies retained their validity and that they were not necessarily connected with war communism. See *Desyatyi Syezd RKP*, p. 191, and *Moya Zhizn*, vol. ii, chapter xxxviii.

[2] *Desyatyi Syezd RKP*, loc. cit.

undeserved.[1] The incident also shows how unreal is the juxta-position, in Stalinist versions, of Lenin the friend and Trotsky the enemy of the peasantry: Lenin's reputation as the well-wisher of the muzhik rests primarily on the New Economic Policy.

Yoffe, whom we know as Trotsky's close friend, remarked in the letter he wrote before his suicide in 1927, that it was Trotsky's major weakness that he did not persist in his wisdom, especially when to be wise was to be alone.[2] One might add that on this occasion Trotsky, rebuked for his wisdom, plunged back into the accepted folly and persisted in it with an ardour which even the fools thought too foolish. After the Central Committee rejected his proposals, he dropped the matter. He did not raise it again or even hint at it at the ninth congress of the party, which met a month later, at the end of March 1920. Instead he appeared as the government's chief economic policy-maker and expounded a master plan for the next phase of war communism. Did he become convinced that the revision of policy he had suggested was unseasonable? Did he consider it impolitic to advocate a reform for which the Mensheviks, too, clamoured? Did he fear that the party as a whole was not in a receptive mood? Probably all these motives had their part in inducing him to act as he did.

The nation's economy continued to decay. The need for radical action became more pressing. As the party had refused to ease the rigours of war communism it had to aggravate them. Trotsky consented to bear the onus and the odium of the job. The Politbureau urgently requested him to take charge of the wrecked transport system and offered to back him to the hilt in any course of action he might take, no matter how severe. Trotsky pleaded incompetence, but agreed to take over tem-porarily the department of transport in addition to that of war.[3] With increased confidence he returned to the theme of mili-tarization of labour. This, he said at the congress, was indis-pensable for the integration and development of the nation's resources under a single economic plan. Planned economy was still far off; but the party and the nation should not expect to

[1] See Trotsky's messages to the Central Committee and the Politbureau of 7 August 1921 and 22 August 1922. *The Archives.*

[2] *The Trotsky Archives.*

[3] See the correspondence between Lenin and Trotsky (1 February and 9 March 1920), ibid.

move towards it by cautious, well-measured steps. In the past Russia had always advanced by violent leaps and bounds; she would continue to do so. Compulsion of labour was, of course, unthinkable under fully fledged socialism; but it 'would reach the highest degree of intensity during the transition from capitalism to socialism'. He urged the congress to approve disciplinary measures, 'the severity of which must correspond to the tragic character of our economic situation': 'deserters from labour' ought to be formed into punitive battalions or put into concentration camps.[1] He also advocated incentive wages for efficient workers and 'Socialist emulation'; and he spoke of the need to adopt the progressive essence of 'Taylorism', the American conception of scientific management and organization of labour, which had been abused by capitalism and rightly hated by the workers, but of which socialism could and should make rational use. These were then startling ideas. At the congress a minority denounced them and indignantly resisted the disciplinarian trend of Trotsky's policy. That minority consisted of the 'libertarians', the 'ultra-lefts', the 'democratic centralists', led by Osinsky, Sapronov, and Preobrazhensky, men with whom Trotsky would one day join hands against Stalin. Now he was their chief antagonist, and he swayed the congress.[2]

Soon afterwards he again expounded and elaborated his policy at a congress of trade unions. He demanded that the unions should discipline the workers and teach them to place the interest of production above their own needs and demands. The Central Council of trade unions was already split into two groups: one supported his 'productionist' attitude; the other, led by Tomsky, felt that the trade unions could not help defending the 'consumptionist' claims of the workers. Trotsky argued that the workers must first produce the resources from which their claims could be met; and that they should remember that they were working for the workers' state, not for the old possessing classes. Most Bolshevik trade unionists knew from experience that such exhortations did not impress hungry men. But since the party had endorsed Trotsky's policy, they could not oppose him in public. At the congress the Mensheviks became the mouthpieces of discontent. They attacked the labour armies. They denied the government the right to conscript

[1] Trotsky, Sochinenya, vol. xv, p. 126.   [2] Devyatyi Syezd RKP, pp. 81–4, 123–36.

workers and deprive them of the freedom to defend their interests. They argued that compulsory labour was inefficient. 'You cannot build a planned economy', exclaimed Abramovich, the Menshevik, 'in the way the Pharaohs built their pyramids.'[1] Abramovich thus coined the phrase, which years later Trotsky was to repeat against Stalin. The Mensheviks were on strong ground; and the fact that their record in the revolution had been poor, even odious, could not detract from the logic and truth of their argument. Trotsky himself could not at heart contradict them when they argued that the wastage of the industrial labour force could not be stopped as long as the peasants were not allowed to sell their crops freely.[2]

His answer to the criticisms was little better than a piece of brilliant sophistry. Its historical interest lies in the fact that this has been perhaps the only frank attempt made in modern times to give a logical justification of forced labour—the actual taskmasters and whippers-in do not bother to produce such justifications. The crux of Trotsky's argument was that under any social order 'man must work in order not to die'; that labour was therefore always compulsory; and that Communists should approach the matter without cant, because they were the first to organize labour for the benefit of society as a whole. He came to deny by implication the significance of the differences in form and degree in which the natural compulsion of labour manifested itself under different social systems. Man had worked as slave, serf, free artisan, independent peasant, and free wage-earner. The natural compulsion of labour had been aggravated or softened by social relations. Man had fought against slavery, serfdom, and capitalism in order to ease it. The Russian Revolution had promised to ease it radically by means of rational economic organization. It was not the revolution's fault that, because of inherited poverty and the devastation of several wars and of blockade, it could not honour its promise. But the Bolsheviks need not have expressly repudiated that promise. This was what Trotsky appeared to do when he told the trade unions that coercion, regimentation, and militarization of labour were no mere emergency measures, and that the workers' state

---

[1] *Tretii Vserossiiskii Syezd Profsoyuzov*, p. 97.

[2] The case for a change in policy which anticipated the N.E.P. was made at the congress by the Menshevik Dallin. Ibid., p. 8.

normally had the right to coerce any citizen to perform any work at any place of its choosing.

> We are now heading towards the type of labour [he stated] that is socially regulated on the basis of an economic plan, obligatory for the whole country, compulsory for every worker. This is the basis of socialism. . . . The militarization of labour, in this fundamental sense of which I have spoken, is the indispensable basic method for the organization of our labour forces. . . . Is it true that compulsory labour is always unproductive? . . . This is the most wretched and miserable liberal prejudice: chattel slavery, too, was productive. . . . Compulsory serf labour did not grow out of the feudal lords' ill-will. It was [in its time] a progressive phenomenon.[1]

Carried away by his desire to justify the measures he sponsored, he, the rebel *par excellence*, the expounder of permanent revolution, came very near to talking like an apologist for past systems of coercion and exploitation.

For a time the Polish war blunted the edge of this controversy. Peril from without once again induced people to accept without murmur policies which, before, had aroused their intense resentment. At the height of the war, Trotsky, surrounded by a team of technicians, made a determined effort to set the railways in motion. By this time the stock of locomotives had been almost entirely wasted. Engineers forecast the exact date— only a few months ahead—when not a single railway in Russia would be working. Trotsky placed the railway men and the personnel of the repair workshops under martial law; and he organized systematic and rapid rehabilitation of the rolling-stock. He went into the repair workshops to tell the workers that the country was paying for their slackness in blood: the paralysis of transport had encouraged the Poles to attack. 'The situation of the worker', he declared, 'is grievous in every respect . . . it is worse than ever. I would deceive you if I were to say that it will be better to-morrow. No, ahead of us are months of heavy struggle until we can lift our country out of this terrible misery and utter exhaustion, until we can stop weighing our bread ration on the chemist's scales.'[2] When the railwaymen's trade union raised objections to his action, he

---

[1] Ibid., pp. 87–96.
[2] See his speech at the Muromsk workshops of 21 June 1920 in *Sochinenya*, vol. xv, p. 368.

S

dismissed its leaders and appointed others who were willing to do his bidding. He repeated this procedure in unions of other transport workers. Early in September he formed the *Tsektran*, the Central Transport Commission, through which he brought the whole field of transport under his control. The Politbureau backed him to the hilt as it had promised. To observe electoral rights and voting procedures in the unions seemed at that moment as irrelevant as it might seem in a city stricken with pestilence. He produced results and surpassed expectations: the railways were rehabilitated well ahead of schedule—'the blood circulation of the economic organism was revived'—and he was acclaimed for the feat.[1]

But no sooner had the Polish war been concluded than the grievances and dissensions exploded anew and with greater force than before. He himself provoked the explosion. Flushed with success, he threatened to 'shake up' various trade unions as he had 'shaken up' those of the transport workers. He threatened, that is, to dismiss the elected leaders of the unions and to replace them by nominees who would place the nation's economic interest above the sectional interests of the workers. He grossly overstepped the mark. Lenin now bluntly dissociated himself from Trotsky and persuaded the Central Committee to do likewise. The Committee openly called the party to resist energetically 'militarized and bureaucratic forms of work': and it castigated that 'degenerated centralism' which rode roughshod over the workers' elected representatives. It called on the party to re-establish proletarian democracy in the trade unions and to subordinate all other considerations to this task.[2] A special commission was formed to watch that these decisions were carried out. Zinoviev presided over it, and, although Trotsky sat on it, nearly all its members were his opponents.[3] As a finishing stroke, the Central Committee forbade Trotsky to speak

[1] For the famous Order no. 1042 concerning the railways see op. cit., pp. 345-7. Later in the year Trotsky was placed at the head of special commissions which took emergency action to rehabilitate the industries of the Donetz valley and of the Urals.

[2] See the report of the Central Committee in *Izvestya Tsentralnovo Komiteta RKP*, no. 26, 1920, and G. Zinoviev, *Sochinenya*, vol. vi, pp. 600 ff.

[3] The Commission consisted of Zinoviev, Tomsky, Rudzutak, Rykov, and Trotsky. Later Shlyapnikov, Lutovinov, Lozovsky, and Andreev were co-opted. Of these only Andreev, who thirty years later was still a member of Stalin's last Politbureau, shared Trotsky's view.

in public on the relationship between the trade unions and the state.

Trotsky, unrepentant, sulked. At the beginning of December, at a closed session of the *Tsektran*, he returned to the attack on trade unionists who, as he said, had been good at conducting strikes in the old days but showed little understanding of the needs of a Socialist economy. He defended his practice of overruling them, made light of the demand for elections in the trade unions, and castigated those who cried out that a new bureaucracy was reviving Tsarist methods of government. 'Bureaucracy . . .', he replied, 'was not a discovery of Tsardom. It has represented a whole epoch in the development of mankind', an epoch by no means closed. A competent, hierarchically organized civil service had its merits; and Russia suffered not from the excess but from the lack of an efficient bureaucracy. He made this point repeatedly, arguing that for the sake of efficiency it was necessary to grant certain limited privileges to the bureaucracy. He thus made himself the spokesman of the managerial groups, and this later enabled Stalin to taunt him plausibly with being the 'patriarch of the bureaucrats'.[1] He was confident, Trotsky said, that he could win popular support for his policy; but the economic and social breakdown left no time for the application of the democratic process, which worked with unbearable slowness, because of the low cultural and political level of the Russian masses. 'What you call bossing and working through nominees is in inverse proportion to the enlightenment of the masses, to their cultural standards, political consciousness, and the strength of our administrative machinery.'[2]

Once again the Central Committee rebuffed him. Trotsky fretfully reminded Lenin and the other members of how often they had privately urged him, the 'trouble-shooter', to act ruthlessly and disregard considerations of democracy. It was disloyal of them, he remarked, to pretend in public that they defended the democratic principle against him.[3]

The deeper ill which afflicted the whole system of government, and of which this tug-of-war was merely a symptom, lay in the

[1] Stalin, *Sochinenya*, vol. vi, p. 29.
[2] Trotsky, *Sochinenya*, vol. xv, p. 422.   [3] *Desyatyi Syezd RKP*, p. 215.

frustration of the popular hopes aroused by the revolution. For
the first time since 1917 the bulk of the working class, not to
speak of the peasantry, unmistakably turned against the Bolsheviks. A sense of isolation began to haunt the ruling group.
To be sure, the working class had not come to regret the revolution. It went on to identify itself with it; and it received with
intense hostility any openly counter-revolutionary agitation.
'October' had so deeply sunk into the popular mind that Mensheviks and Social Revolutionaries now had to preface their
criticisms of the government with an explicit acceptance of the
'achievements of October'. Yet the opposition to current Bolshevik policies was just as intense and widespread. The Mensheviks and Social Revolutionaries, who in the course of three
years had been completely eclipsed and had hardly dared to
raise their heads, were now regaining some popular favour.
People listened even more sympathetically to anarchist agitators violently denouncing the Bolshevik régime. If the Bolsheviks
had now permitted free elections to the Soviets, they would
almost certainly have been swept from power.[1]

The Bolsheviks were firmly resolved not to let things come to
that pass. It would be wrong to maintain that they clung to
power for its own sake. The party as a whole was still animated
by that revolutionary idealism of which it had given such
abundant proof in its underground struggle and in the civil war.
It clung to power because it identified the fate of the republic
with its own fate and saw in itself the only force capable of
safeguarding the revolution. It was lucky for the revolution—
and it was also its misfortune—that in this belief the Bolsheviks
were profoundly justified. The revolution would hardly have
survived without a party as fanatically devoted to it as the
Bolsheviks were. But had there existed another party equally
devoted and equally vigorous in action, that party might, in
consequence of an election, have displaced Lenin's government
without convulsing the young state. No such party existed. The
return of Mensheviks and Social Revolutionaries would have
entailed the undoing of the October Revolution. At the very

[1] Many Bolshevik leaders explicitly or implicitly admitted this. See Lenin,
Sochinenya, vol. xxxii, pp. 160, 176, 230 and *passim*; Zinoviev in *Desyatyi Syezd RKP*,
p. 190. In a private letter to Lunacharsky (of 14 April 1926) Trotsky describes the
'menacing discontent' of the working class as the background to the controversy of
1920–1. *The Trotsky Archives*.

least it would have encouraged the White Guards to try their luck once again and rise in arms. From sheer self-preservation as well as from broader motives the Bolsheviks could not even contemplate such a prospect. They could not accept it as a requirement of democracy that they should, by retreating, plunge the country into a new series of civil wars just after one series had been concluded.

Nor was it by any means likely that a free election to the Soviets would return any clear-cut majority. Those who had supported Kerensky in 1917 had not really recovered from their eclipse. Anarchists and anarcho-syndicalists, preaching a 'Third Revolution', seemed far more popular among the working class. But they gave no effective focus to the opposition; and they were in no sense pretenders to office. Strong in criticism, they possessed no positive political programme, no serious organization, national or even local, no real desire to rule a vast country. In their ranks honest revolutionaries, cranks, and plain bandits rubbed shoulders. The Bolshevik régime could be succeeded only by utter confusion followed by open counter-revolution. The Bolsheviks refused to allow the famished and emotionally unhinged country to vote their party out of power and itself into a bloody chaos.

For this strange sequel to their victory the Bolsheviks were mentally quite unprepared. They had always tacitly assumed that the majority of the working class, having backed them in the revolution, would go on to support them unswervingly until they had carried out the full programme of socialism. Naïve as the assumption was, it sprang from the notion that socialism was the proletarian idea *par excellence* and that the proletariat, having once adhered to it, would not abandon it. That notion had underlain the reasoning of all European schools of Socialist thought. In the vast political literature produced by those schools the question of what Socialists in office should do if they lost the confidence of the workers had hardly ever been pondered. It had never occurred to Marxists to reflect whether it was possible or admissible to try to establish socialism regardless of the will of the working class. They simply took that will for granted. For the same reason it had seemed to the Bolsheviks as clear as daylight that the proletarian dictatorship and proletarian (or Soviet) democracy were only two complementary and inseparable aspects of the same thing: the dictatorship was there to suppress the resistance of the propertied classes; and it derived its strength and historic legitimacy from the freely and democratically expressed opinion of the working classes. Now a conflict arose between the two aspects of the Soviet system. If the working classes were to be allowed to speak and vote freely they would destroy the dictatorship. If the dictatorship, on the other hand, frankly abolished proletarian democracy it would deprive itself of historic legitimacy, even in its own eyes. It would cease to be a proletarian dictatorship in the strict sense. Its use of that title would henceforth be based on the claim that it pursued a policy with which the working class, in its own interest, ought and eventually must identify itself, but with which it did not as yet identify itself. The dictatorship would then at best represent the idea of the class, not the class itself.

The revolution had now reached that cross-roads, well known to Machiavelli, at which it found it difficult or impossible to fix the people in their revolutionary persuasion and was driven 'to take such measures that, when they believed no longer, it might be possible to make them believe by force'. For the Bolshevik party this involved a conflict of loyalties, which was in some respects deeper than any it had known so far, a conflict bearing the seeds of all the turbulent controversies and sombre purges of the next decades.

At this cross-roads Bolshevism suffered a moral agony the like of which is hardly to be found in the history of less intense and impassioned movements. Later Lenin recalled the 'fever' and 'mortal illness' which consumed the party in the winter of 1920–1, during the tumultuous debate over the place of the trade unions in the state. This was an important yet only a secondary matter. It could not be settled before an answer had been given to the fundamental question concerning the very nature of the state. The party was wholly absorbed in the controversy over the secondary issue, because it was not altogether clearly aware of the primary question and was afraid to formulate it frankly in its own mind. But as the protagonists went on arguing they struck the great underlying issue again and again and were compelled to define their attitudes.

It is not necessary here to go into the involved and somewhat technical differences over the trade unions, although the fact that the drama of the revolution revealed itself in a seemingly dry economic argument significantly corresponded to the spirit of the age.[1] Suffice it to say that, broadly speaking, three attitudes crystallized. The faction led by Trotsky (and later by Trotsky and Bukharin) wanted the trade unions to be deprived of their autonomy and absorbed into the machinery of government. This was the final conclusion which Trotsky drew from his conflicts with the trade unions. Under the new dispensation, the leaders of the unions would, as servants of the state, speak for the state to the workers rather than for the workers to the state. They would raise the productivity and maintain the discipline of labour; they would train workers for industrial management; and they would participate in the direction of the country's economy.

At the other extreme the Workers' Opposition, led by Shlyapnikov and Kollontai, protested against the government's and the party's tutelage over the unions. They denounced Trotsky and Lenin as militarizers of labour and promoters of inequality. In quasi-syndicalist fashion they demanded that trade unions, factory committees, and a National Producers' Congress should assume control over the entire economy. While Trotsky argued that the trade unions could not in logic defend the workers against the workers' state, Shlyapnikov and Kollontai already branded the Soviet state as the rampart of a new privileged bureaucracy.

Between these two extremes, Lenin, Zinoviev, and Kamenev spoke for the main body of Bolshevik opinion and tried to strike a balance. They, too, insisted that it was the duty of the trade unions to restrain the workers and to cultivate in them a sense of responsibility for the state and the nationalized economy. They emphasized the party's right to control the unions. But they also wished to preserve them as autonomous mass organizations, capable of exerting pressure on government and industrial management.

Implied in these attitudes were different conceptions of state and society. The Workers' Opposition and the so-called *Decemists* (the Group of Democratic Centralism) were the stalwart defenders of 'proletarian democracy' *vis-à-vis* the dictatorship.

[1] A detailed account of the debate can be found in Deutscher, *Soviet Trade Unions* (*Their place in Soviet labour policy*), pp. 42–59.

They were the first Bolshevik dissenters to protest against the
method of government designed 'to make the people believe by
force'. They implored the party to 'trust its fate' to the working
class which had raised it to power. They spoke the language
which the whole party had spoken in 1917. They were the real
Levellers of this revolution, its high-minded, Utopian dreamers.
The party could not listen to them if it was not prepared to
commit noble yet unpardonable suicide. It could not trust its
own and the republic's fate to a working class whittled down,
exhausted, and demoralized by civil war, famine, and the black
market. The quixotic spirit of the Workers' Opposition was
apparent in its economic demands. The Opposition clamoured
for the immediate satisfaction of the workers' needs, for equal
wages and rewards for all, for the supply, without payment, of
food, clothing, and lodging to workers, for free medical attention, free travelling facilities, and free education.[1] They wanted
to see fulfilled nothing less than the programme of full communism, which was theoretically designed for an economy of
great plenty. They did not even try to say how the government
of the day could meet their demands. They urged the party to
place industry, or what was left of it, once again under the control of those factory committees which had shown soon after the
October Revolution that they could merely dissipate and squan-
der the nation's wealth. It was a sad omen that the people
enveloped in such fumes of fancy were almost the only ones to
advocate a full revival of proletarian democracy.

Against them, Trotsky prompted the party to cease for the
time being the advocacy and practice of proletarian democracy
and instead to concentrate on building up a Producers' Democracy. The party, to put it more plainly, was to deny the workers
their political rights and compensate them by giving them scope
and managerial responsibility in economic reconstruction. At
the tenth congress (March 1921), when this controversy reached
its culmination, Trotsky argued:

The Workers' Opposition has come out with dangerous slogans.
They have made a fetish of democratic principles. They have placed
the workers' right to elect representatives above the party, as it
were, as if the party were not entitled to assert its dictatorship even
if that dictatorship temporarily clashed with the passing moods of

[1] *Desyatyi Syezd RKP*, p. 363; A. M. Kollontai, *The Workers' Opposition in Russia.*

the workers' democracy. . . . It is necessary to create among us the awareness of the revolutionary historical birthright of the party. The party is obliged to maintain its dictatorship, regardless of temporary wavering in the spontaneous moods of the masses, regardless of the temporary vacillations even in the working class. This awareness is for us the indispensable unifying element. The dictatorship does not base itself at every given moment on the formal principle of a workers' democracy, although the workers' democracy is, of course, the only method by which the masses can be drawn more and more into political life.[1]

The days had long passed when Trotsky argued that the Soviet system of government was superior to bourgeois parliamentarianism because under it the electors enjoyed, among other things, the right to re-elect their representatives at any time and not merely at regular intervals; and that this enabled the Soviets to reflect any change in the popular mood closely and instantaneously, as no parliament was able to do. His general professions of faith in proletarian democracy now sounded like mere saving clauses. What was essential was 'the historical birthright of the party' and the party's awareness of it as the 'indispensable unifying element'. Euphemistically yet eloquently enough he now extolled the collective solidarity of the ruling group in the face of a hostile or apathetic nation.

Lenin refused to proclaim the divorce between the dictatorship and proletarian democracy. He, too, was aware that government and party were in conflict with the people; but he was afraid that Trotsky's policy would perpetuate the conflict. The party had had to override trade unions, to dismiss their recalcitrant leaders, to break or obviate popular resistance, and to prevent the free formation of opinion inside the Soviets. Only thus, Lenin held, could the revolution be saved. But he hoped that these practices would give his government a breathing space—his whole policy had become a single struggle for breathing spaces—during which it might modify its policies, make headway with the rehabilitation of the country, ease the plight of the working people, and win them back for Bolshevism. The dictatorship could then gradually revert to proletarian democracy. If this was the aim, as Trotsky agreed, then the party must reassert the idea of that democracy at once and

[1] *Desyatyi Syezd RKP*, p. 192. See also p. 215.

T

initiate no sweeping measures suggesting its abandonment. Even though the régime had so often had recourse to coercion, Lenin pleaded, coercion must be its last and persuasion its first resort.[1] The trade unions ought therefore not to be turned into appendages of the state. They must retain a measure of autonomy; they must speak for the workers, if need be against the government; and they ought to become the schools, not the drill-halls, of communism. The administrator—and it was from his angle that Trotsky viewed the problem—might be annoyed and inconvenienced by the demands of the unions; he might be right against them in specific instances; but on balance it was sound that he should be so inconvenienced and exposed to genuine social pressures and influences. It was no use telling the workers that they must not oppose the workers' state. That state was an abstraction. In reality, Lenin pointed out, his own administration had to consider the interests of the peasants as well as of the workers; and its work was marred by muddle, by grave 'bureaucratic distortions', and by arbitrary exercise of power. The working class ought therefore to defend itself, albeit with self-restraint, and to press its claims on the administration. The state, as Lenin saw it, had to give scope to a plurality of interests and influences. Trotsky's state was implicitly monolithic.

The tenth congress voted by an overwhelming majority for Lenin's resolutions. Bolshevism had already departed from proletarian democracy; but it was not yet prepared to embrace its alternative, the monolithic state.

.   .   .   .

While the congress was in session the strangest of all Russian insurrections flared up at the naval fortress of Kronstadt, an insurrection which, in Lenin's words, like a lightning flash illumined reality.

The insurgents, sailors of the Red Navy, were led by anarchists. Since the end of February they had been extremely restless. There had been strikes in nearby Petrograd; a general strike was expected; and Kronstadt was astir with rumours of alleged clashes between Petrograd workers and troops. The crews of the warships were seized by a political fever reminiscent of the excitement of 1917. At meetings they passed resolutions demanding freedom for the workers, a new deal for the peas-

[1] *Desyatyi Syezd RKP.*, pp. 208 ff.

ants, and free elections to the Soviets. The call for the Third
Revolution began to dominate the meetings, the revolution
which was to overthrow the Bolsheviks and establish Soviet
democracy. Kalinin, President of the Soviet Republic, made a
flat-footed appearance at the naval base; he denounced the
sailors as 'disloyal and irresponsible' and demanded obedience.
A delegation of the sailors sent to Petrograd was arrested there.

Soon the cry 'Down with Bolshevik tyranny!' resounded
throughout Kronstadt. The Bolshevik commissars on the spot
were demoted and imprisoned. An anarchist committee assumed
command; and amid the sailors' enthusiasm the flag of revolt
was hoisted. 'The heroic and generous Kronstadt', writes the
anarchist historian of the insurrection, 'dreamt of the liberation
of Russia. . . . No clear-cut programme was formulated. Freedom and the brotherhood of the peoples of the world were the
watchwords. The Third Revolution was seen as a gradual
transition towards final emancipation; and free elections to
independent Soviets as the first step in this direction. The Soviets
were, of course, to be independent of any political party—a free
expression of the will and the interests of the people.'[1]

The Bolsheviks denounced the men of Kronstadt as counter-
revolutionary mutineers led by a White general. The denunciation appears to have been groundless. Having for so long
fought against mutiny after mutiny, each sponsored or encouraged by the White Guards, the Bolsheviks could not bring
themselves to believe that the White Guards had no hand in this
revolt. Some time before the event, the White émigré press had
indeed darkly hinted at trouble brewing in Kronstadt; and
this lent colour to the suspicion. The Politbureau, at first inclined to open negotiations, finally resolved to quell the revolt.
It could not tolerate the challenge from the Navy; and it was
afraid that the revolt, although it had no chance of growing into
a revolution, would aggravate the prevailing chaos. Even after
the defeat of the White Guards, numerous bands of rebels and
marauders roamed the land from the northern coasts down to
the Caspian Sea, raiding and pillaging towns and slaughtering
the agents of the government. With the call for a new revolution bands of famished Volga peasants had overrun the *guber-
nia* of Saratov, and later in the year Tukhachevsky had to

[1] Alexander Berkman, *Der Aufstand von Kronstadt*, pp. 10–11.

employ twenty-seven rifle divisions to subdue them.[1] Such was the turmoil that leniency towards the insurgents of Kronstadt was certain to be taken as a sign of weakness and to make matters worse.

On 5 March Trotsky arrived in Petrograd and ordered the rebels to surrender unconditionally. 'Only those who do so', he stated, 'can count on the mercy of the Soviet Republic. Simultaneously with this warning I am issuing instructions that everything be prepared for the suppression of the mutiny by armed force. . . . This is the last warning.'[2] That it should have fallen to Trotsky to address such words to the sailors was another of history's ironies. This had been his Kronstadt, the Kronstadt he had called 'the pride and the glory of the revolution'. How many times had he not stumped the naval base during the hot days of 1917! How many times had not the sailors lifted him on their shoulders and wildly acclaimed him as their friend and leader! How devotedly they had followed him to the Tauride Palace, to his prison cell at Kresty, to the walls of Kazan on the Volga, always taking his advice, always almost blindly following his orders! How many anxieties they had shared, how many dangers they had braved together! True, of the veterans few had survived; and even fewer were still at Kronstadt. The crews of the *Aurora*, the *Petropavlovsk*, and other famous warships now consisted of fresh recruits drafted from Ukrainian peasants. They lacked—so Trotsky told himself— the selfless revolutionary spirit of the older classes. Yet even this was in a way symbolic of the situation in which the revolution found itself. The ordinary men and women who had made it were no longer what they had been or where they had been. The best of them had perished; others had become absorbed in the administration; still others had dispersed and become disheartened and embittered. And what the rebels of Kronstadt demanded was only what Trotsky had promised their elder

---

[1] See the correspondence between S. Kamenev, Shaposhnikov, and Smidovich with the commander of the Saratov area, and Tukhachevsky's report to Lenin of 16 July 1921. *The Trotsky Archives*. And here is a characteristic message sent to Lenin from Communists in the sub-Polar region on 25 March 1921: 'The Communists of the Tobolsk region in the North are bleeding white and sending their fiery farewell greetings to the invincible Russian Communist Party, to our dear comrades and our leader Lenin. Perishing here, we carry out our duty towards the party and the Republic in the firm belief in our eventual triumph.' Ibid.

[2] Trotsky, *Sochinenya*, vol. xvii, book 2, p. 518.

brothers and what he and the party had been unable to give.
Once again, as after Brest, a bitter and hostile echo of his own
voice came back to him from the lips of other people; and once
again he had to suppress it.

The rebels ignored his warning and hoped to gain time. This
was the middle of March. The Bay of Finland was still ice-
bound. In a few days, however, a thaw might set in; and then
the fortress, bristling with guns, defended by the whole Red
Navy of the Baltic, assured of supplies from Finland or other
Baltic countries, would become inaccessible, almost invincible.
In the meantime even Communists joined in the revolt, an-
nouncing that they had left 'the party of the hangman Trotsky'.
The fortress, so Trotsky (or was it Tukhachevsky?) resolved,
must be seized before ice floes barred the approach. In feverish
haste picked regiments and shock troops were dispatched to
reinforce the garrison of Petrograd. When the news of the
mutiny reached the tenth congress, it aroused so much alarm
and anger that most of the able-bodied delegates rushed
straight from the conference hall in the Kremlin to place themselves at the head of the shock troops which were to storm the
fortress across the Bay of Finland. Even leaders of the Workers'
Opposition and *Decemists* who, at the congress, had just raised
demands not very different from those the rebels voiced, went
into battle. They, too, held that the sailors had no right to
dictate, hands on triggers, even the justest of demands.

White sheets over their uniforms, the Bolshevik troops, under
Tukhachevsky's command, advanced across the Bay. They were
met by hurricane fire from Kronstadt's bastions. The ice broke
under their feet; and wave after wave of white-shrouded
attackers collapsed into the glacial Valhalla. The death march
went on. From three directions fresh columns stumped and
fumbled and slipped and crawled over the glassy surface until
they too vanished in fire, ice, and water. As the successive
swarms and lines of attackers drowned, it seemed to the men of
Kronstadt that the perverted Bolshevik revolution drowned
with them and that the triumph of their own pure, unadultera-
ted revolution was approaching. Such was the lot of these
rebels, who had denounced the Bolsheviks for their harshness
and whose only aim it was to allow the revolution to imbibe the
milk of human kindness, that for their survival they fought a

battle which in cruelty was unequalled throughout the civil war. The bitterness and the rage of the attackers mounted accordingly. On 17 March, after a night-long advance in a snowstorm, the Bolsheviks at last succeeded in climbing the walls. When they broke into the fortress, they fell upon its defenders like revengeful furies.

On 3 April Trotsky took a parade of the victors. 'We waited as long as possible', he said, 'for our blinded sailor-comrades to see with their own eyes where the mutiny led. But we were confronted by the danger that the ice would melt away and we were compelled to carry out . . . the attack.'[1] Describing the crushed rebels as 'comrades', he unwittingly intimated that what he celebrated was morally a Pyrrhic victory. Foreign Communists who visited Moscow some months later and believed that Kronstadt had been one of the ordinary incidents of the civil war, were 'astonished and troubled' to find that the leading Bolsheviks spoke of the rebels without any of the anger and hatred which they felt for the White Guards and interventionists. Their talk was full of 'sympathetic reticences' and sad, enigmatic allusions, which to the outsider betrayed the party's troubled conscience.[2]

. . . .

The rising had not yet been defeated when, on 15 March, Lenin introduced the New Economic Policy to the tenth congress. Almost without debate the congress accepted it. Silently, with a heavy heart, Bolshevism parted with its dream of war communism. It retreated, as Lenin said, in order to be in a better position to advance. The controversy over the trade unions and the underlying issue at once died down. The cannonade in the Bay of Finland and the strikes in Petrograd and elsewhere had demonstrated beyond doubt the unreality of Trotsky's ideas: and in the milder policies based on the mixed economy of subsequent years there was, anyhow, no room for the militarization of labour.

The controversy had not been mere sound and fury, however. Its significance for the future was greater than the protagonists

---

[1] Trotsky, *Sochinenya*, vol. xvii, book 2, p. 523.

[2] André Morizet, *Chez Lénine et Trotski*, pp. 78–84 and V. Serge, *Mémoires d'un Révolutionnaire*, chapter iv, describe the Kronstadt period from the standpoint of foreign Communists in Russia. Both writers accepted the party's case, although both sympathized with the rebels.

themselves could suppose. A decade later Stalin, who in 1920–1 had supported Lenin's 'liberal' policy, was to adopt Trotsky's ideas in all but name. Neither Stalin nor Trotsky, nor the adherents of either, then admitted the fact: Stalin—because he could not acknowledge that he was abandoning Lenin's attitude for Trotsky's; Trotsky—because he shrank in horror from his own ideas when he saw them remorselessly carried into execution by his enemy. There was hardly a single plank in Trotsky's programme of 1920–1 which Stalin did not use during the industrial revolution of the thirties. He introduced conscription and direction of labour; he insisted that the trade unions should adopt a 'productionist' policy instead of defending the consumer interests of the workers; he deprived the trade unions of the last vestige of autonomy and transformed them into tools of the state. He set himself up as the protector of the managerial groups, on whom he bestowed privileges of which Trotsky had not even dreamt. He ordered 'Socialist emulation' in the factories and mines; and he did so in words unceremoniously and literally taken from Trotsky.[1] He put into effect his own ruthless version of that 'Soviet Taylorism' which Trotsky had advocated. And, finally, he passed from Trotsky's intellectual and historical arguments ambiguously justifying forced labour to its mass application.

In the previous chapter we traced the thread of unconscious historic continuity which led from Lenin's hesitant and shamefaced essays in revolution by conquest to the revolutions contrived by Stalin the conqueror. A similar subtle thread connects Trotsky's domestic policy of these years with the later practices of his antagonist. Both Trotsky and Lenin appear, each in a different field, as Stalin's unwitting inspirers and prompters. Both were driven by circumstances beyond their control and by their own illusions to assume certain attitudes in which circumstances and their own scruples did not allow them to persevere—attitudes which were ahead of their time, out of tune with the current Bolshevik mentality, and discordant with the main themes of their own lives.

[1] At the beginning of 1929, a few weeks after Trotsky's expulsion from Russia, the sixteenth party conference proclaimed 'Socialist emulation', quoting *in extenso* the resolution written by Trotsky and adopted by the party in 1920. The author's name was not mentioned, of course.

516THE PROPHET ARMED

It was only under the threat of the total decomposition of the revolution and of the Russian body politic that Trotsky advanced the idea of complete state control over the working classes. His alert, restless, experimenting mind boldly sought a way out in contradictory directions. In each direction it moved to the ultimate limit, while the main body of Bolshevik opinion marked time. He proposed the New Economic Policy when the party was still rigidly committed to war communism. Then his thought switched in the opposite direction, explored it to the end and reached the alternative conclusion: that the only remedy for the ills of war communism was cast iron discipline of labour. By now the main current of Bolshevik opinion had slowly moved towards the New Economic Policy, which it had compelled him to abandon. It was his clear, consistent, and swift logic—the logic of the great administrator impatient of confusion and bungling—that defeated Trotsky. His mind fixed on his objective, he rushed headlong into controversy, impetuously produced arguments and generalizations, and ignored the movement of opinion until he overreached himself and aroused angry resentment. The self-confident administrator in him got the better of the sensitive political thinker and blinded him to the implications of his schemes. What was only one of many facets in Trotsky's experimental thinking was to become Stalin's alpha and omega.[1]

In his aberration Trotsky remained intellectually honest—honest to the point of futility. He made no attempt to conceal his policy. He called things by their names, no matter how unpalatable. Accustomed to sway people by force of argument and appeal to reason he went on appealing to reason in a most unreasonable cause. He publicly advocated government by coercion, that government which can never be publicly advocated and is practised only *sub silentio*. He hoped to *persuade* people that they needed no government by persuasion. He told them that the workers' state had the right to use forced labour; and he was sincerely disappointed that they did not rush to enrol in the labour camps.[2] He behaved thus absurdly because before

[1] It was probably with these incidents in his mind that Lenin in his last will remarked on Trotsky's 'too far-reaching self-confidence and a disposition to be too much attracted by the purely administrative side of affairs'.

[2] It is a moot point to what extent Trotsky was led astray by his habit of applying European standards to Russia. It was one thing for a government to direct labour

his mind's eye he had no cold machine of coercion slowly and remorselessly grinding its human material, but the monumental and evanescent outlines of a 'Proletarian Sparta', the austere rigours of which were part of the pioneering adventure in social-ism. The very absurdity of his behaviour contained its own antidote. In his candour he gave the people ample notice of the danger threatening them. He indicated the limits to which he was prepared to go. He submitted his policies to public control. He himself did everything in his power to provoke the resistance that frustrated him. To keep politically alive he needed broad daylight. It took Stalin's bat-like character to carry his ideas into execution.

The Bolshevik party still defended the principle of proletarian democracy against Trotsky; but it continued to depart from it in practice.

It was only in 1921 that Lenin's government proceeded to ban all organized opposition within the Soviets. Throughout the civil war the Bolsheviks had harassed the Mensheviks and Social Revolutionaries, now outlawing them, now allowing them to come into the open, and then again suppressing them. The harsher and the milder courses were dictated by circumstances and by the vacillations of those parties in which some groups leaned towards the Bolsheviks and others towards the White Guards. The idea, however, that those parties should be sup-pressed on principle had not taken root before the end of the civil war. Even during the spells of repression, those opposition groups which did not plainly call for armed resistance to the Bolsheviks still carried on all sorts of activities, open and clan-destine. The Bolsheviks often eliminated them from the Soviets or reduced their representation by force or guile. It was through the machinery of the Soviets that Lenin's government organized the civil war; and in that machinery it was not prepared to countenance hostile or neutral elements. But the government still looked forward to the end of hostilities when it would be able to respect the rules of Soviet constitutionalism and to readmit

in an industrialized country and to shift workers, say, from Manchester to Birming-ham or from Stuttgart to Essen, and quite another to direct Ukrainian peasants or Petrograd workers to factories and mines in the Urals and in Siberia, or in the Far North. Direction of labour in a more or less uniform industrial environment may involve a minimum of compulsion. It required a maximum in Russia.

regular opposition. This the Bolsheviks now thought themselves unable to do. All opposition parties had hailed the Kronstadt rising; and so the Bolsheviks knew what they could expect from them. The more isolated they themselves were in the nation the more terrified were they of their opponents. They had half-suppressed them in order to win the civil war; having won the civil war they went on to suppress them for good.

Paradoxically, the Bolsheviks were driven to establish their own political monopoly by the very fact that they had liberalized their economic policy. The New Economic Policy gave free scope to the interests of the individualistic peasantry and of the urban bourgeoisie. It was to be expected that as those interests came into play they would seek to create their own means of political expression or try to use such anti-Bolshevik organizations as existed. The Bolsheviks were determined that none should exist. 'We might have a two-party system, but one of the two parties would be in office and the other in prison'—this dictum, attributed to Bukharin, expressed a view widespread in the party. Some Bolsheviks felt uneasy about their own political monopoly; but they were even more afraid of the alternative. Trotsky later wrote that he and Lenin had intended to lift the ban on the opposition parties as soon as the economic and social condition of the country had become more stable. This may have been so. In the meantime, however, the Bolsheviks hardened in the conviction, which was to play so important a part in the struggles of the Stalinist era, that any opposition must inevitably become the vehicle of counter-revolution. They were haunted by the fear that the new urban bourgeoise (which soon flourished under the N.E.P.), the intelligentsia, and the peasantry might join hands against them in a coalition of over-whelming strength; and they shrank from no measure that could prevent such a coalition. Thus, after its victory in the civil war, the revolution was beginning to escape from its weakness into totalitarianism.

Almost at once it became necessary to suppress opposition in Bolshevik ranks as well. The Workers' Opposition (and up to a point the *Decemists* too) expressed much of the frustration and discontent which had led to the Kronstadt rising. The cleavages tended to become fixed; and the contending groups were inclined to behave like so many parties within the party. It would have been preposterous to establish the rule of a single party and then to allow that party to split into fragments. If Bolshevism were to break up into two or more hostile movements, as the old Social Democratic party had done, would not one of them —it was asked—become the vehicle of counter-revolution?

In the temper of the party congress of 1921 there was indeed something of that seemingly irrational tension which had characterized the congress of 1903. A split similarly cast its shadow ahead—only the real divisions were even more inchoate and confused than in 1903. Now as then Trotsky was not on the side of the controversy to which he would eventually belong. And now as then he was anxious to prevent the split. He therefore raised no objection when Lenin proposed that the congress should prohibit organized groups or factions within the party; and he himself disbanded the faction he had formed during the recent controversy.[1] This was not yet strictly a ban on inner party opposition. Lenin encouraged dissenters to express dissent. He liberally invited them to state their views in the Bolshevik newspapers, in special discussion pages and discussion sheets. He asked the congress to elect the leaders of all shades of opposition to the new Central Committee. But he insisted that opposition should remain diffuse and that the dissenters should not form themselves into solid leagues. He submitted a resolution, one clause of which (kept secret) empowered the Central Committee to expel offenders, no matter how high their standing in the party. Trotsky supported the clause, or, at any rate, raised no objection to it; and the congress passed it. It was against Shlyapnikov, Trotsky's most immitigable opponent, that the punitive clause was immediately directed; and against him it was presently invoked. It did not occur to Trotsky that one day it would be invoked against himself.

The arrangement under which opposition was permitted provided it remained dispersed could work as long as members of the party disagreed over secondary or transient issues. But when the differences were serious and prolonged it was inevitable that members of the same mind should band together. Those who, like the Workers' Opposition, charged the ruling group with being

---

[1] Among the leaders of the faction were, apart from Trotsky and Bukharin, Dzerzhinsky, Andreev, Krestinsky, Preobrazhensky, Rakovsky, Serebriakov, Pyatakov and Sokolnikov.

animated by 'bureaucratic and bourgeois hostility towards the masses' could hardly refrain from concerting their efforts against what they considered to be a sinister and formidably organized influence within the party. The ban on factions could thus at first delay a split only to accelerate it later.

Barely two years were to elapse before Trotsky was to take up and give a powerful resonance to many of the criticisms and demands made by the less articulate leaders of the Workers' Opposition and of the *Decemists*, whom he now helped to defeat, and before he, too, was to cry out for a return to proletarian democracy.

.   .   .   .

It was only a few years since Trotsky had, as an émigré in Vienna, drawn that impressive vista of Russia's past, in which he showed how history had thrown the Russian people into a 'severe environment', exposed them to pressures from wealthy and powerful Europe and to invasions from all directions, and let a Leviathan-like state mould their destinies for them. To feed itself, he then wrote, the Leviathan starved the nation, retarded or accelerated the growth of its social classes, and atrophied its civilization.[1] The revolution was in one of its aspects the people's triumph over the Leviathan. The triumph had seemed complete, for the old state had been reduced to dust and ashes.

Yet the revolution, too, had to draw its nourishment and its vitality from that same 'severe environment'. From this it absorbed all its severity. Rich in world-embracing ideas and aspirations, the new republic was 'poor with the accumulated poverty of over a thousand years'. It mortally hated that poverty. But that poverty was its own flesh and blood and breath.

Trotsky had contrasted 'the spires and the vaulting arches and the gothic lacework' of western European feudalism with the coarse and barbarous vulgarity of Russian feudalism, which could only fill the crevices of its log cabin with moss. He had juxtaposed the rich and complex growth of the Third Estate in Europe with the Russian police-sponsored crafts; the free and cultivated 'bourgeois personality' of the West with the 'snout which every policeman could kick and punch'. Yet from that same log cabin, shattered by revolution and war, he set out with the Bolshevik party to pioneer for socialism. Against all ex-

[1] See above, chapter VII.

pectations, the 'advanced, civilized' West had turned its back on the revolution; and for decades Bolshevism had to entrench itself in its native environment in order to transform it. The brand of socialism which it then produced could not but show the marks of its historic heritage. That socialism, too, was to rise rough and crude, without the vaulting arches and spires and lacework of which Socialists had dreamt. Hemmed in by superior hostile forces, it soon delivered itself up to the new Leviathan-state—rising as if from the ashes of the old. The new state, like the old, was to protect and starve the nation, retard and accelerate its growth, and efface the human personality, the revolutionary-proletarian personality. It was another of history's ironies that Trotsky, the hater of the Leviathan, should have become the first harbinger of its resurrection.

When he was still at the threshold of his career, Trotsky wrote: 'A working class capable of exercizing its dictatorship over society will tolerate no dictator over itself.'[1] By 1921 the Russian working class had proved itself incapable of exercising its own dictatorship. It could not even exercise control over those who ruled in its name. Having exhausted itself in the revolution and the civil war, it had almost ceased to exist as a political factor. Trotsky then proclaimed the party's 'historical birthright', its right to establish a stern trusteeship over the proletariat as well as the rest of society. This was the old 'Jacobin' idea that a small virtuous and enlightened minority was justified in 'substituting' itself for an immature people and bringing reason and happiness to it, the idea which Trotsky had abjured as the hereditary obsession of the *Decembrists*, the *Narodniks*, and the Bolsheviks. This 'obsession', he himself had argued, had reflected the atrophy or the apathy of all social classes in Russia. He had been convinced that with the appearance of a modern, Socialist working class that atrophy had been overcome. The revolution proved him right. Yet after their paroxysms of energy and their titanic struggles of 1917–21 all classes of Russian society seemed to relapse into a deep coma. The political stage, so crowded in recent years, became deserted and only a single group was left on it to speak boisterously on behalf of the people. And even its circle was to grow more and more narrow.

[1] See above, p. 96.

When Trotsky now urged the Bolshevik party to 'substitute' itself for the working classes, he did not, in the rush of work and controversy, think of the next phases of the process, although he himself had long since predicted them with uncanny clear-sightedness. 'The party organization would then substitute itself for the party as a whole; then the Central Committee would substitute itself for the organization; and finally a single dictator would substitute himself for the Central Committee.'

The dictator was already waiting in the wings.

Bibliography

(*This list includes only such sources as have been quoted or directly referred to by the author*).

AKIMOV, V. L., *Materialy dlya Kharakteristiki Razvitya RSDRP*. Geneva, 1905.

ANTONOV–OVSEENKO, V. A., *Zapiski o Grazhdanskoi Voine*, vol. i. Moscow, 1924.

ARSCHINOFF, P., *Geschichte der Machno-Bewegung (1918–1921)*. Berlin, no date.

AVDEEV, N., and others, *Revolutsia 1917 (Khronika Sobytii)*, vol. i–v. Moscow, 1923–6.

AXELROD, P. B., *Pisma P. B. Axelroda i Yu. O. Martova*. Berlin, 1924.

—— *Perepiska G. V. Plekhanova i P. B. Axelroda*. Moscow, 1925.

BADAEV, A. E., *Bolsheviki v Gosudarstvennoi Dume*. Moscow, 1930.

BALABANOFF, A., *My Life as a Rebel*. London, 1938.

BEATTY, BESSIE, *The Red Heart of Russia*. New York, 1918.

BEER, M., *Fifty Years of International Socialism*. London, 1937.

BERKMAN, A., *Der Aufstand von Kronstadt*, Reprint, *Der Monat*. Berlin, no date.

—— *The Bolshevik Myth*. London, 1925.

Bolsheviki, Dokumenty Okhrannovo Otdelenia (Dokumenty po Istorii Bolshevisma s 1903 po 1916 g. byvshevo Moskovskovo Okhrannovo Otdelenia), Ed. M. A. Tsyavlovskii. Moscow, 1918.

Borba za Petrograd, 15 Oktyabrya–6 Noyabrya, 1919, with Foreword by G. Zinoviev. Petrograd, 1920.

BRUPBACHER, F., *60 Jahre Ketzer*. Zürich, 1935.

BRYANT, LOUISE, *Six Red Months in Russia*. London, 1919.

BUBNOV, A., and others, *Grazhdanskaya Voina, 1918–1921*, vols. i–iii. Moscow, 1928.

BUCHANAN, SIR GEORGE, *My Mission to Russia*. London, 1923.

CHEREVANIN, N., *Organisatsionnyi Vopros*, with preface by Martov. Geneva, 1904.

CHERNOV, V., *The Great Russian Revolution*. New Haven, 1936.

—— (Tchernov) *Mes Tribulations en Russie Soviétique*. Paris, 1921.

CZERNIN, COUNT OTTOKAR, *In the World War*. London, 1919.

DAN, F., *Proiskhozhdenie Bolshevisma*. New York, 1946.

DABSKI, JAN, *Pokój Ryski*. Warsaw 1931. (The second edition of J. Dąbski's memoirs, published in Polish at a later date, contains much more information about the background to the Russo-Polish peace treaty of 1921. It was not available during the writing of this book.)

DENIKIN, A. I., GENERAL, *Ocherki Russkoi Smuty*, vols. i–v. Paris–Berlin, 1921–6.

Doklad Russkikh Sotsial-Demokratov Vtoromu Internatsionalu. Geneva, 1896.

DUBNOV, S. M., *History of the Jews in Russia and Poland*. Philadelphia, 1918.

EASTMAN, M., *Leon Trotsky: The Portrait of a Youth.* New York, 1925.

EGOROV, A., *Lvov–Varshava.* Moscow, 1929.

ENGELS, F., *The Peasant War in Germany.* London, 1927.

FRUNZE, M. V., *Sobranie Sochinenii,* vols. i–iii, with preface by Bubnov. Moscow, 1929.

GARVI, P. A., *Vospominanya Sotsial-Demokrata.* New York, 1946.

GORKY, M., *Lénine et le Paysan Russe.* Paris, 1924.

—— *Days with Lenin.* London, 1931.

HARD, WILLIAM, *Raymond Robins' Own Story.* New York, 1920.

History of the Communist Party of the Soviet Union (Bolsheviks); Short Course. Moscow, 1943.

HOFFMANN, MAX, *Die Aufzeichnungen des Generalmajors Max Hoffmann.* Berlin, 1929.

ILIN–ZHENEVSKII, A. F., *Bolsheviki u Vlasti.* Leningrad, 1929.

JAURÈS, J., *L'Armée Nouvelle.* Paris, 1911.

KAKURIN, N., *Kak Srazhalas Revolutsia,* vols. i–ii. Moscow, 1925.

KERENSKY, ALEXANDER, *Izdaleka, Sbornik Statei.* Paris, 1922.

—— *The Crucifixion of Liberty.* London, 1934.

KNOX, SIR ALFRED, Major General, *With the Russian Army 1914–1917.* London, 1921.

KOLLONTAI, A. M., *The Workers' Opposition in Russia.* London, 1923.

KRUPSKAYA, N. K., *Memories of Lenin.* London, 1942.

KÜHLMANN, RICHARD VON, *Erinnerungen.* Heidelberg, 1948.

LATSIS (Sudbars), *Chrezvychainye Komissii po Borbe s Kontrrevolutsiei.* Moscow, 1921.

LENIN, V. I., *Sochinenya,* vols. i–xxxv. Moscow 1941–50. All quotations from Lenin's Works are from this, the fourth edition, unless otherwise stated.

—— *Sobranie Sochinenii.* This is the first edition of Lenin's Works published between 1920–6, of which occasional use has been made for quotation of passages omitted from later editions.

—— *Letters of Lenin.* London, 1937.

Leninskii Sbornik, vols. iv–xx. Moscow, 1925–32.

Lenin's correspondence with Trotsky and other party leaders and military commanders, some of it hitherto unpublished, has been quoted from *The Trotsky Archives.* Harvard.

LLOYD GEORGE, D., *War Memoirs.* London, 1938.

LOCKHART BRUCE, R. H., *Memoirs of a British Agent.* London, 1932.

LUDENDORFF, E., *Meine Kriegserinnerungen 1914–1918.* Berlin, 1919.

LUNACHARSKY, A., *Revolutsionnye Siluety.* Moscow, 1923.

LYADOV, M. N., *Kak Nachala Skladyvatsya R. K. P.* Moscow, 1925.

—— *Iz Zhizni Partii.* Moscow, 1926.

LYADOV, M. N., (M. LYDIN), *Material zur Erläuterung der Parteikrise in der S. D. Arbeiterpartei Rußlands.* Geneva, 1904.

MARTOV, L., MASLOV, P., POTRESOV, A., *Obshchestvennoe Dvizhenie v Rossii v Nachale XX-Veka,* vols. i–ii. Petersburg, 1909–10.

MARTOV, L., (Yu.) *Pisma Axelroda i Martova.* Berlin, 1924.

—— *Istoria Rossiiskoi Sotsial-Demokratii.* Moscow, 1923.

—— *Spasiteli ili Uprazdniteli.* Paris, 1911.

MARX, K. and ENGELS, F., *Selected Correspondence.* London, 1941.

—— *Perepiska Marxa i Engelsa s Russkimi Politicheskimi Deyatelyami.* Moscow, 1947.

MEDEM, VLADIMIR, *Von Mein Leben,* vols. i–ii (Yiddish). New York, 1923.

MILIUKOV, P. N., *Istorya Vtoroi Russkoi Revolutsii.* Sofia, 1921.

—— *Kak Proshli Vybory vo Vtoruyu Gos. Dumu.* Petersburg, 1907.

MILL, JOHN, *Pioneers and Builders,* vols. i–ii (Yiddish). New York, 1946.

Mirnye Peregovory v Brest-Litovske, Records of the peace conference of Brest Litovsk. Editor A. A. Yoffe (V. Krymsky), preface by Trotsky. Moscow, 1920.

MORIZET, A., *Chez Lénine et Trotski.* Paris, 1922.

NOULENS, JOSEPH, *Mon Ambassade en Russie Soviétique,* vols. i–ii. Paris, 1932.

OLGIN, M. J., 'Biographical Notes' in the American edition of Trotsky's *Our Revolution.* New York, 1918.

PALÉOLOGUE, MAURICE, *La Russie des Tsars pendant la Grande Guerre,* vols. i–iii. Paris, 1922.

PARVUS (HELPHAND, A. L.), *Rossia i Revolutsia.* Petersburg, 1906.

PAVLOVICH, *Pismo k Tovarishcham o Vtorom Syezde RSDRP.* Geneva, 1904.

PLEKHANOV, G. V., *God na Rodine,* vols. i–ii. Paris, 1921.

—— *Perepiska Plekhanova i Axelroda.* Moscow, 1925.

POKROVSKY, M. N., *Oktyabrskaya Revolutsia.* Moscow, 1929.

—— *Ocherki po Istorii Oktyabrskoi Revolutsii,* vols. i–ii. Moscow, 1927.

POPOV, N., *Outline History of the C.P.S.U. (b),* vols. i–ii (English translation from 16th Russian edition). London, no date.

POTRESOV, A. N., *Posmertny Sbornik Proizvedenii.* Paris, 1937.

PRICE PHILIPS, M., *My Reminiscences of the Russian Revolution.* London, 1921.

Pyat Let Vlasti Sovietov. Moscow, 1922.

RADEK, K., *Portrety i Pamphlety.* Moscow, 1927.

—— *Pyat Let Kominterna.* Moscow, 1924.

RANSOME, ARTHUR, *Six Weeks in Russia in 1919.* London, 1919.

Raskol na Vtorom Syezde RSDRP i Vtoroi Internatsional (Sbornik Dokumentov). Moscow, 1933.

RASKOLNIKOV, F. F., *Kronshtadt i Piter v 1917 g.* Moscow, 1925.

REED, JOHN, *Ten Days that Shook the World.* London, 1934.

ROSMER, A., *Le Mouvement Ouvrier pendant la Guerre.* Paris, 1936.

SADOUL, JACQUES, *Notes sur la Révolution Bolchevique*. Paris, 1919.

SERGE, V., *Mémoires d'un Révolutionnaire*. Paris, 1951.

SIBIRYAK, *Studencheskoye Dvizhenie v Rossii*. Geneva, 1899.

SLEPKOV, A., *Kronshtadtskii Myatezh*. Moscow, 1928.

SMILGA, I., *Ocherednye Voprosy Stroitelstva Krasnoi Armii*. Moscow, 1921.

STALIN, J. V., *Sochinenya*, vols. i–xiii. Moscow, 1946–51.

Stalin's correspondence with Lenin, Trotsky, and other members of the Politbureau, some of it unpublished, is quoted from *The Trotsky Archives*.

STEINBERG, I., *Als ich Volkskommissar war*. Munich, 1929.

SUKHANOV, N., *Zapiski o Revolutsii*, vols. i–vii. Moscow, 1922.

SVERCHKOV, D., *Na Zarie Revolutsii*. Leningrad, 1925.

TROTSKY, L. D.

—— *The Trotsky Archives* (Houghton Library, Harvard University). The earliest document in this collection is dated Brest Litovsk 31 January 1918; the last bears the date 17 August 1940, three days before the assassination of Trotsky. The Archives consist of four parts:

Section A: contains about 800 letters and messages exchanged between Trotsky, Lenin, and other Soviet leaders (1918–22), and various other unpublished documents;

Section B: contains, in twenty-five dossiers, Trotsky's manuscripts and correspondence up to 1929;

Section C: contains, also in twenty-five dossiers, letters and memoranda from Zinoviev, Yoffe, Lunacharsky, Radek, Rakovsky, Preobrazhensky, Sosnovsky, and many others. Most of this correspondence belongs to the period of Trotsky's exile at Alma Ata. This section also includes many documents relating to the work of the Trotskyist opposition within the Soviet Union;

Section D: contains Trotsky's correspondence with groups and members of the Fourth International in various countries. This section is sealed and is not to be made available for research before 1980.

The references to *The Archives*, which occur in this volume are mainly to Section A. Only in a few instances are documents belonging to Sections B and C referred to. Extensive use of Sections B and C is made by the author in *The Prophet Unarmed*, the next volume in this series.

Sochinenya. (This was planned to be the complete edition of Trotsky's *Works*, but its publication was discontinued in 1927, at the time of Trotsky's expulsion from the party. The following volumes, published in 1925–7, were available to the author:

Vol. II (parts 1 and 2) *Nasha Pervaya Revolutsia*;

Vol. III: (part 1) *Ot Fevralya do Oktyabrya*; (part 2) *Ot Oktyabrya do Bresta;*

Vol. IV: *Politicheskaya Khronika*;

Vol. VI: *Balkany i Balkanskaya Voina*;

Vol. VIII: *Politicheskie Siluety*;

Vol. IX: *Evropa v Voine*;

Vol. XII: *Osnovnye Voprosy Proletarskoi Revolutsii*;
Vol. XIII: *Kommunisticheskii Internatsional*;
Vol. XV: *Khozaistvennoe Stroitelstvo v Sovetskoi Rossii*;
Vol. XVII: (part 2) *Sovietskaya Respublika i Kapitalisticheskii Mir*;
Vol. XX: *Kultura Starovo Mira*;
Vol. XXI: *Kultura Perekhodnovo Vremeni*.

TROTSKY, L. D., *Kak Vooruzhalas Revolutsia*, vols. i–iii. Moscow, 1923–5. (The collection of Trotsky's military writings, orders of the day and speeches.)
—— *Vtoroi Syezd RSDRP (Otchet Sibirskoi Delegatsii)*. Geneva, 1903. (In the signature over this and the next work Trotsky used the initial N., not L.)
—— *Nashi Politicheskie Zadachi*. Geneva, 1904.
—— *Istoria Revolutsii 1905–06*. Petrograd, 1917.
—— *Our Revolution*. New York, 1918.
—— *Itogi i Perspektivy*. Moscow; 1919.
—— *Terrorism i Kommunism*. Petersburg, 1920.
—— *Between Red and White*. London, 1922.
—— *Die Russische Revolution 1905*. Berlin, 1923.
—— *Pyat Let Kominterna*. Moscow, 1924.
—— *Lénine*. Paris, 1924.
—— *Pokolenie Oktyabrya*. Moscow, 1924.
—— *Moya Zhizn*. vols. i–ii, Berlin, 1930.
—— *Permanentnaya Revolutsia*. Berlin, 1930.
—— *History of the Russian Revolution*, vols. i–iii. London, 1932–3.
—— *Vie de Lénine, Jeunesse*. Paris, 1936.
—— *The Stalin School of Falsification*. New York, 1937.
—— *Stalin*. New York, 1946.

(Apart from the sources listed above, the author has quoted extensively from Trotsky's speeches printed in many published records of party and Soviet congresses and in the proceedings of the Central Committee. For Trotsky's early writings the author has drawn *inter alia* on the files of *Iskra*, *Nachalo*, the 'Viennese' *Pravda*, *Golos*, *Nashe Slovo*, &c., sources rarely, if ever, used by previous writers on the history of Russian revolutionary movements. These papers are in the Hoover Library, Stanford University, California.)

TUKHACHEVSKY, M., *Voina Klassov*. Moscow, 1921.

VANDERVELDE, E., *Souvenirs d'un Militant Socialiste*. Paris, 1939.
VOITINSKY, V., *Gody Pobied i Porazhenii*. Berlin, 1923.
VOROSHILOV, K., *Stalin i Krasnaya Armia*. Moscow, 1929.

WHEELER–BENNETT, JOHN W., *Brest Litovsk. The Forgotten Peace*. London, 1938.
WITTE, S. YU., *Vospominania*, vols. i–iii. Petrograd, 1923–4.

ZELIKSON–BOBROVSKAYA, Ts., *Pervaya Russkaya Revolutsia v Peterburge 1905*, vols. i–ii. Moscow, 1925.
ZETKIN, KLARA, *Reminiscences of Lenin*. London, 1929.
ZINOVIEV, G. *Sochinenya*, vols. i–xvi. Moscow, 1924–9.

ZIV, G. A., *Trotsky. Kharakteristika po Lichnym Vospominaniam.* New York, 1921.

The following editions of protocols and verbatim reports have been quoted:

Protokoly Tsentralnovo Komiteta RSDRP (August 1917–February 1918). Moscow, 1929.
    2 Syezd RSDRP. Moscow, 1932.
    5 Syezd RSDRP. Moscow.
    6 Syezd RSDRP. Moscow, 1934.
    7 Syezd RKP (b). Moscow, 1923.
    8 Syezd RKP (b). Moscow, 1933.
    9 Syezd RKP (b). Moscow, 1934.
    10 Syezd RKP (b). Moscow, 1921.
    1 Vserossiiskii Syezd Sovetov. Moscow, 1930.
    3 Vserossiiskii Syezd Sovetov. Petersburg, 1918.
    5 Vserossiiskii Syezd Sovetov. Moscow, 1918.
    3 Vserossiiskii Syezd Profsoyuzov. Moscow, 1920.
    2 Kongress Kommunisticheskovo Internatsionala. Petrograd, 1921.

Newspapers and periodicals:

Ekonomicheskaya Zhizn', Forward—Vorwärts (New York), *Golos* (Paris), *Iskra* ('old' and 'new'), *Izvestya, Izvestya Tsentralnovo Komiteta RKP (b), Krasnaya Letopis, Luch, Nachalo, The New International, Nashe Slovo* (Paris), *Nasha Zarya, Novaya Zhizn, Neue Zeit, Pechat i Revolutsia, Pravda* ('Viennese'), *Pravda, Proletarskaya Revolutsia, Przeglad Socjal-Demokratyczny, Rabocheye Delo* (Geneva, 1899), *Russkaya Gazeta, Rabochyi Put, Ryech, Sotsial-Demokrat, Sotsialisticheskii Vestnik, The Times, Vestnik Russkoi Revolutsii, Voprosy Istorii.*

INDEX

Abramovich, R., 271 n. 1, 313, 337, 500.
Adler, Alfred, 193.
Adler, Friedrich, 185, 186 n. 1, 213.
Adler, Victor, 57, 116, 139, 391; Trotsky on, 185; on Trotsky, 186 n. 4; and war, 213; and Brest Litovsk Peace, 376.
Akimov, V. L., 76.
Alexander II, 1–5, 19.
Alexander III, 19.
Alexeev, General, 337.
Alexinsky, G. A., 216, 220 n. 2, 276.
Anarchists, 270, 505, 510–14.
Andreev, A., 502 n. 3, 519 n. 1.
D'Annunzio, G., 48.
Antonov-Ovseenko, V. A., sets up *Nashe Slovo*, 221; imprisoned in July 1917, 279, 281; in October rising, 298, 306, 311; on orgy of drunkenness, 322–4; taken prisoner, 329; and Constituent Assembly, 373 n. 1; as Commissar of War, 406; in Ukraine, 434–5.
Arakcheev, General, 492.
'August Bloc', 200–1, 205, 218–19.
Austria, 159, 355, 356; Social Democrats of, 185–6; and Brest Litovsk Peace, 364, 388, 394; peace demonstrations in, 372, 374, 376; 1918 collapse of, 428, 449; under Versailles Peace, 455.
Avksentiev, 131.
Axelrod, P. B., 57, 218; as co-editor of *Iskra*, 59 ff.; Trotsky's attachment to, 63–64, 88, 92 n. 2; and Jewish problem, 75; Lenin versus, 78–82; as Menshevik leader, 85, 196–8; and schism in party, 200–1; at Zimmerwald, 225, 232.
Azev, 107 n. 2.

Babeuf, G., 454.
Bakaev, 426.
Bakunin, M., 3.
Balabanov, A., 222, 250.
Balkans, and Balkan wars, 201 ff.
Balmashev, 68.
Barbusse, H., 230.
Bauer, Otto, 186.
Bebel, A., 139, 182, 198 n. 1.
Belinsky, V. G., 48, 52.
Bentham, J., 25.
Berkman, Alexander, 511.

Bernstein, E., 40.
Berzin, J., 308.
Bitsenko, 361.
Black Hundreds, 167.
Blumkin, J., 403.
Bogdanov, A., 125, 139, 193.
Bolshevism, or Bolsheviks, 45, 76–77; origins of, 79–82; and Jacobinism, 91–97; and intelligentsia, 94–95, 106; on prospects of revolution in 1904–5, 112–14; early in 1905, 117–18; and first Soviet, 125–6, 130, 135; and 'permanent revolution', 150, 162–3; and land problem, 155; 'boycotters' in ranks of, 176, 195–6; at London Congress of 1907, 177–80; and 'Europeanization', 180, 191; R. Luxemburg and, 183; their final split with Mensheviks, 194–8; and World War I, 212, 232 ff.; and determinism, 234; after February revolution, 254 ff.; and *Mezhrayonka*, 255–6, 269; at first Congress of Soviets, 262 ff.; in June and July 1917, 268–9, 270–5; ostracized, 277 ff.; defeat Kornilov, 281–2; ascendancy of, 282–3; and Constituent Assembly, 283, 372; and pre-Parliament, 284–6, 294; and armed insurrection, 289 ff., 295 ff.; and proletarian dictatorship, 318–19; and peasantry, 320 ff.; coalesce with Left SR's, 325, 328–9; and coalition government, 330 ff.; and single party system, 336–41, 486–7, 504 ff., 517–18; peace policy of, 346 ff., 355 ff.; and Brest Litovsk Peace, 373–93; and Ukrainian separatism, 376–7; and militarism, 406 ff.; and revolution in Europe, 448–50; and Third International, 448–77; and East and West, 456–8; and revolution by conquest, 471–7; and War Communism, 487–503, 514.
Bonch-Bruevich, General, 408, 494.
Bourderon, 227.
Brest Litovsk Peace, and negotiations, 186 n. 4, 293, 322; preliminaries to, 346–53; conference of, 359–78; break of negotiations, 378–82; German *Diktat*, 386; signed, 393; aftermath of, 394 ff.; annulment of, 428.
Bronstein, Anna, Trotsky's mother, 7, 168, 184.

Bronstein, David, Trotsky's father, 5–7, 17–18, 29–30, 42, 168, 184.

Bronstein, Leon or Lev Davidovich, *see* Trotsky.

Brusilov, General, 460.

Bryant, L., 345.

Bubnov, A. S., 299, 307, 389 ff., 410, 434.

Buchanan, Sir George, 275, 306 n. 2, 347 n. 5, 353 n. 2.

Budienny, S. M., 416 n. 2, 466, 468, 482–3.

Bukharin, N., 148, 176, 191, 235 n. 3; in 1914, 213; edits *Novyi Mir*, 242; on party and 'state, 336, 518; on Constituent Assembly, 340–1; leads opposition to Brest Litovsk Peace, 373, 388 ff., 390 n. 2; and Trotsky's military policy, 410, 425; and trade union controversy, 507, 519 n. 1.

Bulygin, 120.

Bund, the Jewish Socialist Party, 60, 72–76, 200.

Cervantes, 231 n. 1.

Cheka, 392, 400, 403–4, 447, 459.

Chernov, V., 252, 254, 277; and Trotsky, 271–2, 275.

Chernyshevsky, 25.

Chicherin, G., 222–3, 353, 355, 429, 444 n. 2.; and Russo-Polish war, 458–9, 462–3.

Chkheidze, 232–3, 244.

Churchill, Winston, 443, 461.

Civil Wars, Kerensky's troops routed, 327–30; formation of White Guards, 337–8, 405, 416; Entente and, 350–1; rising of Left SR's, 400–4; Czech Legion in, 417–18; after collapse of Central Powers, 428 ff.; strategy of, 432–3, 481–4; Kolchak's main offensive, 433–4; Denikin's main offensive, 434–41, 445–6; Yudenich's advance, 443–5; last act of, 445–6; epilogue and aftermath of, 468, 487 ff.

Clausewitz, K., 228, 229, 405; his influence on Trotsky, 477, 484.

Clemenceau, 429.

Cloots, Anacharsis, 207, 390.

Communist Party, Russian, *see* Bolshevism, or Bolsheviks, Social Democratic Party, especially Congresses of; for non-Russian Communist Parties *see* International, Third.

Constituent Assembly, 245; demand of, in 1904, 111; in 1917, 252, 283; elections to, 319–20; and Soviets,

340–1; dispersal of, 372–3; and civil war, 422.

Constitutional Democrats (Cadets), 137, 141 n. 2; in first Duma, 145; in 1907, 175; and Russian policy in Balkans, 202; in February revolution, 244, 251 ff., 262; and Kornilov, 282, 284–6; and White Guards, 338–40; outlawed, 341. *See also* Liberalism, or Liberals.

Council of Workers' and Peasants' Defence, 423 n. 1.

Councils of Workers', Peasants', and Soldiers' Deputies, *see* Soviets.

Cromwell, O., 77, 267.

Czechoslovak Legion, 399, 417–19.

Czernin, Count Ottokar, 186 n. 4, 362; at Brest Litovsk, 363–4, 370, 376–80.

Dallin, 500 n. 2.

Dan, T., 85, 410; and Trotsky, 88, 106; and schism in party, 200–1; in 1917, 309–10.

Danton, 267, 390–1.

Darwin, Charles, 38, 39 n. 1, 51.

Debs, E., 243.

Decemists (Group of Democratic Centralism), 507–8, 513, 518–20.

De Man, H., 248.

Denikin, General, 337, 415, 428; his base in the Caucasus, 429, 432; his main offensive, 434 ff., 440, 483; analysing causes of his defeat, 445 n. 3; and Poland's independence, 458.

Deutsch, L., 64, 71, 75, 145 n. 1.

Dobrolyubov, 48, 52–53.

Doroshevich, V. M., 16.

Doumergue, President, 252.

Dukhonin, General, 349, 350.

Dumas: 'Bulygin Duma', 120, 127; first, 145; second, 175; third, 175; fourth, 232, 265.

Durnovo, Minister of the Interior, 24, 169.

Dutov, Ataman, 338.

Dybenko, F., 279, 406.

Dzerzhinsky, F., 301 n. 1, 304 n. 1, 307, 333, 438; opposed to Brest Litovsk Peace, 373 ff., 389 ff.; and Russo-Polish war, 465, 470; in trade union controversy, 519 n. 1.

Eastman, Max, 12, 15, 28 n. 2.

Ebert, F., 100 n. 2.

'Economists', 33, 58, 101; at second party congress, 72, 76; Trotsky on, 89.

Engels, Frederick, 18, 39, 391, 396.

Foch, Marshal, 429.
France, and Russia at war, 346–7, 349, 350–1, 356; and Brest Litovsk Peace, 385; intervention of, in Russia, 399, 417, 428–9, 448, 458; and Russo-Polish war, 461 ff.; military doctrines in, 477–8, 484.
Frunze, M., 447, 468, 482, 485.

Gandhi, 456.
Gapon, Father, 112, 157.
Georgia, invasion of, 473–6.
Gerea, Dobrodjanu, 208–9.
Germany, Social Democratic Party of, 182, 192, 197–8, 214, 349; Trotsky's hopes of revolution in, 245–6, 266–7, 449 ff.; peace feelers of, to Russia, 264; 1918 revolution in, 275 n. 1, 292, Lenin on revolution in, 293; and armistice with Russia, 349, 351, 362 ff.; and separate peace in West, 356; annexes Poland and Baltic lands, 363, 369; anti-war movement in, 372, 376; renews attack on Russia, 383 ff., 388; dictates peace terms, 386; enforces them, 394 ff.; suppresses Red Finland, 399; collapses in 1918, 428, 449; communism in, 451–2, 454–5; and Russo-Polish war, 465–6; strategic doctrines of, 484.
Gibbon, E., 228.
Gläser, 230.
Gogol, 48, 49 n. 1.
Goltzman, E., 492.
Gorky, Maxim, 48, 68, 139, 201 n. 1, 313; and Lenin and Trotsky, 180 n. 1, 259–60, 277 n. 1, 430 n. 1.
Great Britain, and Russia at war, 346–7, 349, 350–1, 356; 1907 agreement of, with Russia, 360; and Brest Litovsk Peace, 385 ff.; intervenes in Russia, 399, 417, 440, 448, 458; and Russo-Polish war, 461 ff.; and military doctrine, 483 n. 2, 484.
Grimm, 264.
Guchkov, 243, 251.
Guesde, J., 70, 187, 207, 239.

Haase, H., 182.
Hardie, Keir, 187.
Hašek, J., 230.
Hauptmann, G., 48.
Henderson, A., 475.
Hervé, G., 227.
Herzen, A., 48, 52.
Herzl, T., 75 n. 2.

Hilferding, R., 186.
Hillquit, M., 243.
Hindenburg, Field Marshal, 363, 382.
Hitler, A., 76, 193.
Hoffmann, M., General, 354, 362, 376, 382; and Ludendorff, 363; and Trotsky, 367, 369–71, 379–80; resumes hostilities, 383; suppresses Bavarian Soviets, 455.
Hungary, revolution in, 434, 454–5, 470.

Ibsen, H., 48, 50–51.
Inter-Borough Organization, or *Mezhrayonka*, 254–5, 260, 269, 279.
Internationals:
Second, Socialist, or Social Democratic, 20, 104 n. 2, 159; its pre-1914 leaders and outlook, 187, 211–13; its Copenhagen congress of 1910, 197; its collapse in 1914, 214 ff., 225, 453. *See also* Zimmerwald conference.
Third, or Comintern, 217, origin of, 225, 235; foundation of, 451–4; second congress, 457 n. 2, 467; its policy in Asia, 462.
Iskra, 45, 55, 56; its editors, 59–62, 64 ff.; Trotsky and, 67–9, 89–90, 106–7, 118; and second party congress, 72–82; the 'new' *Iskra*, 85–87, 98; Parvus's contributions to, 100–1, 103 ff.

Jacobinism, or Jacobins, and Marxism, 76; Trotsky on, 91–97, 153, 338, 521; and war, 267; Lenin on, 340.
Japan, at war with Russia, 86, 89, 103–4, 107; invades Siberia, 350, 399, 456.
Jaurès, J., 70, 208, 447; and Russians, 182 n. 2; Trotsky on, 187; assassinated, 213; his influence on Trotsky, 477–80.
Jews and Jewish problem, Trotsky's origin, 5–7; anti-Jewish legislation in Russia, 9–13; and Trotsky's background, 11–12, 13–14, 35, 38, 42, 181; and the West, 20–21; and *Iskra*, 60, 63; at second party congress, 73–76; pogroms, in Russia, 132, 168; and Trotsky in 1917, 326.
Jordania, N., 475.
Judson, General, 352.

Kaledin, General, 337, 448 n. 1.
Kalinin, M., 511.

Kamenev, B., 176, 194; and Viennese *Pravda*, 195, 197; and 'April Theses', 255-6; in July 1917, 273, 274, 276; imprisoned and released, 279, 282; and Lenin in hiding, 289; opposed to October insurrection, 290-5, 299 ff., 304 n. 1; participates in insurrection, 307; leads moderate Bolsheviks, 331-5; at Brest Litovsk, 361, 369.

Kamenev, S., General, 433-4, 435, 439.

Kamkov, B., 400-2.

Kant, I., 38.

Kaplan, F., 422.

Kapp (*Putsch*), 465.

Kautsky, Karl, 94, 139, 475; inspires European socialism, 159; and Trotsky, 181-2, 194, 198.

Kerensky, Alexander, 243, 244, 306 n. 2, 354; as Minister of War, 253, 261, 415; as Premier opposed by Kornilov, 281-2; at Democratic Conference, 284-6; forms his last government, 286; his resignation demanded, 287; opens pre-Parliament, 294; prepares to suppress the Bolsheviks, 297, 306, 308, 347; 'silent rising' against, 300; overthrow of, 310 ff.; attempts to regain power, 327-30; and Constituent Assembly, 372; Trotsky compared with, 402.

Khinchuk, 313.

Khrustalev-Nosar, 131, 139, 147.

Kibalchich, 4.

Kienthal conference, 235, 452.

Klyuchevsky, V. O., 24.

Knox, Sir Alfred, 308 n. 2, 310 n. 3, 347.

Knuniants-Radin, 125, 130.

Kolarov, V., 201, 225.

Kolchak, Admiral, 417, 422, 428, 456 n. 1; his main offensive, 432-4; and Denikin, 437.

Kollontai, Alexandra, 201 n. 1, 223, 242, 299; opposed to Brest Litovsk Peace, 389; leads Workers' Opposition, 507.

Kopp, V., 193.

Kornilov, General, 280-2, 284-5, 337, 347.

Kossior, 374.

Krasin, L., 117-18, 122; and Trotsky in 1905, 124, 126; his 1920 mission to London, 461.

Krasnov, General, 327-8, 330, 428.

Krestinsky, N., 392, 438, 519 n. 1.

Kronstadt, early in 1917, 260-1; in July days, 270 ff.; and Kornilov revolt, 281; sailors of, in Kazan battle, 419-20; rising of, 510-14, 518.

Krupskaya, N., 57, 65, 71.

Krylenko, N., 279, 281, 301, 349; as Commander-in-Chief, 350-1, 408.

Kühlmann, Richard von, 361-3; and Trotsky, 369-71, 382; conducts Brest negotiations, 366 ff.; plays Ukrainian card, 365, 376-80.

Kun, Bela, 404, 417.

Kzhizhanovsky-Clair, 56.

Labour Armies, 494-6.

Lapinsky, 465.

Larin, Y., 219 n. 1, 277, 492.

Lashevich, M., 298; opposed to Trotsky's military policy, 412, 426, 429, 434, 439; on Trotsky in the battle of Petrograd, 445.

Lassalle, F., 35, 164, 267.

Lavrov, 3.

Lazimir, 298.

Ledebour, G., 182.

Lenin, V. I., 19, 24, 45; first heard of, and read by Trotsky, 40, 55; first meeting with Trotsky, 57-59; as co-editor of *Iskra*, 61, 64-66, 78 n. 1; prevents Trotsky's return to Russia, 71; and Jacobinism, 76, 91-97; against the 'veterans', 78 ff.; drafts party statutes, 79-80; gains majority at second congress, 81; as 'new Robespierre', 84, 95-96; defeated by Mensheviks and Plekhanov, 85-86; attacked by Trotsky for his 'substitutism', 89-90; opposed to idea of workers' government in Russia, 113; advocates armed insurrection in 1905, 119; and liberalism, 121; and first Petersburg Soviet, 125 n. 1; on time-table of 1905 revolution, 130 n. 1; on Trotsky in 1905, 136; his reconciliation with Mensheviks, 136-7; edits *Novaya Zhizn*, 139; for 'democratic dictatorship of proletariat and peasantry', 157, 162; and 'boycotters', 176, 195; escapes to Finland, 177; at London congress, 178-9; and Europeanization, 180-1, 191; at Copenhagen congress, 197; proclaims Bolshevik faction to be the party, 198; and Trotsky's *Pravda*, 199; at outbreak of war, 213, 215, 216; edits *Social-Democrat*, 223; at Zimmerwald conference, 225-6; leads Zimmerwald minority, 232 ff.; his differences with Trotsky in 1915-16, 236-8; his return to Russia in 1917,

249; his meeting with Trotsky in May 1917, 255-9; at first Congress of Soviets, 263 ff.; and June demonstrations, 268-9; Lunacharsky on, 269; in July days, 270-5; goes into hiding, 274, 318; advocates insurrection, 289 ff., 295, 299, 301; opposes pre-Parliament, 294; and Trotsky during October rising, 311-12; forms his first government, 325-6; his exclusion from government demanded, 331 ff.; opposed to coalition government, 334-5; and single party system, 336-41, 487, 517-18; his relationship with Trotsky, 341-3; his peace policy, 346 ff., 355; urges Trotsky to go to Brest, 361; and Constituent Assembly, 372-3; advocates acceptance of German peace terms, 373 ff., 383 ff.; his private agreement with Trotsky, 375-6; and co-operation with Entente, 386; his peace policy evaluated, 387 ff.; and Trotsky during Brest period, 389-93; alleged *coup* against, 390 n. 2; and aftermath of Brest 394 ff., 399 ff.: and employment of Tsarist officers, 412, 429-30; attempt on his life, 422; and Tsaritsyn group, 424-5; and Ukraine, 428; on Wilson's proposal for Prinkipo conference, 429; and revolution in Hungary, 434; and crisis in supreme command, 435-6, 438; tension between Trotsky and, 439-40; proposes surrender of Petrograd, 442; founds Comintern, 451-3; and Russo-Polish war, 458-73; and invasion of Georgia, 475; on militarization of labour, 492-3, 502-3; and N.E.P., 497-8, 514; and crisis of 1920-21, 506 ff.; on proletarian democracy, 509-10; as Stalin's unwitting prompter, 515 ff.; bans factions within Bolshevik Party, 519-20.

Leopold (Rupprecht) of Bavaria, 361, 362, 383-4.

Liberalism, or liberals (bourgeois), 86, 107-9; in revolution, 120-1, 134; after the October Manifesto of 1905, 129-30; and Russian state, 151-2; during counter-revolution, 175; and Tsarist policy in Balkans, 202; in western Europe before 1914, 211-12; in 1917 revolution, 280 ff. *See also* Constitutional Democrats.

Liebknecht, Karl, 182-3, 225, 227, 247, 454; assassination of, 275 n. 1, 451.

Litvinov, M., 459,

Lloyd George, D., 461.

Lockhart, Bruce, R. H., 351.

Lomov-Oppokov, G., 299, 307; opposed to Brest Litovsk Peace, 389 ff.

Lopukhin, 169.

Lozovsky, A., 194, 222, 224, 234, 333.

Lubinsky, 377.

Ludendorff, E., 363, 382, 388 n. 1.

Lunacharsky, A., 62, 110, 139; on Lenin and Trotsky, 136, 269, 342; expelled from Bolshevik ranks, 195; defends Trotsky in 1910, 197; sets up party school at Bologna, 201 n. 1; and *Nashe Slovo*, 221, 224; as member of *Mezhrayonka*, 255, 260; on Lenin and Martov, 258 n. 1; at first Congress of Soviets, 265; arrested after July days, 278-9; and October insurrection, 299; and Lenin's first government, 325, 331, 333.

Lutovinov, Y., 502 n. 3.

Luxemburg, Rosa, 94 n. 1, 139, 145 n. 1, 207, 454, 470; and Trotsky, 178, 182-3; assassination of, 275 n. 1, 451.

Lvov, Prince, 243-5, 251, 263, 347.

MacDonald, Ramsay, 187, 475.

Machiavelli, 506.

Maisky, I., 223.

Makhno, Ataman, 416, 434.

Mamontov, 483.

Manuilsky, D. (Bezrabotnyi), 222, 224, 225 n. 2; and Trotsky, 234, member of *Mezhrayonka*, 255, 269.

Markhlevsky, J., 465.

Markin, N., 348.

Martov, Y., 24, 45, 157, 228; as co-editor of *Iskra*, 59 ff., 66; at second party congress, 73 ff.; as Lenin's antagonist, 79 ff.; leads the Mensheviks, 84-85; and Trotsky and Plekhanov, 86-87, 92 n. 2, 106-7; and bourgeois liberalism, 119; reconciled with Lenin, 136-7; and Trotsky in 1905, 139, 146; and 'liquidators', 176; escapes to Finland, 177; at London congress, 178-9; at Paris conference of January 1910, 194; on Trotsky and the 'liquidators', 196-7; and schism in party, 201, 205, 213; and *Golos* and *Nashe Slovo*, 216 ff., 221 ff., his divided loyalties, 224 ff.; and Zimmerwald conference, 225; resigns from *Nashe Slovo*, 235; early in 1917, 258, 265; defends Lenin in July days, 278, 295; leads Menshevik

Martov, Y. (cont.)
exodus from Soviets, 313–14, 336;
breaks negotiations with Bolsheviks,
337; his attitude towards Red Army,
410, 447.

Martynov, 76.

Marx, Karl, 18, 24, 25, 39, 162; his
forecast of Russian revolution, 5;
studied by Trotsky, 43, 70, 153 n. 1,
164; and his Russian followers, 60;
and 'permanent revolution', 156; on
'premature' revolutions, 396.

Maupassant, Guy, 48.

Mehring, Franz, 39, 139, 182–3, 194,
477.

Menshevism, or Mensheviks, 45 n. 1,
76–77; the origins of, 79–82; boycott
Iskra and the Leninist Central
Committee, 84–85; take over Iskra,
85–87, 94; Trotsky's estrangement
from, 87–88; and liberalism, 88, 108,
119; Trotsky's eulogy of, 89 ff.; and
intelligentsia, 94–95, 106; on eve of
1905 revolution, 99, 106, 112–14;
early in 1905, 117–18; and first
Petersburg Soviet, 125–6, 130, 135;
under Trotsky's influence in 1905,
137–9; and theory of 'permanent revolution', 150, 162–3; and problem of
land, 155; 'liquidators' in their ranks,
175–6, 195; at London congress of
1907, 177–80; against Bolshevik
'expropriations', 178–80, 198; and
Europeanization of Russian socialism,
180, 200; Rosa Luxemburg and, 183;
and final split with Bolsheviks, 194–7,
198, 200–1, 205; and World War I,
212, 217 ff., 232 ff, 234; and February
revolution, 244, 251 ff.; and Trotsky
early in 1917, 250; at first Congress of
Soviets, 262 ff.; in June and July,
268–9, 270–5; and anti-Bolshevik
reaction, 277 ff.; and Kornilov
revolt, 281–2; decline of their influence, 282–3; at Democratic Conference, 284–6; and Military Revolutionary Committee, 298; and October
insurrection, 302 ff., 309 ff.; secede
from second Soviet Congress, 313–14;
state terms for coalition with Bolsheviks, 331; shades of opinion
among, 339–40; and Red Army,
410, 447; rule Georgia, 473–5;
opposed to War Communism, 497,
499–500; in 1920–21, 504–5; suppressed by Lenin's government,
517–18.

Menzhinsky, V., 201 n. 1, 425.

Merrheim, 227.

Mezhlauk, V., 420.

Military Revolutionary Committee,
origin of, 298; arms Red Guards,
300; takes control of Petrograd
garrison, 304–5; plans insurrection,
306; stages insurrection, 307–8, 311;
after insurrection, 327.

Miliukov, P., 69 n. 1, 105 n. 1.; wel-
comes Bulygin Duma, 120; on Witte,
134 n. 1; on 'Trotskyism' in 1905,
137; on Russian state, 151; and
Stolypin's terror, 175; promotes
Slavophilism in Balkans, 201, 204;
as Foreign Minister, 243, 247, 251,
347; resigns, 252; calls for imprisonment of Lenin and Trotsky, 264–5,
275; fights Bolsheviks with German
assistance, 399.

Miliutin, V., 288, 301, 304 n. 1, 308,
492; favours coalition government,
333.

Mill, John Stuart, 24, 25, 34.

Millerand, or Millerandism, 70.

Mirbach, Count, 400, 403.

Molotov, see Parvus.

Monatte, Pierre, 227.

Morgari, O., 225.

Muralov, N., 423.

Muraviev, Colonel, 328–9, 417–18.

Mussolini, B., 222.

Napoleon I, 387, 483.

Narodniks (Populists), under Alexander
II, 1–5; after Alexander II, 18–19;
their influence on Trotsky, 23, 25–27,
31–33; and Slavophilism, 52; and
Gleb Uspensky, 52–53; revival of
Narodnik movement, 58, 68; 'substitutism' in Narodnik movement, 2–5,
190, 521. See also Social Revolutionaries.

Nazism, 75 n. 3, 190.

New Economic Policy (N.E.P.), 497–8,
514, 516, 518.

Nicholas II, 20, 24, 87; in 1905, 112;
and Bulygin Duma, 120; issues
October Manifesto, 126–7; 'financial
boycott' of, 141; strikes back in 1906,
145; backs Black Hundreds, 169;
and Stolypin, 175; his overthrow,
249; his execution, 418.

Niessel, General, 353.

Nietzsche, F., 48, 49–50.

Nogin, V., 288, 307, 333, 492; warns
Bolsheviks against 'irresponsible
government', 334.

Nordau, M., 75 n. 2.

Noulens, J., 353.
Novitsky, General, 412.

Okulov, 424, 425.
Olgin, M., 183, 241.
Ordjonikidze, S., 474, 475.
Osinsky, V., 494.

Paléologue, M, 346 n. 2.
Panteleev, Commissar, 420, 426.
Parvus (Helphand, A. L.; other pen-name Molotov), 94 n. 1, 100, 152; character-sketch of, 99–101; his influence on Trotsky, 101–3; about nation-state, 103; on prospects of Russian revolution, 104 ff.; his view on Russian state, 105; writes preface to Trotsky's brochure, 112–13; and Lenin on workers' government, 113; advocates armed insurrection in 1905, 119; co-edits Nachalo, 138; calls for financial boycott of Tsar, 141; in Peter Paul fortress, 145 n. 1; intro-duces Trotsky to Kautsky, 181; Trotsky's break with, 219–20, 276.
Perovskaya, S., 4.
Peshekhonov, 263.
Peter the Great, 152, 189.
Petlura, S., 428.
Pilsudski, J., 378, 458 ff., 468–9.
Plehve, Minister of Interior, 107.
Plekhanov, G. V., 39, 45, 98, 157, 207; on Black Partition, 4; as co-editor o Iskra, 59 ff.; his animosity towards Trotsky, 62, 86–87, 106, 139, 162, 197; at second party congress, 73 ff.; with Lenin against Mensheviks, 78–80; with Mensheviks against Lenin, 85–86; on Lenin as new Robespierre, 96; opposed to 'liqui-dators', 176, 198 n. 3; appeals to International against Lenin, 213; and World War I, 216, 232, 267.
Pobedonostzev, C., 19, 24.
Podvoisky, N., 298, 406, 434.
Pokrovsky, M., 201 n. 1, 222, 255, 361.
Poland, 159; in 1905, 133; Social Democrats of, 177–8; and Brest Litovsk Peace, 363, 367–8, 374, 376–8; Soviets in, 449; concludes secret armistice with Russia, 458; at war with Russia, 458–73.
Politbureau, origin of, 299, 341; dis-cusses Trotsky's military policy, 426 ff., 436, 438–40, 442; and Russo-Polish war, 458–73; and invasion of Georgia, 474–5; and War Commun-ism, 498 ff.

Potresov, A. N., 24, 59, 66, 78, 85, 232.
Pravda ('Viennese', Trotskyist, anti-Bolshevik), 191–9, 210, 234.
Preobrazhensky, E., 499, 519 n. 1.
Pre-Parliament, 283–4, 294.
Price Philips, M., 375, 393.
Pyatakov, Y., 389, 410, 495, 519 n. 1.

Radek, Karl, 213, 215, 223; at Brest Litovsk, 360–1, 378; opposed to peace, 388 ff., 390 n. 2; on Trotsky's role at Brest, 395; on Trotsky as founder of Red Army, 408, 477; and Russo-Polish war, 465, 470.
Rakovsky, Christian, 223, 402, 429; his pre-1914 career, 207–8; at Zimmerwald conference, 225; in 1920 trade union controversy, 519 n. 1.
Raskolnikov, F., 272 n. 1, 279, 420, 423.
Razumnik, Ivan, 188.
Red Army, 389, 399, 404; origins of, 405 ff.; politics of, 408–9, 436–8; Commissars and officers in, 415, 425–6, 429–32; first battles of, 419 ff., under Vatzetis's command, 423; Tsaritsyn group, 423–8; and eighth party congress, 431–2; its strategic position, 432–3; in Kolchak offen-sive, 423–4; in campaign against Denikin, 437 ff.; in Ukraine, 439–40; its morale in crisis, 441–2; and 'road to India', 457; in Russo-Polish war, 461 ff., 488; and revolution abroad, 469 ff.; and militias, 478 ff., 491; its strategic doctrine, 481–5.
Red Guards, arming of, 281, 285–6, 300; in October rising, 305–10; after rising, 327–9; and Brest Litovsk Peace, 399–401, 404; strength of, 405; and Red Army, 407 ff., 411, 416; in Ukraine, 428 ff., 434–5.
Remarque, E. M., 230.
Renner, Karl, 186.
Revolution, permanent, 103; origins of theory of, 112–14; further develop-ment, 118–19; the theory of, sum-marized and analysed, 149–62; and Lenin in 1917, 256–7.
Revolutions:
    French, Great, 84, 111, 115, 120, 294; recalled by Trotsky, 91–97, 134, 338; middle-class in, 152–3; and war, 390–1, 414, 415; and Napoleonic conquest, 469.
    German, of 1848, 120, 153; See also Germany.

Revolutions: (cont.)

Russian, of 1905, eve of, 108, 112;
beginning of, 112-18, 122-3; the
October movement, 125-7, 130-3;
as dress rehearsal for 1917, 140-1;
compared with 1789 and 1848,
153, 249.

Russian, of 1917, outbreak of,
243 ff.; early phase, 249 ff.; turning
point of June, 267 ff.; the July
days, 270-5; subsequent reaction,
279 ff.; Kornilov's attempt at
counter-revolution, 282; October
insurrection, 290-4, 307-14;
'Peace, Land, and Bread' in,
314-22; anti-climax to, 322-4;
terror in, 338-41; and Constituent
Assembly, 372; and self-determination, 377-8; and 1918 upheaval in
Europe, 449-50.

Revolutionary War Council of the
Republic, 422-3, 436.

Ribot, 347.

Robespierre, 84, 153; and Lenin,
91-97, 390-1.

Robins, R., 351, 385 n. 1, 390 n. 2.

Rodzianko, M., 296.

Rosengoltz, A., 420, 423.

Rosmer, A., 227, 241.

Rothstein, Th., 223, 463 n. 3.

Rudzutak, I., 502 n. 3.

Ruskin, John, 48.

Ryazanov, D., 192, 197, 221, 492;
member of Mezhrayonka, 255;
negotiates about coalition government, 331 ff.; opposed to Brest
Litovsk Peace, 389 ff.

Rykov, A., 194, 288, 294, 492, 502 n. 3;
for coalition government, 333.

Sadoul, J., 288 n. 1, 345, 347 n. 6,
351, 361; compares Lenin and Trotsky, 403.

Sapronov, T., 499.

Sazonov, the Social Revolutionary, 107.

Schopenhauer, A., 34 n. 2.

Schulz, German military historian, 477.

Sedov, Lev, or Leon, Trotsky's older
son, 184.

Sedov, Sergei, Trotsky's younger son,
184.

Sedova, Natalya, Trotsky's second wife,
70-71, 101, 241, 373 n. 1; returns to
Russia in 1905, 116, 124; and
Trotsky's deportation in 1906, 170,
174; in Berlin, 181; in Vienna, before
1914, 183-4, 192; during the
revolution, 345.

Semkovsky, 192.

Serebriakov, L., 519 n. 1.

Shaumian, S., 288.

Shchastny, Admiral, 414.

Shchedrin, N. P., 31.

Sherriff, R. C., 230.

Shlyapnikov, G., 424, 502 n. 3; leads
Workers' Opposition, 507 ff., 519.

Shvigovsky, Franz, 23, 25, 30, 36.

Shydlovsky, Senator, 125, 131.

Siberia, early in the century described
by Trotsky, 46-48; 1906 revolts in,
145; Japanese invasion of, 350, 399;
Czech Legion in, 417; civil war in,
433-4; and American-Japanese
rivalry, 456.

Siberian Social Democratic Union, 44,
45 n. 1, 72, 83.

Sklyansky, E. M., 423, 438, 466, 474.

Skobelev, 192, 209, 253, 254.

Skoptsy, 43, 205-6.

Skoropadsky, Hetman, 394.

Slavophilism, or Pan-Slavism, 52, 67,
201-2, 204.

Smilga, I., 426, 434, 439, 480-1.

Smirnov, I. N., 392, 410, 420, 423.

Social Democracy, Russian, or Russian
Social Democratic Party,
foundation of, 34; and Jacobinism, 76, 91-97; splits into
Mensheviks and Bolsheviks 81-
86; its role in 1905 revolution,
118-19; opposed to terrorism,
139; under Stolypin régime, 175;
and February revolution, 244.

Congresses of Russian Social Democratic Workers' Party, later
Communist Party (Bolsheviks):
Minsk 'congress' of 1898, 34, 72.
second congress (1903), 72-82.
fifth (London) congress (1907),
177-80.
sixth congress (1917), 269.
seventh congress (1918), 389,
394-8.
eighth congress (1919), 430-1, 478.
ninth congress (1920), 498-9.
tenth congress (1921), 508-10, 519.

Social (or Socialist) Revolutionary
Party, 68, 130; in Petrograd Soviet
of 1905, 139; in 1914, 212; during
and after February revolution, 250-
1 ff.: at first Congress of Soviets,
262 ff.; in July days, 270-5; and
anti-Bolshevik reaction, 277 ff.; and
Kornilov, 281-2; decline of its
influence, 282-3; at Democratic
Conference, 284-6; and October

revolution, 302 ff.; secedes from second Congress of Soviets, 313–14; in Constituent Assembly, 320, 372; and coalition with Bolsheviks, 331; stages semi-insurrection, 338; shades of opinion in, 339–40; forms anti-Bolshevik government, 422; in 1920–1, 504–5; suppressed by Lenin's government, 517–18.

Social Revolutionaries, Left, 313, 320, 325, 328; join Lenin's government, 335; and separate peace with Germany, 355, 373–93, 400; and Constituent Assembly, 472; rise against Bolsheviks, 390 n. 2, 400–4, 417; opposed to Trotsky's military policy, 410.

Sokolnikov, G., 194, 222, 288, 299, 447; on insurrection, 301; negotiates about coalition government, 331 ff.; supports Brest Litovsk Peace, 374 ff.; signs the peace, 393; defends Trotsky's military policy, 430, 478; in trade union debate, 519 n. 1.

Sokolovskaya, Alexandra, Trotsky's first wife, 25; and young Trotsky, 27–28, 31, 97; on Trotsky's character, 35; marries Trotsky, 42; deported to Siberia, 42–43; urges Trotsky to escape, 55; and Sedova, 71.

Southern Russian Workers' Union, 30–31, 36, 63.

Soviet of Petersburg (1905), its origin, 125 ff.; elects Executive, 130; activities of, 130–6; reprisals against, 139–40; last period of its activity, 140–4; trial of its members, 163–9.

Soviet of Petrograd (1917), 244, 247, 250; backs Lvov's government, 254; and Army, 265; Bolshevik ascendancy in, 282–3; Trotsky elected its President, 286; its role in the October revolution, 297 ff., 304 ff.

Soviets, Councils of Workers', Peasants', and Soldiers' Deputies, first all-Russian Congress of, 262–8; and Constituent Assembly, 283; Bolshevik ascendancy in, 286; preliminaries to second Congress of, 286, 290, 300; as source of power, 291; of Northern Russia, 300; and single party system, 504 ff.; second Congress of, 309–14, 318–19, 346; third Congress of, 373, 375; fifth Congress of, 400–4; seventh Congress of, 446–7.

Spencer, Herbert, 24, 50.

Spentzer, M. F., 12, 16, 20, 33, 184 n. 1.

Stalin, J. V., 135, 155 n. 5, 156 n. 2, 193, 288; on 'permanent revolution', 160; on Trotsky, 176–7; at London congress, 179; on Rosa Luxemburg, 183; versus Lenin, 197; edits Bolshevik Pravda, 199; his meeting with Trotsky in 1913, 209–10; as exponent of 'national revolutionary' Messianic mood, 238; on pre-Parliament, 294; in Politbureau, 299; and October insurrection, 301–2, 304 n. 1, 307; on Constituent Assembly, 341; and Sverdlov and Trotsky, 343, 393; and armistice, 349; supports Brest Litovsk Peace, 374 ff., 384, 388 n. 2; alleged plot against, 390 n. 2; and Left Communists, 392 n. 5; and Tsaritsyn group, 420, 423–8, 431–2; his action against C.-in-C. Vatzetis, 434, 435, 438–9; and campaign against Denikin, 441, 443; awarded Red Banner Order, 446 n. 1; and Orient, 458; and Russo-Polish war, 465, 466, 468; and revolution by conquest, 472, 475, 476; and militias, 481; and Labour Armies, 495; unwittingly inspired by Lenin and Trotsky, 515–17.

Stolypin, P., Prime Minister, 145, 169, 175, 198 n. 1.

Struve, P., 58, 92 n. 2., advocates 'legal Marxism', 108–9; Trotsky versus, 114, 138, 149.

'Substitutism', 2–4, 89–97, 190, 470, 520–2.

Sukhanov, N., 272, 278; on Trotsky in 1917, 284, 287, 300, 325.

Svatopolk-Mirsky, Prince, 107, 109.

Svechin, General, 479.

Sverchkov, D., 130, 147.

Sverdlov, Y. M., 73 n. 1, 288, 299, 304 n. 1; in October rising, 307; and Jewish problem 326; and Trotsky, 327; opposed to coalition government, 333; heads Executive of Soviets, 335; and Stalin and Trotsky, 343; and Brest Litovsk, 384.

Swift, J., 231 n. 1.

Sytin, General, 424.

Tatishchev, Count, 348–9.

Teodorovich, I., 333.

Thermidorians, 84.

Thomas, Albert, 351.

Tikhomirov, 19.

Tolstoy, L., 19, 44.

Tomsky, M., 499, 502 n. 3.

Trepov, General, vice-Minister of Interior, 127-8, 132, 169.

Trotsky, Lev (Leon) Davidovich, birth of, 7-8; childhood, 8-12; at school in Odessa, 12-15; and his father, 17-18, 29-30; schooldays at Nikolayev, 22; his initial indifference to socialism, 20-23; comes under Narodnik influence, 25-27; and Sokolovskaya, 27-28, 31, 42; graduates from school and enters university, 29-30.

his early activities: founds Southern Russian Workers' Union, 30-32, 34; early characteristics, 34-36; in prisons at Nikolayev, Kherson, Odessa, and Moscow, 36-42; deported to Siberia, 42-43; anticipates Lenin's views on party, 45-46; as young journalist and literary critic, 46-55; escapes from Siberia, 55; origin of pseudonym Trotsky, 56; first meeting with Lenin in London, 57-59; under Martov's and Zasulich's influence, 60-61; and Plekhanov, 62, 86-87, 106, 139; promoted by Lenin in *Iskra*, 61-63, 71; his first contributions to *Iskra*, 67-69; early oratorical successes, 69-70; meets Natalya Sedova, 70-71; and Jewish problem at second party congress, 73 ff.; on Zionism, 75; as 'Lenin's cudgel', 76; turns against Lenin, 78 ff.; sides with Mensheviks, 80-81; his motives, 82-83; his report on second congress, 83-84; boycotts *Iskra*, 84; as member of leading Menshevik group, 85; and Menshevik *Iskra*, 86-87; his differences with Mensheviks, 87-88; writes *Our Political Tasks*, 88; attacks Lenin's 'substitutism', 89-90; on Jacobinism and Social Democracy, 91-97; becomes a 'conciliator', 98-99; comes under Parvus's influence, 101 ff.; secedes from Menshevik group, 106; returns to 'new' *Iskra*, 106-7; his prognostications on revolution, 108-12; is backed by Parvus, 112-15; his return to Russia, 116; advocates armed insurrection, 118-19; his controversy with Miliukov, 120-1; as pamphleteer and journalist in 1905, 122-4; his appearance in Petersburg Soviet, 126; and October Manifesto, 127-9; leads Mensheviks in Soviet, 131; and Khrustalev-Nosar, 131; his activity in Soviet, 131-9; addresses Guards Officers, 137-8; edits *Russkaya Gazeta* and *Nachalo*, 138-9; leads Soviet after Khrustalev's arrest, 140 ff.; is arrested, 144; his argument with Martov over tactics in dock, 146; his literary work in prison, 147-9; *The Balance and the Prospects* (the theory of 'permanent revolution'), 149-62; his speech in the dock, 164-8; sentenced to deportation for life, 169; his escape, 172-4.

1907-17: his behaviour during counter-revolution, 176-7; his escape to Finland, 177; at London congress, 178-80; calls for Europeanization, 180-1, 190-1, 520-2; his German and Austrian associates, 182-7; his life in Vienna, 183-4; and leaders of European socialism before 1914, 187; his criticism of Razumnik's book on Russian intelligentsia, 188-91; edits Viennese *Pravda*, 191 ff.; preliminaries to August Bloc, 195-8; at Jena congress of German socialists, 197-8; and Bolshevik *Pravda*, 198-9; his role in August Bloc, 200-1; as war correspondent in Balkans, 201-9; and Rakovsky, 207-8; his 1913 impression of Stalin, 209-10; at outbreak of World War I, 213-14; writes *War and the International*, 214-15; sentenced by German court, 214; contributes to Martov's *Golos*, 216 ff.; charged with pro-Germanism, 216; breaks with August Bloc and with Parvus, 218-20; edits *Nashe Slovo* in Paris, 220 ff.; sees Lenin 'in new light', 224 ff.; his role at Zimmerwald conference, 225-7; inspires French anti-militarists, 227; his military writings, 228-32; his gradual evolution towards Bolshevism, 233-8; advocates United States of Socialist Europe, 236-8; expelled from France, 238 ff.; his adventures in Spain, 239-41.

in 1917: his stay in New York, 241 ff.; his first reaction to February revolution, 243-6; interned in Canada, 246-7; returns to Russia, 248; appointed to Executive of Petrograd Soviet, 250, 253; his first speech in Soviet, 253–4; leads *Mezhrayonka*, 254–5, 260, 269; meets Lenin in May 1917, 255–9; defends Kronstadt sailors; 260–1; at first Congress of Soviets; 263 ff.; and June demonstrations, 268–9; Lunacharsky on, 269; during July days, 270–5; defends Bolsheviks and himself, 275–7; is arrested, 278; his activity in prison, 279 ff.; released on bail, 282; at Democratic Conference, 284–6; elected President of Soviet, 286–7; joins Bolsheviks, 287–8; advocates armed insurrection, 290–4, 299 ff.; his tactics, 296–8, 302–3; opposes pre-Parliament, 294, 297; heads Military Revolutionary Committee, 298 ff.; prepares October insurrection, 299–306; leads insurgents, 307–14; as member of Lenin's first government, 325–7; defeats Kerensky's attempt to regain power, 327–30; his exclusion from government demanded, 331 ff.; opposed to coalition government, 334–5; frees Kerensky's ministers, 336; and single party system, 336–41; his relations with Lenin, 341–3; his conduct as Commissar, 344–5, 348 ff.

during Brest Litovsk period and civil war: his views on separate peace, 357–9; his arrival at Brest, 359, 361–2; conducts negotiations, 364 ff.; and Kühlmann, 369–71; 'neither war nor peace', 372 ff., 383 ff.; and dispersal of Constituent Assembly, 372–3; backed by Central Committee, 375; his private agreement with Lenin, 375–6; and Ukrainians at Brest, 377–8; breaks negotiations, 378–82; and Left Communists, 383, 386–90; votes for peace, 385–6; urges co-operation with Entente, 385–6; and Lenin during Brest period, 389–93; resigns as Commissar for Foreign Affairs, 393; and aftermath of Brest, 394 ff., 399–400; as Commissar of War, 399; suppresses Left Social Revolutionary rising, 402–4; presides over Supreme War Council, 405; founds Red Army, 405–16; conducts campaign against Czechs and Kolchak, 416 ff.; demands trial for Tsar, 418; his ruthlessness, 421,

426; forms Revolutionary War Council, 422; on Sklyansky, 423; and Tsaritsyn group, 423–8; on bureaucracy, 427–8; his Ukrainian plans, 428, 434–5; and Prinkipo conference, 429; his military policy opposed, 429 ff.; and Kolchak offensive, 433–4; his setbacks 435–6, 438; resigns from all posts, 436; his plan of campaign against Denikin, 436–8; tension between him and Lenin, 439–40; during crisis of October 1919, 441–2; takes charge of defence of Petrograd, 442–5; at end of civil war, 446–7; on 1918 European revolution, 450–1, 454–5; and foundation of Comintern, 452–4; urges 'eastern reorientation', 456–8, 462; his attitude in Russo-Polish war, 458–73; at second Comintern congress, 467; on revolutionary conquest, 471–3, 475–7; and invasion of Georgia, 474–5; his military writings, 477–85; stumbles at pinnacle of power, 486, 520–2; initiates militarization of labour, 487–8, 491–6, 498–503, 507; proposes N.E.P. a year before its introduction, 497–8; versus Workers' opposition, 508–9; suppresses Kronstadt rising, 512–14; as Stalin's unwitting prompter, 515 ff.; and ban on factions within Bolshevik Party, 519–20.

Trotsky's pseudonyms: Lvov, 31, Antid-Oto, 46, Trotsky, 56, *Pero* (The Pen), 56, Samokovlieff, 73, Arbuzov, 117, Peter Petrovich, 118, Vikentiev, 124, Yanovsky, 128, N. Takhotsky, 149, P. Tanas, 279.

Trotsky, Nicholas, 216.

Tsektran, Central Transport Commission, 502–3.

Tseretelli, I., 253, 267.

Tukhachevsky, M., 420, 422, 447, 460; in Russo-Polish war, 461, 466, 469; on 'revolution from outside', 472, 482–5; and militias, 481; suppresses peasant rebellion, 511–12; suppresses Kronstadt rising, 513–14.

Turati, Ph., 187.

Ukraine; and Brest Litovsk Peace, 364–5, 376–80, 386 ff.; under German occupation, 394, 396, 399–400; civil war in, 428 ff., 434 ff., 439–40, 458; and Russo-Polish war, 460 ff.

Ulyanov, Alexander, Lenin's older brother, 19, 67.

Ulyanov, Dimitry, Lenin's younger brother, 72 n. 2, 81.

United States of America, Trotsky's impression of, 242-3; and Brest Litovsk Peace, 349, 385; intervention of, in Russia, 350-1, 448; and Japanese expansion in Siberia, 456.

Uritsky, M., 192, 223, 255, 269, 304 n. 1; opposed to Brest Litovsk Peace, 374 ff., 389 ff.; assassinated, 422.

Uspensky, Gleb, 46, 48, 52.

Valden, Colonel, 328.

Vandervelde, E., 187, 225, 248.

Vatzetis, J., 404, 417; Commander-in-Chief, 420, 423, 433-4; dismissed, 435-6, 438.

Volodarsky, V., 242, 255, 299, 301.

Voroshilov, K., 416, 423-8, 431, 435; and strategic doctrine, 482, 485.

War Communism, 487-503.

Wars:

Russo-Japanese of 1904-5, 86, 89, 103-4, 107, 110-11.

Russo-Polish of 1920, 458-73, 497.

First World War, outbreak, 211-13; Trotsky on, 228-32; Russian front in 1917, 265, 296; Russia's withdrawal from, 346 ff.; end of, 428; aftermath of, 476.

Second World War, 161, 476, 480; Trotsky's anticipations of, 484-5. See also Civil Wars.

Wheeler-Bennett, J. W., 354 n. 3, 379 n. 1, 381, 382.

White Armies, or Guards, origin of, 337-8, 405, 416; political outlook of, 339, 445 n. 3; their well-wishers in Red Army, 414; and Tsar, 418; reject Wilson's proposal, 429; strategic position of, 432-3, 483; and foreign intervention, 443, 448; disintegration of, 460; and Kronstadt rising, 511. See also Civil Wars.

Witos, W., 468.

Witte, Count Sergei, Prime Minister, 127, 132, 169; Trotsky's rebuff to, 133-4; Miliukov on, 134 n. 1; in 1905 and after, 139, 145.

Workers' Opposition, 507-10, 513, 518-20.

Wrangel, P., General, 462-3, 468.

Yegorov, A., 460, 461, 466.

Yermolenko, 273.

Yoffe, A., 193, 255, 498; and Brest Litovsk Peace, 360, 361, 389 ff.

Yudenich, N., General, 433, 435, 440, 458; his second offensive, 443-5.

Yureniev, K., 255, 269, 333, 423.

Zalewski, K., 234 n. 1.

Zalutsky, 426.

Zarudny, 279.

Zaslavsky, E. O., 31.

Zasulich, V., shoots at Trepov, 4; co-edits Iskra, 59 ff.; Lenin versus, 78-82; leaning towards liberalism, 88; supports war, 232-3.

Zemstvos, 20, 47, 67-68; dispersed by Plehve, 107, 109; in 1917, 283.

Zetkin, K., 139, 194, 198.

Zhelyabov, A., 4.

Zimmerwald Conference, 225-7, 452, 232 ff.

Zinoviev, G., 176, 218, 255, 444, 502; in July days, 1917, 273, 276; opposes insurrection, 289, 291-5, 299 ff., 304 n. 1; and coalition government, 333, 335; supports Brest Litovsk Peace, 374 ff., 384, 390 n. 2; and military policy, 412, 425, 431-2.

Ziv, G., 25, 28 n. 2, 39 n. 2; on Trotsky at Nikolayev, 30-32, 34, 35; on Trotsky's first marriage, 42; on Trotsky in prison in 1906, 146, 147; on Trotsky in New York in 1917, 241, 243.

Zlydniev, P., 131, 163-4.

Zola, E., 48, 277 n. 1.

Zubatov, Colonel, 112.

Zweig, A., 230.